RACIST SATANIC NETWORK

DR. OLAYINKA BAMGBELU

Copyright @2021 by Dr. Olayinka Bamgbelu

All rights reserved. No part of this book may be reproduced in any form or by any electronic or mechanical means, including information storage and retrieval systems, without permission in writing from the publisher, except by reviewers, who may quote brief passages in a review.

This publication contains the opinions and ideas of its author. It is intended to provide helpful and informative material on the subjects addressed in the publication. The author and publisher specifically disclaim all responsibility for any liability, loss or risk, personal or otherwise, which is incurred as a consequence, directly or indirectly, of the use and application of any of the contents of this book.

WORKBOOK PRESS LLC
187 E Warm Springs Rd,
Suite B285, Las Vegas, NV 89119, USA

Website:	https://workbookpress.com/
Hotline:	1-888-818-4856
Email:	admin@workbookpress.com

Ordering Information:
Quantity sales. Special discounts are available on quantity purchases by corporations, associations, and others.
For details, contact the publisher at the address above.

ISBN-13: 978-1-954753-73-0 (Paperback Version)
          978-1-954753-74-7 (Digital Version)

REV. DATE: 22/03/2021

RACIST SATANIC NETWORK

True Story

By

Yinka Bamgbelu

DEDICATION

"The Negro is an animal, the Negro is bad, the Negro is mean, the Negro is ugly; look, a nigger ……… Mama, the nigger's going to eat me up……….Where shall I hide." Frantz Fanon.

Systemic and structural racism, the pillars of white privilege: The mother of all racist scams, and one of the enduring residues of the original sin (slavery) - Habakkuk.
He is watching them - Proverbs 15:3.
The nemesis is not extinct, and the fact that it tarries isn't proof that it will never come - Habakkuk.
The foundation of Bedford, brick by brick and almost in its entirety, was forged with the proceeds of centuries of merciless, evil racial hatred and fraud.

Before slavery, what?
Aliens – essentially a motley assembly of agricultural labourers from all over mainland Europe – dispossessed the Native Britons and stole their land. The land thieves were subsequently immeasurably transformed by gigantic yields of several centuries of merciless, racial hatred and fraud. They have reinvented themselves and fool the foolish with foolishness on stolen land.

"Many Scots masters were considered among the most brutal, with life expectancy on their plantations averaging a mere four years. We worked them to death then simply imported more to keep the sugar and thus the money flowing. Unlike centuries of grief and murder, an apology cost nothing. So, what does Scotland have to say?" – Herald Scotland, Ian Bell, columnist, Sunday 28 April 2013

"As hard-hearted as a Scot of Scotland." – English saying

"Scotsmen tak a' they can get and a little more if they can." – Scottish saying Before slavery, what?

"I know of no evil that has ever existed, nor can imagine any evil to exist, worse than the tearing of eighty thousand persons annually from their native land, by a combination of the most civilised nations inhabiting the most enlightened part of the globe, but more especially under the sanction of the laws of that Nation which calls herself the most free and the most happy of them all." – Prime Minister William Pitt the Younger, 1792

The book is dedicated to the millions of kidnapped and stolen African children that were mercilessly worked to death or slaughtered during the centuries of evil European terrorism and racist, merciless tyranny.

"It did not become illegal to own a slave in Scotland until 1778. Until then it had been fashionable for wealthy families to have a young black boy or girl 'attending' on them. Scottish newspapers, such as the Edinburgh Evening Courant and the Caledonian Mercury from the 1740s to the 1770s, carried adverts offering slaves for sale or rewards for the capture of escaped slaves." – National Library of Scotland

ACKNOWLEDGEMENT

I am grateful for the patience and support of my publishers.

PREFACE

Vengeance belongs to Christ, and He knows all, and He sees all – Proverbs 15:3.

"I want to draw blood (with it). I'm warning all of you, if you feel vengeful, read this book and you will be alright. It is like homeopathic medicine." – Inter Inventions: Between Defective Memory and Public Lie: A Personal Odyssey in the Republic of Liars – W.S. (Wole Soyinka, not William Shakespeare.

A shallow atheist. When he reads this book, He will realise that He reveals Himself to those who stand where He can come and do so with unalloyed FAITH.

Christianity is 100% FAITH.

***

Before slavery, what?

The real name of Ghislaine Maxwell's father was, Ján Ludvík Hyman Binyamin Hoch, he was from Czechoslovakia. He came to Britain in the 1940s.

The real name of Nigella Lawson's Great Grandfather was Gustav Liebson, and he came to Britain in the 1890s.

Mustafa Mehmet is Turkish; Boris Johnson isn't.

GIGANTIC yields of millions of stolen and destroyed lives, not feudal agriculture, lured Eastern European Jews to Britain, they changed their names, and blended with the huge TRUST FUND.

Facts are sacred.

NORTHAMPTON, ENGLAND: Based on available evidence, GDC-WITNESS, Dr Geraint Evans, Postgraduate Tutor, Oxford, unrelentingly lied under implied oath - Habakkuk 1:4; John 8:44; John 10:10.

A RACIST WHITE CROOK.

CREEPING NORTH KOREA.

FACTS ARE SACRED.

CORBY, ENGLAND: Based on available evidence, GDC-WITNESS, Dr George Rothnie unrelentingly lied under implied oath - Habakkuk 1:4; John 8:44; John 10:10.

A RACIST WHITE CROOK.

CREEPING NORTH KOREA.

FACTS ARE SACRED.

CORBY, ENGLAND: Based on available evidence, GDC-WITNESS, Dr Kevin Atkinson, Scottish Ken, unrelentingly lied under oath - Habakkuk 1:4; John 8:44; John 10:10.

A RACIST WHITE CROOK.

CREEPING NORTH KOREA.

FACTS ARE SACRED.

OXFORD, ENGLAND: Based on available evidence, GDC-WITNESS, British Soldier - Territorial Defence, Dr Stephanie Twidale (TD) unrelentingly lied under oath - Habakkuk 1:4; John 8:44; John 10:10.

A RACIST WHITE CROOK.

CREEPING NORTH KOREA.

FACTS ARE SACRED.

WOLLASTON, ENGLAND: Based on available evidence, GDC-WITNESS, Ms Rachael Bishop, Senior NHS Nurse, unrelentingly lied under oath - Habakkuk 1:4; John 8:44; John 10:10.

A RACIST WHITE CROOK.

CREEPING NORTH KOREA.

FACTS ARE SACRED.

BEDFORD, ENGLAND: Based on available evidence, GDC-INSIDER, Dr Sue Gregory, Officer of the Most Excellent Order of our Empire unrelentingly lied under implied oath - Habakkuk 1:4; John 8:44; John 10:10.

A RACIST WHITE CROOK.

CREEPING NORTH KOREA.

FACTS ARE SACRED.

BEDFORD, ENGLAND: Based on available evidence, GDC-WITNESS, Freemason, Brother, Dr Richard William Hill fabricated reports and unrelentingly lied under oath - Habakkuk 1:4; John 8:44; John 10:10.

A RACIST WHITE CROOK.

CREEPING NORTH KOREA.

FACTS ARE SACRED.

A bastardised, unashamedly mediocre, indiscreetly dishonest, vindictive, potently weaponised, and institutionally RACIST system that his overseen by MASONS (Mediocre Mafia) - Habakkuk.

Then and now, in jurisdictions where the satanic network (Antichrist Racist Freemason) is in charge, their members have power to tell lies under oath.

If the genius atheist, Wole Soyinka could prove that District Judge Paul Ayers, Senior Vice President of the Association of Her Majesty's District Judges was not a functional semi-illiterate and an incompetent liar, and if he could prove that GDC-Witness, Ms Rachael Bishop, Senior NHS Nurse, did not unrelentingly tell lies under oath, and if he could prove that Dr Richard William Hill, Postgraduate Tutor - NHS, did not fabricate reports and unrelentingly told lies under oath, and if he could prove that Stephen Henderson, LLM, Head of MDDUS, was not a functional semi-illiterate closeted racist thug who unrelentingly deviated from the truth on record, and if he could prove that GDC-INSIDER, Dr Sue Gregory (OBE), Officer of the Most Excellent Order of our Empire, did not unrelentingly tell lies under implied oath, and if he could prove that GDC-Witness, Stephanie Twidale, British Army Officer - Territorial Defence, did not unrelentingly tell lies under oath, and if he could prove that Geraint Evans, Postgraduate Tutor, did not unrelentingly tell lies under implied oath, and if he could prove that Kevin Atkinson, Postgraduate Tutor, did not unrelentingly tell lies under oath, and if he could prove that Dr George Rothnie, Deputy Postgraduate Dean, did not deviate from the truth under implied oath, he would confirm the belief of billions, which is that Antichrist Freemasonry Quasi Religion, Antichrist Judaism, Antichrist Islam, and all motley assemblies of exotic religions and FAITHS under the common umbrella of the Governor of the Church of England and commander of THE FAITH are not intellectually flawed Satanic Mumbo Jumbo; it will also confirm that reasoning and vision have boundaries. If reasoning and vision have boundaries, He must have lied when, before the Council, He disclosed pictures His purportedly unbounded mind painted, and He must have also lied when He audaciously stated: "I am the way and the truth and the life. No one comes to the Father except through me." - John 14:6.

If He told the truth before the Council, everything that is not aligned to John 14:6 is travelling in the wrong direction.

FACTS ARE SACRED.
Ignorance is bliss.

You cannot go to Him, but He will come to you if you stand where He can come, and with unalloyed FAITH.

"The supreme vice is shallowness." Wilde
Before SLAVERY, there was ONLY feudal agriculture.
GIGANTIC yields of centuries of merciless, RACIST evil, not agriculture, lured JEWS to Britain
The NHS apparatchiks, led by Sue Gregory (OBE), maliciously lied, and lied and lied again, on record, including under oath.
Sue Gregory (OBE) and her mediocre, racist gang are the thoroughly wretched descendants of thoroughly wretched feudal agricultural labourers (serfs) from mainland Europe who used extreme violence to steal the land of aboriginal Britons. The barbarians were immeasurably transformed by the gigantic yields of centuries of merciless, racist evil, which the European trade in millions of stolen Africans was. They have reinvented themselves with stolen money on stolen land and fool the foolish with foolishness.

Gigantic yields of sadistic, racist evil were the magnet that pulled Eastern Europe Jews to Britain. Before SLAVERY what? Feudal agriculture!

"It was in 1066 that William the Conqueror occupied Britain, stole our land and gained control by granting it to his Norman friends, thus creating a feudal system we have not yet fully escaped." – Tony Benn

Normans stole from others what others had stolen from others. Genetically pure Britons are extinct; all were dispossessed, robbed, and slaughtered.

Tony Benn was dishonest, or he was confused when he implied that he was genetically an aboriginal Briton. Genetically pure aboriginal Britons are extinct. They were dispossessed and robbed of their land by a motley assembly of mainland Europeans – hereditary serfs or descendants of feudal agricultural labourers – who were hugely transformed by the gigantic gains of slavery. They have reinvented themselves.

It is fact and absolute truth that Sir Winston Churchill implied that the average Briton was a moron. More than sixty years later, the OECD seamlessly corroborated the proximate observations of the great man.

Sue Gregory (OBE) was a shepherd of England's young adults.

"FAILING SCHOOLS AND A BATTLE FOR BRITAIN: This was the day the British education establishment's 50 year betrayal of the Nation's children lay starkly exposed in all its ignominy. After testing 166,000 people in 24 education systems, the Organisation for Economic Cooperation and Development (OECD) finds that England young adults are amongst the least literate and numerate in the industrialised world." – The Daily Mail, 09.01.2013

Shepherds of morons are likelier to be morons too.

x

Racist Satanic Network Dear SUE GREGORY (OBE): True Story

"All sections of UK society are institutionally racist." – Sir Bernard Hogan-Howe, London Metropolitan Police

Sue Gregory (OBE) and the other NHS apparatchiks that she shepherded are sections of UK society.

Privileged shepherds of morons shouldn't insert any organ in the mouth of pigs; they should insert balls in the mouth of live PACU, the fish (the organ grinder).

Before GIGANTIC yields of SLAVERY there was only feudal agriculture.

Yields of EVIL, not yields of feudal agriculture, were the magnet for Eastern European Jews.

Before slavery what?

"Agriculture not only gives riches to a nation, but the only riches she can call her own." – Dr Samuel Johnson

"Those who have robbed have also lied." – Dr Samuel Johnson corroborating prophet Habakkuk

INTRODUCTION

"The English think that incompetence is the same thing as sincerity."
– Quentin Crisp

"To disagree with three-fourths of the British public on all points is one of the first elements of sanity, one of the deepest consolations in all moments of spiritual doubt." – Oscar Wilde

Before GIGANTIC yields of SLAVERY there was only feudal agriculture. Yields of EVIL, not the yields of feudal agriculture were the magnet for Eastern European Jews.

The colour bar was crude and cruel. The reasoning bar is spineless cowardice.

"Nothing that you will learn in the course of your studies will be of the slightest possible use to you in after life – save only this – if you work hard and diligently you should be able to detect when a man is talking rot, and that, in my view, is the main, if not the sole, purpose of education." – J.A Smith, Oxford University Professor, Moral Philosophy

Nigel Lawson was born in 1932 to a wealthy Jewish family living at Hampstead. His father, Ralph Lawson (1904–1982), was the owner of a commodity-trading firm in the city of London, while his mother, Joan Elisa Davis, was also from a prosperous family of stockbrokers. His paternal grandfather, Gustav Leibson, a merchant from Mitau (now Jelgava in Latvia), changed his name from Leibson to Lawson in 1925, having become a British citizen in 1911.

Members of the House of Saxe-Coburg and Gotha (a branch of the House of Wettin) did not similarly change their names after they acquired Britain.

The house of Windsor springs from the marriage of Queen Victoria to Prince Albert in 1840. He was the son of the Duke of Saxe-Coburg-Gotha in Germany and his name became that used by the British royal family.

It was founded by King George V by royal proclamation on 17 July 1917, when he changed the name of the British Royal Family from the German Saxe-Coburg and Gotha (a branch of the House of Wettin) to the English Windsor, due to the anti-German sentiment in the British Empire during World War I.

Before slavery, there was only feudal agriculture. The real magnet to Britain for Nigel Lawson's ancestors was the gigantic yields of evil: centuries of merciless, racial hatred, armed robbery, and stealing, including the stealing millions of stolen children. Britain has a huge satellite that extends to every corner of the world. His ancestral Jewish name will make him unacceptable in those parts.

If naturalisation is the reason for change of name, would they have changed their names to Native American names had they emigrated to America?

The ancestors of Tony Benn discarded their real fathers' names and abandoned their true mother's tongue (language is one of the first things to disappear in the metamorphosis or extinction of a people) as soon as they arrived in Britain from mainland Europe with neither luggage, passports nor visas.

Racist Satanic Network Dear SUE GREGORY (OBE), Officer of the Most Excellent Order of the British Empire: True Story

Yinka Bamgbelu did not change his real father's name and retained his true mother's tongue after he became a British citizen. In any case, that wouldn't have helped his case.

Omo ale ti ko gbo ede baba re.

"My only sin is in my skin." – "Black and Blue," Louis Armstrong

So, Sue Gregory (OBE) is almost certainly a direct descendant of thoroughly wretched feudal agricultural labourers from the mainland Europe. The serfs were immeasurably transformed by the gigantic yields of centuries of merciless, racist evil and naked fraud (slavery). They have reinvented themselves on stolen land and fool the foolish with plenty of foolishness.

CHAPTER 1

Dear Sue Gregory,

It is fact that Abiodun Olayinka Bamgbelu was the first Negro to practise dentistry in Bedford, and his surgery was the first ever Negro dental surgery in Bedford.

It is fact that the Negro was admitted onto the Bedford Health Authority's Dentist list on 18 December 1995, only one week before Christmas, and he took over an on-going concern from Danielle Bannister (a Caucasian), and commenced work at the practice on 8 January 1996.

Why did you implicitly instruct Richard Hill, one of your seemingly hereditary racist disciples, to tell lies under oath and state that the Negro had worked in Bedford since 1994? Prior to 1995, the Negro had only seen Bedford on maps.

Andrew Hurst was the privileged barrister that was appointed and instructed by the GDC.
Richard Hill was one of the ablest disciples of Sue Gregory.

They were all white: Homogeneity in the administration of the law is the impregnable secure mask of RACIAL HATRED.
Even Christ faced his own kind, in the Council.
The Negro was surrounded by about a dozen white faces.
If a Negro is surrounded by only white faces, in a Court Room, it is the first sign of a guilty verdict.

JUDICIAL DIVERSITY: ACCELERATING CHANGE "The near absence of women and Black, Asian and minority ethnic judges in the senior judiciary, is no longer tolerable. It undermines the democratic legitimacy of our legal system; it demonstrates a denial of fair and equal opportunities to members of underrepresented groups, and the diversity deficit weakens the quality of justice." Sir Geoffrey Bindman, QC, and Karon Monaghan, QC

DIVERSE MEDIOCRITY IS AKIN TO RAKING MUCK.

It is cruel deceit that our people became equal under white man's law after the abolition of several centuries of Europeans' GIGANTICALLY profitable commerce in millions of stolen children of other people.
"Change occurs slowly. Very often a legal change might take place, but the cultural shift required to really accept its spirit lingers in the wings for decades." Sara Sheridan.
Our visible chains are off, only Christ will remove our true chains, as no people will voluntarily relinquish centuries-old advantages acquired with extreme violence, during several centuries of the evilest terrorism the world will ever know - Habakkuk.

"I know of no evil that has ever existed, nor can imagine any evil to exist, worse than the tearing of eighty thousand persons annually from their native land, by a combination of the most civilised nations inhabiting the most enlightened part of the globe, but more especially under the sanction of the laws of that Nation which calls herself the most free and the most happy of them all." Prime Minister William Pitt the Younger

"Many Scots masters were considered among the most brutal, with life expectancy on their plantations averaging a mere four years. We worked them to death then simply imported more to keep the sugar and thus the money flowing. Unlike centuries of grief and murder, an apology cost nothing. So, what does Scotland have to say?" Herald Scotland: Ian Bell, Columnist, Sunday 28 April 2013

Only fools expected GIANT leaps overnight.

"Progress is not an illusion, it happens, but it is slow and invariably disappointing. There is always a new tyrant waiting to take over from the old - generally not quite so bad, but still a tyrant." George Orwell

The nemesis is not extinct, and the fact that it tarries isn't proof that it will never come – Habakkuk.

"To the American founding fathers, the 'truth that all men are created equal' was 'self-evident'. It'd better be, for it certainly can't be proved. True equality can only exist in heaven; on earth, the belief that all men are created equal is wishful thinking. For men are created unequal in strength, intelligence, character – well, in everything. Earthly inequality is thus a natural order of things, and it can only be distorted by unnatural means. Even then it won't disappear; it'll be replaced by a worse type of inequality or else camouflaged by demagoguery." ALEXANDER BOOT 29 December 2011, DAILY MAIL

"Of black men, the numbers are too great who are now repining under English cruelty." Dr Samuel Johnson.

✵ ✵ ✵

November 18, 2008: GDC CHAMBERS (QUASI-COURT ROOM):

MR RICHARD WILLIAM HILL, Sworn
Examined by MR HURST
THE CHAIRMAN (DR SHIV PABARY, MEMBER OF THE BRITISH EMPIRE): Thank you. Good morning, Mr
Hill.
RICHARD HILL: Good morning.
ANDREW HURST: Mr Hill, my name is Andrew Hurst. I am going to ask you some questions, first of all, on behalf of the General Dental Council.
RICHARD HILL: Right.
ANDREW HURST: This is quite a difficult room in terms of layout, so if you can try and address your answers to the Committee; I will not think you are being rude. When I have finished, Mr Morris, who sits to your left, will ask you some questions on behalf of Mr Bamgbelu. You are Richard William Hill. Is that right?

RICHARD HILL: That's correct, yes.

ANDREW HURST: Your professional address is c/o Bedfordshire Primary Care Trust, Gilbert Hitchcock House, 21 Kimbolton Road, Bedford. Is that right?

RICHARD HILL: That's correct.

ANDREW HURST: And you are a part time Dental Practice Adviser for the Bedfordshire Primary Care Trust and for Luton Primary Care Trust.

RICHARD HILL: That's correct.

ANDREW HURST: Can you tell the Committee what is a Dental Practice Adviser and what does a Dental Practice Adviser do?

RICHARD HILL: There is no strict definition of Dental Practice Adviser. A Dental Practice Adviser essentially carries out activities on behalf of the PCT to whom he or she advises. It can be obviously practice visits, inspections, that type of activity. It will be activities such as organising the emergency dental service locally; it will be advising practitioners on such matters as infection control and, as we have done so in Bedfordshire, writing documents on things like Health & Safety at work, this type of activity. Also part of my role has been, not so much today but has been involved in developing continuous professional development courses. We have organised them over the years on things like infection control, for example, the relationship within a practice between different practitioners and such other matters.

ANDREW HURST: You have mentioned that within your role is to carry out practice inspections and visits. Is that to ensure that dentists are complying with their General Dental Services Terms of Service?

RICHARD HILL: Yes. It is essentially that they comply with those Regulations.

ANDREW HURST: You are also in practice as a general dental practitioner yourself. Is that correct?

RICHARD HILL: That's correct.

ANDREW HURST: At a practice in Hertfordshire.

RICHARD HILL: Yes.

ANDREW HURST: How many days of your working week do you spend doing that?

RICHARD HILL: Usually two, occasionally two and a half.

ANDREW HURST: And obviously, therefore, you are a qualified

dentist, a Bachelor of Dental Surgery. Is that right?

RICHARD HILL: That's right.

ANDREW HURST: And I think you also have a qualification in Bachelor of Laws.

RICHARD HILL: That's correct.

ANDREW HURST: In terms of the Dental Practice Adviser, can you help the Committee with this: is it a role akin to a policeman or is it a role more akin to support?

RICHARD HILL: No, it's more to do with support. I would like to divorce it really from the Dental Reference Service. The Dental Reference Service is more of a policing activity whereas the Dental Practice Adviser acts very much as a link, a bridge, if you like, between the Primary Care Trust and the practitioners there in the field. So, consequently, it is more support. Obviously you will report back to the PCT and the managers at the PCT to inform them of what's happening up there, but when I was first appointed (and I'm going back now to 1991 when it was then the Family Health Service Authority) I was told by the then General Manager that my role was essentially pastoral.

ANDREW HURST: Thank you. Now, as you know, you have been asked to assist with your involvement with Mr Bamgbelu who originally had a practice situated at 21 Grove Place in Bedford.

RICHARD HILL: Yes.

ANDREW HURST: I think it is right to say that you first met Mr Bamgbelu in your professional capacity as a Dental Practice Adviser from around 1994 onwards. Is that right?

RICHARD HILL: That's correct.

ANDREW HURST: I see you have got your statement there.

RICHARD HILL: Yes.

ANDREW HURST: If you do need to refresh your memory from your statement, do please ask and then we can discuss it.

RICHARD HILL: Sure.

ANDREW HURST: To avoid the temptation put it to one side.

RICHARD HILL: Yes, put it on one side.

ANDREW HURST: It is very important that the Committee hear your evidence as you give it rather than as influenced by your statement. Between 1994 and 1997 you were working as a Dental Practice Adviser for Bedfordshire Health. Is that correct?

RICHARD HILL: That's correct.

ANDREW HURST: That is what it was called then anyway.

RICHARD HILL: Yes, it was called that.

ANDREW HURST: Mr Bamgbelu being a single handed practitioner. Is that right?

RICHARD HILL: Correct.

ANDREW HURST: And in that time you undertook routine practice inspections of his practice and offered him professional advice and support.

RICHARD HILL: That's correct, yes.

ANDREW HURST: Just one issue perhaps you could clarify for the Committee at this stage before we go too much further. Is there a technical difference between an inspection and a visit?

RICHARD HILL: It's difficult to say. I think there's an overlap between the two. I think you would visit a practice and you would offer advice, but I suppose you would never be failing to look and consider all the various information that comes to your attention. I would go as far as to say there's an overlap.

ANDREW HURST: An overlap. All right. Would it be fair to say – and please contradict me if this is a wrong way of looking at it – a visit is something a little less formal and more pastoral than an inspection?

RICHARD HILL: Yes, certainly so.

ANDREW HURST: Thank you. I think it is right that you visited Mr Bamgbelu's practice on 22 January 1996.

RICHARD HILL: Yes.

✳ ✳ ✳

"Freedom to report the truth is a basic right to which the court gives a high level of protection, and the author's right to his story includes the right to tell it as he wishes." Lord Toulson

I was the only Negro in the council chambers (Court Room). I was surrounded by the descendants of the carriers of my direct ancestors, the inheritors of the huge yields of several centuries of a GIGANTICALLY profitable trade: The Carrying Trade.

'Negro' has caused too much problem in my life, where shall I hide?

I did not choose Negro, it is what I got, unsolicited. If Negro is a sin or disease, equitable and transparently Just Christ must know that only His father, the maker, should suffer.

"The blame is his who chooses. God is blameless." Plato

Sue Gregory, if you condense the tortuous gibberish between the brainless England young adults you should be able to discern that Richard Hill implied that the Negro had served the NHS in Bedfordshire since 1994.

He was dishonest and he lied under oath. The buck stops with you.

Under Apartheid, only the armed European occupiers could tell lies under oath. In some other jurisdictions in our Commonwealth, members of the racist satanic network (all for one, one for all) are also allowed to tell lies under oath. They agree the verdicts in secret, and playthings out in the open as if they were live and real. They plant their "people," often closet racist thugs, in the committee (Judges) and fool the foolish with foolishness – Habakkuk 1:4.

Incompetent art incompetently imitates life.

Do you think that Richard Hill would have lied on oath with your seemingly tacit approval and support if the Negro had been a white man?

"Michael Jackson would have been found guilty if he'd been black." – Jo Brand, English Actress

Without transparent equality and exact laws for all, only our visible chains are removed. Our true chains will never be voluntarily removed. Substitution is likelier. Substitution is pretend emancipation.

"Transparent equality and exact laws for all." – President Thomas Jefferson

"Anytime you live in a society supposedly based upon law and it doesn't enforce its own laws because the colour of a man's skin happens to be wrong, then I say those people are justified to resort to any means necessary to bring about justice when the government can't give them justice." – Malcolm X

"All sections of the UK Society are institutionally racist." Sir Bernard Hogan-Howe, Knight of the Most Excellent Order of our Empire.

A former Metropolitan Police Chief had access to a lot of classified information.

The American Actress, Megan Markle: "She was the subject of explicit and obnoxious RACIAL HATRED." John Bercow

The former speaker had access to a lot of facts.

Sue Gregory and Richard Hill are shepherds of England's young adults.

"FAILING SCHOOLS AND A BATTLE FOR BRITAIN: This was the day the British education establishment's 50 year betrayal of the Nation's children lay starkly exposed in all its ignominy. After testing 166,000 people in 24 education systems, the Organisation for Economic Cooperation and Development (OECD) finds that England young adults are amongst the least literate and numerate in the industrialised world." – The Daily Mail, 09.01.2013

Shepherds of morons are likelier to be morons too.

Sheep unnaturally shepherd sheep.

Sue Gregory, are you and/or your spouse a member of the racist satanic network?

Do you know whether Richard Hill was a member of the racist satanic network? I noticed that in the council before the council, Richard Hill seemed to wink three or four times to Dr Shiv Pabary (Member of the British Empire), who winked back at him, but only after he had lied under oath, which was a lot of times.

Mr Lagbaja or somebody else said that the White Hall is awash with members of the racist satanic network (all for one, one for all) – is it true?

There was no White Hall before slavery, and there mightn't have been

White Hall had there not been slavery.

"Iain Whyte, author of Scotland and the Abolition of Slavery, insists we have at times ignored our guilty past. He said: 'For many years Scotland's historians harboured the illusion that our nation had little to do with the slave trade or plantation slavery. We swept it under the carpet. This was remarkable in the light of Glasgow's wealth coming from tobacco, sugar and cotton, and Jamaica Streets being found in a number of Scottish towns and cities. It is healthy we are now recognising Scotland was very much involved.' The industries, which saw Glasgow and much of the country flourish, were built on the back of slavery. There were familiar names such as Scot Lyle of Tate and Lyle fame whose fortune was built on slavery. Ewing from Glasgow was the richest sugar producer in Jamaica. The stunning Inveresk Lodge in Edinburgh, now open to the public, was bought by James Wedderburn with money earned from 27 years in Jamaica as a notorious slaver. The Wee Free Church was founded using profits and donations from the slave trade. Even our schools have a dark history. Bathgate Academy was built from money willed by John Newland, a renowned slave master and Dollar Academy has a similar foundation. For many years, the goods and profits from West Indian slavery were unloaded at Kingston docks in Glasgow. Leith in Edinburgh and Glasgow were popular ports from which ambitious Scottish men sailed to make their fortunes as slave masters." – Herald Scotland

The satanic network is everywhere. It controls almost everything except intellect. Without objective basis, it awards itself monopoly of knowledge.

The proceeds of centuries of merciless, racial hatred and fraud kick-started the industrial revolution in Europe and brought European slave merchants and traders - great wealth.

The proceeds of merciless, racial hatred and fraud were used to build cathedrals, churches, courts, castles, and councils. Before slavery, there was only agriculture.

"Agriculture not only gives riches to a nation, but the only riches she can call her own." – Dr Samuel Johnson

Feudal agricultural labourers from mainland Europe dispossessed/robbed aboriginal Britons. They've been transformed and reinvented by slavery.

Only two weeks after the Negro started work in Bedford, on 22 January 1996, Dr Richard Hill visited the surgery that the Negro took over from Danielle Bannister – a tall and elegant but not so sensuous white woman. Essentially, he recommended that the Negro should replace the smaller Kavoklave autoclave that the Negro inherited from his predecessor at the practice (less than a month earlier). The Negro acceded to his request immediately. The Kavoklave was not an issue when their kindred ran the practice that she set up and worked, using the Kavoklave, for several years. Apartheid by stealth!

In order for Evlynne Gilvarry's predecessor at the GDC to corroborate the 2007 allegations by her own kindred, the ugly, seemingly Gallic, flat, fat ass, fat cat linked up with Bedford's "racist mafia" – probably Sue Gregory and the seemingly hereditary racist thugs – and went back to 1996 (almost twelve years) to exhume forgeries, one of which was used to create the following, amongst others, seemingly with the full knowledge and tacit approval of Sue Gregory:

"On 22 January 1996 an Authority Practice Inspection was conducted by then Bedfordshire Health Surgery and a number of deficiencies were identified and notified to you, including the need for an autoclave for sterilisation as opposed to the Kavoclave that was in sole use" (GDC charge 7, 2008).

The GDC charged and found the first ever and only Negro dentist in Bedford guilty of using a Kavoklave instead of autoclave in 1996 in 2008/2009.

The Mediocre GDC (MGDC) of Mediocre Great England (MGE) did not know that a Kavoklave is an autoclave.

The crooked and racist council of England young adults and former England young adults used other people's millions to engage in a war of disinformation with a single Negro, and fool the foolish with foolishness. Oyinbo Olodo! Oyinbo ode!

Part of the reason why England's young adults are amongst the dullest in the industrialised world is because Sue Gregory and Evlynne Gilvarry are their shepherds.

"FAILING SCHOOLS AND A BATTLE FOR BRITAIN: This was the day the British education establishment's 50 year betrayal of the

Nation's children lay starkly exposed in all its ignominy. After testing 166,000 people in 24 education systems, the Organisation for Economic Cooperation and Development (OECD) finds that England young adults are amongst the least literate and numerate in the industrialised world." – The Daily Mail, 09.01.2013

Shepherds of morons, such as Sue Gregory, Helen Falcon, and the seemingly Gallic cougar Evlynne Galvarry, are likelier to be morons too.

Intellectually impotent, deluded and racist, satanic network, descendants of stealer and sellers of human beings - lies that it doesn't lie.

To read more about racist cougars, see Helen Falcon: Community Dentist, Racist Empress of Privileged Dullards, by Abiodun Olayinka Bamgbelu, published in Texas by SBPRA

CHAPTER 2

"Mama, look, a Negro....... Where shall I hide?" Dr Frantz Fanon.

"The one great principle of the English law is, to make business for itself. There is no other principle distinctly, certainly, and consistently maintained through all its narrow turnings. Viewed by this light it becomes a coherent scheme, and not the monstrous maze the laity are apt to think it. Let them but once clearly perceive that its grand principle is to make business for itself at their expense, and surely they will cease to grumble." Charles Dicken

The colour bar was crude and cruel. The reasoning bar is spineless cowardice.

"Our Government is valuable because it is free. What, I beg gentlemen to ask themselves, are the fundamental parts of a free government? I know there are differences of opinion upon this subject, but my own opinion is that freedom does not depend upon the executive government, or upon the administration of justice, or upon any one particular or distinct part, or even upon forms so much as it does on general freedom of speech and writing. What I mean is this: that any man may write and print what he pleases, although he is liable to be punished if he abuses that freedom; this I call perfect freedom in the first instance. I say, it is not the written law of the constitution of England; it is not the law that is to be found in books, that has constituted the true principle of freedom of any country, at any time. No! It is the energy, the boldness of a man's mind, which prompts him to speak, not in private, but in large and popular assemblies, that constitutes, that creates, in a state, the spirit of freedom. This is the principle which gives life to liberty; without, the human character is a stranger to freedom. If you suffer the liberty of speech to be wrested from you; you will then have lost the freedom, the energy, and the boldness of the British character." – The Right Honourable Charles James Fox, English politician

There is reasoning higher than that of privileged dullards who might have been lied to at home and at school that the brain is in the skin.

The Romans and the Jews did not believe Christ, our own God, because they did not understand the notion of infinite reasoning power and believed that anything that they did not understand was wrong and expresses ignorance or lunacy.

He was jailed only because he spoke. The lunatic Jew removed the head of John because he refused to stop speaking. John who baptised the Messiah was not punished for speaking, he was permanently prevented from speaking.

He was lynched like Gadhafi and only because He was invited to disclose pictures His unbounded mind (infinite) painted. He was not asked to expatiate. He was not punished for speaking, he was prevented from disclosing the truth.

The stone that the builders rejected is now the cornerstone – Psalm 118:22; Luke 20:17.

If the land is natural resources poor and the people are rich, the wealth is likelier to be the yield of very high intellect or it must have been stolen.

Andrew Hurst seemed to desire to give the impression of higher intellect based almost entirely upon the skin colour that he neither made nor chose, the fact that he is an England class barrister (some barristers go on to be judges) and was born in a very rich country that is natural resources poor.

One should look at the facts and display the shallow reasoning of the former England young adult and shepherd of England young adults.

At the GDC hearing of 21 November 2008, the mediocre, Negrophobic, and corrupt council within one of the least literate countries in Western Europe, seemingly aided by Sue Gregory, exhumed mummified forgeries from twelve years prior (1996) in pursuance of using them to corroborate an allegation by Rachael Bishop, an England class senior NHS nurse and verifiably dishonest racist thug that seemed consumed by jealousy. The Negro was the first ever and only Negro dentist in Wellingborough, Northamptonshire.

There is no evidence, certainly nonconclusive, that Rachael Bishop was a member of the Northants Patriots, a "battalion" of the BNP (the equivalent of the KKK in the USA), but there is evidence that the racist group was very active and visible in Northamptonshire. In 2020, Northamptonshire yields only food. In 1720, the people of Northamptonshire were fed like battery hens with the gigantic proceeds of merciless, racist evil, which European trade in millions of stolen Africans was.

Seemingly in pursuance of creating deceit, shepherds did not bring stolen Africans home and thereby deceived moron sheep that it was paragon of wisdom who, like Mother Teresa, did virtuous work abroad. Moron sheep believed that shepherds were exceedingly clever benefactors who fed them with the yields of virtue. Sheep saw huge wealth that shepherds brought from abroad. They did not know that the shepherds were merciless, evil, racist murderers, armed robbers, and thieves: people stealers, carriers, sellers, and exploiters.

Till today, the sheep believe that the shepherds are paragons of wisdom who feed them with the yields of virtue.

Everything was spun; everything is being spun. The creators must spin their creations, or else.

"We have the power to turn against our creators." Dr Richard Dawkins.

"Time for Scots to say sorry for slavery.
Herald Scotland:
Ian Bell, Columnist / Sunday 28 April 2013 / Opinion
Sunday 28 April 2013
According to the American founding father, the son of a Caithness Kirk minister had about him of "an air of great simplicity and honesty'". The likes of James Boswell and Laurence Sterne also enjoyed the merchant's company.

To his contemporaries, he was, as the author Adam Hochschild has written, "'a wise, thoughtful man who embodied the Scottish virtues of frugality, sobriety, and hard work'". Oswald was a scholar of theology, philosophy, and history. He collected art, particularly Rubens and Rembrandt, and gave handsomely to charity. Oswald, who learned his trade in Glasgow, also represented Britain in negotiations with the Americans after their war of liberation. He was the cosmopolitan epitome of Enlightenment success. But when he wasn't busy with good works, Oswald waded in blood. The precise number of deaths that can be laid at his door is impossible to calculate. As the leading figure in Grant, Oswald & Co, he had investments in each corner of the '"triangular trade"'. In his own name, Oswald trafficked at least 13,000 Africans, although he never set foot on their continent. By the time he bought Auchincruive House and 100,000 acres in Ayrshire in 1764, he was worth £500,000. Writing in 2005, Hochschild thought this was '"'roughly equivalent"'" to $68 million (about £44m). This is conservative.

Oswald was remarkable, but not unique. Where Glasgow and its merchants in sugar, tobacco, and human life are concerned, there are plenty of names and no shortage of monuments: Dennistoun, Campbell, Glassford, Cochrane, Buchanan, Hamilton, Bogle, Ewing, Donald, Speirs, Dunlop. One way to understand what they wrought is simple: take pleasure in the city"s architecture today and you are likely to be admiring the fruits of slavery.

Glasgow is not alone in that. London, Liverpool and Bristol also have their stories to tell. Edinburgh's once-great banks grew from foundations built on bones. The first Scottish venture into slavery set out from the capital in 1695. Montrose, Dumfries, Greenock and Port Glasgow each tried their hands. In the language of the present age, they were all in it together.

When commerce was coursing around the triangle, most of polite Scotland was implicated. The nobility (and country) rendered bankrupt in 1700 in the aftermath of the Darien Venture was by the mid-1760s contemplating big elegant townhouses and 100,000-acre estates. You could call that a reversal of fortune. Contrary to self-serving myth, it did not happen because of '"frugality, sobriety, and hard work".

Certain things need to be remembered about Scotland and slavery. One is that the mercantile class got stinking rich twice over: despite fortunes made from stolen lives, they were quick to demand compensation when slavery was ended in 1833. Britain's government decided that

£20m, a staggering sum, could be raised. In his 2010 book, The Price of Emancipation, Nicholas Draper reckons Glasgow's mob got £400,000 – in modern terms, hundreds of millions.

Compensation cases also demonstrated that Scots were not merely following an English lead. According to Draper, a country with 10% of the British population accounted for at least 15% of absentee slavers. By another estimate, 30% of Jamaican plantations were run by Scots. For all the pride taken in the abolitionist societies of Glasgow and Edinburgh, the slave-holders did not suffer because of abolition. They were '"compensated"'.

And that wasn't the worst of it. Thanks to Hollywood movies, the slave economy of the American South is still taken as barbarism's benchmark. Few realise that the behaviour of Scots busy getting rich in the slave-holders" empire was actually worse – routinely worse – than the worst of the cottonocracy. You need only count the corpses................."

"American South is still taken as barbarism's benchmark. Few realise that the behaviour of Scots busy getting rich in the slave-holders' empire was actually worse – routinely worse – than the worst of the cottonocracy. You need only count the corpses.

"By the time slavery was brought to an end in America, the country's 400,000 trafficked people had grown to a population of four million. In the British West Indies, only 670,000 survived from two million imported souls. In the American South, slaves were valuable and bred. We worked them to death then simply imported more to keep the sugar and thus the money flowing. Unlike centuries of grief and murder, an apology cost nothing. So, what does Scotland have to say?" – Herald Scotland, Ian Bell, columnist, Sunday 28 April 2013

"It was our arms in the river of Cameroon, put into the hands of the trader, that furnished him with the means of pushing his trade; and I have no more doubt that they are British arms, put into the hands of Africans, which promote universal war and desolation that I can doubt their having done so in that individual instance. I have shown how great is the enormity of this evil, even on the supposition that we take only convicts and prisoners of war. But take the subject in another way, and how does it stand? Think of 80,000 persons carried out of their native country by we know not what means! For crimes imputed! For light or inconsiderable faults! For debts perhaps! For crime of witchcraft! Or a thousand other weak or scandalous pretexts! Reflect on 80,000 persons annually taken off! There is something in the horror of it that surpasses all bounds of imagination." – Prime Minister William Pitt the Younger, 1792

"The grand object of all European traders in kidnapped and stolen Africans was - money, money, money; money was their god! In Africa, the poor wretched natives, blessed with the most fertile and luxuriant soil, are rendered so much the more miserable by the Christians' (European traders in stolen Africans) abominable traffic for slaves and the horrid cruelty and treachery of the petty [African] Kings. The Africans kings were encouraged by their European (Christian) customers who carry them strong liquors to enflame their madness and powder and bad firearms to furnish them with the hellish means of killing and kidnapping. But enough - it is a subject that sours my blood." – Ignatius Sancho, 1778

"I know of no evil that has ever existed, nor can imagine any evil to exist, worse than the tearing of eighty thousand persons annually from their native land, by a combination of the most civilised nations inhabiting the most enlightened part of the globe, but more especially under the sanction of the laws of that Nation which calls herself the most free and the most happy of them all." – Prime Minister William Pitt the Younger, 1792 Before slavery, what?

"Agriculture not only gives riches to a nation, but the only riches she can call her own." – Dr Samuel Johnson

"Truth is the prime attribute of the Deity." – Lord Byron

In the council chambers on 21 November 2008, before the sincerely perceived racist council, the Negro told the council and the former

England young adults that he had not seen or heard of nearly all of the 1996 allegations before the GDC case against him. The mediocre, corrupt, and racist council seemed too dull to discern the absurdity of the exhumed, mummified NHS forgeries from 1996, and the fact that in 2008 they had to go back to 1996.

Why only 1996?

"I had not seen all these before this case, yes." – Negro

The England class racist barrister, Andrew Hurst, did not believe the Negro. He thought he was smart, not knowing that those that he and his kind regularly spin are amongst the dullest adult population in the industrialised world.

"Well, you have, Mr Bamgbelu, because it was part of Mr Hill's statement served on you," said Andrew Hurst.

"No, no, no. I said I had not seen all these before this case," replied the Negro.

Andrew Hurst was wrong, and he immortalised stupidity for eternity.

"There is no sin except stupidity." – Oscar Wilde

"Ignorance, the root and stem of all evil." – Plato

Andrew Hurst talked nonsense with civilised decorum and an imitation upper-class accent. He allowed prior predilection, stereotype, and prejudice to becloud his objective reasoning and judgement.

If you measure me by the dark coat that I neither made nor chose, and cannot change, you are shallow.

"The supreme vice is shallowness." Wilde

If you believe that you are better than me because your father is richer than mine, you are vulgar.

Andrew Hurst, the England class barrister (some barristers go on to become judges), former England young adult and shepherd of England young adults, did not realise that he agreed with the Negro when he stated, "Well, you have, Mr Bamgbelu, because it was part of Mr Hill's statement served on you," as his statement seamlessly corroborated the Negro's when he stated,

"No, no, no. I said I had not seen all these before this case." These are the facts which a seemingly modular bar course, within one of the least literate countries in the industrialised world, prevented Andrew Hurst from discerning.

The allegations against the first ever and only Negro dentist in Bedford and Wellingborough were disclosed to him on 21 October 2008. On 21 November 2008, in the sincerely perceived racist council and before a sincerely perceived racist council, the Negro stated that he had not seen or heard of nearly all the allegations from twelve years prior before the GDC case. The imbecile "barristo," a moron "white boy," danced in muck. Had it been an examination where his skin colour and imitation upper class English accent would not count, he would have failed and failed woefully. Just by the by, the upper-class English accent seems to be one of the most efficient accents for talking rot.

"I am very fond of my pigs; it doesn't stop me from eating them." Archbishop Runcie of Canterbury Cathedral, England.

If one bred pigs for bacon, the stupidest of the pigs should be the first to be butchered and eaten.

"Nothing that you will learn in the course of your studies will be of the slightest possible use to you in after life – save only this – if you work hard and diligently you should be able to detect when a man is talking rot, and that, in my view, is the main, if not the sole, purpose of education." – J.A Smith, Oxford University Professor, Moral Philosophy

"The lawyers have twisted it into such a state of bedevilment that the original merits of the case have long disappeared from the face of the earth. It's about a Will, and the trusts under a Will – or it was, once. It is about nothing but Costs, now. We are always appearing, and disappearing, and swearing, and interrogating, and filing, and cross – filing, and arguing, and scaling, and motioning, and referring, and reporting, and revolving about the Lord Chancellor and all his satellites, and equitably waltzing ourselves off to dusty death, about Costs. That's the great question. All the rest, by some extraordinary means, has smelt away." – Charles Dickens

Before slavery, the areas all around Wimpole Street, London, and beyond were farmlands that were worked by wretched, feudal agricultural labourers from mainland Europe, working for lords, also from mainland Europe, all on stolen aborigine land. So, there was no council on Wimpole Street before slavery, and there wouldn't have been a council on Wimpole Street had there not been slavery.

"All have taken what had other owners, and all have had recourse to arms rather than quit the prey on which they were fastened." Dr Samuel Johnson

Almost everything was stolen, or is the yield of fraud, except agriculture. Everything else is a lie.

"Agriculture not only gives riches to a nation, but the only riches she can call her own." – Dr Samuel Johnson
Sir Winston Churchill, in corroboration of Oscar Wilde and George Bernard Shaw, implied that the average Briton was a moron.
"The best argument against democracy is a five-minute conversation with the average voter." – Sir Winston Churchill
"A typical English man, usually violent, always dull." – Oscar Wilde
"Pardon him, Theodotus: He is a barbarian, and thinks the customs of his tribe and highland are the laws of nature." George Bernard Shaw.
The proceeds of centuries of merciless, racial hatred and fraud kick-started the industrial revolution in Europe and brought European slave merchants and traders great wealth.
Apart from the yield of agriculture, almost everything was directly or indirectly stolen. What else before slavery?

"Sometimes people don't want to hear the truth because they don't want their illusions destroyed." – Friedrich Nietzsche

"Those who have robbed have also lied." – Dr Samuel Johnson corroborating prophet Habakkuk Before slavery, what?

Since He merely spoke and the universe became, the Negro was the first ever member of his race to set up a practice and practise dentistry in

Bedford.

Sue Gregory, a dmf, was the "Field Marshall" of NHS dentistry in Bedford. She seemed very well connected, and seemingly the "cardinal" of crookedness and racial hatred in the politics of dentistry in the UK.

Sue Gregory and Bedfordshire NHS are sections of the UK society.

"All sections of UK society are institutionally racist." – Sir Bernard Hogan-Howe, London Metropolitan Police

"Experience hath shewn, that even under the best forms of government those entrusted with power have, in time, and by slow operations, perverted it into tyranny." – President Thomas Jefferson
"Fight like hell." President Trump

"Gie a Scotsman an inch, and he'll take an 'ell." Scottish saying.

His mother (Trump) was a genetic Scottish wench who stowaway to America without luggage, passport, visa or decent shoes.

In 1720, the land of Bedford, yielded only food. Then, the people of Bedfordshire, almost entirely agricultural labourers from mainland Europe (and indeed everywhere else), were fed like battery hens with the proceeds of merciless, sadistic racial hatred and naked fraud (slavery): the stealing, carrying, and selling of millions of unarmed and defenceless stolen human beings, and millions were worked to death at gun point on cane and cotton plantations of the stolen New World of the West Indies and Americas, not for a little while, but for several continuous centuries of merciless, sadistic, tyrannical cowardice.

As the shepherds did not bring stolen Africans home, the sheep were implicitly deceived that their shepherds were paragons of wisdom who fed them with the yields of virtue. They lied and deceived moron sheep, as they were merciless, racist thugs, armed robbers, and thieves who took possession whenever they mercilessly slaughtered, and dispossessed wherever they robbed.

There were laws then, as there are laws now, but the judiciary of the era was neck deep in fraud, as they were also fed like battery hens with the yields of merciless racial hatred and naked fraud.

"Those who have robbed have also lied." – Dr Samuel Johnson corroborating prophet Habakkuk

Deluded privileged dullards deceive their children and the children of others, who are amongst the dullest young adult populations in the industrialised world, by associating the gigantic yields of several continuous centuries of merciless, sadistic, racial hatred and fraud (slavery) with their personal intellect and industry.

A motley assembly of wretched feudal agricultural labourers (serfs) from all over mainland Europe were transformed by the gigantic yields of several centuries of merciless slavery. They have reinvented themselves, and now fool the foolish.

It is fact and absolute truth that Sir Winston Churchill implied that the average adult Briton was a moron. More than sixty years later, the Organisation for Economic Cooperation and Development seamlessly corroborated the very proximate observations of the great man.

"The best argument against democracy is a five-minute conversation with the average voter." – Sir Winston Churchill

"FAILING SCHOOLS AND A BATTLE FOR BRITAIN: This was the day the British education establishment's 50-year betrayal of the Nation's children lay starkly exposed in all its ignominy. After testing 166,000 people in 24 education systems, the Organisation for Economic Cooperation and Development (OECD) find's that England young adults are amongst the least literate and numerate in the industrialised world." – The Daily Mail, 09.01.2013

Facts are sacred; they can't be overstated.

Shepherds of morons are likelier to be morons too.

Racial hatred is considerably more common that realised. Where this Negro is concerned, he sincerely believes that there is jealousy, but considerably more fear, as it is confirmed that the brain is not in the skin and will concomitantly confirm that some of the millions of Africans that Sue Gregory's racist, murderous, sadistic, savage, armed robber, and thieving ancestors mercilessly worked to death at gun point and/or viciously slaughtered on stolen land of the West Indies and Americas were not all created intellectually inferior.

"Iain Whyte, author of Scotland and the Abolition of Slavery, insists we have at times ignored our guilty past. He said: 'For many years Scotland's historians harboured the illusion that our nation had little to do with the slave trade or plantation slavery.

"'We swept it under the carpet. This was remarkable in the light of Glasgow's wealth coming from tobacco, sugar and cotton, and Jamaica Streets being found in a number of Scottish towns and cities.

"'It is healthy we are now recognising Scotland was very much involved.'

"The industries, which saw Glasgow and much of the country flourish, were built on the back of slavery.

"There were familiar names such as Scot Lyle of Tate and Lyle fame whose fortune was built on slavery. Ewing from Glasgow was the richest sugar producer in Jamaica.

"The stunning Inveresk Lodge in Edinburgh, now open to the public, was bought by James Wedderburn with money earned from 27 years in Jamaica as a notorious slaver.

"The Wee Free Church was founded using profits and donations from the slave trade. Even our schools have a dark history. Bathgate Academy was built from money willed by John Newland, a renowned slave master and Dollar Academy has a similar foundation.

"For many years, the goods and profits from West Indian slavery were unloaded at Kingston docks in Glasgow.

"Leith in Edinburgh and Glasgow were popular ports from which ambitious Scottish men sailed to make their fortunes as slave masters.

"There was a feeling in Scotland that something was wrong, which is not to say we didn't let it go on for 300 years.

"But there was a deep-rooted fear in Britain that the wheels of commerce would grind to a halt without slavery.

"It was only when economists like the Scot Adam Smith suggested slavery hampered freedom of enterprise that the argument took hold that it was no longer financially viable." – Herald Scotland, Ian Bell, columnist, Sunday 28 April 2013

Shepherd deceived sheep that he was a paragon of wisdom who fed sheep with the yield of virtue. Shepherd did not bring stolen Africans home

The land of Bedford yielded only food. The land of Bedford yields only food. Almost everything else was stolen.

"Agriculture not only gives riches to a nation, but the only riches she can call her own." – Dr Samuel Johnson Before slavery, what?

Richard Hill visited the surgery of the first ever and only Negro dentist in Bedford – since he merely spoke, and the world became – in January 1996. He made some recommendations which concerned facts that predated the Negro's takeover of the surgery. The Negro fully acceded to his recommendations.

The seemingly hereditary racist thug came again in April, July, and November 1996, and in April 1997. His reports were all good.

Out of the blue the MGDC (or Mediocre GDC) of MGE (Mediocre Great England) charged the Negro with the content of a report of 02.04.2003, which Richard Hill allegedly produced following a visit to the surgery of the first ever Negro dentist in Bedford – since he merely spoke, and the world became.

In response to a Freedom of Information request, the NHS stated that it visited the surgery of the first ever and only Negro dentist in Bedford, but implied that the report was missing or lost, and further stated that it carried out two visits to the surgery of the Negro the following year, on 22 July 2004, and implicitly conducted a follow up visit on an unknown date.

In 2008, the NHS sent the Negro copies of the visit reports.

"Record of Practice Visits-Bedford PCT. Dear John, Please find attached the record of practice visits that you were chasing up. Sorry for the delay! As you can see, the great majority of practices are not a cause for concern. However, we will need to focus particularly on the Bamgbelu and the alpha practices. Perhaps also beta practice in delta and the gamma practice are worthy of closer attention. Regards, Richard." – NHS email of 6 September 2006

"RECORD OF PRACTICE VISITS: BEDFORD PCT. DENTIST: Mr O Bamgbelu. ADDRESS: Grey Friars Dental Practice 52 Bromham

Road Bedford MK40 2QG. Telephone No: 01234300505. Visit Date: JULY 2004. CONCERNS: No risk assessment, no CoSSH, A Kavoclave type autoclave was present in the surgery. This type of autoclave should not be used as the cycle can be broken into before sterilisation is complete. No other member of staff were present at the visit so could not be questioned as regards the methods of cross infection control used by practice." – NHS visit report of 22 July 2004

"OUTSTANDING ISSUES: Even though the necessary documents have now been seen. I continue to have concerns as to the cross infection control procedures in the practice." – NHS visit report of undisclosed date

The NHS reports that were attached to the first ever and only Negro dentist in Bedford for more than four years were incompetent racist forgeries by moron England young adults and/or former England young adults.

He who His with us is greater than He who is in the world – John 4:4, not through righteousness, but only through non-negotiable and His unsolicited kindness.

If you do not fear He who merely spoke, and the world became, and can speak again, and it will perish, it is proof that you do not know Him.

The reports were withdrawn in their entirety on 16 October 2008, more than four years after the alleged first visit of 22 July 2004.

CASE NO: 69238

IN THE MATTER OF THE GENERAL DENTAL COUNCIL AND ABIODUN BAMGBELU

SUPPLEMENTAL WITNESS STATEMENT OF RICHARD HILL

I, RICHARD HILL, c/o Bedfordshire Primary Care Trust, Gilbert Hitchcock House, 21 Kimbolton Road, Bedford, MK40 2AW WILL SAY AS FOLLOWS:

1. I make this statement supplemental to my statement dated 23.09.2008.

2. I attach as Exhibit SRWH1 a copy of my report dated 22.07.2004, I attach a synopsis of practice visits that makes reference to a practice visit to MR BAMGBELU's practice at 52, Bromham Road, Bedford, MK40 2QG in July 2004. The document is incorrect in recording that

the inspection took place in 2004. No such inspection in fact took place.

3. In 2006 the Healthcare Commission carried out a visit to Bedfordshire PCT and I was asked to provide all my practice visit reports. While collating this information, I noticed that some inspection reports were missing, which included an inspection of Mr Bamgbelu's practice on 02.04.2003. Around that time my department moved and it is possible that some reports had been lost during the move. I did locate some of my draft handwritten notes and referred to these to prepare my inspection report dated 22.07.2004 for MR BAMGBELU's practice which at the time, I understood to be a correct and accurate record of my inspection. Following another move to different premises, I went through some of my files and found my correct inspection report dated which is exhibited to my September 2008 statement as RWH11.

4. The contents of the 22.07.2004 and 02.04.2003 report differ. The reason that the contents differ is because the hand written notes I used to prepare the 22.07.2004 also had a reference to a difference and dates and notes were mixed up. Having reviewed the documents, it became clear to me that the July 2004 was created in error. The contents of the 02.04.2003 report is an accurate reflection of the inspection done at the time and I stand by the contents of the same.

5. I did not undertake any further inspections at Mr Bamgbelu's practice between 2003 and 2007.

6. The content of the synopsis of the practice was correct at the time, but the reason why it does not make reference to the 02.04.2003 inspection is because that report was not found at the time of creating the synopsis of practice visits and reference to the 22.07.2004 visit was inserted.

7. When I undertake practice visits, I take rough notes and write up the report at a later date, usually a couple of days afterwards in order to keep the report as contemporaneous as possible.

8. I attach as Exhibit SRWH2 an anonymised list of consolidation practice visits confirming that Mr Bamgbelu's practice was visited on 02.04.2003. This list has been signed by J BRADBURY, Primary Care contract Manager at Bedfordshire PCT dated 23.09.2008 confirming that an inspection did take place on 02.04.2003.

I confirm that the facts stated in this witness statement consisting of 2 pages are true to the best of my knowledge information and belief.

Signed ....

Dated ....

74222882_1.doc/3 Oct 2008.

The withdrawal statement, which remains live and valid, is based upon falsified information by the NHS.

Sue Gregory, you should admit that it would be reasonable to suggest that you were stupid, as you implicitly endorsed stupidity, and for eternity.

"There is no sin except stupidity." – Oscar Wilde

Sue Gregory, you seemed a power drunk, racist thug that was propped by crude oil and gas money in the same way as your merciless, racist thug armed robber and thieving ancestors were for centuries sustained by the proceeds of stealing and selling millions of kidnapped and stolen human beings.

Before slavery, what?

"Many Scots masters were considered among the most brutal, with life expectancy on their plantations averaging a mere four years. We worked them to death then simply imported more to keep the sugar and thus the money flowing. Unlike centuries of grief and murder, an apology costs nothing. So what does Scotland have to say?" – Herald Scotland, Ian Bell, columnist, Sunday 28 April 2013

There were laws then as there are laws now, but the judiciary of that era was complicit in merciless, racial hatred and fraud, as it was sustained by it.

"I know of no evil that has ever existed, nor can imagine any evil to exist, worse than the tearing of eighty thousand persons annually from their native land, by a combination of the most civilised nations inhabiting the most enlightened part of the globe, but more especially under the sanction of the laws of that Nation which calls herself the most free and the most happy of them all." – Prime Minister William Pitt the Younger

Facts are sacred; they can't be overstated.

"Those who have robbed have also lied." – Dr Samuel Johnson corroborating prophet Habakkuk

Brainless privileged dullards and members of the satanic network, without objective basis, delude themselves that they have the monopoly of knowledge. The bartenders wear charity as a cloak of deceit and swear by the name of Almighty God never to tell lies, but they lie that they don't lie (Songs of David 144).

Sue Gregory, I must sincerely confess to you that I cursed you as follows: "May the French ulcer love you and may the Lord hate you" (a paraphrased Arabian curse).

"On 2 April 2003 Bedford PCT undertook a routine practice inspection of the Bedford Practice that identified concerns." – GDC charge against the Negro of November 2008

The committee that the mediocre, corrupt, and racist GDC seemingly planted found the lone Negro in their midst guilty of the glaringly brainless construction.

The NHS disclosed the report of the alleged visit of 2 April 2003 to the GDC sometime after September 2008. The GDC used it to charge the Negro, and the report was disclosed to the first ever and only Negro dentist in Bedford on 21.10.2008 – after the GDC had charged him with the content, and five years after the alleged visit.

Sue Gregory and the GDC seemed too dull and allowed racial hatred and Negrophobia to becloud their objective reasoning and judgement. They seemed so stupid; they could not detect the absurdity in the brainless charge, as a concern that was disclosed almost six years after the identification of the concern cannot be a concern.

I sincerely called Evlynne Gilvarry, the seemingly Gallic, ugly cougar with the muscular looking ass – like that of Christine Ohuruogu, albeit from a distance – and Sue Gregory, silly and dull, flat, big, muscular ass fat cats.

Richard Hill stated under oath that there was no problem in 2003 or at any other time, to his knowledge, and I fully acceded to his recommendation after his first visit to the surgery of the first ever and only Negro dentist in Bedford, in 1996 and 1997.

"Had there been any problem, I would be asked by the PCT to visit the practice and carry out a formal inspection in that situation. That's normally along with a colleague, so it's a proper and formal procedure. But I have no record of being told that there were any concerns." – Richard Hill, under oath, on 18 November 2008

Irrespective all the available facts, the mediocre, dishonest, and racist council instructed its counsel – Andrew Hurst – to unrelentingly lie under oath. The council seemed to have planted some members of the racist, satanic network in the council committee to guide and guard the blatant dishonesty of Andrew Hurst.

The first ever and only Negro dentist in Bedford practised dentistry in Bedford from Grove Place, Bedford from 8 January 1996 till the end of December 2002. He moved his practice to Bromham Road in December 2002 and started work there in January 2003. In 2003, the first ever and only Negro dentist in Bedford informed the NHS about his move of premises through Richard Hill. Richard Hill visited the Negro at his new premises only once in 2003. The Negro could not recall the exact date of the visit. Richard Hill looked round the surgery, but he did not write anything down, and he did not produce a report. He did not write to the Negro after the visit and the Negro was not provided with a report directly or indirectly or in any way whatsoever.

Under cross examination, the Negro informed the GDC committee that Richard Hill visited his surgery in 2003. Irrespective of this fact, the mediocre and racist council instructed Andrew Hurst to state that the first ever and only Negro dentist in Bedford stated that Richard Hill did not visit his practice in 2003, and implied that the Negro lied. A descendant of merciless, racist thugs, armed robbers, thieves, and human being stealers and sellers, they wrongly accused another solely because of skin colour that he neither chose nor made and could not change – slimy hypocrisy. I sincerely called Andrew Hurst a merciless, racist bas****, but did so only in my mind.

The Negro appeared before the council in the council chambers and was cross examined by David Morris, the counsel that was appointed and instructed by the Medical Protection Society (MPS), who was also the employer of Stephanie Twidale, the chief witness for the prosecution in their racist, incestuous, Negrophobic charade—incompetent art incompetently imitated life.
****

Council chambers, 20 November 2008 (Court Room):

DAVID MORRIS: Now going then, please, to behind tab 20, we have a report of the visit which Mr. Hill said he conducted on the 2 April 2003?

THE NEGRO: Yes.

DAVID MORRIS: Did he conduct a visit on that day?

THE NEGRO: No, I am absolutely sure actually that that did not happen. And I know that when he gave his evidence here yesterday he said he came to see me on the evening of that day. On the evening of that day I was not in Bedford. By that time I had two practices, one at Bedford and one in Wellingborough, and I have evidence which would show that on that day I worked at my Northampton practice, which was in Wellingborough, from about 3 to 6.30, something like that. But I worked from the Bedford surgery from 9 until about 1. So I worked in the morning at Bedford, and he would normally come to see me in the evening, and he said he came to see me in the evening.

DAVID MORRIS: Dealing with the substance of what he said in there, page 3, no disabled access he noted, but you (the practitioner) had some ancillary equipment for home visits, if necessary?

THE NEGRO: Yes, and the PCT then, yes, I remember the PCT, and there was more money then for access to the dental services, and they gave me £5000 just to buy that equipment mobile dental unit, a dental unit that I can take out, and only use to do a small filling and things like that.

DAVID MORRIS: I think by this time, 2003, you moved, hadn't you, from Grove Place to Bromham Road.

THE NEGRO: Yes.

DAVID MORRIS: He mentions that you had a Kavoclave back up, is that accurate?

THE NEGRO: No. By the time I was there in 2003, I didn't have a Kavoclave. I threw the Kavoclave away in 1996, but in 2003 I had about two SCS 2000 type. Yes, I had two SCS 2000 type. By that time they had bought me other one.

DAVID MORRIS: On page 4 he noted that the risk assessment was not seen, nor was controlled substance to help risk assessment. Would that be right as a matter of fact?

THE NEGRO: I did not have – that's quite right, actually, I did not have those there. Risk assessment is something . . . the thing that you say that your stairs are this way; you just make sure the practice is very safe. And it was a new thing then, all this stuff; and COSs as well. All these things were new and I didn't have them there then; but this inspection did not happen.

CHAIRMAN (DR SHIV PABARY, MEMBER OF THE BRITISH

EMPIRE): To clarify what we are talking about, you say no visit took place on that day, but there are bits of that form that you agree with?
THE NEGRO: Yes, I agree with.

CHAIRMAN (DR SHIV PABARY): Are you saying that there was a visit, but later on, or there was no visit at all?
THE NEGRO: No, there was no visit at all on that day.
DAVID MORRIS: No visit on that day, but I think you told us that from time to time he would come and visit your surgery?
THE NEGRO: Yes, there was no visit on that day, but he would have come to my surgery. I can recall that when I moved, yes, he came to me, yes.
CHAIRMAN (DR SHIV PABARY): Just to clarify, the actual issue of this report, is it the date that you dispute. The actual contents, what you just said about risk assessment, are true?
THE NEGRO: Yes.

NEGRO'S PERSPECTIVE:
These are the key facts: Richard Hill visited the Negro's surgery after he moved from Grove Place to Bromham Road in 2003. He did so only once. The Negro could not remember the exact date. He did not write to the Negro after the alleged visit, and the Negro was not provided with a report.

In response to a Freedom of Information request in 2008, the NHS stated that there was a visit to the surgery of the first ever and only Negro dentist in Bedford on 2 April 2003. It stated that it did not have the report, but it stated that the NHS carried out further visits a year later and it had the reports of those visits (visits of 22 July 2004 and a follow up visit of an undisclosed date). The NHS withdrew the merciless, racist reports in their entirety – albeit more than four years after the alleged visit of 22 July 2004. The withdrawal statement of 16 October 2008 is a falsified statement by the NHS. It remains live and valid.

In response to David Morris's question upon the matter, the Negro confirmed that Richard Hill visited his practice when he moved to Bromham Road in 2003:
CHAIRMAN (DR SHIV PABARY): Are you saying that there was a

visit, but later on, or there was no visit at all?

THE NEGRO: No, there was no visit at all on that day.

DAVID MORRIS: No visit on that day, but I think you told us that from time to time he would come and visit your surgery?

THE NEGRO: Yes, there was no visit on that day, but he would have come to my surgery. I can recall that when I moved, yes, he came to me, yes.

NEGRO'S PERSPECTIVE:

"There was no visit on that day" implies that there was no visit on a particular day, but there was a visit on another day. Dr Shiv Pabary, Member of the British Empire, seemed too dull to work that out.

"Sir, he was dull in company, dull in his closet, dull everywhere. He was dull in a new way, and that made many people think him great." – Dr Samuel Johnson

"Why, Sir, Sherry is dull, naturally dull, but it must have taken him a great deal of pain to become what we now see him. Such an excess stupidity, Sir, is not in Nature." – Dr Samuel Johnson

THE NEGRO: Yes, there was no visit on that day, but he would have come to my surgery. I can recall that when I moved, yes, he came to me, yes.

The Negro moved only once, and Richard Hill visited him at his new premises. Modular education within one of the least literate countries in the industrialised world seemed to have fried the brains of the privileged dullards who act as though the brain is inside the skin colour, and in delusion associate the gigantic proceeds of several centuries of merciless racial hatred and naked fraud with intellect and industry.

Before slavery, what?

Before slavery, there was no council, as then the land only yielded food, and it was occupied by agricultural labourers oftener from mainland Europe, and also alien landowners from mainland Europe.

"Agriculture not only gives riches to a nation, but the only riches she can call her own." – Dr Samuel Johnson

Feudal agricultural labourers, from mainland Europe dispossessed/robbed aborigine Britons. They've been transformed and reinvented by SLAV-ERY

"Iain Whyte, author of Scotland and the Abolition of Slavery, insists we have at times ignored our guilty past. He said: 'For many years Scotland's historians harboured the illusion that our nation had little to do with the slave trade or plantation slavery.

"'We swept it under the carpet. This was remarkable in the light of Glasgow's wealth coming from tobacco, sugar and cotton, and Jamaica Streets being found in a number of Scottish towns and cities.

"'It is healthy we are now recognising Scotland was very much involved.'

"The industries, which saw Glasgow and much of the country flourish, were built on the back of slavery. There were familiar names such as Scot Lyle of Tate and Lyle fame whose fortune was built on slavery. Ewing from Glasgow was the richest sugar producer in Jamaica. The stunning Inveresk Lodge in Edinburgh, now open to the public, was bought by James Wedderburn with money earned from 27 years in Jamaica as a notorious slaver. The Wee Free Church was founded using profits and donations from the slave trade. Even our schools have a dark history. Bathgate Academy was built from money willed by John Newland, a renowned slave master and Dollar Academy has a similar foundation. For many years, the goods and profits from West Indian slavery were unloaded at Kingston docks in Glasgow. Leith in Edinburgh and Glasgow were popular ports from which ambitious Scottish men sailed to make their fortunes as slave masters." – Herald Scotland, Ian Bell, columnist, Sunday 28 April 2013

"Those who have robbed have also lied." – Dr Samuel Johnson corroborating prophet Habakkuk

Almost everything was stolen. The proceeds of merciless, racial hatred and fraud (slavery) were used to build cathedrals, courts, churches, castles, and councils.

There was no council at Wimpole Street, London before slavery, and there mightn't have been a council on Wimpole Street had there not been slavery.

The proceeds of centuries of merciless, racial hatred and fraud kick-started the industrial revolution in Scotland and brought Scottish slave merchants and traders, great wealth.

The satanic network is everywhere. It controls almost everything except intellect. Without objective basis, it awards itself the monopoly of knowledge.

Feudal agricultural labourers from mainland Europe dispossessed/robbed aboriginal Britons. They've been transformed and reinvented by slavery.

"Many Scots masters were considered among the most brutal, with life expectancy on their plantations averaging a mere four years. We worked them to death then simply imported more to keep the sugar and thus the money flowing. Unlike centuries of grief and murder, an apology costs nothing. So, what does Scotland have to say?" – Herald Scotland, Ian Bell, columnist, Sunday 28 April 2013

Facts are sacred; they can't be overstated.

"As hard-hearted as a Scot of Scotland." – English saying

"Scotsmen tak a' they can get and a little more if they can." – Scottish saying

"There is no sin except stupidity." – Oscar Wilde

****

The lone Negro in the council chamber was cross examined by Andrew Hurst on 21 November 2008 (Court Room):

ANDREW HURST: We see there 21 April 1997 on our first page; Mr Hill's further inspection visit.

THE NEGRO: Those problems were resolved before '97.

ANDREW HURST: Quite right, but nonetheless Mr Hill is able to in effect sign you off as safe and complying with all the relevant tests by April 1997.

THE NEGRO: Yes.

ANDREW HURST: Then, nothing else happens.

THE NEGRO: Yes.

Dr. Olayinka Bamgbelu

ANDREW HURST: Until arguably April 2003, although we appreciate your answers that you do not accept you were visited in 2003.

THE NEGRO: Yes. It is important to – yes, okay.

ANDREW HURST: We will park that.

THE NEGRO: 2000/2001 is not part of it. In 2003, Mr Hill came to my practice when I moved from Grove Place. He wrote an inspection thing. He did not do it on that day, but even that visit that he did, there is nothing on it that is actually against me.

ANDREW HURST: Quite. That is a point we will look at a bit later on. But taking it at its highest in the report in 2003, the only things he is particularly picking you up for is an absence of some of the documentation, is there not?

THE NEGRO: There were two things. I think he mentioned COSHH.

ANDREW HURST: If you are agreeing with me, you do not necessarily need to go into a long explanation. Can we deal with it this way? We are agreeing that the April 2003 visit to Bromham Road, which you say did not happen but Council says it did, whether it did or did not happen, there is very little that Mr Hill picked up on. It was simply actually to do with documentation, the two things that you remembered.

THE NEGRO: That is right.

ANDREW HURST: No problems in 2004 with Bedford?

THE NEGRO: Yes.

ANDREW HURST: No problems in 2005 with Bedford?

THE NEGRO: Yes.

NEGRO'S PERSPECTIVE:

The Negro confirmed again that Richard Hill visited his practice in 2003.

THE NEGRO: 2000/2001 is not part of it. In 2003, Mr Hill came to my practice when I moved from Grove Place. He wrote an inspection thing. He did not do it on that day, but even that visit that he did, there is nothing on it that is actually against me.

Richard Hill came to my practice in 2003. He did not write anything. They were merciless, racist thugs and cowards – the descendants of racist stealers and sellers of human beings.

What they seemingly would have liked is for there to be proof that the brain is in the skin colour, as that would lessen the guilt of mercilessly killing millions of Negroes and working millions more to death.

The truth is that the brain was not and is not in the skin colour, and many of the millions that the racist bas****s worked to death and sadistically, mercilessly slaughtered in the African bush and armed others to destroy with guns during several centuries of merciless tyranny were created intellectually superior by Almighty God.

They found guns and used them to destroy the world so that morons could thrive.

The "meat" again is that Richard Hill did not give the first ever and only Negro dentist in Bedford any report, and he did not communicate with him directly or indirectly about any visit.

The racist bas****s seemed to desire to create jobs for "fish and chips" solicitors and barristers, albeit England's young adults and/or former England young adults.

"FAILING SCHOOLS AND A BATTLE FOR BRITAIN: This was the day the British education establishment's 50 year betrayal of the Nation's children lay starkly exposed in all its ignominy. After testing 166,000 people in 24 education systems, the Organisation for Economic Cooperation and Development (OECD) finds that England young adults are amongst the least literate and numerate in the industrialised world." – The Daily Mail, 09.01.2013

"The one great principle of English law is to make business for itself." – Charles Dickens

No brain, natural resources poor, only skin colour that the wearer neither made nor chose, and what else? Pure scam! It wouldn't endure, as the future generations would be too dull to keep the charade going seamlessly.

The mediocre, dishonest, and corrupt council instructed the "fish and chips" England class barrister to state as follows:

"Mr Bamgbelu insist that there was no practice visit in 2003" (Andrew Hurst, under oath, in his final statement to the seemingly planted, racist, satanic network committee).

He lied, under oath, because the mediocre and corrupt council within one of the least literate countries in the industrialised world instructed him to do so.

Fools! They delude themselves that racial hatred and thuggery is law.

Before slavery, what? The land that Andrew Hurst was born on yields only food in 2020 and yielded only food in 1720. Then, almost everything else was stolen with made-in-Birmingham guns. Andrew Hurst's ancestors – racist bas****s – stole land and stole human beings to work it (those who will steal human beings will steal anything) and stole anything and everything that they could carry back home from anywhere and everywhere. They were immoral rogues and racist bas****s!

"All have taken what had other owners and all have had recourse to arms rather than quit the prey on which they had fastened." – Dr Samuel Johnson

With the full knowledge and tacit approval of Sue Gregory, Richard Hill, the she-man looking man, stated as follows:

CASE NO: 69238
IN THE MATTER OF THE GENERAL DENTAL COUNCIL AND ABIODUN BAMGBELU
SUPPLEMENTAL WITNESS STATEMENT OF RICHARD HILL
I, RICHARD HILL, c/o Bedfordshire Primary Care Trust, Gilbert Hitchcock House, 21 Kimbolton Road, Bedford, MK40 2AW WILL SAY AS FOLLOWS:
1. I make this statement supplemental to my statement dated 23.09.2008.
2. I attach as Exhibit SRWH1 a copy of my report dated 22.07.2004, I attach a synopsis of practice visits that makes reference to a practice visit to MR BAMGBELU's practice at 52, Bromham Road, Bedford, MK40 2QG in July 2004. The document is incorrect in recording that

the inspection took place in 2004. No such inspection in fact took place.

3. In 2006 the Healthcare Commission carried out a visit to Bedfordshire PCT and I was asked to provide all my practice visit reports. While collating this information, I noticed that some inspection reports were missing, which included an inspection of Mr Bamgbelu's practice on 02.04.2003. Around that time my department moved and it is possible that some reports had been lost during the move. I did locate some of my draft handwritten notes and referred to these to prepare my inspection report dated 22.07.2004 for MR BAMGBELU's prac-

tice which at the time, I understood to be a correct and accurate record of my inspection. Following another move to different premises, I went through some of my files and found my correct inspection report dated which is exhibited to my September 2008 statement as RWH11.

4. The contents of the 22.07.2004 and 02.04.2003 report differ. The reason that the contents differ is because the hand written notes I used to prepare the 22.07.2004 also had a reference to a difference and dates and notes were mixed up. Having reviewed the documents, it became clear to me that the July 2004 was created in error. The contents of the 02.04.2003 report is an accurate reflection of the inspection done at the time and I stand by the contents of the same.

5. I did not undertake any further inspections at Mr Bamgbelu's practice between 2003 and 2007.

6. The content of the synopsis of the practice was correct at the time, but the reason why it does not make reference to the 02.04.2003 inspection is because that report was not found at the time of creating the synopsis of practice visits and reference to the 22.07.2004 visit was inserted.

7. When I undertake practice visits, I take rough notes and write up the report at a later date, usually a couple of days afterwards in order to keep the report as contemporaneous as possible.

8. I attach as Exhibit SRWH2 an anonymised list of consolidation practice visits confirming that Mr Bamgbelu's practice was visited on 02.04.2003. This list has been signed by J BRADBURY, Primary Care contract Manager at Bedfordshire PCT dated 23.09.2008 confirming that an inspection did take place on 02.04.2003.

I confirm that the facts stated in this witness statement consisting of 2 pages are true to the best of my knowledge information and belief.

Signed ....
Dated ....
74222882_1.doc/3 Oct 2008.
NEGRO'S PERSPECTIVE:
"I, RICHARD HILL, c/o Bedfordshire Primary Care Trust, Gilbert Hitchcock House, 21 Kimbolton Road, Bedford, MK40 2AW WILL SAY AS FOLLOWS:
"1. I make this statement supplemental to my statement dated 23.09.2008.
"2. I attach as Exhibit SRWH1 a copy of my report dated 22.07.2004, I attach a synopsis of practice visits that makes reference to a practice visit to MR BAMGBELU's practice at 52, Bromham Road, Bedford, MK40 2QG in July 2004. The document is incorrect in recording that the inspection took place in 2004. No such inspection in fact took place." – Richard Hill, 16 October
2008
In 1720, Bedfordshire, England yielded only food. Then, the people were fed like battery hens with the proceeds of racial hatred and fraud (slavery).

The withdrawal statement seemed to have been the result of the Negro informing Alan Cohen of the Medical Protection Society (MPS) in September 2008 that he was not in the UK on 22 July 2004 and his practice was shut – when the NHS purported to inspect his practice. Then, the Negro did not know that blood is thicker than water, and he was dealing with a racist enemy that was very active in Apartheid South Africa.

I was in Switzerland on July 22, 2004, and my surgery was shut.

"Coincidence is God's way of remaining anonymous." Albert Einstein

He that is with us is greater than the Satanic Network who rules our world, Christ is not anonymous to us, not through righteousness, but only through faith and His unsolicited kindness – John 4:4.

To put things into perceptive, in 2020, the fact that Nigeria and places like that has been a docile cash cow to Shell since 1956 is more relevant to the economic survival of Alan Cohen of the Medical Protection Society (MPS) and his children (and indeed his mother and father too) than anything that is in the part of England in which he was born. In

1720, the proceeds of armed racial hatred and fraud against unarmed and defenceless Africans sustained the ancestors of Alan Cohen of the Medical Protection Society, the proceeds of stealing and selling millions of human beings.

Alan Cohen of the Medical Protection Society's ancestors were racist thugs and thieves. They were the world champions at using guns to slaughter millions of unarmed and defenceless Africans and sadistically working millions more to death. Those whose ancestors used to like to mercilessly kill Africans and work others to death should go and use guns to evict Mr Putin from Crimea – even the Americans would not dare. Using guns to slaughter unarmed and defenceless Africans and mercilessly working stolen Africans to death was risk free.

Oyinbo olodo! Oyinbo ode!

Deluded paper tigers, baseless superiority is their birth right. Their hairs stand on end when they're challenged by our people (AFRICANS); we and our type are the only ones racist bastards will beat up without support of the YANKS.

The withdrawal statement was almost certainly created for Richard Hill by England class whiz kids – geniuses amongst morons. Had he written the report he wouldn't have stated that he carried out an inspection – because he did not.

If the bottommost is world class bottommost, the topmost relative to the bottommost could not be world class topmost.

Facts are sacred.

"The truth allows no choice." Dr Samuel Johnson

So, the whiz kids who wrote the rot for Richard Hill were England class whiz kids, amongst the thickest young adult population in the industrialised world.

"The document is incorrect in recording that the inspection took place in 2004. No such inspection in fact took place." – Richard Hill, 16 October 2008

He realised the alleged incorrectness more than four years after the alleged visit of 22 July 2004. The incorrectness implied poor record keeping.

Part of the reason why seemingly white supremacist thugs hounded Dr Anand Kamath to death was because he was alleged to have kept poor records.

"Worked to death: NHS dentist takes his own life after health bosses threatened to strike him off because he couldn't keep up with paperwork for 10,000 patients' .

"An NHS dentist who was so hardworking he never refused a patient was driven to suicide when health chiefs threatened to strike him off over his record-keeping.

"Dr Anand Kamath, 42, was the only NHS dentist in his area and took on as many people as he could so they would not have to pay to go private.
"But the father-of-three became the subject of an investigation when NHS officials criticised his record-keeping, which had suffered due to his 10,000-strong list of patients.
"Dr Anand Kamath had 10,000 patients on his books but was threatened with being struck off because of minor record keeping errors. His wife Dr Rajni Prasad accused health chiefs of driving her husband to suicide
"His widow told an inquest he felt 'bullied and harassed' after being summoned for a meeting and sent a letter warning he could be reported to the General Dental Council. Now the British Dental Association has called on the NHS to hold an inquiry into his death.
"His wife Dr Rajni Prasad, a dentist who worked alongside him, wept yesterday as she said over-zealous health officials had driven him to his death.
"'It was just too much. They behaved like bullies and drove a loyal NHS servant over the edge,' she said.
"'He just couldn't take the anxiety. He wasn't eating or sleeping after the meeting. When the letter came that was the final straw. He gave

everything to the NHS. He worried about losing everything if they stopped us practising.'

"She added: 'His reward for caring for thousands of patients no other practice would take was to be threatened with the most severe disciplinary action over administrative matters which we agreed straightaway needed improvement.'

"The inquest in Wakefield, Yorkshire, heard last week how Dr Kamath and his wife, 42, had worked for the NHS in Leeds for ten years.

"The pair tried to take on as many patients as possible, giving them a list four times the length of the average practice. For the first four years at Rothwell Dental Surgery Dr Kamath did not take a holiday and rarely took a lunchbreak. At one point, the centre was treating up to 50 people a day.

"Dr Prasad said her husband was a servant to NHS.

"The couple were on a modest contract and could have earned tens of thousands more treating private patients.

"But after two minor complaints, the primary care trust conducted an audit which led to an investigation into record-keeping. The pair were called to a meeting in December where trust officials threatened to report them to the General Dental Council.

"Two days later a letter arrived from the same managers warning of action to suspend them from the list of NHSapproved dentists.

"Soon afterwards, Dr Kamath's wife found him dead at their home in Pudsey near Leeds.

"She told the inquest: 'We were both very stressed and felt vulnerable, harassed and bullied with no support offered.' Wakefield coroner David Hinchliff recorded a verdict of suicide and said unreasonable pressure exerted on Dr Kamath by the trust 'pushed a good man over the edge.'

"Dr Prasad said: 'I told my children dad died after a fall. How could I tell them the awful truth?'

"An NHS England spokesman said: 'We are happy that the investigation that was being undertaken at this practice was following National Clinical Assessment service advice." – Eleanor Harding, The Daily Mail, published 11 August 2013, updated 12 August 2013

Why must one lick a stinking camel toe of a fat and ugly NHS madam manager in order to practice dentistry?

Had I met Kamath before his insanity and self-harm, I would've told him about my own God (Christ), through I am bound to travel by FAITH, travel light, and safe. He, Christ, has the power to anything is an instance.

The sole basis of the power exercised is money. There was nothing in Leeds before slavery apart from agricultural land. Almost everything was stolen with guns against unarmed and defenceless Africans, and not for a little while, but for several centuries of racist tyranny.

"Even if these miserable beings were proved guilty of every crime before you take them off, ought we not to take upon ourselves the office of executioners? And even if we condescend so far, still can we be justified in acquiring them in exchange for our guns, carrying and selling them for great profits, unless we have clear proof that they are criminals? But, if we go much further, if we ourselves tempt them to sell their fellow creatures to us, we may rest assured that they will take care to provide by every possible method a supply of victims increasing in proportions to our demand. Can we, then, hesitate in deciding whether the wars in Africa are their wars or ours? It was our arms in the river of Cameroon, put into the hands of the trader, that furnished him with the means of pushing his trade; and I have no more doubt that they are British arms, put into the hands of Africans, which promote universal war and desolation that I can doubt their having done so in that individual instance. I have shown how great is the enormity of this evil, even on the supposition that we take only convicts and prisoners of war. But take the subject in another way, and how does it stand? Think of 80,000 persons carried out of their native country by we know not what means! For crimes imputed! For light or inconsiderable faults! For debts perhaps! For crime of witchcraft! Or a thousand other weak or scandalous pretexts! Reflect on 80,000 persons annually taken off! There is something in the horror of it that surpasses all bounds of imagination. Admitting that there exists in Africa something like to Courts of justice; yet what an office of humiliation and meanness is it in us, to take upon ourselves to carry into execution the iniquitous sentences of such courts, as if we also were strangers to all religion and to the first principles of justice! But that country, it is said, has been in some degree civilised, and civilised by us. It is said that they have gained some knowledge of the principles of justice." – Prime Minister William

Pitt the Younger, 1792
He, Christ, is transparently just, and he is watching all – Proverbs 15:3.

The nemesis isn't extinct, and the fact that it tarries isn't proof that it will never come.

CHAPTER 3

"No such inspection in fact took place." – Richard Hill, 16 October 2008

The inspection refers to the visit of 22 July 2004, and if there was no visit the alleged follow up visit was also dishonesty under the watch of Sue Gregory, the sincerely perceived closeted racist thug propped up by crude oil and gas money (Bedfordshire yielded and yields only food), in the same way as her merciless, racist thug, armed robber, and thieving ancestors were for centuries sustained by the proceeds of merciless racial hatred and fraud (Europeans' commerce in stolen human beings).

Sue Gregory seemed deluded as she appeared to associate the proceeds of stealing, including stealing and selling human beings (those who will steal human beings will steal anything) with personal intellect and industry.

Oyinbo olodo! Oyinbo ode!

Again, it took the coward, racist thug and f****** idiot more four years to realise that no such inspection took place.

Based entirely upon the request of seemingly hereditary racist Stephanie Twidale, John Hooper contacted Richard Hill, Sue Gregory, and Charlotte Dowling Goodson as follows:

"Richard (Hill), Stephanie Twidale called us a few weeks ago about DRS visits and Charlotte prioritised Mr Bamgbelu's practice; Stephanie has been in touch a few times as her colleagues had highlighted issues from a similar practice in Northants and they would like to review report etc etc prior to visiting. She also wanted to know if there has been a dental inspection there at all and I did not know the answer . . . Cue Richard have you carried out an inspection at this practice, please could you advise Stephanie when she contacts you, and would it be possible to see our reports so we can be more proactive with any other queries. Thanks. With kind regards, John Hooper" (15.08.2006).

Sue Gregory responded to the email, and immediately. She was the only one who did.

"Richard had made visits to Bamgbelu. You would have to ask him for his reports." – Sue Gregory's response to John Hooper's email of 15.08.2006 on 15.08.2006

Sue Gregory, the crooked, racist cougar, seemingly propped up by crude oil and gas money (there are no oil wells or gas fields in Bedford, and there was no White Hall before slavery, and there mightn't be White Hall had there not been slavery), implied that irrespective of her email of 18.05.2005, she had no firm knowledge of visits and reports to the Negro's surgery. The words "visits" and "reports" denote more than one visit and report.

It is my honest belief that Sue Gregory, the seemingly crooked and racist cougar, was dishonest as she lied when she stated that Richard Hill made visits and produced reports other than those of 2003 to the surgery of the first ever and only Negro dentist in Bedford. Richard Hill confirmed this fact when he stated as follows in his belated (more than four years) withdrawal statement of 16.10.2008 – after the alleged visit of 22 July 2004 and follow up of undisclosed date: "I did not undertake any further inspections at Mr Bamgbelu's practice between 2003 and 2007" (Richard Hill).

So, Sue Gregory lied, or she was recklessly confused when she implied that Richard Hill made more than one relevant visit to the practice of the first ever and only Negro dentist in Bedford and produced a report. The shepherds have always lied, and continue to live a lie, and their sheep – amongst the dullest in the industrialised world – have a grossly exaggerated view of their impostor shepherds.

Prior to slavery, the land yielded only food, and it was the only richness that was virtuous, as almost everything else was stolen.

"Agriculture not only gives riches to a nation, but the only riches she can call her own." – Dr Samuel Johnson

Sheep see huge wealth. They know that it is not derived from land nor is it the yield of visible work, so it must have been the product of the extraordinary virtuous work of the extraordinarily wise shepherds from abroad. It was a lie; it is a lie. The shepherds were merciless, opportunistic, racist murderers, armed robbers, and thieves - Habakkuk.

Sheep believed that shepherds were paragons of wisdom who fed them with the yields of virtue. Shepherds dishonestly made sheep believe that the gigantic loot that the shepherds brought from abroad was the yield of virtue. Deceptively, shepherds concealed stolen Africans and merciless, inhuman, racist brutality from moron sheep, and gave the impression that they were "Mother Teresa" who did good work and earned honest pay from abroad. They lied. They were merciless, racist thugs, armed robbers, and thieves - Habakkuk. Whenever they used made-in-Birmingham guns to murder, they robbed, and wherever they used made-in Birmingham guns to dispossess, they took possession. They were ruthless opportunists, racist thugs, armed robbers, and thieves - Habakkuk.

"Many Scots masters were considered among the most brutal, with life expectancy on their plantations averaging a mere four years. We worked them to death then simply imported more to keep the sugar and thus the money flowing. Unlike centuries of grief and murder, an apology cost nothing. So, what does Scotland have to say?" – Herald Scotland, Ian Bell, columnist, Sunday 28 April 2013

"I know of no evil that has ever existed, nor can imagine any evil to exist, worse than the tearing of eighty thousand persons annually from their native land, by a combination of the most civilised nations inhabiting the most enlightened part of the globe, but more especially under the sanction of the laws of that Nation which calls herself the most free and the most happy of them all." – Prime Minister William Pitt the Younger

Before slavery, what?

The entire foundation of the opulence that we all enjoy is forged with the proceeds of several centuries of merciless, racist evil – the kidnapping, stealing, and selling of millions of stolen human beings, not for a little while, but for several continuous centuries of merciless, tyrannical cowardice.

Almost everything was stolen!

There was no industrial revolution before slavery, as it cost a lot of money, and there wouldn't have been an industrial revolution had there not been slavery.

"The fact is that civilisation requires slaves. The Greeks were quite right there. Unless there are slaves to do the ugly, horrible, uninteresting work, culture and contemplation become almost impossible." – Oscar Wilde

"Those who have robbed have also lied." – Dr Samuel Johnson corroborating prophet Habakkuk

Those that the crooked, racist cougar Sue Gregory had to spin are some of the dullest adult population in the industrialised world.

It is fact and absolute truth that Sir Winston Churchill implied that the average Briton was a moron. The OECD seamlessly and objectively corroborated the proximate observation of the great man more than sixty years later.

"The best argument against democracy is a five-minute conversation with the average voter." – Sir Winston Churchill

"FAILING SCHOOLS AND A BATTLE FOR BRITAIN: This was the day the British education establishment's 50-year betrayal of the Nation's children lay starkly exposed in all its ignominy. After testing 166,000 people in 24 education systems, the Organisation for Economic Cooperation and Development (OECD) finds that England young adults are amongst the least literate and numerate in the industrialised world." – The Daily Mail, 09.01.2013

Shepherds of morons are likelier to be morons too.

Part of the reason why England young adults are amongst the dullest in the industrialised world is because Sue Gregory and her type are their shepherds.

Mediocrity and confusion are not in the national interest.

Sue Gregory is significant only because she has the most favourable skin colour and she was born in a rich country. The entire foundation of the wealth is centuries of merciless, opportunistic, racial hatred and naked fraud. It is impossible for the natural talent of Sue Gregory or the virtuous yield of the land upon which she was born to sustain her standard of living.

Before slavery, what?

Sue Gregory, Richard Hill, John Hooper, Charlotte Dowling Goodson, and the NHS are parts of the UK society.

"All sections of UK society are institutionally racist." – Sir Bernard Hogan-Howe, London Metropolitan Police

Richard Hill told the GDC committee that he was not certain that he responded to John Hooper's email of 15.08.2006, and if he did, it must have been a verbal response. Very convenient, an oral response, as it is not verifiable! Crooked, racist bastards!

※ ※ ※ ※

David Morris cross examined Richard Hill in the council chambers on 18 November 2008 (Court Room):

DAVID MORRIS: You are apologising for the delay. You include the synopsis of visits. These are the synopsis of visits that you recall that you carried out. We can see that on p.3 onwards.

RICHARD HILL: Yes. These are the ones that we would have undertaken.

DAVID MORRIS: You say "we" –

THE CHAIRMAN (DR SHIV PABARY, MEMBER OF THE BRITISH EMPIRE): I am sorry, I just need to clarify this. Are you saying that this is the response to that email? This is your response to that email?

RICHARD HILL: I am not sure if it is. There's a long delay and I'm not sure that that would have actually been –

THE LEGAL ADVISER (MR DAVID SWINSTEAD): Mr Morris, might I make this point, that in the request one in 2005 it appears to be referring to Mr Bamgbelu, but the sense (and this is without prejudice, obviously) of the response in 2006 appears to be a reference to numbers of practices. Therefore, there must actually have been a request to Mr

Hill for some sort of detail of all his practice visits and the two cannot be related because one is specific and one is general, all his practices. I would say that without prejudice to anything Mr Hill says. It seemed odd that you put it in that way.

DAVID MORRIS: I think that is a fair comment. It may be an unfair way of putting it to Mr Hill.

THE LEGAL ADVISER (MR DAVID SWINSTEAD): I did not want to stop you, but it did appear to be in another direction.

NEGRO'S PERSPECTIVE:
The email dialogue being referred to was John Hooper's email of 15 August 2006, which he sent to Richard Hill, Sue Gregory, and Charlotte Dowling Goodson, and which Sue Gregory responded to. Sue Gregory's response of the same date was copied to Richard Hill and Charlotte Dowling Goodson. Richard Hill alleged that he did not remember whether he responded immediately to the email, but if he did, it must have been off record. Charlotte Dowling Goodson also did not respond, and certainly not on record – very convenient – but she stated that they were waiting for the reports which had been requested by Stephanie Twidale, and she couldn't remember whether she shared the content of the merciless, racist forgery with Stephanie Twidale, but she believed that Richard Hill must have done so, as it was part of the reason why Richard Hill was ordered to conduct the inspection with Stephanie Twidale.

Dishonesty could be in the national interest, but implausible dishonesty is a stupidity, and stupidity in every form is not in the national interest.

"There is no sin except stupidity." – Oscar Wilde

David Morris cross examined Charlotte Dowling Goodson on 20 November 2008 (Court Room):

DAVID MORRIS: Tab 21. From Richard Hill 6 September 06 to you and others at Bedford; record of practice visits, and we have the entry on that schedule for July 2004, all right?

CHARLOTTE DOWLING GOODSON: Yes.

DAVID MORRIS: And did you, as part of his process then . . . well, I can see the concerns that were raised in that column: no risk assessment, no COSSH, Kavoclave type autoclave, why that shouldn't be used, no other members of practice staff present at visits, and could not be questioned regarding cross infection control by the practice. But did you, as part of this process, receive a copy of what was purported to be the visit record for that date, 22 July 04?

CHARLOTTE DOWLING GOODSON: Not at that time, but we did get copies of the reports and for these visits at a later date. We had been requesting them.

DAVID MORRIS: That is D5, if you can have a look at that, please. (Handed)

CHARLOTTE DOWLING GOODSON: Thank you

(Perused document).

DAVID MORRIS: And I think if I can take you to the feedback, final page, page 5, summary of these concerns: "The practice uses a Kavoclave type autoclave. This is not acceptable. There is also a large turnover of staff and I am not satisfied that staff training is at an acceptable level and have concerns over the cross infection control procedures", and the essential action points set out there. So you would have received that, and that would have informed your concerns at that time about that practice?

CHARLOTTE DOWLING GOODSON: This report was received at a later time. I did not receive it until 2004.

DAVID MORRIS: No.

CHARLOTTE DOWLING GOODSON: But what I also I received was part of the decision making process, and prioritising the practice for an inspection by the DRS.

DAVID MORRIS: And would those concerns, informed in part by that report, have been fed through to Stephanie Twidale prior to her conducting her inspection in February 07?

CHARLOTTE DOWLING GOODSON: I can't remember if I passed them on. I think Richard Hill would have shared those issues with Stephanie as part of the discussion prior to the visit, and that is part of the reason why Richard went with Stephanie to undertake the visit with her.

DAVID MORRIS: It would have made a lot of sense for the information in that report to have been passed on and fed through as necessary preliminary material prior to inspection?

CHARLOTTE DOWLING GOODSON: Yes, it would have been.

DAVID MORRIS: And do you appreciate that now, very recently, Mr. Hill has realised that that report, relating to Mr. Bamgbelu's practice, in fact was an error, in as much as the concerns in it related to wholly different matters?

CHARLOTTE DOWLING GOODSON: No, I was not aware of that.

THE NEGRO'S PERSPECTIVE:

It will be very interesting to know whether prior to 20 November 2008 Sue Gregory knew that Richard Hill had withdrawn the NHS forged reports of 22 July 2004 and the follow up of undisclosed date, and whether she spoke with Richard Hill and/ or Charlotte Dowling Goodson, directly or indirectly or in any way whatsoever, between 16 October 2008 and 19 November 2008.

Descendants of wretched, feudal agricultural labourers (serfs) from mainland Europe stole the land of aboriginal Britons. They were immeasurably transformed by the gigantic yields of merciless, racial hatred and fraud (slavery), and have since reinvented themselves and fool the foolish.

"Mr Morris, might I make this point, that in the request one in 2005 it appears to be referring to Mr Bamgbelu, but the sense (and this is without prejudice, obviously) of the response in 2006 appears to be a reference to numbers of practices. Therefore, there must actually have been a request to Mr Hill for some sort of detail of all his practice visits and the two cannot be related because one is specific and one is general, all his practices. I would say that without prejudice to anything Mr Hill says. It seemed odd that you put it in that way." – David Swinstead, implicitly under oath, on 18 November 2008

By his statement supra, it would be reasonable to suggest that David Swinstead was an intellectually impotent nonentity, propped up by crude oil and gas money, and I don't mean Mr Alex Salmond's "Scottish oil," in exactly the same way as his direct ancestors were for centuries sustained by the proceeds of merciless, racial hatred and naked fraud (slavery).

By the statement, Mr David Swinstead took advantage of the incompetence of David Morris – although I suspect it was a "plant" – by the sincerely perceived white supremacists.

Foolish David Morris, as instructed by Ian Sandler – a former England young adult – somehow came up with the fact that Richard Hill's email of 6 September 2006 was in response to Sue Gregory's email of 18 May 2005.

Moron former England young adult! England class barrister! Some barristers go on to become judges.

Shocking!

"Why, that is, because, dearest, you are a dunce." – Dr Samuel Johnson

It would be extraordinary, would it not, if Richard Hill gave a response to the email of Sue Gregory of more than a year earlier (18 May 2005) and directed the response to John Hooper? David Morris and Ian Sadler's mums couldn't have sent their respective wards to schools in Mediocre Great England where critical reasoning was taught as a subject.

Oyinbo olodo! Oyinbo ode!

Those they regularly spin are amongst the dullest adult population in the industrialised world.

Richard Hill's testimony on oath encompassed every year from 1996 till the racist stitch up inspection by Stephanie Twidale on 22 February 2007.

"Had there been any problem, I would be asked by the PCT to visit the practice and carry out a formal inspection in that situation. That's normally along with a colleague, so it's a proper and formal procedure. But I have no record of being told that there were any concerns." – Richard Hill, under oath, on 18 November 2008

Mr David Swinstead, a dull white supremacist, propped up by crude oil and gas money (and I do not mean Mr Alex Salmond's Scottish oil) in the same was as his murderous, cowardly, ruthless, opportunistic armed robbers and thieving ancestors were for centuries sustained by the proceeds of merciless racial hatred and fraud, was dishonest when he implied that John Hooper's email of 15 August 2006 referred to any other than the lone Negro in their midst.

DIFFICULT to trust the intellect and integrity of legal systems that tampers with COURT TRANSCRIPTS and conceal RACE HATE and MEDIOCRITY.

Facts are sacred.

* * * * *

"It does no harm to throw the occasional man overboard, but it does not do much good if you are steering full speed ahead for the rocks." Sir Ian Gilmour

Based on available evidence, English law is equal, its administration is not - Habakkuk 1:4.

"Change occurs slowly. Very often a legal change might take place, but the cultural shift required to really accept its spirit lingers in the wings for decades." Sara Sheridan

Quasi-Apartheid administration of the law: When their own people commit RACIST CRIMES against our people, racist bastards bury RACIAL HATRED - Habakkuk 1:4; John 8 44; John 10:10.

OYINBO OLE: WHITE THIEVES: HABAKKUK.

No brain.
Poor in natural resources.

Several centuries of stealing and slavery preceded the TRUST FUND. Only the skin colour is indisputably superior.

Facts are sacred.

"The truth allows no choice." Dr Samuel Johnson

"All sections of the UK Society are institutionally racist." Sir Bernard Hogan-Howe

The Judiciary is part of the UK Society.

It is cruel deceit that AFRICANS are no longer inferior under English law. Africans did not become Equal under English law after the 1807 Act.

OYINBO OLE: WHITE THIEVES: HABAKKUK.

"A complaints such as Ms Bishop could trigger an enquiry." Stephen Henderson, Head of MDDUS

A CROOKED RACIST WHITE DUNCE.

Everything about them is superior except their fertility tools and their brains.

"I don't want to talk grammar. I want to talk like a lady." George Bernard Shaw.

WOLLASTON, ENGLAND: Based on available evidence, GDC-Witness, Ms Rachael Bishop, Senior NHS Nurse, unrelentingly lied under oath - Habakkuk 1:4; John 8:44; John 10:10.

A RACIST WHITE CROOK.

OYINBO OLE: WHITE THIEVES: HABAKKUK.

Facts are sacred.

ENGLAND: A CLOSETED RACIST HELL-HOLE.

Whites measure whites with a very different yardstick: Demons will not cast out demons - Matthew 12:27.

Then, racist white bastards carried and sold millions of stolen children of defenceless people; now, they carry natural resources.

SUBSTITUTION: FRAUDULENT EMANCIPATION.

"Moderation is a virtue only among those who are thought to have found alternatives." Henry Kissinger.

There are no oil wells or gas-fields in KEMPSTON, and Bishop's Stortford yields only food: Cecil Rhodes was a THIEF - Habakkuk.

"We shall deal with the racist white bastards when we get out of prison." Robert Mugabe.

The child's sister has since gained a first-class science degree from one of the topmost Universities in the UK; aged saved her from the closeted white supremacist, functional semi-illiterate — Dylan Roof, Fake District Judge, whose white British mother and father did not have very, very strong views about education; an ignorant descendant of professional thieves and owners of stolen and destroyed children of defenceless people

(Kamala's ancestors) — HABAKKUK.

The white British privileged dullard is more familiar with the black Caribbean; the descendants of those who were unnaturally selected, genetically reversed, paired up, bred for labour, and reared like cattle on the plantations of Good Christians (better men who became SAINTS).

The truth cannot be overstated.

OYINBO OLE: WHITE THIEVES: HABAKKUK.

The white British Norwich Solicitor (a Fake District Judge) wanted to use only his indisputably superior skin colour, which he neither made nor chose, to teach Negroes, who secretly look down on his mediocre brain, what his own white British mother and father, who did not have very, very strong views about education, did not know, and which the natural talents of his own relatively duller white British children (OECD) will not exploit.

DELUDED PAPER TIGERS: BASELESS SUPERIORITY IS THEIR BIRTHRIGHT.

Their hairs stand on end when they are challenged by our people; we and our type are the only ones racist bastards could beat up without the support of the YANKS.

An ignorant descendant of industrial-scale professional THIEVES and owners of stolen children of defenceless poor people - Habakkuk

Facts are sacred; they cannot be overstated.

OYINBO OLE: WHITE THIEVES: HABAKKUK.

He is watching them - Proverbs 15:3.

Only Judges (disproportionately, Judges are white) who have no sins (Saints) should judge sinners; latent but very potent Racist Criminals should not judge sinners.

Judges are emissaries of Christ on Earth; Christ is not a closeted Racist white supremacist thug, and He is not a crooked and confused moron — HABAKKUK.

"Someone must be trusted. Let it be the Judges." Lord Denning

We trust only Christ.

Judges are human beings; some human beings are racists.

Facts are sacred.

"Mr Bamgbelu clearly has very, very strong views about education and I understand those views are based upon the fact that he is a successful dentist here in Bedford which he attributes to the fact that his parents cared for him and his education when he was young. They ensured that he had a proper fee paying education……..." The Senior Vice President of the Association of Her Majesty's District Judges — proofed and approved Judgement.

Indiscreet ENVY.

OYINBO OLODO: AN IMBECILE WHITE MAN

The functional semi-illiterate, closeted racist. and indiscreetly envious Freemason Judge seemed obsessed with the material possessions of a mere Negro.

"Look, a Negro. Mama, look, a Negro. Hell, the Negro is getting mad, where shall I hide?

Financial disclosure in a divorce: How can a mere Negro have what I do not have?

A closeted racist spineless worm: Envy is very weak.

Envy is a THIEF.

The American Actress, Megan Markle: "She was the subject of explicit and obnoxious RACIAL HATRED." John Bercow.

The former speaker had access to a lot of classified information.

https://www.youtube.com/watch?v=BlpH4hG7m1A

When ENVY and FAMILIAL RACIAL HATRED copulate, insanity is their offspring.

The cretins who sit before the closeted racist former Norwich Solicitor do not know that his appointment as a Judge was not based on colour blind and measurable objectivity.

The last time he passed through the filter of transparent, colour-blind, and measurable objectivity was when he studied 5th rate law at polytechnic.

They're very lucky, those they need to spin are among the least literate and least numerate in the industrialised world.

The report, by the OECD, warns that the UK needs to take significant action to boost the basic skills of the nation's young people. The 460-page study is based on the first-ever survey of the literacy, numeracy and problem-solving at work skills of 16 to 65-year-olds in 24 countries, with almost 9,000 people taking part in England and Northern Ireland to make up the UK results. The findings showed that England and Northern Ireland have some of the highest proportions of adults scoring no higher than Level 1 in literacy and numeracy - the lowest level on the OECD's scale. This suggests that their skills in the basics are no better than that of a 10-year-old.

AN IMBECILE: AN ADULT WITH THE BASIC SKILLS OF A CHILD.

Apart from creating cushy salaried jobs (quasi-communism) for incontrovertibly functional semi-illiterate Solicitors/Barristers who couldn't hack it in the very competitive real world, what do imbeciles need expensive administration of the law for?

Adults with the basic skills of a foetus will succeed adults with the basic skills of a child, and the former should need only food and shelter.

Our Empire did not evolve; then, almost everything was actively and deliberately stolen - Habakkuk.

OYINBO OLE: WHITE THIEVES: HABAKKUK.

"Affluence is not a birth right." David Cameron

He is relevant only because he is a Judge; theretofore, the incontrovertibly functional semi-illiterate debt-collector Solicitor in NORWICH - was purified NOTHING.

The only evidence of his purportedly higher IQ is the stolen affluence that his ancestors crossed the English Channels, without luggage or decent shoes, to latch onto. They changed their names, blended, and automatically became the rightful inheritors of the yields of several centuries of sadism and savagery: The barbarously racist traffic in millions of stolen children of defenceless people (the evilest terrorism the world will ever know) - Habakkuk.

OYINBO OLE: WHITE THIEVES: HABAKKUK.

He is watching them - Proverbs 15:3.

PERCEPTION IS GRANDER THAN REALITY.

Everything is assumed in favour of the indisputably superior skin colour that the wearer neither made nor chose - Habakkuk; John 8:44; John 10:10.

OYINBO OLE: WHITE THIEVES: HABAKKUK.

No brain.

Poor in natural resources.

Several centuries of stealing and slavery preceded the TRUST FUND.

Only the indisputably superior skin colour is good; the wearer neither made nor chose it.

Facts are sacred; they cannot be overstated.

OYINBO OLE: WHITE THIEVES: HABAKKUK.

Putin sits on the largest gas reserve in the world; did he poison Bob Dudley?

"It is incumbent upon the court and all those professionals involved to conclude court proceedings as quickly as possible. This hopefully ensures that a child has stability, love and affection and the parents working together to ensure that he has the best opportunity of developing academically and emotional." The Senior Vice President of the Association of Her Majesty's District Judges – proofed and approved Judgement.

"Yes, Sir, it does her honour, but it would do nobody else honour. I have indeed, not read it all. But when I take up the end of a web, and find it packthread, I do not expect, by looking further, to find embroidery." Dr Samuel Johnson

AN IMBECILE WHITE FREEMASON DISTRICT JUDGE.

Just as it was at Professor Stephen Hawking's schools, then, at the University of Lagos, Nigeria, the brightest students did not attend lectures at the Faculty of Law.

"In my school, the brightest boys did math and physics, the less bright did physics and chemistry, and the least bright did biology. I wanted to do math and physics, but my father made me do chemistry because he thought there would be no jobs for mathematicians." Dr Stephen Hawking

Sincere immodesty is sincerer than the deceptively schooled insincere modesty.

NIGERIA: SHELL'S DOCILE CASH COW.
There are no oil wells or gas fields in Luton.
Facts are sacred.

Babies with huge oil wells and gas fields near their houses eat only

1.5.day; a closeted racist, functional semi-illiterate former Norwich Solicitor whose white father and mother have never seen crude oil is our District Judge in BEDFORD

OYINBO OLE: WHITE THIEVES: HABAKKUK.

Then, the white ancestors of his white father and mother were fed like battery hens with the yields of stolen children of defenceless poor people - Habakkuk.

Facts are sacred.

NEW HEROD, MATTHEW 2:16: They lie to their duller children that they're GENIUSES, they kill all those who know that they're brainless racist bastards.

Then, like Herod, Kim and MBS, lunatic bastards used to butcher all those who stated and/or printed what they didn't want their moron sheep to know about. The last decapitation in England was in 1827, and beheading was removed from the statute book in 1973.

Freedom of expression was only for those who did not know what they do not want their moron sheep to know about.

He was jailed only because he spoke; the lunatic Jew removed the head of John when he refused to stop speaking. He was not punished for speaking, he was permanently prevented from speaking.

Deluded paper tigers. Baseless superiority is their birth right. Their hairs stand on end when they're challenged by our people. We and our type are the only ones racist bastards will beat up without the support of the YANKS.

He was lynched like Gadhafi and crucified only because He spoke. He was not punished for speaking; he was permanently prevented from speaking.

Illegitimi non carborundum:

Too late for the Negro.

If a pride of hungry lions can see you in the African bush, you're finished, and must return to mother earth as lions' waste.

Once you can see the RACIST BASTARDS, and they know you can see them, you are dead MEAT, as you know, through Christ, what their moron sheep must not know.

They're not immortal; we will go, and they must come - 2 Samuel 12:23.

Certainly, of the body, any integer plus infinity is infinity.

Deluded intellectual cowards: Their indisputably superior skin colour is an asset, they know; our dark coat is curse, we know. Our asset is useless without Freedom of Expression. They, cowardly, stifled Freedom of Expression. Racist bastards invited our people to swords fight, spineless racist bastards seized our swords. They want superiority, their baseless birth right, they don't want Freedom of Expression because they don't want their moron sheep to know that they're brainless racist bastards.

TYPICAL: They want to eat their cakes and have them.

"A typical Englishman, usually violent, and always dull." Wilde

In many parts of the world, Judges are subjectively selected from the finest filtrates of lawyers; better than crap could also be crap.

In some parts of the world, when Solicitors/Barristers fail in practice, thousands do, if they're FREEMASONS, they could become Judges, if not, they could become Politicians or something else.

Ignorant descendants of THIEVES and owners of stolen children of defenceless poor people - Habakkuk.

OYINBO OLE: WHITE THIEVES; HABAKKUK.

Righteousness and deceptively schooled civilised decorum were preceded by several centuries of barbarously racist traffic in millions of stolen children of defenceless people - Habakkuk.

The nemesis is not extinct, and the fact that it tarries isn't the evidence that it will never come - Habakkuk.

A grossly overrated, overhyped, overpopulated, and mediocre trade that is dying slowly and imperceptibly.

PERCEPTION IS GRANDER THAN REALITY.

"The legal system lies at the heart of any society, protecting rights, imposing duties, and establishing a framework for the conduct of almost every social, political, and economic activity. Some argue that the law is in its death throes while others postulate a contrary prognosis that discerns numerous signs of law's enduring strength. Which is it?" Professor Raymond Wacks, Professor Emeritus Hong Kong, Law School.

BEDFORD, ENGLAND: Based on available evidence, GDC-Witness, Freemason, Brother, Dr Richard William Hill fabricated reports and unrelentingly lied under oath - Habakkuk 1:4; John 8:44; John 10:10

A RACIST WHITE CROOK.

OYINBO OLE: WHITE THIEVES: HABAKKUK.

A bastardised, vindictive, indiscreetly dishonest, unashamedly mediocre, potently weaponised, and institutionally racist system that is overseen by MASONS (Mediocre Mafia/ Ultra-righteous New Pharisees) - Habakkuk 1:4; John 8:44; John 10:10.

No brain.

Poor in natural resources.

Several centuries of stealing and slavery preceded the TRUST FUND

Only the skin colour is indisputably superior; the fortunate wearer neither made nor chose it.

Then, righteous and highly civilised racist bastards carried and sold millions of stolen children of defenceless people; now, they carry natural resources.

OYINBO OLE: WHITE THIEVES: HABAKKUK.

SUBSTITUTION: FRAUDULENT EMANCIPATION.

"Moderation is a virtue only among those who are thought to have found alternatives." Henry Kissinger

He is watching them - Proverbs 15:3.

"A complaints such as Mrs Bishop's could trigger an enquiry." Stephen Henderson, Head of MDDUS.

I don't want to talk grammar. I want to talk like a lady." George Bernard Shaw.

A CROOKED RACIST WHITE DUNCE.

A BRAINLESS WHITE MAN.

Google: Stephen Henderson, MDDUS.

"I am very fond of my pigs. It doesn't stop me from eating them." Archbishop Runcie.

If one farmed some pigs for bacon; the stupidest of the pigs should be the first to be butchered.

WOLLASTON, ENGLAND: Based on available evidence, GDC-Witness, Ms Rachael Bishop, Senior NHS Nurse, unrelentingly lied under oath - Habakkuk 1:4; John 8:44; John 10:10.

A RACIST WHITE CROOK.

OYINBO OLE: WHITE THIEVES: HABAKKUK.

He is watching them - Proverbs 15:3.

"It is incumbent upon the court and all those professionals involved to conclude court proceedings as quickly as possible. This hopefully ensures that a child has stability, love and affection and the parents working together to ensure that he has the best opportunity of developing academically and emotional." District Judge Paul Ayers, Senior Vice President of the Association of Her Majesty's District Judges – proofed and approved Judgement

"Yes, Sir, it does her honour, but it would do nobody else honour. I have indeed, not read it all. But when I take up the end of a web, and find it packthread, I do not expect, by looking further, to find embroidery." Dr Samuel Johnson

OUR SEMI-ILLITERATE RACIST FREEMASON YOUR HONOUR.

A CLOSETED RACIST BRAINLESS WHITE MAN.

The only evidence of the purportedly higher IQ of the incontrovertibly functional semi-illiterate white man is the stolen affluence that his ancestors crossed the English Channels, without luggage or decent shoes to latch onto. They changed their names, blended, and deceived the undiscerning that their ancestors were aboriginal Britons who evolved from gorillas in Luton.

Descendants of aliens (genetic aliens) oppress, we, the descendants of the robbed with the yields of the robbery.

The white father and mother of the Senior Vice President of the Association of Her Majesty's District Judges, evidently, didn't care, had they, their closeted racist white son would not have approved and immortalised (for eternity), excessive stupidity at 16, and he'd be a properly educated lawyer, privately educated Antony Blair, Anthony Julius, Geoff Hoon and Rabinder Singh's class, and he might practice proper law in STRAND, instead of daily dialogues with imbeciles, in a District Court, in a Province.

OYINBO OLE: WHITE THIEVES: HABAKKUK.

Apart from creating cushy salaried jobs for Solicitors and Barristers who couldn't hack it in the very real world (Quasi-Communism), what do imbeciles (adults with the basic skills of a child) need very expensive administration of the law for?

The report, by the OECD, warns that the UK needs to take significant action to boost the basic skills of the nation's young people. The 460-page study is based on the first-ever survey of the literacy, numeracy and problem-solving at work skills of 16 to 65-year-olds in 24 countries, with almost 9,000 people taking part in England and Northern Ireland to make up the UK results. The findings showed that England and Northern Ireland have some of the highest proportions of adults scoring no higher than Level 1 in literacy and numeracy - the lowest level on the OECD's scale. This suggests that their skills in the basics are no better than that of a 10-year-old.

Based on available evidence, Dr Richard Dawkins and OECD implied that all the children of District Judge Paul Ayers, Senior Vice President of the Association of Her Majesty's District Judges should be duller than their white father.

Facts are sacred.

"Natural selections will not remove ignorance from future generations." Dr Richard Dawkins

England's young people are near the bottom of the global league table for basic skills. OECD finds 16- to 24-year-olds have literacy and numeracy levels no better than those of their grandparents' generation.

England is the only country in the developed world where the generation approaching retirement is more literate and numerate than the youngest adults, according to the first skills survey by the Organisation for Economic Co-operation and Development.

In a stark assessment of the success and failure of the 720-million-strong adult workforce across the wealthier economies, the economic thinktank warns that in England, adults aged 55 to 65 perform better than 16- to 24-year-olds at foundation levels of literacy and numeracy. The survey did not include people from Scotland or Wales.

The OECD study also finds that a quarter of adults in England have the maths skills of a 10-year-old. About 8.5 million adults, 24.1% of the population, have such basic levels of numeracy that they can manage only one-step tasks in arithmetic, sorting numbers or reading graphs. This is worse than the average in the developed world, where an average of 19% of people were found to have a similarly poor skill base.

"By definition therefore there needs to be a contact order for Mr B so that he knows when he is going to see his son. It is absolutely essential that this occurs and mother agrees with that. She said so several times in her evidence. Mrs Waller agreed that not only should a child have the opportunity of developing relationship with both parents, any sibling should also be there so that inter- sibling relationship could be fostered and nurtured. Obviously in this particular case the children reside in different places. That immediately puts a strain on the children having limited contact with each other. F's sister is very much older than him and she will be further advanced into her adult life. Thus it is not a matter that that sibling relationship can only be fostered by the children being together. Indeed as we all know absence sometimes makes the heart grow fonder. F should have an opportunity of seeing his sister. Wherever he does that it should be done in a friendly and loving environment. If the time comes that his sister goes to university of course his contact with her will be restricted to the time that she is home from university. In years to come when they have both grown up, with their own family they will see less of each other. But it doesn't mean that they don't still love and adore each other as much as they would if they saw each other every day." The Senior Vice President of the Association of Her Majesty's District Judges – proofed and approved Judgement.

https://www.youtube.com/watch?v=BlpH4hG7m1A

Shocking!

"Why, that is, because, dearest, you are a dunce." Habakkuk.

A scatter-head racist plebeian; an overpromoted polytechnic university educated racist bastard. A righteous descendant of industrial-scale professional THIEVES and owners of stolen children of defenceless people (Kamala's ancestors) - Habakkuk.

OYINBO OLE: WHITE THIEVES: HABAKKUK.

The white father and mother of the Senior Vice President of the Association of Her Majesty's District Judges did not care, had they, he'd not have approved and immortalised excessive stupidity at 16, and he'd be a properly educated lawyer, privately educated Anthony Blair, Anthony Julius, Geoff Hoon and Rabinder Singh's class, and he might practice proper law in STRAND.

It's plainly deductible that the white father and mother of the Senior Vice President of the Association of Her Majesty's District Judges couldn't afford to pay for qualitative education; why should we have to come from very far AFRICA to pay for his misfortune and part of its tell-tale signs (sequelae)?

Our ancestors have paid, and they paid more than enough.

"Many Scots masters were considered among the most brutal, with life expectancy on their plantations averaging a mere four years. We worked them to death then simply imported more to keep the sugar and thus the money flowing. Unlike centuries of grief and murder, an apology cost nothing. So, what does Scotland have to say?" Herald Scotland: Ian Bell, Columnist, Sunday 28 April 2013

"I know of no evil that has ever existed, nor can imagine any evil to exist, worse than the tearing of eighty thousand persons annually from their native land, by a combination of the most civilised nations inhabiting the most enlightened part of the globe, but more especially under the sanction of the laws of that Nation which calls herself the most free and the most happy of them all." Prime Minister William Pitt the Younger

OYINBO OLE: WHITE THIEVES: HABAKKUK.

If the Senior Vice President of the Association of Her Majesty's District Judges read his approved Judgement, he was excessively stupid; if he didn't, he lied.

Facts are sacred.

"Of black men, the numbers are too great who are now repining under English cruelty." Dr Samuel Johnson.

Whites are very scared, and not just in Trump's America (75M), and rightly so. Increasingly colour-blind level playing field is gradually unravelling the mother of all racist scams: The centuries-old unspoken myth that the brain is related to skin colour. Only fools expect descendants of THIEVES and owners of stolen children of defenceless poor people to voluntarily relinquish the inherited advantageous position (WHITE PRIVILEGE) that was primarily gained through centuries of extreme violence, and properly organised industrial-scale, armed stealing of moveable and immoveable valuables that had other owners, without a fight.

Descendants of minor Europeans, the descendants of stolen Africans, and motley assemblies of other genetic aliens fight like ferrets in a sack on stolen Indian land.

OYINBO OLE: WHITE THIEVES: HABAKKUK.

"All have taken what had other owners, and all have had a recourse to arms rather than quit the prey on which they were fastened." Dr Samuel Johnson

They persecute our people for the dark coat that we neither made nor chose, and cannot change, and they steal the yields of our Christ's granted talents.

He is watching them, and He is transparently just—Proverbs 15:3.

The nemesis is not extinct; the fact that it tarries isn't proof that it will never come - Habakkuk.

"To deny or belittle this good is, in this dangerous century when the resources and pretensions of power continue to enlarge, a desperate error of intellectual abstraction. More than this, it is a self-fulfilling error, which encourages us to give up the struggle against bad laws and class bound procedures and to disarm ourselves before power. It is to throw away a whole inheritance of struggle about the law and within the forms of law, whose continuity can never be fractured without bringing men and women into immediate danger." - E. P Thompson

"You will bow. You can't beat the system." Kemi Daramola

Jezebel: Esu.

She has got W.C.

Contractor's daughter: Psychotic, imported, dull-faced devil.

I shan't. I know who can - Roman 11; 1 John 4:4.

Then, Birmingham shipped about 200,000 guns annually to West Africa, and after several centuries of unrelenting daily racist terrorism, and properly organised theft of children of defenceless poor people, in 1892, white racist bastards returned to our tribe, in the African bush, IJEBU, only a walking distance from the Atlantic Ocean, and they sadistically used heavy guns to slaughter almost everybody: the REMAINDER - the descendants of those who were CARRIED.

THE ENDURING RESIDUES OF THE ORIGINAL SIN.

ENGLAND: AN INSTITUTIONALLY RACIST HELL-HOLE.

"All sections of the UK Society are institutionally RACIST." Sir Bernard Hogan-Howe.

The Judiciary is part of the UK Society.

"Those who have the power to do wrong with impunity seldom wait long for the will." Dr Samuel Johnson

GOOGLE: MAGBON WAR, 1892.

OYINBO OLE: WHITE THIEVES: HABAKKUK

He is transparently just, and He is watching all - Proverbs 15:3.

The nemesis is not extinct; the fact that it tarries isn't proof that it will never come. Time will unfold the truth.

Then, they used extreme violence to destroy our direct ancestors; now, they use incompetent racist lies to impede our ascent from the huge crater in which made in Birmingham guns buried our ancestors in the African bush.

He is watching them - Proverbs 15:3.

One day, at an unexpected minute, He'd flip.

He has the capacity to get ANGRY, and He has an infinite power to display His anger; He cursed a fig free - Mark 11: 12 - 25.

"Indeed, I tremble for my country when reflect that God is just: that his justice cannot sleep for ever: that considering numbers, nature and natural means only, a revolution of the wheel of fortune, an exchange of situation, is among possible events: that it may become probable by supernatural interference!" Thomas Jefferson

Then, they carried and sold millions of stolen children of defenceless poor people; now, they carry natural resources.

SUBSTITUTION: FRAUDULENT EMANCIPATION.

OYINBO OLE: WHITE THIEVES: HABAKKUK.

"Moderation is a virtue only among those who are thought to have found alternatives." Henry Kissinger.

Facts are sacred; they can't be overstated.

Vengeance belongs to Almighty God; He is watching them - Proverbs 15:3; Habakkuk

The Law Paralysed by Michael Coleade - YouTube

The closeted racist, incontrovertibly functional semi-illiterate, white Senior Vice President of the Association of Her Majesty's District Judges rides a very powerful tiger, deluded, he thinks he's it; dismounted, he'd instantly revert to NOTHING (a former debt-collector Solicitor in Norwich); a brainless descendant of industrial-scale professional thieves and owners of stolen children of defenceless poor people — HABAKKUK

Facts are sacred.

OYINBO OLE: WHITE THIEVES: HABAKKUK.

NIGERIA: SHELL'S DOCILE CASH COW.

The highly luxuriant soil of KEMPSTON yields only food.

Babies with huge oil wells and gas-fields near their houses eat only 1.5/day; a closeted racist, functional semi-illiterate former debt-collector Solicitor in Norwich whose white father and mother have never seen crude oil is our District Judge in BEDFORD.

Majestic appointee.

Majestic stupidity.

"There is no sin except stupidity." Wilde

Freedom of Expression was part of a Queen's speech.

https://www.youtube.com/watch?v=BlpH4hG7m1A

Indisputably superior skin colour, the trust fund (gigantic yields of millions of stolen children of defenceless poor people), and what else?

Ignorance is bliss.

"Those who know the least obey the best. George Farquhar.

The very highly luxuriant soil of Bedfordshire yields only food. The brain of the Polytechnic-educated racist trash yields only confusion; an ignorant descendant of professional thieves and owners of millions of stolen and destroyed innocent human beings — Habakkuk.

No brain.

Poor in natural resources.

Several centuries of stealing and slavery preceded the TRUST FUND. Only the indisputably superior skin colour is good; the wearer neither made nor chose it.

He gave them the indisputably superior skin colour, and they stole almost everything He gave to others - Habakkuk; James 4.

"All have taken what had other owners, and all have resorted to arms rather than quit the prey on which they were fastened." Dr Samuel Johnson

The very greedy, myopic, and shallow racist bastards are not immortal; we are all travellers passing through.

He is watching them - Proverbs 15:3.

OYINBO OLE: WHITE THIEVES: HABAKKUK.

Very greedy, innately racist bastards: There are no oil wells or gas-fields in LUTON. Then, all the people of Luton were fed like battery-hens with the yields of stolen children of defenceless poor people (Kamala's ancestors) - Habakkuk.

He is watching them - Proverbs 15:3.

One day, at an unexpected minute, he'd flip. That is what will happen.

He spoke, and the Universe evolved. He will speak again, and it will perish

A wicked Jew (Herod the Great) jailed, and then decapitated John who baptised Christ, only because he spoke. John was not punished for speaking; John was permanently prevented from speaking.

NEW HEROD: They lied to their simpler children that they are geniuses; they kill all those who know that they are brainless racist bastards -Matthew 2:16.

"Affluence is not a birth right." David Cameron.

Fake righteousness and deceptively schooled civilised decorum were preceded by several centuries of barbarously racist traffic in millions of stolen children of defenceless poor people - Habakkuk.

OYINBO OLE: WHITE THIEVES: HABAKKUK.

Deluded intellectual cowards: Ignorant descendants of racist killers, THIEVES, and owners of stolen children of other people want to force others to see them as they want to be seen, not as they truly are.

There is Freedom of Expression in North Korea; there, one is free to say and/or print only what Kim wants to hear.

In the future, one will be free to say and/or print only what Antichrist Jews and members of the Antichrist Racist Freemasonry Quasi-Religion (Mediocre Mafia), want to hear.

CREEPING NORTH KOREA.

Based on available evidence, Freemasonry Quasi-Religion is intellectually flawed.

Antichrist Racist Freemasonry Quasi-Religion: Half-educated school dropouts and their superiors who have informal access to some very powerful white Judges.

Google: Freemasonry, intellectually flawed.

They use very expensive aprons to decorate the temples of their powerless and useless fertility tools, and carry out indiscreet, vulgar, and Pharisees' charitable works.

OYINBO OLE: WHITE THIEVES: HABAKKUK.

"The good Samaritan had money." Mrs Margaret Thatcher

Indiscreet, vulgar, and Pharisees' charitable works in exchange for what?

Theirs is not a good deal. It was not a good deal then, and it is not a good deal now - Matthew 4:9.

Righteousness without equitable reparation is continuing RACIST FRAUD.

He told the righteous Jew to sell the yields of virtue; He would have told him to return the yields of vice - Matthew 19:21.

Some Jews/Romans lynched and crucified Christ only because He spoke; He disclosed pictures that HIS unbounded mind painted. He was not punished for speaking; He was permanently prevented from speaking.

OYINBO OLE: WHITE THIEVES: HABAKKUK.

"Jews are very good with money." President Donald Trump.

Whose money?

"Fight like hell." President Trump.

Corporal Adolf flipped.

Dr. Olayinka Bamgbelu

"This statement is about a series of letters and emails I have been recieving. I am the above named person. I live at an address provided to police. In this statement I will also mention XXXXXXXXXXXXXXXXXXXXXXXXX a leaseholder for a property I manage at my place work. I am the company director of DOBERN properties based in Ilford. These emails have been sent to my company email address of mail@debern.co.uk, and also letters have been sent to myself at our company ADDress of P.O BOX 1289, ILFORD, IG2 7XZ over the last Two and a half years, I have recieving a series of letters and emails from DR BAMGeLu. DR BAMGBELU is a leasholder for a property I manage at my place of work. Over the period of his leaseholding, DR BAmGelu has continually failed to pay arrears for the property. In march 2016 my company took DR to court and he was ordered to pay outstanding costs of around £20000 since that time and lead up to the case, DR BaMGBelu has been emailing me and posting me letters that are lengthy and accuses me repeatedly of being a racist in emails and letters tact are regularly Ten to twelve pages long, DR BAMGBELU. lists numerous quots from google searches all refrencing ham I am a bigot and a racist. The most recent letter I received from DR BAMGBELU opens with you are jealous and racist Evil combination you hate us we know it" he goes on to say "I would not have knowingly had anything to do with white supremicists." In the last email I recieved from him on 02/09/2016 DR BaMGBELU stated "you are restricted by poor Education within one of the least literate countries in the world". I would be perfectly happy for DR BAMGBElu to contact myself or my company if he has relevant enquiries to his lease holding, however these continuous letters and emails are causing me distress and I feel intimidated. I am not a racist and these accusatios make uncomfortable. All I want is to conduct between us in a normal manner. I want BambGlu to stop emailing me and sending me letters accusing me of being racist and harassing me."
MR ROBERT KINGSTON, SOLICITOR, ACCOUNTANT, AND COMPANY DIRECTOR.

An imbecile Jew!

Corporal Adolf flipped, the rest his history.

"Yes, Sir, it does her honour, but it would do nobody else honour. I have indeed, not read it all. But when I take up the end of a web, and find it packthread, I do not expect, by looking further, to find embroidery."
Dr Samuel Johnson

Idi-Amin expelled the untouchables (DALITS) Britain shipped to Uganda, without luggage or Visas; he seemed to believe that they were thieves. Things didn't turn out well for Uganda.

Hitler Gassed Jews (not all); he seemed to believe that they were thieves.
Germany has, by far, the largest economy in Europe. Germany is the economic powerhouse of Europe. There are not too many Imbecile Jew/Solicitor/Accountant/Company Directors in Germany.

BEDFORD, ENGLAND: Based on available evidence, GDC-Witness, Freemason, Brother, Dr Richard William Hill fabricated reports and unrelentingly lied under oath - Habakkuk 1:4; John 8:44: John 10:10

A RACIST WHITE CROOK.

Facts are sacred.

OYINBO OLE: WHITE THIEVES: HABAKKUK.

When they FORK, which is often, Jews are their GO-TO-PEOPLE.

BLACK HOLOCAUST: The barbarously racist traffic in millions of stolen children of defenceless poor people was the evilest terrorism the world will ever know, in comparison, NAZI HOLOCAUST was a storm in a teacup - Habakkuk.

Gigantic yields of millions of stolen children of defenceless poor people (Kamala's ancestors), not feudal agriculture, lured Eastern European Jews to Britain - Habakkuk.

Facts are sacred.

The truth allows no choice." Dr Samuel Johnson

Bernard Madoff, the undisputed world champion crook, is a Jew.

Based on available evidence, some Jews are imbeciles; imbecile Jews are likelier to be crooked and racist.

Facts are sacred.

"The truth allows no choice." Dr Samuel Johnson

Robert Maxwell was not the real name of the shifty Jew; Ján Ludvík Hyman Binyamin Hoch.

Is Robert Kingston the real name of the Jew?

Paradoxically, the huge profits of black holocaust or the gigantic yields of millions of stolen and destroyed children of defenceless poor people, not feudal agriculture lured Eastern European Jews to Britain; they deceptively changed their names, blended, and latched on to the yields of millions of stolen and destroyed innocent lives (the evilest and most enduring acts of Racist Terrorism the world will ever know) -Habakkuk.

The closeted racist, functional semi-illiterate crooked Judge must one day face the only true Judge, his maker.

https://www.youtube.com/watch?v=BlpH4hG7m1A

"To deny or belittle this good is, in this dangerous century when the resources and pretensions of power continue to enlarge, a desperate error of intellectual abstraction. More than this, it is a self-fulfilling error, which encourages us to give up the struggle against bad laws and class bound procedures and to disarm ourselves before power. It is to throw away a whole inheritance of struggle about the law and within the forms of law, whose continuity can never be fractured without bringing men and women into immediate danger." - E. P Thompson

He is watching them - Proverbs 15:3.

No one is good, absolutely no one - Psalm 53.

The nemesis is not extinct, and the fact that it tarries isn't proof that it will never come – Habakkuk.

✳ ✳ ✳ ✳

RE: English law is equal; its administration is not - Habakkuk 1:4.
Tue, 26 Jan 2021 9:32
Civil Appeals - CMSC (civilappeals.cmsC@justice.gov.uk)To:you Details
Dear Sir/Madam,

Please can you provide your court of appeal reference?

Kind Regards,

Case Management
Civil Appeals Office | HMCTS | Royal Courts Of Justice| London | WC2A 2LL
Web: www.gov.uk/hmcts

With effect from 1st February 2018 the Case Progression team will only answer the phones between the hours of 10am – 12pm and 2pm – 4pm

For information on how HMCTS uses personal data about you please see: https://www.gov.uk/government/organisations/hm-courts-and-tribunals-service/about/personal-information-charter

---

Bamgbelu v GDC/2015.

If our Prime Minister, The Right Honourable Boris Johnson, could prove that District Judge Paul Ayers, Senior Vice President of the Association of Her Majesty's District Judges was not a functional semi-illiterate and an incompetent liar, and if he could prove that GDC-Witness, Ms Rachael Bishop, Senior NHS Nurse, did not unrelentingly tell lies under oath, and if he could prove that Dr Richard William Hill, Postgraduate Tutor - NHS, did not fabricate reports and unrelentingly told lies under oath, and if he could prove that Stephen Henderson, LLM, Head of MDDUS, was not a functional semi-illiterate closeted racist thug who unrelentingly deviated from the truth on record, and if he could prove that GDC-INSIDER, Dr Sue Gregory (OBE), Officer of the Most Excellent Order of our Empire, did not unrelentingly tell lies under implied oath, and if he could prove that GDC-WITNESS, GDC-Witness, Stephanie Twidale, British Army Officer - Territorial Defence, did not unrelentingly tell lies under oath, and if he could prove that Geraint Evans, Postgraduate

Tutor, did not unrelentingly tell lies under implied oath, and if he could prove that Kevin Atkinson, Postgraduate Tutor did not unrelentingly tell lies under oath, and if he could prove that Dr George Rothnie, Deputy Postgraduate Dean, did not deviate from the truth under implied oath, he would confirm the belief of billions, which is that Antichrist Freemasonry Quasi Religion, Antichrist Judaism, Antichrist Islam, and motley assemblies of exotic religions and FAITHS under the common umbrella of the Governor of the Church of England and commander of THE FAITH are not intellectually flawed Satanic Mumbo Jumbo; it will also confirm that reason and vision have boundaries. If reasoning and vision have boundaries, He must have lied when, before the Council, He disclosed the pictures His purportedly unbounded mind painted, and He must have also lied when He audaciously stated: "I am the way and the truth and the life. No one comes to the Father except through me." - John 14:6.

If He told the truth before the Council, everything that is not aligned to John 14:6 is travelling in the wrong direction.

Ignorance is bliss.

"I do not approve of anything that tampers with natural ignorance. Ignorance is like a delicate exotic fruit; touch it and the bloom is gone. The whole theory of modern education is radically unsound. Fortunately, in England, at any rate, education produces no effect whatsoever. If it did, it would prove a serious danger to the upper classes, and probably lead to acts of violence in Grosvenor Square." Oscar Wilde

Based on available evidence, the administration of English law is a weapon of latent but very potent race war.

"Those who have the power to do wrong with impunity seldom wait long for the will." Dr Samuel Johnson.

"To disagree with three – fourths of the British public on all points is one of the first elements of sanity, one of the deepest consolations in all moments of spiritual doubt." Oscar Wilde

Some factual tweets:

Dr George Rothnie (NHS) lied on record.
"The best opportunity of developing academically and emotional." DISTRICT JUDGE BEDFORD
A scatter-head Racist Mason
Superior skin colour concealed dark-black brain; an ignorant descendant of WHITE THIEVES

https://www.youtube.com/watch?v=BlpH4hG7m1A

Dr Kevin Atkinson (Scottish Ken) lied under oath.
"The best opportunity of developing academically and emotional." DISTRICT JUDGE BEDFORD
A scatter-head Racist Mason
Superior skin colour concealed black brain; an ignorant descendant of THIEVES.
https://www.youtube.com/watch?v=BlpH4hG7m1A

Dr Geraint Evans (NHS) lied on record.
"The best opportunity of developing academically and emotional." DISTRICT JUDGE BEDFORD
A scatter-head Racist Mason
Superior skin colour concealed dark black brain; an ignorant descendant of WHITE THIEVES
https://www.youtube.com/watch?v=BlpH4hG7m1A

Dr Stephanie Twidale lied under oath.
"The best opportunity of developing academically and emotional." DISTRICT JUDGE BEDFORD
A scatter-head Racist Mason
Superior skin colour concealed dark black brain; an ignorant descendant

of WHITE THIEVES
https://www.youtube.com/watch?v=BlpH4hG7m1A

Ms Rachael Bishop lied under oath.
"The best opportunity of developing academically and emotional."
DISTRICT JUDGE BEDFORD
A scatter-head Racist Mason
Superior skin colour concealed dark black brain; an ignorant descendant of WHITE THIEVES
https://www.youtube.com/watch?v=BlpH4hG7m1A

Dr Sue Gregory (OBE) lied on record.
"The best opportunity of developing academically and emotional."
DISTRICT JUDGE BEDFORD
A scatter-head Racist Mason
Superior skin colour concealed dark black brain; an ignorant descendant of WHITE THIEVES
https://www.youtube.com/watch?v=BlpH4hG7m1A

Dr Richard Hill fabricated reports
"The best opportunity of developing academically and emotional."
DISTRICT JUDGE BEDFORD
A scatter-head Racist Mason
Superior skin colour concealed dark black brain; an ignorant descendant of WHITE THIEVES
https://www.youtube.com/watch?v=BlpH4hG7m1A

Dr Richard Hill lied under oath.
"The best opportunity of developing academically and emotional."
DISTRICT JUDGE BEDFORD
A scatter-head Racist Mason
Superior skin colour concealed dark black brain; an ignorant descendant of WHITE THIEVES
https://www.youtube.com/watch?v=BlpH4hG7m1A

Dr. Olayinka Bamgbelu

✱ ✱ ✱ ✱ ✱ ✱ ✱

After a High Court hearing in July 2015, the Negro asked for the Transcript of the Court Hearing and Judgement, the usual way.

Re: Confirmation - bamgbelu (Abiodune) v GDC
Tue, 21 Jul 2015 16:48
adeolacole (adeolacole@aol.com)To:ttp Details Slideshow
DTI.jpg (355 KB)

Dear Sir,

I have credited your account with £200. I did not have the case id with me at the bank, so I used Bamgbelu/GDC as the ID.

Please find attached evidence.

Kindly acknowledge the receipt of the sum.

Yours faithfully,

A. Bamgbelu

-----Original Message-----
From: TTP <ttp@dtiglobal.eu>
To: adeolacole <adeolacole@aol.com>
Sent: Tue, 21 Jul 2015 12:06
Subject: Confirmation - bamgbelu (Abiodune) v GDC

Dear Sir/Madam,
Thank you for choosing DTI Global as your nominated tape transcription company. We have received a copy of the court audio for this case, today.
We would be grateful if you could complete and sign the attached

quote, and return it to us with the correct deposit. We will commence transcription once we are in receipt of the signed quotation and the deposit by 3.00pm on the day you wish transcription to begin

We only accept payment by electronic means. To pay the deposit over the telephone, please call 020 7421 4036, quoting the CASE ID 160569.

For bank transfers please use the following details:
National Westminster Bank
56-00-27
27569276
Swift Code/BIC   NWB KGB 2L
IBAN   GB86 NWBK 5600 2727 569276
Account Name   Wordwave International Limited
Reference   CASE ID detailed above

If you are ordering a judgment the timeframes are for production of the draft judgment only. The judgment will need to be approved by the relevant judge before it can be released.

Please note that if you require transcription of a judgment, post judgment discussions or witness evidence in a Court of Appeal, Administrative Court or a transcript of an Application for Permission in the Admin Court, then you will need to make a request in writing to our RCJ Department [020 7421 4036] to rcj@dtiglobal.eu or to RCJ Department, 8th Floor, 165 Fleet Street, London, EC4A 2DY or DX: 414 LDE.

If you would like further information please do not hesitate to contact the Tape Transcription Department on 020 7421 4036.
Regards
TTP Department | DTI
Contracts Administrator, Court Reporting Solutions

Office: +44 (020) 7421-4036

---

165 Fleet Street, London, EC4A 2DY
www.DTIGlobal.com World-class service. Local commitment.

* * * * *

https://www.youtube.com/watch?v=BlpH4hG7m1A

Why is England rich?

Is affluence the yield of the land or Polytechnic-educated brain of the District Judge?

Then, affluence was the yield of several centuries of barbarously racist traffic in millions of stolen children of defenceless people -Habakkuk.

OYINBO OLE: WHITE THIEVES: HABAKKUK

Superiority is their birthright, and any Negro that challenges the centuries-old racist scam will be dealt with.

"Mr Bamgbelu clearly has very, very strong views about education and I understand those views are based upon the fact that he is a successful dentist here in Bedford which he attributes to the fact that his parents cared for him and his education when he was young. They ensured that he had a proper fee paying education........" The Senior Vice President of the Association of Her Majesty's District Judges – proofed and approved Judgement

https://www.youtube.com/watch?v=BlpH4hG7m1A

Indiscreet envy.

Envy is a thief.

When envy and innate RACIAL HATRED copulate, sadism is their offspring.

Facts are sacred; they can't be overstated.

Financial disclosure in a divorce: How can a mere Negro have what I do not have?

"Envy is weak." Yul Brynner

A racist descendant of THIEVES and owners of stolen children of defenceless poor people – Habakkuk.

Their idea of a Negro is FRANK BRUNO, DAVID LAMMY, DIANE ABBOTT and their type: Direct descendants of plantation Negroes: an amalgam of genes, with the African gene being the dominant gene; descendants of stolen human beings who were unnaturally selected, genetically reversed, deliberately bred for hard labour, and reared like cattle on the plantations of righteous Freemasons (very good men who became Saints).

The nemesis is not extinct, the fact that it tarries isn't proof that it will never come.

"All sections of the UK Society are institutionally racist." Sir Bernard Hogan-Howe.

The former Chief of the Metropolitan Police had access to a lot of classified information.

Had his white father and mother had very strong views about education, he'd not have approved and immortal excessive stupidity at 16, and he'd have realised that Jack Dorsey, Mark Zuckerberg and EV Williams, will disseminate any truth to the world, and they're unplayable.

"By definition therefore there needs to be a contact order for Mr B so that he knows when he is going to see his son. It is absolutely essential that this occurs and mother agrees with that. She said so several times in her evidence. Mrs Waller agreed that not only should a child have the opportunity of developing relationship with both parents, any sibling should also be there so that inter- sibling relationship could be fostered and nurtured. Obviously in this particular case the children reside in different places. That immediately puts a strain on the children having limited contact with each other. F's sister is very much older than him and she will be further advanced into her adult life. Thus it is not a matter that that sibling relationship can only be fostered by the children being together. Indeed as we all know absence sometimes makes the heart grow fonder. F should have an opportunity of seeing his sister. Wherever he does that it should be done in a friendly and loving environment. If the time comes that his sister goes to university of course his contact with her will be restricted to the time that she is home from university. In years to come when they have both grown up, with their own family they will see less of each other. But it doesn't mean that they don't still love and adore each other as much as they would if they saw each other every day." The Senior Vice President of the Association of Her Majesty's District Judges – proofed and approved Judgement.

Facts are sacred; they can't be overstated

OYINBO OLODO: A RACIST WHITE DUNCE.

PERCEPTION IS GRANDER THAN REALITY.

https://www.youtube.com/watch?v=BlpH4hG7m1A

Shocking!

"Why, that is, because, dearest, you are a dunce." Habakkuk.

A scatter-head plebeian; an overpromoted polytechnic university educated racist bastard. A righteous descendant of industrial-scale professional THIEVES and owners of stolen children of defenceless people (Kamala's ancestors) - Habakkuk.

OYINBO OLE: WHITE THIEVES: HABAKKUK.

The white father and mother of the Senior Vice President of the Association of Her Majesty's District Judges did not care, had they, he'd not have approved and immortalised excessive stupidity at 16, and he'd be a properly educated lawyer, privately educated Anthony Blair, Anthony Julius, Geoff Hoon and Rabinder Singh's class, and he might practice proper law in STRAND.

It's plainly deductible that the white father and mother of the Senior Vice President of the Association of Her Majesty's District Judges couldn't afford to pay for qualitative education; why should we have to come from very far AFRICA to pay for his misfortune and parts of its tell-tale signs (sequelae)?

Our ancestors have paid, and they paid more than enough.

Dr Richard Dawkins and OECD implied that all the children of the Senior Vice President of the Association of Her Majesty's District Judges should be duller than their white father and his type.

He is relevant only because he's a Judge; I wouldn't have voluntarily bought anything from a closeted racist former debt-collector Solicitor in Norwich.

Only his skin colour is indisputably superior; what else?

He is relevant only because England is rich; the affluence is not the yield of the land or his brain.

Affluence did not evolve; then, it was actively and deliberately stolen.

"Affluence is not a birthright." David Cameron.

NIGERIA (oil/gas) is by far more relevant to the survival of all his children than KEMPSTON. Then, the white ancestors of his white father and mother were fed like battery hens with the yields of stolen children of defenceless poor people - Habakkuk.

Facts are sacred.

In order to maintain the very unfair the advantage that is based on the indisputably superior skin colour that the wearer neither made nor chose, they stifle Freedom of Expression, suppress the truth, and propagate the centuries-old scam that the brain is part of the indisputably superior skin colour that they neither made nor chose.

Whites are very scared, and not just in Trump's America (75M), and rightly so.

Increasingly colour-blind level playing field is gradually unravelling the mother of all racist scams: The centuries-old unspoken myth that the brain is related to skin colour. Only fools expect descendants of THIEVES and owners of stolen children of defenceless poor people to voluntarily relinquish the inherited advantageous position (WHITE PRIVILEGE) that was primarily gained through centuries of extreme violence, and properly organised industrial-scale stealing of human beings, armed stealing of moveable and immoveable valuables that had other owners, without fights.

"Fight like hell." President Trump

If our Prime Minister, The Right Honourable Boris Johnson, could prove that District Judge Paul Ayers, Senior Vice President of the Association of Her Majesty's District Judges was not a functional semi-illiterate and an incompetent liar, and if he could prove that GDC-Witness, Ms Rachael Bishop, Senior NHS Nurse, did not unrelentingly tell lies under oath, and if he could prove that Dr Richard William Hill, Postgraduate Tutor - NHS, did not fabricate reports and unrelentingly told lies under oath, and if he could prove that Stephen Henderson, LLM, Head of MDDUS, was not a functional semi-illiterate closeted racist thug who unrelentingly deviated from the truth on record, and if he could prove that GDC-INSIDER, Dr Sue Gregory (OBE), Officer of the Most Excellent Order of our Empire, did not unrelentingly tell lies under implied oath, and if he could prove that GDC-Witness, Stephanie Twidale, British Army Officer - Territorial Defence, did not unrelentingly tell lies under oath, and if he could prove that Geraint Evans, Postgraduate Tutor, did not unrelentingly tell lies under implied oath, and if he could prove that Kevin Atkinson, Postgraduate Tutor, did not unrelentingly tell lies under oath, and if he could prove that Dr George Rothnie, Deputy Postgraduate Dean, did not deviate from the truth under implied oath, he would confirm the belief of billions, which is that Antichrist Freemasonry Quasi Religion, Antichrist Judaism, Antichrist Islam, and motley assemblies of exotic religions and FAITHS under the common umbrella of the Governor of the Church of England and commander of THE FAITH are not intellectually flawed Satanic Mumbo Jumbo; it will also confirm that reasoning and vision have boundaries. If reasoning and vision have boundaries, He must have lied when, before the Council, when He disclosed pictures His purportedly unbounded mind painted, and He must have also lied when He audaciously stated: "I am the way and the truth and the life. No one comes to the Father except through me." - John 14:6.

If He told the truth before the Council, everything that is not aligned to John 14:6 is travelling in the wrong direction.

FACTS ARE SACRED.
Ignorance is bliss.

Another Prime Minister implied that some Judges are racists, as they seemed to measure their own kindred with a very different yardstick - Apartheid by stealth.

Demons will not cast out demons - Matthew 12:27

FACTS ARE SACRED.

"British Prime Minister attacks racial bias in Universities and the Justice System. 'David Cameron has persuaded a leading labour MP to 'defect' by launching a Government investigation into why black people make up such a high proportion of the prison population. Mr Cameron said Mr Lammy would examine why blacks and ethnic minorities make up nearly a quarter of Crown Court defendants – compared to 14 percent of the population. He added: 'If you are black, you are more likely to be in a prison cell than studying in a University. And if you are black, it seems you're more likely to be sentenced to custody for a crime than if you are white. 'We should investigate why this is and how we can end this possible discrimination. That's why I have asked David Lammy to lead a review. Mr Lammy, who is a qualified barrister, said: 'I am pleased to accept the Prime Minister's invitation." Mr Paul Dacre, Daily Mail, 31.01.2016

FACTS ARE SACRED.

Then, Mr David Cameron had full access to all classified information.

"Someone must be trusted. Let it be the Judges." Lord Denning

Judges are human beings; some human beings are RACISTS.

RACIAL HATRED is not a myth, and it is considerably more common than ordinarily realised.

"White supremacy is REAL, and it needs to be shattered." Dr Cornel West

The American Actress, Megan Markle: "She was the subject of explicit and obnoxious RACIAL HATRED." John Bercow

The speaker had access to a lot of information.

"FAILING SCHOOLS AND A BATTLE FOR BRITAIN: This was the day the British education establishment's 50-year betrayal of the Nation's children lay starkly exposed in all its ignominy. After testing 166,000 people in 24 education systems, the Organisation for Economic Cooperation and Development (OECD) finds that England young adults are amongst the least literate and numerate in the industrialised world." Daily Mail, 09.01.2013

Young adults have LORDS.

LORDS of morons are likelier to be morons too.

All sections of the UK Society are institutionally RACIST." Sir Bernard

Hogan-Howe.

Sir Bernard Hogan-Howe had access to a lot of classified information.

RACIST JUDGES are very careful, they remove their masks only when they feel it is very safe to do so; they are becoming very dull so their safety net in unsafe.

"It is incumbent upon the court and all those professionals involved to conclude court proceedings as quickly as possible. This hopefully ensures that a child has stability, love and affection and the parents working together to ensure that he has the best opportunity of developing academically and emotional." The Senior Vice President of the Association of Her Majesty's District Judges – proofed and approved Judgement.

A RACIST WHITE FOOL'S APPROVAL.

Sheep unnaturally shepherd sheep.

"Mediocrity weighing mediocrity in the balance, and incompetence applauding its brother ...." Wilde

Prior to COVID, what was in Norwich for functional semi-illiterate Solicitors to do?

PERCEPTION IS GRANDER THAN REALITY

He WILL lose in everything on a colour-blind level playing field. Sincere immodesty is sincerer than insincere modesty. Only his skin colour is indisputably superior; he neither made nor chose it.

"The truth allows no choice." Dr Samuel Johnson

Freedom of Expression is ESSENTIAL for the continuing refinement and improvement of our system.

"Freedom of Expression is the cornerstone of our democracy." Jacob

Rees-Mogg.

The Senior Vice President of the Association of Her Majesty's District Judges approved what his white father and mother spoke, which his polytechnic educated supervisors in Luton authorised.

His Honour Judge Perusko studied law at Polytechnic.

Facts are sacred.

* * * * *

Dr Richard Hill fabricated reports
NIGERIA: SHELL'S CASH COW
Babies with huge oilwells near their houses eat 1.5/day; a closeted racist semi-illiterate white man whose father and mother have never seen crude oil is our Judge in BEDFORD.
https://www.youtube.com/watch?v=BlpH4hG7m1A

* * * * *

NORTHAMPTON, ENGLAND: Based on available evidence, GDC-WITNESS, Dr Geraint Evans, Postgraduate Tutor, Oxford, unrelentingly lied under implied oath - Habakkuk 1:4; John 8:44; John 10:10.

A RACIST WHITE CROOK.

CREEPING NORTH KOREA.

FACTS ARE SACRED.

CORBY, ENGLAND: Based on available evidence, GDC-WITNESS, Dr George Rothnie unrelentingly lied under implied oath - Habakkuk 1:4; John 8:44; John 10:10.

A RACIST WHITE CROOK.

CREEPING NORTH KOREA.

FACTS ARE SACRED.

CORBY, ENGLAND: Based on available evidence, GDC-WITNESS, Dr Kevin Atkinson, Scottish Ken, unrelentingly lied under oath - Habakkuk 1:4; John 8:44; John 10:10.

A RACIST WHITE CROOK.

CREEPING NORTH KOREA.

FACTS ARE SACRED.

OXFORD, ENGLAND: Based on available evidence, GDC-WITNESS, British Soldier - Territorial Defence, Dr Stephanie Twidale (TD) unrelentingly lied under oath - Habakkuk 1:4; John 8:44; John 10:10.

A RACIST WHITE CROOK.

CREEPING NORTH KOREA.

FACTS ARE SACRED.

WOLLASTON, ENGLAND: Based on available evidence, GDC-WITNESS, Ms Rachael Bishop, Senior NHS Nurse, unrelentingly lied under oath - Habakkuk 1:4; John 8:44; John 10:10.

A RACIST WHITE CROOK.

CREEPING NORTH KOREA.

FACTS ARE SACRED.

BEDFORD, ENGLAND: Based on available evidence, GDC-INSIDER, Dr Sue Gregory, Officer of the Most Excellent Order of our Empire unrelentingly lied under implied oath - Habakkuk 1:4; John 8:44; John 10:10.

A RACIST WHITE CROOK.

CREEPING NORTH KOREA.

FACTS ARE SACRED.

BEDFORD, ENGLAND: Based on available evidence, GDC-WITNESS, Freemason, Brother, Dr Richard William Hill fabricated reports and unrelentingly lied under oath - Habakkuk 1:4; John 8:44; John 10:10.

A RACIST WHITE CROOK.

CREEPING NORTH KOREA.

FACTS ARE SACRED.

A bastardised, unashamedly mediocre, indiscreetly dishonest, vindictive, potently weaponised, and institutionally RACIST system that his overseen by MASONS (Mediocre Mafia) - Habakkuk.

Then and now, in jurisdictions where the satanic network (Antichrist Racist Freemason) is in charge, their members have power to tell lies under oath.

"The supreme vice is shallowness." Wilde

Christ before the crooked, shallow, and intellectually insufficient Council.

"Then the people who had arrested Christ led him to the home of Caiaphas, the high priest, where the teachers of religious law and other leaders had gathered. Meanwhile, Peter was following behind and eventually came to the courtyard of the high priest's house. He went in and sat with the guards and waited to see what was going to happen to Christ. Inside the leading priests and the entire Council was trying to find witnesses who would lie about Jesus, so they could put him to death. But even though they found many who agreed to give false witness, there was no testimony that they could use. Finally, two men were found who declared, "This man said, 'I am able to destroy the Temple of God and rebuild it in three days.'" Then the high priest stood up and said to Christ, "Well, aren't you going to answer to these charges? What do you have to say for yourself?" But Jesus remained silent. Then the high priest said to him, "I demand in the name living God that you will tell us whether you are the Messiah, the son of God." Jesus replied, "Yes, it is as you say. And in the future, you will see me, the son of Man, sitting at God's right hand in place of power and coming back in clouds of heaven." Then the high priest tore his clothing to show his horror, shouting, "Blasphemy! Why do you need other witnesses? You have heard his blasphemy. What is your verdict?" "Guilty!" they shouted. "He must die!" Then they spit in Christ's face and hit him with their fists and slapped him, saying "Prophesy to us, you Messiah! Who hit you that time?" as stated in the Book of Matthew.

The Council lied. The Council's Judges lied.

He was not asked to expatiate. He was lynched like Gadhafi and crucified only because He spoke. He was not punished for speaking, He was permanently prevented from speaking, and His offence was extracted from the response He gave to their question.

Then lunatics killed the Judge because He stated what they didn't like. Now, half-educated school dropouts and their superiors who have informal access to some very powerful white Judges – destroy anyone who disagrees with their brainless Satanic Mumbo Jumbo and/or refuses to bow down to low life racist trash, genetic aliens with camouflage English names, only because they have the indisputably superior skin colour; they neither made nor chose the most favourable asset.

Righteous descendants of industrial-scale professional THIEVES and owners of stolen children of defenceless poor people (the evilest racist terrorism the world will ever know) – Habakkuk.

As they seemed to have been lied to at home and/or school that their indisputably superior skin colour is the greatest creation of Almighty God, everything good is assumed in favour of their asset as human beings, and they will be considerably diminished as human being without it.

White privilege is a fraudulent scam.

White Privilege is a racist scam: The mother of all racist scam. They are scared because if it universally found out that intellect is unrelated to their indisputably superior skin colour, the centuries-old elaborate scam will unravel.

"Gracia Negrito." Cavani, Manchester United.

A cheap racist slur is by far better than unrelenting persecutory Negrophobia and Negrophobic Perjury.

RACISM: ZERO TOLERANCE IN GREAT BRITAIN.

Fake Zero Tolerance: Incompetent art incompetently imitates life.

Almost everything is a spin.

"Racism is rife in most of the organisations across Britain." The Mayor of London.

The Mayor of London has access to a lot of classified information.

If the white man, the Senior Vice President of the Association of Her Majesty's District Judges, read his approved Judgement, he was excessively stupid; if he didn't, he lied.

FACTS ARE SACRED.

He will not defend himself on a colour-blind level playing field. His skin colour is indisputably superior; what else?

It is plainly deductible that the white father and mother of the Senior Vice President of the Association of Her Majesty's District Judges did not care, had they, he'd not have approved and immortalised (for eternity) excessive stupidity at 16, and he'd be a properly educated lawyer, privately educated Anthony Blair, Anthony Julius, Geoff Hoon and Rabinder Singh's class, and he might practice proper law in STRAND.

Then, after several centuries of daily, merciless racist tyranny (the evilest racist terrorism the world will ever know), in 1892, they returned to our tribe in the African bush (IJEBU), and they used heavy guns to sadistically slaughter almost everybody.

Facts are sacred.

GOOGLE: MAGBON 1892.

Now, they impede our ascent from the very deep crater in which made in Birmingham guns buried our direct ancestors, in the African bush, during several centuries of the evilest racist terrorism the world will ever know - Habakkuk.

Fake righteousness and deceptively schooled civilised decorum were preceded by several centuries of barbarously racist traffic in millions of stolen children of defenceless poor people – Habakkuk.

Facts are sacred.

"England is like a prostitute who, having sold her body all her life, decides to quit and close her business, and then tells everybody she wants to be chaste and protect her flesh as if it were jade." He Manzi, Chinese politician

OYINBO OLE: WHITE THIEVES: HABAKKUK

He is watching them - Proverbs 15:3.

They persecute our people for the dark coat that we neither made nor chose, and cannot change, and they steal the yields of our Christ granted talents.

The nemesis isn't extinct, and the fact that it tarries isn't proof that it will never come - Habakkuk.

If you are a functional semi-illiterate, and you have power, you are likely to stifle Freedom of Expression, and conceal intellectual impotence.

NEW HEROD, MATTHEW 2:16: They lie to their duller children that they're geniuses, and they kill all those who know that they're brainless racist bastards.

He rides a very powerful tiger, deluded, he thinks he is it, dismounted, the closeted racist, functional semi-illiterate former debt-collector Solicitor in Norwich will instantly revert to NOTHING.

The want superiority, their baseless birth right; they don't want Freedom of Expression - Apartheid by stealth. They want to eat their cakes and have them.

If they were truly superiorly created by Almighty God, they would embrace the basic right to disclose any true picture the mind paints.

"There is not a truth existing which I fear... or would wish unknown to the whole world." Thomas Jefferson

Deluded intellectual cowards: They want baseless superiority that is based on the indisputably superior skin colour that they neither made mor chose, they don't want Freedom of Expression because they don't want their people to know about what they secretly do to our people.

Bedford, England: Based on available evidence, Freemason, Brother, Dr Richard William Hill fabricated reports and unrelentingly lied under oath – Habakkuk 1:4; John 8:44; John 10:10.

A RACIST WHITE CROOK.

A bastardised, unashamedly mediocre, vindictive, indiscreetly dishonest, potently weaponised, and institutionally racist system that is overseen by the Antichrist Racist MASONS (Mediocre Mafia) – Habakkuk 1:4.

Facts are sacred.

BORIS JOHNSON: Give is the legal tools, and we will deal with our irreconcilable enemies: The spineless (worms) half-educated school dropouts and their superiors who use expensive aprons to decorate the temples of their powerless and useless fertility tools.

They swear by the name of Almighty God never to tell lies but they lie that they don't lie – Psalm 144.

"Give us the tools, and we will finish the job." Sir Winston Churchill.

In some parts of the world, Judges, nearly all, are MASONS; some of them are thicker than a gross of planks.

https://www.youtube.com/watch?v=BlpH4hG7m1A

Facts are sacred.

In some parts of the world, Antichrist Racist Freemasons, half-educated school dropouts and their superiors who have informal access to some very powerful Judges, are above all laws (Christ's and Man's) – Habakkuk 1:4.

The closeted racist, dodgy, Antichrist Racist Freemason Judges are not immortal, and they must leave, and they WILL inevitably face the transparent Justice of Christ.

And He ordered us to preach to the people, and solemnly to testify that this is the One who has been appointed by God as Judge of the living and the dead - Acts 10:42.

Ignorant fools: Righteous descendants of industrial-scale professional THIEVES and owners of stolen children of defenceless poor people – Habakkuk.

He is watching them, and He is transparently just – Proverbs 15:3.

"I tremble for my country when I reflect that God is just; that his justice cannot sleep forever." Thomas Jefferson

The nemesis is not extinct, and the fact that it tarries isn't proof that it will never come.

Antichrist Racist Freemasons wear vulgar Pharisees' charitable works as cloaks of deceit, and they use very expensive aprons to decorate the temples of their powerless and useless fertility tools; they have informal access to some very powerful white Judges – Habakkuk 1:4.

"The good Samaritan had money." Mrs Margaret Thatcher (1925 – 2013).

Presumably, the Good Samaritans money was the yield of transparent virtue.

He told the righteous Jew to sell the yields of virtue, give the proceeds to the poor, and follow Him; He'd have told the rich Pharisee to return the yields of vice to the rightful owners – Matthew 19:21.

The Grand Antichrist Masons' Temple to Baal, 60 Great Queen St, Holborn, London WC2B 5AZ, was built in the 1700s (18th century), at a height of the barbarously racist traffic in millions of stolen children of defenceless poor people – Habakkuk.

Righteousness without equitable reparation is continuing racist fraud.

Deluded and conceited, like the Pharisees, they baselessly awarded themselves the monopoly knowledge and become impervious and intolerant to other views, and they usurped power, their job is to interpret the laws prescribed by the servants of the people, but they impose their will with illegal parallel power (unelected). They lie to their duller children that they're geniuses, and they kill all those who know they're not – Matthew 2:16.

He jailed him only because he spoke; the lunatic Jew removed John's head when he refused to stop speaking – Matthew 14.

He was lynched like Gadhafi and was crucified only because He spoke: He disclosed pictures His unbounded painted.

Then, like Herod, MBS and Kim, they used to butcher those who stated and/or printed what they did not want their moron sheep to know. The last decapitation in England was in 1827, and beheading was removed from the statute book in 1973, and the same year (1973), Kenneth Baker banned caning.

Why remove the heads of your enemies if it is illegal to flog them?

They lied to their duller children that they are geniuses, when, in fact, the power to economically strangulate and/or inflict bodily sufferings on their enemies is the principal leverage of the hands-off racist killers; they will lose, all the time, on a colour-blind and level playing field – Matthew 26, 27.

They lied to their moron sheep that they were geniuses, and they killed all those who knew that they were brainless racist bastards. Their sole objective is to shepherd their moron sheep unchallenged.

"Of black men, the numbers are too great who are now repining under English cruelty." Dr Samuel Johnson.

https://www.facebook.com/rotimi.osunsan/videos/3088536551193798

https://www.youtube.com/watch?v=BlpH4hG7m1A&feature=youtu.be

"They may not have been well written from a grammatical point of view, but I am confident I had not forgotten any of the facts." Dr Geraint Evans, Postgraduate Tutor, Oxford.

Northampton England, Rowtree Dental Care: Based on available evidence, Geraint Evans, Welsh Dunce, GDC-WITNESS, unrelentingly lied under oath – Habakkuk 1:4; John 8:44: John 10:10.

A RACIST WHITE CROOK.

Facts are sacred.

They deter the expression of the truth by indirect threat to take life and/or economically strangulate, induce insanity, and take life indirectly.

They have the power to destroy the body that they did not make and cannot make, and what is inferior to it, they do not have power to do anything about the vivid revelation that He is who He say He is, and He WILL get what He wants.

We are forked: His Knight attacks the Queen and King, and only the Queen can move.

Harold Shipman was a hands-on direct killer, but there was no racist bone in him, and he poisoned only his own kindred.

They are hands-off racist killers, as only our people are dying in the latent but very potent, raging, and unspoken race war: The enduring residues of the original sin.

OYINBO OLE: WHITE THIEVES: HABAKKUK.

When their own people commit racist crimes against our own people, their principal objective is to spin racist lies to their people, or bury he racist lies, or bury the victim. They're not immortal, we will go, and racist bastards must come – 2 Samuel 12:23.

It is impossible to conceal their incompetent racist lies, and save face, without killing the victim.

"White supremacy is real, and it needs to be shattered." Dr Cornel West.

OYINBO OLE: WHITE THIEVES: HABAKKUK

No brain.
Poor in natural resources.

The closeted white supremacist thugs have power over the body and what is inferior to it, nateril possessions

If one bred some white pigs for bacon, the stupidest of the white pigs should be the first to be butchered,

https://youtu.be/rayVcfyu9Tw

"Those who have the power to do wrong with impunity seldom wait long for the will." Dr Samuel Johnson.

They're very hardened racist thugs, and those they need to spin are among the least literate and least numerate adults in the industrialised world - OECD.

Facts are sacred.

"FAILING SCHOOLS AND A BATTLE FOR BRITAIN: This was the day the British education establishment's 50-year betrayal of the Nation's children lay starkly exposed in all its ignominy. After testing 166,000 people in 24 education systems, the Organisation for Economic Cooperation and Development (OECD) finds that England young adults are amongst the least literate and numerate in the industrialised world." Daily Mail, 09.01.2013

Young adults have LORDS.

LORDS of morons are likelier to be morons too.

The report, by the OECD, warns that the UK needs to take significant action to boost the basic skills of the nation's young people. The 460-page study is based on the first-ever survey of the literacy, numeracy and problem-solving at work skills of 16 to 65-year-olds in 24 countries, with almost 9,000 people taking part in England and Northern Ireland to make up the UK results. The findings showed that England and Northern Ireland have some of the highest proportions of adults scoring no higher than Level 1 in literacy and numeracy - the lowest level on the OECD's scale. This suggests that their skills in the basics are no better than that of a 10-year-old.

AN IMBECILE: AN ADULT WITH THE BASIC SKILLS OF A CHILD.

When Solicitors and/or Barristers fail in Law Practice, thousands do, if they're MASONS, they could become Judges, and if not, they become Politicians or something else.

Apart fron creating cushy salaried jobs for Solicitors and Barristers

Google: Dr Anand Kamath, dentist.

Based on very proximate observations and direct experiences, the instinct of the privileged dullard is Apartheid by stealth.

Freedom of expression was a natural right in our tribe in the African bush (IJEBU) – before their ancestors found ours in the African bush, in the 15th century.

"The liberty of the individual is no gift of civilization. It was greatest before there was any civilization." SIGMUND FREUD

They want superiority, their birth right

"Gracia Negrito." Cavani, Manchester United.

A cheap racist slur is a crime; unrelenting persecutory Negrophobia and Negrophobic perjury are not: Zero tolerance for racial intolerance, indeed. Incompetent art incompetently imitates life. They use sticky plaster to treat chronic gangrene that is centuries old. The enduring residue of the original sin.

They are very lucky; those they need to spin are among the least literate and least numerate in the industrialised world. They spin their people in layers, and they have been spun for centuries.

The report, by the OECD, warns that the UK needs to take significant action to boost the basic skills of the nation's young people. The 460-page study is based on the first-ever survey of the literacy, numeracy and problem-solving at work skills of 16 to 65-year-olds in 24 countries, with almost 9,000 people taking part in England and Northern Ireland to make up the UK results. The findings showed that England and Northern Ireland have some of the highest proportions of adults scoring no higher than Level 1 in literacy and numeracy - the lowest level on the OECD's scale. This suggests that their skills in the basics are no better than that of a 10-year-old.

AN IMBECILE: AN ADULT WITH THE BASIC SKILLS OF A CHILD.

"Racism is rife in most of the organisations across Britain." The Mayor of London

The Mayor of London has access to a lot of classified information.

"All sections of the UK Society are institutionally racist." Sir Bernard Hogan-Howe

"Racism is alive and well and living in Tower Hamlets, in Westminster and, yes, sometimes in the judiciary." Judge Peter Herbert, Officer of the Most Excellent Order of the British Empire (OBE)

They want to eat their cakes and have them; one needs power to do that.

Facts are sacred, they can't be overstated.

Their skin colour is indisputably superior, ours is a curse. It is impossible to defend ourselves against those who visibly better than us without Freedom of Expression.

Their indisputably superior skin colour is not the greatest creation of Almighty God.

White supremacy is a centuries-old scam; based on available evidence, its beneficiaries, including some Racist Judges guard it.

FACTS ARE SACRED.

"Those who have the power to do wrong with impunity seldom wait long for the will." Dr Samuel Johnson.

CREEPING NORTH KOREA.

Based on observations and direct experiences, functional semi-illiterate Judges, nearly all, are RACISTS.

NIGERIA: SHELL'S DOCILE CASH COW.

Babies with huge oil wells and gas fields near their houses eat only 1.5/day; a closeted racist, incontrovertibly functional semi-illiterate former Norwich Solicitor whose white father and mother have never seen crude oil is our District Judge in BEDFORD.

Then, righteous, civilised, and Christian racist bastards carried and sold millions of stolen children of defenceless poor people, now, they carry natural resources.

SUBSTITUTION: FRAUDULENT EMANCIPATION.

There are no oil wells or gas fields in Luton.

FACTS ARE SACRED.

"Moderation is virtue only among those who are thought to have found alternatives." Henry Kissinger.

"To deny or belittle this good is, in this dangerous century when the resources and pretensions of power continue to enlarge, a desperate error of intellectual abstraction. More than this, it is a self-fulfilling error, which encourages us to give up the struggle against bad laws and class bound procedures and to disarm ourselves before power. It is to throw away a whole inheritance of struggle about the law and within the forms of law, whose continuity can never be fractured without bringing men and women into immediate danger." - E. P Thompson

MONEY is meat, and it is not the yield of the brain of the polytechnic-educated fake Judge. The highly luxuriant soil of Kempston yields only food. His white ancestors were THIEVES and owners of stolen children - Habakkuk.

https://www.youtube.com/watch?v=BlpH4hG7m1A

A righteous descendant of racists, THIEVES, and owners of stolen children of defenceless poor people - Habakkuk.

The land yields only food. The District Judge is a functional semi-illiterate. It is plainly deductible that his white ancestors were THIEVES - Habakkuk.

"Gracia Negrito." Cavani, Manchester United

A cheap racist slur is a crime; fabricating reports and unrelentingly telling lies under oath isn't.

Racism: Zero Tolerance in Britain. Incompetent art incompetently imitates life.

Righteousness without equitable reparation is continuing racist fraud.

Intelligence is a function of genetic mix; education will polish only what genetic mix presents to it. Antichrist Racist Freemasons do not control genetic mix; intelligence is the exclusive preserve of Christ.

Those who shipped millions of guns to West Africa, among those who had no means to treating penetrative gunshot wounds, during several centuries of barbarously racist traffic in millions of stolen children of defenceless poor people, were neither civilised nor intelligent.

Parts of the resultant effects of several centuries of merciless racist terrorism is that imbeciles thrive in Great Britain. What's great about that?

"It is incumbent upon the court and all those professionals involved to conclude court proceedings as quickly as possible. This hopefully ensures that a child has stability, love and affection and the parents working together to ensure that he has the best opportunity of developing academically and emotional." The Senior Vice President of the Association of Her Majesty's District Judges – proofed and approved Judgement.

"Yes, Sir, it does her honour, but it would do nobody else honour. I have indeed, not read it all. But when I take up the end of a web, and find it packthread, I do not expect, by looking further, to find embroidery." Dr Samuel Johnson

Semi-illiterate District Judge of imbeciles.

The report, by the OECD. warns that the UK needs to take significant action to boost the basic skills of the nation's young people. The 460-page study is based on the first-ever survey of the literacy, numeracy and problem-solving at work skills of 16 to 65-year-olds in 24 countries, with almost 9,000 people taking part in England and Northern Ireland to make up the UK results. The findings showed that England and Northern Ireland have some of the highest proportions of adults scoring no higher than Level 1 in literacy and numeracy - the lowest level on the OECD's scale. This suggests that their skills in the basics are no better than that of a 10-year-old.

AN IMBECILE: AN ADULT WITH THE BASIC SKILLS OF A CHILD.

The only evidence of his purportedly higher IQ is the stolen affluence that his ancestors crossed the English Channels, in dinghy boats, without luggage or decent shoes, to latch onto.

They want baseless superiority; they don't want Freedom of Expression because they don't want their people to know about what we truly feel about what they do to our people inside Antichrist Britain. They like to eat their cakes and have them - Apartheid by stealth.

Based on very proximate observations and direct experiences, the natural instinct of the privileged dullard is Apartheid by stealth.

FACTS ARE SACRED.

"I think I will ask our legal adviser for any advice he may have. My view is that there are six or seven of us here who had the admission down, but we cannot find it in the transcript and there is wordings that imply that there was, but it is not in black and white....." Dr Shiv Pabary, Member of the British Empire (MBE) and Justice of Peace (JP)

Moron Member of our Empire (MMBE) and Justice of Incompetent Racist Lies (JIRL)

"The truth allows no choice." Dr Samuel Johnson

* * * * *

Re Meeting 9th March
Mon, 8 Mar 2010 20:20
George Rothnie georgerothnie@hotmail.com
To adeolacole@aol.com
Hi Ola,
We are scheduled to meet tomorrow evening at my surgery about 5.30ish. Unfortunately something has cropped up which necessytates me having to postpone the meeting. I'm really sorry it's such short notice.
I will contact you in the week to arrange another date.
Once agaim my apologies.

George

Dr George Rothnie (Scottish George), Deputy Postgraduate Dean Oxford.

Everything is baselessly assumed in favour of the indisputably superior skin colour that the wearer neither made nor chose - Apartheid by stealth.

https://www.youtube.com/watch?v=BlpH4hG7m1A&feature=youtu.be

"They may not have been well written from a grammatical point of view but I am confident I had not forgotten any of the facts." Dr Geraint Evans, Postgraduate Tutor, Oxford

https://youtu.be/rayVcfyu9Tw

Natural selection will not remove ignorance from future generations." Dr Richard Dawkins.

England's young people are near the bottom of the global league table for basic skills. OECD finds 16- to 24-year-olds have literacy and numeracy levels no better than those of their grandparents' generation.

England is the only country in the developed world where the generation approaching retirement is more literate and numerate than the youngest adults, according to the first skills survey by the Organisation for Economic Co-operation and Development.

In a stark assessment of the success and failure of the 720-million-strong adult workforce across the wealthier economies, the economic thinktank warns that in England, adults aged 55 to 65 perform better than 16- to 24-year-olds at foundation levels of literacy and numeracy. The survey did not include people from Scotland or Wales.

The OECD study also finds that a quarter of adults in England have the maths skills of a 10-year-old. About 8.5 million adults, 24.1% of the population, have such basic levels of numeracy that they can manage only one-step tasks in arithmetic, sorting numbers or reading graphs. This is worse than the average in the developed world, where an average of 19% of people were found to have a similarly poor skill base.

Everything about them is superior except their brain; they know. Their people are everywhere, and they kill Negroes, who refuse to accept that their brains are superior because their skin colour is indisputably superior, albeit hands-off.

OYINBO OLE: WHITE THIEVES: HABAKKUK

No brain.

Poor in natural resources.

Several centuries of stealing and SLAVERY preceded the TRUST FUND - Habakkuk.

Only the indisputably superior skin colour is good.

Facts are sacred.

The report, by the OECD, warns that the UK needs to take significant action to boost the basic skills of the nation's young people. The 460-page study is based on the first-ever survey of the literacy, numeracy and problem-solving at work skills of 16 to 65-year-olds in 24 countries, with almost 9,000 people taking part in England and Northern Ireland to make up the UK results. The findings showed that England and Northern Ireland have some of the highest proportions of adults scoring no higher than Level 1 in literacy and numeracy - the lowest level on the OECD's scale. This suggests that their skills in the basics are no better than that of a 10-year-old.

AN IMBECILE: AN ADULT WITH THE BASIC SKILLS OF A CHILD.

Apart from creating cushy salaried jobs (quasi-communism) for incontrovertibly functional semi-illiterate Solicitors/Barristers who couldn't hack it in the very competitive real world, what do imbeciles need expensive administration of the law for?

"Many Scots masters were considered among the most brutal, with life expectancy on their plantations averaging a mere four years. We worked them to death then simply imported more to keep the sugar and thus the money flowing. Unlike centuries of grief and murder, an apology cost nothing. So, what does Scotland have to say?" Herald Scotland: Ian Bell, Columnist, Sunday 28 April 2013

"I know of no evil that has ever existed, nor can imagine any evil to exist, worse than the tearing of eighty thousand persons annually from their native land, by a combination of the most civilised nations inhabiting the most enlightened part of the globe, but more especially under the sanction of the laws of that Nation which calls herself the most free and the most happy of them all." Prime Minister William Pitt the Younger

OYINBO OLE: WHITE THIEVES: HABAKKUK.

If the Senior Vice President of the Association of Her Majesty's District Judges read his approved Judgement, he was excessively stupid; if he didn't, he lied.

"Time for Scots to say sorry for slavery
Herald Scotland:
Ian Bell, Columnist / Sunday 28 April 2013 / Opinion
Sunday 28 April 2013

According to the American founding father, the son of a Caithness Kirk minister had about him "an air of great simplicity and honesty'". The likes of James Boswell and Laurence Sterne also enjoyed the merchant's company.

To his contemporaries, he was, as the author Adam Hochschild has written, "'a wise, thoughtful man who embodied the Scottish virtues of frugality, sobriety, and hard work'". Oswald was a scholar of theology, philosophy, and history. He collected art, particularly Rubens and Rembrandt, and gave handsomely to charity. Oswald, who learned his trade in Glasgow, also represented Britain in negotiations with the Americans after their war of liberation. He was the cosmopolitan epitome of Enlightenment success. But when he wasn't busy with good works, Oswald waded in blood. The precise number of deaths that can be laid at his door is impossible to calculate. As the leading figure in Grant, Oswald & Co, he had investments in each corner of the "'triangular trade'". In his own name, Oswald trafficked at least 13,000 Africans, although he never set foot on their continent. By the time he bought Auchincruive House and 100,000 acres in Ayrshire in 1764, he was worth £500,000. Writing in 2005, Hochschild thought this was ""roughly equivalent"" to $68 million (about £44m). This is conservative.

Oswald was remarkable, but not unique. Where Glasgow and its merchants in sugar, tobacco, and human life are concerned, there are plenty of names and no shortage of monuments: Dennistoun, Campbell, Glassford, Cochrane, Buchanan, Hamilton, Bogle, Ewing, Donald, Speirs, Dunlop. One way to understand what they wrought is simple: take pleasure in the city"s architecture today and you are likely to be admiring the fruits of slavery.

Glasgow is not alone in that. London, Liverpool and Bristol also have their stories to tell. Edinburgh's once-great banks grew from foundations built on bones. The first Scottish venture into slavery set out from the capital in 1695. Montrose, Dumfries, Greenock and Port Glasgow each tried their hands. In the language of the present age, they were all in it together.

When commerce was coursing around the triangle, most of polite Scotland was implicated. The nobility (and country) rendered bankrupt in 1700 in the aftermath of the Darien Venture was by the mid-1760s contemplating big elegant townhouses and 100,000-acre estates. You could call that a reversal of fortune. Contrary to self-serving myth, it did not happen because of "'frugality, sobriety, and hard work".

Certain things need to be remembered about Scotland and slavery. One is that the mercantile class got stinking rich twice over: despite fortunes made from stolen lives, they were quick to demand compensation when slavery was ended in 1833. Britain's government decided that £20m, a staggering sum, could be raised. In his 2010 book, The Price of Emancipation, Nicholas Draper reckons Glasgow's mob got £400,000 – in modern terms, hundreds of millions.

Compensation cases also demonstrated that Scots were not merely following an English lead. According to Draper, a country with 10% of the British population accounted for at least 15% of absentee slavers. By another estimate, 30% of Jamaican plantations were run by Scots. For all the pride taken in the abolitionist societies of Glasgow and Edinburgh, the slave-holders did not suffer because of abolition. They were "'compensated'".

And that wasn't the worst of it. Thanks to Hollywood movies, the slave economy of the American South is still taken as barbarism's benchmark. Few realise that the behaviour of Scots busy getting rich in the slave-holders" empire was actually worse – routinely worse – than the worst of the cottonocracy. You need only count the corpses................"

Ghislaine Maxwell's father's real name was Ján Ludvík Hyman Binyamin Hoch, and he came from Czechoslovakia in the 1940s.

The real name of Nigel Lawson's grandfather was Gustav Liebson, and he came from Latvia in the 1890s.

Gigantic yields of millions of stolen and destroyed lives, not feudal agriculture, lured Eastern European Jews to Britain.

FACTS ARE SACRED.

Incontrovertibly functional semi-illiterate white District Judge, what is your father's real name, and where did your father's father come from? Or did the white ancestors of your white father and mother evolve from gorillas in KEMPSTON?

Ignorance is bliss.

Genetic aliens with camouflage English names oppress, we, the direct descendants of the robbed with the yields of the robbery - Habakkuk.

"All have taken what had other owners, and all have had recourse to arms rather than quit the prey on which they were fastened - Dr Samuel Johnson

Brainless descendants of extremely nasty racist murderers, THIEVES, and owners of stolen children of defenceless poor people – Habakkuk

Fake righteousness and deceptively schooled civilised decorum were preceded by several centuries of merciless racist evil: The evilest terrorism the world will ever know.

Righteousness without equitable reparation is continuing racist fraud.

"Those who know the least obey the best." George Farquhar

Facts are sacred.

The principal parts of the delusion of the White Privileged Dullard are that he believes, without colour blind, and measurable objectivity that he was superiorly created by Almighty God, and that Christ is impotent and irrelevant. So, in his actions, he's answerable only to the bendable, and breakable administration of English Law.

It's cruel deceit that our people became equal under English law after the 1807 Act. The European economically cannibalistic commerce in millions of stolen children of defenceless poor people carried on for several decades after 1807. Coincidentally, Charles Darwin was born only two years after the Abolition Act of 1807 was recorded in the statute book.

In pursuance of an appeal against the decision of Sir Mr, Justice Haddon-Cave, QC, KBE, I asked for the transcript of the case and judgement.

Re: Bamgbelu v GDC
Wed, 12 Aug 2015 16:32
adeolacole adeolacole@aol.comHide
To ttp@dtiglobal.eu
Dear Rachael Wilson,
Thank yours.
Your account has been credited with the sum (£24.94) as requested.
I look forward to receiving from you.
Very sincerely,
A. Bamgbelu
-----Original Message-----
From: TTP <ttp@dtiglobal.eu>
To: 'adeolacole' <adeolacole@aol.com>
Sent: Tue, Aug 11, 2015 2:26 pm
Subject: Bamgbelu v GDC

Dear Sirs
Bamgbelu v GDC
The transcript in the above matter has now been completed.
As per our quotation, we do require full payment before releasing the transcript. I can confirm there is currently £24.94 outstanding on your account. Upon receipt of this amount, we will release the transcript to you.
To pay over the telephone immediately, please contact our finance team on 020 7421 4036, quoting the case id reference 160569. For bank transfers please use the following details:
National Westminster Bank
56-00-27
27569276
Swift Code/BIC XXXXXXXXXXXXXX
IBAN XXXXXXXXXXXXXXX

Account Name XXXXXXXXXXXXXXXXX
Reference CASE ID detailed above
A formal invoice will be sent to you within the next week.
We look forward to hearing from you soon.
Rachael Wilson | DTI
Court Contracts Administrator, Court Reporting Solutions
rachael.wilson@DTIGlobal.eu
Office: +44 (0) 207 421 4036
Direct: +44 (0) 207 421 4066

---

165 Fleet Street | London | EC4A 2DY | UK | DX: 414 LDE
www.DTIGlobal.com World-class service. Local commitment.

* * * *

On receiving the transcript of the case, I immediately sent it to the Royal Court of Appeal.

* * * *

-----Original Message-----
From: Civil Appeals - CMSC <civilappeals.cmsC@hmcts.gsi.gov.uk>
To: 'adeolacole@aol.com' <adeolacole@aol.com>
Sent: Fri, 14 Aug 2015 12:23
Subject: C1/2015/2250 BAMGBEL v The General Dental Council

Good Afternoon,

Thank you for your letter dated 12th August 2015 enclosing the Proceedings of the hearing on 23rd June 2015.

Unfortunately, we do need the Transcript of Judgement and not the proceedings if you could arrange for this to be sent by the 19th August 2015.

Also just a note, that we do only require one set of documents. (So you don't keep coping).

Thank you for your help in this matter, and look forward to hearing from you shortly.
Kind Regards
Ann-Marie Smith
Casemanagement Section A
Civil Appeals Office Room E323
Royal Court of Justice
Strand
London
WC2A 2LL
DX 44450 STRAND
Tel: 0207 073 4832
Fax: 0207 947 6736
civilappeals.cmsa@hmcts.gsi.gov.uk

✳ ✳ ✳ ✳

Re: C1/2015/2250 BAMGBEL v The General Dental Council
Fri, 14 Aug 2015 14:00
adeolacole (adeolacole@aol.com)
To:civilappeals.cmsC Details

Dear Ann - Marie Smith,
Thank you very much for yours, which I opened a moment ago.

The Judgement of the case would have to be approved by the Lord Justice. The time it will take the Lord Justice to do this, and return it to the Transcript producer, before it is forwarded to me - is unknown to me, and beyond my control. If it reaches me before 19.08.2015, I will be in the position to send it to you as ordered.

I would be very grateful if you would kindly let me know if you would accept the receipt of the transcript (judgement) of the case electronically, additionally?

"Also just a note, that we do only require one set of documents. (So you don't keep coping)."

I suspect that you do not mean that I am not coping, but meant - to write 'copying' and missed the 'y'. If I am wrong, and I am not coping, I'd try harder.

I will send the judgement to the court as soon as it comes to hand. Again, when that happens is beyond my control.

Very sincerely,

A.   Bamgbelu

✻ ✻ ✻ ✻

Re: C1/2015/2250 BAMGBEL v The General Dental Council
Fri, 14 Aug 2015 18:09
   adeolacole adeolacole@aol.comHide
To   civilappeals.cmsC@hmcts.gsi.gov.uk
Dear Ann - Marie Smith,

Thank you very much for yours.

I contacted transcription contractors, and I was advised the Judgement (transcript) is currently with the Lord Justice.

I will forward it to you as soon as it comes to hand. Please find attached the relevant correspondence.

Fri, 14 Aug 2015 14:11
RE: Bamgbelu v GDC
From TTP ttp@dtiglobal.euhide details
To   'adeolacole' adeolacole@aol.com

Dear Sirs

Thank you for your email.

The Judgment is currently with the Judge for approval, your email has been noted and once it has been completed you will be sent a quote for a copy.

Please contact our RCJ team at RCJ@dtiglobal.eu if you have any queries in regards to this Judgment.

Kind Regards

Rachael Wilson | DTI
Court Contracts Administrator, Court Reporting Solutions
rachael.wilson@DTIGlobal.eu

www.DTIGlobal.com World-class service. Local commitment.

Once again, I will forward the judgement as soon as it comes to hand.

Very sincerely,

A. Bamgbelu

-----Original Message-----
From: Civil Appeals - CMSC <civilappeals.cmsC@hmcts.gsi.gov.uk>
To: 'adeolacole' <adeolacole@aol.com>
Sent: Fri, 14 Aug 2015 15:36
Subject: RE: C1/2015/2250 BAMGBEL v The General Dental Council
Good Afternoon

Thank you for your email, We have granted an extension of time for the

Transcript of Judgment until 28th August 2015, if you haven't received the Transcript by then, please inform us and yes we can accept the receipt of the transcript electronically.

Please accept my apologies; I did miss off the "Y" in copying. (I'm so sorry).

Have a Good Weekend

Kind Regards

Ann-Marie Smith
Casemanagement Section A
Civil Appeals Office Room E323
Royal Court of Justice
Strand
London
WC2A 2LL
DX 44450 STRAND
Tel: 0207 073 4832
Fax: 0207 947 6736
civilappeals.cmsa@hmcts.gsi.gov.uk

-----Original Message-----
From: Civil Appeals - CMSC <civilappeals.cmsC@hmcts.gsi.gov.uk>
To: 'adeolacole@aol.com' <adeolacole@aol.com>
Sent: Fri, 14 Aug 2015 12:23
Subject: C1/2015/2250 BAMGBEL v The General Dental Council
Good Afternoon,

Thank you for your letter dated 12th August 2015 enclosing the Proceedings of the hearing on 23rd June 2015.

Unfortunately, we do need the Transcript of Judgement and not the proceedings if you could arrange for this to be sent by the 19th August 2015.

Also just a note, that we do only require one set of documents. (So you don't keep coping).

Thank you for your help in this matter, and look forward to hearing from you shortly.

Kind Regards

Ann-Marie Smith
Casemanagement Section A
Civil Appeals Office Room E323
Royal Court of Justice
Strand
London
WC2A 2LL
DX 44450 STRAND
Tel: 0207 073 4832
Fax: 0207 947 6736
civilappeals.cmsa@hmcts.gsi.gov.uk

From: adeolacole [mailto:adeolacole@aol.com]
Sent: 14 August 2015 14:01
To: Civil Appeals - CMSC
Subject: Re: C1/2015/2250 BAMGBEL v The General Dental Council

Dear Ann - Marie Smith,

Thank you very much for yours, which I opened a moment ago.

The Judgement of the case would have to be approved by the Lord

Justice. The time it will take the Lord Justice to do this, and return it to the Transcript producer, before it is forwarded to me - is unknown to me, and beyond my control. If it reaches me before 19.08.2015, I will be in the position to send it to you as ordered.

I would be very grateful if you would kindly let me know if you would accept the receipt of the transcript (judgement) of the case electronically, additionally?

"Also just a note, that we do only require one set of documents. (So you don't keep coping)."

I suspect that you do not mean that I am not coping, but meant - to write 'copying' and missed the 'y'. If I am wrong, and I am not coping, I'd try harder.

I will send the judgement to the court as soon as it comes to hand. Again, when that happens is beyond my control.

Very sincerely,

A. Bamgbelu

※ ※ ※ ※ ※

-----Original Message-----
From: Civil Appeals - CMSC <civilappeals.cmsC@hmcts.gsi.gov.uk>
To: 'adeolacole' <adeolacole@aol.com>
Sent: Fri, 14 Aug 2015 15:36
Subject: RE: C1/2015/2250 BAMGBEL v The General Dental Council
Good Afternoon
Thank you for your email, We have granted an extension of time for the Transcript of Judgment until 28th August 2015, if you haven't received the Transcript by then, please inform us and yes we can accept the receipt of the transcript electronically.

Please accept my apologies; I did miss off the "Y" in copying. (I'm so sorry).
Have a Good Weekend
Kind Regards
Ann-Marie Smith
Casemanagement Section A
Civil Appeals Office Room E323
Royal Court of Justice
Strand
London
WC2A 2LL
DX 44450 STRAND
Tel: 0207 073 4832
Fax: 0207 947 6736
civilappeals.cmsa@hmcts.gsi.gov.uk

✻ ✻ ✻ ✻

My mind is finer than this system, and I do not believe in it, and I am bound by it; it is not what I chose, it is what I got, unsolicited. Disclosure of the difference will convince you that you are travelling in the wrong direction.

It is illogical and immoral to persecute fellow human beings because of visible and/or invisible characteristics they did not chose and cannot change,

The fundamental basis of this system is intellectually flawed. Reasoning and vision are unbounded. He is who He says He is, and He told the truth when He disclosed pictures His infinite mind and vision painted before the Council.

The Transcribed Judgement was sent to the Royal Court in August; it was approved about seven months later, in March 2016, why?

Justice delayed is Justice denied.

In some parts of the world, delay usually means sexing up, alterations, doctoring, or other forms of adjustments by those who believe that they are above all laws (Christ's and Man's).

"Those who have the power to do wrong with impunity seldom wait long for the will." Dr Samuel Johnson

He is watching them, and He is transparently just – Proverbs 15:3.

They continue to persecute our people for the dark coat that we neither made nor chose, and cannot change, and they steal the yields of our Christ granted talents.

"The blame is his who chooses. God is blameless." Plato.

The nemesis is not extinct, and the fact that it tarries isn't proof that it will never come.

He is watching them – Proverbs 15:3

New Herod, Matthew 2:16: They lie to their simpler children that they're geniuses, and they kill all those who know that they're brainless racist bastards.

They believe that they're superior to our people, and they do not want to face the test of colour blind and measurable objectivity – Apartheid by stealth.

They want to eat their cakes and have them.

We accept the glaringly obvious fact, which is that their skin colour is indisputably superior; we know that they're not intellectually superior. Several centuries of Europeans' commerce in stolen children of defenceless poor people reversed our people - Habakkuk.

Based on available evidence, irreversible genetic damage is the most enduring residue of the original sin: Several centuries of Europeans' barbarously racist commerce in millions of stolen children of defenceless poor people – Habakkuk.

Percentage of children in the UK hitting educational targets at 5, in descending order:
1. Asian (Indian)
2. Asian (Any other Asian)
3. White (British)
4. White (Irish)
5. Mixed (any other)
6. Mixed (white and black African)
7. Chinese
8. Mixed (White and black Caribbean)
9. Black (African heritage)
10. Asian (Any other Asian)
11. Black (Caribbean heritage)
12. Black (other)
13. Asian (Bangladeshi)
14. White (Any other white)
15. Any other ethnic group
16. Asian (Pakistani)
17. White (Traveller of Irish heritage)
18. White (Gypsy/ Roma)
Source: Centre Forum, Daily Mail, 04.04.2016

Children in the UK hitting educational targets at 16, in descending order:
1. Chinese
2. Asian (Indian)
3. Asian (Any other Asian)
4. Mixed (White and Asian)
5. White (Irish)
6. Mixed (Any other)
7. Any other ethnic group
8. Asian (Bangladeshi)
9. Parent/pupil preferred not to say

10. Mixed (White and black African)
11. White (Any other white)
12. Black (African heritage)
13. White (British)
14. Asian (Pakistani)
15. Black (other)
16. Mixed (White and black Caribbean)
17. Black (Caribbean heritage)
18. White (Traveller of Irish heritage)
19. White (Gypsy/ Roma)
Source: Centre Forum, Daily Mail, 04.04.2016

Genetic damage is the most enduring residue of several centuries of barbarously racist traffic in millions of stolen children of defenceless poor people - Habakkuk.

Facts are sacred.
"Give me liberty or give death." Patrick Henry.

On the plantations of highly civilised European Christians in the Americas and West Indies, the brightest among the stolen Africans rebelled as only fools will surrender to indefinite servitude; they were mechanically deselected. The not so diverse, common genetic pool of the stolen Africans was further weakened by the deselection (reversed natural selection) of the brightest genes. Of the rest, the brightest among the placid did not voluntarily make baby slaves as the owners of the cows owned their calves and, more importantly, it would have been excessively stupid and selfish to bring slave babies to Hell on Earth and leave them there. Thousands were raped by the Christians, and they were made richer by thousands of mulatto slave babies. The common genetic pool of the enslaved was further weakened.

The European Christians selected the prettiest among their possessions for their personal enjoyment, and the prettiest slaves became mulatto-slave-babies' factory. The ugly and/or dull Africans were artificially paired up and deliberately bred for labour by highly civilised and enlightened European Christians.

"I know of no evil that has ever existed, nor can imagine any evil to exist, worse than the tearing of eighty thousand persons annually from their native land, by a combination of the most civilised nations inhabiting the most enlightened part of the globe, but more especially under the sanction of the laws of that Nation which calls herself the most free and the most happy of them all." Prime Minister William Pitt the Younger

Slavery decommissioned natural selection, and reversed evolution for the captors and their descendants, and, more for the captives and their descendants.

Based on available evidence, White Privilege is Antichrist, and a centuries-old fraudulent racist scam.

Based on available evidence, the English law is equal; its administration is not.

Based on very proximate observations and direct experiences, the administration of English law is Antichrist, and intellectually flawed – Habakkuk 1:4.

"Freedom of expression is a basic right." Lady Hale

Facts are sacred.

"Freedom of expression is the cornerstone of our democracy." Jacob Rees-Mogg.

The administration of the law is the MEAT of the law.

"Rightful liberty is unobstructed action according to our will within limits drawn around us by the equal rights of others. I do not add 'within the limits of the law' because law is often but the tyrant's will, and always so when it violates the rights of the individual." Thomas Jefferson

If Sir, Mr Justice Haddon-Cave QC, KBE, Knight Commander of the Most Excellent Order of our Empire, could prove that District Judge Paul Ayers, Senior Vice President of the Association of Her Majesty's District Judges was not a functional semi-illiterate and an incompetent liar, and if he could prove that GDC-Witness, Ms Rachael Bishop, Senior NHS Nurse, did not unrelentingly tell lies under oath, and if he could prove that Dr Richard William Hill, Postgraduate Tutor - NHS, did not fabricate reports and unrelentingly told lies under oath, and if he could prove that Stephen Henderson, LLM, Head of MDDUS, was not a functional semi-illiterate closeted racist thug who unrelentingly deviated from the truth on record, and if he could prove that GDC-INSIDER, Dr Sue Gregory (OBE), Officer of the Most Excellent Order of our Empire, did not unrelentingly tell lies under implied oath, and if he could prove that GDC-WITNESS, GDC-Witness, Stephanie Twidale, British Army Officer - Territorial Defence, did not unrelentingly tell lies under oath, and if he could prove that Geraint Evans, Postgraduate Tutor, did not unrelentingly tell lies under implied oath, and if he could prove that Kevin Atkinson, Postgraduate Tutor did not unrelentingly tell lies under oath, and if he could prove that Dr George Rothnie, Deputy Postgraduate Dean, did not deviate from the truth under implied oath, he would confirm that his white kindred were not RACIST CRIMINALS, and he would also confirm the belief of billions of people, which is that Antichrist Freemasonry Quasi Religion, Antichrist Judaism, Antichrist Islam, and motley assemblies of exotic religions and FAITHS under the common umbrella of the Governor of the Church of England and commander of THE FAITH are not intellectually flawed Satanic Mumbo Jumbo; it will also confirm that reasoning and vision have boundaries. If reasoning and vision have boundaries, He must have lied when, before the Council, He disclosed the pictures His purportedly unbounded mind painted, and He must have also lied when He audaciously stated: "I am the way and the truth and the life. No one comes to the Father except through me." - John 14:6.

If Christ told the truth before the Council, everything that is not aligned to John 14:6 is travelling in the wrong direction.

Ignorance is bliss.

"I do not approve of anything that tampers with natural ignorance. Ignorance is like a delicate exotic fruit; touch it and the bloom is gone. The whole theory of modern education is radically unsound. Fortunately, in England, at any rate, education produces no effect whatsoever. If it did, it would prove a serious danger to the upper classes, and probably lead to acts of violence in Grosvenor Square." Oscar Wilde

They were all white.

Based on observations and direct experiences, homogeneity in the administration of English law is the impregnable secure mask of RACIAL HATRED.

A Prime Minister implied that some White Judges were RACISTS, as he seemed to believe what many black people know, which is that some white Judges measure their own white kindred with a very different yardstick – Apartheid by stealth.

Demons will not cast out demons – Matthew 12:27.

"Someone must be trusted. Let it be the Judges." Lord Denning.

Judges are human beings. Some human beings are RACISTS.

"British Prime Minister attacks racial bias in Universities and the Justice System. 'David Cameron has persuaded a leading labour MP to 'defect' by launching a Government investigation into why black people make up such a high proportion of the prison population. Mr Cameron said Mr Lammy would examine why blacks and ethnic minorities make up nearly a quarter of Crown Court defendants – compared to 14 percent of the population. He added: 'If you are black, you are more likely to be in a prison cell than studying in a University. And if you are black, it seems you're more likely to be sentenced to custody for a crime than if you are white. 'We should investigate why this is and how we can end this possible discrimination. That's why I have asked David Lammy to lead a review. Mr Lammy, who is a qualified barrister, said: 'I am pleased to accept the Prime Minister's invitation." Mr Paul Dacre, Daily Mail, 31.01.2016

Then, Mr David Cameron had full access to all classified information.

Facts are sacred.

* * * * *

Re: C1/2015/2250 BAMGBEL v The General Dental Council
Mon, 7 Sep 2015 10:52
adeolacole adeolacole@aol.com
To civilappeals.cmsC@hmcts.gsi.gov.uk, ttp@dtiglobal.eu
Dear Anne - Marie Smith,
The extended time has elapsed. I have not disregarded it. The Judgement is still at the RCJ, undergoing approval by the Lord Justice. It is impossible to do anything until this process is complete.
I will forward the approved judgement to you as soon as it comes to hand.
Very sincerely,
A. Bamgbelu

Whites are very scared, and not just in Trump's America (75M), and rightly so. Increasingly colour-blind level playing field is gradually unravelling the mother of all racist scams: The centuries-old unspoken myth that the brain is related to skin colour. Only fools expect descendants of THIEVES and owners of stolen children of defenceless poor people to voluntarily relinquish the inherited advantageous position (WHITE PRIVILEGE) that was primarily gained through centuries of extreme violence, and properly organised industrial-scale, armed stealing of moveable and immoveable valuables that had other owners, without a fight.

Re: C1/2015/2250 BAMGBEL v The General Dental Council
Thu, 10 Sep 2015 11:02
adeolacole adeolacole@aol.comHide
To   civilappeals.cmsC@hmcts.gsi.gov.uk
Dear Anne Marie Smith,

I acknowledge the Civil Appeal Court's second class letter of 08.09.2015, it reached me today.

The date the judgement part of the transcript is sent to you depends entirely upon when the Lord Justice approves it. I hope this will be before the reset date.

I will keep you posted.

Very sincerely,

A.   Bamgbelu

Re: C1/2015/2250 BAMGBEL v The General Dental Council
Wed, 14 Oct 2015 12:52
adeolacole adeolacole@aol.comHide
To   civilappeals.cmsC@hmcts.gsi.gov.uk
Dear Ann Marie Smith,

The further extension granted by the court lapsed on 09.10. 2015. I did not defy your order, as I have been advised that the order is yet to be approved by the Noble Lord.

Paragraph 40 Magna Carta: "To no one will we sell, to no one deny or delay right or justice."

As soon as the approved judgement comes to hand, I shall forward it to you, in earnest.

I am grateful for your patience.

Very sincerely,

A. Bamgbelu

adeolacole@aol.com

Re: C1/2015/2250
Mon, 19 Oct 2015 12:25
adeolacole (adeolacole@aol.com)To:civilappeals.cmsC Details

Dear Jade Lestrade - Thomas,

Thank you very much for yours.

The transcript of the judgement was sent to the Lord Justice for approval by TTP only because it was ordered by me. I will let you have a copy of the judgement as soon as possible upon its approval.

The attached correspondence should fulfil your request for proof of ordering the transcript of judgement. The transcript of the hearing is with the Appeal Court; only the approved judgement is outstanding, as it is yet to be approved by the Lord Justice.

I hope my explanation meets your requirement for proof of ordering the judgement. Again, the judgement was sent to the Lord Justice following its order by me. If my explanation does not fulfil your requirement for proof, kindly expatiate and I shall fully accede to your further request.

Once again, please find attached, infra, correspondence, which should make my explanation clearer.

I will be very willing to assist further if desired.

Very sincerely,
A. Bamgbelu

Fri, 14 Aug 2015 14:11
RE: Bamgbelu v GDC
From TTP ttp@dtiglobal.euhide details
To 'adeolacole' adeolacole@aol.com
Dear Sirs
Thank you for your email.
The Judgment is currently with the Judge for approval, your email has been noted and once it has been completed you will be sent a quote for a copy.
Please contact our RCJ team at RCJ@dtiglobal.eu if you have any queries in regards to this Judgment.
  Kind Regards
Rachael Wilson | DTI
Court Contracts Administrator, Court Reporting Solutions
rachael.wilson@DTIGlobal.eu
www.DTIGlobal.com World-class service. Local commitment.

  Mon, 12 Oct 2015 13:13
RE: Bamgbelu v GDC
From TTP ttp@dtiglobal.euhide details
To 'adeolacole' adeolacole@aol.com
Yes we will
Diane Fleuty | DTI
Operations Manager, Court Reporting Solutions
Diane.Fleuty@dtiglobal.eu
Office: +44 (0)20 7421 4027

165 Fleet St | London, EC4A 2DY
www.DTIGlobal.com World-class service. Local commitment.

-----Original Message-----
From: Civil Appeals - CMSC <civilappeals.cmsC@hmcts.gsi.gov.uk>
To: 'adeolacole' <adeolacole@aol.com>
Sent: Mon, 19 Oct 2015 10:35
Subject: C1/2015/2250
Thank you for your email dated 14th October.

The time for filing your outstanding transcript of judgment has been extended until 30th October 2015.

You must also provide proof of ordering said transcript by this date.

Kind regards,
Jade Lestrade-Thomas
Civil Appeals Office
Room E311
The Royal Courts of Justice
Strand, London
WC2A 2LL
Tel: 0207 073 4832
Fax: 0207 947 7679
civilappeals.cmsc@hmcts.gsi.gov.uk

The pattern seemed to be the same everywhere. In my correspondence 14, August 2015, I attached the correspondence of RCJ. In the correspondence, RCJ, stated, 'The Judgment is currently with the Judge for approval, your email has been noted and once it has been completed you will be sent a quote for a copy."

Fri, 14 Aug 2015 14:11
RE: Bamgbelu v GDC
From TTP ttp@dtiglobal.euhide details
To 'adeolacole' adeolacole@aol.com
Dear Sirs
Thank you for your email.

The Judgment is currently with the Judge for approval, your email has been noted and once it has been completed you will be sent a quote for a copy.

Please contact our RCJ team at RCJ@dtiglobal.eu if you have any queries in regards to this Judgment.

Kind Regards
Rachael Wilson | DTI
Court Contracts Administrator, Court Reporting Solutions
rachael.wilson@DTIGlobal.eu
www.DTIGlobal.com World-class service. Local commitment.

*****

On August 14, 2015, the Civil Appeal Court was informed that the transcript of the Judgement was with the High Court Judge for approval.

Several weeks later, the Court wanted me to provide proof that I had ordered the transcript.

Incompetent art incompetently imitated life.
Reductio ad absurdum.

"Tactics." Diane Abbott

Then, highly civilised European Christians shipped about 200, 000 made in Birmingham guns to West Africa annually, among natives who evolved differently, in completely different ecosystems, and who had no means or knowledge of treating penetrative gunshot wounds: Highly civilised and Christians indeed. Now, without equitable reparation, they impede our ascent from the deep holes in which their ancestors buried ours – Habakkuk.

He is watching them – Proverbs 15:3.

After several centuries of daily racist terrorism and artificially fomented wars, the euphemism for properly organised, industrial-scale armed stealing of the children of defenceless poor people, in 1892, armed racist bastards returned to our tribe in the African bush (IJEBU), only a walking distance from the Atlantic Ocean, and used heavy guns, on wheels, to slaughter almost everybody.

Now, they sadistically, impede our ascent from the deep crater in which made in Birmingham guns buried our ancestors in the African bush.

He is watching them – Proverbs 15:3.

The nemesis is not extinct, and the fact that it tarries isn't proof that it will never come.

-----Original Message-----
From: Civil Appeals - CMSC <civilappeals.cmsC@hmcts.gsi.gov.uk>
To: 'adeolacole' <adeolacole@aol.com>
Sent: Mon, 19 Oct 2015 10:35
Subject: C1/2015/2250
Thank you for your email dated 14th October.

The time for filing your outstanding transcript of judgment has been extended until 30th October 2015.
You must also provide proof of ordering said transcript by this date.

Kind regards,
Jade Lestrade-Thomas
Civil Appeals Office
Room E311
The Royal Courts of Justice
Strand, London
WC2A 2LL
Tel: 0207 073 4832
Fax: 0207 947 7679
civilappeals.cmsc@hmcts.gsi.gov.uk

Dr Richard Hill fabricated reports
NIGERIA: SHELL'S CASH COW
Babies with huge oilwells near their houses eat 1.5/day; a closeted racist semi-illiterate white man whose father and mother have never seen crude oil is our Judge in BEDFORD.
https://www.youtube.com/watch?v=BlpH4hG7m1A

NORTHAMPTON, ENGLAND: Based on available evidence, GDC-WITNESS, Dr Geraint Evans, Postgraduate Tutor, Oxford, unrelentingly lied under implied oath - Habakkuk 1:4; John 8:44; John 10:10.

A RACIST WHITE CROOK.

CREEPING NORTH KOREA.

FACTS ARE SACRED.

CORBY, ENGLAND: Based on available evidence, GDC-WITNESS, Dr George Rothnie unrelentingly lied under implied oath - Habakkuk 1:4; John 8:44; John 10:10.

A RACIST WHITE CROOK.

CREEPING NORTH KOREA.

FACTS ARE SACRED.

CORBY, ENGLAND: Based on available evidence, GDC-WITNESS, Dr Kevin Atkinson, Scottish Ken, unrelentingly lied under oath - Habakkuk 1:4; John 8:44; John 10:10.

A RACIST WHITE CROOK.

CREEPING NORTH KOREA.

FACTS ARE SACRED.

OXFORD, ENGLAND: Based on available evidence, GDC-WITNESS, British Soldier - Territorial Defence, Dr Stephanie Twidale (TD) unrelentingly lied under oath - Habakkuk 1:4; John 8:44; John 10:10.

A RACIST WHITE CROOK.

CREEPING NORTH KOREA.

FACTS ARE SACRED.

WOLLASTON, ENGLAND: Based on available evidence, GDC-WITNESS, Ms Rachael Bishop, Senior NHS Nurse, unrelentingly lied under oath - Habakkuk 1:4; John 8:44; John 10:10.

A RACIST WHITE CROOK.

CREEPING NORTH KOREA.

FACTS ARE SACRED.

BEDFORD, ENGLAND: Based on available evidence, GDC-INSIDER, Dr Sue Gregory, Officer of the Most Excellent Order of our Empire unrelentingly lied under implied oath - Habakkuk 1:4; John 8:44; John 10:10.

A RACIST WHITE CROOK.

CREEPING NORTH KOREA.

FACTS ARE SACRED.

BEDFORD, ENGLAND: Based on available evidence, GDC-WITNESS, Freemason, Brother, Dr Richard William Hill fabricated reports and unrelentingly lied under oath - Habakkuk 1:4; John 8:44; John 10:10.

A RACIST WHITE CROOK.

CREEPING NORTH KOREA.

FACTS ARE SACRED.

The most effective method of covering up RACIAL HATRED is to kill the victim.

https://www.facebook.com/rotimi.osunsan/videos/3088536551193798

A bastardised, unashamedly mediocre, indiscreetly dishonest, vindictive, potently weaponised, and institutionally RACIST system that his overseen by MASONS (Mediocre Mafia) - Habakkuk.

Facts are sacred; they can't be overstated.

OYINBO OLE: WHITE THIEVES: HABAKKUK.

Nigeria: Shell's docile cash cow.

Babies with huge oilwells near their houses eat only 1.5/day; a closeted racist, functional semi-illiterate former debt collector Solicitor in Norwich whose white father and mother have never seen crude oil is our District Judge in Bedford.

Then, the highly luxuriant soil of Norwich yields only food.

Then, they carried and sold millions of stolen children of defenceless poor people; now, they carry natural resources - Habakkuk.

Substitution is fraudulent emancipation.

He is watching them – Proverbs 15:3.

"Moderation is a virtue only among those who are thought to have found alternatives." Henry Kissinger

They are properly organised racist criminals who use a bastardised, indiscreetly racist administration of the law as a weapon of a latent but very potent race war.

We know what their moron sheep must not know; we are dead MEATS.

MATTHEW 2:16, NEW HEROD: They lie to their duller children that they're geniuses; they kill all those who know that they're brainless racist bastards.

They stalk our people like prey, and they hunt in packs.

He is watching them – Proverbs 15:3.

https://factsaresacred89.medium.com/county-courts-courtserve-live-court-listings-f6736242a059

"To deny or belittle this good is, in this dangerous century when the resources and pretensions of power continue to enlarge, a desperate error of intellectual abstraction. More than this, it is a self-fulfilling error, which encourages us to give up the struggle against bad laws and class bound procedures and to disarm ourselves before power. It is to throw away a whole inheritance of struggle about the law and within the forms of law, whose continuity can never be fractured without bringing men and women into immediate danger." - E. P Thompson

The nemesis is not extinct; the fact that it tarries is not proof that it will never come – Habakkuk.

"Of black men, the numbers are too great who are now repining under English cruelty." Dr Samuel Johnson.

He is watching them – Proverbs 15:3.

BEDFORD, ENGLAND: District Judge, which part of Bedford County Court preceded the sadistic commerce in millions of stolen children of defenceless poor people – Habakkuk?

Then, there were laws: Then, the yields of millions of stolen and destroyed children of defenceless poor people were used to build Courts and pay the wages of Judges who sent those who stole money to prisons built with stolen money – Habakkuk.

Facts are sacred.

They want superiority; they don't want Freedom of Expression because they don't want their moron sheep to know about what they secretly do to our people. Deluded, conceited, and spineless cowards, they want to eat their cakes and have them.

OYINBO OLE: WHITE THIEVES: HABAKKUK.

"I think I will ask our legal adviser for any advice he may have. My view is that there are six or seven of us here who had the admission down, but we cannot find it in the transcript and there is wordings that imply that there was, but it is not in black and white….." Dr Shiv Pabary, Member of the Most Excellent Order of Empire (MBE) and Justice of Peace (JP)

Moron Member of our Empire (MMBE) and Justice of Incompetent Racist Lies (JIRL).

Facts are sacred.

https://www.youtube.com/watch?v=BlpH4hG7m1A&feature=youtu.be

"They may not have been well written from a grammatical point of view, but I am confident I had not forgotten any of the facts." Dr Geraint Evans, Postgraduate Tutor, Oxford

https://youtu.be/rayVcfyu9Tw

"It is incumbent upon the court and all those professionals involved to conclude court proceedings as quickly as possible. This hopefully ensures that a child has stability, love and affection and the parents working together to ensure that he has the best opportunity of developing academically and emotional." The Senior Vice President of the Association of Her Majesty's District Judges – proofed and approved Judgement.

Based on proximate observations and direct experiences, semi-illiterate Judges, nearly all, are RACISTS.

A RACIST WHITE FOOL'S APPROVAL!

When semi-illiterate Solicitors/Barristers fail in practice, thousands do, if they are MASONS, they could become Judges, if not, they could become Politicians or something else.

It is plainly deductible that the white father and mother of the Senior Vice President of the Association of Her Majesty's District Judges did not care, had they, their white son wouldn't have approved and immortalised excessive stupidity for eternity, and he'd be a properly educated lawyer, privately educated Anthony Blair, Anthony Julius, Geoff Hoon, and Rabinder Singh's Class, and he might practice proper law in STRAND.

Unlike her little brother, age saved the child's sister from the Closeted-Racist-Dylan–Roof-Freemason-Judge. She thanks her stars that the incontrovertibly functional semi-illiterate, closeted racist white man did not have anything to do with her education.
In her GCSE, she gained the following grades:
English Language A*
English Literature A*
Mathematics A*
Additional Mathematics A*
Physics A*
Chemistry A*
Biology A*
History A*
Latin A
Spanish A
Advanced Level Mathematics A
The academic height that the white father and mother of the closeted racist white District Judge cannot know, and which the natural talents of his own children will not exploit.
The brain isn't skin colour; then, we were robbed with guns.
The child sister has since gained a First-Class Science Degree from one of the topmost Universities in the UK, and she's gainfully engaged, batting for her Country. Christ saved her from the evil clutches of the Closeted Racist Freemason Thugs.

It's plainly deductible that the white children of the white Senior Vice President of the Association of Her Majesty's District Judges were inferiorly created by Almighty God, certainly intellectually - OECD.

Facts are sacred.

"The truth allows no choice." Dr Samuel Johnson

If the Prime Minister, the Right Honourable Boris Johnson, could use cogent facts and hard evidence to prove that all the white children of the incontrovertibly functional semi-illiterate Senior Vice President of the Association of Her Majesty's District Judges were not inferiorly created by Almighty God, he would also confirm the belief of billions of people, which is that Antichrist Freemasonry Quasi Religion, Antichrist Judaism, Antichrist Islam, and motley assemblies of exotic religions and FAITHS under the common umbrella of the Governor of the Church of England and commander of THE FAITH are not intellectually flawed Satanic Mumbo Jumbo; it will also confirm that reasoning and vision have boundaries. If reasoning and vision have boundaries, He must have lied when, before the Council, He disclosed the pictures His purportedly unbounded mind painted, and He must have also lied when He audaciously stated: "I am the way and the truth and the life. No one comes to the Father except through me." - John 14:6.

If Christ told the truth before the Council, everything that is not aligned to John 14:6 is travelling in the wrong direction.

https://www.youtube.com/watch?v=BlpH4hG7m1A&feature=youtu.be

Ignorance is bliss.

"I do not approve of anything that tampers with natural ignorance. Ignorance is like a delicate exotic fruit; touch it and the bloom is gone. The whole theory of modern education is radically unsound. Fortunately, in England, at any rate, education produces no effect whatsoever. If it did, it would prove a serious danger to the upper classes, and probably lead to acts of violence in Grosvenor Square." Oscar Wilde

Re Meeting 9th March
Mon, 8 Mar 2010 20:20
George Rothnie georgerothnie@hotmail.comHide
To adeolacole@aol.com
Hi Ola,
We are scheduled to meet tomorrow evening at my surgery about 5.30ish. Unfortunately something has cropped up which necessytates me having to postpone the meeting. I'm really sorry it's such short notice.
I will contact you in the week to arrange another date.
Once agaim my apologies.
George

Dr George Rothnie: Deputy Postgraduate Dean, Oxford.

"By definition therefore there needs to be a contact order for Mr B so that he knows when he is going to see his son. It is absolutely essential that this occurs and mother agrees with that. She said so several times in her evidence. Mrs Waller agreed that not only should a child have the opportunity of developing relationship with both parents, any sibling should also be there so that inter- sibling relationship could be fostered and nurtured. Obviously in this particular case the children reside in different places. That immediately puts a strain on the children having limited contact with each other. F's sister is very much older than him and she will be further advanced into her adult life. Thus it is not a matter that that sibling relationship can only be fostered by the children being together. Indeed as we all know absence sometimes makes the heart grow fonder. F should have an opportunity of seeing his sister. Wherever he does that it should be done in a friendly and loving environment. If the time comes that his sister goes to university of course his contact with her will be restricted to the time that she is home from university. In years to come when they have both grown up, with their own family they will see less of each other. But it doesn't mean that they don't still love and adore each other as much as they would if they saw each other every day." The Senior Vice President of the Association of Her Majesty's District Judges – proofed and approved Judgement.

"Yes, Sir, it does her honour, but it would do nobody else honour. I have indeed, not read it all. But when I take up the end of a web, and find it packthread, I do not expect, by looking further, to find embroidery." Dr Samuel Johnson

Antichrist Racist Freemasons teach their members secret handshakes, not grammar; the former is easier to master.

OYINBO OLODO: A RACIST WHITE DUNCE

Majestic appointee.
Majestic stupidity.
"There is no sin except stupidity." Wilde.

https://www.youtube.com/watch?v=BlpH4hG7m1A&feature=youtu.be

Freedom of Expression was part of a Queen's speech.

"Freedom of Expression is the cornerstone of our democracy." Jacob Rees-Mogg.

https://www.youtube.com/watch?v=BlpH4hG7m1A

Shocking!

"Why, that is, because, dearest, you are a dunce." Habakkuk.

A scatter-head racist plebeian; an overpromoted polytechnic university educated racist bastard. A righteous descendant of industrial-scale professional THIEVES and owners of stolen children of defenceless people (Kamala's ancestors) - Habakkuk.

Nigeria: Shells docile cash cow.
Kempston yields only food.
Babies with huge oil wells and gas-fields near their houses eat 1.5/ day; a closeted racist former debt-collector Solicitor in Norwich whose

white father and mother have never seen crude oil is our District Judge in Bedford.

Then, the white ancestors of his white father and mother were fed like battery hens with the yields of stolen children of defenceless poor people – Habakkuk.

OYINBO OLE: WHITE THIEVES: HABAKKUK.

Then, racist bastards carried and sold millions of stolen children of defenceless poor people; now, they carry natural resources.

SUBSTITUTION: FRAUDULENT EMANCIPATION.

"Moderation is a virtue only among those who are thought to have found alternatives." Henry Kissinger.

"Mr Bamgbelu clearly has very, very strong views about education and I understand those views are based upon the fact that he is a successful dentist here in Bedford which he attributes to the fact that his parents cared for him and his education when he was young. They ensured that he had a proper fee paying education…….." The Senior Vice President of the Association of Her Majesty's District Judges – proofed and approved Judgement

https://www.youtube.com/watch?v=BlpH4hG7m1A

Indiscreet envy.

Envy is a thief.

When envy and innate RACIAL HATRED copulate, insanity is their offspring.

Financial disclosure in a divorce: How can a mere Negro have what I do not have?

"Envy is weak." Yul Brynner

OYINBO OLE: WHITE THIEVES: HABAKKUK.

No brain.
The land yields only food: Poor in natural resources.
Several centuries of stealing and slavery preceded the TRUST FUND – Habakkuk.
Only the skin colour is indisputably superior; the wearer neither made nor chose it.

Straight faced, righteous, and ignorant descendants of THIEVES and owners of stolen children of defenceless poor people - Habakkuk.

He is watching them – Proverbs 15:3.

"All have taken what had other owners, and all have resorted to arms rather than quit the prey on which they were fastened." Dr Samuel Johnson

The very greedy, myopic, and shallow racist white bastards are not immortal; we are all travellers passing through.

He is watching them - Proverbs 15:3.

OYINBO OLE: WHITE THIEVES: HABAKKUK.

Very greedy, innately racist white bastards: There are no oil wells or gas-fields in LUTON. Then, all the people of Luton were fed like battery-hens with the yields of stolen children of defenceless poor people (Kamala's ancestors) - Habakkuk.

He is watching them - Proverbs 15:3.

One day, at an unexpected minute, he'd flip. That is what will happen. He spoke, and the Universe evolved. He will speak again, and it will perish

A wicked Jew (Herod the Great) jailed, and then decapitated John who baptised Christ, only because he spoke. John was not punished for speaking; John was permanently prevented from speaking.

NEW HEROD: They lied to their simpler children that they are geniuses; they kill all those who know that they are brainless racist white bastards -Matthew 2:16.

"Affluence is not a birth right." David Cameron.

Fake righteousness and deceptively schooled civilised decorum were preceded by several centuries of barbarously racist traffic in millions of stolen children of defenceless poor people - Habakkuk.

OYINBO OLE: WHITE THIEVES: HABAKKUK.

Deluded intellectual cowards: Ignorant descendants of racist killers, THIEVES, and owners of stolen children of other people want to force others to see them as they want to be seen, not as they truly are.

There is Freedom of Expression in North Korea; there, one is free to say and/or print only what Kim wants to hear.

In the future, one will be free to say and/or print only what Antichrist Jews and members of the Antichrist Racist Freemasonry Quasi-Religion (Mediocre Mafia), want to hear.

CREEPING NORTH KOREA.

Based on available evidence, Freemasonry Quasi-Religion is intellectually flawed.

AntiChrist Racist Freemasonry Quasi-Religion: Half-educated school dropouts and their superiors who have informal access to some very powerful white Judges.

They use very expensive aprons to decorate the temples of their powerless and useless fertility tools, and carry out indiscreet, vulgar, and Pharisees' charitable works.

OYINBO OLE: WHITE THIEVES: HABAKKUK.

"The good Samaritan had money." Mrs Margaret Thatcher

Indiscreet, vulgar, and Pharisees' charitable works in exchange for what? Theirs is not a good deal. It was not a good deal then, and it is not a good deal now - Matthew 4:9.

Righteousness without equitable reparation is continuing RACIST FRAUD.

He told the righteous Jew to sell the yields of virtue; He'd have told him to return the yields of vice - Matthew 19:21.

Some Jews/Romans lynched and crucified Christ only because He spoke; He disclosed pictures that HIS unbounded mind painted. He was not punished for speaking; He was permanently prevented from speaking.

OYINBO OLE: WHITE THIEVES: HABAKKUK.

"Jews are very good with money." President Donald Trump.

Whose money?

Corporal Adolf flipped.

"This statement is about a series of letters and emails I have been recieving. I am the above named person. I live at an address provided to police. In this statement I will also mention XXXXXXXXXXXXXXXXXXXXXXXXX a leaseholder for a property I manage at my place work. I am the company director of DOBERN properties based in Ilford. These emails have been sent to my company email address of mail@debern.co.uk, and also letters have been sent to myself at our company ADDress of P.O BOX 1289,

ILFORD, IG2 7XZ over the last Two and a half years, I have recieving a series of letters and emails from DR BAMGeLu. DR BAMGBELU is a leasholder for a property I manage at my place of work. Over the period of his leaseholding, DR BAmGelu has continually failed to pay arrears for the property. In march 2016 my company took DR to court and he was ordered to pay outstanding costs of around £20000 since that time and lead up to the case, DR BaMGBelu has been emailing me and posting me letters that are lengthy and accuses me repeatedly of being a racist in emails and letters tact are regularly Ten to twelve pages long, DR BAMGBELU. lists numerous quots from google searches all refrencing ham I am a bigot and a racist. The most recent letter I received from DR BAMGBELU opens with you are jealous and racist Evil combination you hate us we know it" he goes on to say "I would not have knowingly had anything to do with white supremicists." In the last email I recieved from him on 02/09/2016 DR BaMGBELU stated "you are restricted by poor Education within one of the least literate countries in the world". I would be perfectly happy for DR BAMGBElu to contact myself or my company if he has relevant enquiries to his lease holding, however these continuous letters and emails are causing me distress and I feel intimidated. I am not a racist and these accusatios make uncomfortable. All I want is to conduct between us in a normal manner. I want BambGlu to stop emailing me and sending me letters accusing me of being racist and harassing me." MR ROBERT KINGSTON, SOLICITOR, ACCOUNTANT, AND COMPANY DIRECTOR.

"Yes, Sir, it does her honour, but it would do nobody else honour. I have indeed, not read it all. But when I take up the end of a web, and find it packthread, I do not expect, by looking further, to find embroidery." Dr Samuel Johnson

An imbecile Jew!

"Jews are very good with money." President Trump

Whose money?

Ghislaine Maxwell's father, Ján Ludvík Hyman Binyamin Hoch, came from Czechoslovakia in the 1940s, he and Judas Iscariot were Jews.

Bernard Madoff and Robert Kingston, the latter, probably camouflage English names, are Jews.

Gigantic yields of millions of stolen children of defenceless poor people (BLACK HOLOCAUST), not feudal agriculture, lured Eastern European Jews to Great Britain.
Before slavery, what?
Facts are sacred.
Corporal Adolf flipped, the rest his history.

NORTHAMPTON, ENGLAND: Based on available evidence, GDC-WITNESS, Dr Geraint Evans, Postgraduate Tutor, Oxford, unrelentingly lied under implied oath - Habakkuk 1:4; John 8:44; John 10:10.

A RACIST WHITE CROOK.

CREEPING NORTH KOREA.

FACTS ARE SACRED.

OYINBO OLE: WHITE THIEVES: HABAKKUK.
Fish and chips system that is overseen by Freemasons; when their people commit RACIST CRIMES against our people, they criminally bury RACIAL HATRED – Apartheid by stealth – Habakkuk 1:4.
He is watching them – Proverbs 15:3.
They're not immortal, and one day, the Antichrist closeted racist bastards must face transparent Justice.
The Father judges no one, He has given all judgment to the Son - John 5:22.

CORBY, ENGLAND: Based on available evidence, GDC-WITNESS, Dr George Rothnie unrelentingly lied under implied oath - Habakkuk 1:4; John 8:44; John 10:10.

A RACIST WHITE CROOK.

CREEPING NORTH KOREA.

FACTS ARE SACRED.

OYINBO OLE: WHITE THIEVES: HABAKKUK.
Fish and chips system that is overseen by Freemasons; when their people commit RACIST CRIMES against our people, they criminally bury RACIAL HATRED – Apartheid by stealth – Habakkuk 1:4.
He is watching them – Proverbs 15:3.
They're not immortal, and one day, the Antichrist closeted racist bastards must face transparent Justice.
The Father judges no one, He has given all judgment to the Son - John 5:22.

CORBY, ENGLAND: Based on available evidence, GDC-WITNESS, Dr Kevin Atkinson, Scottish Ken, unrelentingly lied under oath - Habakkuk 1:4; John 8:44; John 10:10.

A RACIST WHITE CROOK.

CREEPING NORTH KOREA.

FACTS ARE SACRED.

OYINBO OLE: WHITE THIEVES: HABAKKUK.
Fish and chips system that is overseen by Freemasons; when their people commit RACIST CRIMES against our people, they criminally bury RACIAL HATRED – Apartheid by stealth – Habakkuk 1:4.
He is watching them – Proverbs 15:3.
They're not immortal, and one day, the Antichrist closeted racist bastards must face transparent Justice.

The Father judges no one, He has given all judgment to the Son - John 5:22.

OXFORD, ENGLAND: Based on available evidence, GDC-WITNESS, British Soldier - Territorial Defence, Dr Stephanie Twidale (TD) unrelentingly lied under oath - Habakkuk 1:4; John 8:44; John 10:10.

A RACIST WHITE CROOK.

CREEPING NORTH KOREA.

FACTS ARE SACRED.

OYINBO OLE: WHITE THIEVES: HABAKKUK.
Fish and chips system that is overseen by Freemasons; when their people commit RACIST CRIMES against our people, they criminally bury RACIAL HATRED – Apartheid by stealth – Habakkuk 1:4.
He is watching them – Proverbs 15:3.
They're not immortal, and one day, the Antichrist closeted racist bastards must face transparent Justice.
The Father judges no one, He has given all judgment to the Son - John 5:22.

"A complaints such as Mrs Bishop's could trigger an enquiry." Stephen Henderson, Head of MDDUS.

"Yes, Sir, it does her honour, but it would do nobody else honour. I have indeed, not read it all. But when I take up the end of a web, and find it packthread, I do not expect, by looking further, to find embroidery." Dr Samuel Johnson

OYINBO ODE: A CROOKED RACIST WHITE DUNCE

Freemasons teach their members secret handshakes, not grammar; the former considerably easier to master.

WOLLASTON, ENGLAND: Based on available evidence, GDC-WITNESS, Ms Rachael Bishop, Senior NHS Nurse, unrelentingly lied under oath - Habakkuk 1:4; John 8:44; John 10:10.

A RACIST WHITE CROOK.

CREEPING NORTH KOREA.

FACTS ARE SACRED.

OYINBO OLE: WHITE THIEVES: HABAKKUK.
Fish and chips system that is overseen by Freemasons; when their people commit RACIST CRIMES against our people, they criminally bury RACIAL HATRED – Apartheid by stealth – Habakkuk 1:4.
He is watching them – Proverbs 15:3.
They're not immortal, and one day, the Antichrist closeted racist bastards must face transparent Justice.
The Father judges no one, He has given all judgment to the Son - John 5:22.

BEDFORD, ENGLAND: Based on available evidence, GDC-INSIDER, Dr Sue Gregory, Officer of the Most Excellent Order of our Empire unrelentingly lied under implied oath - Habakkuk 1:4; John 8:44; John 10:10.

A RACIST WHITE CROOK.

CREEPING NORTH KOREA.

FACTS ARE SACRED.

OYINBO OLE: WHITE THIEVES: HABAKKUK.
Fish and chips system that is overseen by Freemasons; when their people commit RACIST CRIMES against our people, they criminally bury RACIAL HATRED – Apartheid by stealth – Habakkuk 1:4.
He is watching them – Proverbs 15:3.

They're not immortal, and one day, the Antichrist closeted racist bastards must face transparent Justice.

The Father judges no one, He has given all judgment to the Son - John 5:22.

BEDFORD, ENGLAND: Based on available evidence, GDC-WITNESS, Freemason, Brother, Dr Richard William Hill fabricated reports and unrelentingly lied under oath - Habakkuk 1:4; John 8:44; John 10:10.

A RACIST WHITE CROOK.

CREEPING NORTH KOREA.

FACTS ARE SACRED.

OYINBO OLE: WHITE THIEVES: HABAKKUK.
Fish and chips system that is overseen by Freemasons; when their people commit RACIST CRIMES against our people, they criminally bury RACIAL HATRED – Apartheid by stealth – Habakkuk 1:4.

He is watching them – Proverbs 15:3.

They're not immortal, and one day, the Antichrist closeted racist bastards must face transparent Justice.

The Father judges no one, He has given all judgment to the Son - John 5:22.

A bastardised, unashamedly mediocre, indiscreetly dishonest, vindictive, potently weaponised, and institutionally RACIST system that his overseen by MASONS (Mediocre Mafia) - Habakkuk.

Based on available evidence, the administration of English seemed to be a properly organised RACIST SCAM.

He is watching them – Proverbs 15:3.

* * * * *

Dr Anand Kamath was threatened with reportage to the GDC, and he killed himself. Insanity always precedes self-destruction.

Google: Dr Anand Kamath, dentist.

Deluded and conceited, they believe they're better than us, but they don't want colour-blind, measurable objectivity, and Freedom of Expression because they know they're not.

The affluence that they implicitly brag about was stolen. Then, almost everything was stolen - Habakkuk.

Affluence did not evolve; then, it was actively and deliberately stolen - Habakkuk.

"Affluence is not a birth right." David Cameron.

Facts are sacred.

On September 24, 2007, I attended a GDC hearing in London. The hearing concerned a complaint by Ms Rachael Bishop and Bedfordshire PCT.

WOLLASTON, ENGLAND: Based on available evidence, GDC-WITNESS, Ms Rachael Bishop, Senior NHS Nurse, unrelentingly lied under oath - Habakkuk 1:4; John 8:44; John 10:10.

A RACIST WHITE CROOK.

CREEPING NORTH KOREA.

FACTS ARE SACRED.

OYINBO OLE: WHITE THIEVES: HABAKKUK.
Fish and chips system that is overseen by Freemasons; when their people commit RACIST CRIMES against our people, they criminally bury RACIAL HATRED – Apartheid by stealth – Habakkuk 1:4.

He is watching them – Proverbs 15:3.

They're not immortal, and one day, the Antichrist closeted racist bastards must face transparent Justice.

The Father judges no one, but he has given all judgment to the Son - John 5:22.

Based on available evidence, Bedfordshire PCT (NHS) unrelentingly lied under implied oath.

"Lies are told all the time." Sir Michael Havers, Attorney General, 1980.

Facts are sacred.

"All sections of the UK Society are institutionally RACIST." Sir Bernard Hogan-Howe.

Bedfordshire PCT (NHS) was part of the UK Society.

In the GDC hearing, on September 24, 2007, unbeknownst to the only Negro in the entire process, three NHS fabrications were live, valid, and accessible to white people.

"Mama, look a Negro......Where shall I hide." Frantz Fanon.

1) The fabricated NHS report of July 22, 2004. It was abruptly withdrawn on October 16, 2008, after I informed the Medical Protection Society that I was not in the UK on July 22, 2004, and I had evidence. If there's evidence that some of one's white ancestors were industrial-scale professional THIEVES and owners of stolen children of defenceless poor people, it would be naïve not to expect incompetent mendacity complicated by RACIAL HATRED to be part of one's genetic inheritances – Habakkuk. Facts are sacred.

2) The fabricated follow up report of undisclosed date. The closeted

racist white bastards forgot to fabricate a date to the fabricated follow-up report. The NHS fabrication was abruptly withdrawn on October 16, 2008 but only after I informed the MPS that I was not in the UK on July 22, 2004.

3) The fabricated email address, adeola@aol.com. For very obvious reasons, Charlotte Dowling (Goodson) Loughborough Business Studies graduate, never used her creation, and the NHS used it only once. The correspondence that was deliberately sent to a wrong address was not intended to reach me, and it didn't. The fabricated email address remains live and valid.

If one bred some white pigs for bacon, the stupidest of the white pigs should be the first to be butchered.

"I am very fond of my pigs; it doesn't stop me from eating them." Archbishop Runcie.

NIGERIA: SHELL'S DOCILE CASH COW.

The highly luxuriant soil of Bedfordshire yields only food. Based on available evidence, Nigeria (oil/gas) is by far more relevant to the economic survival of all the children of Charlotte Dowling (Goodson) than Bedford. Then, the white ancestors of the white father and mother of Charlotte Dowling (Goodson) were fed like battery hens with the yields of stolen children of defenceless poor people.

OYINBO OLE: WHITE THIEVES: HABAKKUK.

No brain.
Poor in natural resources.
Several centuries of stealing and slavery preceded the TRUST FUND -Habakkuk.
Only the skin colour is indisputably superior; the wearer neither made nor chose it.
Facts are sacred.

Deluded paper tigers: Baseless superiority is their birth right. Their hairs stand on end when they're challenged by our people (AFRICANS); we and our type are the only ones racist bastards will beat up without the support of the YANKS.

Antichrist Racist Freemasons should forcibly evict Putin from Crimea; he forcibly stole it.

Deluded intellectual cowards: They want superiority, their birth right; they don't want Freedom of Expression. They don't want their people to know about what they secretly do to our people. They want to eat their cakes and have them.

"A typical English man, usually violent and always dull." Wilde.

BEDFORD, ENGLAND: Based on available evidence, GDC-WITNESS, Freemason, Brother, Dr Richard William Hill fabricated reports and unrelentingly lied under oath - Habakkuk 1:4; John 8:44; John 10:10.

A RACIST WHITE CROOK.

CREEPING NORTH KOREA.

FACTS ARE SACRED.

OYINBO OLE: WHITE THIEVES: HABAKKUK.
Fish and chips system that is overseen by Freemasons; when their people commit RACIST CRIMES against our people, they criminally bury RACIAL HATRED – Apartheid by stealth – Habakkuk 1:4.
He is watching them – Proverbs 15:3.

They're not immortal, and one day, the Antichrist closeted racist bastards must face transparent Justice.

The Father judges no one, He has given all judgment to the Son - John 5:22.

In the GDC hearing of September 24, 2007, the GDC stated that the NHS visited my practice on April 02, 2003 and it produced an adverse report.

After the GDC hearing of September 24, 2007, I used the Freedom of information Act to ask the NHS for the report of April 02, 2003, as I was not aware of it.

The NHS stated that it did not have the report of April 02, 2003, and under Exemption 12, of the Freedom of Information Act, it was not bound to produce the report that it did not have. The NHS further stated that it carried out follow up inspections, the first of which was on July 22, 2004, and the NHS sent me its report of July 22, 2004 and the follow up report of undisclosed date.

The very adverse reports of July 22, 2004 and the follow up report of undisclosed date were incompetent racist fabrications – by the NHS (Richard William Hill); I was not in the UK on July 22, 2004, and my surgery was shut, and I had evidence. On October 16, 2008, about a year after the NHS responded to my Freedom of Information request, and only after I had informed the MPS (Medical Protection Society) that I was not in the UK on July 22, 2004, the NHS abruptly withdrew its incompetent racist fabrications.

OYINBO OLE: WHITE THIEVES: HABAKKUK.

"Coincidence is Christ's way of remaining anonymous." Albert Einstein Paraphrased.

For better for stay, for worse for leave.

Three weeks before the commencement of the GDC hearing of November 17, 2008, Kemi Daramola filed for divorce.

She prayed to Christ at Brick Hill Baptist Church in Bedford, and pays hefty tithe (quasi-protection money), and the Antichrist Racist Freemasonry Quasi-Religion (The Builders), in Kempston answered her prayers.

The stone that the builders rejected is now the cornerstone – Psalm 118:22; Luke 20:17.

Which part of Bedfordshire Masonic Centre, the keep, Bedford Rd, Kempston, Bedford MK42, preceded the barbarously racist traffic in millions of stolen children of defenceless poor people – Habakkuk?

OYINBO OLE: WHITE THIEVES: HABAKKUK.

Before slavery, what?

Righteousness and deceptively schooled civilised decorum were preceded by several centuries of barbarously racist traffic in millions of stolen children of defenceless poor people – Habakkuk.

Facts are sacred.

"England is like a prostitute who, having sold her body all her life, decides to quit and close her business, and then tells everybody she wants to be chaste and protect her flesh as if it were jade." He Manzi, Chinese politician

BEDFORD, ENGLAND: Based on available evidence, GDC-INSIDER, Dr Sue Gregory, Officer of the Most Excellent Order of our Empire unrelentingly lied under implied oath - Habakkuk 1:4; John 8:44; John 10:10.

A RACIST WHITE CROOK.

CREEPING NORTH KOREA.

FACTS ARE SACRED.

OYINBO OLE: WHITE THIEVES: HABAKKUK.
Fish and chips system that is overseen by Freemasons; when their

people commit RACIST CRIMES against our people, they criminally bury RACIAL HATRED – Apartheid by stealth – Habakkuk 1:4.

He is watching them – Proverbs 15:3.

They're not immortal, and one day, the Antichrist closeted racist bastards must face transparent Justice.

The Father judges no one, He has given all judgment to the Son - John 5:22.

NIGERIA: SHELL'S DOCILE CASH COW.

The highly luxuriant soil of Freemasons' Kempston yields only food. Then, all the people of Kempston were fed like battery hens with the yields of millions of stolen children of defenceless poor people – Habakkuk.

OYINBO OLE: WHITE THIEVES: HABAKKUK.

Babies with huge oil wells and gas fields near their houses eat only 1.5/day, in NIGERIA; a closeted racist functional semi-illiterate former debt collector Solicitor in Norwich whose white father and mother have never seen crude oil is our District Judge in Bedford. Then, the white ancestors of his white father and mother were fed like battery hens with the yields of millions of stolen children of defenceless poor people.

"A complaints such as Mrs Bishop's could trigger an enquiry." Stephen Henderson, Head of MDDUS.

"Yes, Sir, it does her honour, but it would do nobody else honour. I have indeed, not read it all. But when I take up the end of a web, and find it packthread, I do not expect, by looking further, to find embroidery." Dr Samuel Johnson

OYINBO ODE: A CROOKED RACIST WHITE DUNCE

Freemasons teach their members secret handshakes, not grammar; the former considerably easier to master.

WOLLASTON, ENGLAND: Based on available evidence, GDC-WITNESS, Ms Rachael Bishop, Senior NHS Nurse, unrelentingly lied under oath - Habakkuk 1:4; John 8:44; John 10:10.

A RACIST WHITE CROOK.

CREEPING NORTH KOREA.

FACTS ARE SACRED. Harold Shipman was a killer, but he had no racist bone I him, as he killed only his own white kindred.

Dr Anand Kamath (42) was threatened with reportage to the GDC, he killed himself. Only our people are dying in this latent but very potent undeclared race war.

https://www.facebook.com/rotimi.osunsan/videos/3088536551193798

OYINBO OLE: WHITE THIEVES: HABAKKUK.
Fish and chips system that is overseen by Freemasons; when their people commit RACIST CRIMES against our people, they criminally bury RACIAL HATRED – Apartheid by stealth – Habakkuk 1:4.
He is watching them – Proverbs 15:3.
They're not immortal, and one day, the Antichrist closeted racist bastards must face transparent Justice.
The Father judges no one, He has given all judgment to the Son - John 5:22.

They want superiority, their birth right; they don't want Freedom of Expression because they don't want their people to know what they secretly do to our people.

"By definition therefore there needs to be a contact order for Mr B so that he knows when he is going to see his son. It is absolutely essential that this occurs and mother agrees with that. She said so several times in her evidence. Mrs Waller agreed that not only should a child have the opportunity of developing relationship with both parents, any sibling should also be there so that inter- sibling relationship could be fostered and nurtured. Obviously in this particular case the children reside in different places. That immediately puts a strain on the children having limited contact with each other. F's sister is very much older than him and she will be further advanced into her adult life. Thus it is not a matter that that sibling relationship can only be fostered by the children being together. Indeed as we all know absence sometimes makes the heart grow fonder. F should have an opportunity of seeing his sister. Wherever he does that it should be done in a friendly and loving environment. If the time comes that his sister goes to university of course his contact with her will be restricted to the time that she is home from university. In years to come when they have both grown up, with their own family they will see less of each other. But it doesn't mean that they don't still love and adore each other as much as they would if they saw each other every day." The Senior Vice President of the Association of Her Majesty's District Judges – proofed and approved Judgement.

"Yes, Sir, it does her honour, but it would do nobody else honour. I have indeed, not read it all. But when I take up the end of a web, and find it packthread, I do not expect, by looking further, to find embroidery." Dr Samuel Johnson

Sincerely perceived brainless nonsense.

A righteous functional semi-illiterate: A closeted racist descendant of industrial-scale professional THIEVES and owners of stolen children of defenceless poor people - Habakkuk.

Facts are sacred.

Sheep unnaturally shepherd sheep.

"Mediocrity weighing mediocrity in the balance, and incompetence applauding its brother ...." Wilde

Antichrist Racist Freemasons teach their members secret handshakes, not grammar; the former is easier to master.

OYINBO OLODO: A RACIST WHITE DUNCE

https://www.youtube.com/watch?v=BlpH4hG7m1A

Shocking!

"Why, that is, because, dearest, you are a dunce." Habakkuk.

A scatter-head racist plebeian; an overpromoted polytechnic university educated racist bastard. A righteous descendant of industrial-scale professional THIEVES and owners of stolen children of defenceless people (Kamala's ancestors) - Habakkuk.

Nigeria: Shells docile cash cow.
Kempston yields only food.
Babies with huge oil wells and gas-fields near their houses eat 1.5/day; a closeted racist former debt-collector Solicitor in Norwich whose white father and mother have never seen crude oil is our District Judge in Bedford.

Then, the white ancestors of his white father and mother were fed like battery hens with the yields of stolen children of defenceless poor people – Habakkuk.

OYINBO OLE: WHITE THIEVES: HABAKKUK.

Then, racist bastards carried and sold millions of stolen children of defenceless poor people; now, they carry natural resources.

SUBSTITUTION: FRAUDULENT EMANCIPATION.

"Moderation is a virtue only among those who are thought to have found alternatives." Henry Kissinger.

No brain.
Poor in natural resources.

Several centuries of stealing and slavery preceded the TRUST FUND. Only the skin colour is indisputably superior.

Facts are sacred.

"Mr Bamgbelu clearly has very, very strong views about education and I understand those views are based upon the fact that he is a successful dentist here in Bedford which he attributes to the fact that his parents cared for him and his education when he was young. They ensured that he had a proper fee paying education........" The Senior Vice President of the Association of Her Majesty's District Judges – proofed and approved Judgement

"Envy is weak." Yul Brynner

Sincerely perceived brainless nonsense.

Patronage rather than colour-blind measurable objectivity unfairly granted polytechnic-educated functional semi-illiterate former debt collector Solicitor in Norwich the platform to display hereditary prejudice.

A racist descendant of very hardened, industrial-scale professional THIEVES and owners of stolen children of defenceless poor people.

After several centuries of merciless, daily tyranny: The organised stealing of the children of other people, in 1892, racist bastards returned to our tribe, in the African bush (IJEBU), and they used heavy guns on wheels to sadistically slaughter almost everyone.

Facts are sacred.

"The truth allows no choice." Dr Samuel Johnson

Google: Magbon, 1892.

https://www.youtube.com/watch?v=BlpH4hG7m1A

Indiscreet envy.

Envy is a thief.

When envy and innate RACIAL HATRED copulate, insanity is their offspring.

Financial disclosure in a divorce: How can a mere Negro have what I do not have

OYINBO OLE: WHITE THIEVES: HABAKKUK.

No brain.
The land yields only food: Poor in natural resources.
Several centuries of stealing and slavery preceded the TRUST FUND – Habakkuk.
Only the skin colour is indisputably superior; the wearer neither made nor chose it.

Straight faced, rightcous, and ignorant descendants of THIEVES and owners of stolen children of defenceless poor people - Habakkuk.

He is watching them – Proverbs 15:3.

The report, by the OECD warns that the UK needs to take significant action to boost the basic skills of the nation's young people. The 460-page study is based on the first-ever survey of the literacy, numeracy and problem-solving at work skills of 16 to 65-year-olds in 24 countries, with almost 9,000 people taking part in England and Northern Ireland to make up the UK results. The findings showed that England and Northern Ireland have some of the highest proportions of adults scoring no higher than Level 1 in literacy and numeracy - the lowest level on the OECD's scale. This suggests that their skills in the basics are no better than that of a 10-year-old.

AN IMBECILE: AN ADULT WITH THE BASIC SKILLS OF A CHILD.

Apart from creating cushy salaried jobs for Solicitors and Barristers who couldn't hack it in the very competitive real world (quasi-communism), what do imbeciles need very expensive administration of the law for?

Adults with the basic skills of a foetus will succeed adults with the basic skills of a child; the former will need only food and shelter.

"We have the power to turn against our creators." Dr Richard Dawkins

CONFLICT OF INTEREST: The creators of IMBECILES punish those who can't relate to imbecility.

https://www.youtube.com/watch?v=BlpH4hG7m1A&feature=youtu.be

"They may not have been well written from a grammatical point of view, but I am confident I had not forgotten any of the facts." Dr Geraint Evans, Postgraduate Tutor, Oxford

https://youtu.be/rayVcfyu9Tw

Dr Rowan Williams was very suspicious of the Builders: Charitable Mediocre Mafia.

Based on available evidence, the Grand Masonic Temple to Baal, 60 Great Queen St, Holborn, London WC2B 5AZ, was built in London, in the 1700s, at a height of the barbarously racist traffic in millions of stolen children of defenceless poor people - Habakkuk.

They do indiscreet and vulgar Pharisees' charitable works in exchange for what?

Then, theirs was not a good deal, and now, theirs isn't a good deal – Matthew 4:9.

Freemason, Brother Jimmy Savile did not fix anything for NOTHING.

Antichrist Racist Freemasons: Charitable half-educated school dropouts and their superiors who have informal access to some very powerful white Judges – Habakkuk 1:4.

WOLLASTON, ENGLAND: Based on available evidence, GDC-WITNESS, Ms Rachael Bishop, Senior NHS Nurse, unrelentingly lied under oath - Habakkuk 1:4; John 8:44; John 10:10.

A RACIST WHITE CROOK.

CREEPING NORTH KOREA.

FACTS ARE SACRED.

OYINBO OLE: WHITE THIEVES: HABAKKUK.
Fish and chips system that is overseen by Freemasons; when their people commit RACIST CRIMES against our people, they criminally bury RACIAL HATRED – Apartheid by stealth – Habakkuk 1:4.
He is watching them – Proverbs 15:3.
They're not immortal, and one day, the Antichrist closeted racist bastards must face transparent Justice.
The Father judges no one, but he has given all judgment to the Son - John 5:22.

"The good Samaritan had money." Mrs Margaret Thatcher (1925 – 2013).

Presumably, the money of the good Samaritan was the yield of transparent virtue.

MATTHEW 19:21: He told the righteous Jew to sell the yields of transparent virtue, give the proceeds to the poor, and follow Him; He'd have told the rich Pharisee to return the yields of vice.

Righteousness without equitable reparation is continuing racist fraud.

Deluded and conceited intellectual cowards: They want superiority, but they do not want Freedom of Expression. They want to eat their cakes and have them. Their indisputably superior skin colour is an asset, and they know it; they neither made nor chose it. Our own dark coat is a curse, and we know it. Our asset is useless without Freedom of Expression, they know it so, they stifle Freedom of Expression. Spineless racist cowards (worms); they invited us to a sword fight, and they seized our swords. Their ancestors were the world champions at, directly and indirectly, using guns to mercilessly slaughter unarmed Africans.

Facts are sacred.

He is watching them – Proverbs 15:3

The nemesis is not extinct, and the fact that it tarries isn't proof that it will never come – Habakkuk.

"Many Scots masters were considered among the most brutal, with life expectancy on their plantations averaging a mere four years. We worked them to death then simply imported more to keep the sugar and thus the money flowing. Unlike centuries of grief and murder, an apology cost nothing. So, what does Scotland have to say?" Herald Scotland: Ian Bell, Columnist, Sunday 28 April 2013

"I know of no evil that has ever existed, nor can imagine any evil to exist, worse than the tearing of eighty thousand persons annually from their native land, by a combination of the most civilised nations inhabiting the most enlightened part of the globe, but more especially under the sanction of the laws of that Nation which calls herself the most free and the most happy of them all." Prime Minister William Pitt the Younger

"Time for Scots to say sorry for slavery.
Herald Scotland:
Ian Bell, Columnist / Sunday 28 April 2013 / Opinion
Sunday 28 April 2013
According to the American founding father, the son of a Caithness Kirk minister had about him of "an air of great simplicity and honesty"". The likes of James Boswell and Laurence Sterne also enjoyed the merchant's

company.

To his contemporaries, he was, as the author Adam Hochschild has written, "'a wise, thoughtful man who embodied the Scottish virtues of frugality, sobriety, and hard work'". Oswald was a scholar of theology, philosophy, and history. He collected art, particularly Rubens and Rembrandt, and gave handsomely to charity. Oswald, who learned his trade in Glasgow, also represented Britain in negotiations with the Americans after their war of liberation. He was the cosmopolitan epitome of Enlightenment success. But when he wasn't busy with good works, Oswald waded in blood. The precise number of deaths that can be laid at his door is impossible to calculate. As the leading figure in Grant, Oswald & Co, he had investments in each corner of the "'triangular trade'". In his own name, Oswald trafficked at least 13,000 Africans, although he never set foot on their continent. By the time he bought Auchincruive House and 100,000 acres in Ayrshire in 1764, he was worth £500,000. Writing in 2005, Hochschild thought this was ""roughly equivalent"" to $68 million (about £44m). This is conservative.

Oswald was remarkable, but not unique. Where Glasgow and its merchants in sugar, tobacco, and human life are concerned, there are plenty of names and no shortage of monuments: Dennistoun, Campbell, Glassford, Cochrane, Buchanan, Hamilton, Bogle, Ewing, Donald, Speirs, Dunlop. One way to understand what they wrought is simple: take pleasure in the city"s architecture today and you are likely to be admiring the fruits of slavery.

Glasgow is not alone in that. London, Liverpool and Bristol also have their stories to tell. Edinburgh's once-great banks grew from foundations built on bones. The first Scottish venture into slavery set out from the capital in 1695. Montrose, Dumfries, Greenock and Port Glasgow each tried their hands. In the language of the present age, they were all in it together.

When commerce was coursing around the triangle, most of polite Scotland was implicated. The nobility (and country) rendered bankrupt in 1700 in the aftermath of the Darien Venture was by the mid-1760s contemplating big elegant townhouses and 100,000-acre estates. You could call that a reversal of fortune. Contrary to self-serving myth, it did not happen because of "'frugality, sobriety, and hard work'".

Certain things need to be remembered about Scotland and slavery. One is that the mercantile class got stinking rich twice over: despite fortunes made from stolen lives, they were quick to demand compensation when slavery was ended in 1833. Britain's government decided that £20m, a staggering sum, could be raised. In his 2010 book, The Price of Emancipation, Nicholas Draper reckons Glasgow's mob got £400,000 – in modern terms, hundreds of millions.

Compensation cases also demonstrated that Scots were not merely following an English lead. According to Draper, a country with 10% of the British population accounted for at least 15% of absentee slavers. By another estimate, 30% of Jamaican plantations were run by Scots. For all the pride taken in the abolitionist societies of Glasgow and Edinburgh, the slave-holders did not suffer because of abolition. They were '"compensated"'.

And that wasn't the worst of it. Thanks to Hollywood movies, the slave economy of the American South is still taken as barbarism's benchmark. Few realise that the behaviour of Scots busy getting rich in the slave-holders" empire was actually worse – routinely worse – than the worst of the cottonocracy. You need only count the corpses................."

Before slavery, what?

OYINBO OLE: WHITE THIEVES: HABAKKUK.

* * * * *

I attended GDC hearings in London from November 17, 2008 to November 21, 2008 (5 days). During the hearings, unbeknownst to the only Negro in the process, NHS's fabrications were live and valid.

1) The NHS fabricated report of July 22, 2004 had been withdrawn; it was withdrawn on October 16, 2008.
2) The NHS fabricated report of undisclosed date had been withdrawn; it was withdrawn on October 16, 2008.
3) Unbeknownst to the only Negro in the process, the NHS fabricated email address of January 04, 2007 was live and valid.
4) Unbeknownst to the only Negro in the process, the NHS

termination letter of July 30, 2007 was live and valid.

"Those who have the power to do wrong with impunity seldom wait long for the will." Dr Samuel Johnson.

NEW HEROD, MATTHEW 2:16: They lie to their moron sheep that they are geniuses; they kill all those who know they're brainless racist bastards.

If some of one's ancestors were industrial scale professional THIEVES and owners of stolen children of defenceless poor people, it'd be naïve not to expect incompetent mendacity to be part of one's genetic inheritances – Habakkuk.

OYINBO OLE: WHITE THIEVES: HABAKKUK.

"Racism is rife in most of the organisations across Britain." The Mayor of London

The Negro attended a GDC hearing in London February 09, 2009. The hearing was adjourned.

After the hearing of February 09, 2009, and several months before the recommencement of the hearing, the jobbers, racists, and loafers at GDC, Business Studies Type who spend other people's money on themselves and their friends, deliberately published in its Gazette that the hearing had concluded, and the Negro had been found guilty.

"Those who have the power to do wrong with impunity seldom wait long for long for the will." Dr Samuel Johnson

The real name of Nigel Lawson's grandfather was Gustav Liebson; he came from Latvia in the 1890s.

Mustafa is Turkish; Boris Johnson isn't.

The real name of Ghislaine Maxwell's father was, ,; he came from Czechoslovakia in 1940.

Essentially, genetic alien jobbers, loafers, and racists at the GDC, Business Studies type who think they are wonderful because they spend other people's money on themselves and their friends, are relevant only because England is rich, and affluence is not the yield of the land or their business studies intellect. Then, almost everything was stolen – Habakkuk.

"All have taken what had other owners, and all have had recourse to arms rather than quit the prey on which they were fastened." Dr Samuel Johnson.

OYINBO OLE: WHITE THIEVES: HABAKKUK.

"Affluence is not a birth right." David Cameron

The Negro attended GDC hearings in London, from June 15, 2009 to June 19, 2009.

Seemingly, in synchrony by probably the Antichrist Racist Freemason killers, albeit hand's off, the Negro was invited simultaneously ordered to attend a divorce hearing in Bedford, on June 19, 2009.

Dr Shipman was a killer, but he had no racist bone in him; he poisoned only his own white kindred.

They (Antichrist Racist Freemasons) kill only our people, albeit hands off.

Google: Dr Richard Bamgboye, GP

Google: Dr Anand Kamath, dentist.

On September 14 and 15, 2009, I attended GDC hearings in London.

Dr. Olayinka Bamgbelu

On September 1, 2010, I attended a GDC hearing in London.

On August 17, 2011, I attended a GDC hearing in London.

On 22, November 2013, I attended a GDC hearing in London.

On 14, February 2014, I attended a GDC hearing in London.

On April 03, 2014, I attended a GDC hearing in London.

When the transcript of the hearing of April 03, 2014 was sexed up, I realised that I had crossed swords with medusas with many heads, and with immortal, I discerned the plot to kill me, and ran for my life.

The racist white bastards will get me in end, and I am ready; I know too many things their moron sheep must know so, I am:

"A dead man walking." Claudio Ranieri.

I shall go, and they must come – 2 Samuel 12:23.

Any integer plus infinity is infinity. The endless state of non-being is our common destiny.

RE: GDC IOC review hearing on 3 April 2014
Tue, 25 Mar 2014 15:30
Andrew Richardson Andrew.Richardson@capsticks.comHide
To adeolacole adeolacole@aol.com
CC James Penry-Davey James.Penry-Davey@capsticks.com

Dear Mr Bamgbelu
Please see the attached letter for your attention.
Kind regards
Andrew Richardson
Paralegal
DD 0208 780 4872
E andrew.richardson@capsticks.com

W www.capsticks.com

Re: GDC HEARING OF 03.04.2014
Fri, 4 Apr 2014 18:33
 adeolacole adeolacole@aol.comHide
To   amanda.borland@nhs.net

Dear Amanda Borland,

I hereby give notice that I wish to terminate my NHS contract, as it is practically impossible for me to continue, during the interim suspension and beyond that date. The interim suspension based entirely upon the perceived tone of free speech was a constructive erasure - with unfortunately no leave to appeal. I sincerely perceive unfairness, but life must go on. I will advice my patients accordingly, and we will continue to practically assist all our patients with securing other services.

I am very grateful for the opportunity to serve.

As advised we will ask our emergency patients to try the 8-8 centre.

Very sincerely,

A. BAMGBELU

GDC CHARGES AGAINST THE NEGRO.
At the GDC hearing of 17th December 2014, which concerned Mr Bamgbelu, the Professional Conduct Committee of the General Dental Council (PCC-GDC), the following charges were considered:
1. Between approximately 26 September 2013 and 20 November 2013 you sent emails and a letter to Mr A (identified in Schedule A1*) and in your communications you made one or more: (a) abusive or, in the alternative, offensive comments as set out in Schedule 1*, which included one or more such comments: (i) referring to nationality, race or ethnicity; (ii) using sexual language or content; (b) threatening comments as set out in Schedule 2*; (c) offensive comments referring to nationality, race or ethnicity as set out in Schedule 3*; (d) offensive comments using sexual

language or content as set out in Schedule 4*. * Unidentified Person

2. On or around 19 December 2013 you sent a letter to Mrs B (identified in Schedule A*) and in your letter you made: (a) one or more abusive or, in the alternative, offensive comments as set out in Schedule 5*; (b) an offensive comment using sexual language or content as set out in Schedule 6*.

3. Your conduct at each of paragraphs 1 and 2 was intentionally abusive, threatening or offensive, or such that you were aware that it may be abusive, threatening or offensive.

4. Between approximately 23 January and 27 January 2014 you communicated by email with Mr C (identified in Schedule B*) and in your emails you (a) made an abusive or, in the alternative, offensive comment as set out in Schedule 7; (b) repeated the comment at paragraph 4(a) in emails sent on 24 January 2014 and 26 January 2014; (c) made one or more offensive comments referring to nationality, race or ethnicity as set out in Schedule 8*

5. On 31 March 2014 you communicated by email with Mrs D (identified in Schedule B) and in your emails you (a) made one or more abusive or, in the alternative, offensive comments as set out in Schedule 9*; (b) made one or more offensive comments referring to nationality, race, ethnicity or religion as set out in Schedule 10*; 9 (c) made an offensive comment using sexual language or content as set out in Schedule 11*; (d) repeated the comments at each of paragraphs 5(a), 5(b) and 5(c) in an email you sent at 22:31 on 31 March 2014.

6. Your conduct at each of paragraphs 4 and 5 was intentionally abusive or offensive, or such that you were aware that it may be abusive or offensive.

7. Between 14 February 2014 and 10 April 2014 you sent one or more emails to an employee of the General Dental Council (GDC) and/or a legal advisor to the GDC in which you used emotional and/or abusive language in breach of Condition 7 of an Interim Order for conditions that were imposed on your registration on 14 February 2014.

8. At a hearing before the General Dental Council's (GDC) Interim Orders Committee (the Committee) on 10 April 2014 you provided to the Committee a copy of an email sent to you by Capsticks Solicitors (Capsticks), which was not a complete and/or accurate copy of the original email in that: (a) words had been removed from the original

email, in particular: (i) 'due to expire on 19 February 2014 do not cover the provision'; (ii) 'until such time as you have appropriate'; (iii) 'in place please confirm, by return, that you'; (b) words had been underlined when they were not underlined in the original email, in particular: (i) 'dental treatment'; (ii) 'indemnity cover.'

9. In respect of the copy email that you provided on 10 April 2014, you said to the Committee: (a) 'I have not cut anything out of it'; (b) 'That is the email that was sent to me.'

10. Your conduct at paragraph 9 was: (a) misleading; (b) dishonest, in that you knew that the copy email you provided on 10 April 2014 was not a complete and/or accurate copy of the original email.

11. You have failed to co-operate with the GDC's investigation into your fitness to practise in that, despite requests made by or on behalf of the GDC, you have not agreed to undergo a health assessment/medical examination.

GOOGLE: INCOMPETENT LIARS: SOME LAWYERS.
GOOGLE: THE WHITE JUDGE LIED.

The first seven (1 – 7) of the charges concerned emails that my Bamgbelu sent to others. Charges 8 – 10 concerned incompetently created dishonesty by white British imbeciles. Charge 11 concerned health assessment (any Negro that believes some white people are decorticate racist bastards must be a lunatic). The enduring residues of the ORIGINAL SIN.

"To disagree with three – fourths of the British public on all points is one of the first elements of sanity, one of the deepest consolations in all moments of spiritual doubt." Oscar Wilde

How can a mere Negro disagree with members of the superior race; he must be a lunatic?

White Privilege: Part of the enduring residues of the ORIGINAL SIN.

There was no hearing on April 10, 2014; the legal transcript was sexed-up.

The report, by the OECD, warns that the UK needs to take significant action to boost the basic skills of the nation's young people. The 460-page study is based on the first-ever survey of the literacy, numeracy and problem-solving at work skills of 16 to 65-year-olds in 24 countries, with almost 9,000 people taking part in England and Northern Ireland to make up the UK results. The findings showed that England and Northern Ireland have some of the highest proportions of adults scoring no higher than Level 1 in literacy and numeracy - the lowest level on the OECD's scale. This suggests that their skills in the basics are no better than that of a 10-year-old.

AN IMBECILE: AN ADULT WITH THE BASIC SKILLS OF A CHILD.

Facts are sacred; they can't be overstated.

Apart from creating cushy salaried jobs for Solicitors and Barristers who couldn't hack it in the very competitive real world (Quasi-Communism), what do imbeciles need very expensive administration of the law for?

Based on available evidence, sexed-up legal transcripts are not uncommon in the administration of English law - Habakkuk 1:4; John 8:44; John 10:10.

OYINBO OLE: WHITE THIEVES: HABAKKUK.

"It does no harm to throw the occasional man overboard, but it does not do much good if you are steering full speed ahead for the rocks." Sir Ian Gilmour

"Those who have the power to do wrong with impunity seldom wait long for the will." Dr Samuel Johnson

"You will bow. You can't beat the system." Kemi Daramola.

I shan't, and I know who can – Romans 11; John 4:4.

CHAPTER 4

"In 2006 the Healthcare Commission carried out a visit to Bedfordshire PCT and I was asked to provide all my practice visit reports. While collating this information, I noticed that some inspection reports were missing, which included an inspection of Mr Bamgbelu's practice on 02.04.2003. Around that time my department moved and it is possible that some reports had been lost during the move. I did locate some of my draft handwritten notes and referred to these to prepare my inspection report dated 22.07.2004 for MR BAMGBELU's practice which at the time, I understood to be a correct and accurate record of my inspection. Following another move to different premises, I went through some of my files and found my correct inspection report dated which is exhibited to my September 2008 statement as RWH11." – Richard Hill, 16 October 2008

NEGRO'S PERSPECTIVE:
"In 2006 the Healthcare Commission carried out a visit to Bedfordshire PCT and I was asked to provide all my practice visit reports. While collating this information, I noticed that some inspection reports were missing, which included an inspection of Mr Bamgbelu's practice on 02.04.2003." – Richard Hill, 16 October 2008

In the synopsis of reports that Richard Hill produced and sent to John Hooper on 6 September 2006, there were nineteen reports. The author was the first ever and only Negro dentist in Bedford. When the objective examination ends, the true examination begins for the Negro.

Richard Hill alleged that some of the nineteen reports were missing, and not unexpectedly, the missing report included the report for the lone Negro in their midst.

Richard Hill alleged that he noticed that the 2 April 2003 report that belonged to the lone Negro in their midst was missing.

Had Richard Hill's mama exposed him to qualitative education, which included critical reasoning, he would have detected the absurdity in his brainless construction.

Richard Hill was dishonest, as he told racist lies seemingly with the full knowledge and tacit approval of Sue Gregory.

By stating that he created the reports of 22 July 2004 and the follow up of unknown date from handwritten drafts, Richard Hill was intellectually too dull to realise that he implied these reports were missing too. They hate us with seemingly latent, sadistic passion, which only genetics could reasonably justify. Our children are in trouble, but they do not know – some of them think lion cubs are cats. The only black that they like unconditionally is crude oil. In 2020, Bedfordshire yields only food. In 1720, Bedfordshire yielded only food – almost everything else was stolen with guns against unarmed and defenceless peoples on almost every square inch of the unarmed and defenceless world.

"Many Scots masters were considered among the most brutal, with life expectancy on their plantations averaging a mere four years. We worked them to death then simply imported more to keep the sugar and thus the money flowing. Unlike centuries of grief and murder, an apology cost nothing. So, what does Scotland have to say?" – Herald Scotland, Ian Bell, columnist, Sunday 28 April 2013

"Those who have robbed have also lied." – Dr Samuel Johnson corroborating prophet Habakkuk

Under oath, "some missing reports" mutated to "two or three missing reports." The intellectually impotent former England young adult (white skin and what else?) seemed too dull to detect the absurdity in his brainless construction. No brain, natural resources poor, only skin colour that the wearer neither made nor chose, and what else? Pure scam!

Two or three missing reports implied that Richard Hill was not sure of the number of missing reports. If Richard Hill was unsure of the number of missing reports in 2006, it seemed extraordinary that he remained unsure of the number of missing reports in November 2008.

Reductio ad absurdum!

Two or three reports implied a minimum of two reports and a maximum of three reports. There was only one Negro amongst the nineteen dentists in the synopsis, and, not unexpectrdly, all the three allegedly missing reports belonged to the Negro.

Richard Hill alleged that the 2 April 2003 report was missing or lost.
Richard Hill implied that the 22 July 2004 report was missing or lost.
Richard Hill implied that the follow up report of unknown or undisclosed date was also missing.

Racial hatred is not a myth, and Dylann Roof's use of guns to mercilessly slaughter unarmed and defenceless Africans was not a conspiracy theory. He seemed to have been would up at home.

The allegedly missing three reports seemed to belong to the lone Negro in their midst. Extraordinary, isn't it?

✳ ✳ ✳ ✳

David Morris cross examined Richard Hill under oath on 18 November 2008 (Court Room):
DAVID MORRIS: At that time I think some of your inspection visit reports were missing.
RICHARD HILL: Two or three were missing. The reason was and the reason I suspect why that was missing was because we had moved office, I had moved office in 2002, 2004 and 2006 and the problem is that I work for one session a week and I am at the office quite often only once every other week; the other time I'm on the road visiting. What happens is that when there's a move, other people are responsible for putting all my files into boxes and then re-filing them at the other location simply because I'm not there.
DAVID MORRIS: So when we look at the 2003 report that we have behind tab 20, it had got lost and is it the case that this is a contemporaneous document—

RICHARD HILL: Yes.

DAVID MORRIS: – or might it have been a document reconstituted from memory following the loss of an earlier document?

RICHARD HILL: This would have been contemporaneous. Well, when I say contemporaneous, what I would do, without support, would be to make some notes and then complete it normally the next day. This was carried out of an evening. We try to be flexible. Most of our inspections/visits are carried out at lunch time and most practitioners are happy for that; it means that we can actually have myself and one or two PCT members of staff visit as well so that we can have, if you like, a holistic approach to the whole practice, not just seeing if people comply but trying to sort of find ways in which we can support the practitioner in the future. So it is a multifaceted approach. In this particular case, we visited in the evening because Mr Bamgbelu was finding that much more convenient. I don't know whether that was because he was at dual locations he could only make it in the evening, but we would normally do it lunch time. Unfortunately, in those circumstances you do not get any support because people finish at 5 o'clock and I go straight from practice. I finish in my practice probably mid afternoon and then I arrange for that visit to be carried out in the evening.

DAVID MORRIS: So this visit that you have documented here behind tab 20, you would have had this pro forma with you, would you?

RICHARD HILL: Yes, I would take it with me.

DAVID MORRIS: Because you now have this pro forma, would there be any need to make any notes?

RICHARD HILL: I would make sort of relevant notes which are not covered by these, sort of anything to do with dentist problems, worries, that sort of thing, concerns.

NEGRO'S PERSPECTIVE:

"Two or three were missing. The reason was and the reason I suspect why that was missing was because we had moved office, I had moved office in 2002, 2004 and 2006 and the problem is that I work for one session a week and I am at the office quite often only once every other week; the other time I'm on the road visiting. What happens is that when there's a move, other people are responsible for putting all my files into boxes and then re-filing them at the other location simply because I'm not there." – Richard Hill, under oath, on 18 November 2008

Exceedingly irritating, dishonest, tortuous gibberish; f****** rot by a merciless, closeted white supremacist and a coward!

The satanic network is everywhere, and they control almost everything except intellect.

"Nothing that you will learn in the course of your studies will be of the slightest possible use to you in after life – save only this – if you work hard and diligently you should be able to detect when a man is talking rot, and that, in my view, is the main, if not the sole, purpose of education." – J.A. Smith, Oxford University Professor, Moral Philosophy

"The great enemy of the clear language is INSINCERITY (DISHONESTY). When there is a gap between one's real and one's declared aims, one turns as it were instinctively to long words and exhausted idioms, like a cuttlefish squirting ink. In our age there is no such thing as 'keeping out of politics'. All issues are political issues, and politics itself is a mass of lies, evasions, folly, HATRED and schizophrenia. When the general atmosphere is bad, language must suffer." – George Orwell

"This would have been contemporaneous. Well, when I say contemporaneous, what I would do, without support, would be to make some notes and then complete it normally the next day. This was carried out of an evening. We try to be flexible. Most of our inspections/visits are carried out at lunch time and most practitioners are happy for that; it means that we can actually have myself and one or two PCT members of staff visit as well so that we can have, if you like, a holistic approach to the whole practice, not just seeing if people comply but trying to sort of find ways in which we can support the practitioner in the future. So it is a multifaceted approach. In this particular case, we visited in the evening because Mr Bamgbelu was finding that much more convenient. I don't know whether that was because he was at dual locations he could only make it in the evening, but we would normally do it lunch time. Unfortunately, in those circumstances you do not get any support because people finish at 5 o'clock and I go straight from practice. I finish in my practice probably mid afternoon and then I arrange for that visit to be carried out in the evening." – Richard Hill

THE NEGRO'S PERSPECTIVE:
Richard Hill, the cretin disciple of Sue Gregory, was seemingly propped up by crude oil and gas money in exactly the same way as his merciless, racist thug, armed robber, and thieving ancestors were for centuries sustained by the proceeds of racial and fraud (slavery). In 2015, Bedfordshire yields only food. In 1715, Bedfordshire yielded only food – almost everything else was stolen. He allegedly moved office in 2002, 2004, 2006, and 2008 – and things are likelier to get lost or missing because cretin England young adults move the files for cretin former England young adults, which causes orderly recorded keeping failing.

Sir Winston Churchill implied that the average Briton was a moron. More than sixty years later, the OECD corroborated the proximate observation of the great man.

"The best argument against democracy is a five-minute conversation with the average voter." – Sir Winston Churchill

"FAILING SCHOOLS AND A BATTLE FOR BRITAIN: This was the day the British education establishment's 50-year betrayal of the Nation's children lay starkly exposed in all its ignominy. After testing 166,000 people in 24 education systems, the Organisation for Economic Cooperation and Development (OECD) finds that England young adults are amongst the least literate and numerate in the industrialised world." – The Daily Mail, 09.01.2013

Part of the reasons why England young adults are amongst the dullest in the industrialised world is because Sue Gregory, Richard Hill, and their type are their shepherds. No brain, natural resources poor, only skin colour that the wearer neither made nor chose, and what else? Pure scam! The charade will not endure. The future generations will be too dull to keep things going seamlessly. Time will unfold the truth.

"Ignorance, the root and stem of all evil." – Plato

"Natural selection will not remove ignorance from future generations."
– Dr Richard Dawkins

They found guns and used them to destroy the world so that semi-illiterate and innumerate England young adults could thrive in the future.

There were no offices in Bedford before slavery. There mightn't have been offices in Bedford had there not been slavery. The foundation of Bedford, almost in its entirety, was forged with the proceeds of merciless, racial hatred and naked fraud - Habakkuk.

Richard Hill implied that he kept poor records. Part of the reasons why Anand Kamath was mercilessly hounded to death by seemingly white supremacist thugs was because he was alleged to have kept poor records.
Google: Anand Kamath.

For several years in his native India. He came to England, and within some few years, he was driven round the bend, and killed himself. Better life, indeed.

"Dr Anand Kamath felt 'bullied and harassed' by an investigation into his record-keeping, which had suffered because of the amount of patients he treated." –11 Aug 2013, Nick Owens and Martyn Halle

It sincerely crossed my mind that Sue Gregory and her type were in charge and behind the scenes of the merciless murder of the Indian dentist Dr Anand Kamath, albeit hands off.
We are chemicals, and we are controlled by chemicals!
Unbearable pressures and stress caused altered and reduced monoamines in the brain which led to insanity, suicide, and death.

The hands-off killers of Dr Anand Kamath did not consider the fragility of his mind and seemed oblivious to the fact that the doses of stress they forced him to take were too much for him.

Merciless, racist bastards!

He is watching them, and He is transparently just – Proverbs 15:3.

A principle of criminal law is that the defendant "takes his victim as he finds him." This is often enunciated with the example of a hypothetical victim of an assault who is particularly susceptible to a severe head injury following a minor blow due to an abnormally "thin skull." A defendant cannot escape responsibility for the victim's death as a result of that abnormality should he strike him on the head. This general principle was described in: R V Hayward (1908) and confirmed more recently in R V Blaue (1975).

"Two or three were missing. The reason was and the reason I suspect why that was missing was because we had moved office, I had moved office in 2002, 2004 and 2006 and the problem is that I work for one session a week and I am at the office quite often only once every other week; the other time I'm on the road visiting. What happens is that when there's a move, other people are responsible for putting all my files into boxes and then refiling them at the other location simply because I'm not there." – Richard Hill, under oath, 18 November 2008

Richard Hill should go to Peckham in London and blow his f****** brainless rot to brunos. "You know what I mean?" He should find a bitch, preferably with golden fangs, who could bark and blow his two-yearly f****** rot to it! He is likelier to be very delighted that he was talking to one of the topmost former England young adults.

"England young adults are amongst the least literate and numerate in the industrialised world." – The OECD

If the bottommost part of a whole is world class bottommost, the topmost part of that whole cannot be world class topmost.

Descendants of wretched, feudal, agricultural labourers (serfs) from mainland Europe who used violence to dispossess and steal the land of aboriginal Britons (who were immeasurably transformed by the gigantic yields of several continuous centuries of merciless racial hatred and naked fraud—slavery) have reinvented themselves on stolen land and they fool the foolish with foolishness.

"It was in 1066 that William the Conqueror occupied Britain, stole our land and gained control by granting it to his Norman friends, thus creating a feudal system we have not yet fully escaped." – Tony Benn

Normans stole from others what others had stolen from others. Genetically pure Britons are extinct; all were dispossessed, robbed, and slaughtered.

Tony Benn was dishonest, or he was confused when he implied that he was genetically an aboriginal Briton. Genetically pure aboriginal Britons are extinct. They were dispossessed and robbed of their land by a motley assembly of mainland Europeans – hereditary serfs or descendants of feudal agricultural labourers – who were hugely transformed by the gigantic gains of slavery. They have reinvented themselves.

Richard Hill, the sincerely perceived moron England young adult, implied that all the missing reports belonged to the first ever and only Negro dentist in Bedford – since He merely spoke, and the world became.
The alleged 2 April 2003 report was missing.
The alleged 22 July 2004 report was missing, so it was reconstituted from a handwritten draft, which contains other matters. Pretty extraordinary!
The alleged follow up visit of undisclosed date was missing, so it was reconstituted from a handwritten draft, which contains other matters.

Pretty extraordinary!

"Around that time my department moved and it is possible that some reports had been lost during the move. I did locate some of my draft handwritten notes and referred to these to prepare my inspection report dated 22.07.2004 for MR BAMGBELU's practice which at the time, I understood to be a correct and accurate record of my inspection. Following another move to different premises, I went through some of my files and found my correct inspection report dated which is exhibited to my September 2008 statement as RWH11." – Richard Hill, 16 October 2008

Richard Hill was dishonest, as it was impossible to reconstitute entire reports from handwritten drafts which contained matters that were unrelated to the records in the main body of the report.

Mendacem memorem esse opportet!

※ ※ ※

David Morris cross examined Richard Hill in the council before a seemingly planted committee of white supremacists on 18 November 2008 (Court Room):

DAVID MORRIS: So this visit that you have documented here behind tab 20, you would have had this pro forma with you, would you?

RICHARD HILL: Yes, I would take it with me.

DAVID MORRIS: Because you now have this pro forma, would there be any need to make any notes?

RICHARD HILL: I would make sort of relevant notes which are not covered by these, sort of anything to do with dentist problems, worries, that sort of thing, concerns.

NEGRO'S PERSPECTIVE:

Mendacem memorem esse opportet!

"Politicians never rise beyond the level of misrepresentation, and actually condescend to prove, to discuss, to argue. How different from the temper of a true liar, with her frank, fearless statements, her superb irresponsibility, her healthy, natural disdain of proof of any kind! After all what is a fine lie? Simply that which is its own evidence. If a woman is sufficiently unimaginative to produce evidence in support of a lie, she might just as well speak the truth at once. No! Politicians won't do. Something may, perhaps, be urged on behalf of the BAR. The mantle of the Sophist has fallen on its members. Their feigned ardours and unrealistic rhetoric are delightful. They can make the worse appear the better cause, as though they were fresh from Leontine schools, and have been known to wrest from the reluctance juries' triumphant verdicts of

Satanic Network

acquittal for their clients." — The Decay of Lying: A Protest by Oscar Wilde

Richard Hill was dishonest as he maliciously lied under oath before a seemingly planted committee of white supremacists – all seemingly propped up by crude oil and gas money in

CHAPTER 5

David Swinstead is a shepherd of England young adults.

Google: David Swinstead Barrister.

So, Richard Hill said that his response of 6 September 2006 was not to Sue Gregory's email of more than a year earlier (of 18 May 2005). Bizarrely, the seemingly she-man who wiggles his ass from side to side, in relative high frequency, when he walks - also said that he was not sure whether his email of 6 September 2006 was to John Hooper's email of 15 August 2006. He lied under oath. The mediocre, dishonest, and racist council seemed to have "planted" white supremacists in the crooked committee to see Richard Hill's racist perjury through.

* * * *

David Morris cross examined Richard Hill under oath in the council chambers on 18 November 2008:
DAVID MORRIS: Yes. (To the witness) I think I ought to show you another email and, I am sorry, I do not think it is copied in our bundle. I have not had it copied in order to hand up. Can I just show it to my learned friend and then, if he is content, I will just read it out. (Same done) Sir, it was exhibited but it does not appear to be in your bundle. We will have copies made of it, but so as not to delay matters I will read it to you. It is not particularly long. It is from Sue Gregory, dated 15 August 2006 to John Hooper, Sue Gregory (again), Richard Hill and a copy to Charlotte Dowling.
"Subject: RE DRS Visit - Mr Bamgbelu
John [that is John Hooper]

I know that Richard has done practice visits to Bamgbelu in the past, he will need to let you have the details. Sue."

I am sorry, I am taking this out of order. The original message is this:

"From: John Hooper, Sent: 15 August 2006, to: Sue Gregory (HPCT); Richard Hill (HPCT), Cc: Charlotte Dowling
(Goodson)
Subject: DRS Visit – Bamgbelu
Sue/Richard

Stephanie Twidale called us a few weeks ago about DRS visits and Charlotte prioritised Mr Bamgbelu's practice. Stephanie has been in touch a few times as her colleagues had highlighted issues from a similar practice in Northants and they would like to review report etc. etc. prior to visiting.

She also wanted to know if there has been a dental inspection there at all and I did not know the answer . . . Cue Richard have you carried out an inspection at this practice. Please could you advise Stephanie when she contacts you, and would it be possible to see our reports so we can be more proactive with any other queries."

I will show the witness that. (Same done) (To the witness) I do not want take an unfair point, but going back to the May 2005 email, can you recall when and what your response might have been to that?

RICHARD HILL: I don't have any record of a response. There might have been an oral response, but there was certainly nothing in writing.

DAVID MORRIS: And if it was an oral response, can you recall what the nature of that was? Please do not guess if you have absolutely no recollection.

RICHARD HILL: I daren't guess. No, I have no idea.

DAVID MORRIS: But looking at the records that we do have, would it be fair to surmise this, that following the original concern back in 1996/1997 you had been keeping informal contact with Mr Bamgbelu—
RICHARD HILL: Yes.

DAVID MORRIS: —and there had been no continuing cross infection control/cleanliness issue?

RICHARD HILL: There had been nothing brought to my attention. We were happy – well, I was happy that things had stabilised and I was not informed of any complaints through the complaints department of the PCT that there were concerns. I am sure I would have been informed because what happens is if there is a typical number of complaints on a particular issue, let's say a number of people phone over a period of time saying the surgery was dirty or the practitioner was not wearing gloves, this type of thing, you see a pattern emerge and then I would be asked by the PCT to visit the practice and carry out a formal inspection in that situation. That's normally along with a colleague, so it's a proper and formal procedure. But I have no record of being told that there were any concerns.

NEGRO'S PERSPECTIVE:
Richard Hill confirmed that the bizarre suggestion by David Morris (a former England young adult) that his email of 6 September 2006 was in response to Sue Gregory's email of 18 May 2005, more than a year earlier was confusion. Stupid reasoning and stupid questions, my moron former England young adult.

"FAILING SCHOOLS AND A BATTLE FOR BRITAIN: This was the day the British education establishment's 50 year betrayal of the Nation's children lay starkly exposed in all its ignominy. After testing 166,000 people in 24 education systems, the Organisation for Economic Cooperation and Development (OECD) finds that England young adults are amongst the least literate and numerate in the industrialised world." – The Daily Mail, 09.01.2013

Richard Hill, David Morris, and Ian Sadler were shepherds of England's young adults.

Are shepherds of morons, morons too?
If the bottommost part of the whole is world class bottommost, the topmost part relative to that bottommost cannot be world class topmost.
Richard Hill also bizarrely implied that his email of 6 September 2006 was not in response to John Hooper's email of 15 August 2006. How?
Again, John Hooper's email of 15 August 2006 to Richard Hill, Sue Gregory, and Charlotte Dowling Goodson is as follows: "Richard (Hill), Stephanie Twidale called us a few weeks ago about DRS visits and Charlotte prioritised Mr Bamgbelu's practice; Stephanie has been in touch a few times as her colleagues had highlighted issues from a similar practice in

Northants and they would like to review report etc etc prior to visiting. She also wanted to know if there has been a dental inspection there at all and I did not know the answer . . . Cue Richard have you carried out an inspection at this practice, please could you advise Stephanie when she contacts you, and would it be possible to see our reports so we can be more pro active with any other queries. Thanks. With kind regards, John Hooper."

Richard Hill's response of 6 September 2006, only three weeks later, was directed to John Hooper, and copies were sent to Sue Gregory and Charlotte Dowling Goodson as follows:

"Record of Practice Visits-Bedford PCT. Dear John, Please find attached the record of practice visits that you were chasing up. Sorry for the delay! As you can see, the great majority of practices are not a cause for concern. However, we will need to focus particularly on the Bamgbelu and the alpha practices. Perhaps also beta practice in delta and the gamma practice are worthy of closer attention. Regards, Richard" (email of 6 September 2006).

"RECORD OF PRACTICE VISITS: BEDFORD PCT. DENTIST: Mr O Bamgbelu. ADDRESS: Grey Friars Dental Practice 52 Bromham Road Bedford MK40 2QG. Telephone No: 01234300505. Visit Date: JULY 2004. CONCERNS: No risk assessment, no CoSSH, A Kavoclave type autoclave was present in the surgery. This type of autoclave should not be used as the cycle can be broken into before sterilisation is complete. No other member of staff were present at the visit so could not be questioned as regards the methods of cross infection control used by practice." – Report of 22 July 2004

"OUTSTANDING ISSUES: Even though the necessary documents have now been seen. I continue to have concerns as to the cross infection control procedures in the practice." – Follow up report of unknown date

If as alleged by Richard Hill his email and attached report were not in direct response to John Hooper's email of 15 August 2006, it must have been in response to another email or request by John Hooper. That fact does not make sense. The sincerely perceived white supremacist privileged dullards seemed to allow prior predilection and prejudice to becloud their objective reasoning and judgement. They immortalised imbecility for eternity.

Richard Hill apologised to John Hooper for a delay. The maximum delay possible could only be less than three weeks, as the alleged further request by John Hooper must have succeeded his request of 15 August 2006.

The father and mother of some privileged dullards did not attend schools where critical reasoning was properly taught as a subject.

Richard Hill implied that the alleged request by John Hooper, which allegedly succeeded his email of 15 August 2006, was in relation to the alleged CQC inspection.

Brainless, white supremacists!

He immortalised the stupidity of a privileged dullard, seemingly propped up by crude oil and gas money (there are no oil wells or gas fields in Bedfordshire) in the same way as his merciless, racist thug ancestors were for centuries sustained by the proceeds of cowardice (using guns to slaughter and rob unarmed and defenceless Africans)—merciless racial hatred and naked fraud (slavery)!
Before slavery, what?
Almost everything was stolen!
"Those who have robbed have also lied." – Dr Samuel Johnson corroborating prophet Habakkuk
In 2020, Bedfordshire yields only food. In 1720, Bedfordshire yielded only food.
"Agriculture not only gives riches to a nation, but the only riches she can call her own." – Dr Samuel Johnson Almost everything else was stolen.

"In 2006 the Healthcare Commission carried out a visit to Bedfordshire PCT and I was asked to provide all my practice visit reports. While collating this information, I noticed that some inspection reports were missing, which included an inspection of Mr Bamgbelu's practice on 02.04.2003. Around that time my department moved and it is possible that some reports had been lost during the move. I did locate some of my draft handwritten notes and referred to these to prepare my inspection report dated 22.07.2004 for MR BAMGBELU's practice which at the time, I understood to be a correct and accurate record of my inspection. Following another move to different premises, I went through some of my files and found my correct inspection report dated which is exhibited to my September 2008 statement as RWH11." – Richard Hill, 16 October 2008

"In 2006 the Healthcare Commission carried out a visit to Bedfordshire PCT and I was asked to provide all my practice visit reports." – Richard Hill's withdrawal statement of 16 October 2008

John Hooper is the "I" that Richard Hill referred to in his statement supra. The phantom further request by John Hooper was never disclosed, and no one else mentioned it except Richard Hill.

Richard Hill was too dull to detect the absurdity in his brainless construction. He is a mere descendant of wretched, feudal, agricultural labourers from mainland Europe who stole the land of native Britons (they were immeasurably transformed by the proceeds of centuries of merciless, racial hatred and naked fraud). The descendants of wretched peasants have reinvented themselves with the yields of centuries of evil, and now fool the foolish with foolishness.

"American South is still taken as barbarism's benchmark. Few realise that the behaviour of Scots busy getting rich in the slave-holders' empire was actually worse – routinely worse – than the worst of the cottonocracy. You need only count the corpses.

By the time slavery was brought to an end in America, the country's 400,000 trafficked people had grown to a population of four million. In the British West Indies, only 670,000 survived from two million imported souls. In the American South, slaves were valuable and bred. We worked them to death then simply imported more to keep the sugar and thus the money flowing. Unlike centuries of grief and murder, an apology costs nothing. So what does Scotland have to say?" – Herald Scotland, Ian Bell, columnist, Sunday 28 April 2013

"It was our arms in the river of Cameroon, put into the hands of the trader, that furnished him with the means of pushing his trade; and I have no more doubt that they are British arms, put into the hands of Africans, which promote universal war and desolation that I can doubt their having done so in that individual instance. I have shown how great is the enormity of this evil, even on the supposition that we take only convicts and prisoners of war. But take the subject in another way, and how does it stand? Think of 80,000 persons carried out of their native country by we know not what means! For crimes imputed! For light or inconsiderable faults! For debts perhaps! For crime of witchcraft! Or a thousand other weak or scandalous pretexts! Reflect on 80,000 persons annually taken off! There is something in the horror of it that surpasses all bounds of imagination." – Prime Minister William Pitt the Younger, 1792

The vicious, racist thugs, merciless murderers, armed robbers, and thieves are no longer here, but their sadistic genes seem to continue to flow through the veins of some of those who remain here.

Merciless, sadistic bas****s!

Before slavery, what?

Sue Gregory was exceedingly well connected. Their people are almost everywhere: the GDC, the BDA, the CQC, the Health Commission, the NCAS, and others. The sole basis of the power of the seemingly white supremacists in these organisations is money, and the entire foundation of the money is racial hatred and fraud (slavery).

Before slavery, what?

"I know of no evil that has ever existed, nor can imagine any evil to exist, worse than the tearing of eighty thousand persons annually from their native land, by a combination of the most civilised nations inhabiting the most enlightened part of the globe, but more especially under the sanction of the laws of that Nation which calls herself the most free and the most happy of them all." – Prime Minister William Pitt the Younger

There were laws then as there are laws now, but the judiciary of that era was neck deep in merciless, racist evil, as it was fed like battery hens with the proceeds of racial hatred and fraud.

The proceeds of racist evil were used to build courts and prisons and paid the wages of judges who sent those who stole money to prisons that stolen money built.

"Iain Whyte, author of Scotland and the Abolition of Slavery, insists we have at times ignored our guilty past.

"He said: 'For many years Scotland's historians harboured the illusion that our nation had little to do with the slave trade or plantation slavery.

"'We swept it under the carpet. This was remarkable in the light of Glasgow's wealth coming from tobacco, sugar and cotton, and Jamaica Streets being found in a number of Scottish towns and cities.

"'It is healthy we are now recognising Scotland was very much involved.'

"The industries, which saw Glasgow and much of the country flourish, were built on the back of slavery.

"Proceeds of centuries of merciless, racial hatred and fraud kick-started the industrial revolution in Scotland and brought Scottish slave merchants and traders great wealth.

"There were familiar names such as Scot Lyle of Tate and Lyle fame whose fortune was built on slavery. Ewing from Glasgow was the richest sugar producer in Jamaica. The stunning Inveresk Lodge in Edinburgh, now open to the public, was bought by James Wedderburn with money earned from 27 years in Jamaica as a notorious slaver. The Wee Free Church was founded using profits and donations from the slave trade. Even our schools have a dark history. Bathgate Academy was built from money willed by John Newland, a renowned slave master and Dollar Academy has a similar foundation. For many years, the goods and profits from West Indian slavery were unloaded at Kingston docks in Glasgow. Leith in Edinburgh and Glasgow were popular ports from which ambitious Scottish men sailed to make their fortunes as slave masters." – Herald Scotland, Ian Bell, columnist, Sunday 28 April 2013

The proceeds of merciless, racial hatred and naked fraud were used to build cathedrals and courts, castles, churches, prisons and councils.

They were merciless racist thugs, armed robbers, and thieves.

The satanic network is everywhere. It controls almost everything except intellect. Without objective basis, it awards itself the monopoly of knowledge. It's a scam!

Richard Hill implied that the further request that John Hooper allegedly made, which had no evidence of, and which succeeded his first request for reports at the behest of Stephanie Twidale of August 15, 2008, solely concerned the Health Care Commission visit which took place after 6 September 2006.

F****** rot!

It is torture most unbearable to freely educate a Negro and punish him for thinking freely.

"Nothing that you will learn in the course of your studies will be of the slightest possible use to you in after life – save only this – if you work hard and diligently you should be able to detect when a man is talking rot, and that, in my view, is the main, if not the sole, purpose of education." – J.A. Smith, Oxford University Professor, Moral Philosophy

If Richard Hill's mama told him that the brain is in his skin colour, she lied to him. "Yesterday," millions of kidnapped and stolen Africans were real money. Today, it is crude oil and gas. "Yesterday," the Niger area yielded millions of the former. Today, the Niger area yields trillions of pounds of the latter. That is the "meat."

Substitution is fraudulent emancipation.
Feudal agricultural labourers from mainland Europe dispossessed/robbed aboriginal Britons. They've been transformed and reinvented by slavery.
John Hooper did not state that he made a further request after his email of 15 August 2006. There is no evidence of any such request. Neither Sue Gregory nor Charlotte Dowling Goodson mentioned any such request.

Richard Hill, the one-dimensionally educated moron who seemed to baselessly award himself intellectual superiority (they are the best in everything, but only where there are no colour-blind objective measurements), seemed too dull to realise that if John Hooper made the phantom further request after 15 August 2006 but before 6 September 2006, it implied that he was unaware of the alleged Health Care Commission visit.
Immortalised, racist dishonesty!

The Negro is an oral surgeon, so he failed dental materials at school. Brainless nonsense.

Oyinbo olodo! Oyinbo ode!

The half-educated school dropout spies of the white collar white supremacists are amongst the dullest adult population in the industrialised world. They hate our people with passion, but only secretly. The only black that they like is crude oil.

The entire foundation of Bedfordshire is racial hatred and fraud.

Before slavery, what?

Some people are very lucky that their ancestors accurately foresaw that their descendants would become world class dull in the distant future, so when they came by guns, they went on merciless, racist, armed robbery raids all over only the unarmed and defenceless world.

"I did locate some of my draft handwritten notes and referred to these to prepare my inspection report dated 22.07.2004 for MR BAMGBELU's practice which at the time, I understood to be a correct and accurate record of my inspection. Following another move to different premises, I went through some of my files and found my correct inspection report dated which is exhibited to my September 2008 statement as RWH11."
– Richard Hill, 16 October 2008

Richard Hill, the incompetently mendacious and moronic former England young adult and shepherd of England young adults, seemed too dull to realise that the correctness and accuracy which he allegedly understood at the alleged time have basis.

The f****** idiot, Richard Hill, the seemingly brainless white supremacist, also did not realise that as he later allegedly found, the alleged report, which had extraordinarily hidden itself in the files for donkey's, it implied poor record keeping.

Facts are sacred; they can't be overstated.

Part of the reasons why seemingly white supremacist thugs mercilessly murdered Anand Kamath, albeit hands off, was because he was adjudged have kept poor records.

"Worked to death: NHS dentist takes his own life 'after health bosses threatened to strike him off because he couldn't keep up with paperwork for 10,000 patients'.

"Dr Anand Kamath was investigated over minor record keeping problems . . .

"His wife and fellow dentist Dr Rajni Prasad accused health chiefs of driving her husband to suicide.

"Dr Prasad said they felt 'very vulnerable and harassed and bullied' by Trust.

"An NHS dentist who was so hardworking he never refused a patient was driven to suicide when health chiefs threatened to strike him off over his record-keeping. Dr Anand Kamath, 42, was the only NHS dentist in his area and took on as many people as he could so they would not have to pay to go private. But the father-of-three became the subject of an investigation when NHS officials criticised his record-keeping, which had suffered due to his 10,000-strong list of patients. Dr Anand Kamath had 10,000 patients on his books but was threatened with being struck off because of minor record keeping errors. His wife Dr Rajni Prasad accused health chiefs of driving her husband to suicide." – Eleanor Harding, The Daily Mail, 11 August 2013, updated: 12 August 2013

The sole basis of the power of merciless, racist bas****s such as Sue Gregory and Richard Hill is money. The entire foundation of the money was forged with the proceeds of merciless racial hatred and naked fraud: the kidnapping, stealing, carrying, and selling of millions of unarmed and defenceless human beings, unprovoked.

Many of the millions of our ancestors who were stolen from Africa at gun point, and who were mercilessly f***** body and soul and worked to death, were created intellectually superior to their murderous cowards and racist captors.

"Those who have robbed have also lied." – Dr Samuel Johnson corroborating prophet Habakkuk

"The contents of the 22.07.2004 and 02.04.2003 report differ. The reason that the contents differ is because the hand written notes I used to prepare the 22.07.2004 also had a reference to a difference and dates and notes were mixed up. Having reviewed the documents, it became clear to me that the July 2004 was created in error. The content of the 02.04.2003 report is an accurate reflection of the inspection done at the time and I stand by the contents of the same." – Richard Hill, 16 October 2008

Richard Hill, the brainless and racist former England young adult and shepherd of England young adults, did not realise that his moronic tortuous gibberish supra implied that he created the 2004 reports as replacement for the allegedly missing 2003 report.

It became clear to the moron former England young adult and shepherd of England young adults – after close to five years – that he had created records for the first ever and only Negro dentist in Bedford in error. He should go to Peckham, London and find a black bitch bruno, preferably with gold teeth, and feed rot to. He should stay here and blow rot, as in other parts of our Commonwealth the probability that he will be blown into quarks within the native and customary laws – that is, legally – is not below zero, and His Excellency, Jean-Claude Juncker, has no ready power to do anything about it.

Descendants of wretched, feudal agricultural labourers dispossessed the aborigines; they were transformed and reinvented by gigantic yields of sadistic slavery. They now fool the foolish with foolishness.
Before slavery, what?
F****** idiot!
Oyinbo olodo! Oyinbo ode!
"Nothing that you will learn in the course of your studies will be of the slightest possible use to you in after life – save only this – if you work hard and diligently you should be able to detect when a man is talking rot, and that, in my view, is the main, if not the sole, purpose of education." – J.A. Smith, Oxford University Professor, Moral Philosophy

Richard Hill, the former England young adult, shepherd of England young adults, the f****** moron, with a thick, muscular ass like that of Christine Ohuruogu, but not as big, which he wiggled before me on Bromham Road and/or at 52 Bromham Road, Bedford – like a she-man, in a "come and get me if you dare" fashion – reasoned like a quality CQC manager, and he expressed his reasoning worse than an imbecile. Even if one were a man's shit hole f*****, why should anyone f*** a muscular shit hole or prick breaker of a scruffy, racist thug?

Thu, 3 Sep 2015 20:00
RE: Outstanding statutory annual registration fee invoice: payment due – FINAL REMINDER
From cqc (NHS SHARED BUSINESS SERVICES LTD (BRISTOL)) SBS-B.cqc@nhs.net
To adeolacole adeolacole@aol.com
Hello,
Thank you for your below email
Kindly request you to provide your contact details (telephone number) so we can contact you and explain.
If any query please let me know
Thanks and Regards, Kanchan Jaisinghani
Collections
Debt Management Team
Shared Business Services
Tel 0303-123-1155
Fax 0117-933-8890
E-mail: sbs-b.cqc@nhs.net
Website: www.sbs.nhs.uk
Government Business Award Winner
Central Government Supplier of the Year 2011.

Sue Gregory and Richard Hill and their type are shepherds of England's young adults.

"FAILING SCHOOLS AND A BATTLE FOR BRITAIN: This was the day the British education establishment's 50 year betrayal of the Nation's children lay starkly exposed in all its ignominy. After testing 166,000 people in 24 education systems, the Organisation for Economic Cooperation and Development (OECD) finds that England young adults are amongst the least literate and numerate in the industrialised world." – The Daily Mail, 09.01.2013

Shepherds of morons are likelier to be morons too.

"The content of the 02.04.2003 report is an accurate reflection of the inspection done at the time and I stand by the contents of the same." – Richard Hill, 16 October 2008

The alleged accuracy must have a verifiable basis. Richard Hill, the seemingly imbecile former England young adult and shepherd of England's young adults, seemed too dull to work that out. Richard Hill's mama did not send him to schools where critical reasoning was taught as a subject.

"CASE NO: 69238
"IN THE MATTER OF THE GENERAL DENTAL COUNCIL AND ABIODUN BAMGBELU
"SUPPLEMENTAL WITNESS STATEMENT OF RICHARD HILL
"I, RICHARD HILL, c/o Bedfordshire Primary Care Trust, Gilbert Hitchcock House, 21 Kimbolton
Road, Bedford, MK40 2AW WILL SAY AS FOLLOWS:
"1. I make this statement supplemental to my statement dated 23.09.2008.
"2. I attach as Exhibit SRWH1 a copy of my report dated 22.07.2004, I attach a synopsis of practice visits that makes reference to a practice visit to MR BAMGBELU's practice at 52, Bromham Road, Bedford, MK40 2QG in July 2004. The document is incorrect in recording that the inspection took place in 2004. No such inspection in fact took place." – Richard Hill, 16 October 2008

The alleged incorrectness, which took Richard Hill almost five years to detect and was solely for the first ever and only Negro dentist in Bedford, since He merely spoke and the world became must also have a verifiable basis.

"The contents of the 22.07.2004 and 02.04.2003 report differ. The reason that the contents differ is because the hand written notes I used to prepare the 22.07.2004 also had a reference to a difference and dates and notes were mixed up." – Richard Hill, 16 October 2008

"Mixed up" – by a messed up, f******, racist bas****!

"The great enemy of the clear language is INSINCERITY (DISHONESTY). When there is a gap between one's real and one's declared aims, one turns as it were instinctively to long words and exhausted idioms, like a cuttlefish squirting ink. In our age there is no such thing as 'keeping out of politics'. All issues are political issues, and politics itself is a mass of lies, evasions, folly, HATRED and schizophrenia. When the general atmosphere is bad, language must suffer." – George Orwell

"Mediocrity weighing mediocrity in balance, and incompetence applauding its brother that is the spectacle which artistic activity of England affords us from time to time." – Oscar Wilde

"No advance in wealth, no softening of manners, no reform or revolution has ever brought human equality a millimeter nearer." – George Orwell

For good record keeping, especially where the lifetime sacrifice of the first ever and only Negro dentist in Bedford was concerned, Richard Hill, the former England young adult and shepherd of England young adults, must have employed handwritten drafts that had the Negro's name and the name and address of his practice.

The f****** fool, with a muscular ass which he wiggled from side to side in relative high frequency, and walked in short strides with also relatively high frequency, the bas****, the descendant of f****** serfs (mere feudal, agricultural labourers from mainland Europe who were immeasurably transformed by gigantic yields of merciless racial hatred and naked fraud – slavery – seem to have reinvented themselves on stolen land, and they now fool the foolish with foolishness) was pretending to be "somebody." No! He is not! They are descendants of aliens from mainland Europe on stolen land.

"I hate a fellow whom pride, or cowardice, or laziness drives into a corner, and who does nothing when he is there but sit and growl; let him come out as I do, and bark." – Dr Samuel Johnson

"Too often the strong, silent man is silent only because he does not know what to say, and is reputed strong only because he has remained silent." – Sir Winston Churchill

"It was in 1066 that William the Conqueror occupied Britain, stole our land and gained control by granting it to his Norman friends, thus creating a feudal system we have not yet fully escaped." – Tony Benn

Normans stole from others what others had stolen from others. Genetically pure Britons are extinct; all were dispossessed, robbed, and slaughtered.

Tony Benn was dishonest, or he was confused when he implied that he was genetically an aboriginal Briton. Genetically pure aboriginal Britons are extinct. They were dispossessed and robbed of their land by a motley assembly of mainland Europeans – hereditary serfs or descendants of feudal agricultural labourers – who were hugely transformed by the gigantic gains of slavery. They have reinvented themselves.

If the bottommost are world class bottommost, the topmost relative to the bottommost could not be world class topmost. Morons are easier to spin.

Shepherds deceived sheep that they were paragons of wisdom who fed them with the yields of virtue. They didn't bring millions of stolen Africans, home.

"The contents of the 22.07.2004 and 02.04.2003 report differ. The reason that the contents differ is because the hand written notes I used to prepare the 22.07.2004 also had a reference to a difference and dates and notes were mixed up." – Richard Hill, 16 October 2008

Had Richard Hill's mama sent him to schools where logical reasoning was taught as a subject, the f****** brainless, seemingly hereditary racist rotter blower would have considered the following: It would be considered stupid to use handwritten drafts for the first ever and only Negro dentist in Bedford or indeed anyone else – unless Richard Hill was absolutely sure that they referred to him and to his practice. The withdrawal of the adverse report laden with cross infection issues fitted the Negro, but did not belong to him.

Richard Hill was dishonest and intellectually incompetent. The seemingly hereditary serf was too dull to realise that it was impossible to create the report of 22 July 2004 and the follow up of undisclosed date from the handwritten drafts, which he implied were correctly labelled, even if they had been correctly labelled.

* * *

Under oath, Richard Hill, the merciless, racist thug, was cross examined by his kindred, David Morris, and he stated as follows (Court Room):

DAVID MORRIS: Just in terms of the April 2003 visit, I think you have mentioned the Health Care Commission and you were asked to provide details of all your practice visit reports back in 2006.
RICHARD HILL: Yes.
DAVID MORRIS: At that time I think some of your inspection visit reports were missing.
RICHARD HILL: Two or three were missing. The reason was and the reason I suspect why that was missing was because we had moved office, I had moved office in 2002, 2004 and 2006 and the problem is that I work for one session a week and I am at the office quite often only once every other week; the other time I'm on the road visiting. What happens is that when there's a move, other people are responsible for putting all my files into boxes and then re-filing them at the other location simply because I'm not there.
DAVID MORRIS: So when we look at the 2003 report that we have behind tab 20, it had got lost and is it the case that this is a contemporaneous document—
RICHARD HILL: Yes.
DAVID MORRIS: —or might it have been a document reconstituted from memory following the loss of an earlier document?
RICHARD HILL: This would have been contemporaneous. Well, when I say contemporaneous, what I would do, without support, would be to make some notes and then complete it normally the next day. This was carried out of an evening. We try to be flexible. Most of our inspections/visits are carried out at lunch time and most practitioners are happy for that; it means that we can actually have myself and one or

Satanic Network

two PCT members of staff visit as well so that we can have, if you like, a holistic approach to the whole practice, not just seeing if people comply but trying to sort of find ways in which we can support the practitioner in the future. So it is a multifaceted approach. In this particular case, we visited in the evening because Mr Bamgbelu was finding that much more convenient. I don't know whether that was because he was at dual locations he could only make it in the evening, but we would normally do it lunch time. Unfortunately, in those circumstances you do not get any support because people finish at 5 o'clock and I go straight from practice. I finish in my practice probably mid afternoon and then I arrange for that visit to be carried out in the evening.

DAVID MORRIS: So this visit that you have documented here behind tab 20, you would have had this pro forma with you, would you?

RICHARD HILL: Yes, I would take it with me.

DAVID MORRIS: Because you now have this pro forma, would there be any need to make any notes?

RICHARD HILL: I would make sort of relevant notes which are not covered by these, sort of anything to do with dentist problems, worries, that sort of thing, concerns.

NEGRO'S PERSPECTIVE:

The f****** dunce, Richard Hill, an exceedingly dull former England young adult and shepherd of England young adults who seemed propped up by crude oil and gas money in the same way as his merciless, racist ancestors were for centuries sustained by the proceeds of evil (slavery), immortalised dishonesty for eternity.

It is impossible to create the reports of 22 July 2004 and the follow up of undisclosed date from alleged, implicitly correctly labelled, handwritten drafts "which are not covered by these, sort of anything to do with dentist problems, worries, that sort of thing, concerns."

Oyinbo olodo! Oyinbo ode!

No brain, natural resources poor, only skin colour that the wearer neither made nor chose, and what else? Pure scam!

Like Sue Gregory, Richard Hill seemed exceedingly dull, and covered hereditary simplicity with the cloak of the most favourable skin colour, which they neither made nor chose, but wear as if it were a first-class degree from Oxford University.

Dr. Olayinka Bamgbelu

"The first-class degree at Oxford, where I have examined, is an overrated mark." – Lord Dacre (Hugh Trevor-Roper): Baron Dacre of Glanton, (15 January 1914 – 26 January 2003), English historian, and Professor of Modern History at the University of Oxford.

CHAPTER 6

"The contents of the 22.07.2004 and 02.04.2003 report differ. The reason that the contents differ is because the hand written notes I used to prepare the 22.07.2004 also had a reference to a difference and dates and notes were mixed up." – Richard Hill, 16 October 2008

Why should the content of a single report of the alleged visit of 2 April 2003 be expected to be like two reports (visit and follow up) of 22 July 2004 and a follow up of undisclosed date? And why should two reports from 2004 (visit and follow up) replace a single report from 2003? Why were the 2004 reports (visit and follow up) never found, particularly the parts that were recorded in the pro forma?

Reductio ad absurdum!

Oyinbo olodo! Oyinbo ode!

"Why, Sir, Sherry is dull, naturally dull, but it must have taken him a great deal of pain to become what we now see him. Such an excess stupidity, Sir, is not in Nature." – Dr Samuel Johnson

I'd rather be shot dead through my shit hole than be intellectually defeated by a brainless white boy (Richard Hill). He seemed so dull; he must have been created dull by Almighty God and born duller by his mama.

"Sir, he was dull in company, dull in his closet, dull everywhere. He was dull in a new way, and that made many people think him great." – Dr Samuel Johnson

The imbecile racist thug also seemed so dull he did not realise that because he allegedly created the 2004 reports from handwritten drafts, it implied that the reports were missing and that they were never found.

I am Abiodun Olayinka Bamgbelu. I am not Frank Bruno, Chris Eubanks, or Diane Abbott. Our people were never carried.

Sue Gregory's ancestors – merciless, murderous cowards and racist bas****s, armed robbers, and thieves – slaughtered many (thousands) in our tribe in the African bush with made-in-Birmingham guns and the f****** bas****s armed others to slaughter scores of thousands more, but they did not carry many, as our people fought to the last with bare hands. They believed that Sue Gregory's racist ancestors were goddamn cannibals, and those that were carried invariably ended up in the white man's pot as roast beef, and returned to mother earth as white man's waste.

So, it is actual fact and absolute truth that some of Sue Gregory's ancestors were goddamn cannibals, racist thugs, armed robbers, and thieves who ate some of the Africans that they kidnapped, stole, and carried.

"Ancient Britons were cannibals. So now we can admit the truth: that other 'gentle native peoples' ate each other." – Damian Thompson, Society

"The contents of the 22.07.2004 and 02.04.2003 report differ. The reason that the contents differ is because the hand written notes I used to prepare the 22.07.2004 also had a reference to a difference and dates and notes were mixed up." – Richard Hill, 16 October 2008

By the statement supra, Richard Hill implied that he created two reports for 2004 (22 July and follow up report of unknown date) as replacements for a single report for 2003 (2 April); immortalised stupidity!

"There is no sin except stupidity." – Oscar Wilde

Richard Hill implied that the visits of 2004 (visit and follow up) did not succeed the visit of 2 April 2003, as he created the latter in place of the missing former. Furthermore, it would not make sense if the alleged two visits and reports for 2004 succeeded the alleged visit of 2 April 2003 – for the following reasons:

• Prior to the report of the alleged visit of 2 April 2003, the last report was that of April 1997. The report was good.

• The visit of 2003 was instigated by the first ever and only Negro dentist in Bedford. He informed Richard Hill that he had moved premises, and he visited the new premises on a date in 2003. If he truly produced a report and sent it to the Negro, there wouldn't be a dispute about the date, and the belated endorsement by the NHS was bizarre. The alleged NHS Data Base that implicitly inaccurately recorded the date and/or practice alleged visited on 22 July 2004, and implicitly did not record the date of the alleged follow up visit, is more bizarre. It is incompetent racist dishonesty.

It is a fact and absolute truth that Richard Hill and the NHS are sections of the UK society.

"All sections of UK society are institutionally racist." – Sir Bernard Hogan-Howe, London Metropolitan Police.

"I attach as Exhibit SRWH2 an anonymised list of consolidation practice visits confirming that Mr Bamgbelu's practice was visited on 02.04.2003. This list has been signed by J BRADBURY, Primary Care contract Manager at Bedfordshire PCT dated 23.09.2008 confirming that an inspection did take place on 02.04.2003." – Richard Hill, 16 October 2008

The fact that the NHS could endorse the report and verify that the visit took place implies that the NHS kept better records than the racist "white boy" that seemed propped up by crude oil and gas money in the same way as his merciless, racist thug, armed robber, and thieving ancestors were for centuries sustained by the proceeds of evil and fraud (slavery). The April 02, 2003 report was endorsed more than six years after it was created, and the July 22, 2004 and follow up of undisclosed date were not similarly endorsed. Had they been Negroes, they'd have been jailed – for Perjury.

The cornerstone of almost everything was forged with the proceeds of merciless, racist evil and fraud (slavery). Before slavery, what?

Shepherds did not bring stolen Africans home, and as the sheep knew that the gigantic wealth was not the yield of the land or the products of the industry of those that lived on the land, it must have come from abroad, and since the shepherds were righteous people who went to church services every Sunday and preached against stealing, the gigantic loot from abroad must have been the yield of the exceedingly brilliant shepherds abroad. Nah! The bas****s were evil racist thugs, armed robbers, and thieves. They deceived the sheep that they fed like battery hens with the yield of armed robbery and merciless racist evil, which they concealed from them.

"Many Scots masters were considered among the most brutal, with life expectancy on their plantations averaging a mere four years. We worked them to death then simply imported more to keep the sugar and thus the

money flowing. Unlike centuries of grief and murder, an apology costs nothing. So what does Scotland have to say?" – Herald Scotland, Ian Bell, columnist, Sunday 28 April 2013

The descendants of thoroughly wretched, feudal agricultural labourers from mainland Europe dispossessed the aboriginal Britons and stole their land. They were immeasurably transformed by the racist evil of slavery. They have reinvented themselves and fool the foolish.

There is no reason in logic or ordinary fact why the alleged visits of 2004 (visit of 22 July 2004 and follow up of unknown date) took place.

The fact that the report of the alleged visit of 2 April 2003 was not given to the Negro, and almost five years after the alleged visit (the NHS stated that it did not have the report in a response to a Freedom of Information request), implies that the report was insignificant.

"I attach as Exhibit SRWH2 an anonymised list of consolidation practice visits confirming that Mr Bamgbelu's practice was visited on 02.04.2003. This list has been signed by J BRADBURY, Primary Care contract Manager at Bedfordshire PCT dated 23.09.2008 confirming that an inspection did take place on 02.04.2003." – Richard Hill, 16 October 2008

It was extraordinary that the absurdity of the fact that the report was endorsed almost six years after the alleged visit was ignored.

We are slaves, as only our visible chains are off, the innately racist white bastards will never remove our true chains. They set up a circus called legal process, lied with abandon, and paid themselves hundreds of thousands of pounds for shameless incompetence. They were decorous, spoke with upper class English accent, and they were very polite; they were racist bastards and incompetent liars. They immortalised excessive stupidity.

In order to protect regular bread, the only option left for the Negro was to pretend that excessively stupid white people were innately superior geniuses and tell lies openly before man and God. If you merely think it, you say it to Christ, and if you believes He is who He says He is, you cannot deny Him in pursuance of bowing to the Racist Satanic Network; He did not bow in exchange for the greatest offer.

Then, our own God declined the offer of the ruler of the world – Matthew 4:9.

They persecute our people for the dark coat that we neither made nor chose, and they steal the yields of our Christ granted talents. He sees all, and He knows all, and He is transparently just so, we must wait to his Justice as vengeance belongs only to Christ – Proverbs 15:3; Habakkuk.

Our people are powerless, and we have been robbed to penniless since economically cannibalistic European Christians found our ancestors in the African bush in the 15th century, and they stole almost everything He gave to our people.

Then, very highly civilised European Christians shipped hundreds of thousands of guns to West Africa, among those who did not have the surgical skills to treat penetrative gunshot wounds, they reversed natural selection and evolution, and distorted natural order. Their guns in the hands of some Africans made it possible to weaker men to kill stronger men, and it made it possible for foolish men to kill wiser men, and steal all their children, and barter stolen lives with civilised European Christians: The exchange of stolen children for guns and gin.

Righteousness and deceptively schooled upper class civilised decorum deceives man, not Christ, as they were preceded by several centuries of merciless racist evil: The evilest terrorism the world will ever know - Habakkuk.

They impede our ascent, and concomitantly our children's ascent from the deep crater in which made in Birmingham guns buried our direct ancestors, in the Africa bush. Then, they used guns to cover the face of Christ; now, they use incompetent racist lies to cover the face of a Just God – Habakkuk; John 8:44; John 10:10.

Then, any mere Negro who disagreed with the owners of stolen children of other people would be frog-marched to the woods, by highly civilised European Christians, at gunpoint and hanged from a tall tree without a hood.

He is watching them; only Christ is a righteous Judge, and only He will judge all, including Crooked and Racist Judges – Matthew 25: 31- 46.

The nemesis is not extinct; the fact that it tarries is not proof that it will never come. Time will, inevitably, unfold the truth, which is that He is who He says He is - Habakkuk.

They are in decline, and they use sticky plaster to treat chronic gangrene. Their merciless racist evil cannot be repaired because it involves accepting that their minds were coarser than that of a mere Negro, and it will uncover part of the evidence that the brain is not part of the skin colour, and that white privilege based on subjectivity is naked fraud.

Based on very proximate observations and direct experiences, one of the great fears of the white privileged dullard is to be openly defeated in a debate by a mere Negro.

To accept that one is stupider than stupid white people in exchange for regular bread is to tell Christ to His face that He is not who He says He is. If you want me to say that He is not who He says He is, it means you want to kill me, and the life of this lucky sperm is not that precious; it is impossible deny the owner of everlasting life, I seek His love more than all.

"When you have to kill a man, it costs nothing to be polite." Sir Winston Churchill.

So, they can take my life if they want, I hope they'd be polite, and they can steal my possession, which is inferior to my life, but it is impossible for Jupiter and all its thunders to do anything about the irreversible certainty (beyond belief) that He is who says He is.

When they fork, which is often, genius Jews are their go-to people.

"Jews are intelligent and creative, Chinese are intelligent but not creative, Indians are servile, and African are morons." Professor Watson - DNA, paraphrased

Professor Watson: A closeted racist genetic Scot. One dimensionally educated Antichrist lunatic professor, he found DNA, he did not make it, and he must leave, and leave for eternity, and what he found be here will be for as long as its maker wants.

"The supreme vice is shallowness." Wilde

I know what their moron sheep must not know, which is that they're impostors, experts of deceptions, and professional scammers who have fooled the world with foolishness for centuries; one way to tie the loose end is to kill, and I am ready. My only regret is that I have children; I know that He will send helpers to them. Again, I hope the racist bastards will be polite killers. If they are not:

Ekan ni omo okunrin nku – African bush saying.

Translation: It is impossible to kill a man twice.

He is who He says He is, and He doesn't care about the views of mere travellers passing through, as He will never leave.

The most effective method of covering up RACIAL HATRED is to kill the victim.

https://www.facebook.com/rotimi.osunsan/videos/3088536551193798

A bastardised, unashamedly mediocre, indiscreetly dishonest, vindictive, potently weaponised, and institutionally RACIST system that his overseen by MASONS (Mediocre Mafia) – Habakkuk; John 8:44; John 10:10.

Facts are sacred; they can't be overstated.

"It does no harm to throw the occasional man overboard, but it does not do much good if you are steering full speed ahead for the rocks." Sir Ian Gilmour

Based on available evidence, White Privilege is Antichrist, and a centuries-old fraudulent racist scam.

Based on available evidence, the English law is equal; its administration is not.

Based on available evidence, whites measure whites with a very different yardstick – Apartheid by stealth.

Demons will not cast out demons – Matthew 12:27.

Based on very proximate observations and direct experiences, the administration of English law is Antichrist, and intellectually flawed – Habakkuk 1:4.

Facts are sacred.

"Freedom of expression is a basic right." Lady Hale

"Freedom of expression is the cornerstone of our democracy." Jacob Rees-Mogg.

The administration of the law is the MEAT of the law.

"Rightful liberty is unobstructed action according to our will within limits drawn around us by the equal rights of others. I do not add 'within the limits of the law' because law is often but the tyrant's will, and always so when it violates the rights of the individual." Thomas Jefferson

If Cambridge University Educated Rich Man's son, Sir, Mr Justice Haddon-Cave QC, KBE, Knight Commander of the Most Excellent Order of our Empire, could prove that District Judge Paul Ayers, Senior Vice President of the Association of Her Majesty's District Judges was not a functional semi-illiterate and an incompetent liar, and if he could prove that GDC-Witness, Ms Rachael Bishop, Senior NHS Nurse, did not unrelentingly tell lies under oath, and if he could prove that Dr Richard William Hill, Postgraduate Tutor - NHS, did not fabricate reports and unrelentingly told lies under oath, and if he could prove that Stephen Henderson, LLM, Head of MDDUS, was not a functional semi-illiterate closeted racist thug who unrelentingly deviated from the truth on record, and if he could prove that GDC-INSIDER, Dr Sue Gregory (OBE), Officer of the Most Excellent Order of our Empire, did not unrelentingly tell lies under implied oath, and if he could prove that GDC-WITNESS, GDC-Witness, Stephanie Twidale, British Army Officer - Territorial Defence, did not unrelentingly tell lies under oath, and if he could prove that Geraint Evans, Postgraduate Tutor, did not unrelentingly tell lies under implied oath, and if he could prove that Kevin Atkinson, Postgraduate Tutor did not unrelentingly tell lies under oath, and if he could prove that Dr George Rothnie, Deputy Postgraduate Dean, did not deviate from the truth under implied oath, he would confirm that his white kindred were not RACIST CRIMINALS, and he would also confirm the belief of billions of people, which is that Antichrist Freemasonry Quasi Religion, Antichrist Judaism, Antichrist Islam, and all motley assemblies of exotic religions and FAITHS under the common umbrella of the Governor of the Church of England and commander of THE FAITH are not intellectually flawed Satanic Mumbo Jumbo; it will also confirm that reasoning and vision have boundaries. If reasoning and vision have boundaries, He, our own God, must have lied when, before the Council, He disclosed the pictures His purportedly unbounded mind painted, and He must have also lied when He audaciously stated: "I am the way and the truth and the life. No one comes to the Father except through me." - John 14:6.

If Christ told the truth before the Council, everything that is not aligned to John 14:6 is travelling in the wrong direction.

Ignorance is bliss.

"I do not approve of anything that tampers with natural ignorance. Ignorance is like a delicate exotic fruit; touch it and the bloom is gone. The whole theory of modern education is radically unsound. Fortunately, in England, at any rate, education produces no effect whatsoever. If it did, it would prove a serious danger to the upper classes, and probably lead to acts of violence in Grosvenor Square." Oscar Wilde

Dr Anand Kamath was threatened with reportage to the GDC, they drove the poor fellow round the bend, turned him into a lunatic, and killed him hands-off; lunatic Anand Kamath killed the brilliant dentist who came to England for better life, and ended up in after life leaving a wife and three children – John 8:44; John 10:10.
A bloody waste of God's creation; He is watching all – Proverbs 15:3.
The mens rea is in the belly of the actus reus. One day, stealthily murderers will be uncovered, and those who drive others round the bend, which induced insanity, and caused them to kill themselves will be liable for murder or manslaughter depending on established intent.

Merely a threat of being reported to the closeted racist thugs at the GDC, 37, Wimpole Street, London, and the Indian bailed, and for eternity, leaving a wife and three children.
Anand Kamath: Poor fellow, he hoped to find better life in Serengeti, and he misread his hosts; he mistook lions, merciless carnivores, for cuddly dogs who eat tinned food from the Supermarket. He knows the truth now, but it is too late. He desired better life; he ended up in after life. He driven to insanity, and he killed himself. The brilliant dentist was killed hands-off. The brilliant dentist was not told about Christ at home and/or at School, so he was unaware of the Racist Satanic Network, the

real rulers of the world. He was killed legally, hands-off.

The racist bastards want to kill me too, and they must, as their survival depends on it, but only hands-on. Like Kamath, they manufactured incompetent racist lies, and threatened me with reportage to the GDC.

F*** you, f*** you, and f*** you, I said, but only behind their backs, as they control the Police Force, and have the power to inflict bodily suffering is an evil, and no philosopher can endure it patiently.

"For there was ever no philosopher that could endure toothache patiently." William Shakespeare.

Even, our own God zipped it after He was kidnapped and fragged before the Courts, He wanted us to know that bodily suffering before death, not death, is an evil.

Then, at Anglican Church Grammar School, in the 70s, we used to floor their type in man-to-man fist fights. Now, if it were legal to do so, it would cross my mind to floor the closeted racist functional semi-illiterate Judge, in 8.46, but the thought wouldn't stay there.

I am not Anand Kamath; I know that He is who He says He is, and He is greater than all the Satanic networks in the universe. He that is with us is greater than He who rules the world so, we have overwhelming leverage – John 4:4. If they play with a straight bat we will show them what they cannot see in what they are looking at, and uncover part of His face.

We do not believe that He is who He says He is, we know that He is. He has revealed part of His face to us not in dreams or vision, but as vividly as the words I here write, and we, mere infants before Christ, have completely decoded the part of infinity that He disclosed to us.

Reasoning and vision are unbounded. He told the truth before the Council when, before the Council, He disclosed pictures that His unbounded mind painted.

It is glaringly obvious that He is who He says He is, and that John 14:6 is non-negotiable.

Genetics: The Holy Grail.

He who controls genetic – mix controls everything, education can only polish what genetic mix presents to it, and the fact that one man is better than another is not proof that both men are not crap.

Better than crap could also be crap.

Professor Watson – DNA, the genetic Scot, evidently believes that he smarter than Negroes, who isn't?

If we are not smart, why are we rich?

Shepherds did not bring stolen children of other people home, they took them to the stolen New Worlds, and they lied to their moron sheep that they were paragons of wisdom and virtue who, like Mother Teresa, did only righteous works in AFRICA.

"I know of no evil that has ever existed, nor can imagine any evil to exist, worse than the tearing of eighty thousand persons annually from their native land, by a combination of the most civilised nations inhabiting the most enlightened part of the globe, but more especially under the sanction of the laws of that Nation which calls herself the most free and the most happy of them all." Prime Minister William Pitt the Younger.

"Many Scots masters were considered among the most brutal, with life expectancy on their plantations averaging a mere four years. We worked them to death then simply imported more to keep the sugar and thus the money flowing. Unlike centuries of grief and murder, an apology cost nothing. So, what does Scotland have to say?" Herald Scotland: Ian Bell, Columnist, Sunday 28 April 2013.

"Time for Scots to say sorry for slavery.
Herald Scotland:
Ian Bell, Columnist / Sunday 28 April 2013 / Opinion
Sunday 28 April 2013
According to the American founding father, the son of a Caithness Kirk minister had about him of "an air of great simplicity and honesty"'. The likes of James Boswell and Laurence Sterne also enjoyed the merchant's company.

To his contemporaries, he was, as the author Adam Hochschild has written, "'a wise, thoughtful man who embodied the Scottish virtues of frugality, sobriety, and hard work'". Oswald was a scholar of theology, philosophy, and history. He collected art, particularly Rubens and Rembrandt, and gave handsomely to charity. Oswald, who learned his trade in Glasgow, also represented Britain in negotiations with the Americans after their war of liberation. He was the cosmopolitan epitome of Enlightenment success. But when he wasn't busy with good works,

Oswald waded in blood. The precise number of deaths that can be laid at his door is impossible to calculate. As the leading figure in Grant, Oswald & Co, he had investments in each corner of the "'triangular trade'". In his own name, Oswald trafficked at least 13,000 Africans, although he never set foot on their continent. By the time he bought Auchincruive House and 100,000 acres in Ayrshire in 1764, he was worth £500,000. Writing in 2005, Hochschild thought this was ""roughly equivalent"" to $68 million (about £44m). This is conservative.

Oswald was remarkable, but not unique. Where Glasgow and its merchants in sugar, tobacco, and human life are concerned, there are plenty of names and no shortage of monuments: Dennistoun, Campbell, Glassford, Cochrane, Buchanan, Hamilton, Bogle, Ewing, Donald, Speirs, Dunlop. One way to understand what they wrought is simple: take pleasure in the city"s architecture today and you are likely to be admiring the fruits of slavery.

Glasgow is not alone in that. London, Liverpool and Bristol also have their stories to tell. Edinburgh's once-great banks grew from foundations built on bones. The first Scottish venture into slavery set out from the capital in 1695. Montrose, Dumfries, Greenock and Port Glasgow each tried their hands. In the language of the present age, they were all in it together.

When commerce was coursing around the triangle, most of polite Scotland was implicated. The nobility (and country) rendered bankrupt in 1700 in the aftermath of the Darien Venture was by the mid-1760s contemplating big elegant townhouses and 100,000-acre estates. You could call that a reversal of fortune. Contrary to self-serving myth, it did not happen because of "'frugality, sobriety, and hard work".

Certain things need to be remembered about Scotland and slavery. One is that the mercantile class got stinking rich twice over: despite fortunes made from stolen lives, they were quick to demand compensation when slavery was ended in 1833. Britain's government decided that £20m, a staggering sum, could be raised. In his 2010 book, The Price of Emancipation, Nicholas Draper reckons Glasgow's mob got £400,000 – in modern terms, hundreds of millions.

Compensation cases also demonstrated that Scots were not merely following an English lead. According to Draper, a country with 10% of the British population accounted for at least 15% of absentee slavers.

By another estimate, 30% of Jamaican plantations were run by Scots. For all the pride taken in the abolitionist societies of Glasgow and Edinburgh, the slave-holders did not suffer because of abolition. They were '"compensated"'.

And that wasn't the worst of it. Thanks to Hollywood movies, the slave economy of the American South is still taken as barbarism's benchmark. Few realise that the behaviour of Scots busy getting rich in the slave-holders" empire was actually worse – routinely worse – than the worst of the cottonocracy. You need only count the corpses................."

They are racist killers, descendants of racist hands-on killers, who are more civilised than their butcher ancestors, and believe that hands-off killing is civilised and legal.

Then, like Herod, Kim, and MBS, they used to butcher those who stated and/or printed what they did not want their moron sheep to know. The last decapitation in England was in 1827, and beheading was removed from the Statute book in 1973, and the same year, Kenneth Baker banned caning in England. Why remove the heads of those you can't cane?

"There is now less flogging in our great schools than formerly, but then less is learned there; so that what the boys get at one end, they lose at the other." Dr Samuel Johnson

Some whites are very scared, and not just in Trump's America (75M), and rightly so. Increasingly colour-blind level playing field is gradually unravelling the mother of all racist scams: The centuries-old unspoken myth that the brain is related to skin colour. Only fools expect descendants of THIEVES and owners of stolen children of defenceless poor people to voluntarily relinquish the inherited advantageous position (WHITE PRIVILEGE) that was primarily gained through centuries of extreme violence, and properly organised industrial-scale, armed stealing of moveable and immoveable valuables that had other owners, including human beings, without a fight.

Re Meeting 9th March
Mon, 8 Mar 2010 20:20
George Rothnie georgerothnie@hotmail.com
To adeolacole@aol.com

Hi Ola,

We are scheduled to meet tomorrow evening at my surgery about 5.30ish. Unfortunately something has cropped up which necessytates me having to postpone the meeting. I'm really sorry it's such short notice.

I will contact you in the week to arrange another date.

Once agaim my apologies.

George

Dr George Rothnie (Scottish George), Deputy Postgraduate Dean Oxford. An imbecile Scotsman; a brainless white man.

Everything is baselessly assumed in favour of the indisputably superior skin colour that the wearer neither made nor chose - Apartheid by stealth.

https://www.youtube.com/watch?v=BlpH4hG7m1A&feature=youtu.be

"They may not have been well written from a grammatical point of view but I am confident I had not forgotten any of the facts." Dr Geraint Evans, Postgraduate Tutor, Oxford

https://youtu.be/rayVcfyu9Tw

When they fork, which is often, Genius Jews are their GO-TO people. When Jews realise that they can't spin the intellectual impotence of the closeted racist bastards, in order to continue to cover His face and conceal the truth from the world, they jail and/or kill those He vividly revealed himself to.

We shall go, and they must come – 2 Samuel 12:23.

He was jailed only because he spoke; the lunatic Jew removed the head of John only because he refused to stop speaking. John was not punished for speaking; he was prevented from speaking.

New Herod, Matthew 2:16: They lie to their duller children that they are geniuses, and they kill all those who know that they're brainless racist bastards.

Had they not controlled the Police Force, we would have told them everything.

Then and now, in jurisdictions where the satanic network (Antichrist Racist Freemason) is in charge, their members have power to tell lies under oath: Persecutory Negrophobia and Negrophobic Perjury.

"The supreme vice is shallowness." Wilde

Our own God (Christ) before the crooked, shallow, and intellectually insufficient Council:

"Then the people who had arrested Christ led him to the home of Caiaphas, the high priest, where the teachers of religious law and other leaders had gathered. Meanwhile, Peter was following behind and eventually came to the courtyard of the high priest's house. He went in and sat with the guards and waited to see what was going to happen to Christ. Inside the leading priests and the entire Council was trying to find witnesses who would lie about Jesus, so they could put him to death. But even though they found many who agreed to give false witness, there was no testimony that they could use. Finally, two men were found who declared, "This man said, 'I am able to destroy the Temple of God and rebuild it in three days.'" Then the high priest stood up and said to Christ, "Well, aren't you going to answer to these charges? What do you have to say for yourself?" But Jesus remained silent. Then the high priest said to him, "I demand in the name living God that you will tell us whether you are the Messiah, the son of God." Jesus replied, "Yes, it is as you say. And in the future, you will see me, the son of Man, sitting at God's right hand in place of power and coming back in clouds of heaven." Then the high priest tore his clothing to show his horror, shouting, "Blasphemy! Why do you need other witnesses? You have heard his blasphemy. What is your verdict?" "Guilty!" they shouted. "He must die!" Then they spit in Christ's face and hit him with their fists and slapped him, saying "Prophesy to us, you Messiah! Who hit you that time?" as stated in the Book of Matthew.

The Council lied. The Council's Judges lied.

He was not asked to expatiate. He was lynched like Gadhafi and crucified only because He spoke. He was not punished for speaking, He was permanently prevented from speaking, and His offence was extracted from the response He gave to their question: The classic modus operandi of the SATANIC NETWORK.

Then lunatics killed the Judge because He stated what they didn't like. Now, half-educated school dropouts and their superiors who have informal access to some very powerful white Judges – destroy anyone who disagrees with their brainless Satanic Mumbo Jumbo and/or refuses to bow down to low life racist trash, genetic aliens with camouflage English names, only because they have the indisputably superior skin colour; they neither made nor chose the most favourable asset.

Righteous descendants of industrial-scale professional THIEVES and owners of stolen children of defenceless poor people (the evilest racist terrorism the world will ever know) – Habakkuk.

As they seemed to have been lied to at home and/or school that their indisputably superior skin colour is the greatest creation of Almighty God, everything good is assumed in favour of their asset as human beings, and they will be considerably diminished as human being without it.

White privilege is a fraudulent racist scam.

He is watching them – Proverbs 15:3.

David Morris cross examined Richard Hill, under oath, on 18 November 2008 (Court Room):
DAVID MORRIS: It is really just the date, as I said, that is a concern

because Mr Bamgbelu's recollection is that on that date, 2 April 2003, certainly in the evening he would have been in his Wellingborough practice.

RICHARD HILL: As I said, we cross referenced it with our database which their Contracts Manager was able to do to corroborate that date, otherwise it would have been changed on the database.

THE NEGRO'S PERSPECTIVE:

On 29 September 2008, when the NHS retrospectively endorsed the alleged visit of 2 April 2003, the NHS reports of 22 July 2004 and follow up of undisclosed date were live and valid, and the NHS must have implicitly endorsed them too, and Richard Hill must have had access to the alleged NHS Data Base when he created the reports, extraordinarily from draft notes, which contained other matters, in September 2006.

Endorsed racist lies!

The sole basis of the power of some people is money. The entire foundation of the money was forged with the proceeds of evil, merciless, opportunistic, racial hatred and fraud – not for a little while, but for several continuous centuries of merciless, tyrannical cowardice.

No brain, natural resources poor, only skin colour that the wearer neither made nor chose, and what else? Pure scam!

"Many Scots masters were considered among the most brutal, with life expectancy on their plantations averaging a mere four years. We worked them to death then simply imported more to keep the sugar and thus the money flowing. Unlike centuries of grief and murder, an apology costs nothing. So what does Scotland have to say?" – Herald Scotland, Ian Bell, columnist, Sunday 28 April 2013

"As hard-hearted as a Scot of Scotland." – English saying

"Scotsmen tak a' they can get and a little more if they can." – Scottish saying

"I know of no evil that has ever existed, nor can imagine any evil to exist, worse than the tearing of eighty thousand persons annually from their native land, by a combination of the most civilised nations inhabiting the most enlightened part of the globe, but more especially under the sanction of the laws of that Nation which calls herself the most free and the most happy of them all." – Prime Minister William Pitt the Younger

In 2020, Bedfordshire yields only food. In 1720, Bedfordshire yielded only food. Then, the people of Bedfordshire were fed like battery hens with the yield of merciless, racist evil (slavery) – not for a little while, but for several centuries of merciless, vicious, racist tyranny.

The Industrial Revolution cost money, and the money was stolen. Evil, racist slavery was neither revolution nor evolution – it was merciless destruction of the creations of Almighty God. He is just. Nemesis is not extinct. The fact that it tarries is not the conclusive evidence of the fact that it will never come.

"The fact is that civilisation requires slaves. The Greeks were quite right there. Unless there are slaves to do the ugly, horrible, uninteresting work, culture and contemplation become almost impossible." – Oscar Wilde

There was no White Hall before the merciless, opportunistic, racist evil of slavery. There mightn't have been a White Hall had there not been the merciless, opportunistic, racist evil of slavery.

There was no White House before the merciless, opportunistic, racist evil of slavery. There mightn't have been a White House had there not been the merciless, opportunistic, evil of slavery.

As shepherds didn't bring stolen Africans home, the moron sheep believed that shepherds were saintly Mother Teresa who did virtuous work abroad.

"I tremble for my country when I reflect that God is just; that his justice cannot sleep forever." – President Thomas Jefferson

CHAPTER 7

So, to associate affluence whose entire foundation is racial hatred and fraud with intellect and industry is spin, which spins the least literate and numerate adult population in the industrialised world but is insufficient to spin the whole world.

"FAILING SCHOOLS AND A BATTLE FOR BRITAIN: This was the day the British education establishment's 50 year betrayal of the Nation's children lay starkly exposed in all its ignominy. After testing 166,000 people in 24 education systems, the Organisation for Economic Cooperation and Development (OECD) finds that England young adults are amongst the least literate and numerate in the industrialised world." – The Daily Mail, 09.01.2013

Shepherds of morons are likelier to be morons too.

Sue Gregory, the seemingly crooked, evil, racist bastard and her type, are the shepherds of England young adults.

The charade will not endure, as the future generation will be considerably duller, and be illiterate and innumerate, and will be too dull to keep the charade going seamlessly. Time will inevitably unfold the truth.

"Natural selection will not remove ignorance from the future generation." – Dr Richard Dawkins

"Ignorance, the root and stem of all evil." – Plato

Some "court" hearings are the delusive immortalisation of the grandeur of the "glorious" evil past.

Incompetent art incompetently imitates life.

Jonathan Martin, a closeted racist GDC jobber and incompetent liar, was instructed by his employer to talk rot on oath. The moron England young adult stated as follows, under oath, in a pretend hearing where significant parts of the charges were based upon merciless, racist, falsified information:

"I nearly cried at my desk. I was taken aback that a registrant could send that, no matter whatever provocation he thought he was under. That made me stop and think was there anything I was doing as a case worker that was causing this sort of behaviour from a registrant? Then I thought for a few minutes and I had to recompose myself and I said, no, I was dealing with the matter best as I could and that there was behaviour being exhibited by me which could cause such an offensive comment to be put in an email. There was one point where the cumulative effect of this did make me think was there anything I was not doing properly but I can assure the Committee, I am sure my manager and my head of department" (Jonathan Martin, GDC, October 2014).

F****** rot!

Oyinbo olodo! Oyinbo ode!

"Nothing that you will learn in the course of your studies will be of the slightest possible use to you in after life – save only this – if you work hard and diligently you should be able to detect when a man is talking rot, and that, in my view, is the main, if not the sole, purpose of education." – J.A. Smith, Oxford University Professor, Moral Philosophy

The moronic England young adult Jonathan Martin – propped up by crude oil and gas money in the same way as his evil, merciless racist ancestors were for centuries sustained by the proceeds of sadism and savagery and merciless, racist evil – should have cried, and wept buckets, and he should have rested his huge head in or on the cleavage of Sue Gregory's seemingly four-fifths deflated, wrinkling, elongated, ugly, and gigantic mammary glands, with fat and blood but no muscle. Sue Gregory, the merciless, racist cougar, in her 7th or 8th decade, certainly has no more milk.

"Truth, Sir, is a cow that will yield such people no more milk, and so they are gone to milk the bull." – Dr Samuel Johnson

Sue Gregory's ancestors were evil, racist thugs and opportunistic thieves.

"The American dispute between us and the French is therefore only the quarrel of robbers for the spoils of a passenger, but as robbers have confederacy, which they are obliged to observe as members of a gang, so the English and the French may have relative rights, and do injustice to each other, while both are injuring the Indians. And such, indeed, is the present contest: they have parted the Northern continent of America between them, and are now disputing their boundaries, and are endeavouring the destruction of the other by the help of the Indians, whose interest it is that both should be destroyed." – Dr Samuel Johnson

Drs Anand Kamath and Richard Bamgboye did not nearly die; they were mercilessly hounded to death by people like Sue Gregory and Jonathan Martin of the GDC, and they f****** died.

Equity demands that their killers, albeit hands off, should die too, and in some other jurisdiction within our Commonwealth, they may, but only legally, within the native and customary laws – and the laws of Moses: "a tooth for a tooth."

The sole basis of their (Jonathan Martin, Sue Gregory, and their white supremacist type) merciless, evil powers is money. There was no council before the merciless, evil trade in stolen Africans. There might have been no council had there not been the merciless, evil trade in stolen human beings.

Almost everything was stolen!

Prior to slavery, the land yielded only food. The land yields only food.

"Agriculture not only gives riches to a nation, but the only riches she can call her own." – Dr Samuel Johnson

"Iain Whyte, author of Scotland and the Abolition of Slavery, insists we have at times ignored our guilty past. He said: 'For many years Scotland's historians harboured the illusion that our nation had little to do with the slave trade or plantation slavery.

"'We swept it under the carpet. This was remarkable in the light of Glasgow's wealth coming from tobacco, sugar and cotton, and Jamaica Streets being found in a number of Scottish towns and cities.

"'It is healthy we are now recognising Scotland was very much involved.'

The industries, which saw Glasgow and much of the country flourish, were built on the back of slavery. There were familiar names such as Scot Lyle of Tate and Lyle fame whose fortune was built on slavery. Ewing from Glasgow was the richest sugar producer in Jamaica. The stunning Inveresk Lodge in Edinburgh, now open to the public, was bought by James Wedderburn with money earned from 27 years in Jamaica as a notorious slaver. The Wee Free Church was founded using profits and donations from the slave trade. Even our schools have a dark history. Bathgate Academy was built from money willed by John Newland, a renowned slave master and Dollar Academy has a similar foundation. For many years, the goods and profits from West Indian slavery were unloaded at Kingston docks in Glasgow. Leith in Edinburgh and Glasgow were popular ports from which ambitious Scottish men sailed to make their fortunes as slave masters." – Ian Bell, Herald Scotland, 28 April 2013

The satanic network is everywhere. It controls almost everything except intellect. Without objective basis, it awards itself the monopoly of knowledge.

The proceeds of centuries of merciless, racial hatred and fraud kick-started the industrial revolution in Scotland and brought Scottish slave merchants and traders great wealth.

Feudal agricultural labourers from mainland Europe dispossessed/robbed aboriginal Britons. They've been transformed and reinvented by slavery.

"It was in 1066 that William the Conqueror occupied Britain, stole our land and gained control by granting it to his Norman friends, thus creating a feudal system we have not yet fully escaped." – Tony Benn

Normans stole from others what others had stolen from others. Genetically pure Britons are extinct; all were dispossessed, robbed, and slaughtered.

Tony Benn was dishonest, or he was confused when he implied that he was genetically an aboriginal Briton. Genetically pure aboriginal Britons are extinct. They were dispossessed and robbed of their land by a motley assembly of mainland Europeans – hereditary serfs or descendants of feudal agricultural labourers – who were hugely transformed by the gigantic gains of slavery. They have reinvented themselves.

Some people associate race, and particularly affluence whose entire foundation is racial hatred and fraud, with intellect and industry. It is a lie! Civilised European Christians used guns, only guns, to gang rape and loot unarmed and defenceless Africa.

Facts are sacred.

"The truth allows no choice." Dr Samuel Johnson

Before the trade in millions of stolen human beings, what?

Oyinbo olodo! Oyinbo ode!

The following is from Mark 10:17-31 (the English Standard Version, or ESV):

The Rich Young Man

And as he was setting out on his journey, a man ran up and knelt before him and asked him, "Good Teacher, what must I do to inherit eternal life?" And Jesus said to him, "Why do you call me good? No one is good except God alone. You know the commandments: 'Do not murder, Do not commit adultery, Do not steal, Do not bear false witness, Do not defraud, Honour your father and mother.'" And he said to him, "Teacher, all these I have kept from my youth." And Jesus, looking at him, loved him, and said to him, "You lack one thing: go, sell all that you have and give to the poor, and you will have treasure in heaven; and come, follow me." Disheartened by the saying, he went away sorrowful, for he had great possessions.

And Jesus looked around and said to his disciples, "How difficult it will be for those who have wealth to enter the kingdom of God!" And the disciples were amazed at his words. But Jesus said to them again, "Children, how difficult it is to enter the kingdom of God! It is easier for a camel to go through the eye of a needle than for a rich person to enter the kingdom of God." And they were exceedingly astonished, and said to him. "Then who can be saved?" Jesus looked at them and said, "With man it is impossible, but not with God. For all things are possible with God." Peter began to say to him, "See, we have left everything and followed you." Jesus said, "Truly, I say to you, there is no one who has left house or brothers or sisters or mother or father or children or lands, for my sake and for the gospel, who will not receive a hundredfold now in this time, houses and brothers and sisters and mothers and children and lands, with persecutions, and in the age to come eternal life. But many who are first will be last, and the last first."

"'You lack one thing: go, sell all that you have and give to the poor, and you will have treasure in heaven; and come, follow me.' Disheartened by the saying, he went away sorrowful, for he had great possessions." – Christ

Had the "rich young man" been a stealer and seller of millions of stolen human beings, Christ would have asked him to return the stolen goods.

The ancestors of Sue Gregory were thieves – merciless, evil, opportunistic, racist thugs and thieves. Christ wouldn't have asked them to sell stolen goods and give the yield of fraud to poor people; he would have asked them to return the loot from several centuries of merciless tyranny to the descendants of those that they robbed.

The bottom line is money. It is actual fact and absolute truth that Sue Gregory's ancestors were racist thugs and thieves, the evil stealers and sellers of millions of stolen human beings.

Almost everything was stolen.

Before slavery, what?

"When we consider the vastness of the continent of Africa; when we reflect how all other countries have for some centuries past been advancing in happiness and civilisation; when we think how in this same period all improvement in Africa has been defeated by her intercourse with Britain; when we reflect that it was we ourselves that have degraded them to that wretched brutishness and barbarity which we now plead as the justification for our guilt; how the slave trade has enslaved their minds, blackened their character, and sunk them so low in the scale of animal beings that some think apes are of a higher class, and fancy the Orang–outang has given them the go-by. What mortification must we feel at having so long neglected to think of our guilt, or attempt at reparation! It seems indeed, as if we had determined to forbear from all interference until the measure of folly and wickedness was so full and complete, until the policy which eventually belongs to vice was become so plain and glaring that not an individual in this country should refuse to join the abolition. It seems as if we had waited until the persons most interested should be tired out with the folly nefariousness of the trade, and should unite in petitioning against it." – William Wilberforce, 1789

"Even if these miserable beings were proved guilty of every crime before you take them off, ought we not to take upon ourselves the office of executioners? And even if we condescend so far, still can we be justified in acquiring them in exchange for our guns, carrying and selling them for great profits, unless we have clear proof that they are criminals? But, if we go much further, if we ourselves tempt them to sell their fellow creatures to us, we may rest assured that they will take care to provide by every possible method a supply of victims increasing in proportions to our demand. Can we, then, hesitate in deciding whether the wars in Africa are their wars or ours? It was our arms in the river of Cameroon, put into the hands of the trader, that furnished him with the means of pushing his trade; and I have no more doubt that they are British arms, put into the hands of Africans, which promote universal war and desolation that I can doubt their having done so in that individual instance. I have shown how great is the enormity of this evil, even on the supposition that we take only convicts and prisoners of war. But take the subject in another way, and how does it stand? Think of 80,000 persons carried out of their native country by we know not what means! For crimes imputed! For light or inconsiderable faults! For debts perhaps! For crime of witchcraft! Or a thousand other weak or scandalous pretexts! Reflect on 80,000 persons annually taken off! There is something in the horror of it that surpasses all bounds of imagination. Admitting that there exists in Africa something like to Courts of justice; yet what an office of humiliation and meanness is it in us, to take upon ourselves to carry into execution the iniquitous sentences of such courts, as if we also were strangers to all religion and to the first principles of justice! But that country, it is said, has been in some degree civilised, and civilised by us. It is said that they have gained some knowledge of the principles of justice." – Prime Minister William Pitt the Younger, 1792

"I know of no evil that has ever existed, nor can imagine any evil to exist, worse than the tearing of eighty thousand persons annually from their native land, by a combination of the most civilised nations inhabiting the most enlightened part of the globe, but more especially under the sanction of the laws of that Nation which calls herself the most free and the most happy of them all." – Prime Minister William Pitt the Younger

"Many Scots masters were considered among the most brutal, with life expectancy on their plantations averaging a mere four years. We worked them to death then simply imported more to keep the sugar and thus the money flowing. Unlike centuries of grief and murder, an apology costs nothing. So what does Scotland have to say?" – Herald Scotland, Ian Bell, columnist, Sunday 28 April 2013

They continue to persecute our people because of the darker coat that we neither made nor chose, and they steal the yields of our Christ granted talents. Where shall we hide?

From, appeared from nowhere, and directly and/or indirectly, and rained hell fire on our people, daily, for several centuries our people lived in hell on earth. They, and those they armed, murdered, robbed, and dispossessed, and carried away other people children, every day.

Had it not been for the unquenchable libido of the Negro, and industrial-scale sex machine in the African bush, the racist bastards would have wiped us out, and steal our land just as they did in Australia and America.

After Christopher Columbus and his gang of land grabbers disembarked in America, things did turn out well for the native Americans.

Now, descendants of minor Europeans, and the descendants of stolen Africans and motley assemblies of other genetic aliens fight like ferrets in a sack on stolen Indian land.

Then, they stole almost everything He gave to others – Habakkuk, James 4.

He is watching them – Proverbs 15:3.

"All have taken what had other owners and have had recourse to arms rather than quit the prey they were fastened." Dr Samuel Johnson.

There were fires in Soweto but there was simultaneous industrial-scale sex machine. So, when racist bastards killed 40, our people breed 4000. Demography is a weapon of war.

Sex in a Negro's game: Continuing population growth in the face of merciless, racist persecution inevitably liberated South Africa.

It is a fact and the absolute truth that Sue Gregory is part of the UK society.

"All sections of UK society are institutionally racist." – Sir
Bernard Hogan-Howe, London Metropolitan Police
"Those who have robbed have also lied." – Dr Samuel Johnson corroborating prophet Habakkuk

Habakkuk's Complaint:
How long, Lord, must I call for help, but you do not listen? Or cry out

to you, "Violence!" but you do not save? Why do you make me look at injustice? Why do you tolerate wrongdoing? Destruction and violence are before me; there is strife, and conflict abounds. Therefore, the law is paralysed, and justice never prevails.

The wicked hem in the righteous, so that justice is perverted.

The Lord's Answer

"Look at the nations and watch— and be utterly amazed. For I am going to do something in your days that you would not believe, even if you were told. I am raising up the Babylonians, that ruthless and impetuous people, who sweep across the whole earth to seize dwellings not their own. They are a feared and dreaded people; they are a law to themselves and promote their own honour. Their horses are swifter than leopards, fiercer than wolves at dusk. Their cavalry gallops headlong; their horsemen come from afar. They fly like an eagle swooping to devour; they all come intent on violence. Their hordes advance like a desert wind and gather prisoners like sand. They mock kings and scoff at rulers. They laugh at all fortified cities; by building earthen ramps they capture them. Then they sweep past like the wind and go on— guilty people, whose own strength is their god."

Habakkuk's Second Complaint

Lord, are you not from everlasting? My God, my Holy One, you will never die. You, Lord, have appointed them to execute judgment; you, my Rock, have ordained them to punish. Your eyes are too pure to look on evil; you cannot tolerate wrongdoing. Why then do you tolerate the treacherous? Why are you silent while the wicked swallow up those more righteous than themselves? You have made people like the fish in the sea, like the sea creatures that have no ruler. The wicked foe pulls all of them up with hooks, he catches them in his net, he gathers them up in his dragnet; and so, he rejoices and is glad. Therefore, he sacrifices to his net and burns incense to his dragnet, for by his net he lives in luxury and enjoys the choicest food. Is he to keep on emptying his net, destroying nations without mercy? I will stand at my watch and station myself on the ramparts; will look to see what he will say to me, and what answer I am to give to this complaint.

The Lord's Answer

Then the Lord replied: "Write down the revelation and make it plain on tablets so that a herald may run with it. For the revelation awaits an appointed time; it speaks of the end and will not prove false. Though it lingers, wait for it; it will certainly come and will not delay. See, the enemy is puffed up; his desires are not upright—but the righteous person will live by his faithfulness. Indeed, wine betrays him; he is arrogant and never at rest. Because he is as greedy as the grave and like death is never satisfied, he gathers to himself all the nations and takes captive all the peoples. Will not all of them taunt him with ridicule and scorn, saying, 'Woe to him who piles up stolen goods and makes himself wealthy by extortion! How long must this go on?' Will not your creditors suddenly arise? Will they not wake up and make you tremble? Then you will become their prey. Because you have plundered many nations, the peoples who are left will plunder you. For you have shed human blood; you have destroyed lands and cities and everyone in them. 'Woe to him who builds his house by unjust gain, setting his nest on high to escape the clutches of ruin! You have plotted the ruin of many peoples, shaming your own house and forfeiting your life. The stones of the wall will cry out, and the beams of the woodwork will echo it. Woe to him who builds a city with bloodshed and establishes a town by injustice! Has not the Lord Almighty determined that the people's labour is only fuel for the fire, that the nations exhaust themselves for nothing? For the earth will be filled with the knowledge of the glory of the Lord as the waters cover the sea.'

"'Woe to him who gives drink to his neighbours pouring it from the wineskin till they are drunk, so that he can gaze on their naked bodies! You will be filled with shame instead of glory. Now it is your turn! Drink and let your nakedness be exposed!

The cup from the Lord's right hand is coming around to you, and disgrace will cover your glory. The violence you have done to Lebanon will overwhelm you, and your destruction of animals will terrify you. For you have shed human blood; you have destroyed lands and cities and everyone in them.'

"Of what value is an idol carved by a craftsman? Or an image that teaches lies? For the one who makes it trusts in his own creation; he makes idols that cannot speak. Woe to him who says to wood, 'Come to life!' Or to lifeless stone, 'Wake up!' Can it give guidance? It is covered with gold and silver; there is no breath in it."

The Lord is in his holy temple; let all the earth be silent before him.

The following is from Habakkuk 3 (New International Version, or NIV):

Habakkuk's Prayer

A prayer of Habakkuk the prophet. On shigionoth.

Lord, I have heard of your fame; I stand in awe of your deeds, Lord.

Repeat them in our day, in our time make them known; in wrath remember mercy.

God came from Teman, the Holy One from Mount Paran. His glory covered the heavens, and his praise filled the earth.

His splendour was like the sunrise; rays flashed from his hand, where his power was hidden.

Plague went before him; pestilence followed his steps.

He stood, and shook the earth; he looked, and made the nations tremble. The ancient mountains crumbled and the age-old hills collapsed— but he marches on forever.

I saw the tents of Cushan in distress, the dwellings of Midian in anguish.

Were you angry with the rivers, Lord? Was your wrath against the streams?

Did you rage against the sea when you rode your horses and your chariots to victory?

You uncovered your bow, you called for many arrows.

You split the earth with rivers; the mountains saw you and writhed.

Torrents of water swept by; the deep roared and lifted its waves on high.

Sun and moon stood still in the heavens at the glint of your flying arrows, at the lightning of your flashing spear.

In wrath you strode through the earth and in anger you threshed the nations.

You came out to deliver your people, to save your anointed one. You crushed the leader of the land of wickedness, you stripped him from head to foot.

With his own spear you pierced his head when his warriors stormed out to scatter us, gloating as though about to devour the wretched who were in hiding.

You trampled the sea with your horses, churning the great waters.

I heard and my heart pounded, my lips quivered at the sound; decay crept into my bones, and my legs trembled. Yet I will wait patiently for the day of calamity to come on the nation invading us.

Though the fig tree does not bud and there are no grapes on the vines, though the olive crop fails, and the fields produce no food, though there are no sheep in the pen and no cattle in the stalls, yet I will rejoice in the Lord, I will be joyful in God my Saviour.

The Sovereign Lord is my strength; He makes my feet like the feet of a deer; he enables me to tread on the heights.

✴ ✴ ✴ ✴

The instinct of a closeted white supremacist thug like Sue Gregory is soft but durable apartheid by stealth.

The brain is not in the skin.

Almost everything was stolen.

Before slavery, what?

Stephanie Twidale, the seemingly obsessively libidinous, racist cougar (I used to do stuff with dirty old gals – postmenopausal European cougars – dirty bas****s – like her for valuable consideration, of course, and aided by Burantashi, derived from the bark of the African tree Pausinystalia yohimbe, when I was a boy/man in Lagos; the ugly cougars should all be found, charged, and jailed for paedophilia, as it wasn't only old men that f***** unripe and unready tubes; European cougars, as old and as ugly as Stephanie Twidale, did in West Africa, and still do) asked to see the previous reports of visits to the surgery of the first ever and only Negro dentist in Bedford prior to her visit to the surgery of the first ever and only Negro dentist in Bedford. The big gal later denied that she did not see the reports.

"We cannot go back to the saint. There is far more to be learned from sinners." Wilde

Then, overwhelmed by the ignorance of youth, we learned from European sinners, and we have gone back to the SAINTS, at least, we hope. Only Christ is a righteous Judge. We beg Him for mercy.

Stephanie Twidale was a racist thug, and she unrelentingly lied on oath before a "fish and chips" committee of former England young adults – shepherds of England young adults.

Those the privileged dullards regularly spin are amongst the dullest adult population in the industrialised world, which confirms that the past was stolen with guns.

It is a fact and the absolute truth that Sir Winston Churchill implied that the average Briton was a moron. More than sixty years later, the OECD objectively and seamlessly corroborated the proximate observation of the great man.

"The best argument against democracy is a five-minute conversation with the average voter." – Sir Winston Churchill

"England young adults are amongst the least literate and numerate in the industrialised world." – OECD.

Are shepherds of morons, morons too?

Based entirely upon the request by Stephanie Twidale, John Hooper (NHS) sent an email to Richard Hill and copied Sue Gregory and Charlotte Dowling Goodson into the email.

"Richard (Hill), Stephanie Twidale called us a few weeks ago about DRS visits and Charlotte prioritised Mr Bamgbelu's practice; Stephanie has been in touch a few times as her colleagues had highlighted issues from a similar practice in Northants and they would like to review report etc etc prior to visiting. She also wanted to know if there has been a dental inspection there at all and I did not know the answer . . . Cue Richard have you carried out an inspection at this practice, please could you advise Stephanie when she contacts you, and would it be possible to see our reports so we can be more pro active with any other queries. Thanks. With kind regards, John Hooper." – NHS email of 15.08.2006

Sue Gregory responded to the email. Charlotte Dowling Goodson alleged that she did not, at least not on record, and Richard Hill alleged that he was not sure whether he did, but if he responded, it was conveniently not on a record.

Crooked, racist bas****s!

"Richard has done visits to Bamgbelu, he would have to provide you with reports of his visits." – Sue Gregory, 15 August 2006

* * * *

David Morris cross examined Richard Hill under oath in the council chambers on 18 November 2008 (Court Room):

DAVID MORRIS: Yes. (To the witness) I think I ought to show you another email and, I am sorry, I do not think it is copied in our bundle. I have not had it copied in order to hand up. Can I just show it to my learned friend and then, if he is content, I will just read it out. (Same done) Sir, it was exhibited but it does not appear to be in your bundle. We will have copies made of it, but so as not to delay matters I will read it to you. It is not particularly long. It is from Sue Gregory, dated 15 August 2006 to John Hooper, Sue Gregory (again), Richard Hill and a copy to Charlotte Dowling.

"Subject: RE DRS Visit - Mr Bamgbelu

John [that is John Hooper]

I know that Richard has done practice visits to Bamgbelu in the past, he will need to let you have the details. Sue."

I am sorry, I am taking this out of order. The original message is this:

"From: John Hooper, sent: 15 August 2006 to: Sue Gregory (HPCT); Richard Hill (HPCT), Cc: Charlotte Dowling (Goodson). Subject: DRS Visit – Bamgbelu.

"Sue/Richard

Stephanie Twidale called us a few weeks ago about DRS visits and Charlotte prioritised Mr Bamgbelu's practice. Stephanie has been in touch a few times as her colleagues had highlighted issues from a similar practice in Northants and they would like to review report etc. etc. prior to visiting.

She also wanted to know if there has been a dental inspection there at all and I did not know the answer . . . Cue Richard have you carried out an inspection at this practice. Please could you advise Stephanie when she contacts you, and would it be possible to see our reports so we can be more proactive with any other queries."

I will show the witness that. (Same done) (To the witness) I do not want take an unfair point, but going back to the May 2005 email, can you recall when and what your response might have been to that?

RICHARD HILL: I don't have any record of a response. There might have been an oral response, but there was certainly nothing in writing.

DAVID MORRIS: And if it was an oral response, can you recall what the nature of that was? Please do not guess if you have absolutely no recollection.

RICHARD HILL: I daren't guess. No, I have no idea.

NEGRO'S PERSPECTIVE:
Richard Hill implied that he spoke only the truth under oath. He was dishonest, as he lied, but the racist satanic network seemed to be there (they are almost everywhere) to protect their own.

Incompetent art incompetently imitates life.

They swear by the name of Almighty God never to tell lies; they lie that they don't lie – Psalm 144.

Those privileged dullards regularly spin are amongst the dullest adult population in the industrial world.

"FAILING SCHOOLS AND A BATTLE FOR BRITAIN: This was the day the British education establishment's 50-year betrayal of the Nation's children lay starkly exposed in all its ignominy. After testing 166,000 people in 24 education systems, the Organisation for Economic Cooperation and Development (OECD) finds that England young adults are amongst the least literate and numerate in the industrialised world." – The Daily Mail, 09.01.2013

Morons have shepherds. Shepherds of morons are likelier to be morons too.

"To disagree with three-fourths of the British public on all points is one of the first elements of sanity, one of the deepest consolations in all moments of spiritual doubt." – Oscar Wilde

The descendants of wretched, feudal agricultural labourers from mainland Europe who dispossessed and robbed the aborigines were transformed by the gigantic proceeds of merciless, racist evil (slavery) and have reinvented themselves and seem to associate the proceeds of merciless sadism and savagery with personal intellect and industry. It is a lie! It is a scam!

Sheep have grossly exaggerated views of their shepherds. Sheep were deceived into believing that shepherds were paragons of wisdom who fed them with the yields of virtue. As shepherds did not bring stolen Africans home, sheep did not know that shepherds were extremely nasty, evil, racist thugs who fed them with the yields of merciless, racist evil (slavery).

"American South is still taken as barbarism's benchmark. Few realise that the behaviour of Scots busy getting rich in the slave-holders' empire was actually worse – routinely worse – than the worst of the cottonocracy. You need only count the corpses. By the time slavery was brought to an end in America, the country's 400,000 trafficked people had grown to a population of four million. In the British West Indies, only 670,000 survived from two million imported souls. In the American South, slaves were valuable and bred. We worked them to death then simply imported more to keep the sugar and thus the money flowing.

Unlike centuries of grief and murder, an apology cost nothing. So, what does Scotland have to say?" – Herald Scotland, Ian Bell, columnist, Sunday 28 April 2013

Under oath, Charlotte Dowling Goodson implied that she was aware of John Hooper's request for reports. She did not relate the requests to the alleged Health Commission visit.

I was the only Negro in the process; I felt swamped by aliens. Homogeneity in the administration of English law is the impregnable secure mask of RACIAL HATRED.

There were laws during Europeans' gigantically profitable commerce in millions of stolen Africans. Then, the yields of other people children were used to build magnificent courts and pay the wages of Judges who sent those who stole money to prisons built with stolen money – Habakkuk.

Affluence did not evolve; then, it was actively and deliberately stolen- Habakkuk.

Before slavery, what?

"Affluence is not a birth right." David Cameron.

* * * *

David Morris cross examined Charlotte Dowling Goodson on 20 November 2008 (Habakkuk):

DAVID MORRIS: But as far as Mr. Bamgbelu and his Bedford practice is concerned, had there been any DRS inspections of his premises before Miss Twidale went in 2007?

CHARLOTTE DOWLING GOODSON: Not of those premises, no.

DAVID MORRIS: You mentioned also yesterday that there had been concerns raised, both in Bedford and Northampton, about Mr. Bamgbelu's practices in those respective PCT areas. Northampton we know about because we have heard evidence about the inspection, the visit that took place there. I just want your help as far as Bedford is concerned. I think at that stage when those were raised . . . let's take it in stages. Can I just first of all take you to a document D2 which . . .

CHAIRMAN (DR SHIV PABARY, MEMBER OF THE BRITISH EMPIRE): I do not think that the committee has that document. Have you got that?

CHARLOTTE DOWLING GOODSON: Yes I have.

DAVID MORRIS: I think this was an e mail you received in 2005 from Sue Gregory, a colleague of yours at Bedford, is that right?

CHARLOTTE DOWLING GOODSON: That is correct, yes. She's the Consultant Dental Public Health at Bedfordshire.

DAVID MORRIS: And talks of Vicky Harrison from Northamptonshire telephoning you with some continuing concerns about Mr. Bamgbelu's other practice on her patch: "Most of these relate to cross infection control and include disposing of clinical waste. I know that we had a number of concerns about his practice in Bedford, and he had both money and support to get things right. Please let me know about any outstanding concerns and when his practice was last inspected." I think at that stage your understanding was that those concerns were ones that were raised way back in 1996, and sort of led to visits from Mr. Hill which was sorted out I think by the end of 1996/7?

CHARLOTTE DOWLING GOODSON: As far as I am aware, yes, it was 95/96; it was prior to my involvement with the

PCT.

DAVID MORRIS: Now, I do not think much happened as a result of that inquiry until 2006, August, is that right?

CHARLOTTE DOWLING GOODSON: I believe that is correct, yes.

DAVID MORRIS: Because we then got another e mail dated . . . it's D4.

CHAIRMAN (DR SHIV PABARY): Do you have a copy for Mrs Dowling (Handed).

DAVID MORRIS: Again, from Sue Gregory in August 2006, no, sorry, John Hooper 2006. John Hooper is another colleague at Bedford, is that correct?

CHARLOTTE DOWLING GOODSON: That's correct; he was one of the managers in my team.

DAVID MORRIS: Referring to, "Stephanie Twidale calling us a few weeks ago and she wanted to know if there had been a dental inspection there at all (I think that's Bedfordshire) and I didn't know the answer. Cue Richard, have you carried out an inspection at this practice. Please could you advise Stephanie when she contacts you." That is the next time this matter arose, is that right?

CHARLOTTE DOWLING GOODSON: That is correct, yes.

DAVID MORRIS: And then I think in response to that, do we get an e mail from Richard Hill, which we have behind tab 21 in volume 1.

CHARLOTTE DOWLING GOODSON: Sorry, can I have the tab again.

DAVID MORRIS: Tab 21. From Richard Hill 6 September 06 to you and others at Bedford; record of practice visits, and we have the entry on that schedule for July 2004, all right?

CHARLOTTE DOWLING GOODSON: Yes.

DAVID MORRIS: And did you, as part of his process then . . . well, I can see the concerns that were raised in that column: no risk assessment, no COSSH, Kavoclave type autoclave, why that shouldn't be used, no other members of practice staff present at visits, and could not be questioned regarding cross infection control by the practice. But did you, as part of this process, receive a copy of what was purported to be the visit record for that date, 22 July 04?

CHARLOTTE DOWLING GOODSON: Not at that time, but we

did get copies of the reports and for these visits at a later date. We had been requesting them.

DAVID MORRIS: That is D5, if you can have a look at that, please. (Handed)

CHARLOTTE DOWLING GOODSON: Thank you

(Perused document).

DAVID MORRIS: And I think if I can take you to the feedback, final page, page 5, summary of these concerns: "The practice uses a Kavoclave type autoclave. This is not acceptable. There is also a large turnover of staff and I am not satisfied that staff training is at an acceptable level and have concerns over the cross infection control procedures", and the essential action points set out there. So you would have received that, and that would have informed your concerns at that time about that practice?

CHARLOTTE DOWLING GOODSON: This report was received at a later time. I did not receive it until 2004.

DAVID MORRIS: No.

CHARLOTTE DOWLING GOODSON: But what I also I received was part of the decision making process, and prioritising the practice for an inspection by the DRS.

DAVID MORRIS: And would those concerns, informed in part by that report, have been fed through to Stephanie Twidale prior to her conducting her inspection in February 07?

CHARLOTTE DOWLING GOODSON: I can't remember if I passed them on. I think Richard Hill would have shared those issues with Stephanie as part of the discussion prior to the visit, and that is part of the reason why Richard went with Stephanie to undertake the visit with her.

DAVID MORRIS: It would have made a lot of sense for the information in that report to have been passed on and fed through as necessary preliminary material prior to inspection?

CHARLOTTE DOWLING GOODSON: Yes, it would have been.

DAVID MORRIS: And do you appreciate that now, very recently, Mr. Hill has realised that that report, relating to Mr. Bamgbelu's practice, in fact was an error, in as much as the concerns in it related to wholly different matters?

CHARLOTTE DOWLING GOODSON: No, I was not aware of that.

NEGRO'S PERSPECTIVE:
"No, I was not aware of that."

Of course, she'd say that she was not aware of the RACIST FABRICATIONS that she had used to persecute the Negro, for years.

The Negro stayed up at night, in his late teens to early twenties, to figure out krebs cycle, amelogenesis, and thousands of other useless nonsenses that white people invented for us, and a brainless white woman who couldn't spell odontogenesis, torpedoed the Negro's lifetime sacrifice.

What they want is automatic intellectual superiority, their baseless birth right; He gave them the indisputably superior skin colour, and they stole almost everything He gave to others – James 4; Habakkuk.

"Education is what remains after you have forgotten what you learned at school." Albert Einstein

Self-education is the 'MEAT' of education.

Sue Gregory was a racist thug and an intellectually incompetent nonentity, seemingly propped up by crude oil and gas money in the same way as her evil, merciless, racist ancestors were for centuries sustained by the proceeds of merciless sadism and savagery. The sadistic savages are no longer here but based upon very proximate observations of Sue Gregory and her type, it seems their sadistic genes continue to flow through the veins of their direct descendants that remain here.

Oyinbo olodo! Oyinbo ode!

"And talks of Vicky Harrison from Northamptonshire telephoning you with some continuing concerns about Mr. Bamgbelu's other practice on her patch: 'Most of these relate to cross infection control and include disposing of clinical waste. I know that we had a number of concerns about his practice in Bedford, and he had both money and support to get things right. Please let me know about any outstanding concerns and when his practice was last inspected.' I think at that stage your understanding was that those concerns were ones that were raised way back in 1996, and sort of led to visits from Mr. Hill which was sorted out I think by the end of 1996/7?" – David Morris, 20 November 2008

Had Sue Gregory's mama sent her to schools within one of the least literate countries in the industrialised world where critical reasoning was taught as a subject, the merciless, racist cougar with seemingly four-fifths deflated humungous mammary glands (f****** libido killer) would have realised the rot she was blowing.

If Victoria Harrison, another dmf (diseased, missing and filled teeth), informed her about issues in the surgery of the first ever and only Negro dentist in Wellingborough in 2005, and she asked to see previous reports, and 2003 and 2004 reports were live at that time and implicitly not missing in 2005. What happened to her request?

Mendacem memorem esse oportet.

Community Dentistry is the softest part of soft dentistry.

Google: Helen Falcon (Community Dentist): Racist Empress of privileged dullards.

There was no evidence of a response by Charlotte Dowling Goodson and Richard Hill that Sue Gregory directed her email to—at least, nothing was disclosed.

The alleged concerns were concealed from the first ever and only Negro dentist in Wellingborough.

Brainless, diseased, missing, and filled teeth wanted to stitch the Negro up within their teeth science. Awon oyinbo olodo! Owon oyinbo ode!

The land yielded only food. No brain, natural resources poor, only skin colour that the wearer neither made nor chose, and what else? Pure scam!

"Agriculture not only gives riches to a nation, but the only riches she can call her own." – Dr Samuel Johnson

The descendants of wretched, feudal agricultural labourers dispossessed the aborigines; they were transformed and reinvented by the gigantic yields of sadistic slavery. Before slavery, what?

So, no one except Richard Hill knew anything about the Health Commission request. Their people seemed to be everywhere, so when they need to f*** the Negro up, they can call for help from members of the gang hiding as moles within the BDA, the CQC, the Health Commission, the GDC, the NCAS, and the like.

Some people join satanic gangs (all for one, one for all). Secret information gathered by England young adults and former England young adults fuel their secret network. Since membership of their satanic gang is neither meritocratic nor open, they are forced to be reliant upon some truth, some half-truths, and plenty of lies. They wear charity as a cloak of deceit and swear by the name of Almighty God never to tell lies, but they lie that they do not lie (Songs of David 144).

The descendants of wretched agricultural labourers have been immeasurably transformed by the gigantic yields of the merciless, evil trade in stolen human beings (slavery) and they have reinvented themselves on stolen land but seem to retain the intellects of serfs.

Even if it could be proved that there was a request by John Hooper for reports in pursuance of the Health Commission visit (it couldn't, but for argument sake, if there was such a request), the brain that the "white boy" inherited from Richard Hill's mama was not open enough to consider the following:

- As his response was to John Hooper, it means that John Hooper made the request.
- If John Hooper made the unknown or undisclosed request on an unknown date, it must mean that he was not aware of the need to make such a request simultaneously with the request he made on 15.08.2006 solely for the use of Stephanie Twidale prior to visiting the surgery of the first ever and only Negro dentist in Bedford, and the unknown request of unknown date could not annul John Hooper's request of 15.08.2006. The phantom request did not diminish the fact of the NHS's incompetent, racist forgeries, seemingly created with the inherited intellects of wretched, feudal agricultural labourers from mainland Europe who were transformed by slavery, and who reinvented themselves and fool the foolish with foolishness— terrorism on stolen land.

"It was in 1066 that William the Conqueror occupied Britain, stole our land and gained control by granting it to his Norman friends, thus creating a feudal system we have not yet fully escaped." – Tony Benn

Normans stole from others what others had stolen from others. Genetically pure Britons are extinct; all were dispossessed, robbed, and

slaughtered.
Facts are sacred.
"The truth allows no choice." Dr Samuel Johnson.

"FAILING SCHOOLS AND A BATTLE FOR BRITAIN: This was the day the British education establishment's 50-year betrayal of the Nation's children lay starkly exposed in all its ignominy. After testing 166,000 people in 24 education systems, the Organisation for Economic Cooperation and Development (OECD) finds that England young adults are amongst the least literate and numerate in the industrialised world." – The Daily Mail, 09.01.2013

Shepherds of morons are likelier to be morons too.

If the bottommost are world class bottommost, the topmost relative to the bottommost could not be world class topmost. Morons easier to spin.

So, Richard Hill was asked by John Hooper to provide all his reports in pursuance of a Health Commission visit and he produced nineteen reports. Unfortunately, the she-man-looking man who wiggles his ass from side to side in relatively high frequency and walked in short strides, then, suddenly discovered that two or three (the crooked descendant of wretched agricultural labourers on stolen land was not certain; before slavery, what?) of the reports were missing, and one of the missing reports was the 02.04.2003 report for the first ever and only Negro dentist in Bedford.

There was one Negro dentist amongst nineteen, and two or three missing reports, all of which belonged to the Negro, and this seemed extraordinary. Three missing reports (100 percent of the missing reports) were supposedly for the first ever and only Negro in Bedford. That was far beyond extraordinary. They were likelier to be intelligently designed by hereditary racist thugs, but with the intellects of serfs. No brain, natural resources poor, only skin colour that the wearer neither made nor chose, and what else? Pure scam! Before slavery, what?

The 02.04.2003 report for the Negro was missing.

The 22.07.2004 report for the Negro was missing, but the handwritten draft, which contained other matters, was found.

The report of the follow up visit of the 22.07.2004 for the Negro of unknown date was missing, but the handwritten draft, which contained other matters, was found.

Richard Hill was a racist crook and an incompetent liar, but because he was an historical imbecile, he did not realise that his ancestors were thoroughly wretched agricultural labourers from mainland Europe who were immeasurably transformed by the gigantic yields of merciless evil, and have reinvented themselves, but will always give the game away when they write down what they truly think, as the intellect of serfs is genetic.

The slave raiders and traders used guns, not brains.

Before slavery, the land yielded only food, and was occupied by thousands of feudal, agricultural labourers and landowners, and from mainland Europe, and therefore on stolen land.

"Agriculture not only gives riches to a nation, but the only riches she can call her own." – Dr Samuel Johnson

So, Richard Hill, your ancestors were racist thugs, armed robbers, and thieves; guns used against unarmed and defenceless Africa and Africans, not brains, were their tools.

Almost everything was stolen!

Merciless, racist bastards!

"The grand object of all European traders in kidnapped and stolen Africans was - money, money, money; money was their god! In Africa, the poor wretched natives, blessed with the most fertile and luxuriant soil, are rendered so much the more miserable by the Christians' (European traders in stolen Africans) abominable traffic for slaves and the horrid cruelty and treachery of the petty [African] Kings. The Africans kings were encouraged by their European (Christian) customers who carry them strong liquors to enflame their madness and powder and bad firearms to furnish them with the hellish means of killing and kidnapping. But enough - it is a subject that sours my blood." – Ignatius Sancho, 1778

"It was our arms in the river of Cameroon, put into the hands of the trader, that furnished him with the means of pushing his trade; and I have no more doubt that they are British arms, put into the hands of Africans, which promote universal war and desolation that I can doubt their having done so in that individual instance. I have shown how great is the enormity of this evil, even on the supposition that we take only convicts and prisoners of war. But take the subject in another way, and how does it stand? Think of 80,000 persons carried out of their native country by we know not what means! For crimes imputed! For light or inconsiderable faults! For debts perhaps! For crime of witchcraft! Or a thousand other weak or scandalous pretexts! Reflect on 80,000 persons annually taken off! There is something in the horror of it that surpasses all bounds of imagination." – Prime

Minister William Pitt the Younger, 1792

Again, it is hereditary serfs' reasoning to suggest that handwritten drafts of two missing 2004 reports were used to create the replacement for a single 2003 report. It is incompetent dishonesty, and it is immortal. Dishonesty on record is a very accurate measure of intelligence.

Again, it is impossible to use handwritten drafts that contained other matters to create entire reports. Oyinbo olodo! Oyinbo ode!

"Politicians never rise beyond the level of misrepresentation, and actually condescend to prove, to discuss, to argue. How different from the temper of a true liar, with her frank, fearless statements, her superb irresponsibility, her healthy, natural disdain of proof of any kind! After all what is a fine lie? Simply that which is its own evidence. If a woman is sufficiently unimaginative to produce evidence in support of a lie, she might just as well speak the truth at once. No! Politicians won't do. Something may, perhaps, be urged on behalf of the BAR. The mantle of the Sophist has fallen on its members. Their feigned ardours and unrealistic rhetoric are delightful. They can make the worse appear the better cause, as though they were fresh from Leontine schools, and have been known to wrest from the reluctance juries triumphant verdicts of acquittal for their clients." – The Decay of Lying: A Protest by Oscar Wilde

Richard Hill, a disciple of Sue Gregory, was exceedingly dull, racist, and dishonest. He seemed even duller than a quality CQC manager of Mediocre Great England.

Thu, 3 Sep 2015 20:00

RE: Outstanding statutory annual registration fee invoice: payment due – FINAL REMINDER

Dr. Olayinka Bamgbelu

From cqc (NHS SHARED BUSINESS SERVICES LTD (BRISTOL)) SBS-B.cqc@nhs.net

To adeolacole adeolacole@aol.com

Hello,

Thank you for your below email

Kindly request you to provide your contact details (telephone number) so we can contact you and explain.

If any query please let me know

Thanks and Regards, Kanchan Jaisinghani

Collections

Debt Management Team

Shared Business Services

Tel 0303-123-1155

Fax 0117-933-8890

E-mail: sbs-b.cqc@nhs.net

Website: www.sbs.nhs.uk Government Business Award Winner

Central Government Supplier of the Year 2011

Losers are duller than winners, but Sir Major banged Egg Winner, so he is a winner too.

Dull, racist, and dishonest Richard Hill was not as dull as the Scottish "professor," the postgraduate dean deputy of Helen Falcon at Oxford and Wessex Deaneries, who stated the following:

Mon, 8 Mar 2010 20:20

Re Meeting 9th March

From George Rothnie georgerothnie@hotmail.com To adeolacole adeolacole@aol.com

Hi Ola,

We are scheduled to meet tomorrow evening at my surgery about 5.30ish. Unfortunately something has cropped up which necessytates me having to postpone the meeting. I'm really sorry it's such short notice.

I will contact you in the week to arrange another date.

Once agaim my apologies.

George

Richard Hill must be brighter than the postgraduate tutor of Oxford and Wessex Deaneries who worked underneath, not just under, Helen Falcon – Geraint Evans, the Welsh Dunce the Younger.

A Yoruba proverb says, "An imbecile man who works underneath a very powerful woman must do his work with his prick, not his brain."

"Mr Bamgbelu has sent me lengthy e mails following the meeting and has copied me correspondence he has sent to others and including his indemnity society. He has gone to great lengths to question my integrity and honesty. The records of the meetings he was given were in note form, this was made clear to him. He has used facts such as the miss spelling of the dean's surname and my stating a meeting took place at 12 pm not 12 noon to undermine their value." – Geraint Evans, postgraduate tutor for Oxford and Wessex Deaneries

What type of work was Miss Spelling doing underneath Mrs Helen Falcon? Is s/he a lesbo or what?
F****** Miss Spelling! Oyinbo olodo! Oyinbo ode!

"Throughout the discussion of the notes he made derogatory comments about the wording and accuracy. He suggested that they were written some time after the visits and that my memory was inaccurate. The notes as stated previously were written within 24 hours of each meeting when fresh in my memory. They may not have been well written from a grammatical point of view but I am confident I had not forgotten any of the facts." – Geraint Evans, imbecile postgraduate tutor for Oxford and Wessex Deaneries who works underneath Helen Falcon

Geraint Evans is an exceedingly dull postgraduate tutor for Oxford and Wessex Deaneries within Mediocre Great England.

"Sir, he was dull in company, dull in his closet, dull everywhere. He was dull in a new way, and that made many people think him great." – Dr Samuel Johnson

The privileged shepherds of moron sheep should not put their tiny pricks in the mouths of dead pigs; they should put their balls in the mouth of a live, BIG PACU, the nutcrackers, the testicles eaters, with human-like teeth.
https://www.youtube.com/watch?v=BlpH4hG7m1A&feature=youtu.be

"They may not have been well written from a grammatical point of view, but I am confident I had not forgotten any of the facts." Dr Geraint Evans, Postgraduate Tutor, Oxford.

A brainless white man; a racist Welsh thug from valleys of Wales.

"The earth contains no race of human beings so totally vile and worthless as the Welsh……..." Walter Savage Landor.

In the 90s, I practiced dentistry in Newport Gwent, Tredegar and Cwmbran, all in South Wales.

Based on observations, then, in the valleys of Wales, there were thousands of sheep and people; all the sheep but not all the people were incestuously conceived, and all sheep but not all the people were excessively stupid.

"The Welsh man prays to God, on his knees, in a Church every Sunday, and preys on his friends the rest of the week." English saying

There are controlled by SATAN through demons; they don't know.

https://youtu.be/rayVcfyu9Tw

Google: Geraint Evans dentist.

CHAPTER 8

When Solicitors and barristers fail in practice, thousands do, if they're Masons, they could become Judges, if not, they could become Politicians or something else.

Richard Hill never stated at any time that he visited another practice in Bedford on 22.07.2004 and conducted a follow up at the same practice on an unknown date.

The report, by the OECD warns that the UK needs to take significant action to boost the basic skills of the nation's young people. The 460-page study is based on the first-ever survey of the literacy, numeracy and problem-solving at work skills of 16 to 65-year-olds in 24 countries, with almost 9,000 people taking part in England and Northern Ireland to make up the UK results. The findings showed that England and Northern Ireland have some of the highest proportions of adults scoring no higher than Level 1 in literacy and numeracy - the lowest level on the OECD's scale. This suggests that their skills in the basics are no better than that of a 10-year-old.

AN IMBECILE: AN ADULT WITH THE BASIC SKILLS OF A CHILD.

Imbeciles have shepherds; shepherds of imbeciles are likely to be imbeciles too.

Apart from creating cushy salaried jobs for Solicitors and barristers who couldn't hack it in the very competitive real world (quasi-communism), what do imbeciles need very expensive administration of the law for?

A grossly overrated, overpopulated, overhyped, and mediocre trade that is dying slowly and imperceptibly.

"The legal system lies at the heart of any society, protecting rights, imposing duties, and establishing a framework for the conduct of almost every social, political, and economic activity. Some argue that the law is in its death throes while others postulate a contrary prognosis that discerns numerous signs of law's enduring strength. Which is it?" Professor Raymond Wacks, Emeritus Professor, Hong Kong Law School

* * * * *

CASE NO: 69238
IN THE MATTER OF THE GENERAL DENTAL COUNCIL AND ABIODUN BAMGBELU
SUPPLEMENTAL WITNESS STATEMENT OF RICHARD HILL
I, RICHARD HILL, c/o Bedfordshire Primary Care Trust, Gilbert Hitchcock House, 21 Kimbolton Road, Bedford, MK40 2AW WILL SAY AS FOLLOWS:

1. I make this statement supplemental to my statement dated 23.09.2008.

2. I attach as Exhibit SRWH1 a copy of my report dated 22.07.2004, I attach a synopsis of practice visits that makes reference to a practice visit to MR BAMGBELU's practice at 52, Bromham Road, Bedford, MK40 2QG in July 2004. The document is incorrect in recording that the inspection took place in 2004. No such inspection in fact took place.

It is the Negro's honest belief that in the council's chamber on 18.11.2008, David Morris maliciously told racist lies when he invited Richard Hill to state that he visited another practice in Bedford on 22.07.2004 and conducted a follow up at the same practice on an unknown date.

David Morris was the counsel that was appointed and instructed by the Medical Protection Society (MPS). The Medical Protection Society was the employer of dull, dishonest, and racist Stephanie Twidale, and Stephanie Twidale, who was an employee of the organisation that was active in South Africa during Apartheid ("Killings in Soweto, my people are dying"), was the chief witness for the prosecution (GDC), and she jointly conducted an inspection of the practice of the first ever and only Negro in Bedford with Richard Hill on 22.02.2007. On that date, unbeknownst to the Negro, three NHS forgeries were live, valid, and accessible: the forged reports of 2004 and a forged email address.

Before me, beside me and behind me, they were all white or nearly white or well advances in their metamorphosis of becoming white.

I was the only Negro in the packed court room (Council Chamber).

Edumare gba wa o: He that we must return to have mercy to.

✱ ✱ ✱ ✱ ✱

David Morris cross examined Richard Hill in the council chambers on 18 November 2008 (Court Room):

DAVID MORRIS: Coming back then to divider 21, it would appear much more likely that that email was a response to that email of August 2006. I am grateful, happy to be corrected on that. But then we look at the synopsis of visits that you compiled and we see the relevant one on p.3 to Mr Bamgbelu at the new premises at Bromham Road dated July 2004 with concerns set out there. I think it is right that in fact that was an error on your part.

RICHARD HILL: It was an administrative error which we acknowledge.

DAVID MORRIS: So (a) there was no visit in July 2004.

RICHARD HILL: No, it was April 2003 which we discussed was, again, a pastoral type of visit.

DAVID MORRIS: And (b) the concerns listed there were not relevant to Mr Bamgbelu's practice.

RICHARD HILL: Not at all.

DAVID MORRIS: They were another practice.

RICHARD HILL: They were another practice that did not refer to him. It did in error, but it was not about him.

DAVID MORRIS: But, unfortunately, that synopsis was sent off to the Bedford PCT in the form of John Hooper, Charlotte Dowling and Sue Gregory.

RICHARD HILL: Yes, although I don't think they acted upon that as regards the Dental Reference Service visit. I think these were required more so for the Health Care Commission which is why there was a whole series. Prior to this, a few months earlier, I carried out a similar exercise for Luton PCT, which I also advise, because they had an imminent visit from the Health Care Commission.

NEGRO'S PERSPECTIVE:

So, in the court dialogue supra, under oath, David Morris actively invited Richard Hill to state that he visited another practice on 22.07.2004 and implicitly carried out a follow up at the same practice on an unknown date. Deluded, the believe that they are very intelligent, so, their brainless trickery must be plausible: Lies that could truths or alternative truths.

"Alternative truth." Mayor Giuliani. The fellow is relevant only because America is very rich. He looks like one of the waiters in an Italian Restaurant in Geneva, they could be genetically related.

In the Court Room (GDC Chambers), the next day, 19.11.2008, behind Richard Hill's back, David Morris implied that Richard Hill stated voluntarily, without prompting, that he visited another practice on 22.07.2004, and implicitly carried out a follow up visit to the same practice on an unknown date.

It is my honest belief that David Morris maliciously lied, implicitly on oath, in pursuance of the indirect best interest of his own kindred, albeit servant of a common master.

So, the prosecutor was white, and the defence was white. The Negro did not choose the defence, white people did.

Homogeneity in the administration of English law is the impregnable secure mask of RACIAL HATRED – Habakkuk 1:4; John 8:44; John 10:10.

* * * * *

David Morris cross examined Stephanie Twidale under oath on 19 November 2008 (Court Room):

DAVID MORRIS: This is a report by Richard Hill dated 22 July 2004. Might you have seen that before the inspection?
DR STEPHANIE TWIDALE: No, I have never seen this before.

NEGRO'S PERSPECTIVE:

She lied, and she unrelentingly did, under oath. Her ancestors lied too; they industrial-scale professional THIEVES and owners of owners of stolen children defenceless poor people – Habakkuk; John 8:44; John 10:10.

Had she been black, she'd have been in trouble.

"Michael Jackson would have jailed if he'd been black." Jo Brand, English Actress.

Again, it is very important to note that David Morris was appointed and instructed by the Medical Protection Society (MPS), and that the Medical Protection Society (MPS) employed Dr Stephanie Twidale, and Dr Stephanie Twidale was the chief witness for the prosecution (GDC), and Dr Stephanie Twidale together with Dr Richard Hill inspected the surgery of the first ever and only Negro dentist on 22.02.2007, and at the inspection, unbeknownst to the Negro, three NHS forgeries were live, valid, and accessible (the NHS forged report of 22.07.2004, the NHS forged follow up report of unknown date, and the NHS forged email address). The NHS abruptly withdrew its forged reports more than four years later. The withdrawal statement of 16.10.2008 is an NHS racist forgery.

They do whatever they like to our people and the expect us to nod our heads in agreement, like automatons with brand new dura cells, in exchange for regular bread.

They should get lost.

"Those who have the power to do wrong with impunity seldom wait long for the will." Dr Samuel Johnson

F*** the wrinkled buttocks racist cougar. She looked like someone who had been to the GAMBIA to sit on black hard rocks.

Stephanie Twidale reminded the Negro of the wicked Welsh women that a poet encountered.

"The ordinary women of Wales are generally short and squat, ill-favoured and nasty." David Mallet, Scottish Poet

It is crude and cruel, and a bloody waste of time to invite use to a demonic, Antichrist, mediocre administration of law where only white people could tell under oath.

They want superiority but they don't want objective intellectual challenge. They want to eat their cakes and have it.

OYINBO OLE: WHITE THIEVES: HABAKKUK.

Demons they consult do not know that association with Christ is a game changer, as He knows all, sees all, and can do all, and in an instant, and His power resides in mere words. He who merely spoke, and the universe became can speak again and it will perish.

The NHS is a section of the UK society.

"All sections of UK society are institutionally racist." – Sir Bernard Hogan-Howe, London Metropolitan Police

The proceeds of centuries of merciless, racial hatred and fraud kick-started the industrial revolution in Europe and brought European slave merchants and traders, great wealth.

The foundation stones of almost everything was forged with the proceeds of several centuries of merciless, racial hatred and fraud.

Facts are sacred.

There was no NHS before slavery, and there wouldn't have been an NHS had there not been slavery.

Then land yielded only food, and now, the land yields only food. Then, almost everything else was stolen.

"Agriculture not only gives riches to a nation, but the only riches she can call her own." – Dr Samuel Johnson

"Those who have robbed have also lied." – Dr Samuel Johnson corroborating prophet Habakkuk

"Iain Whyte, author of Scotland and the Abolition of Slavery, insists we have at times ignored our guilty past.

"He said: 'For many years Scotland's historians harboured the illusion that our nation had little to do with the slave trade or plantation slavery.

'We swept it under the carpet. This was remarkable in the light of Glasgow's wealth coming from tobacco, sugar and cotton, and Jamaica Streets being found in a number of Scottish towns and cities.

"'It is healthy we are now recognising Scotland was very much involved.'

"The industries, which saw Glasgow and much of the country flourish, were built on the back of slavery.

"There were familiar names such as Scot Lyle of Tate and Lyle fame whose fortune was built on slavery. Ewing from Glasgow was the richest sugar producer in Jamaica.

"The stunning Inveresk Lodge in Edinburgh, now open to the public, was bought by James Wedderburn with money earned from 27 years in Jamaica as a notorious slaver.

"The Wee Free Church was founded using profits and donations from the slave trade. Even our schools have a dark history. Bathgate Academy was built from money willed by John Newland, a renowned slave master and Dollar Academy has a similar foundation.

"For many years, the goods and profits from West Indian slavery were unloaded at Kingston docks in Glasgow.

"Leith in Edinburgh and Glasgow were popular ports from which ambitious Scottish men sailed to make their fortunes as slave masters." – Ian Bell, Herald Scotland, 28 April 2013

The entire foundation of Scotland, and indeed almost everywhere else, was forged by the yield of several centuries of sadistic, merciless, racial hatred and naked fraud.

The proceeds of racial hatred and fraud were used to build courts, cathedrals, courts, schools, castles, and councils.

Before slavery, what?

Feudal agricultural labourers from mainland Europe dispossessed/robbed aboriginal Britons. They've been transformed and reinvented by slavery; now, Dalits and mutated to Maharajahs, and they fool the foolish with foolishness.

Everything was spun; everything is spinning.

Incompetent art always incompetently imitates life.

David Morris maliciously lied implicitly under oath and in pursuance of the best interest of his own kindred and a common servant of his "employer" (the MPS) when he implied that the only way Dr Stephanie Twidale could know about previous reports was if she saw them.

*****

GDC Chambers (Court Room), 19.11.2008:

DAVID MORRIS: This is a report by Richard Hill dated 22 July 2004. Might you have seen that before the inspection?
DR STEPHANIE TWIDALE: No, I have never seen this before.

*****

Those regularly spun are amongst the dullest adult population in the industrialised world - OECD.

Even if it could be proved that dull, dishonest, and racist Dr Stephanie Twidale told the truth under oath, there is incontrovertible evidence that she maliciously lied under oath when she was 'absolutely' certain. Seeing a thing is not the only way of knowing about a thing.
Stevie Wonder knows about a lot of things.
She who can hear but cannot see is likelier to know more than she who can see but cannot hear.
When he was the home secretary, the Right Honourable David Blunkett did not see anything, but he heard so much, and knew much more.
David Morris, the pretend defence counsel, and his own kindred, Dr Stephanie Twidale, were aware of the fact that John Hooper (of the NHS) asked Richard Hill for the previous reports of visits to the surgery of the first ever and only Negro dentist in Bedford upon the request to review them prior to visiting the surgery of the first and only Negro dentist in Bedford.

"Richard (Hill), Stephanie Twidale called us a few weeks ago about DRS visits and Charlotte prioritised Mr Bamgbelu's practice; Stephanie has been in touch a few times as her colleagues had highlighted issues from a similar practice in Northants and they would like to review report etc etc prior to visiting. She also wanted to know if there has been a dental inspection there at all and I did not know the answer . . . Cue Richard have you carried out an inspection at this practice, please could

Satanic Network

you advise Stephanie when she contacts you, and would it be possible to see our reports so we can be more pro active with any other queries. Thanks. With kind regards, John Hooper." – NHS, 15.08.2006

The NHS (John Hooper) sent the email supra to Richard Hill, Sue Gregory, and Charlotte Dowling Goodson.

So, according to the NHS (John Hooper) the prioritisation of the surgery of the first ever and only Negro dentist in Bedford was done in the summer of 2006, but only after repeated calls by Dr Stephanie Twidale.

Stephanie Twidale, the seemingly grandma, seemed obsessed with me. She had a 'come and get me if you dared look.'
Sincerity is the supreme virtue. I used to do stuff with wilting and wrinkling European grand mummies like her (who seemed at the start of mummification in readiness for eternity) in Africa when I was a boy/man university student. We exchanged huge, black hard rocks for harder currencies with dirty old bas****s who desired the almost violent turgidity at the inception of manhood and the war-like encounters with "organic" Negro boys at the bloom of manhood, which their husbands never had or had had and had lost. There is time for everything. The time for grand-mummies like Stephanie Twidale is gone; it is time for the more sensuous and turgid grandchildren of grand-mummies, all within the law.

"We cannot go back to saints. There is far more to be learned from sinners." Wilde

We cannot go back to sinners; there are worthier things to learn from saints. We want to make paradise, as hell on earth and hell in after life is the full definition of a tragedy.

The NHS (John Hooper) informed Richard Hill to expect to hear from Stephanie Twidale. David Morris, the England class barrister (some barristers go on to become judges), seemed too dull to realise that if the NHS told Richard Hill to expect to hear from Stephanie Twidale, it meant that the NHS had given Stephanie Twidale the contact details of

Richard Hill. Indeed, the alleged contemporaneous records of Stephanie Twidale confirmed that she was given Richard Hill's contact details in the summer of 2006.

Some privileged dullards like David Morris seem to associate gigantic yields of several centuries of merciless racial hatred and fraud with personal intellect and industry. It is a lie!
Almost everything was stolen.
Before slavery, what?
It is delusion and a gross distortion of facts to associate gigantic yields of centuries of merciless, racist evil with intellect and industry.
Those regularly spun are amongst the dullest adult population in the industrialised world.
David Morris, the crooked and mediocre England class barrister, and his own kindred, Dr Stephanie Twidale, were also aware of the following statements that were made by Dr Stephanie Twidale:

"Yes please we would like a surgery inspection. At the point at which I was informed that Richard Hill had been there some months before hand and had some concerns." Stephanie Twidale (TD), British Soldier – Territorial Defence.

"Having discussed with the PCT they told me that Mr Hill had made previous visits not that long before from which there had been some queries, and they felt perhaps it would be sensible for Mr Hill to come along as well with me to be a second person and follow up on his previous visits to the practice." Stephanie Twidale (TD), British Soldier – Territorial Defence.

"I spoke to Dr Sue Gregory, Consultant in Dental Public Health at the Bedfordshire PCT to impart the information and was informed that Richard Hill, Dental Practice adviser to Bedfordshire PCT, had carried out a previous Surgery inspection at Bromham Road that had raised some concerns." Stephanie Twidale (TD), British Soldier – Territorial Defence.

"Then I know it came through that Richard Hill had been in before about 6 months ago, I think they said, and it was probably sensible for him to go as the second person, a second appropriate second person to do a follow up. The actual timings of bits of those I am afraid I can't REMEMBER." Stephanie Twidale (TD), British Soldier – Territorial Defence.

"At the point at which I was informed that Richard Hill had been there some months before hand and had some concerns" (Dr Stephanie Twidale)." Stephanie Twidale (TD), British Soldier – Territorial Defence.

So, seeing a report is not the only way of knowing about a report, and there is evidence of the fact that the probability of the fact that Dr Stephanie Twidale told the truth is very low.

Truly, I'd love to be white only for a while, just to enjoy the sweetness of whiteness. Real white, not Michael Jackson.

The legal process must have cost millions of pounds (2007 -2014); they don't care as long as the money is swelling the pockets of whites.

Other people spend other people's money on themselves and their friends.

"A government that robs Peter to pay Paul can always depend on the support of Paul." George Bernard Shaw.

* * * * *

GDC Chambers, Court Room, 19.11.2008:
DAVID MORRIS: Sir, you will recall Mr Hill's evidence was that this is a report mistakenly attributed to Mr Bamgbelu's practice when it in fact relates to something that was a mistake?
THE CHAIRMAN (DR SHIV PABARY, MEMBER OF THE BRITISH EMPIRE): Was this where there was a lot of cancellations? I remember something in evidence.

NEGRO'S PERSPECTIVE:
The "Sir" was a mark of respect, and it was meant to beautify incompetent lies, and fool the foolish, under oath.
"The English think that incompetence is the same thing as sincerity."

– Quentin Crisp

Those regularly spun are amongst the dullest adult population in the industrialised world - OECD.

"FAILING SCHOOLS AND A BATTLE FOR BRITAIN: This was the day the British education establishment's 50 year betrayal of the Nation's children lay starkly exposed in all its ignominy. After testing 166,000 people in 24 education systems, the Organisation for Economic Cooperation and Development (OECD) finds that England young adults are amongst the least literate and numerate in the industrialised world." – The Daily Mail, 09.01.2013

Shepherds of morons are likelier to be morons too!

If the bottommost part of a whole is world class bottommost, the topmost part of that whole cannot be world class topmost.

DAVID MORRIS: Sir, you will recall Mr Hill's evidence was that this is a report mistakenly attributed to Mr Bamgbelu's practice when it in fact relates to something that was a mistake?

THE CHAIRMAN (DR SHIV PABARY, MEMBER OF THE BRITISH EMPIRE): Was this where there was a lot of cancellations? I remember something in evidence.

The statement that David Morris made was unrelated to response that their Indian gave. Their Indian was a scatter-head dunce.

"Sir, you will recall Mr Hill's evidence was that this is a report mistakenly attributed to Mr Bamgbelu's practice when it in fact relates to something that was a mistake?" David Morris

There was no mistake; theirs was persecutory Negrophobia and Negrophobic perjury that Christ uncovered. I was in Switzerland on July 22, 2004, and my surgery was shut.

Had I been in the UK, and even if my surgery were shut, it'd have been my words against his, and innately racist whites will believe innately racist whites all the time.

Based on available evidence, white Judges measure whites with a very different yardstick – Apartheid by stealth.

Only brainless Negroes expect demons cannot cast out demons –

Matthew 12:27.

"Was this where there was a lot of cancellations? I remember something in evidence." Dr Shiv Pabary, Member of the Most Excellent Order of Empire and Justice of Peace.

There was nowhere in the transcript where there was a lot of cancellations, and there was nowhere anywhere where there was a lot of cancellations. The Indian was excessively dull, and he was made the figure head of the process for that reason. He was engaged because of his memory, he was engaged because he was a VERY THICK INDIAN, and to add colour, other than black and whites to the process.

A brainless Uncle Tom, with his near perfect imitation moneyed-class class (robber barons) accent, he was well advanced in the metamorphosis of becoming a Higher Upper Class English man. He walked the Oxbridge walk, stirred and sipped his tea like the Higher Upper Class, and dipped his ginger nut in his tea like an Indian.

The fellow was purified froth.

"A typical English man, usually violent and always dull." Wilde

"I think I will ask our legal adviser for any advice he may have. My view is that there are six or seven of us here who had the admission down, but we cannot find it in the transcript and there is wordings that imply that there was, but it is not in black and white….." Dr Shiv Pabary, Member of the Most Excellent Order Empire (MBE) and Justice of Peace (JP)

"Yes, Sir, it does her honour, but it would do nobody else honour. I have indeed, not read it all. But when I take up the end of a web, and find it packthread, I do not expect, by looking further, to find embroidery." Dr Samuel Johnson

MORON MEMBER OF OUR EMPIRE (MMBE) AND JUSTICE OF INCOMPETENT RACIST LIES (JIRL)

A brainless Indian, albeit a near perfect higher upper class English man.

The spinal cord of the brainless Indian seemed to be his highest centre.

Majestic appointee.
Majestic stupidity.

"There is no sin except stupidity." Wilde

"Freedom of expression is the cornerstone of our democracy." Jacob Rees-Mogg.

Freedom of expression was part of the Queen's speech.

DO SOME MEMBERS OF OUR EMPIRE HAVE ALZHEIMER'S DISEASE?

"My view is that there are six or seven of us here who had the admission down." Dr Shiv Pabary, MBE, JP.
Based on available evidence, Dr Shiv Pabary, MBE, JP, their Indian, effectively the Chief Justice of the legal process, lied or he was recklessly confused when he stated, "My view is that there are six or seven of us here who had the admission down."

"We cannot find it in the transcript and there is wordings that imply that there was, but it is not in black and white." Dr Shiv Pabary, Member of the Most Excellent Order Empire (MBE) and Justice of Peace (JP)
Their very, very THICK Indian stated that they couldn't find racist lies in transcript, an imbecile INDIAN contradicted himself when, he stated, "there is wordings that imply that there was, but it is not in black and white....."
They are controlled by Antichrist demons; they don't know.
If it's in the transcript, and if the had wordings, those wordings must have been recorded in any other place order than in the transcript, and the wordings were not in black and white, they must have been in other colour or colours.

INDIAN VOODOO: ALL ANTICHRIST ARE CONTROLLED BY DEMONS
The brother of Dr Shiv Pabary, Member of the Most Excellent Order Empire (MBE) and Justice of Peace (JP), is autistic, he seemed wonky too, certainly mentally. Their father and mother could be siblings or cousins.
Charles Darwin married his first cousin, and expectedly, their children, not all, were physically and/or mentally wonky. Charles Darwin was born in 1809. The yields of slavery directly or indirectly sustained he and his

family. The descendant of THIEVES and owners of stolen children of defenceless Africans should have studied the effects of decommissioned natural selection and reversed evolution on millions of kidnapped children of defenceless people.

Based on available evidence, irreversible genetic damage is the most enduring residue of the original sin: Several centuries of Europeans' barbarously racist commerce in millions of stolen children of defenceless poor people – Habakkuk.

Percentage of children in the UK hitting educational targets at 5, in descending order:
1. Asian (Indian)
2. Asian (Any other Asian)
3. White (British)
4. White (Irish)
5. Mixed (any other)
6. Mixed (white and black African)
7. Chinese
8. Mixed (White and black Caribbean)
9. Black (African heritage)
10. Asian (Any other Asian)
11. Black (Caribbean heritage)
12. Black (other)
13. Asian (Bangladeshi)
14. White (Any other white)
15. Any other ethnic group
16. Asian (Pakistani)
17. White (Traveller of Irish heritage)
18. White (Gypsy/ Roma)
Source: Centre Forum, Daily Mail, 04.04.2016

Children in the UK hitting educational targets at 16, in descending order:
1. Chinese
2. Asian (Indian)
3. Asian (Any other Asian)
4. Mixed (White and Asian)

5. White (Irish)
6. Mixed (Any other)
7. Any other ethnic group
8. Asian (Bangladeshi)
9. Parent/pupil preferred not to say
10. Mixed (White and black African)
11. White (Any other white)
12. Black (African heritage)
13. White (British)
14. Asian (Pakistani)
15. Black (other)
16. Mixed (White and black Caribbean)
17. Black (Caribbean heritage)
18. White (Traveller of Irish heritage)
19. White (Gypsy/ Roma)
Source: Centre Forum, Daily Mail, 04.04.2016

Genetic damage is the most enduring residue of several centuries of barbarously racist traffic in millions of stolen children of defenceless poor people - Habakkuk.

Facts are sacred.
"Give me liberty or give death." Patrick Henry.

On the plantations of highly civilised European Christians in the Americas and West Indies, the brightest among the stolen Africans rebelled as only fools will surrender to indefinite servitude; they were mechanically deselected. The not so diverse, common genetic pool of the stolen Africans was further weakened by the deselection (reversed natural selection) of the brightest genes. Of the rest, the brightest among the placid did not voluntarily make baby slaves as the owners of the cows owned their calves and, more importantly, it would have been excessively stupid and selfish to bring slave babies to Hell on Earth and leave them there. Thousands were raped by the Christians, and they were made richer by thousands of mulatto slave babies. The common genetic pool of the enslaved was further weakened.

The European Christians selected the prettiest among their possessions for their personal enjoyment, and the prettiest slaves became mulatto-slave-babies' factory. The ugly and/or dull Africans were artificially paired up and deliberately bred for labour by highly civilised and enlightened European Christians.

Some people accurately foresaw that their descendants would be amongst the dullest adult population in the industrialised world, so when they found guns, they turned them against the unarmed and defenceless world, and looted it. Whenever they slaughtered, they dispossessed, and wherever they robbed, they took possession. They were merciless, racist thugs, armed robbers, and thieves.

"Those who have robbed have also lied." – Dr Samuel Johnson corroborating prophet Habakkuk

DIFFICULT to trust the intellect and integrity of legal systems that tampers with COURT TRANSCRIPTS, and display RACE HATE and MEDIOCRITY.

"Was this where there was a lot of cancellations? I remember something in evidence." – Dr Shiv Pabary Kuli olodo! Kuli ode!

The honourable and distinguished Member of the Empire reasoned like an imbecile, and he expressed his reasoning worse than an imbecile.

DAVID MORRIS: Mr Hill said yesterday that while he made an error and he thought there had been an inspection on 22 July 2004, and in fact that was not right, it referred to another practice. In chatting with Richard Hill, presumably you did before going round, did he mention any previous inspections that he had done?

NEGRO'S PERSPECTIVE:

"Mr Hill said yesterday that while he made an error and he thought there had been an inspection on 22 July 2004, and in fact that was not right, it referred to another practice." – David Morris, the former England young adult, maliciously lying on oath, as he was the one who told Richard Hill to say that

He is an England class barrister because he is one of the topmost amongst England young adults, but he seemed a racist thug and a dunce.

"England young adults are amongst the least literate and numerate in the industrialised world." – The OECD

If the bottommost of a whole is world class bottommost, the topmost of that whole cannot be world class topmost.

Before slavery, what?

David Morris was dishonest again, and indiscreetly so, under oath. Dishonesty on record is an accurate depiction of intelligence.

Under oath, David Morris implied he was not aware of the fact that Stephanie Twidale had had discussions with Richard Hill and/or others about previous visits to the surgery of the first ever and only Negro dentist in Bedford that she expressly sought. He was dishonest, as he maliciously lied.

"In chatting with Richard Hill, presumably you did before going round, did he mention any previous inspections that he had done?" – David Morris, England class barrister

Stephanie Twidale, the crooked and racist soldier and former England young adult, a shepherd of England young adults, returned an incompetently mendacious question with a recklessly dishonest and immortalised answer.

"In examinations those who do not wish to know ask questions of those who cannot tell." – Walter Raleigh

"I never spoke to Richard Hill, nor had I ever met him before we arrived at the practice together. It was a classic two people standing outside a building saying: 'Are you? Oh yes, right fine.' We had never met and we did not speak beforehand. The only people I spoke to beforehand would be John Hooper and some e-mail correspondence with John, with Charlotte Dowling and with the Consultants in public health, Sue Gregory. I didn't actually have any contact with Richard at all." – Stephanie Twidale Stephanie Twidale, the dull, dishonest, and racist cougar and "pretend soldier," lied unrelentingly under oath.

David Morris and Stephanie Twidale and some of those sitting before them in the Negrophobic charade legal process, who may be members of the satanic network, are aware of the following facts: Stephanie Twidale asked to see reports prior to visiting the surgery of the first ever and only Negro dentist in Bedford, and it was during one of her calls that the NHS prioritised the surgery of the first ever and only Negro dentist in Bedford, and she recklessly lied on oath about that fact. She seemed obsessed with me. It was as if she fantasied about me. No wonder she was wearing a G-string for her gigantic, ugly, old ass, which was made uglier by the pinkish string that sought to reveal rather than conceal the wilting and wrinkling anatomy of the grand Mumsie.

What a f****** dirty, old, racist bat! Hypocrite!

They hate the Negro, but they love the Negro's huge black prick. It should be all or none.

On 30 November 2006, Sue Gregory, the cardinal of crookedness, sent correspondence to Stephanie Twidale and Richard Hill as follows: "Dear Stephanie, Just to confirm that I have spoken to Richard Hill and he will join you for the DRS visit on Thursday 22nd February to Mr Bamgbelu's Bedford Practice, commencing at 9 a.m. We will endeavour to share any issues the PCT may have with you PRIOR to the 22nd. Kind regards, Sue."

It is actual fact and absolute truth that Sue Gregory, OBE, was dishonest and/or complicit in dishonesty.

Under oath at the GDC hearing of 19 November 2008, Stephanie Twidale and David Morris were aware of the NHS correspondence of 30 November 2006, and they had full access to it.

Under oath at the GDC hearing of 20 November 2008, about two years after Sue Gregory's correspondence of 30 November 2006, Charlotte Dowling Goodson (of the NHS) seamlessly corroborated Sue Gregory when she stated that Richard Hill was asked to conduct the inspection of the surgery of the first ever and only Negro dentist in Bedford because of his report of 22.07.2004 and the succeeding report of unknown date.

"We got the report (the report of 22.07.2004), we had been requesting them. I can't remember if I passed them to DRO. I think DPA would have shared those issues with DRO as part of the discussion prior to the visit and that is part of the reason why

DPA went with DRO to undertake the visit with her." Hereditary aliens on stolen land!

The descendants of feudal agricultural labourers (serfs) from mainland Europe used violence to steal the land of native Britons (and later used the same tactics to steal the land of Native Americans) and were immeasurably transformed by the gigantic yields of several centuries of merciless, evil, racist terrorism. Hereditary aliens have reinvented themselves on stolen land and fool the foolish with foolishness. It's a scam! It won't endure, as the future generations will be too dull to keep things going seamlessly. Time will unfold the truth.

"It was in 1066 that William the Conqueror occupied Britain, stole our land and gained control by granting it to his Norman friends, thus creating a feudal system we have not yet fully escaped." – Tony Benn

Normans stole from others what others had stolen from others. Genetically pure Britons are extinct; all were dispossessed, robbed, and slaughtered.

"The American dispute between us and the French is therefore only the quarrel of robbers for the spoils of a passenger, but as robbers have confederacy, which they are obliged to observe as members of a gang, so the English and the French may have relative rights, and do injustice to each other, while both are injuring the Indians. And such, indeed, is the present contest: they have parted the Northern continent of America between them, and are now disputing their boundaries, and are endeavouring the destruction of the other by the help of the Indians, whose interest it is that both should be destroyed." – Dr Samuel Johnson

In the same way as the Normans stole Britain from the motley assembly of mainland Europeans who had stolen it from the aborigines, a motley assembly of mainland Europeans used better guns to steal America from the British and the French, who had stolen it from the Native Americans.

"All have taken what had other owners and all have had recourse to arms rather than quit the prey on which they had fastened." – Dr Samuel Johnson

Dr Stephanie Twidale, the dull, dishonest, and racist cougar, changed her tack when it became apparent that she was complicit in merciless, racist fraud, and lies under oath confirmed rather than concealed her dishonesty.

Oyinbo olodo! Oyinbo ode!

The sole basis of the power of Stephanie Twidale is money. The entire foundation of the money is gigantic proceeds of several centuries of armed racial hatred and fraud against unarmed and defenceless Africans.

Dr Stephanie Twidale lied that she did not have any contact with Richard Hill prior to visiting the surgery of the first ever and only Negro dentist in Bedford.

Only Richard Hill visited the surgery of the first ever and only Negro dentist in Bedford, so the discussions that Stephanie Twidale stated that she had with others must have been based upon original information from Richard Hill: "Yes please we would like a surgery inspection. At the point at which I was informed that Richard Hill had been there some months before hand and had some concerns.

"Having discussed with the PCT they told me that Mr Hill had made previous visits not that long before from which there had been some queries, and they felt perhaps it would be sensible for Mr Hill to come along as well with me to be a second person and follow up on his previous visits to the practice.

"I spoke to Dr Sue Gregory, Consultant in Dental Public Health at the Bedfordshire PCT to impart the information and was informed that Richard Hill, Dental Practice adviser to Bedfordshire PCT, had carried out a previous Surgery inspection at Bromham Road that had raised some concerns.

"Then I know it came through that Richard Hill had been in before about 6 months ago, I think they said, and it was probably sensible for him to go as the second person, a second appropriate second person to do a follow up. The actual timings of bits of those I am afraid I can't REMEMBER.

"At the point at which I was informed that Richard Hill had been there some months before hand and had some concerns."

Sue Gregory, OBE, seemed to be the cardinal of dishonesty. They were racist thugs and cowards. Sue Gregory, the alleged Deputy Chief Dental Officer at White Hall, and Stephanie Twidale, Dental Reference Officer, are shepherds of England young adults.

"FAILING SCHOOLS AND A BATTLE FOR BRITAIN: This was the day the British education establishment's 50 year betrayal of the Nation's children lay starkly exposed in all its ignominy. After testing 166,000 people in 24 education systems, the Organisation for Economic Cooperation and Development (OECD) finds that England young adults are amongst the least literate and numerate in the industrialised world." – The

Daily Mail, 09.01.2013

Shepherds of morons are likelier to be morons too.

Dr. Olayinka Bamgbelu

CHAPTER 9

"Freedom to report the truth is a basic right to which the court gives a high level of protection, and the author's right to his story includes the right to tell it as he wishes." Lord Toulson

"It is incumbent upon the court and all those professionals involved to conclude court proceedings as quickly as possible. This hopefully ensures that a child has stability, love and affection and the parents working together to ensure that he has the best opportunity of developing academically and emotional."District Judge Paul Ayers, Senior Vice President of the Association of Her Majesty's District Judges – proofed and approved Judgement

"Yes, Sir, it does her honour, but it would do nobody else honour. I have indeed, not read it all. But when I take up the end of a web, and find it packthread, I do not expect, by looking further, to find embroidery." Dr Samuel Johnson

OUR SEMI-ILLITERATE RACIST FREEMASON YOUR HONOUR.

A CLOSETED RACIST BRAINLESS WHITE MAN.

The only evidence of the purportedly higher IQ of the incontrovertibly functional semi-illiterate white man is stolen affluence that his ancestors crossed the English Channels, without luggage or decent shoes to latch onto. They changed their names, blended, and deceived the undiscerning that their ancestors were aboriginal Britons who evolved from gorillas in Luton.

Descendants of aliens (genetic aliens) oppress, we, the descendants of the robbed with the yields of the robbery.

"All have taken what had other owners, and all have had recourse to arms rather than quit the prey they were fastened to." Dr Samuel Johnson

Everything is subjectively assumed in favour of his indisputably superior skin colour; he neither made nor chose it - Apartheid by stealth.

The last time he passed through a colour-blind and transparently objective filter system was when he studied 5th rate law at Polytechnic, and it shows.

A CLOSETED RACIST WHITE DUNCE.

Facts are sacred.

An impostor and an expert of deception; he has coasted along for decades, seemingly guided and guarded by the AntiChrist Racist Quasi-Religion (Mediocre Mafia/ New Pharisees), and has sold confusion to the undiscerning in exchange for valuable consideration.

In an open dialogue former Justice Ruth Bader Ginsburg (1933 - 2020), Lady Hale lamented funding.

My Lady, what's the value of several layers of unashamed mediocrity and confusion?

New Herod, Matthew 2:16: They lie to their stupider children that they're geniuses; they 'kill' we, their enemies, who know that they're brainless racist bastards.

Deluded intellectual cowards: They want superiority, their baseless birthright; they don't want Freedom of Expression because they don't want their simpler children to know about what they do to our people - Habakkuk.

A typical English man seemed to want to eat his cake and have it:

Reductio ad absurdum - A logical fallacy.

"A typical English man, usually violent and always dull." Wilde

Matthew 19:21: He told the righteous Jew to sell the yields of transparent virtue and give the proceeds to the poor. Had the Jew been a scammer who sold confusion for cash, Christ would have told him to return the cash to the scammed, and sin no more.

The Good Samaritan had money." Mrs Margaret Thatcher (1925 -2013).

The money of the Good Samaritan was, presumably, the yield of transparent virtue.

Half-educated school dropouts and their superiors decorate the temples of their powerless and useless fertility tools with expensive aprons, and have informal access to some very powerful white Judges - Habakkuk 1:4.

They want a segregated world (Prince Hall's Mason), in terms of opportunities and rights, where human beings are graded according to the colour of the skin that they neither made nor chose; a world based on the embroidery on the aprons they use to decorate the temples of their powerless and useless fertility tools.

Based on very proximate observations and direct experiences, the natural instinct of some white privileged dullards is Apartheid by stealth.

They do vulgar Pharisees' charitable works in exchange for what?

Their offer is not a good deal - Matthew 4:9.

Brother Jimmy Savile did not fix anything for NOTHING.

Google: Freemasonry, intellectually flawed.

When Freedom of Expression becomes a basic right, we shall show the closeted racist dim-wits what they could't see in the supernatural thing that they're looking at.

The Grand Masons' Temple to Baal, 60 Great Queen St, Holborn, London WC2B 5AZ, was built in the 1700s (18th Century), at a height of the barbarously racist traffic in millions of stolen children of defenceless poor people - Habakkuk.

Righteousness without equitable reparation is continuing racist fraud.

Then, Judges, nearly all, were MASONS; some of them were thicker than a gross of planks.

Charitable AntiChrist Racist Freemasonry Quasi-Religion teaches its members the cultist-like, and quasi-voodoo, handshake, not grammar; the former is considerably easier to master.

Based on available evidence, Dr Richard Dawkins and OECD implied that all the children of District Judge Paul Ayers, Senior Vice President of the Association of Her Majesty's District Judges should be duller than their white father.

Facts are sacred.

"Natural selections will not remove ignorance from future generations." Dr Richard Dawkins

England's young people are near the bottom of the global league table for basic skills. OECD finds 16- to 24-year-olds have literacy and numeracy levels no better than those of their grandparents' generation.

England is the only country in the developed world where the generation approaching retirement is more literate and numerate than the youngest adults, according to the first skills survey by the Organisation for Economic Co-operation and Development.

In a stark assessment of the success and failure of the 720-million-strong adult workforce across the wealthier economies, the economic thinktank warns that in England, adults aged 55 to 65 perform better than 16- to 24-year-olds at foundation levels of literacy and numeracy. The survey did not include people from Scotland or Wales.

The OECD study also finds that a quarter of adults in England have the maths skills of a 10-year-old. About 8.5 million adults, 24.1% of the population, have such basic levels of numeracy that they can manage only one-step tasks in arithmetic, sorting numbers or reading graphs. This is worse than the average in the developed world, where an average of 19% of people were found to have a similarly poor skill base.

Just as it was at Professor Stephen Hawking's schools, then, at the University of Lagos, the brightest students did not attend lectures at the Faculty of Law.

"In my school, the brightest boys did math and physics, the less bright did physics and chemistry, and the least bright did biology. I wanted to do math and physics, but my father made me do chemistry because he thought there would be no jobs for mathematicians." Dr Stephen Hawking

They secretly hate Freedom of Expression because they don't want their people to know about what they, secretly, do to our people.

Oxford, England: GDC-Witness, Dr Stephanie Twidale (TD), British Army Officer - Territorial Defence, unrelentingly lied under oath - Habakkuk 1:4; John 8:44; John 10:10.

A RACIST WHITE CROOK.

Her white ancestors lied too; they were industrial-scale professional THIEVES and owners of stolen children of defenceless poor people - Habakkuk.

OYINBO OLE: WHITE THIEVES: HABAKKUK.

Unlike her little brother, age saved the child's sister from the Closeted-Racist-Dylan–Roof-Freemason-Judge. She thanks her stars that the incontrovertibly functional semi-illiterate, closeted racist white man did not have anything to do with her education.

In her GCSE, she gained the following grades:
English Language A*
English Literature A*
Mathematics A*
Additional Mathematics A*
Physics A*
Chemistry A*
Biology A*
History A*
Latin A
Spanish A
Advanced Level Mathematics A

The academic height that the white father and mother of the closeted racist white District Judge cannot know, and which the natural talents of his own children will not exploit.

The brain isn't skin colour; then, we were robbed with guns.

The child sister has since gained a First-Class Science Degree from one of the topmost Universities in the UK, and she's gainfully engaged, batting for her Country. Christ saved her from the evil clutches of the Closeted Racist Freemason Thugs.

It's plainly deductible that the white children of the white Senior Vice President of the Association of Her Majesty's District Judges were inferiorly created by Almighty God, certainly intellectually - OECD.

Facts are sacred.

"The truth allows no choice." Dr Samuel Johnson.

BEDFORD, ENGLAND: Based on available evidence, GDC-WITNESS, Freemason, Brother, Dr Richard William Hill fabricated reports and unrelentingly lied under oath - Habakkuk 1:4; John 8:44; John 10:10.

A RACIST WHITE CROOK.

Facts are sacred.

English law is equal; its administration isn't.

Based on available evidence, the administration of English law is a very potent weapon of a raging but latent RACE WAR.

"All sections of the UK Society are institutionally racist." Sir Bernard Hogan-Howe.

The former Chief of the Metropolitan Police had access to a lot of classified information.

"By definition therefore there needs to be a contact order for Mr B so that he knows when he is going to see his son. It is absolutely essential that this occurs and mother agrees with that. She said so several times in her evidence. Mrs Waller agreed that not only should a child have the opportunity of developing relationship with both parents, any sibling should also be there so that inter- sibling relationship could be fostered and nurtured. Obviously in this particular case the children reside in different places. That immediately puts a strain on the children having limited contact with each other. F's sister is very much older than him and she will be further advanced into her adult life. Thus it is not a matter that that sibling relationship can only be fostered by the children being together. Indeed as we all know absence sometimes makes the heart grow fonder. F should have an opportunity of seeing his sister. Wherever he does that it should be done in a friendly and loving environment. If the time comes that his sister goes to university of course his contact with her will be restricted to the time that she is home from university. In years to come when they have both grown up, with their own family they will see less of each other. But it doesn't mean that they don't still love and adore each other as much as they would if they saw each other every day." The

Senior Vice President of the Association of Her Majesty's District Judges – proofed and approved Judgement.

A BRAINLESS WHITE MAN; ENGLAND'S CLASS JUDGE.

An ignorant descendant of THIEVES and owners of stolen children – Habakkuk.

https://www.youtube.com/watch?v=BlpH4hG7m1A

Shocking!

"Why, that is, because, dearest, you are a dunce." Habakkuk.

A scatter-head plebeian; an overpromoted polytechnic university educated racist bastard. A righteous descendant of industrial-scale professional THIEVES and owners of stolen children of defenceless people (Kamala's ancestors) - Habakkuk.

OYINBO OLE: WHITE THIEVES: HABAKKUK.

The white father and mother of the Senior Vice President of the Association of Her Majesty's District Judges did not care, had they, he'd not have approved and immortalised excessive stupidity at 16, and he'd be a properly educated lawyer, privately educated Anthony Blair, Anthony Julius, Geoff Hoon and Rabinder Singh's class, and he might practice proper law in STRAND.

David Morris cross examined Richard Hill on 18 November 2008 (Court Room):

DAVID MORRIS: And (b) the concerns listed there were not relevant to Mr Bamgbelu's practice.
RICHARD HILL: Not at all.

DAVID MORRIS: They were another practice.
RICHARD HILL: They were another practice that did not refer to him. It did in error, but it was not about him.

NEGRO'S PERSPECTIVE:
So, David Morris, the top England young adult or former top England young adult, implicitly lied on oath.
They artificially created jobs for themselves and destroyed the lone Negro in their midst.
Racist bas****s!
No brain, natural resources poor, only skin colour that the wearer neither made nor chose, and what else? Pure scam! The charade wouldn't endure, as the future generation will be too dull to keep things going seamlessly. Time will unfold the truth.
"The one great principle of English law is to make business for itself."
– Charles Dickens
DR STEPHANIE TWIDALE: I never spoke to Richard Hill, nor had I ever met him before we arrived at the practice together. It was a classic two people standing outside a building saying: "Are you? Oh yes, right fine." We had never met and we did not speak beforehand. The only people I spoke to beforehand would be John Hooper and some e-mail correspondence with John, with Charlotte Dowling and with the Consultants in public health, Sue Gregory. I didn't actually have any contact with Richard at all.

NEGRO'S PERSPECTIVE:
What exactly is the point of a seemingly dishonest, confused, and unequal apartheid legal system where only white people can tell lies under oath? It's almost a scam!
"I didn't actually have any contact with Richard at all." – Stephanie Twidale, territorial defence (TD), maliciously telling
Negrophobic lies
Oyinbo olodo! Oyinbo ode!
It is actual fact and absolute truth that Dr Stephanie Twidale is part of the UK society.

"All sections of UK society are institutionally racist." – Sir Bernard

Hogan-Howe, London Metropolitan Police

Dr Stephanie Twidale, one of Sue Gregory's disciples, lied about almost everything under oath. The ugly, post-menopausal, racist cougar with gigantic, seemingly three-fourths deflated mammary glands with no milk, or at least not a lot of it, lied unrelentingly under oath. It was as if part of the perks for officers of the Territorial Defence Force was a buffet of lies, under oath, in any court in the land, especially where a mere Negro was concerned.

Thuggery is not law.
The sincerely perceived merciless, racist cougar seemed to be an old cow with no more milk in her wilting breasts.

"Truth, Sir, is a cow which will yield such people no more milk, and so they are gone to milk the bull." – Dr Samuel Johnson
What some people want is to associate the gigantic yields of centuries of merciless, racial hatred and fraud with their own personal intellect and industry. David Morris dribbles himself, and immortally, with unashamed mediocrity, Negrophobia, and confusion. Those that they regularly spin are amongst the dullest adult population in the industrialised world.
Sir Winston Churchill implied that the average Briton was a moron. More than sixty years after the proximate observation of the great man, the OECD objectively corroborated his statement when upon objective assessment it found that England's young adults are amongst the dullest in the industrialised world.
David Morris is a former England young adult, and a shepherd of England young adults.
Dr Stephanie Twidale did not disclose that she contacted Richard Hill in 2006 after she was given his contact details and he was told to expect to hear from her.

Dr Stephanie Twidale was a dishonest, racist thug, and a pretend territorial defender.

The English channels are the most important defence. Everything else is a lie!

Dr. Olayinka Bamgbelu

"If the Almighty were to rebuild the world and asked me for advice, I would have English Channels round every country. And the atmosphere would be such that anything which attempted to fly would be set on fire."
– Sir Winston Churchill

If Dr Stephanie Twidale and/or her children and spouse could openly prove that their matriarch was not a racist thug, they must sue the Negro. They wouldn't because the ugly, racist cougar, with gigantic, seemingly three-fourths deflated boobs, and seemingly with no milk, was a racist and a liar.
Oyinbo olodo! Oyinbo ode!
Not all liars are racist, but all racists are malicious liars.
But, beside 2006, Stephanie Twidale (TD) lied on oath when she stated that she did not have any contact with Richard Hill at any time in 2007 prior to their joint inspection of the surgery of the first ever and only Negro dentist in Bedford on 22 February 2007.
The following is an email from Dr Stephanie Twidale (15.02.2007 at 6.28 p.m.) to Richard Hill, copied to Mr John Hooper, Dr Sue Gregory, and Dr Steven Claydon:

"Dear Richard, Just to confirm that I have agreed with John Hooper that we go ahead with the Surgery inspection part of the DRS monitoring programme as arranged for 9.00am on Thursday 22 Feb. However the patient and record card/radiograph examination part of the process will now be delayed until after April, as Mr Bamgbelu has already exceeded his UDA target for the current year. I spoke to Mr Bamgbelu this afternoon, and he has asked that I arrange that date with him at the visit next week. I am assuming that I will see you at the practice at 9.00am, as arranged. Di you want to meet up outside first, or should we go in independently? It might look as if we are 'ganging up' if we met first. Also I gather that parking is a problem. If you need to discuss further, please phone xxxxxxxxx or xxxxxxxxxxxx (2 phone numbers)."

In some jurisdictions, members of the satanic network and their spouses can lie on oath, as long as they do charitable works and/or pay protection money.

February 15, 2007 was before Stephanie Twidale and Richard Hill jointly inspected the surgery of the first ever Negro dentist in Bedford. The wrinkling, ugly, and old racist bat with the ugly, huge ass, which was made uglier by what looked like a G-string, lied under oath.

Some people leave youth unworn and try to dress in it when it does not suit them anymore. What appeared to be G-string did not seem to suit the shapeless (overeating), gigantic, ugly ass of Stephanie Twidale.

They are the best in everything, but only where there are no objective measurements, and there is an element of conflict of interest in that fact.

The following is an email to Mr John Hooper, copied to Dr Richard Hill, Dr Sue Gregory, and Dr Steven Claydon on 09.02.2007:

"John, I telephoned Mr Bamgbelu this morning to confirm arrangements for the New Style Monitoring visit (surgery inspection, patient examinations and radiographs/record card checks) due on Thu 22 Feb. This is our normal procedure, 2 weeks beforehand. Mr Bamgbelu told me that there will be no patients to examine, as he is already 100 UDA over his target, so is doing no more NHS work until 01 April. He refuses to get four patients in for me to see, even if he does not treat them himself that day – he tells me I am welcome to seee private patients, whom he is continuing to treat – but of course that is not part of our remit. He is apparently still expecting me to come and do the surgery inspection at 0900 – Richard Hill is accompanying me for that. I would also be able to do radiograph/record card check part of the process – but no patient would be seen. I imagine you would be unhappy with that situation – I certainly am – but the onus is on you as PCT I am afraid to decide what to do now."

They had been lied to at hone and/or at school that their brains are inside their indisputably superior skin colour, and they know that the Negro will not agree to the baseless and brainless nonsense.

February 9, 2007 was prior to 22 February 2007 when Stephanie Twidale and Richard Hill jointly visited the surgery of the first ever and only Negro dentist in Bedford. She lied unrelentingly under oath.

The legal process seemed to be incompetent art incompetently imitating life.

They seem to agree on everything in secret and play it out in the open as if it were live and real. They select the committee and plant their "people" in it. In the spirit of fairness, they select independents, oftener laymen and always former England young adults, and therefore dull persons. So, they have people in place to deliver the verdicts that they had agreed prior to the hearing.

The satanic network—all for one, one for all. Without objective basis, it awards itself the monopoly of knowledge and lies that it doesn't lie (Psalm 144).

✸ ✸ ✸ ✸ ✸ ✸ ✸

GENERAL DENTAL COUNCIL
FITNESS TO PRACTISE COMMITTEE
Monday 17 November 2008
37 Wimpole Street
London, W1G 8DQ
Chairman – Mr Shiv Pabary
Case of: BAMGBELU, Abiodun Olayinka (Registration No: 69238)
DAY ONE
Transcript of the shorthand notes of T A Reed & Co. Ltd.
Tel No: 01992 465900
TA REED & CO. LTD
GENERAL DENTAL COUNCIL
FITNESS TO PRACTISE COMMITTEE
Monday 17 November 2008 Chairman: Mr Shiv Pabary Committee:
Mrs Catherine Brady
Mrs Mary Harley
Mr Anthony Kravitz
Mr Jacques Lee

Legal Adviser: Mr David Swinstead

NEGRO'S PERPECTIVE:

NORTHAMPTON, ENGLAND: Based on available evidence, GDC-WITNESS, Dr Geraint Evans, Postgraduate Tutor, Oxford, unrelentingly lied under implied oath - Habakkuk 1:4; John 8:44; John 10:10.

A RACIST WHITE CROOK.

CREEPING NORTH KOREA.

FACTS ARE SACRED.

CORBY, ENGLAND: Based on available evidence, GDC-WITNESS, Dr George Rothnie unrelentingly lied under implied oath - Habakkuk 1:4; John 8:44; John 10:10.

A RACIST WHITE CROOK.

CREEPING NORTH KOREA.

FACTS ARE SACRED.

CORBY, ENGLAND: Based on available evidence, GDC-WITNESS, Dr Kevin Atkinson, Scottish Ken, unrelentingly lied under oath - Habakkuk 1:4; John 8:44; John 10:10.

A RACIST WHITE CROOK.

CREEPING NORTH KOREA.

FACTS ARE SACRED.

OXFORD, ENGLAND: Based on available evidence, GDC-WITNESS, British Soldier - Territorial Defence, Dr Stephanie Twidale (TD) unrelentingly lied under oath - Habakkuk 1:4; John 8:44; John

10:10.

A RACIST WHITE CROOK.

CREEPING NORTH KOREA.

FACTS ARE SACRED.

WOLLASTON, ENGLAND: Based on available evidence, GDC-WITNESS, Ms Rachael Bishop, Senior NHS Nurse, unrelentingly lied under oath - Habakkuk 1:4; John 8:44; John 10:10.

A RACIST WHITE CROOK.

CREEPING NORTH KOREA.

FACTS ARE SACRED.

BEDFORD, ENGLAND: Based on available evidence, GDC-INSIDER, Dr Sue Gregory, Officer of the Most Excellent Order of our Empire unrelentingly lied under implied oath - Habakkuk 1:4; John 8:44; John 10:10.

A RACIST WHITE CROOK.

CREEPING NORTH KOREA.

FACTS ARE SACRED.

BEDFORD, ENGLAND: Based on available evidence, GDC-WITNESS, Freemason, Brother, Dr Richard William Hill fabricated reports and unrelentingly lied under oath - Habakkuk 1:4; John 8:44; John 10:10.

A RACIST WHITE CROOK.

CREEPING NORTH KOREA.

FACTS ARE SACRED.

A bastardised, unashamedly mediocre, indiscreetly dishonest, vindictive, potently weaponised, and institutionally RACIST system that his overseen by MASONS (Mediocre Mafia) - Habakkuk.

Then and now, in jurisdictions where the satanic network (Antichrist Racist Freemason) is in charge, their members have power to tell lies under oath.

"The supreme vice is shallowness." Wilde
To convince the Negro and their public (amongst the dullest adult population in the industrialised world according to the OECD), they selected a Member of the British Empire (MBE) as the chairman.

The chairman was Dr Shiv Pabary, MBE, and the token Indian – of tried and tested methods in occupied East and South Africa. He implied that he did not know Dr Stephanie Twidale directly, but he did not state whether he knew her indirectly.

Mrs Catherine Brady, a dentist, admitted, albeit well into the 2008 hearing, that she was very close to two of the three dentist witnesses who testified for the GDC against the lone Negro in their midst. The three dentists who testified against the lone Negro in their midst are:

- Dr Stephanie Twidale, the chief witness for the mediocre, Negrophobic, and corrupt council. At the hearings, she was an employee of the Medical Protection Society, who appointed and instructed David Morris in their seemingly incestuous, racist charade. The sole basis of their power is money. The entire foundation of the money was forged with the proceeds of merciless, racial hatred and fraud: the stealing, carrying, and selling of millions of stolen human beings. Before slavery, there was no council at Wimpole Street; there were only farmlands and feudal agricultural labourers working on stolen land. The gigantic yields of merciless, evil slavery immeasurably transformed wretched serfs. They have reinvented them and fool the foolish with foolishness. In 1720, Wimpole Street yielded only food. Then, those who lived there were fed like battery hens with the proceeds of merciless, racial hatred and fraud.

No brain, natural resources poor, only skin colour that the wearer neither made nor chose, and what else? Pure scam! Some people associate the proceeds of merciless, racial hatred and fraud with their own personal intellect and industry. It is a lie! Slavery and slavery alone transformed wretched agricultural labourers and their descendants! Almost everything was stolen.

Before slavery, what?
"I know of no evil that has ever existed, nor can imagine any evil to exist, worse than the tearing of eighty thousand persons annually from their native land, by a combination of the most civilised nations inhabiting the most enlightened part of the globe, but more especially under the sanction of the laws of that Nation which calls herself the most free and the most happy of them all." – Prime Minister William Pitt the Younger, 1792

"Many Scots masters were considered among the most brutal, with life expectancy on their plantations averaging a mere four years. We worked them to death then simply imported more to keep the sugar and thus the money flowing. Unlike centuries of grief and murder, an apology costs nothing. So what does Scotland have to say?" – Herald Scotland, Ian Bell, columnist, Sunday 28 April 2013

- Dr Richard Hill, NHS, a dull, dishonest, racist, incompetent, and incapable liar and forger. Deluded, they award the monopoly of intellect to themselves, and expect everyone to see them as they see themselves. In 2015 and 1715, Bedfordshire yielded only food; almost everything else was stolen.

- Dr Kevin Atkinson (Scottish Ken), a dull, dishonest, openly jealous, and racist Scotsman. He is an intellectually incompetent and very nasty Scotsman. At grammar school (Jogs), to mercilessly beat a fellow like Kevin Atkinson was sweeter than sex, which was exceedingly rare. Scotsmen mercilessly slaughtered and worked to death more Negroes in the plantations than any other European race. He was down south to make it, and seemed to be raking it in through mediocrity and confusions. Dr Samuel Johnson expected Kevin Atkinson and millions of his type to migrate southwards in search of a better life, but he implied that he expected them to be semi-illiterates and therefore to work in agriculture.

"Agriculture not only gives riches to a nation, but the only riches she can call her own." – Dr Samuel Johnson

"Their (the Scots) learning is like bread in a besieged town: everyone gets a little, but no man gets a full meal." – Dr Samuel Johnson

"Norway, too, has noble wild prospects; and Lapland is remarkable for its prodigious noble wild prospects. But, Sir, let me tell you, the noblest prospect which a Scotchman ever sees, is the high road that leads him to England!" – Dr Samuel Johnson

"Many Scots masters were considered among the most brutal, with life expectancy on their plantations averaging a mere four years. We worked them to death then simply imported more to keep the sugar and thus the money flowing. Unlike centuries of grief and murder, an apology costs nothing. So what does Scotland have to say?" – Herald Scotland, Ian Bell, columnist, Sunday 28 April 2013

"As hard-hearted as a Scot of Scotland." – English saying

"Scotsmen tak a' they can get and a little more if they can."

– Scottish saying Before slavery, what?
Scotsmen were seemingly natural born Negro destroyers and killers.

The Scottish, racist bas****s killed millions of Africans and worked millions more to death during several continuous centuries of merciless, tyrannical cowardice.

Kevin Atkinson's Scottish ancestors were amongst the world champions at using guns or arming others to use guns to mercilessly slaughter millions of unarmed and defenceless Africans. Those who used to like using guns to slaughter Africans or arm others to mercilessly and indiscriminately slaughter innocent human beings should go and use guns to eject Mr Putin from Crimea. Even the Americans wouldn't dare. The merciless, racist, Scottish bas****s are no longer here, but their sadistic genes seem to continue to flow through the veins of some of those who remain here, almost certainly including Kevin Atkinson.

It is a fact and the absolute truth that the foundation of Scotland, almost in its entirety, was forged by the gigantic proceeds of several centuries of merciless, racial hatred and fraud.

"American South is still taken as barbarism's benchmark. Few realise that the behaviour of Scots busy getting rich in the slave-holders' empire was actually worse – routinely worse – than the worst of the cottonocracy. You need only count the corpses.

"By the time slavery was brought to an end in America, the country's 400,000 trafficked people had grown to a population of four million. In the British West Indies, only 670,000 survived from two million imported souls. In the American South, slaves were valuable and bred. We worked them to death then simply imported more to keep the sugar and thus the money flowing.

"Unlike centuries of grief and murder, an apology costs nothing. So what does Scotland have to say?" – Herald Scotland, Ian Bell, columnist, Sunday 28 April 2013

The proceeds of centuries of merciless, racial hatred and fraud kick-started the industrial revolution in Scotland and brought Scottish slave merchants and traders great wealth.

The satanic network is everywhere. It controls almost everything except intellect. Without objective basis, it awards itself the monopoly of knowledge.

"Iain Whyte, author of Scotland and the Abolition of Slavery, insists we have at times ignored our guilty past.

"He said: 'For many years Scotland's historians harboured the illusion that our nation had little to do with the slave trade or plantation slavery.

"'We swept it under the carpet. This was remarkable in the light of Glasgow's wealth coming from tobacco, sugar and cotton, and Jamaica Streets being found in a number of Scottish towns and cities.

"'It is healthy we are now recognising Scotland was very much involved.'

"The industries, which saw Glasgow and much of the country flourish, were built on the back of slavery.

"There were familiar names such as Scot Lyle of Tate and Lyle fame whose fortune was built on slavery. Ewing from Glasgow was the richest sugar producer in Jamaica.

"The stunning Inveresk Lodge in Edinburgh, now open to the public, was bought by James Wedderburn with money earned from 27 years in Jamaica as a notorious slaver.

"The Wee Free Church was founded using profits and donations from

Satanic Network

the slave trade. Even our schools have a dark history. Bathgate Academy was built from money willed by John Newland, a renowned slave master and Dollar Academy has a similar foundation.

"For many years, the goods and profits from West Indian slavery were unloaded at Kingston docks in Glasgow.

"Leith in Edinburgh and Glasgow were popular ports from which ambitious Scottish men sailed to make their fortunes as slave masters." – Herald Scotland, Ian Bell, columnist, Sunday 28 , April 2013

Feudal agricultural labourers from mainland Europe dispossessed/robbed aboriginal Britons. They've been transformed and reinvented by slavery.

Mrs Catherine Brady, the stout cougar, built like a barn door and carrying three-fourths deflated "elephants" on her chest with little or no milk, was good friends and/or village neighbours with the dull, verifiably dishonest, and racist Kevin Atkinson and Stephanie Twidale. She implied that she did not know Richard Hill.

"Truth, Sir, is a cow which will yield such people no more milk, and so they are gone to milk the bull." – Dr Samuel Johnson

If the racist "cow" had any milk, it must be very little, as she was mediocre, dishonest, seemingly a hereditary racist, and/or confused.

The remaining members of the committee were Mrs Mary Harley (lay member, judge), Mr Anthony Kravitz (dentist member of the committee), and Mr Jaques Lee (lay member, judge).

So, the GDC chose the jury without any input from their Negro victim. They are above board, so Negro shouldn't worry, especially as civilised people do not tell lies and they do not steal except by mistake. The Right Honourable Dianne Abbott's ancestors must have believed that, and for their belief they spent several entire generations picking cotton and cutting cane, and millions were mercilessly slaughtered; millions more were worked to death, only because they were the only ones with guns, as some of their victims were created intellectually superior to their merciless, racist captors.

I am Abiodun Olayinka Bamgbelu only because my ancestors were born free and lived freely until the Europeans found us in the fifteenth century. European Christians and those they armed slaughtered too many in our tribe (IJEBU), only a walking distance from the Atlantic Ocean, but they did not carry many, as our people believed that white people were after their meat (Cannibals).

Mr David Swinstead's ancestors used made-in-Birmingham guns to slaughter many in our tribe in the African bush, and armed other with extremely feared made-in-Birmingham guns and the hell fire that they used to spit, but Mr David Swinstead's ancestors, who were extremely cruel and merciless, racist bas****s, did not carry many, as our ancestors chose to die in Africa rather than end up on white men's dinner tables as roast beef.

Mr David Swinstead seemed to have a grossly exaggerated self-view. The view of those whose ancestors were never carried is oftener different from those who had been genetically modified through several centuries of sadistic, merciless, racial hatred and terrorism on the plantations. They are likelier to believe that Mr David Swinstead is superior because of the skin colour that he neither made not chose, or that the riches, which are not the yield of the land, are derived from intellect and industry and are therefore virtuous. Only stupid people and concomitantly shallow people reason like that.

"The supreme vice is shallowness" – Wilde

"There is no sin except stupidity." – Oscar Wilde
"American South is still taken as barbarism's benchmark. Few realise that the behaviour of Scots busy getting rich in the slave-holders' empire was actually worse – routinely worse – than the worst of the cottonocracy. You need only count the corpses.

"By the time slavery was brought to an end in America, the country's 400,000 trafficked people had grown to a population of four million. In the British West Indies, only 670,000 survived from two million imported souls. In the American South, slaves were valuable and bred. We worked them to death then simply imported more to keep the sugar and thus the money flowing.

"Unlike centuries of grief and murder, an apology costs nothing. So what does Scotland have to say?" Herald Scotland, Ian Bell, columnist, Sunday 28 April 2013

"When we consider the vastness of the continent of Africa; when we reflect how all other countries have for some centuries past been advancing in happiness and civilisation; when we think how in this same period all improvement in Africa has been defeated by her intercourse with Britain; when we reflect that it was we ourselves that have degraded them to that wretched brutishness and barbarity which we now plead as the justification for our guilt; how the slave trade has enslaved their minds, blackened their character, and sunk them so low in the scale of animal beings that some think apes are of a higher class, and fancy the Orang–outang has given them the go-by. What mortification must we feel at having so long neglected to think of our guilt, or attempt at reparation! It seems indeed, as if we had determined to forbear from all interference until the measure of folly and wickedness was so full and complete, until the policy which eventually belongs to vice was become so plain and glaring that not an individual in this country should refuse to join the abolition. It seems as if we had waited until the persons most interested should be tired out with the folly nefariousness of the trade, and should unite in petitioning against it." – William Wilberforce, 1789

"The grand object of all European traders in kidnapped and stolen Africans was - money, money, money; money was their god! In Africa, the poor wretched natives, blessed with the most fertile and luxuriant soil, are rendered so much the more miserable by the Christians' (European traders in stolen Africans) abominable traffic for slaves and the horrid cruelty and treachery of the petty [African] Kings. The Africans kings were encouraged by their European (Christian) customers who carry them strong liquors to enflame their madness and powder and bad fire-arms to furnish them with the hellish means of killing and kidnapping. But enough - it is a subject that sours my blood." – Ignatius Sancho, 1778

"It was our arms in the river of Cameroon, put into the hands of the trader, that furnished him with the means of pushing his trade; and I have no more doubt that they are British arms, put into the hands of Africans, which promote universal war and desolation that I can doubt their having done so in that individual instance. I have shown how great is the enormity of this evil, even on the supposition that we take only convicts and prisoners of war. But take the subject in another way, and how does it stand? Think of 80,000 persons carried out of their native country by we know not what means! For crimes imputed! For light or inconsiderable faults! For debts perhaps! For crime of witchcraft! Or a thousand other weak or scandalous pretexts! Reflect on 80,000 persons annually taken off! There is something in the horror of it that surpasses all bounds of imagination." – Prime Minister William Pitt the Younger, 1792

So, associating gigantic yields of several centuries of merciless racial hatred and unrelenting evil terrorism against unarmed and defenceless Africans is continuing deceit. There was no CNN or BBC then, and as shepherds did not bring stolen human beings home, moron sheep were deceived into believing that they were fed with the yield of virtue by paragons of wisdom. It is a lie! Mr David Swinstead's ancestors were merciless, racist bas****s; they were evil armed robbers, people stealers, carriers, and sellers, and thieves. That is the truth.

"Truth is the chief attribute of the Deity." – Lord Byron

"Those who have robbed have also lied." – Dr Samuel Johnson corroborating prophet Habakkuk

CHAPTER 10

Council chambers, 19 November 2008:
THE LEGAL ADVISER (MR DAVID SWINSTEAD): Mr Morris, can you make it absolutely clear for everybody that I think you are referring to the document behind divider 21, and it is the Schedule Record of Practice which is the second part, is that right?

NEGRO'S PERSPECTIVE:

Apart from Dr Shiv Pabary, who seemed far advanced in his metamorphosis of becoming an advanced Caucasian and European, and Mr Lee, who was Chinese-like, everyone else was Caucasian (not necessarily genetically aboriginal Britons; for example, Nigel Lawson is genetically from Latvia and Mr David Swinstead looked like a Russian), everyone else was advanced Caucasian and European, and everyone seemed at one. The verdict seemed agreed, and the hearing seemed to be incompetent art incompetently imitating life. They were white supremacists, racist thugs, and cowards.

So, "everybody" depicted the lone Negro in their midst.

They were very 'fake polite', but they were RACIST CROOKS.

DAVID MORRIS: That is right, sir.
THE LEGAL ADVISER (MR DAVID SWINSTEAD): Sorry, do I look behind it?
DAVID MORRIS: Yes, if you look behind tab 21. Richard Hill sent an e-mail to his colleagues at the PCT, Bedford PCT.
THE LEGAL ADVISER (MR DAVID SWINSTEAD): It is page 3

behind page 21, I think you have said. There is a table and there is a reference there which I think you suggested to Mr Hill was not actually a report of Mr Bamgbelu's practice, is that right?

DAVID MORRIS: That is right. It was a report, we have the report here.

NEGRO'S PERSPECTIVE:

The question by David Swinstead: "There is a table and there is a reference there which I think you suggested to Mr Hill was not actually a report of Mr Bamgbelu's practice, is that right?"

The answer by David Morris: "That is right. It was a report, we have the report here." Acerebral rot!

The whole show was designed to spin me. Their children will be stupider and nastier; our children are in trouble.

"Nothing that you will learn in the course of your studies will be of the slightest possible use to you in after life – save only this – if you work hard and diligently you should be able to detect when a man is talking rot, and that, in my view, is the main, if not the sole, purpose of education." – J.A. Smith, Oxford University Professor, Moral Philosophy

* * * * * * *

THE LEGAL ADVISER (MR DAVID SWINSTEAD): So the Committee understand what the status of D5 is?

DAVID MORRIS: It is my fault, I should have clarified this with Mr Hill yesterday, but D5 is a report drafted by Mr Hill in error, which he accepted yesterday, in error attributing it as an inspection of Mr Bamgbelu's practice at Bromham Road Bedford. When, in fact, it was not, and the substance of the contents were from another practice.

NEGRO'S PERSPOECTIVE:

OYINBO OLE: WHITE THIEVES: HABAKKUK.

Mistakes do happen, don't they?

"It is my fault, I should have clarified this with Mr Hill yesterday." – David Morris

By similar mistake, "civilised and Christian Scotchmen" slaughtered millions of innocent Africans and mercilessly worked millions more to death.

David Morris, a closeted racist thug and coward that seemed propped up by crude oil and gas money (the land on which he was born yields and yielded only food) in the same way as his ancestors were for centuries sustained by the gigantic yields of merciless, evil, racial hatred and fraud, should go and blow his rot to the likes of the Right Honourable Dianne Abbott. She might believe him, as her ancestors were stolen, carried, and sold, and her genes had been tamed by centuries of merciless, racist brutality on cane and cotton plantations by the extremely nasty, merciless, racist bastard ancestors of David Morris.

I do not believe anything that comes out of his mouth. That is why I am Abiodun Olayinka Bamgbelu; my ancestors were never carried.

The sole basis of the power that David Morris displayed was money, and the entire foundation of the money is the gigantic yields of several centuries of merciless, racial hatred and fraud.

"I know of no evil that has ever existed, nor can imagine any evil to exist, worse than the tearing of eighty thousand persons annually from their native land, by a combination of the most civilised nations inhabiting the most enlightened part of the globe, but more especially under the sanction of the laws of that Nation which calls herself the most free and the most happy of them all." – Prime Minister William Pitt the Younger

"Many Scots masters were considered among the most brutal, with life expectancy on their plantations averaging a mere four years. We worked them to death then simply imported more to keep the sugar and thus the money flowing. Unlike centuries of grief and murder, an apology costs nothing. So what does Scotland have to say?" – Herald Scotland, Ian Bell, columnist, Sunday 28 April 2013

Before slavery, what?

"Those who have robbed have also lied." – Dr Samuel Johnson

corroborating prophet Habakkuk

* * * * *

THE LEGAL ADVISER (MR DAVID SWINSTEAD): Was there a visit to another practice?
DAVID MORRIS: That is how he put it yesterday.
NEGRO'S PERSPECTIVE:
David Morris lied on oath. In some jurisdictions, members of the racist, satanic network can tell lies on oath.
David Morris implicitly told Richard Hill to state that he visited another practice in Bedford on 22 February 2007 and carried out a follow up visit at the same practice on an unknown date.
OYINBO OLE: WHITE THIEVES: HABAKKUK.
Then racist white bastards righteously carried and sold millions of stolen children of defenceless poor people; now, they carry natural resources.
SUBSTITUTION: FRAUDULENT EMANCIPATION.
"Moderation is a virtue only among those who are thought to have found alternatives." Henry Kissinger.

* * * * * *

David Morris cross examined Richard Hill on 18 November 2008:
DAVID MORRIS: And (b) the concerns listed there were not relevant to Mr Bamgbelu's practice.
RICHARD HILL: Not at all.
DAVID MORRIS: They were another practice.
RICHARD HILL: They were another practice that did not refer to him. It did in error, but it was not about him.

NEGRO'S PERSPECTIVE:

OYINBO OLE: WHITE THIEVES: HABAKKUK.
Defence or Prosecution, whites will always side with whites.
If David Morris goes to Peckham in London and finds a bruno with gold teeth and feeds her the rot supra, the bitch wouldn't discern that

he was a racist bastard, a descendant of merciless, evil racist bastards, who seemingly on cue told Richard Hill to state that he visited another practice on 22.07.2004 and carried out a follow up at the same practice on an unknown date.

David Morris was an incompetent liar. Not all liars are racists, but all racists are malicious liars.

* * * * *

DAVID MORRIS: So (a) there was no visit in July 2004.
RICHARD HILL: No, it was April 2003 which we discussed was, again, a pastoral type of visit.
DAVID MORRIS: And (b) the concerns listed there were not relevant to Mr Bamgbelu's practice.
RICHARD HILL: Not at all.
DAVID MORRIS: They were another practice.
RICHARD HILL: They were another practice that did not refer to him. It did in error, but it was not about him.

NEGRO'S PERSPECTIVE:
So, David Morris, a former England young adult and shepherd of England young adults, told Richard Hill, almost on cue, to state that the report of 22.07.2004 and the follow up of unknown date belonged to another practice.

Richard Hill had never independently made such a reckless statement, as he might have suspected (correctly) that the Negro would unpick the rot. David Morris was a dunce. Some have said he was a member of the racist, satanic network, which Mr Lagbaja or somebody else stated was a refuge of privileged dullards propped up by the gigantic yields of several centuries of merciless, racist evil and naked fraud.

If one were to Google "David Morris barrister," the following amongst others would come up: Christ Is Our God: It Is Mathematics: Deducible Originalism by Yinka Bamgbelu (2015). Mr David Morris, English lawyer/barrister: "It is my fault, I should have clarified this with Mr Hill yesterday, but D5 is a report drafted by Mr Hill in error."

If David Morris were indeed a member of a racist, satanic network, the next time he goes to their secret meeting, he should give other members pen and paper and ask them to write a short essay, no more than a thousand words, titled "My Day" in their handwriting. If, unlike Stephanie Twidale (TD), Nicholas Peacock, Jonathan Anslow, and the Right Honourable Gordon Brown, they could write legibly, it would become immediately apparent that some of them are created and born morons. The postgraduate tutor for Oxford and Wessex Deaneries, Geraint Evans, from the valleys of Wales or near there, implied that his father and grandfather were members of the merciless, evil, racist satanic network.

"Mr Bamgbelu has sent me lengthy e mails following the meeting and has copied me correspondence he has sent to others and including his indemnity society. He has gone to great lengths to question my integrity and honesty. The records of the meetings he was given were in note form, this was made clear to him. He has used facts such as the miss spelling of the dean's surname and my stating a meeting took place at 12 pm not 12 noon to undermine their value." – Geraint Evans, postgraduate tutor for Oxford and Wessex Deaneries

F****** Miss Spelling was a shepherd of England young adults.
"FAILING SCHOOLS AND A BATTLE FOR BRITAIN: This was the day the British education establishment's 50-year betrayal of the Nation's children lay starkly exposed in all its ignominy. After testing 166,000 people in 24 education systems, the Organisation for Economic Cooperation and Development (OECD) finds that England young adults are amongst the least literate and numerate in the industrialised world." – The Daily Mail, 09.01.2013

Shepherds of morons are likelier to be morons too.

OYINBO OLE: WHITE THIEVES: HABAKKUK.
David Morris of Outer Temple Chambers, Strand, London is a top

former England young adult and a shepherd of England young adults. If the bottommost part of a whole is world class bottommost, it is very unlikely that the topmost part of that whole will be world class topmost.

"Sometimes people don't want to hear the truth because they don't want their illusions destroyed." – Friedrich Nietzsche

"Throughout the discussion of the notes he made derogatory comments about the wording and accuracy. He suggested that they were written some time after the visits and that my memory was inaccurate. The notes as stated previously were written within 24 hours of each meeting when fresh in my memory. They may not have been well written from a grammatical point of view, but I am confident I had not forgotten any of the facts." – Geraint Evans, the Welsh Dunce the Younger and postgraduate tutor for Oxford and Wessex Deaneries of Mediocre Great England (MGE)

Pretty extraordinary!

Geraint Evans, the postgraduate tutor for Oxford and Wessex Deaneries, was an accurate reflection of the intellect and integrity of Helen Falcon, a not atypical "fish and chips" postgraduate dean within Mediocre Great England (MGE).

Mon, 8 Mar 2010 20:20
Re Meeting 9th March
From George Rothnie georgerothnie@hotmail.com To adeolacole adeolacole@aol.com

Hi Ola,

We are scheduled to meet tomorrow evening at my surgery about 5.30ish. Unfortunately something has cropped up which necessytates me having to postpone the meeting. I'm really sorry it's such short notice.

I will contact you in the week to arrange another date.

Once agaim my apologies.

George

George Rothnie (Scottish George) was appointed by Helen Falcon who, like Nigel Lawson (former chancellor), is a genetic Eastern European with a camouflage English name. Nigel Lawson is genetically Estonian, and Helen Falcon is allegedly genetically Czechoslovakian.

Nigel Lawson, Helen Falcon, Dianne Abbott, Chris Eubanks, Ed and

David Milliband, and almost everyone else except Michael Portillo have discarded or lost their real fathers' names and have abandoned or forgotten their real mothers' tongues. In the metamorphosis of extinction, language is the first to disappear.

Awon omo ale ti won ko gbo ede baba nla won!

"To disagree with three-fourths of the British public on all points is one of the first elements of sanity, one of the deepest consolations in all moments of spiritual doubt." – Oscar Wilde

"The English think that incompetence is the same thing as sincerity." – Quentin Crisp

"Truth, Sir, is a cow which will yield such people no more milk, and so they are gone to milk the bull." – Dr Samuel Johnson

I am Abiodun Olayinka Bamgbelu. Even if I Anglicised or completely discarded the name of my ancestors, I could not change the colour of my face.

I'm white inside, but that doesn't help my case, as I am judged by merciless, racist bastards by the colour of my face.

"Michael Jackson would have been found guilty if he'd been black." – Jo Brand

George Rothnie, Scottish dunce the elder, albeit postgraduate dean deputy of Oxford and Wessex Deaneries and a shepherd of England's young adults, is a natural born Negro destroyer and a direct descendant of Scottish natural born Negro killers.

Scotchman George Rothnie's ancestors, almost certainly duller than he, at least on paper as they did not go to Edinburgh University, were the most brutal and most efficient killers of Negroes during the centuries of gigantically profitable evil, which slavery was. Ironically, George Rothnie's ancestors were also very efficient sex machines, as the bastards raped millions of Negro maidens and beautiful Negro boys, and fathered tens of thousands of mulattoes (bastards) on the slave plantations in the West Indies, America, and Africa.

The merciless, evil, racist bastards are no longer here, but based upon very proximate observations of George Rothnie and Kevin Atkinson, it is my honest belief that their sadistic genes continue to flow through the veins of some of their direct descendants that remain here.

"American South is still taken as barbarism's benchmark. Few realise that the behaviour of Scots busy getting rich in the slave-holders' empire was actually worse – routinely worse – than the worst of the cottonocracy. You need only count the corpses.

Before slavery, the Scots did not invent anything.

"The fact is that civilisation requires slaves. The Greeks were quite right there. Unless there are slaves to do the ugly, horrible, uninteresting work, culture and contemplation become almost impossible." – Oscar Wilde

So, to associate affluence whose entire foundation is racial hatred and fraud with intellect and industry is spin, which spins the least literate and numerate adult population in the industrialised world, but it is insufficient to spin the whole world.

Dr Samuel Johnson accurately foresaw that Scotchmen would migrate to England in search of a better life, but as he also stated that they were functional semi-illiterates (like George Rothnie), he implied that he expected them to work in agriculture.

"Agriculture not only gives riches to a nation, but the only riches she can call her own." – Dr Samuel Johnson
"Their (the Scots) learning is like bread in a besieged town: everyone gets a little, but no man gets a full meal." – Dr Samuel Johnson
"Norway, too, has noble wild prospects; and Lapland is remarkable for its prodigious noble wild prospects. But, Sir, let me tell you, the noblest prospect which a Scotchman ever sees, is the high road that leads him to England!" – Dr Samuel Johnson

CHAPTER 11

It is the truth that in his withdrawal statement of 16.10.2008, Richard Hill neither stated nor implied that he visited another practice on 22.07.2004 and conducted a follow up at the same practice on another day. He stated as follows:

"I, RICHARD HILL, c/o Bedfordshire Primary Care Trust, Gilbert Hitchcock

House, 21 Kimbolton Road, Bedford, MK40 2AW WILL SAY AS FOLLOWS:

"1. I make this statement supplemental to my statement dated 23.09.2008.

"2. I attach as Exhibit SRWH1 a copy of my report dated 22.07.2004, I attach a synopsis of practice visits that makes reference to a practice visit to MR BAMGBELU's practice at 52, Bromham Road, Bedford, MK40 2QG in July 2004. The document is incorrect in recording that the inspection took place in 2004. No such inspection in fact took place" (Richard Hill, 16.10.2008).

"No such inspection in fact took place" is objective and unambiguous.

Again, to orientate the reader: David Morris was a barrister that was appointed and instructed by the Medical Protection Society (MPS), and he who pays the piper dictates the tune.

Stephanie Twidale (TD), who together with Richard Hill inspected the surgery of the first ever and only Negro dentist in Bedford on 22.02.2007, was an employee of the Medical Protection Society (MPS) and also the chief witness for the GDC in their mediocre, indiscreetly dishonest, racist, and Negrophobic charade.

David Morris, the "pretend defence," was a fool and a dishonest, racist thug. He desired to help his kindred, Richard Hill, as he detected the glaring absurdity in the immortalised, brainless construction of his equally, seemingly hereditary racist kindred.

If "no such practice inspection took place" on 22.07.2004, it concomitantly means that there was no follow up visit on an unknown date, which means that the reports were racist fabrications for the first ever and only Negro dentist in Bedford.

Richard Hill would never have voluntarily stated that he visited another practice on 22.07.2004 and carried out a follow up visit at the same practice on an unknown date, as he might have sensed where the mines were laid if he were to immortalise such a statement. He took the cue from David Morris, probably because he spoke with an upper class English accent and was wearing brand new shoes and a very expensive looking suit.

Richard Hill grossly overrated David Morris.

David Morris, the racist and dishonest imposter and seemingly schooled expert of deception, was too stupid and too shallow to consider the following:

"There is no sin except stupidity." – Oscar Wilde

"The supreme vice is shallowness." – Oscar Wilde

David Morris, England class barrister, seemed too dull to discern the absurdities in his incompetent mendacity.

Oyinbo olodo! Oyinbo ode!

Richard Hill stated that he was allegedly asked by John Hooper (of the NHS) to provide all his reports for the alleged impending Health Commission visit. Sue Gregory, Charlotte Dowling Goodson, Stephanie Twidale, and John Hooper made no mention of the alleged Health Commission visit, and there is no evidence of the alleged request for reports for the alleged visit.

"In 2006 the Healthcare Commission carried out a visit to Bedfordshire PCT and I was asked to provide all my practice visit reports. While collating this information, I noticed that some inspection reports were missing, which included an inspection of Mr Bamgbelu's practice on 02.04.2003. Around that time my department moved and it is possible that some reports had been lost during the move. I did locate some of my draft handwritten notes and referred to these to prepare my inspection report dated 22.07.2004 for MR BAMGBELU's practice which at the time, I understood to be a correct and accurate record of my inspection. Following another move to different premises, I went through some of my files and found my correct inspection report dated 02.04.2003 which is exhibited to my September 2008 statement as RWH11." – Richard Hill, 16.10.2008

Richard Hill lied, and did so incompetently. He immortalised mendacity for eternity. Dishonesty on record is a very accurate measure of intelligence. Richard Hill is a very accurate reflection of the intellect and integrity of Sue Gregory.

"Politicians never rise beyond the level of misrepresentation, and actually condescend to prove, to discuss, to argue. How different from the temper of a true liar, with her frank, fearless statements, her superb irresponsibility, her healthy, natural disdain of proof of any kind! After all what is a fine lie? Simply that which is its own evidence. If a woman is sufficiently unimaginative to produce evidence in support of a lie, she might just as well speak the truth at once. No! Politicians won't do. Something may, perhaps, be urged on behalf of the BAR. The mantle of the Sophist has fallen on its members. Their feigned ardours and unrealistic rhetoric are delightful. They can make the worse appear the better cause, as though they were fresh from Leontine schools, and have been known to wrest from the reluctance juries triumphant verdicts of acquittal for their clients." – The Decay of Lying: A Protest by Oscar Wilde

Richard Hill produced nineteen reports for nineteen principal dentists and their dental surgeries, all in Bedford. He sent the reports to John Hooper three weeks after he asked for reports based entirely upon the demand of Dr Stephanie Twidale.

The following is an email from Mr John Hooper of Bedfordshire PCT

(BPCT) to Dr Sue Gregory and Dr Richard Hill and copied to Mrs Charlotte Dowling, all of the BPCT: "Richard (Hill), Stephanie Twidale called us a few weeks ago about DRS visits and Charlotte prioritised Mr Bamgbelu's practice; Stephanie has been in touch a few times as her colleagues had highlighted issues from a similar practice in Northants and they would like to review report etc etc prior to visiting. She also wanted to know if there has been a dental inspection there at all and I did not know the answer . . . Cue Richard have you carried out an inspection at this practice, please could you advise Stephanie when she contacts you, and would it be possible to see our reports so we can be more proactive with any other queries. Thanks. With kind regards, John Hooper" (15.08.2006).

Three weeks later, on 06.09.2006, Richard Hill produced nineteen reports. In his production of the reports, he allegedly realised that a minimum of two and a maximum of three reports were missing, and one of them belonged to the lone Negro in their midst (the first ever and only Negro dentist in Bedford).

Had David Morris's mama sent him to schools in Mediocre Great England (MGE) where critical reasoning was taught as a subject, he would have detected the absurdities in the extraordinary construction.

It was extraordinary and dishonest that in October 2008 when Richard Hill signed the withdrawal statement, he was not certain of the number of reports that were allegedly missing in the summer of 2006, when he was asked for reports.

Had David Morris's mama sent him to schools in Mediocre Great England (MGE) where critical reasoning was taught as a subject, he would have realised that based upon statements by Richard Hill, all the missing reports belonged to the first ever and only Negro dentist in Bedford:

The missing report of 02.04.2003 belonged to the Negro.

The missing report of 22.07.2004, which was created from handwritten drafts, which contained other matters, belonged to the Negro.

• The missing report of the follow up of the 22.07.2004 visit, which was created from handwritten drafts, which contained other matters, belonged to the Negro.

David Morris, the dull and dishonest England class barrister, was too dull to detect the absurdity in the brainless construction.

"Nothing that you will learn in the course of your studies will be of the slightest possible use to you in after life – save only this – if you work hard and diligently you should be able to detect when a man is talking rot, and that, in my view, is the main, if not the sole, purpose of education." – J.A. Smith, Oxford University
Professor, Moral Philosophy

If David Morris's mama brought up the England class barristo to believe that the brain is in the skin, she lied to him. Many of the millions of Africans that his merciless, racist thug ancestors viciously slaughtered and armed others to slaughter, and the millions more that were sadistically worked to death, were created intellectually superior to their "Christian and civilised" European captors and persecutors.

Oyinbo olodo! Oyinbo ode!

He is the brainless descendant of racist thugs, armed robbers, and thieves who used guns to dominate and terrorise for centuries unarmed and defenceless Africans who were not in the position to return fire for fire, and die fighting, but with dignity in defence of their children, women, and meagre possessions.

A nrin nile, inu bi elesin. A nje fo sun, inu bi eleran!

"Many Scots masters were considered among the most brutal, with life expectancy on their plantations averaging a mere four years. We worked them to death then simply imported more to keep the sugar and thus the money flowing. Unlike centuries of grief and murder, an apology costs nothing. So what does Scotland have to say?" – Herald Scotland, Ian Bell, columnist, Sunday 28 April 2013

"Even if these miserable beings were proved guilty of every crime before you take them off, ought we not to take upon ourselves the office of executioners? And even if we condescend so far, still can we be justified in acquiring them in exchange for our guns, carrying and selling them for great profits, unless we have clear proof that they are criminals? But, if we go much further, if we ourselves tempt them to sell their fellow creatures to us, we may rest assured that they will take care to provide by every possible method a supply of victims increasing in proportions to our demand. Can we, then, hesitate in deciding whether the wars in Africa are their wars or ours? It was our arms in the river of Cameroon, put into the hands of the trader, that furnished him with the means of pushing his trade; and I have no more doubt that they are British arms, put into the hands of Africans, which promote universal war and desolation that I can doubt their having done so in that individual instance. I have shown how great is the enormity of this evil, even on the supposition that we take only convicts and prisoners of war. But take the subject in another way, and how does it stand? Think of 80,000 persons carried out of their native country by we know not what means! For crimes imputed! For light or inconsiderable faults! For debts perhaps! For crime of witchcraft! Or a thousand other weak or scandalous pretexts! Reflect on 80,000 persons annually taken off! There is something in the horror of it that surpasses all bounds of imagination. Admitting that there exists in Africa something like to Courts of justice; yet what an office of humiliation and meanness is it in us, to take upon ourselves to carry into execution the iniquitous sentences of such courts, as if we also were strangers to all religion and to the first principles of justice! But that country, it is said, has been in some degree civilised, and civilised by us. It is said that they have gained some knowledge of the principles of justice." – Prime Minister William Pitt the Younger, 1792

"In 2006 the Healthcare Commission carried out a visit to Bedfordshire PCT and I was asked to provide all my practice visit reports. While collating this information, I noticed that some inspection reports were missing, which included an inspection of Mr Bamgbelu's practice on 02.04.2003. Around that time my department moved and it is possible that some reports had been lost during the move. I did locate some of my draft handwritten notes and referred to these to prepare my inspection report dated 22.07.2004 for MR BAMGBELU's practice which at the time, I understood to be a correct and accurate record of my inspection. Following another move to different premises, I went through some of my files and found my correct inspection report dated 02.04.2003 which is exhibited to my September 2008 statement as RWH11." – Richard Hill, 16.10.2008

So, Richard Hill used a handwritten draft to create two reports (22.07.2004 and follow up of unknown date) as a replacement for a single missing report of 02.04.2003.

"Around that time my department moved and it is possible that some reports had been lost during the move. I did locate some of my draft handwritten notes and referred to these to prepare my inspection report dated 22.07.2004 for MR BAMGBELU's practice which at the time, I understood to be a correct and accurate record of my inspection. Following another move to different premises, I went through some of my files and found my correct inspection report dated 02.04.2003 which is exhibited to my September 2008 statement as RWH11." – Richard Hill, 16.10.2008

Had David Morris's mama sent him to schools in Mediocre Great England where critical reasoning was taught as a subject, he would have detected the absurdity in Richard Hill's statement, that he lost or misplaced the single report of 02.04.2003 and used two allegedly handwritten drafts of two missing or lost reports of 2004 (visit of 22.07.2004 and follow up of unknown date), which contained other matters not in the main body of the reports, to reconstitute the entire reports of 2004 (visit and follow up) as a replacement for the similarly missing or lost, but single, 2003 report.

Reductio ad absurdum!
Oyinbo olodo! Oyinbo ode!

According to Richard Hill, the following reports were missing or lost: The main report for 02.04.2003, which concerned a single visit to the surgery of the first ever and only Negro dentist in Bedford; the usual handwritten draft report for 02.04.2003, which concerned a single visit to the surgery of the first ever and only Negro dentist in Bedford; and the main report for 22.07.2004 and follow up report, which concerned the visit of 22.07.2004 and a follow up of unknown date, to the surgery of the first ever and only Negro dentist in Bedford.

The handwritten draft report for 22.07.2004 and handwritten draft follow up report, which concerned the visit of 22.07.2004 and a follow up of unknown date to the surgery of the first ever and only Negro dentist in Bedford, were found. Hurrah!

Had David Morris's mama sent him to schools in Mediocre Great England (MGE) where critical reasoning was taught as a subject, he would have realised that he endorsed imbecility by Richard Hill, a racist rotter blower and descendant of killers, stealers, carriers, and sellers of millions of stolen Africans.

Awon oyinbo ole! Awon oyinbo olosa! Awon oyinbo jaguda! Whenever they slaughtered, they dispossessed, and wherever they robbed, they took possession. They stole everything from almost everyone and everywhere.

Richard Hill was dull, dishonest, and racist. He was an accurate reflection of Sue Gregory.

David Morris was dull, dishonest, and racist. He seemed to be a reflection of the English bar.
It is a fact and the absolute truth that Richard Hill, Sue Gregory, the NHS, Davis Morris, and the English bar are sections of the UK society.
"All sections of UK society are institutionally racist." – Sir Bernard Hogan-Howe, London Metropolitan Police

David Morris cross examined Richard Hill in the council chambers on 18 November 2008:
DAVID MORRIS: Just in terms of the April 2003 visit, I think you have mentioned the Health Care Commission and you were asked to provide details of all your practice visit reports back in 2006.
RICHARD HILL: Yes.
DAVID MORRIS: At that time I think some of your inspection visit reports were missing.
RICHARD HILL: Two or three were missing. The reason was and the reason I suspect why that was missing was because we had moved office,

I had moved office in 2002, 2004 and 2006 and the problem is that I work for one session a week and I am at the office quite often only once every other week; the other time I'm on the road visiting. What happens is that when there's a move, other people are responsible for putting all my files into boxes and then re-filing them at the other location simply because I'm not there.

DAVID MORRIS: So when we look at the 2003 report that we have behind tab 20, it had got lost and is it the case that this is a contemporaneous document—

RICHARD HILL: Yes.

DAVID MORRIS: —or might it have been a document reconstituted from memory following the loss of an earlier document?

RICHARD HILL: This would have been contemporaneous. Well, when I say contemporaneous, what I would do, without support, would be to make some notes and then complete it normally the next day. This was carried out of an evening. We try to be flexible. Most of our inspections/visits are carried out at lunch time and most practitioners are happy for that; it means that we can actually have myself and one or two PCT members of staff visit as well so that we can have, if you like, a holistic approach to the whole practice, not just seeing if people comply but trying to sort of find ways in which we can support the practitioner in the future. So it is a multifaceted approach. In this particular case, we visited in the evening because Mr Bamgbelu was finding that much more convenient. I don't know whether that was because he was at dual locations he could only make it in the evening, but we would normally do it lunch time. Unfortunately, in those circumstances you do not get any support because people finish at 5 o'clock and I go straight from practice. I finish in my practice probably mid afternoon and then I arrange for that visit to be carried out in the evening.

DAVID MORRIS: So this visit that you have documented here behind tab 20, you would have had this pro forma with you, would you?

RICHARD HILL: Yes, I would take it with me.

DAVID MORRIS: Because you now have this pro forma, would there be any need to make any notes?

RICHARD HILL: I would make sort of relevant notes which are not covered by these, sort of anything to do with dentist problems, worries, that sort of thing, concerns.

NEGRO'S PERSPECTIVE:
Again, it is impossible to create the entire reports of 2004 (visit and follow-up) from handwritten drafts which contained other matters, albeit "relevant notes which are not covered by these, sort of anything to do with dentist problems, worries, that sort of thing, concerns."

Dull, dishonest, and racist England class barrister David Morris attached himself to incompetent mendacity for eternity.

Dr Stephen Hawking implied that boys in his school (not all) who went on to become barristers were morons, as they were implicitly duller than those who did biology (Dr Richard Dawkins), who he, upon very proximate observation, adjudged to be the least bright.

"In my school, the brightest boys did math and physics, the less bright did physics and chemistry, and the least bright did biology. I wanted to do math and physics, but my father made me do chemistry because he thought there would be no jobs for mathematicians." – Dr Stephen Hawking

David Morris was a dull, dishonest, and racist England class barrister that seemed less bright than the least bright who did biology (Dr Richard Dawkins). Some of the brightest barristers go on to become to become judges.

Many of the millions of our ancestors that David Morris's ancestors, merciless, racist thugs and evil bastards, mercilessly slaughtered and armed others to viciously kill and work to death, were created intellectually superior by Almighty God.

"Many Scots masters were considered among the most brutal, with life expectancy on their plantations averaging a mere four years. We worked them to death then simply imported more to keep the sugar and thus the money flowing. Unlike centuries of grief and murder, an apology costs nothing. So what does Scotland have to say?" – Herald Scotland, Ian Bell, columnist, Sunday 28 April 2013

Dr Anand Kamath was not worked to death; he was hounded to death.

THE LEGAL ADVISER (MR DAVID SWINSTEAD):
Effectively, so that the address is incorrect because it is a different

surgery, is that right?

DAVID MORRIS: The address is incorrect, the name of the practitioner is incorrect?

THE LEGAL ADVISER (MR DAVID SWINSTEAD): The name of the practitioner is incorrect?

DAVID MORRIS: Yes. He listed, when being chased for previous inspections he listed it in that schedule, and he accepted yesterday that there was no such visit in 2004.

THE CHAIRMAN (DR SHIV PABARY): This was not put to Mr Hill yesterday.

DAVID MORRIS: The actual report was not, but we went through the schedule, but for completeness I should have put it to him yesterday. (To the witness) You have not seen that before and you did not have any discussion with Mr Hill about it?

DR STEPHANIE TWIDALE: None at all.

NEGRO'S PERSPECTIVE:
David Morris, the dull, dishonest, and racist England class barrister (some barristers go on to become judges), the descendant of merciless, racist stealers, carriers, and sellers of millions of stolen human beings, was too dull to detect the reckless and indiscreet absurdities in Richard Hill's statement infra: "I did locate some of my draft handwritten notes and referred to these to prepare my inspection report dated 22.07.2004 for MR BAMGBELU's practice which at the time, I understood to be a correct and accurate record of my inspection."

Oyinbo olodo! Oyinbo ode!
Richard Hill lied about everything, and incompetently and recklessly did so on record. Richard Hill was a very accurate reflection of Sue Gregory.

"I understood to be a correct and accurate record of my inspection."
The accuracy and correctness which Richard Hill described must have had basis, and the fact that it took more than four years to withdraw the racist forgeries implied that the correctness and accuracy described by the former England young adult must have had a very strong basis.

The basis of the accuracy must have been rechecked when the NHS gave response to the Freedom of Information request in January 2008.

Richard Hill, former England young adult and shepherd of England young adults, was a moron. Only stupid people tell lies on record.

"There is no sin except stupidity." – Oscar Wilde

David Morris was too dull to realise that the fact that Richard Hill expected the reports to be similar implied that he created two separate allegedly missing reports from 2004 as a replacement for a single allegedly missing report for 2003.

Oyinbo olodo! Oyinbo ode!

"The contents of the 22.07.2004 and 02.04.2003 report differ. The reason that the contents differ is because the hand written notes I used to prepare the 22.07.2004 also had a reference to a difference and dates and notes were mixed up. Having reviewed the documents, it became clear to me that the July 2004 was created in error. The content of the 02.04.2003 report is an accurate reflection of the inspection done at the time and I stand by the contents of the same." – Richard Hill, 16.10.2008

"The content of the 02.04.2003 report is an accurate reflection of the inspection done at the time and I stand by the contents of the same." – Richard Hill, who does not know what accuracy is, and was an incompetent pillar of dishonesty

Those regularly spun are amongst the dullest adult population in the industrialised world. Shepherds of morons are likelier to be morons too.

The sole basis of the power exercised is money. In 2020, the land in Bedfordshire yields only food. In 1720, the land in Bedfordshire yielded only food. Then, the people were fed like battery hens with the gigantic yields of merciless, evil, racial hatred and fraud: the proceeds of stealing, carrying, and selling millions of stolen human beings.

Almost everything was stolen.

Before slavery, what?

Dr. Olayinka Bamgbelu

CHAPTER 12

OYINBO OLE: WHITE THIEVES: HABAKKUK

No brain.
Poor in natural resources.
Several centuries of stealing and slavery preceded the HUGE TRUST FUND
Only the skin colour is indisputably superior; the wearer neither made nor chose it.

OYINBO OLE: WHITE THIEVES: HABAKKUK.

Apart from creating cushy salaried jobs for Solicitors and Barristers who couldn't hack it in the very competitive real world (Quasi-Communism), what do imbeciles (adults with the basic skills of a child) need very expensive administration of the law for?

The report, by the OECD, warns that the UK needs to take significant action to boost the basic skills of the nation's young people. The 460-page study is based on the first-ever survey of the literacy, numeracy and problem-solving at work skills of 16 to 65-year-olds in 24 countries, with almost 9,000 people taking part in England and Northern Ireland to make up the UK results. The findings showed that England and Northern Ireland have some of the highest proportions of adults scoring no higher than Level 1 in literacy and numeracy - the lowest level on the OECD's scale. This suggests that their skills in the basics are no better than that of a 10-year-old.

Based on available evidence, Dr Richard Dawkins and OECD implied that all the children of District Judge Paul Ayers, Senior Vice President of the Association of Her Majesty's District Judges should be duller than their white father.

Facts are sacred.

"Natural selections will not remove ignorance from future generations." Dr Richard Dawkins

England's young people are near the bottom of the global league table for basic skills. OECD finds 16- to 24-year-olds have literacy and numeracy levels no better than those of their grandparents' generation.

England is the only country in the developed world where the generation approaching retirement is more literate and numerate than the youngest adults, according to the first skills survey by the Organisation for Economic Co-operation and Development.

In a stark assessment of the success and failure of the 720-million-strong adult workforce across the wealthier economies, the economic thinktank warns that in England, adults aged 55 to 65 perform better than 16- to 24-year-olds at foundation levels of literacy and numeracy. The survey did not include people from Scotland or Wales.

The OECD study also finds that a quarter of adults in England have the maths skills of a 10-year-old. About 8.5 million adults, 24.1% of the population, have such basic levels of numeracy that they can manage only one-step tasks in arithmetic, sorting numbers or reading graphs. This is worse than the average in the developed world, where an average of 19% of people were found to have a similarly poor skill base.

"By definition therefore there needs to be a contact order for Mr B so that he knows when he is going to see his son. It is absolutely essential that this occurs and mother agrees with that. She said so several times in her evidence. Mrs Waller agreed that not only should a child have the opportunity of developing relationship with both parents, any sibling should also be there so that inter- sibling relationship could be fostered and nurtured. Obviously in this particular case the children reside in different places. That immediately puts a strain on the children having limited contact with each other. F's sister is very much older than him and she will be further advanced into her adult life. Thus it is not a matter that that sibling relationship can only be fostered by the children being together. Indeed as we all know absence sometimes makes the heart grow fonder. F should have an opportunity of seeing his sister. Wherever he does that it should be done in a friendly and loving environment. If the time comes that his sister goes to university of course his contact with her will be restricted to the time that she is home from university. In years to come when they have both grown up, with their own family they will see less of each other. But it doesn't mean that they don't still love and adore each other as much as they would if they saw each other every day." The Senior Vice President of the Association of Her Majesty's District Judges – proofed and approved Judgement.

https://www.youtube.com/watch?v=BlpH4hG7m1A

Shocking!

"Why, that is, because, dearest, you are a dunce." Habakkuk..

NIGERIA: SHELL'S DOCILE CASH COW.

Babies with huge oil wells near their houses eat only 1.5/day; a semi-illiterate former debt-collector Solicitor in Norwich whose white father and mother have never seen crude oil is our District Judge in Bedford.

OYINBO OLE: WHITE THIEVES: HABAKKUK

Then, racist bastards carried and sold millions of stolen children of defenceless poor people; now, they carry natural resources.

Substitution is fraudulent emancipation.

There are no oil wells or gas fields in KEMPSTON.

"Moderation is a virtue only among those who are thought to have found alternatives." Henry Kissinger

A scatter-head racist; an overpromoted polytechnic university educated racist dunce. A righteous descendant of industrial-scale professional THIEVES and owners of stolen children of defenceless people (Kamala's ancestors) - Habakkuk.

He rides a powerful tiger, deluded, he thinks he is it, dismounted, he'd instantly revert to nothing.

The only evidence of his purportedly higher IQ is the stolen affluence that his white ancestors crossed the English Channels, without luggage or decent shoes, to latch onto.

Before slavery, what?

OYINBO OLE: WHITE THIEVES: HABAKKUK

He sat on skulls of stolen children of defenceless people, more skulls than the millions at the doorsteps of Pol Pot, in a building that destroyed lives yielded; future flats.

OYINBO OLE: WHITE THIEVES: HABAKKUK.

The white father and mother of the Senior Vice President of the Association of Her Majesty's District Judges did not care, had they, he'd not have approved and immortalised excessive stupidity at 16, and he'd be a properly educated lawyer, privately educated Anthony Blair, Anthony Julius, Geoff Hoon and Rabinder Singh's class, and he might practice proper law in STRAND.

Deluded intellectual cowards: Ignorant descendants of racist killers, THIEVES, and owners of stolen children of other people want to force others to see them as they want to be seen, not as they truly are.

There is Freedom of Expression in North Korea; there, one is free to say and/or print only what Kim wants to hear.

In the future, one will be free to say and/or print only what Antichrist Jews and members of the Antichrist Racist Freemasonry Quasi-Religion (Mediocre Mafia), want to hear.

CREEPING NORTH KOREA.

Based on available evidence, Freemasonry Quasi-Religion is intellectually flawed.

Antichrist Racist Freemasonry Quasi-Religion: Half-educated school dropouts and their superiors who have informal access to some very powerful white Judges.

Google: Freemasonry, intellectually flawed.

They use very expensive aprons to decorate the temples of their powerless and useless fertility tools, and carry out indiscreet, vulgar, and Pharisees' charitable works.

OYINBO OLE: WHITE THIEVES: HABAKKUK.

"The good Samaritan had money." Mrs Margaret Thatcher

Indiscreet, vulgar, and Pharisees' charitable works in exchange for what?

Theirs is not a good deal. It was not a good deal then, and it is not a good deal now - Matthew 4:9.

Righteousness without equitable reparation is continuing RACIST FRAUD.

He told the righteous Jew to sell the yields of virtue; He would have told him to return the yields of vice - Matthew 19:21.

Some Jews/Romans lynched and crucified Christ only because He spoke; He disclosed pictures that HIS unbounded mind painted. He was not punished for speaking; He was permanently prevented from speaking.

OYINBO OLE: WHITE THIEVES: HABAKKUK.

"Jews are very good with money." President Donald Trump.

Whose money?

"Fight like hell." President Trump.

Corporal Adolf flipped.

"This statement is about a series of letters and emails I have been recieving. I am the above named person. I live at an address provided to police. In this statement I will also mention XXXXXXXXXXXXXXXXXXXXXXXXXX a leaseholder for a property I manage at my place work. I am the company director of DOBERN properties based in Ilford. These emails have been sent to my company email address of mail@debern.co.uk, and also letters have been sent to myself at our company ADDress of P.O BOX 1289, ILFORD, IG2 7XZ over the last Two and a half years, I have recieving a series of letters and emails from DR BAMGeLu. DR BAMGBELU is a leasholder for a property I manage at my place of work. Over the period of his leaseholding, DR BAmGelu has continually failed to pay arrears for the property. In march 2016 my company took DR to court and he was ordered to pay outstanding costs of around £20000 since that time and lead up to the case, DR BaMGBelu has been emailing me and posting me letters that are lengthy and accuses me repeatedly of being a racist in emails and letters tact are regularly Ten to twelve pages long, DR BAMGBELU. lists numerous quots from google searches all refrencing ham I am a bigot and a racist. The most recent letter I received from DR BAMGBELU opens with you are jealous and racist Evil combination you hate us we know it" he goes on to say "I would not have knowingly had anything to do with white supremicists." In the last email I recieved from him on 02/09/2016 DR BaMGBELU stated "you are restricted by poor Education within one of the least literate countries in the world". I would be perfectly happy for DR BAMGBElu to contact myself or my company if he has relevant enquiries to his lease holding, however these continuous letters and emails are causing me distress and I feel intimidated. I am not a racist and these accusatios make uncomfortable. All I want is to conduct

between us in a normal manner. I want BambGlu to stop emailing me and sending me letters accusing me of being racist and harassing me."
MR ROBERT KINGSTON, SOLICITOR, ACCOUNTANT, AND COMPANY DIRECTOR.

An imbecile Jew!

Corporal Adolf flipped, the rest his history.

"Yes, Sir, it does her honour, but it would do nobody else honour. I have indeed, not read it all. But when I take up the end of a web, and find it packthread, I do not expect, by looking further, to find embroidery."
Dr Samuel Johnson

Idi-Amin expelled the untouchables (DALITS) Britain shipped to Uganda, without luggage or Visas; he seemed to believe that they were thieves. Things didn't turn out well for Uganda.

Hitler Gassed Jews (not all); he seemed to believe that they were thieves. Germany has, by far, the largest economy in Europe. Germany is the economic powerhouse of Europe. There are not too many Imbecile Jew/Solicitor/Accountant/Company Directors in Germany.

BEDFORD, ENGLAND: Based on available evidence, GDC-Witness, Freemason, Brother, Dr Richard William Hill fabricated reports and unrelentingly lied under oath - Habakkuk 1:4; John 8:44: John 10:10

A RACIST WHITE CROOK.

Facts are sacred.

OYINBO OLE: WHITE THIEVES: HABAKKUK.

When they FORK, which is often, Jews are their GO-TO-PEOPLE.

BLACK HOLOCAUST: The barbarously racist traffic in millions of stolen children of defenceless poor people was the evilest terrorism the world will ever know, in comparison, NAZI HOLOCAUST was a storm in a teacup - Habakkuk.

Gigantic yields of millions of stolen children of defenceless poor people (Kamala's ancestors), not feudal agriculture, lured Eastern European Jews to Britain - Habakkuk.

Facts are sacred.

The truth allows no choice." Dr Samuel Johnson

Bernard Madoff, the undisputed world champion crook, is a Jew.

Based on available evidence, some Jews are imbeciles; imbecile Jews are likelier to be crooked and racist.

Facts are sacred.

"The truth allows no choice." Dr Samuel Johnson

Robert Maxwell was not the real name of the shifty Jew; Ján Ludvík Hyman Binyamin Hoch.

Is Robert Kingston the real name of the Jew?

Paradoxically, the huge profits of black holocaust or the gigantic yields of millions of stolen and destroyed children of defenceless poor people, not feudal agriculture lured Eastern European Jews to Britain; they deceptively changed their names, blended, and latched on to the yields of millions of stolen and destroyed innocent lives (the evilest and most enduring acts of Racist Terrorism the world will ever know) -Habakkuk.

The closeted racist, functional semi-illiterate crooked Judge must one day face the only true Judge, his maker.

https://www.youtube.com/watch?v=BlpH4hG7m1A

"To deny or belittle this good is, in this dangerous century when the resources and pretensions of power continue to enlarge, a desperate error of intellectual abstraction. More than this, it is a self-fulfilling error, which encourages us to give up the struggle against bad laws and class bound procedures and to disarm ourselves before power. It is to throw away a whole inheritance of struggle about the law and within the forms of law, whose continuity can never be fractured without bringing men and women into immediate danger." - E. P Thompson

He is watching them - Proverbs 15:3.

I was admitted onto the Bedford Dentist List on 18.12.1995. I started work there on 08.01.1996. I was the first ever and only Negro dentist. Unbeknownst to me, I walked into the lion's den. I took over an on-going concern which had been there for several years. Two weeks later, on 22.01.1996, Richard Hill came to my practice and made some recommendations, which I fully acceded to.

About thirteen years later, the NHS and the GDC exhumed merciless, racist lies to corroborate the blatant dishonesties of their own kindred: the senior NHS nurse's allegations of May 2007. Unbeknownst to the first ever and only Negro dentist in Bedford and Wellingborough, in May 2007 three NHS forgeries were live, valid, and accessible: the NHS forged report of 22.07.2004, the NHS forged follow up report of unknown date, and the NHS forged email address. More than four years after the alleged visit of 22.07.2004, the NHS withdrew its recklessly forged reports. The withdrawal statement is an NHS forgery which remains live and valid.

Before slavery, what?

I was taken back to 1996 on 21 November 2008 by merciless, racist bas****s!

Before slavery, there was only agriculture. Everything else was stolen.

"Agriculture not only gives riches to a nation, but the only riches she can call her own." – Dr Samuel Johnson

"Those who have robbed have also lied." – Dr Samuel Johnson corroborating prophet Habakkuk

Negro being cross examined by Andrew Hurst, counsel to the GDC, on 21 November 2008:

ANDREW HURST: I want to take you to 1996 and back to Bedford.
NEGRO: Yes.
ANDREW HURST: We have heard the evidence from Mr Hill.
NEGRO: Yes.
ANDREW HURST: You have heard him speak about you. You remember him?
NEGRO: Yes.
ANDREW HURST: And you remember he came to visit you on a number of occasions in 1996, yes?
NEGRO: Yes. I think he came to see me about two or three times in '96, yes.
ANDREW HURST: It is also right that Mr Hill told you, in July of 1996 certainly, that several complaints had been received about you.
NEGRO: In July '96?
ANDREW HURST: He told you that.
NEGRO: No.
ANDREW HURST: So you are saying to the Committee "Mr Hill never told me that any complaints had been received about me."
NEGRO: Mr Hill might have told me there are some complaints who received by the . . . sorry, by the BDA. I was new in the practice then. But Mr Hill did not . . . in fact, they came to my practice, he came to my practice on 21/1/96, two or three weeks after I started the practice, because some complaints had been received. So that was the only reason why he came to my practice. All the visits that he made on 22/1/96 was not a routine visit.
ANDREW HURST: To come back to the question, are you saying to the Committee that Mr Hill never said to you that complaints had been received about your practice?
NEGRO: He might have told me . . . 1996 is a very long time . . . that I had—
NEGRO'S PERPECTIVE:
Rachael Bishop (Caucasian), the dull, dishonest, and racist England class senior NHS nurse, could not remember 2007 in 2008, and that was OK for the racist thugs.
Andrew Hurst cross examined the senior NHS nurse on 17 November

2008:

ANDREW HURST: What did you think when he came back to you and you were concerned about the gloves? Did you say anything?

SENIOR NHS NURSE: I can't exactly remember. It's not very conducive to talking when you have half a tooth missing really, so it wasn't that easy. To be honest I can't really remember if I said anything. No, I can't remember.

ANDREW HURST: What was Mr Bamgbelu doing after he had come back to you? Was he continuing to work on your mouth?

SENIOR NHS NURSE: Yes, he continued to work on my mouth and preparing the rest of the tooth for the cap.

ANDREW HURST: Whilst that was going on was there any conversation between you or did Mr Bamgbelu say anything that you can remember?

SENIOR NHS NURSE: No, I think his receptionist came in and they were talking about the ceiling leaking and about getting that fixed, but his receptionist's first language isn't English and Mr Bamgbelu, I struggled to understand him on occasions. So I can't recall any.

ANDREW HURST: You cannot now recall any conversation that Mr Bamgbelu had or you had whilst he was continuing to treat or prepare for the crown at that stage?

SENIOR NHS NURSE: No. Is it possible to look at my statement just to refresh my memory, or not?

ANDREW HURST: Certainly I have no objection to that if you would like to look at your statement.

THE CHAIRMAN (DR SHIV PABARY, MEMBER OF THE BRITISH EMPIRE): Mr Morris?

DAVID MORRIS: Sir, I do not think the witness can be prevented from refreshing her memory at this stage.

THE LEGAL ADVISER (MR DAVID SWINSTEAD): Can you remember when you made the statement?

SENIOR NHS NURSE: Yes, I can. I wrote the letter—

THE LEGAL ADVISER (MR DAVID SWINSTEAD): Not the letter, the statement; when did you make that, roughly?

SENIOR NHS NURSE: Six months ago, roughly.

THE LEGAL ADVISER (MR DAVID SWINSTEAD): 26 August I have a date; is that right in fact?

ANDREW HURST: Sir, that is certainly the date it was signed.

THE LEGAL ADVISER (MR DAVID SWINSTEAD): The point is a technical point, that clearly when you made your statement the matters were fresher in your mind than they are now.

SENIOR NHS NURSE: Yes, they were. It does feel like a very long time ago and the letter was written initially so that is actually the most accurate.

THE LEGAL ADVISER (MR DAVID SWINSTEAD): Your reference would be to your statement. Perhaps you can answer this question. You wrote a letter; did you have the letter with you when you made your statement or not?

SENIOR NHS NURSE: No.

THE LEGAL ADVISER (MR DAVID SWINSTEAD): You did not.

SENIOR NHS NURSE: I had access to it and I quickly re-read it when I made my statement, just to refresh my memory.

THE LEGAL ADVISER (MR DAVID SWINSTEAD): The important point is that the events were fresher in your memory logically then than now?

SENIOR NHS NURSE: Yes.

THE LEGAL ADVISER (MR DAVID SWINSTEAD): And you do not have any objection, Mr Morris?

DAVID MORRIS: Sir, the statement was made on 26 August of this year, which is 15 months from the relevant event and the witness has to establishment that the matters were fresh in her mind at that date, and that is rather difficult to do given the 15-month gap.

SENIOR NHS NURSE: I actually signed it quite a long while after it was made; it took a long while coming through the post and preparation and that sort of thing, so it wasn't actually made on that date.

THE CHAIRMAN (DR SHIV PABARY): Can you remember when it was made? A few months before that?

SENIOR NHS NURSE: Yes, it was about six months ago and Mrs O'Shea came to my home and took the statement, but in preparation it was quite a long time between that and actually signing it and returning it.

DAVID MORRIS: That will take us back to May of this year, which is 12 months since the index event, so I question as to how it can be that matters were fresh in her mind at that time.

Dr. Olayinka Bamgbelu

THE LEGAL ADVISER (MR DAVID SWINSTEAD): The issue is not that they were fresh, but fresher is how the law currently deals with this matter; that they were fresher logically than they are today. Secondly, giving evidence before this Committee is not primarily simply a memory test and if the witness would be assisted by referring to the document then my advice to the Committee is that she should be able to do so. Do you contest that?

Aided by her allegations of 30.05.2007 and the GDC-commissioned statement that she signed on 26.08.2008, the dull, dishonest, and racist senior NHS nurse had forgotten almost everything of several months later. Her ancestors accurately foresaw that as the land yielded only food, they used guns to terrorise unarmed and defenceless world, especially in Africa. Whenever they mercilessly slaughtered, they dispossessed, and wherever they robbed, they took possession. They were merciless, evil, racist thugs, sadistic savages, armed robbers, and thieves. They destroyed the creations of Almighty God so that morons could thrive in the distant future.

If there is God, He is just.

"I tremble for my country when I reflect that God is just; that his justice cannot sleep forever." – President Thomas Jefferson

Dr Konstantina Tranganiti (Caucasian) could not remember 2007 in 2008.

"I cannot recall whether Miss Bishop presented with any facial injuries or swelling. During my examination Miss Bishop was able to open her mouth sufficiently in order for me to check her teeth." – Dr Konstantina Traganiti, June 2008

Dr Konstantina Traganiti examined and treated the senior NHS nurse in June 2007.

So, their own kindred could not remember 2007 in 2008.

Dr Stepahnie Twidale (TD) could not remember 2007 in 2008.

"If I REMEMBER, we arrived and Mr Bamgbelu had a patient I think in the chair, or shortly after. So I THINK we arrived." – Dr Stephanie Twidale, under oath, on 19.11.2008 Mumsie olodo! F****** rotter blower! Oyinbo olodo!

"Possibly. I can't remember what kind of – I know on the left of the store room was a reception door. I think it probably is, I think that is probably the store room. I can't REMEMBER." – Dr Stephanie Twidale, under oath, on 19.11.2008

"It may be on a cardboard box on a cupboard, I can't REMEMBER whether the cardboard box was on the floor or on the cupboard I am afraid now." – Dr Stephanie Twidale, under oath, on 19.11.2008

"Yes I did. Once I received the e-mail I rang the practice. I can't REMEMBER whether I reached him the first time I phoned, or whether I needed to arrange a time to phone back, that may have been the case. I am afraid I can't REMEMBER that." – Dr Stephanie Twidale, under oath, on 19.11.2008 Stephanie Twidale could not remember 2007 in 2008 irrespective of the fact that she allegedly kept contemporaneous records. The racist thugs expected the Negro to remember 1996 in 2008 without notes of any kind, in pursuance of corroborating the allegations by their dishonest kindred more than a decade later. They are merciless, racist bastards who are incontrovertibly the goddamned descendants of vicious, racist bastards: the stealers, carriers, and sellers of millions of stolen human beings.

"I know of no evil that has ever existed, nor can imagine any evil to exist, worse than the tearing of eighty thousand persons annually from their native land, by a combination of the most civilised nations inhabiting the most enlightened part of the globe, but more especially under the sanction of the laws of that Nation which calls herself the most free and the most happy of them all." – Prime Minister William Pitt the Younger

"Many Scots masters were considered among the most brutal, with life expectancy on their plantations averaging a mere four years. We worked them to death then simply imported more to keep the sugar and thus the money flowing. Unlike centuries of grief and murder, an apology costs nothing. So what does Scotland have to say?" – Herald Scotland, Ian Bell, columnist, Sunday

28 April 2013

"As hard-hearted as a Scot of Scotland." – English saying

"Scotsmen tak a' they can get and a little more if they can."

– Scottish saying Before slavery, what?

ANDREW HURST: Sorry? Are you accepting now he might have told you about it?

NEGRO: He might have told me, yes.

ANDREW HURST: If we go to our file 1, divider 15. We have there a report of a practice visit.

NEGRO: Yes.

ANDREW HURST: And that relates to 29 July 1996.

NEGRO: Yes.

ANDREW HURST: What we have is some text, but then we have an awful lot of things which have been blanked out.

NEGRO: Yes.

ANDREW HURST: I want to show you the document. Just look at my divider. This is an unredacted one. (Same handed) If you want to read to yourself.

NEGRO: There is a paragraph, Sir, which would be in your fifth paragraph. There is a note there made by Mr Hill.

ANDREW HURST: Yes. You read that to yourself. (Pause) Having read that—

NEGRO: What date? The 29th?

ANDREW HURST: Yes. Having read that to yourself, do you accept that Mr Hill made you aware of his knowledge that several complaints had been received about you?

NEGRO: Yes, I still do not accept that. Why don't I accept that? It is possible that he told me that some complaints have been made against me. But I was aware as well that I had received one or two complaints. In fact, in the whole of that year, 1996, I only had three complaints against me.

ANDREW HURST: The question simply is this. You have heard Mr Hill and you have heard how he has been complimentary about your clinical skills.

NEGRO: Yes.

NEGRO'S PERSPECTIVE:

Richard Hill complimenting me doesn't add anything to me. If a moron England young adult or former young adult thinks the Negro is fantastic, it adds nothing to him. If a moron England young adult or former young adult thinks the Negro is a lunatic, it takes nothing from the Negro, as the Negro remains a Negro and the hereditary moron remains a moron. In 2015, there are no oil wells or gas fields in Bedfordshire. In 1715, the people of Bedfordshire were fed like battery hens with the yields of racist evil and merciless racial hatred and fraud.

Bedfordshire yielded only food and yields only food. Almost everything else was stolen. Before slavery what?

"Agriculture not only gives riches to a nation, but the only riches she can call her own." – Dr Samuel Johnson

"All sections of UK society are institutionally racist." – Sir Bernard Hogan-Howe, London Metropolitan Police

"I know of no evil that has ever existed, nor can imagine any evil to exist, worse than the tearing of eighty thousand persons annually from their native land, by a combination of the most civilised nations inhabiting the most enlightened part of the globe, but more especially under the sanction of the laws of that Nation which calls herself the most free and the most happy of them all." – Prime Minister William Pitt the Younger, 1792

"Many Scots masters were considered among the most brutal, with life expectancy on their plantations averaging a mere four years. We worked them to death then simply imported more to keep the sugar and thus the money flowing. Unlike centuries of grief and murder, an apology costs nothing. So what does Scotland have to say?" – Herald Scotland, Ian Bell, columnist, Sunday 28 April 2013 Evil, merciless, racist bastards!

"Those who have robbed have also lied." – Dr Samuel Johnson corroborating prophet Habakkuk

Andrew Hurst, England class barrister, was amongst the topmost former England young adults and a shepherd of England young adults.

"FAILING SCHOOLS AND A BATTLE FOR BRITAIN: This was the day the British education establishment's 50 year betrayal of the Nation's children lay starkly exposed in all its ignominy. After testing 166,000 people in 24 education systems, the Organisation for Economic Cooperation and Development (OECD) finds that England young adults are amongst the least literate and numerate in the industrialised world." – The Daily Mail, 09.01.2013

Shepherds of morons are likelier to be morons too.

Andrew Hurst: If the bottommost part of a whole is world class bottommost, the topmost part of that whole is unlikely to be world class topmost.

"To disagree with three-fourths of the British public on all points is one of the first elements of sanity, one of the deepest consolations in all moments of spiritual doubt." – Oscar Wilde "The English think that incompetence is the same thing as sincerity." – Quentin Crisp

"Truth, Sir, is a cow which will yield such people no more milk, and so they are gone to milk the bull." – Dr Samuel Johnson

Normans didn't steal Britain from the aborigines. They stole land from other mainland Europeans which had been stolen from the natives.

ANDREW HURST: I have shown you a note where he has recorded that he made you aware of his knowledge that several complaints had been received. Having looked at that note, and knowing Mr Hill as you do, would you be prepared to accept that Mr Hill is indeed right in his note of 1996 that he did indeed make you aware of several complaints having been received?

NEGRO: I will not expect him just to lie about it, so yes.

ANDREW HURST: Having had a think about it now, do you think it is quite possible, or indeed likely, that . . . Mr Hill did make you aware that several complaints had been received?

NEGRO: Just like I said in the past, the only reason they came to my practice was because some people had complained. And it depends on what you mean by "several." That was why he was advising me about my staff, my equipment and so on and so on. But it is quite possible that 12 years ago I am sure that he might have told me that some complaints were made against me. But I cannot recall him saying "several," because as far as I was concerned in 1996 I received only three complaints against me.

NEGRO'S PERSPECTIVE:

I was the first ever and only Negro dentist in Bedford. I took over an on-going concern in 1996. The racist bastards exhumed mummified forgeries only from 1996 to corroborate the allegation of a functional semi-illiterate England class senior NHS nurse.

Twelve year old allegations were not a crime in Bobby's Zimbabwe unless one was a member of the MDC.

Intellectually impotent racist bastards!

Testis unus; testis nullius.

The descendants of thoroughly wretched, feudal agricultural labourers (serfs) from mainland Europe stole the land of aboriginal Britons, and they were immeasurably transformed by the gigantic yields of merciless, racist evil (slavery). They have reinvented themselves on stolen land and fool the foolish with foolishness. Many retain the intellects of serfs.

Members of the House of Saxe-Coburg-Gotha came to Britain by boat. Had Andrew Hurst, the imbecile former England young adult and shepherd of England young adults, understood what he read in Richard Hill's statement of 23.09.2008, the brainless moron would not be talking rot.

I met the f***** at the urinals in or under 37 Wimpole Street. We did the business but not side by side, but as much as Andrew Hurst tried to conceal his prick, I managed to catch a glimpse. His was no prick at all, as it looked more like a gigantic clitoris. I did see his balls, which were concealed in what looked like a Tescos F/F boxer short, so there was no way of confirming whether he was a transvestite.

Somebody said that he studied law at Oxford University where he might have put his prick in the mouths of dead pigs. If privileged shepherds of England young adults are truly brave, they should insert their balls into the mouth of pacu, the organ grinder.

The proceeds of centuries of merciless, racial hatred and fraud kickstarted the industrial revolution in Europe and brought European slave merchants and traders great wealth.

The satanic network is everywhere. It controls almost everything except intellect. Without objective basis, it awards itself the monopoly of knowledge.

"Iain Whyte, author of Scotland and the Abolition of Slavery, insists we have at times ignored our guilty past.

"He said: 'For many years Scotland's historians harboured the illusion that our nation had little to do with the slave trade or plantation slavery.

"'We swept it under the carpet. This was remarkable in the light of Glasgow's wealth coming from tobacco, sugar and cotton, and Jamaica Streets being found in a number of Scottish towns and cities.

"'It is healthy we are now recognising Scotland was very much involved.'

"The industries, which saw Glasgow and much of the country flourish, were built on the back of slavery.

"There were familiar names such as Scot Lyle of Tate and Lyle fame whose fortune was built on slavery. Ewing from Glasgow was the richest sugar producer in Jamaica.

"The stunning Inveresk Lodge in Edinburgh, now open to the public, was bought by James Wedderburn with money earned from 27 years in Jamaica as a notorious slaver.

"The Wee Free Church was founded using profits and donations from the slave trade. Even our schools have a dark history. Bathgate Academy was built from money willed by John Newland, a renowned slave master and Dollar Academy has a similar foundation.

"For many years, the goods and profits from West Indian slavery were unloaded at Kingston docks in Glasgow.

"Leith in Edinburgh and Glasgow were popular ports from which ambitious Scottish men sailed to make their fortunes as slave masters." – Ian Bell, Herald Scotland, 28 April 2013

The proceeds of merciless evil, racial hatred, and fraud were used to build cathedrals, courts, castles, and councils.

Before slavery, Wimpole Street was farmland and yielded only food.

"Agriculture not only gives riches to a nation, but the only riches she can call her own." – Dr Samuel Johnson

Feudal agricultural labourers from mainland Europe dispossessed/robbed aboriginal Britons. They've been transformed and reinvented by slavery.

ANDREW HURST: So do we understand each other that you are prepared to accept that Mr Hill did tell you that complaints had been received?

NEGRO: Yes.

ANDREW HURST: Certainly more than one, if we use "complaints" in the plural?

NEGRO: Yes, that was my year one. That was the reason just for his visits.

ANDREW HURST: And those complaints related to things like the appearance, standard and cleanliness of the surgery, the absence of clinical clothing being worn by you and your staff and standards of hygiene. That was the kind of thing he was telling you about in 1996.

NEGRO: Yes, in 1996 I wore a white coat then. He did not complain to me about my own— yes, I have no evidence, no letter that they complained about me personally.

ANDREW HURST: Not Mr Hill complaining about you. The question is very specific; it is that Mr Hill told "you" that other people had complained about those sorts of things. Do you accept that that is in fact the case: Mr Hill did tell you that other people had complained to you about those sorts of things?

NEGRO: Mr Hill might have told me that people complained about my staff, clothing and things, not me, no. So he told me about the staff that I had just acquired in a new business, that I had never done before. I acquired two or three girls. He told me that the patients complained about one or two of the staffs, about the way they talk to them— these are people I did not know and that I had just acquired . . . and perhaps talked about things as well. But it was a new thing to me. I had just acquired a new practice. I think then that after that I changed one of the girls. Yes, I changed one of the girls.

ANDREW HURST: I want to see if I can agree on this. In 1996 Mr Hill would have told you – now that you accept he did tell you about the fact that more than one complaint had been received about your surgery in 1996 – and that you accept that Mr Hill told you about complaints which related to the appearance, standard and cleanliness of the surgery; issues about the absence of clinical clothing being worn by you and your staff and standards of hygiene. That was the sort of thing he passed on to you, is it not?

NEGRO'S PERSPECTIVE:

Andrew Hurst was a racist and unintelligent "white boy," propped up by crude oil and gas money in exactly the same way as his ancestors were for centuries sustained by the proceeds of merciless racist evil and naked fraud.

In November 2008, the f****** idiot with a giant clitoris like prick (likkle tin) that he urinates through expected me to remember what Richard Hill told me in 1996, off the top of my head. His Excellency, Field Marshall and Messenger of God Teodoro Obiang Nguema Mbasogo was not that brutal to Lieutenant Simon Mann, the alleged mercenary, armed robber, and thief who allegedly was financed by Sir Mark Thatcher in pursuance of stealing oil from Africa. Elder comrade Bobby of Zimbabwe also treated Lieutenant Simon Mann reasonably in Zimbabwe after he was kidnapped and later sold to His Excellency, Field Marshall and Messenger of God Teodoro Obiang Nguema Mbasogo for $10,000,000 worth of crude oil. Bobby never misses a deal.

"We shall deal with the racist bastards when we get out of prison."
Robert Mugabe

Had Andrew Hurst's mama sent him to schools where critical reasoning was taught as a subject, he would have realised that Richard Hill's letters to me (I was not given any report) after his visits in 1996, which formed part of his statement of 23.09.2008, are the most accurate evidence of what he told me more than twelve years prior.

Stupid, racist thug!

"There is no sin except stupidity." – Oscar Wilde

NEGRO: Yes, but I cannot recall that, and I am not sure he made any mention about my own clothing. He might have made mention about the structure of my practice; the way things were; maybe over how clean it was, and so on. But there was no mention about my own clothing, because I wore a white coat. I have always worn a white coat.
ANDREW HURST: Leaving aside your own clothing, do you accept that he may have mentioned the absence of clinical clothing being worn by people other than you?
NEGRO: That is right.
ANDREW HURST: So you accept that.
NEGRO: Yes.
ANDREW HURST: You accept that he would have passed on that there had been complaints about the standards of hygiene, yes?
NEGRO: It is actually depends – depends what you mean by that. If you mean by "standards of hygiene" the surgery was not clean and swept, things like that – yes; I do not think that would be right. But if you talked about the standard of hygiene in terms of the staff not wearing uniform and so on, yes.
ANDREW HURST: All right. So you accept about the staff and their uniform.
NEGRO: Yes.
NEGRO'S PERSPECTIVE:
I couldn't recall 1996 in 2008, and I would not have been asked to do so had I been a white man. No part of Richard Hill's report or letters about that period concerned uniforms.
There was something deeper going on.

Theirs is a trinity of guilt, shame, and fear (GSF).

If it could be proved that the brain was in the skin, it should lessen the guilt if millions of Africans who were mercilessly slaughtered and millions more who were worked to death by Andrew Hurst's ancestors were proved to be intellectually inferior to their evil, racist, and allegedly "civilised Christian" persecutors.

The brain is not in the skin. If it were, Andrew Hurst would not be so dull. Oyinbo olodo! Oyinbo ode!

"Many Scots masters were considered among the most brutal, with life expectancy on their plantations averaging a mere four years. We worked them to death then simply imported more to keep the sugar and thus the money flowing. Unlike centuries of grief and murder, an apology costs nothing. So what does Scotland have to say?" – Herald Scotland, Ian Bell, columnist, Sunday 28 April 2013

"I know of no evil that has ever existed, nor can imagine any evil to exist, worse than the tearing of eighty thousand persons annually from their native land, by a combination of the most civilised nations inhabiting the most enlightened part of the globe, but more especially under the sanction of the laws of that Nation which calls herself the most free and the most happy of them all." – Prime Minister William Pitt the Younger

✼ ✼ ✼ ✼ ✼ ✼

ANDREW HURST: And you accept about the physical state of the premises, the structural stuff.

NEGRO: Yes.

ANDREW HURST: But you do not think he passed on a complaint about your own clothing.

NEGRO: No.

ANDREW HURST: Or about the cleanliness of the surgery.

NEGRO: No.

ANDREW HURST: But you do recall having complaints in 1996.

NEGRO: Yes.

ANDREW HURST: I do not want to know what they were.

NEGRO: Yes. In 1996, when I took over the practice, I realised later—because when I took over the practice I bought it just for a bit of money, but the lady had four thousand patients, and I had four thousand.

THE CHAIRMAN (DR SHIV PABARY, MEMBER OF THE BRITISH EMPIRE): Mr Bamgbelu, I think this is what the Legal Assessor is going to advise. The question is quite specific: "Did you have complaints?" and it was a yes or no.

NEGRO: Yes, I had complaints in 1996. I had three complaints in 1996.

THE LEGAL ADVISER (MR DAVID SWINSTEAD): Can I say that I think it is helpful if you try to just answer the question. You were going to go on to make a point about the patients and the number. I think you told us something about that yesterday, which I think you put into context of what happened when you first took over the practice, and there were four thousand patients. Just answer, because you may be in danger of repeating a point which you may have made yesterday, and the Committee may well have understood that these are the problems, when you started that. So I think if you would just answer.

NEGRO: Okay.

ANDREW HURST: Just the three in 1996.

NEGRO: Yes.

ANDREW HURST: I would like you to look at this. Sir, it is RWH7 and it is exhibited to Mr Hill's statement. (Same handed) It may assist the Legal Assessor, unless it is difficult for the Legal Assessor to read it without the risk of anyone else seeing it. We deal with it more as a memory refreshing document, rather than anything else. (To the witness) Just take a look at that.

NEGRO: Yes.

ANDREW HURST: This is a document served with Mr Hill's statement. It is part of these proceedings. Okay?

NEGRO: Yes.

ANDREW HURST: I am not going to read them all out.

NEGRO: Okay.

ANDREW HURST: Be sure to listen carefully to the question, so you do not say anything you do not need to talk about. The first item is January 1996.

NEGRO: Yes.

ANDREW HURST: Under the column we see a complaint about

the general appearance of the waiting room, reception area scruffy and unwelcoming and the nurse not wearing uniform.

NEGRO: Yes.

ANDREW HURST: And the action taken refers to the Dental Adviser, which is Mr Hill.

NEGRO: Yes.

ANDREW HURST: It refers to Mr Hill visiting you on 22 January.

NEGRO: Yes.

ANDREW HURST: Setting out the recommended actions to be taken by the dentist.

NEGRO: Yes.

ANDREW HURST: This is a note that Mr Hill has compiled.

NEGRO: Yes.

ANDREW HURST: So is this a good example where you now do remember that Mr Hill would have passed on to you: "Now listen, Mr Bamgbelu, we have had a complaint about the state of the premises and the uniforms in relation to your staff."

NEGRO: Yes.

ANDREW HURST: He told you about it and in fact something was going to be done about it. I did not get this complaint. This complaint did not come to me directly. Do not worry.

THE LEGAL ADVISER (MR DAVID SWINSTEAD): You talked a number of times about three complaints.

NEGRO: Yes.

THE LEGAL ADVISER (MR DAVID SWINSTEAD): Are they complaints that came to you directly?

NEGRO: Yes.

THE LEGAL ADVISER (MR DAVID SWINSTEAD): Or complaints that came via Mr Hill? I am not trying to trick you.

NEGRO: They are the complaints that were passed to me by the then Health Authority.

NEGRO'S PERSPECTIVE:

OYINBO OLE: WHITE THIEVES: HABAKKUK
Then, racist bastards carried and sold millions of stolen children of defenceless poor people; now, they carry natural resources.

Dr. Olayinka Bamgbelu

SUBSTITUTION: FRAUDULENT EMANCIPATION.
"Moderation is a virtue only among those who are thought to have found alternatives." Henry Kissinger

"F*** you!" I exclaimed, but only inside!

Trick me with what? Skin colour, brain, or an imitation upper-class accent?

If David Morris's mama had sent the shepherd of England young adults to schools where logical reasoning was taught as a subject, he'd have realised that Richard Hill did not pass any complaint to the first ever and only Negro dentist in Bedford about twelve years prior.
Apart from skin colour, what?
Before slavery what?
No brain, natural resources poor, only skin colour that the wearer neither made nor chose, and what else? Pure scam!
Almost everything was stolen!
"Those who have robbed have also lied." – Dr Samuel Johnson corroborating prophet Habakkuk

✳ ✳ ✳ ✳ ✳

THE LEGAL ADVISER (MR DAVID SWINSTEAD): Are those separate to those that Mr Hill mentioned to you? Because you are talking about the points you have just been answering Mr Hurst about.
NEGRO: When Mr Hill came to me on 22/01/96, he was new to me then. He advised me about things that I should do, but I cannot remember him telling me that those advice were due to some complaints. He was just coming to help me, because I had just joined the practice.

NEGRO'S PERSPECTIVE:
Had David Swinstead been cleverer, he would have been able to pick the following up from Richard Hill's statement of 23.09.2008: I was not given report after his visits. He sent me letters and there was no mention of particular complaints in any of the letters.

Satanic Network

I was the first ever and only Negro dentist in Bedford.

What they want is superiority based upon skin the colour that they neither made nor chose, but they want it by stealth.

The natural instinct of the privileged dullard is soft but durable apartheid by stealth.

ANDREW HURST: Okay. I am asking you very specifically, because a moment ago you accepted that Mr Hill had told you that there had been a complaint about the appearance of the building and also about something to do with the fact that the staff or the nurse was not wearing the appropriate uniform. You agreed with me that he did pass that one on to you.

NEGRO: Yes.

NEGRO'S PERSPECTIVE:

I couldn't remember 1996 in 2008. I was the first ever and only Negro dentist in Bedford. Richard Hill did not mention uniforms in any of his letters to me, and he did not provide me with reports. They had painted a picture of stereotypical dirty Negro, and I must fit into it. My staff did all the cleaning, and they were all white and worked hard.

"Prior to Sandhurst, cadets were sent to Mons Officer Cadet School in the UK for a period of three months. The objective of the Mons training was to separate cadets for either a long or a short training course. The older cadets were sent on the short course, while the younger or more able cadets were sent to Sandhurst. The Mons training was to be my first experience outside my native country and nothing in my interactions with expatriates in Africa prepared me for the culture shock I experienced in those first few months in Britain. The first shock was the freezing cold. However, this was a condition that I could and did adapt to. What was harder to adapt to, was the overt and covert racism that infected the entire British society. There are several facets of racism: first, the conviction that blacks were innately inferior to whites and secondly, intolerance for blacks who failed to conform to a restricted number of stereotypes. From my observations, there were two acceptable 'African Types'; the 'funny' African who grinned incessantly and was incapable of taking offense and secondly, the 'ignorant' African, who understood nothing, appreciated his own ignorance, and was profoundly grateful for whatever attention was bestowed on him by the all-knowing Whites." – Col. Benjamin Adekunle (Black Scorpion), Commander of the Third Marine Commando of the Nigerian Army during the Biafran War (1967 to 1969)

"All sections of UK society are institutionally racist." – Sir Bernard Hogan-Howe, London Metropolitan Police

✻ ✻ ✻ ✻ ✻ ✻ ✻

ANDREW HURST: Here we see in our document . . . sorry, the Committee do not have it, but I am sure you will appreciate there are some things we ought not to distribute. Here is a record of that sort of thing, is it not, on 21 January?
NEGRO: Yes.

NEGRO'S PERSPECTIVE:
Andrew Hurst maliciously lied implicitly under oath, or he was confused when he implied on 21.11.2008 that Richard Hill visited my practice on 21.01.1996.
The imbecile "white boy" was a f****** rotter blower!
"Nothing that you will learn in the course of your studies will be of the slightest possible use to you in after life – save only this – if you work hard and diligently you should be able to detect when a man is talking rot, and that, in my view, is the main, if not the sole, purpose of education." – J.A. Smith, Oxford University Professor, Moral Philosophy

✻ ✻ ✻ ✻ ✻ ✻ ✻

ANDREW HURST: The next one, just looking at it for a moment, in the column marked 2, there is something that says "dentist did not wear a coat." Do you see that?
NEGRO: Yes.
ANDREW HURST: Then the action taken is that "the visit was carried out by the Dental Adviser, on 15 April 1996.

NEGRO: Yes.

NEGRO'S PERSPECTIVE:
Cultural difference! "Yes" meant "next" or "move on," you brainless rotter blower.

ANDREW HURST: Going back to this, and as you make the point very fairly, Mr Bamgbelu, it was a long time ago.

NEGRO: Yes.

ANDREW HURST: Almost eight years ago; more than eight years ago.

NEGRO: It was more than that.

NEGRO'S PERSPECTIVE:
Imbecile barrister of Mediocre Great England (MGE)! The former England young adult and shepherd of England young adults could not write legibly, so it was impossible to know whether he could spell. He could read, but he had not fully acquired the consistent capacity to understand what he had read, and his mental arithmetic was crap.

2008 minus 1996 equals eight—init or isn't it? Eight plus eight is sixteen, isn't it? F****** CSE arithmetic!

Andrew Hurst: f****** idiot, an innumerate and illiterate former England young adult and a shepherd of England young adults.

"FAILING SCHOOLS AND A BATTLE FOR BRITAIN: This was the day the British education establishment's 50 year betrayal of the Nation's children lay starkly exposed in all its ignominy. After testing 166,000 people in 24 education systems, the Organisation for Economic Cooperation and Development (OECD) finds that England young adults are amongst the least literate and numerate in the industrialised world." – The Daily Mail, 09.01.2013

Shepherds of morons are likelier to be morons too.

ANDREW HURST: A lot more. Sorry. I have got it the wrong way round. We are talking of 12. Just looking at this now, do you think it is actually likely that Mr Hill would have said to you, "Mr Bamgbelu, someone else mentioned that you appeared not to be wearing a coat when they saw you."

NEGRO: No.

ANDREW HURST: So he did not pass this one to you.

NEGRO No. Would you allow me to please answer that?

ANDREW HURST: Yes. If I cut you off, please do?

NEGRO: That complaint was 9/01/96. That was only a few days after I joined the practice. The complaint was said to have been made orally. It did not come to me. I was not aware of it. Mr Hill did not come to me until four months or three months later. So yes, I did not know about it. So when Mr Hill came in April, he was not in any way, as far as I recall, talking about the oral complaint made by one patient a week after I joined the practice. That was not passed on to me, because I cannot recall that.

ANDREW HURST: Over the page, 11 January 1996; an issue about standard of hygiene, an oral complaint.

NEGRO: Yes.

ANDREW HURST: Do you remember Mr Hill passing that on to you.

NEGRO: No, I do not remember Mr Hill passing this message of 11/01/96, about 10 days after I joined practice, about the staff that I acquired at the practice. I was not aware of it.

NEGRO'S PERSPECTIVE:

Had Andrew Hurst's mama sent him to schools in Mediocre Great England (MGE) where the capacity to read and comprehend the English language was properly taught, he would have realised upon reading that Richard Hill did not pass any message to the first ever and only Negro dentist in Bedford.

The sole basis of the power displayed is money. In 2015, Bedfordshire yielded only food. In 1715, the people of Bedfordshire were fed like battery hens with the proceeds of evil, racial hatred and fraud.

Before slavery, what?

ANDREW HURST: 9 February 1996: "Standard of hygiene, lack

of privacy and condition of the building. Staff did not wear uniforms. Waiting area and treatment room filthy."

NEGRO: Yes.

NEGRO'S PERSPECTIVE:

It was persecutory Negrophobia and racist thuggery by descendants of merciless Negro murderers, stealers, carriers, sellers, and sadistic savages, armed robbers, and thieves! They are of racist bastards, murderous cowards, armed robbers, and thieves!

Andrew Hurst seemed too shallow to detect the absurdity in his naked racial hatred. February 9, 1996 was only a month after the first ever and only Negro dentist took over the surgery. In order to corroborate the allegation by blatantly dishonest Rachael Bishop in 2008, they were racist rot from only 1996. What about 1997, 1998, 1999, 2000, 2001, 2002, 2003, 2004, 2005, 2006, 2007, and 2008? If Rachael Bishop was not unrelentingly dishonest under oath, she must sue the Negro.

In 2020, there are no oil wells or gas fields in Wollaston. In 1720, the people of Wollaston were fed like battery hens with the yields of merciless, racial hatred and fraud. Before slavery, what?

✱ ✱ ✱ ✱ ✱ ✱

ANDREW HURST: Written complaints.

NEGRO: Yes.

ANDREW HURST: Was that passed on to you by Mr Hill?

NEGRO: Mr Hill did not pass on that to me. If you look on the action taken, it was not passed on to me, no. I was not aware of it. I have not seen all these before this case, yes.

ANDREW HURST: Well, you have, Mr Bamgbelu, because it was part of Mr Hill's statement served on you.

NEGRO: No, no, no. I said I had not seen all these before this case.

NEGRO'S PERSPECTIVE:

There is reasoning higher than that of privileged dullards who might have been lied to at home and at school that the brain is in the skin.

The Romans and the Jews did not believe Christ, our own God, because they did not understand the notion of infinite reasoning power and believed that anything that they did not understand was wrong and expresses ignorance or lunacy.

If the land is natural resources poor and the people are rich, the wealth is likelier to be the yield of very high intellect or it must have been stolen.

Andrew Hurst seemed to desire to give the impression of higher intellect based almost entirely upon the skin colour that he neither made nor chose, the fact that he is an England class barrister (some barristers go on to be judges), and because he was born in a very rich country that is natural resources poor. This should not be evidence of the fact that he is intelligent.

One should look at the fact and display the shallow reasoning of the former England young adult and shepherd of England young adults.

At the GDC hearing of 21 November 2008, the mediocre, Negrophobic, and corrupt council within one of the least literate countries in Western Europe (seemingly aided by Sue Gregory) exhumed mummified forgeries from twelve years prior, 1996, in pursuance of using them to corroborate the allegation by Rachael Bishop, an England class senior NHS nurse, a verifiably dishonest racist thug that seemed consumed by jealousy. The Negro was the first ever and only Negro dentist in Wellingborough, Northamptonshire. There is no evidence, certainly none conclusive, that Rachael Bishop was a member of the Northants Patriots, a "battalion" of the BNP (the equivalent of the KKK in the USA), but there is evidence that the racist group was very active and visible in Northamptonshire. In 2015, Northamptonshire yields only food. In 1715, the people of Northamptonshire were fed like battery hens with the gigantic proceeds of merciless, racist evil, which the European trade in millions of stolen Africans was.

The fabricated the July 22, 2004 report and the follow up of undisclosed date to fit seamlessly with the cooked up 2007 report; Christ uncovered the plot so, they had to go back 13 years to January 1996, only a few days after I took over the practice.

What do they have that is tangible that was not stolen?

Before slavery, what?

Nigeria (oil//gas) is by far more relevant to the economic survival of the white father and mother of Andrew Hurst than Luton. Then, the white ancestors of his white father and mother were fed like battery-hens with thev yields of stolen lives.

OYINBO OLE: WHITE THIEVES: HABAKKUK.

Seemingly in pursuance of creating deceit, shepherds did not bring stolen Africans home and thereby deceived moron sheep that they were the paragons of wisdom who like Mother Teresa did virtuous work abroad. Moron sheep believed that the shepherds were exceedingly clever benefactors who fed them with the yields of virtue. The sheep saw the huge wealth that the shepherds brought from abroad, but they did not know that the shepherds were merciless, evil, racist murderers, armed robbers, and thieves: people stealers, carriers, sellers, and exploiters.

Till today, the sheep believe that the shepherds are paragons of wisdom who feed them with the yields of virtue.

"American South is still taken as barbarism's benchmark. Few realise that the behaviour of Scots busy getting rich in the slave-holders' empire was actually worse – routinely worse – than the worst of the cottonocracy. You need only count the corpses.

"By the time slavery was brought to an end in America, the country's 400,000 trafficked people had grown to a population of four million. In the British West Indies, only 670,000 survived from two million imported souls. In the American South, slaves were valuable and bred. We worked them to death then simply imported more to keep the sugar and thus the money flowing.

"Unlike centuries of grief and murder, an apology costs nothing. So what does Scotland have to say?" – Herald Scotland, Ian Bell, columnist, Sunday 28 April 2013

"It was our arms in the river of Cameroon, put into the hands of the trader, that furnished him with the means of pushing his trade; and I have no more doubt that they are British arms, put into the hands of Africans, which promote universal war and desolation that I can doubt their having done so in that individual instance. I have shown how great is the enormity of this evil, even on the supposition that we take only convicts and prisoners of war. But take the subject in another way, and how does it stand? Think of 80,000 persons carried out of their native country by we know not what means! For crimes imputed! For light or inconsiderable faults! For debts perhaps! For crime of witchcraft! Or a thousand other weak or scandalous pretexts! Reflect on 80,000 persons annually taken off! There is something in the horror of it that surpasses all bounds of imagination." – Prime Minister William Pitt the Younger, 1792

"The grand object of all European traders in kidnapped and stolen Africans was - money, money, money; money was their god! In Africa, the poor wretched natives, blessed with the most fertile and luxuriant soil, are rendered so much the more miserable by the Christians' (European traders in stolen Africans) abominable traffic for slaves and the horrid cruelty and treachery of the petty [African] Kings. The Africans kings were encouraged by their European (Christian) customers who carry them strong liquors to enflame their madness and powder and bad firearms to furnish them with the hellish means of killing and kidnapping. But enough - it is a subject that sours my blood." – Ignatius Sancho, 1778

"I know of no evil that has ever existed, nor can imagine any evil to exist, worse than the tearing of eighty thousand persons annually from their native land, by a combination of the most civilised nations inhabiting the most enlightened part of the globe, but more especially under the sanction of the laws of that Nation which calls herself the most free and the most happy of them all." – Prime Minister William Pitt the Younger, 1792

Before slavery, what?
OYINBO OLE: WHITE THIEVES: HABAKKUK.
"Truth is the prime attribute of the Deity." – Lord Byron

In the council chambers on 21 November 2008, before the sincerely perceived racist council, the Negro told the council and the former England young adults that he had not seen or heard of nearly all of the 1996 allegations before the GDC case against him. The mediocre, corrupt, and racist council seemed too dull to discern the absurdity of the exhumed and mummified NHS forgeries from 1996, and the fact that in 2008 they had to go back to 1996.

Why only 1996?
"I had not seen all these before this case, yes." – Negro

The England class and racist barrister Andrew Hurst did not believe the Negro. He thought he was smart, not knowing that those that he and his type regularly spin are amongst the dullest adult population in the industrialised world.

"Well, you have, Mr Bamgbelu, because it was part of Mr Hill's statement served on you." – Andrew Hurst

"No, no, no. I said I had not seen all these before this case." – Negro

Andrew Hurst was wrong, and he immortalised stupidity for eternity.

"There is no sin except stupidity." – Oscar Wilde

"Ignorance, the root and stem of all evil." – Plato

Andrew Hurst talked nonsense with civilised decorum and an imitation upper-class accent. He allowed prior predilection, stereotype, and prejudice to becloud his objective reasoning and judgement.

Andrew Hurst, the England class barrister (some barristers go on to become judges), former England young adult and shepherd of England young adults, did not realise that he agreed with the Negro when he stated, "Well, you have, Mr Bamgbelu, because it was part of Mr Hill's statement served on you," as his statement seamlessly corroborated the Negro when he stated, "No, no, no. I said I had not seen all these before this case."

These are the facts which the seemingly modular bar course, within one of the least literate countries in the industrialised world, prevented Andrew Hurst from discerning.

The allegations against the first ever and only Negro dentist in Bedford and Wellingborough were disclosed to him on 21 October 2008. On 21 November 2008, in the sincerely perceived racist council before a sincerely perceived racist council, the Negro stated that he had not seen or heard of nearly all the allegations from twelve years prior before the GDC case. The imbecile barristo, a moron "white boy," danced in muck. Had it been an examination where his skin colour and imitation upper class English accent would not count, he would have failed and failed woefully. Just by the by, the upper-class English accent seems to be one of the most efficient accents for talking rot.

"Nothing that you will learn in the course of your studies will be of the slightest possible use to you in after life – save only this – if you work hard and diligently you should be able to detect when a man is talking rot, and that, in my view, is the main, if not the sole, purpose of education." – J.A.

Smith, Oxford University Professor, Moral Philosophy

"The lawyers have twisted it into such a state of bedevilment that the original merits of the case have long disappeared from the face of the earth. It's about a Will, and the trusts under a Will – or it was, once. It is about nothing but Costs, now. We are always appearing, and disappearing, and swearing, and interrogating, and filing, and cross – filing, and arguing, and scaling, and motioning, and referring, and reporting, and revolving about the Lord Chancellor and all his satellites, and equitably waltzing ourselves off to dusty death, about Costs. That's the great question. All the rest, by some extraordinary means, has smelt away." – Charles Dickens

Before slavery, the areas all around Wimpole Street, London and beyond were farmlands that were worked by wretched, feudal agricultural labourers from mainland Europe, working for lords, also from mainland Europe, all on stolen aborigine land. So, there was no council on Wimpole Street before slavery, and there wouldn't have been a council on Wimpole Street had there not been slavery.

Almost everything was stolen, or is the yield of fraud, except agriculture. Everything else is a lie.

"Agriculture not only gives riches to a nation, but the only riches she can call her own." – Dr Samuel Johnson

* * * * * *

ANDREW HURST: Okay. You told the Committee that you have never – "In relation to Patient A, I was not aggressive or rough. I do a lot of crowns for people. I never had any allegations like this, although I must say that some people misinterpret my speech impediment and find it strange."
NEGRO: Yes.
ANDREW HURST: This morning, when Mr Morris was asking you questions, you said: "I did not get complaint about aggressive treatment or rough treatment that I can recall."
NEGRO: Yes.
ANDREW HURST: Without reading it out, would you accept that Mr

Satanic Network

Hill has recorded here in April 1996 a written complaint which referred to the rough manner in which the patient was examined and the abusive language used by the dentist?

NEGRO: Yes.

NEGRO'S PERSPECTIVE:

Cultural difference! By "yes," the Negro meant "move on, you f****** stupid white boy with giant clitoris that pretends to be a prick."

Richard Hill did not record anything "here" or "there." The imbecile barrister of Mediocre Great England (MGE) was dishonest and/or recklessly confused.

ANDREW HURST: Do you accept, first of all, that is what Mr Hill has recorded?

NEGRO: I would like to tell you first that . . .

THE LEGAL ADVISER (MR DAVID SWINSTEAD): No.

Please answer the question.

NEGRO'S PERSPECTIVE:

The huge, seemingly acromegaly-headed, dull, dishonest, and racist baabaa believed that it was possible or wise to pour fine wine into a dirty and leaky wine sack.

If Mr David Swinstead could prove that he was not dishonest and/or recklessly confused, he must sue the Negro.

Had the imbecile baabaa worked harder at school, he could have been a QC at 2 Bedford Row, and would almost certainly have been able to discern when an imbecile barrister like the GDC counsel Andrew Hurst was talking rot.

"Nothing that you will learn in the course of your studies will be of the slightest possible use to you in after life – save only this – if you work hard and diligently you should be able to detect when a man is talking rot, and that, in my view, is the main, if not the sole, purpose of education." – J.A. Smith, Oxford University
Professor, Moral Philosophy

"In examinations, those who do not wish to know ask questions of those who cannot tell." – Walter Raleigh

Moron baabaa or Mr David Swinstead, sir, it is impossible to answer stupid questions in the council before a seemingly council of racist thugs, but it is possible to do so outside the council with sarcasm, insults, and humour.

Sir, had you worked harder at the schools that David Morris's mama sent you to, you'd have been able to detect that the fella, the pretend barrister (Andrew Hurst), was talking rot.

THE CHAIRMAN (DR SHIV PABARY, MEMBER OF THE BRITISH EMPIRE): It is important.

NEGRO'S PERSPECTIVE:

A McDalit arrives in England from India or Bangladesh. He then eats three or four sausages (make it five), eats plenty of "cadavers" or pretend "fish and chips," and buys himself a Mercedes-Benz motor car with the proceeds of mediocrity and confusion. The satanic network sees sincerity and merit in incompetence. He is recommended for a very high title and becomes a tool of the satanic network.

"The English think that incompetence is the same thing as sincerity." – Quentin Crisp

The deluded, myopic, and racist satanic network is a shepherd of morons, without an objective basis, and it awards itself the monopoly of knowledge. LIARS!

Meritocracy was irrelevant within the racist satanic network as the money they shared was the proceeds of stealing and selling human beings.

Dr Shiv Pabary, the sincerely perceived Moron Member of the British Empire (MMBE), seemed to believe that if two upper class barristers who talked rot with upper class English accents (the kuli didn't know that) said something, and a mere Negro disagrees, the Negro must be wrong and mad. The Romans and the Jews thought so too in the council. They were too dull and had not realised the notion of infinite reasoning power. Kuli olodo! Kuli ode!

"To disagree with three-fourths of the British public on all points is one of the first elements of sanity, one of the deepest consolations in all moments of spiritual doubt." – Oscar Wilde

"He who joyfully marches to music in rank and file has already earned my contempt. He has been given a large brain by mistake, since for him the spinal cord would suffice." – Albert Einstein

"The best argument against democracy is a five-minute conversation with the average voter." – Sir Winston Churchill

Sir Winston Churchill implied that the average British adult was a moron.

Dr Shiv Pabary, Member of the British Empire, is a shepherd of England young adults.

✻ ✻ ✻ ✻ ✻

ANDREW HURST: And it is probably more in your interest to listen to the question.
NEGRO: No.

NEGRO'S PERSPECTIVE:
Andrew Hurst, Mediocre Great England (MGE) class barrister: typical racist, ignorant "white boy!"

In order to conceal the evil past, Andrew Hurst's mama seemed to have lied to him that in any dialogue with a mere Negro who was not born "here" and does not impersonate the accent of those that were born "here," and the Negro must be wrong or display lunacy. Oyinbo olodo! Oyinbo ode!

Andrew Hurst's mama did not want him to know that his ancestors used made-in-Birmingham guns, not brains, to loot the world. Whenever the racist bastards murdered, they dispossessed, and wherever they robbed, they took possession. They were murderous cowards, racist thugs, armed robbers, and thieves.

"All have taken what had other owners, and all have had recourse to arms rather than quit the prey on which they had fastened." – Dr Samuel Johnson

"Those who have robbed have also lied." – Dr Samuel Johnson

Any Negro that disagrees with a moron "white boy" must be inattentive. He should come with me to Lagos and repeat that. It will cross my mind, but it wouldn't stay there, to amalgamate his olfactory protuberance with his olfactory lobe with a left hook, then left and right upper cuts in combination, in exactly the same way that Lord Lugard amalgamated Northern and Southern Nigeria in 1914, in pursuance of stealing raw materials and natural resources, but as I always carried a peace tool, I always sought peace, and might pull up my shirt to reveal my peace tool, and give a hint that I could grant him eternal and everlasting peace.

✼ ✼ ✼ ✼ ✼

ANDREW HUSRT: Sorry? You do not accept that he has written it down here?
NEGRO: No.

NEGRO'S PERSPECTIVE:
If Richard Hill, the she-man-like man, did not write it down here, and he could not write it up there, where could he have written it?
F****** idiot!
Oyinbo olodo! Oyinbo ode!
The former England young adult and shepherd of England young adults was not sent to schools in Mediocre Great England (MGE) by Andrew Hurst's mama where the consistent capacity to read and comprehend the English language was properly taught. Had she sent her ward to such a school, he'd have realised on 21 November 2008 that Richard Hill did not write anything down or up or underground in 1996.
F****** moron, brainless "white boy!"
I'd rather be fed bullets through my shit hole and die instantly than be intellectually defeated by a stupid "white boy" like Andrew Hurst.
"There is no sin except stupidity." – Oscar Wilde

✼ ✼ ✼ ✼ ✼ ✼

ANDREW HURST: He has written it down, has he not?
NEGRO: These statements were recovered by Mrs Sally Wright.

NEGRO'S PERSPECTIVE:
The England class imbecile barrister, who seemed to conceal imbecility beneath the cloak of the most favourable skin colour and embellished all with an imitation upper-class accent, which is one of the most efficient accents for talking nonsense, read Richard Hill's signed statement of 23.09.2008, and he did not understand it, and he talked nonsense with

civilised decorum and a nearly pure upper-class English accent. Shi* is shi* in any accent.

Those regularly spun are amongst the dullest adult population in the industrialised world. Being a barrister, albeit an England class barrister, Andrew Hurst is amongst the topmost former England young adults and a shepherd of England young adults.

"FAILING SCHOOLS AND A BATTLE FOR BRITAIN: This was the day the British education establishment's 50-year betrayal of the Nation's children lay starkly exposed in all its ignominy. After testing 166,000 people in 24 education systems, the Organisation for Economic Cooperation and Development (OECD) finds that England young adults are amongst the least literate and numerate in the industrialised world." – The Daily Mail, 09.01.2013

Shepherds of morons are likelier to be morons too.

If the bottommost part of a whole is world class bottommost, the topmost part of that whole is unlikely to be world class topmost.

Oyinbo olodo! Oyinbo ode!

The ancestors of some people accurately foresaw that their descendants would be dull in the distant future, so when they found guns they used them to slaughter millions of creations of Almighty God, and armed others to mercilessly kill millions more, and worked millions more still until they succumbed to unbearable, inhuman labour, solely in pursuance of the comfort of their descendants in the distant future.

God Almighty is watching all (Proverbs 15:3).

"Many Scots masters were considered among the most brutal, with life expectancy on their plantations averaging a mere four years. We worked them to death then simply imported more to keep the sugar and thus the money flowing. Unlike centuries of grief and murder, an apology costs nothing. So what does Scotland have to say?" – Herald Scotland, Ian Bell, columnist, Sunday 28 April 2013

Dr. Olayinka Bamgbelu

Merciless, racist bas****s!

"When we consider the vastness of the continent of Africa; when we reflect how all other countries have for some centuries past been advancing in happiness and civilisation; when we think how in this same period all improvement in Africa has been defeated by her intercourse with Britain; when we reflect that it was we ourselves that have degraded them to that wretched brutishness and barbarity which we now plead as the justification for our guilt; how the slave trade has enslaved their minds, blackened their character, and sunk them so low in the scale of animal beings that some think apes are of a higher class, and fancy the Orang–outang has given them the go-by. What mortification must we feel at having so long neglected to think of our guilt, or attempt at reparation! It seems indeed, as if we had determined to forbear from all interference until the measure of folly and wickedness was so full and complete, until the policy which eventually belongs to vice was become so plain and glaring that not an individual in this country should refuse to join the abolition. It seems as if we had waited until the persons most interested should be tired out with the folly nefariousness of the trade, and should unite in petitioning against it." – William Wilberforce, 1789

Civilised Christians! Yeah right!

For centuries, they poured millions of guns, including made in-Birmingham guns, amongst those who had no means of treating penetrative gunshot wounds.

F****** merciless, sadistic barbarians!

"He (the Briton) is a barbarian and believes the customs of his tribe and Island are the laws of nature." – Judge Bernard Shaw

"Even if these miserable beings were proved guilty of every crime before you take them off, ought we not to take upon ourselves the office of executioners? And even if we condescend so far, still can we be justified in acquiring them in exchange for our guns, carrying and selling them for great profits, unless we have clear proof that they are criminals? But, if we go much further, if we ourselves tempt them to sell their fellow creatures to us, we may rest assured that they will take care to provide by every possible method a supply of victims increasing in proportions to our demand. Can we, then, hesitate in deciding whether the wars in Africa are their wars or ours? It was our arms in the river of Cameroon, put into the hands of the trader, that furnished him with the means of pushing his trade; and I have no more doubt that they are British arms, put into the hands of Africans, which promote universal war and desolation that I can doubt their having done so in that individual instance. I have shown how great is the enormity of this evil, even on the supposition that we take only convicts and prisoners of war. But take the subject in another way, and how does it stand? Think of 80,000 persons carried out of their native country by we know not what means! For crimes imputed! For light or inconsiderable faults! For debts perhaps! For crime of witchcraft! Or a thousand other weak or scandalous pretexts! Reflect on 80,000 persons annually taken off! There is something in the horror of it that surpasses all bounds of imagination. Admitting that there exists in Africa something like to Courts of justice; yet what an office of humiliation and meanness is it in us, to take upon ourselves to carry into execution the iniquitous sentences of such courts, as if we also were strangers to all religion and to the first principles of justice! But that country, it is said, has been in some degree civilised, and civilised by us. It is said that they have gained some knowledge of the principles of justice." – Prime Minister William Pitt the Younger, 1792

"Agriculture not only gives riches to a nation, but the only riches she can call her own." – Dr Samuel Johnson

The land yielded and yields only food; almost everything else was stolen or has fraud as its foundation.

"Those who have robbed have also lied." – Dr Samuel Johnson corroborating prophet Habakkuk Before slavery, what?

ANDREW HURST: Hold on. Perhaps you misunderstand the question. First of all because the Committee do not have the document we are looking at, all right?
NEGRO: Yes.

NEGRO'S PERSPECTIVE:
Any Negro who dared disagree with mediocre and racist "white boy,"

albeit England class barrister, is unilaterally, without cogent, objective basis, adjudged to be ignorant and/or a lunatic.

The Romans and the Jews in the crooked council were shallower than England class barristers (some barristers go on to become judges) as they lynched our own God, Christ, like Gadhafi, merely because he spoke what they did not understand.

"Do you accept, first of all, that is what Mr Hill has recorded?" – Andrew Hurst, England class barrister that was appointed and instructed by the GDC

"Hold on. Perhaps you misunderstand the question. First of all because the Committee do not have the document we are looking at, all right?" – Andrew Hurst, England class barrister that was appointed and instructed by the GDC

When the f*** is there going to be a second of all?
Oyinbo olodo! Oyinbo ode!
When ignorance and arrogance copulate, insanity is their offspring.

I told the imbecile England class barrister the answer to his brainless confusion, but delivered the answer tainted with an original Ijebu Ode accent. He did not believe me because I am not white, and I was not as advanced as Shiv Pabary in the metamorphosis to becoming a white man.

In the 1890s, Andrew Hurst's ancestors used heavy guns to slaughter tens of thousands of my direct ancestors in the Jebu Massacre, which was basically caused by the greed of the British and their desire to cross into the hinterlands to steal natural resources without paying passage duty.

In West Africa in 1892 the British authorities were encountering problems in their dealings with the Ijebu tribe. The tribe, proud, isolated, and determined, lived between fifty and sixty miles northeast of Lagos on the Magbon River, and Jebu Ode was the tribal capital.

The tribal lands straddled important trade routes from the interior and the tribe received an income by charging customs dues. The Ijebu, a Yoruba-speaking tribe, did not want foreigners to cross the tribal territory.

In 1890 the Egirin market a few miles west of Epe on Lagos Lagoon had been closed by the Awujale, ruler of the Ijebu, cutting off the Lagos people from a source of up-country goods and commodities. Lagos had been a Crown Colony since 1886 and although envoys from the British governor in Lagos persuaded the ruler to re-open the market, a mood of hostility towards the British prevailed amongst the Ijebu.

In May 1891 the British Acting Governor, Captain C.M. Denton C.M.G., left Lagos with an escort of Hausa constables (Hausas are from the Islamic north of Nigeria) to visit Jebu Ode to make agreements allowing the free passage of trade goods through Ijebu territory. However, the Awujale refused to agree to the British requests and he also rejected the British presents given to him by Denton, doubtless fearing that to accept them would obligate him in some way.

London then instructed Lagos to obtain an apology from the Awujale for the perceived "insult" to Denton, and to insist on free right of way through the Awujale's territory. In January 1892 a representative of the Awujale went to Lagos to agree to the British demands, and in return the British granted the Ijebu 500 pounds annually to compensate for the loss of customs revenue. However, the tribe was unhappy with this outcome as it did not wish to change its traditional methods and practices, particularly when threatened by foreigners.

A white missionary was allowed through Jebu territory but the second one who tried received a rough time and was sent back, as was a party of Ibadan porters attempting to come south through Jebu Ode. London now authorized the use of force, quickly sending out some special service officers from England to act as a military staff. One of these was Captain Edward Roderick ("Roddy") Owen of the Lancashire Fusiliers, a famous jockey at British race meetings.

Troops from along the West African coast were concentrated at Lagos. The Gold Coast Constabulary sent 150 men from Accra, and the 1st Battalion of the West India Regiment (the British garrison regiment for West Africa) sent a company from Sierra Leone. These troops joined 150 "Lagos Hausas" (mainly escaped slaves from the north of Nigeria that had been recruited and trained into an efficient unit now titled the Lagos Constabulary) and some irregulars from Ibadan, north of Jebu country.

The Inspector-General of the Gold Coast Constabulary, Colonel F.C. Scott C.B., was the force commander and on 12 May 1892 he moved his 450 armed men and 340 carriers by a flotilla of vessels and canoes up Lagos Lagoon, and landed at Epe without opposition. Scott's men had three seven-pounder field guns, two Nordenfeldt guns (hand-cranked multi-barrel weapons that fired in waves of rounds), two rocket troughs, and a Maxim gun as fire support. At Leckie, near Epe, another 186 carriers were recruited.

(The West Indians were expert at using rockets, either for drawing enemy fire by firing them into likely ambush locations, or for setting village thatched roofs alight.)

The Jebus were believed to have up to 8,000 men and some old Snider rifles, but the tribe was not rated highly as fighters. This assumption was mistaken. The British left Epe on 16 May and marched to Pobo, where it burned four villages but took eight casualties. The next day the force reached Atumba and had to fight hard for half an hour. One Briton was killed and one wounded whilst twelve Africans were wounded. The Jebus lost heavily to machine-gun fire.

The advance continued with the Ibadan irregulars scouting ahead and the Gold Coasters and Lagos Hausa alternating daily as advance and rear guard. All Jebu villages found were torched. Colonel Scott was anxious to prove that the Gold Coasters and Hausas could fight as effectively as the regular West Indians, and so the latter were kept tucked away in the main column. The track to Jebu Ode that the British were following was the main trade route, and the outer edges where feet had tramped for hundreds of years were well rutted down, leaving a triangle of earth in the middle which had to be straddled by the marchers. Thick bush on either side forced the British column into a single file two miles long, allowing the Jebu to easily pick off soldiers and then disappear, leaving a corpse or wounded man blocking the track. As yet no white man had ever used this route and the Jebu fought hard to preserve that tradition.

On 19 May the Jebu made a determined stand on the north bank of a ford over the Yemoyi River, five miles south of Jebu Ode. The river here was forty yards wide and sometimes over four feet deep (the Jebu had dug it deeper for this battle to create a difficult obstacle), and above and below the ford the river narrowed and ran through impenetrable bush. The southern approach to the ford ran through a gorge that prevented the British from manoeuvring off the track. The enemy warriors were located on both sides of the river, and the narrowness of the track being used made it extremely difficult for the British to bring up and concentrate their heavy weapons. The Ijebu were determined to prevent the British from crossing the ford and as warriors were shot down or ran out of bullets fresh relays of men from the rear replaced them.

Scott ordered his Hausa advance guard across the river but they did not want to move. It was believed that the Jebu had made a human sacrifice to the goddess of the river in order to obtain the goddess's support in repelling the invaders. Finally a machine gun was brought up to the river bank and Scott ordered the West Indian Regiment Company under Major George Colquhoun Madden to storm the ford. The crossing was successful, and once the Hausa had observed that the river goddess was inactive then they too crossed and engaged the Jebu. By now the guns and rockets had struggled up the congested track and these fired into likely Jebu positions until resistance ceased.

The remainder of the force now crossed the ford and advanced half a mile to Imagbodon village where Scott took stock of the situation. Since they had left Epe the British had lost fifty-six men killed and thirty more wounded, including three white officers, one of them being Roddy Owen, at the river crossing. Although the Jebu had lost around 700 warriors at the ford, mainly to machine-gun fire, thousands more remained at large ready to fight.

Therefore, the next morning as the march resumed, Scott's advance guard was surprised to meet envoys from the Awujale offering submission. The Ijebu admitted to losing a thousand warriors and seven chiefs and were anxious to stop the burning of any more villages. The tribe accepted defeat and, in the words of the Awujale, they were "no fit for fight with white man."

A few hours later Jebu Ode had a Union flag flying over it, the Awujale's palace was being used as the British officers' mess, and the surrounding buildings housed the soldiers. Scott banned looting but this order antagonised the Ibadan irregulars who had to be disarmed. Flying columns marched along the trade routes declaring them open, and Roddy Owen, commanding the one that went north to Oru, destroyed the Ijebu toll gates there. The West Indians marched back to Lagos declaring that south-westerly route open also.

Before marching away and leaving a garrison in Jebu Ode, the British burned part of the city including the Fetish House. The Ijebu were great believers in dark practices and had slaughtered thousands of sacrificial victims in order to placate evil spirits (good spirits could be ignored as they did no harm). After ritual torture the victims were beheaded, buried alive, or nailed to trees by their heads. After the latter the bodies were thrown into a special pond but the skulls were left adorning the trees in the fetish groves.

Everybody except the casualties was pleased with the outcome of this little war. The Colonial Office was particularly gratified that the total cost of the expeditionary force was less than 5,000 pounds sterling. Scott returned to the Gold Coast as Sir Francis Scott, Knight Commander of St. Michael and St. George (K.C.M.G.). Major Madden became a Companion of the Distinguished Service Order (D.S.O.) and Captains Owen and the Honourable Arthur Stewart Hardinge, Royal Scots Fusiliers, were given Brevet promotions to Major.

British troops in the war, but not the Ibadan irregulars, were awarded the East & West Africa Medal with a clasp dated 1892.

The British also beheaded scores of thousands of nobles and serfs. For every nobleman decapitated, hundreds of serfs were also beheaded, and theirs were in not rituals or appeasement of gods; theirs were oftener vindictive revenge and silencing opposition, as the cleverest people are likelier to be opinionated. It created reverse natural selection, where very dull and compliant morons thrived.

In 1893, scores of Ijebu girls gave birth to Mulattos, including some of my direct family. So, I could be white inside.

"FAILING SCHOOLS AND A BATTLE FOR BRITAIN: This was the day the British education establishment's 50-year betrayal of the Nation's children lay starkly exposed in all its ignominy. After testing 166,000 people in 24 education systems, the Organisation for Economic Cooperation and Development (OECD) finds that England young adults are amongst the least literate and numerate in the industrialised world." – The Daily Mail, 09.01.2013

Morons beget morons!

The British beheaded or used heavy axes to remove the heads of dead bodies. Oliver Cromwell was exhumed and beheaded.

Prior to Europeans landing in Africa in the fifteenth century and slavery, our people sacrificed only animals to appease the gods, and what they desired usually came to pass: rain, a good harvest, abatement of epidemics and attacks by carnivores, and others.

When appeasement with animals did not remove the merciless tyranny of slavery, our ancestors believed that the gods of the evil of slavery demanded something more, and the ultimate they had to sacrifice was human beings.

Europeans introduced millions of guns amongst those who had no means of treating penetrative gunshot wounds, and in several hundred years, scores of millions of human beings were slaughtered by Europeans and with European guns in Africa, and millions more were mercilessly worked to death on cane, cotton, and tobacco plantations in faraway land.

"Many Scots masters were considered among the most brutal, with life expectancy on their plantations averaging a mere four years. We worked them to death then simply imported more to keep the sugar and thus the money flowing. Unlike centuries of grief and murder, an apology costs nothing. So what does Scotland have to say?" – Herald Scotland, Ian Bell, columnist, Sunday 28 April 2013

"It was our arms in the river of Cameroon, put into the hands of the trader, that furnished him with the means of pushing his trade; and I have no more doubt that they are British arms, put into the hands of Africans, which promote universal war and desolation that I can doubt their having done so in that individual instance. I have shown how great is the enormity of this evil, even on the supposition that we take only convicts and prisoners of war. But take the subject in another way, and how does it stand? Think of 80,000 persons carried out of their native country by we know not what means! For crimes imputed! For light or inconsiderable faults! For debts perhaps! For crime of witchcraft! Or a thousand other weak or scandalous pretexts! Reflect on 80,000 persons annually taken off! There is something in the horror of it that surpasses all bounds of imagination." – Prime Minister William Pitt the Younger, 1792

"I know of no evil that has ever existed, nor can imagine any evil to exist, worse than the tearing of eighty thousand persons annually from their native land, by a combination of the most civilised nations inhabiting the most enlightened part of the globe, but more especially under the sanction of the laws of that Nation which calls herself the most free and the most happy of them all." – Prime Minister William Pitt the Younger, 1792

In the fifteen years between 1792 and 1807, when the Abolition Act entered the statute book (the saviour of Africa, William Pitt the Younger, died in 1806), at the 80,000 Africans per annum, about 1,200,000 Africans were carried and sold by Europeans in exchange for guns.

In the wars that were deliberately fomented to steal human beings and other resistant activities, about 640,000 Africans were mercilessly slaughtered in the African bush with European guns. So, in the fifteen years between 1792 and 1807, about 10,000,000 Africans were slaughtered in the African bush (9,600,000).

So, unrelenting, merciless tyranny induced psychosis and human sacrifices.

Beheadings in Britain:

Waltheof, Earl of Northumbria (1076) – Executed at Winchester by order of William I for taking part in the Revolt of the Earls

Sir William Wallace (1305) – famous Scottish resistance fighter, hanged, drawn, and quartered by order of Edward I

Piers Gaveston (1312) – Executed near Warwick by Thomas, 2nd Earl of Lancaster in the Baron's Revolt

Thomas, 2nd Earl of Lancaster, Lord High Steward (1322) – Executed at Pontefract by Edward II of England

Edmund FitzAlan, 9th Earl of Arundel (1326) – Executed at Hereford by Queen Isabella, Regent for Edward III

Edmund of Woodstock, 1st Earl of Kent, Lord Wardens of the Cinque Ports (1330) – Executed at Winchester by Queen Isabella, Regent for Edward III

Sir Robert Hales, Lord High Treasurer (1381) – Executed at Tower Hill by rebels during the Peasants' Revolt

Simon of Sudbury, Lord Chancellor, Archbishop of Canterbury, and Bishop of London (1381) – Executed at Tower Hill by rebels during the Peasants' Revolt

Richard Lyons, London Merchant and Financier (1381) – Beheaded in London by rebels during the Peasants' Revolt

Sir John Cavendish, Chief Justice of the King's Bench, Chancellor of the University of Cambridge (1381) – Executed in Bury St Edmunds by rebels during the Peasants' Revolt

Wat Tyler (1381) – Beheaded in London by order of the Lord Mayor of London during the Peasants' Revolt

John Ball (1381) – Hanged, drawn, and quartered at St Albans after the Peasants' Revolt

Sir Simon de Burley, KG (1388) – Executed on Tower Hill by the Merciless Parliament for supporting Richard II of England

John de Beauchamp (1388) – Executed on Tower Hill by the Merciless Parliament for supporting Richard II of England

Sir John Berners (1388) – Executed on Tower Hill by the Merciless Parliament for supporting Richard II of England

Richard FitzAlan, 11th Earl of Arundel, KG (1397) – Executed at Tower Hill by order of Richard II of England

William le Scrope, 1st Earl of Wiltshire, Sir John Bussy, and Sir Henry Green (1399) – Executed in Bristol Castle by the Duke of Hereford (soon to be Henry IV of England)

Ralph de Lumley, 1st Baron Lumley (1400) – Executed at Cirencester during reign of Henry IV for the Epiphany Rising

Thomas le Despenser, 1st Earl of Gloucester (1400) – Executed at Bristol by order of Henry IV for the Epiphany Rising

John Holland, 1st Duke of Exeter, KG, Lord Great Chamberlain and Justice of Chester (1400) – Executed at Pleshey Castle, Essex by order of Joan Fitzalan, Countess of Hereford, with the approval of her son-in-law Henry IV, for the Epiphany Rising

John Montacute, 3rd Earl of Salisbury, KG (1400) – Executed at Cirencester during reign of Henry IV for the Epiphany Rising

Thomas Holland, 1st Duke of Surrey, KG, Earl Marshal (1400) – Executed at Cirencester during reign of Henry IV for the Epiphany Rising

Sir Benard Brocas (1400) – Beheaded at Tyburn during reign of Henry IV for the Epiphany Rising

Thomas Percy, 1st Earl of Worcester (1403) – Executed by order of Henry IV (Hanged, drawn, and quartered)

Sir Richard Vernon (1403) – Executed by order of Henry IV (Hanged, drawn, and quartered)

Sir Richard Venables (1403) – Executed by order of Henry IV (Hanged, drawn, and quartered)

Thomas de Mowbray, 4th Earl of Norfolk, Earl Marshal (1405) – Executed at York by order of Henry IV for treason

Richard le Scrope, Archbishop of York (1405) – Executed at York by order of Henry IV for treason

Sir William de Plumpton (1405) – Executed by order of Henry IV for treason

Richard of Conisburgh, 3rd Earl of Cambridge (1415) – Executed at Southampton by order of Henry V of England for his involvement in the Southampton Plot

Henry Scrope, 3rd Baron Scrope of Masham, KG (1415) – Executed at Southampton by order of Henry V of England for his involvement in the Southampton Plot

William de la Pole (1450) – Beheaded at sea, possibly by order of Richard Plantagenet, 3rd Duke of York

James Fiennes, 1st Baron Saye and Sele (1450) – Beheaded in London by rebels led by Jack Cade

James Touchet, 5th Baron Audley (1459) – Executed after Battle of Blore Heath for being a Lancastrian

Richard Neville, 5th Earl of Salisbury, KG, PC, Lord Chancellor (1460) – Executed after the Battle of Wakefield for being a Yorkist

Edmund, Earl of Rutland (1460) – Executed by order of Lord Clifford for being a Yorkist (stabbed to death during the Battle of Wakefield and later decapitated)

Thomas Thorpe, speaker (1461) – Beheaded by a London mob

Thomas Courtenay, 14th Earl of Devon (1461) – Executed after the Battle of Towton for being a Lancastrian

Sir Owen Tudor (1461) – Executed after the Battle of Towton for being a Lancastrian

James Butler, 5th Earl of Ormond, 1st Earl of Wiltshire (1461) – Executed after the Battle of Towton for being a Lancastrian

Sir Thomas Kyriell (1461) – Executed by order of Margaret of Anjou after the Second Battle of St Albans for being a Yorkist

William Bonville, 1st Baron Bonville (1461) – Executed by order of Margaret of Anjou after the Second Battle of St Albans for being a Yorkist

John de Vere, 12th Earl of Oxford (1462) – Executed by order of John Tiptoft, 1st Earl of Worcester

Lord Aubrey de Vere, son of John de Vere, 12th Earl of Oxford (1462) – Executed at Tower Hill by order of John Tiptoft, 1st Earl of Worcester

Henry Beaufort, 3rd Duke of Somerset (1464) – Beheaded after the Battle of Hexham for being a Lancastrian

Robert Hungerford, 3rd Baron Hungerford (1464) –

Beheaded at Newcastle after the Battle of Hexham for being a Lancastrian

Thomas de Ros, 9th Baron de Ros (1464) – Beheaded at Newcastle after the Battle of Hexham for being a Lancastrian

Sir Philip Wentworth (1464) – Beheaded at Middleham after the Battle of Hexham for being a Lancastrian

Sir William Tailboys (1464) – Executed after Battle of Hexham for being a Lancastrian

Sir Humphrey Neville (1469) – Executed at York by order of Edward IV for being a Lancastrian

Sir Charles Neville, brother of above (1469) – Executed at York by order of Edward IV for being a Lancastrian

Richard Woodville, 1st Earl Rivers, Lord High Treasurer and Lord Warden of the Cinque Ports (1469) – Executed by order of Richard Neville, 16th Earl of Warwick for being a Yorkist

Sir John Woodville, son of above (1469) – Executed by order of Richard Neville, 16th Earl of Warwick for being a Yorkist

Sir Henry Courtenay (1469) – Executed for treason at Salisbury for being a Lancastrian; brother of Sir Hugh Courtenay and the 14th and 15th Earls of Devon who were all executed for being Lancastrians (in 1471, 1461, and 1471 respectively)

William Herbert, 1st Earl of Pembroke (1469) – Executed after Battle of Edgecote Moor for being a Yorkist

Sir Richard Herbert (1469) – Executed after Battle of Edgecote Moor for being a Yorkist, also illegitimate son of the above

Humphrey Stafford, 1st Earl of Devon (1469) – Captured and executed in Bridgewater for being a Yorkist

Richard Welles, 7th Baron Welles (1470) – Executed on battlefield of Losecote by order of Edward IV for being a Lancastrian

Sir Thomas Dymoke (1470) – Executed on battlefield of Losecote by order of Edward IV for being a Lancastrian

Robert Welles, 8th Baron Willoughby de Eresby (1470) – Son of Richard Welles; executed after Battle of Losecoat by order of Edward IV for being a Lancastrian

John Tiptoft, 1st Earl of Worcester, Lord High Treasurer (1470) – Executed at Tower Hill by order of Henry VI for being a Yorkist

Edmund Beaufort, 4th Duke of Somerset (1471) – Beheaded after the

Battle of Tewkesbury for being a Lancastrian

John Courtenay, 15th Earl of Devon (1471) – Beheaded after the Battle of Tewkesbury for being a Lancastrian

Sir Hugh Courtenay (1471) – Beheaded after the Battle of Tewkesbury for being a Lancastrian

Sir Gervase Clifton (1471) – Beheaded after the Battle of Tewkesbury for being a Lancastrian

John Delves (1471) – Beheaded after the Battle of Tewkesbury for being a Lancastrian (The eldest son of Sir John Delves, who was killed in the battle)

Sir Thomas Tresham, MP for Buckinghamshire, Huntingdonshire, and Northamptonshire, High Sheriff of Cambridgeshire and Huntingdonshire, High Sheriff of Sussex, High Sheriff of Surrey, Comptroller of the Household, and Speaker of the House of Commons (1471) – Beheaded after the Battle of Tewkesbury for being a Lancastrian

Sir John Langstrother, Grand Prior of the Hospital of St John of Jerusalem (1471) – Beheaded after the Battle of Tewkesbury for being a Lancastrian

Sir Thomas Neville, the Bastard of Fauconberg (1471) – Executed at Middleham Castle or Southampton by order of Edward IV for being a Lancastrian

Sir Thomas Vaughan (1483) – Executed by order of Richard III even though he was a Yorkist

William Hastings, 1st Baron Hastings (1483) – Executed near Tower Chapel by order of Richard III for being a Lancastrian

Henry Stafford, 2nd Duke of Buckingham, Lord High Constable (1483) – Beheaded at Shrewsbury by order of Richard III for being too close to the crown and also for being a Lancastrian

Anthony Woodville, 2nd Earl Rivers, Chief Butler of England (1483) – Executed at Pontefract castle by order of Richard III for being a Lancastrian and uncle of the below

Sir Richard Grey (1483) – Executed at Pontefract Castle by order of Richard III for being a Lancastrian and nephew of the above

Sir Thomas St Leger (1483) – Beheaded at Exeter for rebellion against his brother-in-law Richard III

William Catesby (1485) – Beheaded at Leicester by order of Henry VII of England after the Battle of Bosworth for being a Yorkist

Sir William Stanley (1495) – Executed at Tower Hill by order of Henry VII of England for supporting the pretender Perkin Warbeck

James Tuchet, 7th Baron Audley (1497) – Executed at Tower Hill by order of Henry VII of England for opposing taxation

Edward Plantagenet, 17th Earl of Warwick, Heir to the English Throne from 9 April 1484 – March 1485 (1499) – Executed at Tower Hill by order of Henry VII of England

Sir James Tyrrell (1502) – Executed at Tower Hill by order of Henry VII of England for treason

Sir John Wyndham (1502) – Executed at Tower Hill by order of Henry VII of England for treason

Sir Edmund Dudley, Speaker of the House of Commons (1510) – Executed at Tower Hill by order of Henry VIII of England for extortion

Sir Richard Empson, Speaker of the House of Commons, Chancellor of the Duchy of Lancaster (1510) – Executed at Tower Hill by order of Henry VIII of England for extortion

Sir Andrew Barton, High Admiral of Scotland (1511) – executed on capture as a pirate, according to ballads

Edmund de la Pole, 3rd Duke of Suffolk (1513) – Executed at Tower Hill by order of Henry VIII of England as Yorkist claimant to throne

Edward Stafford, 3rd Duke of Buckingham, KG, Lord High Steward and Lord High Constable (1521) – Executed at Tower Hill by order of Henry VIII of England as claimant to throne

Sir Rhys ap Gruffydd (1531) – Executed at Tower Hill by order of Henry VIII of England for conspiracy with Scotland

Saint John Fisher, Catholic Bishop of Rochester (1535) – Executed at Tower Hill by order of Henry VIII of England for refusing to take Oath of Supremacy

Sir Thomas More, Lord Chancellor, Chancellor of the Duchy of Lancaster, Speaker of the House of Commons (1535) – Executed at Tower Hill by order of Henry VIII of England for refusing to take Oath of Supremacy

Anne Boleyn, Queen of England and Henry's Wife (1536) – Executed by sword at the Tower of London by order of Henry VIII of England for High Treason

George Boleyn, Viscount Rochford (1536) – Executed at Tower Hill by order of Henry VIII of England for High Treason

Sir Henry Norris, Groom of the Stool (1536) – Executed at Tower Hill by order of Henry VIII of England for High Treason

Sir William Brereton, KB, Groom of the Privy Chamber (1536) – Executed at Tower Hill by order of Henry VIII of England for High Treason

Sir Francis Weston, Gentleman of the Privy Chamber (1536) – Executed at Tower Hill by order of Henry VIII of England for High Treason

Mark Smeaton (1536) – Executed at Tower Hill by order of Henry VIII of England for High Treason

Thomas Darcy, 1st Baron Darcy de Darcy, KG (1537) – Beheaded at Tower Hill by order of Henry VIII of England for being in the Pilgrimage of Grace

John Hussey, 1st Baron Hussey of Sleaford, Chief Butler of England (1537) – Beheaded at Lincoln by order of Henry VIII of England for being in the Pilgrimage of Grace

Sir Nicholas Tempest (1537) – Hung, drawn, and quartered by order of Henry VIII of England for being in Bigod's Rebellion

Sir Edward Neville (1538) – Beheaded at Tower Hill by order of Henry VIII of England for being in Bigod's Rebellion

Henry Pole, 11th Baron Montacute (1539) – Executed at Tower Hill by order of Henry VIII of England for being in Exeter Conspiracy

Henry Courtenay, 1st Marquess of Exeter, KG, PC, Lord Warden of the Stannaries (1539) – Executed at Tower Hill by order of Henry VIII of England for being in Exeter Conspiracy

Sir Nicholas Carew, KG, PC, Master of the Horse (1539) – Executed at Tower Hill by order of Henry VIII of England for being in Exeter Conspiracy

Sir Thomas Dingley (1539) – Executed at Tower Hill by order of Henry VIII of England for being implicated in the Pilgrimage of Grace

Blessed Sir Adrian Fortescue (1539) – Executed by order of Henry VIII of England for Catholicism

Richard Whiting, Abbot of Glastonbury (1539) – Executed on Glastonbury Tor by order of Thomas Cromwell (hung, drawn, and quartered)

Thomas Cromwell, 1st Earl of Essex, KG, PC, Secretary of State, Master of the Rolls, Lord Privy Seal, Governor of the Isle of Wight, Justice in Eyre, Lord Great Chamberlain (1540) – Executed at Tower Hill by order of Henry VIII of England for treason

Walter Hungerford, 1st Baron Hungerford of Heytesbury (1540) – Executed at Tower Hill by order of Henry VIII of England for high treason and buggery

Leonard Grey, 1st Viscount Grane, Lord Deputy of Ireland (1541) – Executed at Tower Hill by order of Henry VIII of England for High Treason after allowing the escape of his nephew Gerald FitzGerald, 11th Earl of Kildare

Margaret Pole, 8th Countess of Salisbury (1541) – Executed at Tower Green by order of Henry VIII of England for high treason

Sir Thomas Culpepper (1541) – Executed at Tyburn by order of Henry VIII for high treason (adultery with the queen)

Catherine Howard, Queen of England and Henry's Wife (1542) – Executed at Tower Green by order of Henry VIII of England for High Treason

Jane Boleyn, Viscountess Rochford, Wife of executed George Boleyn, Viscount Rochford, and sister-in-law of Anne Boleyn (1542) – Executed at Tower Green by order of Henry VIII of England for High Treason

Sir John Neville of Chevet (1546) – Executed by order of Henry VIII of England

Henry Howard, Earl of Surrey, KG, Earl Marshal (1547) – Executed at Tower Hill during the reign of Henry VIII of England for treason

Thomas Seymour, 1st Baron Seymour of Sudeley, Master-General of the Ordnance, Lord Warden of the Cinque Ports, Lord High Admiral, also was the husband of Henry VIII's sixth wife and widow Catherine Parr and the brother of Henry's third wife Jane Seymour (1549) – Beheaded for treason at Tower Hill during the reign of Edward VI of England

Edward Seymour, 1st Duke of Somerset, KG, PC, Earl Marshal, Lord High Treasurer, Lord High Admiral, Lord Protector of England in the period between the death of Henry VIII in 1547 and his own indictment in 1549 (1552) – Executed at Tower Hill during the reign of Edward VI of England for plotting murder of John Dudley

Sir Thomas Arundell of Lanherne, Gentleman of the Privy Chamber (1552) – Beheaded at Tower Hill during the reign of Edward VI of England for treason

Sir Michael Stanhope, Chief Gentleman of the Privy Chamber (1552) – Beheaded at Tower Hill during the reign of Edward VI of England for treason

John Dudley, 1st Duke of Northumberland, KG, Vice-Admiral, Lord Admiral, Governor of Boulogne, President of the Council in the Marches, Lord Great Chamberlain, Grand Master of the Royal Household, Earl Marshal of England, Lord President of the Council, Warden General of the Scottish Marches (1553) – Executed at Tower Hill by order of Mary I for supporting Lady Jane Grey

Sir John Gates KB (1553) – Executed at Tower Hill by order of Mary I for supporting Lady Jane Grey

Sir Thomas Palmer (1553) – Executed at Tower Hill by order of Mary I for supporting Lady Jane Grey

Lady Jane Grey, Queen of England 10–19 July 1553 and Heir to the English and Irish Thrones 21 June – 10 July 1553 (1554) – Executed at Tower Green by Mary I as claimant to throne

Lord Guilford Dudley, Son of John Dudley, 1st Duke of Northumberland and Royal Consort of England 10–19 July 1553 (1554) – Executed at Tower Hill by order of Mary I for supporting Lady Jane Grey

Henry Grey, 1st Duke of Suffolk, KG, Father of the above, Lord Lieutenant of Leicestershire, Justice in Eyre (1554) – Executed at Tower Hill by order of Mary I for rebellion

Sir Thomas Wyatt the Younger (1554) – Executed at Tower Hill by order of Mary I for rebellion

Thomas Howard, 4th Duke of Norfolk, KG, Earl Marshal (1573) – Executed at Tower Hill by order of Elizabeth I of England for Ridolfi plot

Thomas Percy, 7th Earl of Northumberland (1572) – Executed at York during the reign of Elizabeth I of England for taking part in the Rising of the North

Sir Thomas Doughty (1578) – Executed by order of Sir Francis Drake

Edward Arden (1583) – Executed at Tyburn during the reign of Elizabeth I of England for high treason (hanged, drawn, and quartered)

Sir Francis Throckmorton (1584) – Executed during the reign of Elizabeth I of England

Mary, Queen of Scots, Queen of Scots and Queen consort of France (1587) – Executed during the reign of Elizabeth I of England for treason

Robert Devereux, 2nd Earl of Essex, KG, Master of the Horse, Earl Marshal, Lord Lieutenant of Ireland, Custos Rotulorum of Pembrokeshire, Custos Rotulorum of Staffordshire, MasterGeneral of the

Ordnance (1601) – Executed at Tower Hill during the reign of Elizabeth I of England for High Treason

Sir Christopher Blount (1601) – Executed at Tower Hill during the reign of Elizabeth I of England for High Treason

Sir Charles Danvers (1601) – Executed at Tower Hill during the reign of Elizabeth I of England for High Treason

Sir Walter Raleigh, Lord Warden of the Stannaries, Lord Lieutenant of Cornwall, Vice-Admiral of Devon, Captain of the Yeomen of the Guard, Governor of Jersey (1618) – Executed in the Old Palace Yard, Westminster by orders of James VI

Mervyn Touchet, 2nd Earl of Castlehaven (1631) – Executed at Tower Hill for aiding buggery

Thomas Wentworth, 1st Earl of Strafford, KG, Custos Rotulorum of the West Riding of Yorkshire, Lord Lieutenant of Yorkshire, Lord Deputy of Ireland, Lord Lieutenant of Ireland (1641) – Executed at Tower Hill on orders of Parliament

Archbishop William Laud, Archbishop of Canterbury (1645) – Executed at Tower Hill on orders of Parliament

Sir John Hotham the Younger (2 January 1645) – Executed at Tower Hill on orders of Parliament for betraying the parliamentarians to the Royalists

Sir John Hotham, 1st Baronet the Elder, of Scarborough (died 3 January 1645) – Father of above, executed for betraying the parliamentarians to the Royalists

Charles I of England and Scotland (1649) – Executed in Whitehall, London by order of Cromwell's Parliament

James Hamilton, 1st Duke of Hamilton, KG, Master of the Horse, Lord Chancellor of Scotland (1649) – Executed by order of Cromwell's Parliament for being a Royalist

Arthur Capell, 1st Baron Capell of Hadham (1649) – Executed by order of Cromwell's Parliament for being a Royalist

Henry Rich, 1st Earl of Holland, KG, Master of the Horse, Captain of the Yeomen of the Guard, Lord Lieutenant of Berkshire, Lord Lieutenant of Middlesex, Justice in Eyre (1649) – Executed in London by order of Cromwell's Parliament for being a Royalist

Sir Henry Hyde (1650) – Beheaded in London by order of Cromwell's Parliament for being a Royalist

Eusebius Andrews (1650) – Beheaded on Tower Hill for treason as a Royalist

James Stanley, 7th Earl of Derby, KG, Lord Lieutenant of Cheshire, Lancashire, Vice-Admiral of Cheshire (1651) – Executed at Bolton by order of Cromwell's Parliament for being a Royalist

Sir John Penruddock (1619–1655) – Executed at Exeter by order of Cromwell's Parliament for being a Royalist

Sir Henry Slingsby, 1st Baronet (1658) – Beheaded on Tower Hill, London by order of Cromwell's Parliament for being a Royalist

Reverend Dr. John Huett (1658) – Beheaded on Tower Hill, London by order of Cromwell's Parliament for being a Royalist

Gregory Clement (1660) (MP) – Hanged, drawn, and quartered at Charing Cross by Charles II as a regicide

Oliver Cromwell (1661) – Posthumously beheaded by order of Charles II

Sir Henry Vane the Younger (1662) – Executed at Tower Hill by order of Charles II for the death of his father Charles I

John Twyn (1663) – Hanged, drawn, quartered, and beheaded (and head displayed on a Ludgate spike) for publishing an anonymous pamphlet justifying the right of rebellion against the king

William Howard, 1st Viscount Stafford (1680) – Executed at Tower Hill for treason

Saint Oliver Plunkett (1681) – Hung, drawn, and quartered in London for treason

William Russell, Lord Russell, Member of Parliament for Tavistock and Tavistock (1683) – Executed for being involved with the Rye House Plot

Algernon Sidney (1683) – Executed at Tower Hill for being involved with the Rye House Plot

Sir Thomas Armstrong, Member of Parliament for Stafford (1684) – Executed by order of Judge Jeffreys for supporting Monmouth

James Scott, 1st Duke of Monmouth (1685) – Executed at Tower Hill in reign of James II after the Battle of Sedgemoor for treason

Lady Alice Lisle (1685) – Executed at Winchester by Judge Jeffreys during the Bloody Assizes for harbouring Monmouth rebels

Sir John Fenwick (1697) – Jacobite Rebel executed at Tower Hill in reign of William III for treason

Wingina (1586) – Roanoke Indian chief executed by first English settlers in the New World

Wituwamat (1623) – Neponset warrior killed and beheaded by the Plymouth Colony Pilgrim/soldier Miles Standish

Metacomet (1676) – New England Indian chief "King Philip" executed for resisting white settlement

Blackbeard (1718) – Famous pirate beheaded after capture at Ocracoke Island

* * * * *

Andrew Hurst cross examined the Negro in the council:

ANDREW HURST: So we can take it in stages. Surely you do agree with me that we are all looking at a piece of paper with 24 April 96 written on it.

NEGRO: Yes.

NEGRO'S PERSPECTIVE:

The imbecile barrister remembered the "fish and chips" bar course that forged him.

Only imbecile Negroes or utopian fantasists would expect changes by giant leaps instead of by steps.

"Knowledge advances by steps, not by leaps." – Thomas Babington, the First Baron Maucalay

* * * * *

ANDREW HURST: That a written complaint has been received, and the key areas of complaint are the rough manner in which the patient was examined and abusive language used by the dentist.

NEGRO: Yes.

Dr. Olayinka Bamgbelu

✳ ✳ ✳ ✳ ✳ ✳

NEGRO'S PERSPECTIVE:
Cultural difference! "Yes" expressed pent up anger and irritation for a thoroughly stupid "white boy" that seamed propped up by crude oil and gas money in exactly the same way as his murderous coward, racist thug, armed robber, and thieving ancestors were for centuries sustained by the proceeds of stealing and selling millions of human beings.

✳ ✳ ✳ ✳ ✳

ANDREW HURST: So you accept, first of all, that Mr Hill has made a record to that effect. I am not asking you whether it is true or not. I am not asking you where it has come from or anything else at the moment. I would just like you to confirm, for the sake of record, that that is what is written down on Mr Hill's record.

NEGRO'S PERSPECTIVE:
The intellectually impotent racist bas**** was exceedingly irritating! Overrated rubbish! The land yielded only food and yields only food. No brain, natural resources poor, only skin colour that the wearer neither made nor chose, and what else? Pure scam!

Thoroughly dull England class barrister: Some barristers go on to become judges.

"Sir, he was dull in company, dull in his closet, dull everywhere. He was dull in a new way, and that made many people think him great." – Dr Samuel Johnson

✳ ✳ ✳ ✳ ✳

DAVID MORRIS: Just before the witness answers, can I have a word with my learned friend? (Pause)

NEGRO'S PERSPECTIVE:
David Morris, the pretend defence, belatedly understood the simple English comprehension that his kindred and colleague struggled with. He was a racist thug and coward that seemed planted by Ian Sadler. Before slavery, the Great College Street, Westminster area was farmlands, worked by serfs for lords who had stolen the land from native Britons.

"It was in 1066 that William the Conqueror occupied Britain, stole our land and gained control by granting it to his Norman friends, thus creating a feudal system we have not yet fully escaped." – Tony Benn

Normans stole from others what others had stolen from others. Genetically pure Britons are extinct; all were dispossessed, robbed, and slaughtered.

Tony Benn was dishonest, or he was confused when he implied that he was genetically an aboriginal Briton. Genetically pure aboriginal Britons are extinct. They were dispossessed and robbed of their land by a motley assembly of mainland Europeans – hereditary serfs or descendants of feudal agricultural labourers – who were hugely transformed by the gigantic gains of slavery. They have reinvented themselves.

Racist, satanic networks are everywhere, and they seem to control everything except intellect. Meritocracy was irrelevant in their gang as the money (loot) they used to share was the proceeds of merciless, evil, racial hatred and fraud.

* * * * *

ANDREW HURST: Mr Morris has made a very helpful suggestion. Let us leave Mr Hill out of it for the moment as to who may have compiled the document, all right?
NEGRO: Yes.
ANDREW HURST: Somebody at the PCT has created a record which says 24 April 1996: "Rough manner in which patient examined, abusive language used by the dentist."
NEGRO: Yes.
NEGRO'S PERSPECTIVE:
The imbecile barrister did not realise that his question implied that it was impossible for nobody to create records.

Oyinbo olodo! Oyinbo ode!
Reductio ad absurdum!
F****** rotter blower!

"Nothing that you will learn in the course of your studies will be of the slightest possible use to you in after life – save only this – if you work hard and diligently you should be able to detect when a man is talking rot, and that, in my view, is the main, if not the sole, purpose of education." – J.A. Smith, Oxford University Professor, Moral Philosophy

※ ※ ※ ※ ※ ※

ANDREW HURST: You accept that someone has made that record.
NEGRO: Yes.

NEGRO'S PERSPECTIVE:

If no one is a f****** hole in the air, and it could not write, someone must have written it. Init? Oyinbo olodo! Oyinbo ode!

"In my school, the brightest boys did math and physics, the less bright did physics and chemistry, and the least bright did biology. I wanted to do math and physics, but my father made me do chemistry because he thought there would be no jobs for mathematicians." – Dr Stephen Hawking

Dr Stephen Hawking implied that those who did biology (Dr Richard Dawkins) were morons, and further implied that those that he did not classify, such as those who did law, were worse than morons.

Geniuses could see clearer and farther.

Andrew Hurst, the dull, dishonest, and racist former England young adult and shepherd of England young adults, seemed not to have done logical reasoning or enhanced mathematics or physics in the schools that Andrew Hurst's mama sent him to within one of the least literate countries in the industrialised world.

The privileged shepherds of morons should not insert their pricks in the mouths of dead pigs. They should insert their balls in the mouth of pacu, the organ grinder.

✳ ✳ ✳ ✳ ✳ ✳ ✳

ANDREW HURST: I am sorry if I misled you.

NEGRO'S PERSPECTIVE:
"I am sorry if I misled you" is different from "I am sorry I misled you."

Those regularly spun are amongst the dullest adult population in the industrialised world.

Andrew Hurst, the brainless moron, seemingly a pretend barrister, should go to Peckham in South London. He might find some brunos there with gold teeth. He should blow his f****** rot to the wretched bitches; they are likelier to believe him.

The imbecile barrister within one of the least literate countries in the industrialised world did not mislead me. A brainless "white boy" cannot mislead me. How?
If those who sit beside and before him in magnificent buildings up and down the land are cretins like him, they wouldn't know that he misled them, and he wouldn't either. Ignorance is bliss!
"Ignorance, the root and stem of all evil." – Plato
"Ignorance is like a delicate exotic fruit; touch it and the bloom is gone." – Oscar Wilde
Former England young adults like Andrew Hurst are the shepherds of England young adults.
Obo ngbobo gun igi ope. Monkey carries monkey up a hollow and fragile pawpaw tree in the African bush.
"I know of no evil that has ever existed, nor can imagine any evil to exist, worse than the tearing of eighty thousand persons annually from their native land, by a combination of the most civilised nations inhabiting the most enlightened part of the globe, but more especially under the sanction of the laws of that Nation which calls herself the most free and the most happy of them all." – Prime Minister William Pitt the Younger
There were laws then as there are laws now, but the judiciary of that era was neck deep in racial hatred and fraud, as it was fed like battery hens with the proceeds of racial hatred and naked fraud. Then, the proceeds

of naked fraud were used to build magnificent courts and prisons and paid the wages of judges who sent those who stole money to prisons that stolen money built.

CHAPTER 13

"The supreme vice is shallowness." – Oscar Wilde

Christ went before the crooked, shallow, and intellectually insufficient council.

"Then the people who had arrested Christ led him to the home of Caiaphas, the high priest, where the teachers of religious law and other leaders had gathered. Meanwhile, Peter was following behind and eventually came the Courtyard of the high priest's house. He went in and sat with the guards, and waited to see what was going to happen to Christ. Inside the leading priests and the entire Council were trying to find witnesses who will lie about Jesus, so they could put him to death. But, even though they found many who agreed to give false witness, there was no testimony that they could use. Finally two men were found who declared, 'This man said, "I am able to destroy the Temple of God and rebuild it in three days."' Then the high priest stood up and said to Christ, 'Well aren't you going to answer to these charges? What do you have to say for yourself?' But Jesus remained silent. Then the high priest said to him, 'I demand in the name living God that you will tell us whether you are the Messiah, the son of God.' Jesus replied, 'Yes it is as you say. And in the future you will see me, the son of Man, sitting at God's right hand in place of power and coming back in clouds of heaven.' Then the high priest tore his clothing to show his horror, shouting, 'Blasphemy! Why do you need other witnesses?

You have heard his blasphemy. What is your verdict?' 'Guilty!' they shouted. 'He must die!' Then they spit in Christ's face and hit him with their fists and slapped him, saying 'Prophesy to us, you Messiah! Who hit you that time?'" (as stated in the book of Matthew).

The council lied.

The council's judges lied.

If the width of Christ's mind is infinity, why was it impossible that he painted a different picture before the council and told the truth?

Only the pure in spirit shall see God, so part of the indivisible trinity must be pure in spirit.

We are all different. The picture we paint and the widths of our imaginations and realities are based upon the stretch of our individual minds. We are all who we are. We are the inheritors of our inheritances.

No one should pay for superficial or deeper attributes that they did not choose, did not make, and cannot change.

It is a fact and the absolute truth that the GDC is part of the UK society.

"All sections of UK society are institutionally racist." – Sir Bernard Hogan-Howe, London Metropolitan Police

"Many Scots masters were considered among the most brutal, with life expectancy on their plantations averaging a mere four years. We worked them to death then simply imported more to keep the sugar and thus the money flowing. Unlike centuries of grief and murder, an apology costs nothing. So what does Scotland have to say?" – Herald Scotland, Ian Bell, columnist, Sunday 28 April 2013

The merciless, sadistic savages, murderous cowards, racist thugs, armed robbers, and thieves are no longer here, but based upon very proximate observations and direct experiences, it is my sincerest belief that their sadistic genes continue to flow through the veins of some of those who remain here.

Before slavery, what?

The chairman of the council committee was Dr Shiv Pabary, Member of the British Empire. The Honourable Member was verifiably dull, dishonest, and racist.

Evidence:

Dr Shiv Pabary was an ignorant dentist, but he did not know because Dr Anthony Kravitz and all their friends in the crooked council and outside it were like him.

"My dear Algy, you talk exactly as if you were a dentist. It is very vulgar to talk like a dentist when one isn't a dentist. It produces a false impression." – Oscar Wilde

Dr Shiv Pabary, Member of the British Empire, desired to know whether the study casts of the teeth of Rachael Bishop, England young adult and England class senior NHS nurse, were preoperative cast or post-operative. The Moron Member of the Empire blew rot with alacrity.

"Nothing that you will learn in the course of your studies will be of the slightest possible use to you in after life – save only this – if you work hard and diligently you should be able to detect when a man is talking rot, and that, in my view, is the main, if not the sole, purpose of education." – J.A. Smith, Oxford University Professor, Moral Philosophy

Dr Shiv Pabary seemed intellectually disorientated and mentally imbalanced. The post-operative cast was irrelevant for the desired purpose. Common sense alone should have been enough to work that out. The Moron Member of the British Empire (MMBE) reasoned with only his spinal cord.

"He who joyfully marches to music in rank and file has already earned my contempt. He has been given a large brain by mistake, since for him the spinal cord would suffice." – Albert Einstein

He posed his question to a fellow who alleged that he was an expert dentist from Harley Street in London. The fellow must be amongst the topmost former England young adults and concomitantly a shepherd of England young adults.

"FAILING SCHOOLS AND A BATTLE FOR BRIT-AIN: This was the day the British education establishment's 50 year betrayal of the Nation's children lay starkly exposed in all its ignominy. After testing 166,000 people in 24 education systems, the Organisation for Economic Cooperation and Development (OECD) finds that England young adults are amongst the least literate and numerate in the industrialised world." – The Daily Mail, 09.01.2013

Dr Shiv Pabary, Member of the British Empire (MBE), is one of the shepherds of England young adults.

Shepherds of morons are likelier to be morons too.

If the bottommost part of a whole is world class bottommost, the topmost part of that whole is unlikely to be world class topmost.

*****

Dialogue between Dr Shiv Pabary, MBE, and the Harley Street expert with the mediocre and corrupt council on 17 November 2008:

DR SHIV PABARY (JUDGE): The models that you saw, what models were they? I just want to know whether they were preoperative models.

DR ROGER GOULDEN: They are not dated and my assumption is that they are preoperative and I assume that because the second dentist, Miss Traganiti referred to all of the enamel being removed and all of the enamel is not removed on these models, so my assumption is that these are preoperative. But they are undated and unmarked.

NEGRO'S PERSPECTIVE:

"But they are undated and unmarked." – Dr Roger Goulden

There is absolutely nothing golden about rot. Which date did the imbecile former England young adult expect on the model? Was it the date the impression was taken, which the laboratory was not bound to know, or the date the impression reached the laboratory, or the date the laboratory cast the impression, or the date the laboratory sent the cast, or the date the cast reached the dentist, or what?

Dentistry lucrative but too soft; many stupid people are dentists.
Oyinbo olodo! Oyinbo ode!
It is a fact and the absolute truth that Dr Roger Goulden maliciously lied and was dishonest or recklessly confused when he stated that the study casts were not marked.

Some deluded but very powerful privileged dullards do not believe in God, so they are oblivious to the notion of infinite reasoning power.

"They are not dated and my assumption is that they are preoperative and I assume that because the second dentist, Miss Traganiti referred to all of the enamel being removed and all of the enamel is not removed on these models, so my assumption is that these are preoperative." – Dr Roger Goulden

The imbecile baabaa, Dr Roger Goulden, former England young adult and shepherd of England young adults, did not seem to realise that by stating that "all of the enamel is not removed on these models," he implied that some of the enamel had been removed on the primary model.

What?

Shocking!

"Why, that is, because, dearest, you are a dunce." – Dr Samuel Johnson

✱ ✱ ✱ ✱ ✱ ✱ ✱ ✱

DR SHIV PABARY (JUDGE): What I am trying to get at is, can you be sure that they were models that were taken before the tooth was prepared or are they models that were taken after the tooth was prepared?

DR ROGER GOULDEN: I am 99 per cent certain it was before they were prepared.

DR SHIV PABARY (JUDGE): We had better look at them and give them an exhibit number.

DR ROGER GOULDEN: There is a name but no date.

NEGRO'S PERSPECTIVE:

The name on the models was a mark. The date the impressions were taken was in the patient's file.

Those regularly spun are amongst the dullest in the industrialised world.

Before slavery, the Harley Street, London area was farmland, and thoroughly wretched, feudal agricultural labourers (serfs) worked the land that their lordships, also from mainland Europe, had stolen from aboriginal Britons. Slavery immeasurably transformed the lives of their lordships and their quasi slaves (serfs). Their descendants have reinvented themselves on stolen land and fool the foolish with foolishness.

"It was in 1066 that William the Conqueror occupied Britain, stole our land and gained control by granting it to his Norman friends, thus creating a feudal system we have not yet fully escaped." – Tony Benn

Normans stole from others what others had stolen from others. Genetically pure Britons are extinct; all were dispossessed, robbed, and slaughtered.

Tony Benn was dishonest, or he was confused when he implied that he was genetically an aboriginal Briton. Genetically pure aboriginal Britons are extinct. They were dispossessed and robbed of their land by a motley assembly of mainland Europeans – hereditary serfs or descendants of feudal agricultural labourers – who were hugely transformed by the gigantic gains of slavery. They have reinvented themselves.

We are all genetic aliens on stolen land.

So, sir, please let me tell you, sir, Dr Roger Goulden, the foundation of Wimpole Street is forged by the bones of many millions of kidnapped, stolen, carried, and sold human beings. There was only farmland in the area of Wimpole Street before slavery. There wouldn't have been Wimpole Street in its current form had there not been slavery.

Almost everything was stolen.

"Those who have robbed have also lied." – Dr Samuel Johnson corroborating prophet Habakkuk

"Truth is the prime attribute of the Deity." – Lord Byron

"The grand object of all European traders in kidnapped and stolen Africans was - money, money, money; money was their god! In Africa, the poor wretched natives, blessed with the most fertile and luxuriant soil, are rendered so much the more miserable by the Christians' (European traders in stolen Africans) abominable traffic for slaves and the horrid cruelty and treachery of the petty [African] Kings. The Africans kings were encouraged by their European (Christian) customers who carry them strong liquors to enflame their madness and powder and bad fire-arms to furnish them with the hellish means of killing and kidnapping. But enough - it is a subject that sours my blood." – Ignatius Sancho, 1778

According to the United Nations and several human rights organizations, many of the conflicts on the African continent can be traced to the desire to control its mineral resources (money, money, and money; money is the god of the shallow).

"It was our arms in the river of Cameroon, put into the hands of the trader, that furnished him with the means of pushing his trade; and I have no more doubt that they are British arms, put into the hands of Africans, which promote universal war and desolation that I can doubt their having done so in that individual instance. I have shown how great is the enormity of this evil, even on the supposition that we take only convicts and prisoners of war. But take the subject in another way, and how does it stand? Think of 80,000 persons carried out of their native country by we know not what means! For crimes imputed! For light or inconsiderable faults! For debts perhaps! For crime of witchcraft! Or a thousand other weak or scandalous pretexts! Reflect on 80,000 persons annually taken off! There is something in the horror of it that surpasses all bounds of imagination." –Prime Minister William Pitt the Younger, 1792

****

Another dishonesty and/or confusion expressed by the sincerely perceived Moron Member of the British Empire (MMBE) was during the cross examination of the dull, dishonest, and racist England class senior NHS nurse in the council before the council on 17 November 2008.

The senior NHS nurse asked to see the letter of allegation, which she wrote on 30 May 2007, only a day after her last visit to the surgery of the first ever and only Negro dentist in Wellingborough.

The council commissioned another statement about a year later. The council has so far failed or refused to disclose the date when it sent dull, dishonest, and racist England class pretend lawyers from Mills and Reeve Solicitors to the senior NHS nurse's house to take new statements, which more or less dishonestly "sexed up" her original letter of allegation. Nevertheless, the senior NHS nurse signed her statement on 26 August 2008.

The fact that the crooked council read and did not detect the glaring absurdities in the statement that it commissioned, and was willing to immortalise it for eternity, confirmed to me that the council was a "fish and chips" council seemingly run by "fish and chips" gals and factory workers, all propped up by crude oil and gas money in exactly the same way as their merciless, racist thug, and thieving ancestors were for centuries sustained by the proceeds of evil in its purest form – "Evil, Ne plus ultra."

The mediocre and corrupt council within one of the least literate countries in the industrialised world maliciously created artificial jobs for "fish and chips" solicitors, albeit England young adults that it shepherds.

"The one great principle of the English law is to create jobs for itself." – Charles Dickens

Sir Winston Churchill implied that the average Briton was a moron, and the OECD seemed to seamlessly corroborate the proximate observations of the great man, albeit more than sixty years later.

"The best argument against democracy is a five-minute conversation with the average voter." – Sir Winston Churchill

Under oath, the senior NHS nurse rejected the elementary, reckless rot that the crooked and racist council created for her. The council seemingly made her to contradict herself under oath by making her confirm that she acceded to the statement that she signed on 26 August 2008. They were all white, almost, and I was the only Negro in the council chambers.

✶ ✶ ✶ ✶ ✶ ✶

The senior NHS nurse was cross examined in the council chambers on 17 November 2008:

ANDREW HURST: You cannot now recall any conversation that Mr Bamgbelu had or you had whilst he was continuing to treat or prepare for the crown at that stage?
SENIOR NHS NURSE: No. Is it possible to look at my statement just to refresh my memory, or not?
ANDREW HURST: Certainly I have no objection to that if you would like to look at your statement.
THE CHAIRMAN (DR SHIV PABARY, MEMBER OF THE BRITISH EMPIRE): Mr Morris?
DAVID MORRIS: Sir, I do not think the witness can be prevented from refreshing her memory at this stage.
THE LEGAL ADVISER (MR DAVID SWINSTEAD): Can you remember when you made the statement?
SENIOR NHS NURSE: Yes, I can. I wrote the letter—
THE LEGAL ADVISER (MR DAVID SWINSTEAD): Not the letter, the statement; when did you make that, roughly?
SENIOR NHS NURSE: Six months ago, roughly.
THE LEGAL ADVISER (MR DAVID SWINSTEAD): 26 August I have a date; is that right in fact?
ANDREW HURST: Sir, that is certainly the date it was signed.
THE LEGAL ADVISER (MR DAVID SWINSTEAD): The point is a technical point, that clearly when you made your statement the matters were fresher in your mind than they are now.
SENIOR NHS NURSE: Yes, they were. It does feel like a very long time ago and the letter was written initially so that is actually the most

accurate.

THE LEGAL ADVISER (MR DAVID SWINSTEAD): Your reference would be to your statement. Perhaps you can answer this question. You wrote a letter; did you have the letter with you when you made your statement or not?

SENIOR NHS NURSE: No.

THE LEGAL ADVISER (MR DAVID SWINSTEAD): You did not.

SENIOR NHS NURSE: I had access to it and I quickly re-read it when I made my statement, just to refresh my memory.

THE LEGAL ADVISER (MR DAVID SWINSTEAD): The important point is that the events were fresher in your memory logically then than now?

SENIOR NHS NURSE: Yes.

THE LEGAL ADVISER (MR DAVID SWINSTEAD): And you do not have any objection, Mr Morris?

DAVID MORRIS: Sir, the statement was made on 26 August of this year, which is 15 months from the relevant event and the witness has to establishment that the matters were fresh in her mind at that date, and that is rather difficult to do given the 15-month gap.

SENIOR NHS NURSE: I actually signed it quite a long while after it was made; it took a long while coming through the post and preparation and that sort of thing, so it wasn't actually made on that date.

THE CHAIRMAN (DR SHIV PABARY, MEMBER OF BRITISH EMPIRE): Can you remember when it was made? A few months before that?

SENIOR NHS NURSE: Yes, it was about six months ago and Mrs O'Shea came to my home and took the statement, but in preparation it was quite a long time between that and actually signing it and returning it.

DAVID MORRIS: That will take us back to May of this year, which is 12 months since the index event, so I question as to how it can be that matters were fresh in her mind at that time.

THE LEGAL ADVISER (MR DAVID SWINSTEAD): The issue is not that they were fresh, but fresher is how the law currently deals with this matter; that they were fresher logically than they are today. Secondly, giving evidence before this Committee is not primarily simply a memory test and if the witness would be assisted by referring to the document then my advice to the Committee is that she should be able to do so. Do you contest that?

DAVID MORRIS: I do not contest that.

THE CHAIRMAN (DR SHIV PABARY, MEMBER OF THE BRITISH EMPIRE): In that case we will let Patient A look at the statement.

ANDREW HURST: Sir, also dealing with the ground as well in relation to the statement that is being brought, is it right that you wrote out a list of your concerns or you wrote a letter dated 30 May 2007?

SENIOR NHS NURSE: Yes.

ANDREW HURST: Although the Committee do not have a copy of that and you do not have a copy of that, that is something that you exhibited to your statement at the time that you signed it on 26 August 2008.

SENIOR NHS NURSE: Yes. I did write a letter to the health authority, a complaint letter, and that was done directly after my treatment, so that would have been at that specific time and probably the freshest and most relevant thing really.

ANDREW HURST: The Committee are content that you should be able to refresh your memory. (Statement handed to the witness) This is the original. Mr Morris might like to see it as well. (Same shown to Mr Morris) Before you look at it, can you confirm that it is your real name on the top of it?

SENIOR NHS NURSE: Yes.

ANDREW HURST: That each page is dated and signed by you.

SENIOR NHS NURSE: Yes.

ANDREW HURST: Also at the very end of it there appears this endorsement: "I believe the facts stated in this witness statement consisting of 11 pages are true to the best of my knowledge and belief."

SENIOR NHS NURSE: Yes.

ANDREW HURST: Please do not read the statement out loud, but if you would like to, because you have been given leave to refresh your memory, go first of all to paragraph 18 which is towards the bottom of page 4. Just read that paragraph to yourself. (The witness read)

SENIOR NHS NURSE: Yes.

NEGRO'S PERSPECTIVE:

Incompetent art incompetently imitated life.

So, it is actual fact and absolute truth that Dr Shiv Pabary, Member of the British Empire (MBE), was dishonest as he maliciously lied or he was recklessly confused when he stated as follows: "In that case we will let Patient A look at the statement." Based upon very proximate observations and direct experiences, it is my sincerest belief that parts of the administration of the English law is mediocre, Negrophobic, and dishonest.

Another immortalised dishonesty by Dr Shiv Pabary is as follows: At the GDC hearing of Wednesday 17, June 2009, Mr Shiv Pabary (The Chairman of the PCC-GDC), stated

"I think I will ask our legal adviser for any advice he may have. My view is that there are six or seven of us here who had the admission down, but we cannot find it in the transcript and there is wording s that imply that there was, but it is not in black and white. It might be useful to clarify that by recalling Mr Bamgbelu and see. As to second matter, I think it will help the Committee if there is confusion with the situation with the nurse taking the waste out. We are happy to hear that if it is okay."

Leaving aside the thoroughly shameless employment of the English language in the English land by a Member of the British Empire, a fact which is increasingly becoming common amongst privileged dullards in England, Dr Shiv Pabary also immortalised blatant dishonesty, and did so for eternity.

Mon, 8 Mar 2010 20:20
Re Meeting 9th March
From George Rothnie georgerothnie@hotmail.com
To adeolacole adeolacole@aol.com
Hi Ola,
We are scheduled to meet tomorrow evening at my surgery about 5.30ish. Unfortunately something has cropped up which necessytates me having to postpone the meeting. I'm really sorry it's such short notice.

I will contact you in the week to arrange another date.

Once agaim my apologies. George

George Rothnie, the deputy postgraduate dean for Oxford and Wessex Deaneries, is an accurate reflection of the intellect and integrity of Helen Falcon.

George Rothnie works underneath Helen Falcon as the postgraduate dean deputy of Oxford and Wessex Deaneries of Mediocre Great England.

A Yoruba proverb states: "An imbecile man who works underneath a very powerful woman must be doing his work with his prick, not his brain."

Some people found guns, and they mercilessly used them to destroy millions of creations of Almighty God so that stupid people could thrive in the distant future.

Crass!

Many of the millions of Africans who were slaughtered and worked to death were created intellectually superior by Almighty God.

"There is no sin except stupidity." – Oscar Wilde Before slavery, what?

※ ※ ※ ※ ※ ※ ※

Wed, 2 Sep 2015 8:31

RE: Outstanding statutory annual registration fee invoice: payment due – FINAL REMINDER

From cqc (NHS SHARED BUSINESS SERVICES LTD (BRISTOL)) SBS-B.cqc@nhs.net To adeolacole adeolacole@aol.com

Hello,

Thank you for your below email. Please be advise a invoice is raised by Care Quality Commission for an annual registration and raised for Primary care (Dental Service) - 3 locations as below

1-21906121052 BROMHAM ROAD BEDFORD BEDFORDSHIRE MK40 2QG

1-219061275 24 PARK ROAD WELLINGBOROUGH NORTHAMPTONSHIRE NN8 4PW

1-219061290 226 ABINGTON AVENUE ABINGTON NORTHAMPTON NORTHAMPTONSHIRE NN1

4PR

Kindly provide the payment details as the invoice is overdue by several days.

If any query please let me know

Thanks and Regards, Kanchan Jaisinghani

Collections

Debt Management Team

Shared Business Services

Tel 0303-123-1155

Fax 0117-933-8890

E-mail: sbs-b.cqc@nhs.net

Website: www.sbs.nhs.uk

Government Business Award Winner

Central Government Supplier of the Year 2011.

* * * * *

How for Christ's sake did I end up amongst this thoroughly sh** people?

She-men and/or privileged shepherds of England's young adults who insert their tiny pricks (gigantic clitorises) in the mouths of dead pigs when they are high on tablets or other roots and weeds, if they are truly brave or really high, should insert their balls (the two together) into the mouth of pacu, the organ grinder.

"The first class at Oxford where I have examined is an overrated mark." – Lord Dacre (Hugh Trevor-Roper), 1981

The CQC: a "Government Business Award Winner."

Sir Major was a winner too, as he banged egg winner, majorly, on a number of occasions, and from behind the majority of times.

The CQC manager of Mediocre Great England (MGE) was a moron.

"Mr Bamgbelu has sent me lengthy e mails following the meeting and has copied me correspondence he has sent to others and including his indemnity society. He has gone to great lengths to question my integrity and honesty. The records of the meetings he was given were in note form, this was made clear to him. He has used facts such as the miss spelling of the dean's surname and my stating a meeting took place at 12 pm not 12 noon to undermine their value." – Geraint Evans, the postgraduate tutor for Oxford and Wessex Deaneries of Mediocre Great England (MGE)

Miss Spelling from the valleys of the least literate province of England was a very accurate depiction of the intellect and integrity of Helen Falcon, the short and stout racist cougar.

"The ordinary women of Wales are generally short and squat, ill-favoured and nasty." – David Mallet

"England young adults are amongst the least literate and numerate in the industrialised world." – The OECD

Helen Falcon: the topmost amongst bottommost; an unchecked, semi-illiterate, destructive shepherd of England young adults.

Miss Spelling worked underneath Mrs Helen Falcon. Is Geraint Evans's tiny prick, based upon the size of the bulge in his tight trousers, a gigantic clitoris? What work was Miss Spelling doing under Mrs Helen Falcon? Are they lesbos or what?

Some people accurately foresaw that their descendants would be dull in the distant future, so when they found guns, they went on armed robbery raids all over the world.

Before slavery, what?

"Throughout the discussion of the notes he made derogatory comments about the wording and accuracy. He suggested that they were written some time after the visits and that my memory was inaccurate. The notes as stated previously were written within 24 hours of each meeting when fresh in my memory. They may not have been well written from a grammatical point of view, but I am confident I had not forgotten any of the facts." – Geraint Evans, the postgraduate tutor for Oxford and Wessex Deaneries of Mediocre Great England (MGE)

Many of the millions of human beings who were mercilessly slaughtered were created intellectually superior to the merciless, racist bastards – the alleged civilised Christian captors and persecutors.

Descendants of wretched agricultural labourers from mainland Europe who dispossessed native Britons and stole their land were immeasurably transformed by the gigantic yields of proceeds of centuries of merciless evil (Ne plus ultra of evil). They have reinvented themselves on stolen land, and fool the foolish with foolishness.

No brain, natural resources poor, only skin colour, which the wearer neither made nor chose, and what else? It is a scam, and it won't endure.

Before slavery, what?

The short and stout, crooked, racist cougar, Mrs Helen Falcon, postgraduate dean for Oxford and Wessex Deaneries of Mediocre Great England (MGE), and her functional semi-illiterate disciples (Kevin Atkinson, George Rothnie, and Geraint Evans), and the GDC and the CQC, are shepherds of England young adults.

Those regularly spun are amongst the dullest adult population in the industrialised world.

"FAILING SCHOOLS AND A BATTLE FOR BRITAIN: This was the day the British education establishment's 50-year betrayal of the Nation's children lay starkly exposed in all its ignominy. After testing 166,000 people in 24 education systems, the Organisation for Economic Cooperation and Development (OECD) finds that England young adults are amongst the least literate and numerate in the industrialised world." – The Daily Mail, 09.01.2013

Shepherds of moron are likely to be morons too.

In 2020, Northamptonshire yields only food. In 1720, all the people of Northamptonshire were fed like battery hens with the proceeds of racist evil.

"I think I will ask our legal adviser for any advice he may have. My view is that there are six or seven of us here who had the admission down, but we cannot find it in the transcript and there is wording s that imply that there was, but it is not in black and white. It might be useful to clarify that by recalling Mr Bamgbelu and see. As to second matter, I think it will help the Committee if there is confusion with the situation with the nurse taking the waste out. We are happy to hear that if it is okay." – Dr Shiv Pabary, chairman of the GDC Committee What a load of brainless, tortuous gibberish!

"The great enemy of the clear language is INSINCERITY (DISHONESTY). When there is a gap between one's real and one's declared aims, one turns as it were instinctively to long words and exhausted idioms, like a cuttlefish squirting ink. In our age there is no such thing as 'keeping out of politics'. All issues are political issues, and politics itself is a mass of lies, evasions, folly, HATRED and schizophrenia. When the general atmosphere is bad, language must suffer." – George Orwell

Dr Shiv Pabary maliciously lied, and the Honourable Member of the British Empire immortalised dishonesty on record for eternity.

The fella talked nonsense with alacrity, civilised decorum, and delivered rot with a near perfect but nevertheless imitation upper class English accent.

I sincerely called Dr Shiv Pabary a f****** rotter blower, but only in my mind!

"Nothing that you will learn in the course of your studies will be of the slightest possible use to you in after life – save only this – if you work hard and diligently you should be able to detect when a man is talking rot, and that, in my view, is the main, if not the sole, purpose of education." – J.A. Smith, Oxford University Professor, Moral Philosophy

CHAPTER 14

Another one of Dr Shiv Pabary's dishonesties or reckless confusions is as follows: At the GDC hearings of 19 November 2008, Dr Shiv Pabary asked Dr Stephanie Twidale questions. It is my honest belief that Dr Shiv Pabary displayed mediocrity, confusion, and indiscreet dishonesty.

In a correspondence of 15.08.2006, the NHS stated that it selected the surgery of the first ever and only Negro dentist in Bedford for priority during one of Stephanie Twidale's calls to the NHS. Stephanie Twidale, a seemingly closeted racist cougar, was obsessed with a Negro that she had never met. She was rubbish is every way, including intellectually. It will be impossible for anyone to use cogent evidence to prove me wrong. She seemed significant only because of skin colour, and the fact that she was born in a rich country, albeit after slavery, as before slavery the land yielded only food.

"Agriculture not only gives riches to a nation, but the only riches she can call her own." – Dr Samuel Johnson Before slavery, what?

Stephanie Twidale was given Richard Hill's contact details in the summer of 2006, and her alleged contemporaneous records confirmed that fact.

Dr Stephanie Twidale was unrelentingly dishonest under oath. Not all liars are racists, but all racists are malicious liars.

Dr Stephanie Twidale, territorial defence officer (TD), is a section of the UK society.

"All sections of UK society are institutionally racist." – Sir Bernard Hogan-Howe, London Metropolitan Police

"Richard (Hill), Stephanie Twidale called us a few weeks ago about DRS visits and Charlotte prioritised Mr Bamgbelu's practice; Stephanie has been in touch a few times as her colleagues had highlighted issues from a similar practice in Northants and they would like to review report etc etc prior to visiting. She also wanted to know if there has been a dental inspection there at all and I did not know the answer . . . Cue

Richard have you carried out an inspection at this practice, please could you advise Stephanie when she contacts you, and would it be possible to see our reports so we can be more pro active with any other queries. Thanks. With kind regards, John Hooper." – NHS, 15.08.2006

Three weeks later, on 06.09.2006, Richard Hill produced a report which was a forgery. It was withdrawn more than four years later. The withdrawal statement is another NHS forgery which remains live and valid.

Stephanie Twidale did not disclose any direct contact with Richard Hill in 2006, but she disclosed contacts with him in 2007, which she stupidly denied under oath. Oyinbo olodo! Oyinbo ode!

"There is no sin except stupidity." – Oscar Wilde

Stephanie Twidale was so dull she couldn't have acquired such a level of dullness in several lifetimes. She must have been created very dull by Almighty God, and born duller by her mummy.

A ghastly woman!

"Sir, he was dull in company, dull in his closet, dull everywhere. He was dull in a new way, and that made many people think him great." – Dr Samuel Johnson

It is very important to note that on 09.02.2007, prior to visiting the surgery of the first ever and only Negro dentist on 22.02.2007, Dr Stephanie Twidale informed Dr Richard Hill and others that she was not happy with me. In Stephanie Twidale's email of 09.02.2007 to Mr John Hooper, copied to Dr Richard Hill, Dr Sue Gregory, and Dr Steven Claydon, she stated, "John, I telephoned Mr Bamgbelu this morning to confirm the arrangements for the New style monitoring visit (surgery inspection, patient examinations radiograph/ record card checks) due on Thu 22 Feb. This is our normal procedure, 2 weeks beforehand. Mr Bamgbelu told me that there would be no patients to examine, as he is 'already 100 UDAs over his target, so is doing no more NHS work until 01 April.' He refuses to get four patients in for me to see, even if he does not treat them himself that day – he tells me I am welcome to see private patients, whom he is continuing to treat – but of course that is not part of our remit. He is apparently still expecting me to come to do the Surgery Inspection at 0900 –Richard Hill is accompanying me for that. I would also be able to do the radiograph/record card check part of the process – but no patients would be seen. I imagine you would be unhappy with that situation – I certainly am – the onus is on you as PCT I am afraid to decide what to do now. We could put the whole thing off again until April or even do the surg insp now, and patients in April – records/rads could be done at either visit. However this was flagged up by yourselves as a priority, and he has already had it postponed once from January, because he "booked it for the wrong practice", and wasn't in Bedford on the day originally arranged. I have been in negotiations over this whole priority visit since August, and I feel he is just putting us off again. Stephanie."

Stephanie Twidale seemed obsessed with me. If she desired me, she could have had me, but not for nothing. Her mouth smelt of urea, which meant she did not floss regularly, and her ass was ugly and was made uglier still by what looked like a G-string to protect such a gigantic ass. She was ugly all over.

She sent an email to Richard Hill on 09.02.2007, and she lied on oath that she did not have any contact with him before meeting him in front of the surgery of the first ever and only Negro dentist in Bedford on 22.02.2007.

She further sent an email to him on 15.02.2007, prior to visiting the Negro's surgery on 22.02.2007. The dull, dishonest, racist, ugly, and nasty cougar lied with reckless abandon, and immortalised racial hatred, guarded by dishonesty, till Thy Kingdom Come.

The email from Dr Stephanie Twidale (15.02.2007 at 6.28 p.m.) to Richard Hill, copied to Mr John Hooper, Dr Sue Gregory, and Dr Steven Claydon, read: "Dear Richard, Just to confirm that I have agreed with John Hooper that we go ahead with the Surgery inspection part of the DRS monitoring programme as arranged for 9.00am on Thursday 22 Feb. However the patient and record card/radiograph examination part of the process will now be delayed until after April, as Mr Bamgbelu has already exceeded his UDA target for the current year. I spoke to Mr Bamgbelu this afternoon, and he has asked that I arrange that date with him at the visit next week. I am assuming that I will see you at the practice at 9.00am, as arranged. Di you want to meet up outside first, or should we go in independently? It might look as if we are "ganging up" if we met first. Also I gather that parking is a problem. If you need to discuss further, please phone xxxxxxxxx or xxxxxxxxxxxx (2 phone numbers)."

Irrespective of the contacts supra, the crooked, racist cougar maliciously lied that she did not have any contact with Richard Hill. The stupid big gal was trying to dissociate herself from their racist forgeries.

Oyinbo olodo! Oyinbo ode!

✱ ✱ ✱ ✱ ✱ ✱

David Morris cross examined Stephanie Twidale on 19 November 2008:

DAVID MORRIS: This is a report by Richard Hill dated 22 July 2004. Might you have seen that before the inspection?

STEPHANIE TWIDALE: No, I have never seen this before.

NEGRO'S PERSPECTIVE:

The former England young adults implied that the only way of knowing about the content of a report that Stephanie Twidale expressly sought and was produced at her request for her use was if she actually saw it, and they expressed such nonsense on record. Brainless nonsense!

"Nothing that you will learn in the course of your studies will be of the slightest possible use to you in after life – save only this – if you work hard and diligently you should be able to detect when a man is talking rot, and that, in my view, is the main, if not the sole, purpose of education." – J.A. Smith, Oxford University Professor, Moral Philosophy

David Morris and Stephanie Twidale are former England young adults and shepherds of England young adults.

Everything is relative. David Morris is an England class barrister, and only because he was amongst the topmost England young adults who became a former England young adult and a shepherd of England young adults.

Strand, including the offices of the Outer Temple Chambers, and indeed the Royal Courts of Justice, did not exist before slavery, as then England yielded only food, and food consumption was not for sale.

"Sometimes people don't want to hear the truth because they don't want their illusions destroyed." – Friedrich Nietzsche

"Agriculture not only gives riches to a nation, but the only riches she can call her own." – Dr Samuel Johnson

The Industrial Revolution was centuries after Europeans disembarked in Africa in 1445. There was no industrial revolution before slavery, and there wouldn't have been an industrial revolution had there not been slavery, as gigantic yields of the merciless evil of slavery (evil, Ne plus ultra) paid for it.

"The fact is that civilisation requires slaves. The Greeks were quite right there. Unless there are slaves to do the ugly, horrible, uninteresting work, culture and contemplation become almost impossible." – Oscar Wilde

The proceeds of centuries of merciless racial hatred and fraud kick-started the industrial revolution in Europe and brought European slave merchants and traders, great wealth.

Before slavery, what?

Feudal agricultural labourers from mainland Europe dispossessed/robbed aboriginal Britons. They've been transformed and reinvented by slavery.

The GDC hearing was not an intellectual debate; it was seemingly a white supremacist chaos probably aimed at concealing part of the guilt and shame of the past, which is that many of the millions who were mercilessly slaughtered with made-in Birmingham guns and the millions more worked to death were created intellectually superior by Almighty God.

So, David Morris of Outer Temple Chambers, Strand, London (before slavery, there was only farmland in Strand, absolutely nothing else) was dishonest as he maliciously lied when he implied that the only way Stephanie Twidale could know about reports that she expressly sought was only if she physically saw them.

* * * * * * *

DAVID MORRIS: This is a report by Richard Hill dated 22 July 2004. Might you have seen that before the inspection?

STEPHANIE TWIDALE: No, I have never seen this before.

NEGRO'S PERSPECTIVE:

David Morris dishonestly implied that he was unaware of the following fact: the surgery of the first ever and only Negro dentist was selected as priority during one of several telephone calls by Stephanie Twidale to the

NHS about the Negro.

"Richard (Hill), Stephanie Twidale called us a few weeks ago about DRS visits and Charlotte prioritised Mr Bamgbelu's practice; Stephanie has been in touch a few times as her colleagues had highlighted issues from a similar practice in Northants and they would like to review report etc etc prior to visiting. She also wanted to know if there has been a dental inspection there at all and I did not know the answer . . . Cue Richard have you carried out an inspection at this practice, please could you advise Stephanie when she contacts you, and would it be possible to see our reports so we can be more pro active with any other queries. Thanks. With kind regards, John Hooper." – NHS, 15.08.2006

The NHS directly offered to share the reports of visits to the surgery of the first ever and only Negro dentist in Bedford that she sought with her.

"Dear Stephanie, Just to confirm that I have spoken to Richard Hill and he will join you for the DRS visit on Thursday 22nd February to Mr Bamgbelu's Bedford Practice, commencing at 9 a.m. We will endeavour to share any issues the PCT may have with you PRIOR to the 22nd. Kind regards, Sue." – NHS, 30.11.2006

"Sue" was Sue Gregory, the sincerely perceived Satanic Empress (SE) of racist evil. Deluded, she seemed to associate the gigantic yields of several centuries of merciless, racist evil (Evil, Ne plus ultra) with personal intellect and industry. Fact: no brain, natural resources poor, only skin colour that the wearer neither made nor chose, and what else? Pure scam!

Some people accurately foresaw that the average one amongst their descendants would be morons in the distant future, so when they found guns, they went on armed robbery and dispossession raids all over only the unarmed and defenceless world.

Whenever they murdered, they dispossessed, and wherever they robbed, they took possession. They were merciless, racist thugs, armed robbers, and thieves.

"It was our arms in the river of Cameroon, put into the hands of the trader, that furnished him with the means of pushing his trade; and I have no more doubt that they are British arms, put into the hands of Africans, which promote universal war and desolation that I can doubt their having done so in that individual instance. I have shown how great is the enormity of this evil, even on the supposition that we take only convicts and prisoners of war. But take the subject in another way, and how does it stand? Think of 80,000 persons carried out of their native country by we know not what means! For crimes imputed! For light or inconsiderable faults! For debts perhaps! For crime of witchcraft! Or a thousand other weak or scandalous pretexts! Reflect on 80,000 persons annually taken off! There is something in the horror of it that surpasses all bounds of imagination." – Prime Minister William Pitt the

Younger, 1792 Before slavery, what?

Apart from the yield of agriculture, almost everything was stolen – directly or indirectly.

"Agriculture not only gives riches to a nation, but the only riches she can call her own." – Dr Samuel Johnson

"Those who have robbed have also lied." – Dr Samuel Johnson corroborating prophet Habakkuk

Sir Winston Churchill implied that the average Briton was a moron. The Organisation for Economic Cooperation and Development seamlessly corroborated the very proximate observations of the great man.

"The best argument against democracy is a five-minute conversation with the average voter." – Sir Winston Churchill "FAILING SCHOOLS AND A BATTLE FOR

BRITAIN: This was the day the British education establishment's 50 year betrayal of the Nation's children lay starkly exposed in all its ignominy. After testing 166,000 people in 24 education systems, the Organisation for Economic Cooperation and Development (OECD) finds that England young adults are amongst the least literate and numerate in the industrialised world." – The Daily Mail, 09.01.2013

Shepherds of morons are likelier to be morons too.

Not to digress too far, but David Morris of Outer Temple Chambers, Strand, London (before slavery, Strand was agricultural land) was dishonest when he implied that he was not aware of the fact that Stephanie Twidale acknowledged on oath and/or on record that she had several discussions with the NHS. Stephanie Twidale stated on oath that she did not have ANY contact with Richard Hill prior to 22.02.2007, but did with two NHS administrators (Charlotte Dowling Goodson and John Hooper), and more importantly Sue Gregory (OBE), who was the only dentist amongst the seemingly hereditary, racist thugs, which reasonably implied that her discussions were with her professional colleagues Sue Gregory (OBE) and Richard Hill, although she lied under oath that she did not have any discussions with Richard Hill prior to meeting him in the front of the surgery of the first ever and only Negro dentist in Bedford.

Prior to visiting the surgery of the first ever and only dentist in Bedford on 22.02.2007, Stephanie Twidale (TD) confirmed on oath and/or on other records that she had several discussions with Sue Gregory and NHS administrators (Charlotte Dowling Goodson and John Hooper).

"The only people I spoke to beforehand would be John Hooper and some e-mail correspondence with John, with Charlotte Dowling and with the Consultants in public health, Sue Gregory. I didn't actually have any contact with Richard at all." – Stephanie Twidale, 19 November 2008

Stephanie Twidale stated as follows and otherwise on record: "Yes please we would like a surgery inspection. At the point at which I was informed that Richard Hill had been there some months before hand and had some concerns."

"Having discussed with the PCT they told me that Mr Hill had made previous visits not that long before from which there had been some queries, and they felt perhaps it would be sensible for Mr Hill to come along as well with me to be a second person and follow up on his previous visits to the practice."

"I spoke to Dr Sue Gregory, Consultant in Dental Public Health at the Bedfordshire PCT to impart the information and was informed that Richard Hill, Dental Practice adviser to Bedfordshire PCT, had carried out a previous Surgery inspection at Bromham Road that had raised some concerns."

"Then I know it came through that Richard Hill had been in before about 6 months ago, I think they said, and it was probably sensible for him to go as the second person, a second appropriate second person to do a follow up. The actual timings of bits of those I am afraid I can't REMEMBER."

"At the point at which I was informed that Richard Hill had been there some months before hand and had some concerns."

"I spoke to Dr Sue Gregory, Consultant in Dental Public Health at the Bedfordshire PCT to impart the information and was informed that Richard Hill, Dental Practice adviser to Bedfordshire PCT, had carried out a previous Surgery inspection at Bromham Road that had raised some concerns."

If Stephanie Twidale (TD) told the truth, it further confirmed that Sue

Gregory (OBE) was dishonest, as she lied to her.

Oyinbo olodo! Oyinbo ode!

The descendants of wretched, feudal agricultural labourers from mainland Europe were immeasurably transformed by the gigantic yields of merciless slavery (Evil, Ne plus ultra). They have reinvented themselves with stolen money on stolen land.

Pure scam!

Not all liars are racist, but all racists are malicious liars.

Stephanie Twidale (TD) and Sue Gregory (OBE) are sections of the British society and shepherds of England's young adults.

"England young adults are amongst the least literate and numerate in the industrialised world." – The OECD, The Daily

Mail, 09.01.2013

Shepherds of morons are likelier to be morons too.

"All sections of UK society are institutionally racist." – Sir

Bernard Hogan-Howe, London Metropolitan Police

"The best argument against democracy is a five-minute conversation with the average voter." – Sir Winston Churchill

The average voter was an average adult like Sue Gregory (OBE) and Stephanie Twidale (TD). Sir Winston Churchill implied that the average adult in his era was a moron.

"Sometimes people don't want to hear the truth because they don't want their illusions destroyed." – Friedrich Nietzsche

Richard Hill, another merciless, racist thug and disciple of Sue Gregory (OBE), unrelentingly lied on oath in the mediocre and crooked council before a mediocre and crooked committee, all within one of the least literate countries in the industrialised world, and he confirmed, also on oath, that Stephanie Twidale (TD) maliciously lied when she stated on oath that she did not have any contact with him prior to meeting him in front of the surgery of the first ever and only Negro dentist in Bedford on 22.02.2007. They were racist thugs and cowards, and descendants of merciless, racist murderers, armed robbers, and thieves. No brain, natural resources poor, only skin colour that the wearer neither made nor chose, and what else? Pure scam!

"Many Scots masters were considered among the most brutal, with life expectancy on their plantations averaging a mere four years. We worked them to death then simply imported more to keep the sugar and thus the

money flowing. Unlike centuries of grief and murder, an apology costs nothing. So what does Scotland have to say?" – Herald Scotland, Ian Bell, columnist, Sunday 28 April 2013

"As hard-hearted as a Scot of Scotland." – English saying

"I know of no evil that has ever existed, nor can imagine any evil to exist, worse than the tearing of eighty thousand persons annually from their native land, by a combination of the most civilised nations inhabiting the most enlightened part of the globe, but more especially under the sanction of the laws of that Nation which calls herself the most free and the most happy of them all." – Prime Minister William Pitt the Younger

* * * * *

Andrew Hurst, GDC barrister, cross examined Richard Hill (NHS) in the council before the council committee on 18 November 2008:

ANDREW HURST: Thank you. Now obviously during the course of the run up to the visit of 22 February there was some communication between you and Stephanie Twidale.

RICHARD HILL: Yes.

NEGRO'S PERSPECTIVE:

"I didn't actually have any contact with Richard at all." – Stephanie Twidale (TD), under oath, on 19.11.2008

She lied and lied again under oath. Seemingly, the white supremacist satanic network were beside and before the ugly racist cougar with three-fourths deflated mammary glands with no milk in the Negrophobic charade, the pretend legal process.

"Those who have robbed have also lied." – Dr Samuel Johnson corroborating prophet Habakkuk Oyinbo olodo! Oyinbo ode!

"Lies are told in criminal cases. Lies are told in civil cases. Lies are told all the time." – Sir Michael Havers, Attorney General.

Stephanie Twidale: the extremely nasty, ugly, racist cougar lied on oath.

So, Stephanie Twidale was dishonest as she maliciously immortalised Negrophobic lies when she stated she did not have any contact with Richard Hill prior to meeting him in front of the surgery of the first ever

Negro dentist in Bedford on 22.02.2007.

They are deluded racist thugs with grossly exaggerated senses of self-worth. They are the descendants of thoroughly wretched, feudal agricultural labourers from mainland Europe who stole the land of the aboriginal Britons. They were immeasurably transformed by the gigantic yields of merciless evil – Ne plus ultra (slavery). They have reinvented themselves and fool the foolish with foolishness.

No brain, natural resources poor, only skin colour that the wearer neither made nor chose, and what else? Pure scam!

England's young adults are amongst the least literate and numerate in the industrialised world according to the OECD. Are shepherds of morons, morons too?

Before slavery, what?

* * * * *

DAVID MORRIS: Sir, you will recall Mr Hill's evidence was that this is a report mistakenly attributed to Mr Bamgbelu's practice when it in fact relates to something that was a mistake?

THE CHAIRMAN (DR SHIV PABARY, MEMBER OF THE BRITISH EMPIRE): Was this where there was a lot of cancellations? I remember something in evidence.

NEGRO'S PERSPECTIVE:

F****** rotter blower!

Dr Shiv Pabary lied under oath or he was recklessly confused. He reasoned like a lunatic and expressed his reasoning like a lunatic who was an imbecile before being afflicted by lunacy.

"Nothing that you will learn in the course of your studies will be of the slightest possible use to you in after life – save only this – if you work hard and diligently you should be able to detect when a man is talking rot, and that, in my view, is the main, if not the sole, purpose of education." – J.A. Smith, Oxford University Professor, Moral Philosophy

DAVID MORRIS: Mr Hill said yesterday that while he made an error and he thought there had been an inspection on 22 July 2004, and in fact that was not right, it referred to another practice. In chatting with Richard Hill, presumably you did before going round, did he mention

any previous inspections that he had done?
NEGRO'S PERSPECTIVE:
David Morris was dishonest as he implied that on 19.11.2008, he was not aware of or did not have full access to at least the following: an email from Dr Sue Gregory to Dr Stephanie Twidale, Dr Richard Hill, and Mrs Charlotte Dowling Goodson: "Dear Stephanie, Just to confirm that I have spoken to Richard Hill and he will join you for the DRS visit on Thursday 22nd February to Mr Bamgbelu's Bedford Practice, commencing at 9 a.m. We will endeavour to share any issues the PCT may have with you PRIOR to the 22nd. Kind regards, Sue."

✶ ✶ ✶ ✶ ✶

Andrew Hurst, GDC barrister, cross examined Richard Hill (NHS) in the council before the council committee on 18 November 2008:
ANDREW HURST: Thank you. Now obviously during the course of the run up to the visit of 22 February there was some communication between you and Stephanie Twidale.
RICHARD HILL: Yes.

NEGRO'S PERSPECTIVE:

There was no evidence, certainly none conclusive, that David Morris was a member of the satanic network.
Google "David Morris, barrister." The following is part of what comes up: Christ Is Our God: It Is Mathematics: Deducible Originalism by Yinka Bamgbelu (2015).
Mr David Morris, English lawyer/barrister: "It is my fault, I should have clarified this with Mr Hill yesterday, but D5 is a report drafted by Mr Hill in error."
The satanic network: They wear charity as a cloak of deceit and swear by the name of Almighty God never to tell lies, but they lie that they do not lie (Songs of David 144).
Meritocracy was irrelevant within the satanic network as the loot they used to share was the proceeds of merciless, racial hatred and fraud (slavery).

Satanic Network

"Those who have robbed have also lied." – Dr Samuel Johnson corroborating prophet Habakkuk

STEPHANIE TWIDALE: I never spoke to Richard Hill, nor had I ever met him before we arrived at the practice together. It was a classic two people standing outside a building saying: "Are you? Oh yes, right fine" we had never met and we did not speak beforehand. The only people I spoke to beforehand would be John Hooper and some e-mail correspondence with John, with Charlotte Dowling and with the Consultants in public health, Sue Gregory. I didn't actually have any contact with Richard at all.

NEGRO'S PERSPECTIVE:

Again, Stephanie Twidale lied on oath. Members of the satanic network were seemingly beside and before her in an indiscreetly dishonest Negrophobic charade.

In August 2006, the NHS told Richard Hill to expect to expect Stephanie Twidale (TD) to contact him. She was given his contact details.

Stephanie Twidale (TD) was dishonest, as she lied on oath when she stated that she did not have any contact with Richard Hill at any time until she met him in front of the surgery of the first ever and only Negro dentist in Bedford on 22.02.2007.

Stephanie Twidale, the post-menopausal ugly cougar with an uglier ass (which was made uglier still by what appeared to be a G-string, which reasonably suggested that she was still active in the stuff department), and with four-fifths deflated, gigantic mammary glands that seemed to have little or no milk, was an incompetent, racist liar.

"Truth, Sir, is a cow which will yield such people no more milk, and so they are gone to milk the bull." – Dr Samuel Johnson

The slave raiders and traders did not use their brains; they used made-in-Birmingham guns against unarmed and defenceless people, absolutely unprovoked. Almost everything was stolen. Those who will steal human beings will steal anything.

Before slavery, what?

Stephanie Twidale (TD) disclosed that she had contact with Richard Hill in 2007, prior to visiting the surgery of the first ever and also Negro dentist in Bedford. The scatter head racist cougar denied the disclosed fact on oath, but Richard Hill contradicted her on oath, in their "fish and chips," white supremacist, Negrophobic charade.

Oyinbo olodo! Oyinbo ode!

ANDREW HURST: Thank you. Now obviously during the course of the run up to the visit of 22 February there was some communication between you and Stephanie Twidale.

RICHARD HILL: Yes.

Some people found guns and used them to destroy millions of creations of Almighty God so that stupid people could thrive in the distant future. Crass!

CHAPTER 15

On 19.11.2008, Dr Shiv Pabary and Dr Anthony Kravitz were dishonest implicitly under oath, as they lied when they implied that they understood the workings of a dental suction motor. Dr Stephanie Twidale did not either, albeit forty years after had she left dental school (1969). She seemed old in years and young in hours, as she implicitly had wasted useful and irreversible time.

Oyinbo olodo! Oyinbo ode!

There was a dialogue between Dr Anthony Kravitz and Stephanie Twidale in the council chambers on 19.11.2008. Dr Anthony Kravitz desired to let me know that Stephanie Twidale, the dull, dishonest, and racist post-menopausal cougar, was very experienced.

Very experienced doing what? Instead, the sincerely perceived racist tall dwarf presented a picture of elementary past, and poor mental arithmetic and very ignorant dentists. They go to BDA to do meetings about shepherding England young adults.

※ ※ ※ ※ ※ ※

Dr Stephanie Twidale was questioned by Dr Anthony Kravitz, in the council chambers on 19.11.2008:

DR ANTHONY KRAVITZ: Good afternoon. I do declare an interest that I do know who you are, but for the purposes of this meeting I need to ask you some questions about yourself. When did you qualify?

DR STEPHANIE TWIDALE: 1969.

DR ANTHONY KRAVITZ: When did you become a Dental Reference Officer?

DR STEPHANIE TWIDALE: I have to count back. 11 years ago, so that is 1999, I think.

DR ANTHONY KRAVITZ: 1997, if it was 11 years ago.

DR STEPHANIE TWIDALE: 1997, sorry that sounds right.

DR ANTHONY KRAVITZ: What did you do between 1969 and 1997?

DR STEPHANIE TWIDALE: I spent my first 11 years working in the schools dental service and then the community dental service as a dental officer, then senior dental officer. Then an assistant area dental officer. I then went into general practice and opened a practice from scratch and kept that one and sold it after 11 years as a three surgery practice. That was purely NHS. 12 months before I sold that practice I opened up a second practice from scratch in my home village and sold that again as a 3 surgery practice, when I decided to join the dental reference service.

DR ANTHONY KRAVITZ: So to summarise that it would be fair to ask you that you have had experience as a practice owner working within the general dental services?

DR STEPHANIE TWIDALE: Yes, I worked from 1980 through to 1997.

DR ANTHONY KRAVITZ: From 1998?

DR STEPHANIE TWIDALE: From 19 –

DR ANTHONY KRAVITZ: 78? You qualified in 1969?

DR STEPHANIE TWIDALE: Qualified in 1969, 11 years in the community which took me to 1980, then from 1980 through to 1997 that is 17 years, yes.

DR ANTHONY KRAVITZ: You were experienced in working in the pre 1990 contract and the post 1990 contract, but not the 2006 contract?

DR STEPHANIE TWIDALE: That is correct.

DR ANTHONY KRAVITZ: You describe to the Committee the changes to the way you worked, I think you were saying from just before the April 2006 contract and that has developed since then?

DR STEPHANIE TWIDALE: Yes.

DR ANTHONY KRAVITZ: Between when you joined in 1997 and whenever it was in 2005 or 2006, did you undertake some practice inspections in those days?

DR STEPHANIE TWIDALE: Yes.

DR ANTHONY KRAVITZ: In what context would they be undertaken?

DR STEPHANIE TWIDALE: Again when the Primary Care Trust

asked for an independent inspection other than by their dental practice adviser.

DR ANTHONY KRAVITZ: Would you be using some sort of check list for those inspections?

DR STEPHANIE TWIDALE: In the days when I first joined the Reference Service, no, there was not a full check list. The check lists started developing during that period. I can't remember when, in an endeavour to make sure that Reference Officer reports were, even though they were independent at least they were all running to the same, singing from the same song sheets basically. Particularly, when it became a question of trying to make sure that what we were asking for was similar to what the dental practice advisers were asking for, so the practitioners did not get conflicting opinions.

DR ANTHONY KRAVITZ: Are you able to give the Committee a ball park type of figure of the number of practice inspections you would undertake each year?

DR STEPHANIE TWIDALE: Not a lot, probably about 3 or 4.

DR ANTHONY KRAVITZ: So would it be fair from that to say that your experience may be somewhere in the region of 20 to 30 practices before you went to this particular practice?

DR STEPHANIE TWIDALE: Yes, probably.

DR ANTHONY KRAVITZ: Thank you. My other question actually relates to the final questions put by the GDC's counsel. I am a little confused, I have to say, about this aspirator motor venting and the filter. If I say to you my understanding of an aspirator, the motor is just acting like a vacuum cleaner from the mouth, would that be your understanding as well, of what the motor does?

DR STEPHANIE TWIDALE: Yes.

DR ANTHONY KRAVITZ: Therefore the "gunge," if we can call it that, would go from the mouth, and would go out, if it was a mobile unit, into a canister of some sort and in a non mobile unit it would be evacuated somewhere else out of the surgery, would that be correct?

DR STEPHANIE TWIDALE: Yes.

DR ANTHONY KRAVITZ: I am not clear then what the relevance would be of a filter or not, on the motor. Why would you report, if the motor was actually sitting separately. I am not talking about the safety aspect of a motor sitting on the top of the cardboard box or not, that remains to be proved or otherwise by the Committee, but the actual output from the motor, what the difference would be of a motor sitting on a box or sitting inside the aspirator unit with a view to bacteria contamination being dispersed. Where would the filter fit in that?

DR STEPHANIE TWIDALE: We did not consider the filter at all. That question has been asked of me this morning, so I have not, you know, the question of a filter did not arise. The more I am being questioned, you know I am thinking about and being asked about this, this morning, the more to be honest I am not positive in my own mind now that may be the motor itself in terms of it is or is it not going to vent noxious substances, let us be honest I am not sure now. I am getting more and more confused about this myself. We were certainly very unhappy about it, and we both felt at the time that where it was (A) not appropriate, but (B) could be the source of infection. It may be that technically we are wrong on that, I would not like to comment, or put any further opinion on that other than to say it may be that if from an infection point of view it was not a problem, certainly from a safety point of view and appropriateness point of view we felt it should not be there. In terms of filters we did not actually pick up the question of filters, that is something that has come up this morning.

DR ANTHONY KRAVITZ: We need to be absolutely clear because this point has been raised previously before you gave the evidence. The only part now you are saying that you are clear in your mind that you are unhappy about was the safety aspect of where this thing was perched, if I can use that word, you did not use that word. If I say it was put on a cardboard box. That you are clear in your own mind you felt was unsafe?

DR STEPHANIE TWIDALE: Unsafe and totally inappropriate, yes.

DR ANTHONY KRAVITZ: But you are not now clear whether in fact it posed a risk so far as contamination to patients by bacteria or viruses or other obnoxious substances?

DR STEPHANIE TWIDALE: I think at this stage I would wish to take technical advice on that before I wish to on oath comment further.

DR ANTHONY KRAVITZ: OK. Thank you very much.

NEGRO'S PERSPECTIVE:

Only the aspirator motor vented, and it had a bacteria filter. Everything else was brainless nonsense. The Negro did not install the aspirator, and he did not place it on anything. The UK supplier did that, and the engineer was Caucasian. The Negro only paid for the service.

The descendants of thoroughly wretched, feudal agricultural labourers (serfs) from the mainland who stole the land of the aboriginal Britons, and lived solely off the land, were transformed by the gigantic yields of evil – Ne plus ultra (slavery). The have reinvented themselves on stolen land with affluence whose entire foundation is merciless, racial hatred and fraud, and they fool the foolish.

Before slavery, what?

"Agriculture not only gives riches to a nation, but the only riches she can call her own." – Dr Samuel Johnson

The Industrial Revolution succeeded slavery by centuries. The Industrial Revolution was absolutely impossible without slavery. The yield of agriculture could not have paid for it.

The proceeds of centuries of merciless, racial hatred and fraud kick-started the industrial revolution in Europe and brought European slave merchants and traders, great wealth.

Irrespective of the fact that the dull, dishonest, and racist cougar (Stephanie Twidale) declared ignorance upon the subject on oath, although she was condescending at the Negro's practice akin to someone who had been lied to that the brain was in the skin (an historical imbecile who did not realise that some Negroes secretly look down on her type), Dr Shiv Pabary (in the future his children might change Shiv to Steve), Member of the British Empire, expressed confusion, and asked the confused cougar who had declared ignorance, and surrendered to her kindred, but was "charging" about like an intellectual lunatic and imposed baseless superiority that was based on skin colour that she neither made nor chose at the inspection of 22.02.2007; a mere hereditary serf and descendant of merciless, racist thugs and thieves, on stolen land and with stolen wealth (before slavery, what?), to answer stupid questions.

Dr. Olayinka Bamgbelu

* * * * *

Dr Shiv Pabary questioned Dr Stephanie Twidale on oath in the council about the aspirator motor on 19.11.2008:

DR SHIV PABARY (MEMBER OF THE BRITISH EMPIRE): I am going to come back to the aspirator again, I am afraid. The reason is there are three charges here that are not admitted. The first one is the aspirator was broken, was it broken?

DR STEPHANIE TWIDALE: No, the motor on the correct motor, or the original motor supplied with the aspirator was broken. He had put in - Mr Bamgbelu had connected in in some way a replacement motor, so the aspirator was functional.

DR SHIV PABARY (MEMBER OF THE BRITISH EMPIRE): The second charge says that another aspirator was stored uncovered on top of the cupboard. Now you give evidence that there was a cardboard box. The charge actually says it was stored uncovered on top of a cupboard. Do you remember a cupboard?

DR STEPHANIE TWIDALE: It may have been a cardboard box on a cupboard, I can't remember whether the cardboard box was on the floor or on the cupboard I am afraid now.

NEGRO'S PERSPECTIVE:
She couldn't remember—of course she couldn't. Had the ugly, racist cougar remembered more, she could have done better at school.

Some thoroughly wretched, feudal agricultural labourers (serfs) used guns to mercilessly slaughter millions of creations of Almighty God so that in the distant future a McDalit from India and a descendant of wretched, feudal agricultural labourers could subjugate heredity (familial intelligence) and talk rot within a council that the proceeds of merciless, racial hatred and fraud built.

Before slavery, there was no council building, as the land yielded only food. The Wimpole Street area was farmland before slavery. The lands were stolen by mainland Europeans from the aborigines, and those who worked on it were mainland Europeans too. Almost everything not attributable to agriculture was stolen -Habakkuk.

DR SHIV PABARY (MEMBER OF THE BRITISH EMPIRE): There was something on the floor and the aspirator was actually sitting on top of this?

DR STEPHANIE TWIDALE: The aspirator motor was actually sitting on top of a cardboard box. It may well be that the cardboard box, I am trying from my memory now to actually picture – I can picture some parts of the surgery and it may well have been that there was a cupboard with the cardboard box with the motor.

NEGRO'S PERSPECTIVE:
The Negro paid a UK engineer to supply and install an aspirator motor. The Negro did nothing else. For that he was hounded like a fox, and their power is money, and as the land yielded and yields only food, the entire foundation of the money is racial hatred and fraud – centuries of it.

Before slavery, what?

※ ※ ※ ※ ※ ※

DR SHIV PABARY: The last question about the aspirator is the aspirator vent, it says the aspirator vent was unsafely sited. Is your evidence now that you are not sure where it was venting out?
DR STEPHANIE TWIDALE: I didn't – we didn't identify a problem with the vent from the aspirator as supplied with the dental unit. The problem that we had was with this replacement, temporary replacement motor.

NEGRO'S PERSPECTIVE:
Stephanie Twidale, the dull and racist post-menopausal cougar with four-fifths deflated mammary glands, was dishonest as she maliciously lied that there was a temporary replacement motor.
Oyinbo olodo! Oyinbo ode!
Some people associate the proceeds of evil (merciless, racial hatred and fraud) with personal intellect and industry. Before slavery, what?
The duller Indian (Dr Shiv Pabary) did not realise that Stephanie Twidale had thrown in the towel. She was extremely irritating at the inspection of 22.02.2007. That a silly big gal like her could do dentistry is evidence that one has underachieved in life.

Stephanie Twidale was unrelentingly dishonest under oath. She was a racist thug. She was a perjurer, a liar, and a racist thug, but she was surrounded by her own people in a dishonest legal process within one of the least literate countries in the industrialised world, irrespective of the huge gains made during centuries of killing, stealing, and working millions of fellow human beings to death at Birmingham-made gun point.

Centuries of the European trade in millions of stolen Africans, including little children, was the purest form of evil: Ne plus ultra.

Centuries of gigantic, stolen affluence seemed to have distorted the realities of some people.

"Those who have robbed have also lied." – Prophet Habakkuk

DR SHIV PABARY (MEMBER OF THE BRITISH EMPIRE): Your evidence is the vent for that replacement motor was?

DR STEPHANIE TWIDALE: Well, I am having difficulty with, I have to say, a lack of sufficient technical knowledge now of aspirator motors to know whether the motor itself would vent. Mr Hill and I were both under the impression that the motor itself would vent. There is enough questions been put to me this morning, that I am questioning whether in fact we were correct in that. I would need technical advice. The actual vent for the aspirating system we did not identify. We did not specifically look for it, but we did not anticipate a problem with the original system, the problem was with this replacement motor.

✱ ✱ ✱ ✱ ✱ ✱

NEGRO'S PERSPECTIVE:

Stephanie Twidale was a dishonest, racist, intellectual lunatic, all wrapped up in the most favourable skin colour, and further disguised with an imitation upper class accent.

On the day, 19.11.2008, the ugly cougar with the giant ugly ass that seemed to be made uglier by what looked like an ugly G–string (at her seventh, nearly eighth decade) stated as follows upon the same subject: she and Richard Hill were under the impression that the aspirator motor itself would vent. The intellectually impotent racist thug also stated that she was not sure that they were correct upon the fact that the aspirator motor vented (she brought Richard Hill along for that purpose – to rope him into stupid, incompetent, and racist lies). She said she would need technical advice, which implied that the advice that Dr Anthony Kravitz gave her was not technical; in fairness to her, the tall dwarf talked rot. Some people used guns to kill millions of people, and armed others to slaughter millions more, and worked many millions more to death so that their moron descendants could thrive in the distant future. Crass! The stupid woman (Oyinbo olodo) also said that they (Stephanie Twidale and Richard Hill) did not identify the actual vent of the aspirator system.

She also said, "We did not specifically look for it, but we did not anticipate a problem with the original system, the problem was with this replacement motor." The statement by the merciless, racist cougar has no meaning. She talked nonsense, and interspersed it with key words – just like Helen Falcon.

Stephanie Twidale was an intellectual lunatic, and a very dishonest racist thug. She blew plenty of rot and talked nonsense! Oyinbo ode!

"Nothing that you will learn in the course of your studies will be of the slightest possible use to you in after life – save only this – if you work hard and diligently you should be able to detect when a man is talking rot, and that, in my view, is the main, if not the sole, purpose of education." – J.A. Smith, Oxford University

Professor, Moral Philosophy

Without objective basis, they award themselves the monopoly of knowledge. They are the descendants of thoroughly wretched, merciless, and racist, agricultural labourers who used guns to loot and destroy the world.

* * * * * *

DR SHIV PABARY (MEMBER OF THE BRITISH EMPIRE): Thank you very much for that. The legal adviser has just pointed out that the charge actually reads: "Another aspirator was stored

uncovered"?
DR STEPHANIE TWIDALE: No, that is incorrect.

* * * * *

Stephanie Twidale's dialogue with Mrs Mary Harley (council's judge) upon the same subject is as follows:
MRS MARY HARLEY: The aspirator vent itself, could you comment on where that was situated? Not the motor, it is the actual venting of the aspirator?

NEGRO'S PERSPECTIVE:
"Not the motor, it is the actual venting of the aspirator?" –
Mrs Mary Harley, council's judge Brainless nonsense!
Some thoroughly wretched, feudal agricultural labourers from mainland Europe found guns and used them to mercilessly slaughter millions of unarmed and defenceless people, and worked to death millions more. This should not be evidence of the fact that all their descendants are immune from imbecility. "It was our arms in the river of Cameroon, put into the hands of the trader, that furnished him with the means of pushing his trade; and I have no more doubt that they are British arms, put into the hands of Africans, which promote universal war and desolation that I can doubt their having done so in that individual instance. I have shown how great is the enormity of this evil, even on the supposition that we take only convicts and prisoners of war. But take the subject in another way, and how does it stand? Think of 80,000 persons carried out of their native country by we know not what means! For crimes imputed! For light or inconsiderable faults! For debts perhaps! For crime of witchcraft! Or a thousand other weak or scandalous pretexts! Reflect on 80,000 persons annually taken off! There is something in the horror of it that surpasses all bounds of imagination." – Prime
Minister William Pitt the Younger, 1792 Before slavery, what?
In order to get the money, one needs to pretend and play along that stupidity isn't stupidity! Oyinbo olodo!
"To disagree with three-fourths of the British public on all points is one of the first elements of sanity, one of the deepest consolations in all

moments of spiritual doubt." – Oscar Wilde

Only the motor vented. Mrs Mary Harley was confused and ignorant, but skin colour elevated above her God's granted talent.

STEPHANIE TWIDALE: To be honest I am not sure. We accepted the aspirator system as incorporated into Mr Bamgbelu's set of cabinetry which was all very self contained and I am assuming it was all in there. What we were concerned about was this replacement motor, the actual aspirator itself we accepted the system. I am not sure where it was.

NEGRO'S PERSPECTIVE:

Stephanie Twidale talked nonsense: tortuous, meaningless, gibberish by the racist cougar with the gigantic, ugly ass.

She accepted what she assumed was in there! Oyinbo olodo! Oyinbo ode! Idiot!

Stephanie Twidale said she was not sure where the venting of the aspirator was, but the confused racist thug, a descendant of merciless, racist murderers, told Dr Shiv Pabary that they (Stephanie Twidale and Richard Hill) felt that the aspirator motor vented.

"Well, I am having difficulty with, I have to say, a lack of sufficient technical knowledge now of aspirator motors to know whether the motor itself would vent. Mr Hill and I were both under the impression that the motor itself would vent." – Stephanie Twidale in response to questions by Dr Shiv Pabary

I was charged with not cooperating with a lunatic madam. How should one relate to a lunatic racist cougar? They did not teach that in dental school.

"Why, Sir; to be sure when you wish a man to have that belief which you think is of infinite advantage, you wish well to him; but your primary consideration is your own quiet. If a madman were to come into this room with a stick in his hand, no doubt we should pity the state of his mind; but our primary consideration would be to take care of ourselves. We should knock him down first, and pity him afterwards." – Dr Samuel Johnson

Thoroughly stupid, racist cougar!
"There is no sin except stupidity." – Oscar Wilde

✹ ✹ ✹ ✹ ✹ ✹

MRS MARY HARLEY: You do not feel there were any problems associated with where the aspirator itself was venting?
STEPHANIE TWIDALE: We had no concerns over the original equipment as it was set up had his motor not broken and he had been unable to have it repaired. I don't think we would have raised any queries.

NEGRO'S PERSPECTIVE:
Stephanie Twidale and Mrs Mary Harley were intellectually disorientated and mentally imbalanced.

One of the beauties of the upper class accent and the most favourable skin colour is that they beautify stupidity.

"My dear Algy, you talk exactly as if you were a dentist. It is very vulgar to talk like a dentist when one isn't a dentist. It produces a false impression." – Oscar Wilde

The natural instinct of the privileged dullard is soft but durable apartheid by stealth.

Upon the same subject of the aspirator, Stephanie Twidale, the dull, dishonest, and racist cougar with the gigantic, ugly ass that was made uglier by what appeared to be a G-string, was cross examined by David Morris – who was appointed and instructed by her employer, the Medical Protection Society, who were very active in racist, apartheid South Africa. Stephanie Twidale was the principal witness for the GDC in their mediocre, seemingly hereditary Negrophobic charade.

✹ ✹ ✹ ✹ ✹

David Morris cross examined Stephanie Twidale in the council chambers on 19 November 2008:
DAVID MORRIS: As far as the aspirator was concerned, I think you explained that there was an aspirator machine there which was not

working, itself was not working, but it was put back into use by the use of another aspirator motor, is that right?

STEPHANIE TWIDALE: Yes.

DAVID MORRIS: So there was a functioning aspirator within the surgery?

STEPHANIE TWIDALE: Yes.

DAVID MORRIS: The additional motor that was required to get it going was, as you say, stored I think on, in fact, a cardboard box?

STEPHANIE TWIDALE: Yes.

DAVID MORRIS: The aspirator vented within the surgery rather than outside the surgery?

STEPHANIE TWIDALE: Well, yes the motor would have vented, because it was not enclosed at all, would have vented straight into the surgery.

NEGRO'S PERSPECTIVE:

Stephanie Twidale, a former England young adult and a shepherd of England's young adults, couldn't have done very well at school. She seemed a scatter head hereditary moron – a descendant of wretched agricultural labourers (serfs) from mainland Europe who were immeasurably transformed by the gigantic yields of centuries of merciless evil, which slavery was, and have reinvented themselves with stolen money on stolen land, and fool the foolish that the yields of evil, racial hatred and fraud are the evidence of their personal intellect and industry. They give the game away when they display the intellects of serfs.

Before slavery, what?

"Those who have robbed have also lied." – Dr Samuel Johnson corroborating prophet Habakkuk

"Well, yes the motor would have vented, because it was not enclosed at all, would have vented straight into the surgery." –

Stephanie Twidale

Stephanie Twidale stated or implied the following: The aspirator motor vented; had the aspirator been enclosed it wouldn't have vented, which implicitly means that had the aspirator been enclosed, the enclosure would have prevented the aspirator motor from venting bacteria directly into the surgery.

Stephanie Twidale seemed exceedingly dull. She reasoned like an imbecile and expressed her reasoning worse than an imbecile.

The Negro – the first ever and only Negro dentist in Bedford since He merely spoke and the world became – was a villain because he did not understand the lunatic, dull, and racist cougar with the huge ugly ass, which was made uglier by what appeared to be a G-string (which implied that she was still very active in the stuff department), that was sent to inspect his practice.

In response to questions by David Morris, Stephanie Twidale, the lunatic, racist madam who wore skin colour as a cloak of deceit, stated that the aspirator vented.

"Not the motor, it is the actual venting of the aspirator?" – Mrs Mary Harley, council's judge

The judge was thoroughly confused, but she has the most favourable skin colour and spoke with an upper class accent.

F****** brainless rot; intellectual torture!

"Nothing that you will learn in the course of your studies will be of the slightest possible use to you in after life – save only this – if you work hard and diligently you should be able to detect when a man is talking rot, and that, in my view, is the main, if not the sole, purpose of education." – J.A. Smith, Oxford University Professor, Moral Philosophy

"Sometimes people don't want to hear the truth because they don't want their illusions destroyed." – Friedrich Nietzsche

"In examinations, those who do not wish to know ask questions of those who cannot tell." – Walter Raleigh

"Well, I am having difficulty with, I have to say, a lack of sufficient technical knowledge now of aspirator motors to know whether the motor itself would vent. Mr Hill and I were both under the impression that the motor itself would vent." – Stephanie Twidale in response to questions by Dr Shiv Pabary

"Well, yes the motor would have vented, because it was not enclosed at all, would have vented straight into the surgery." – Stephanie Twidale

In the plantations, any unfortunate Negro who disagreed with an armed Caucasian was either shot dead or frog marched to the woods and hanged without a hood.

Today, any Negro that disagrees with a dull, dishonest, and racist Caucasian is dragged before a mediocre and racist council and is suffocated with lies.

Verdicts precede offence, and stereotype and baseless prior predilection beclouds objective reasoning and judgement.

The basis of the power of the oppressors is money. The entire foundation of the money is merciless racial hatred and fraud.

"To disagree with three-fourths of the British public on all points is one of the first elements of sanity, one of the deepest consolations in all moments of spiritual doubt." –
Oscar Wilde
Before slavery, what?
"Agriculture not only gives riches to a nation, but the only riches she can call her own." – Dr Samuel Johnson

✻ ✻ ✻ ✻ ✻ ✻

DAVID MORRIS: Were you aware whether or not the vent had a filter which would filter out any bacteria?
STEPHANIE TWIDALE: I would not expect the motor itself to have a filter on it. It may have had some form of filter. If so –
DAVID MORRIS: Not the motor itself, but the actual vent device?

NEGRO'S PERSPECTIVE:
These characters (David Morris and Stephanie Twidale) are imbeciles. They are just lucky that they have the most favourable skin colour and upper class accents, and more importantly, some wretched feudal agricultural labourers (serfs) who lived off sustenance farming found guns and used them to loot and destroy the world. Apart from those, what else?

"The grand object of all European traders in kidnapped and stolen Africans was - money, money, money; money was their god! In Africa, the poor wretched natives, blessed with the most fertile and luxuriant soil, are rendered so much the more miserable by the Christians' (European traders in stolen Africans) abominable traffic for slaves and the horrid cruelty and treachery of the petty [African] Kings. The Africans kings were encouraged by their European (Christian) customers who carry them strong liquors to enflame their madness and powder and bad firearms to furnish them with the hellish means of killing and kidnapping.

But enough - it is a subject that sours my blood." – Ignatius Sancho, 1778

"Many Scots masters were considered among the most brutal, with life expectancy on their plantations averaging a mere four years. We worked them to death then simply imported more to keep the sugar and thus the money flowing. Unlike centuries of grief and murder, an apology costs nothing. So what does Scotland have to say?" – Herald Scotland, Ian Bell, columnist, Sunday

28 April 2013

"As hard-hearted as a Scot of Scotland." – English saying

"Scotsmen tak a' they can get and a little more if they can."

– Scottish saying Before slavery, what?

They are extremely wicked people, the descendants of merciless, sadistic savages, armed robbers, and thieves.

Our children are in trouble, as those who will be in charge in the future will be worse.

✱ ✱ ✱ ✱ ✱

DAVID MORRIS: Were you aware whether or not the vent had a filter which would filter out any bacteria?

STEPHANIE TWIDALE: I would not expect the motor itself to have a filter on it. It may have had some form of filter. If so –

NEGRO'S PERSPECTIVE:

Only the motor vented, and it had a bacteria filter.

"I would not expect the motor itself to have a filter on it. It may have had some form of filter. If so –." – Stephanie Twidale Meaningless balderdash.

Stephanie Twidale seemed so dull. Her mummy couldn't have sent her to a school within one of the least literate countries in the industrialised world where critical reasoning was taught. Had she, she would have realised enclosing a motor in a cupboard would not prevent it from venting into the surgery room, and deeper reasoning should have made her realise that motors have filters over vents.

"Well, yes the motor would have vented, because it was not enclosed at all, would have vented straight into the surgery." – Stephanie Twidale

The most valuable asset of Stephanie Twidale as a human being was her skin colour. Apart from that, she was nothing. No brains, natural resources poor, only skin colour that the wearer neither made nor chose, and what else? Pure scam!

Before slavery, what?

"Agriculture not only gives riches to a nation, but the only riches she can call her own." – Dr Samuel Johnson

Everything is relative. Stephanie Twidale was an England class Dental Reference Office—a former England young adult and a shepherd of England's young adults. She was amongst the topmost in her "class," and based upon that fact, she was a shepherd of England's young adults.

✱ ✱ ✱ ✱ ✱ ✱ ✱

STEPHANIE TWIDALE: Oh the aspirator itself would have done, our concern was the open unprotected motor that was likely to vent.

NEGRO'S PERSPECTIVE:

The dull, dishonest (perjurer), racist cougar, with a huge, ugly ass which was made uglier by what looked like a G-string, implied in response to David Morris's question that she expected another part of the aspirator, not the motor, to have a bacteria filter. The thoroughly stupid and extremely dull and ugly old bat implied that the aspirator motor would not have vented into the surgery room had it been in an enclosure and protected.

Idiot! Exceedingly dull and dishonest, intellectually disorientated, and mentally imbalanced racist thug!

"Why, Sir, Sherry is dull, naturally dull, but it must have taken him a great deal of pain to become what we now see him. Such an excess stupidity, Sir, is not in Nature." – Dr Samuel Johnson

Stephanie Twidale was so dull; she seemed even duller than a CQC manager, albeit within one of the least literate countries in the industrialised world.

Stephanie Twidale, the dull, dishonest, and racist cougar was so dull that she seemed even duller than Geraint Evans, a postgraduate tutor for Oxford and Wessex Deaneries: "Mr Bamgbelu has sent me lengthy e mails following the meeting and has copied me correspondence he has sent to others and including his indemnity society. He has gone to great lengths to question my integrity and honesty. The records of the meetings he was given were in note form, this was made clear to him. He has used facts such as the miss spelling of the dean's surname and my stating a meeting took place at 12 pm not 12 noon to undermine their value" (Geraint Evans, a postgraduate tutor for Oxford and Wessex Deaneries, in a report to the council of 30.05.2010).

Miss Spelling worked underneath Mrs Helen Falcon, postgraduate dean for Oxford and Wessex Deaneries. Oyinbo olodo! Oyinbo ode!

"Throughout the discussion of the notes he made derogatory comments about the wording and accuracy. He suggested that they were written some time after the visits and that my memory was inaccurate. The notes as stated previously were written within 24 hours of each meeting when fresh in my memory. They may not have been well written from a grammatical point of view but I am confident I had not forgotten any of the facts." – Geraint Evans, a postgraduate tutor for Oxford and Wessex Deaneries, in a report to the NHS of 28.05.2010

Geraint Evans was an accurate reflection of the intellect and integrity of Helen Falcon, the postgraduate dean for Oxford and Wessex Deaneries.

A Yoruba proverb states: "If an imbecile man works underneath a very powerful woman, he must do his work with his prick, not his brain."

Stephanie Twidale was so dull that she seemed duller than the postgraduate dean's deputy for Oxford and Wessex Deaneries who, like Geraint Evans, worked underneath Helen Falcon.

Mon, 8 Mar 2010 20:20
Re Meeting 9th March
From George Rothnie georgerothnie@hotmail.com To adeolacole adeolacole@aol.com
Hi Ola,
We are scheduled to meet tomorrow evening at my surgery about 5.30ish. Unfortunately something has cropped up which necessytates me having to postpone the meeting. I'm really sorry it's such short notice.
I will contact you in the week to arrange another date.
Once agaim my apologies. George

Geraint Evans, Kevin Atkinson, and George Rothnie are accurate reflections of the intellect and integrity of Helen Falcon, the postgraduate dean for Oxford and Wessex Deaneries, within one of the least literate countries in the industrialised world.

Like Sue Gregory and Richard Hill, Helen Falcon, Kevin Atkinson,

Geraint Evans, and George Rothnie are amongst the shepherds of England's young adults.

"FAILING SCHOOLS AND A BATTLE FOR BRITAIN: This was the day the British education establishment's 50-year betrayal of the Nation's children lay starkly exposed in all its ignominy. After testing 166,000 people in 24 education systems, the Organisation for Economic Cooperation and Development (OECD) finds that England young adults are amongst the least literate and numerate in the industrialised world." – The Daily Mail, 09.01.2013

Shepherds of morons are likelier to be morons too.

Stephanie Twidale: Hereditary alien and dishonest, racist thug on stolen land. She is a descendant of wretched, feudal agricultural labourers (serfs) from mainland Europe who stole the land of the aboriginal Britons and they were immeasurably transformed by the gigantic yields of the merciless, racist evil which slavery was. They have reinvented themselves on stolen land and fool the foolish.

"It was in 1066 that William the Conqueror occupied Britain, stole our land and gained control by granting it to his Norman friends, thus creating a feudal system we have not yet fully escaped." – Tony Benn

Normans stole from others what others had stolen from others. Genetically pure Britons are extinct; all were dispossessed, robbed, and slaughtered.

Tony Benn was dishonest or he was confused when he implied that he was genetically an aboriginal Briton. Genetically pure aboriginal Britons are extinct. They were dispossessed and robbed of their land by a motley assembly of mainland Europeans – hereditary serfs or descendants of feudal agricultural labourers – who were hugely transformed by the gigantic gains of slavery. They have reinvented themselves.

At the inspection of 22.02.2007, she stank like an old lady, and her mouth oozed the odour of urea, which suggested that she did not floss regularly.

"Britons stank." W.S.

W.S: Wole Soyinka, not William Shakespeare.

He should know; at least one of his wives, and many of his concubines were Britons.

* * * * * *

DAVID MORRIS: Would that vent air from the patient's mouth, or would that vent air just drawn in from the room?

STEPHANIE TWIDALE: It would vent from the patient's mouth.

NEGRO'S PERSPECTIVE:

The air in the patient's mouth is atmospheric air. David Morris and the crooked, racist cougar, Stephanie Twidale, were confused. It is confusion that any part of the aspirator system other than the motor vents or needs a bacteria filter.

DAVID MORRIS: Were you aware whether or not the vent had a filter which would filter out any bacteria?

STEPHANIE TWIDALE: I would not expect the motor itself to have a filter on it. It may have had some form of filter. If so – DAVID MORRIS: Not the motor itself, but the actual vent device?

STEPHANIE TWIDALE: Oh the aspirator itself would have done, our concern was the open unprotected motor that was likely to vent.

NEGRO'S PERSPECTIVE:

Stephanie Twidale and her type are racist murderers. It was her kind of overwhelming, intellectual impotence and confusion that caused a chemical imbalance (monoamines) in Dr Anand Kamath, Dr Richard Bamgboye, and others (all cut down in their prime) which induced transient insanity, which caused them to kill themselves. Were they killed hands off by the likes of the merciless, dull, racist, and dishonest Stephanie Twidale? The mens rea may lay hidden in the belly of the actus reus.

David Morris and Stephanie Twidale were confused. Only the motor vented and it had a bacteria filter. Based entirely upon skin colour that they neither made nor chose, they awarded themselves the monopoly of knowledge. The wretched, feudal, and sustenance agricultural labourers (serfs) from the mainland who stole the land of the native Britons used guns, not brains, to loot the world. It transformed their lives for the better, and transformed the lives of their victims for the worse.

Racial hatred is not a myth, and it is not extinct.

"All sections of UK society are institutionally racist." – Sir Bernard Hogan-Howe, London Metropolitan Police

The following is from Sancho, a British house Negro rather than a field Negro (Malcolm X's definition). It is a letter to Laurence Sterne during the merciless evil of slavery. Sancho told the novelist that he had read of opposition to slavery in the work of only one author other than Sterne, Sir George Ellison:

"REVEREND SIR,

"It would be an insult on your humanity (or perhaps look like it) to apologize for the liberty I am taking.—I am one of those people whom the vulgar and illiberal call 'Negurs.'—The first part of my life was rather unlucky, as I was placed in a family who judged ignorance the best and only security for obedience.—A little reading and writing I got by unwearied application.—The latter part of my life has been—thro' God's blessing, truly fortunate, having spent it in the service of one of the best families in the kingdom.—My chief pleasure has been books.—Philanthropy I adore . . .

"In your tenth discourse, page seventy-eight, in the second volume—is this very affecting passage—'Consider how great a part of our species—in all ages down to this—have been trod under the feet of cruel and capricious tyrants, who would neither hear their cries, nor pity their distresses.—Consider slavery—what it is—how bitter a draught—and how many millions are made to drink it!'—Of all my favorite authors, not one has drawn a tear in favor of my miserable black brethren—excepting yourself, and the humane author of Sir George Ellison.

"—I think you will forgive me;—I am sure you will applaud me for beseeching you to give one half-hour's attention to slavery, as it is at this day practised in our West Indies.—That subject, handled in your striking manner, would ease the yoke (perhaps) of many—but if only of one—Gracious God!—what a feast to a benevolent heart!"

CHAPTER 16

Dr Shiv Pabary was dishonest or recklessly confused when he implied that the private crown that the new dentist of the senior NHS nurse made for her did not have metal showing.

DAVID MORRIS: Is it the case that maybe through a combination of passage of time and your upset about the appearance of the crown that you had received from Mr Bamgbelu that when you give us your best recollection now about all these matters about which I have challenged you, that recollection is faulty.

SENIOR NHS NURSE: I think it would be fair to acknowledge that so far after the event I can't remember in such detail the events that actually took place when I had the treatment; but to suggest that I am here today giving evidence in front of you – and I have written a letter of complaint, the first one I have ever written – and I've had to leave my children overnight and all of this because there is a little bit of silver showing on my back teeth is absurd really. I am here because I was genuinely that concerned to write that letter.

DAVID MORRIS: You say it is absurd. You found it very upsetting and you took exception to the dentist who provided you with it.

SENIOR NHS NURSE: The tooth at the moment has more silver showing probably than Mr Bamgbelu's did and I didn't take exception to that dentist. It is nothing to do with the appearance of the tooth. I opted to have a white one as opposed to a silver one. If that was the only real concern, around appearance, that wouldn't be a motive for me writing a letter of complaint.

DAVID MORRIS: You say that your current crown shows more metal than was visible after Mr Bamgbelu inserted his.

SENIOR NHS NURSE: There is some metal visible. It's hard to say.

DAVID MORRIS: Help us, please. If we look at the records for Miss Triginiti's treatment of you, your subsequent dentist, and we find them behind tab 4, page 3 of the notes read from the bottom upwards and we see that on 12 June you had a temporary aluminium crown placed; do you see that?

SENIOR NHS NURSE: Yes.

DAVID MORRIS: Then on 26 June you had a crown fitted.

SENIOR NHS NURSE: Yes.

DAVID MORRIS: On 26 March a note: "She wanted to prepare a new one but white – crown jacket porcelain. I informed her about the cost and she agreed."

SENIOR NHS NURSE: Yes, I have a white one but there is metal showing where she had to drill the top to make it fit because it is a tight fit.

DAVID MORRIS: Is the one that you currently had fitted one that has no metal aluminium in it at all?

SENIOR NHS NURSE: No, it's one with metal in it. I'm sure it is.

THE CHAIRMAN (DR SHIV PABARY, MEMBER OF THE BRITISH EMPIRE): Mr Morris, using my dental knowledge, it is very, very difficult for anybody to establish that without examining Miss A at this point in time, but I have read what it says "white – crown jacket porcelain"; but, Mr Morris, I think the evidence is that there is nothing showing. I presume it is probably a bonded crown which has metal and porcelain on top, but I think without examination it is very difficult to ascertain.

DAVID MORRIS: Thank you. I have no more questions.

NEGRO'S PERSPECTIVE:

"Mr Morris, using my dental knowledge, it is very, very difficult for anybody to establish that without examining Miss A at this point in time, but I have read what it says 'white – crown jacket porcelain'; but, Mr Morris, I think the evidence is that there is nothing showing. I presume it is probably a bonded crown which has metal and porcelain on top, but I think without examination it is very difficult to ascertain." – Dr Shiv Pabary

Their Indian reasoned like an imbecile again, and he expressed his reasoning worse than an imbecile.

Which dental knowledge? To do dentistry, he only had to be better than the England's young adults or England's former young adults.

The following are the facts: Dr Shiv Pabary did not tell the truth when he stated "I think the evidence is that there is nothing showing. I presume it is probably a bonded crown which has metal and porcelain on top."

Kuli olodo!

The word "presume" depicts uncertainty. The word "probably" depicts uncertainty.

The evidence by the senior NHS nurse is as follows: "The tooth at the moment has more silver showing probably than Mr Bamgbelu's did and I didn't take exception to that dentist. It is nothing to do with the appearance of the tooth. I opted to have a white one as opposed to a silver one."

"Yes, I have a white one but there is metal showing where she had to drill the top to make it fit because it is a tight fit." – Senior
NHS nurse

That is the evidence. Everything else is nonsense!

Dr Shiv Pabary, the chairman of the GDC committee, seemed confused and talked a lot of nonsense. The entire case was organised, anarchical racism.

"I think I will ask our legal adviser for any advice he may have. My view is that there are six or seven of us here who had the admission down, but we cannot find it in the transcript and there is wordings that imply that there was, but it is not in black and white. It might be useful to clarify that by recalling Mr Bamgbelu and see. As to second matter, I think it will help the Committee if there is confusion with the situation with the nurse taking the waste out. We are happy to hear that if it is okay." – Dr Shiv Pabary, Member of the British Empire, 17.06.2009

Some wretched, merciless, racist thugs found guns and used them to slaughter (directly and indirectly) millions of unarmed and defenceless people, and worked millions more to death at gun point in the cane and cotton plantations of the Americas and West Indies, so that in the distant future a dull Indian could be a chairman within the GDC. Crass!

Before slavery, what?

"American South is still taken as barbarism's benchmark. Few realise that the behaviour of Scots busy getting rich in the slaveholders' empire was actually worse – (routinely worse) – than the worst of the cottonocracy. You need only count the corpses.

"By the time slavery was brought to an end in America, the country's 400,000 trafficked people had grown to a population of four million.

In the British West Indies, only 670,000 survived from two million imported souls. In the American South, slaves were valuable and bred. We worked them to death then simply imported more to keep the sugar and thus the money flowing. Unlike centuries of grief and murder, an apology costs nothing. So what does Scotland have to say?" – Ian Bell, Herald Scotland, 28 April 2013

"It was our arms in the river of Cameroon, put into the hands of the trader, that furnished him with the means of pushing his trade; and I have no more doubt that they are British arms, put into the hands of Africans, which promote universal war and desolation that I can doubt their having done so in that individual instance. I have shown how great is the enormity of this evil, even on the supposition that we take only convicts and prisoners of war. But take the subject in another way, and how does it stand? Think of 80,000 persons carried out of their native country by we know not what means! For crimes imputed! For light or inconsiderable faults! For debts perhaps! For crime of witchcraft! Or a thousand other weak or scandalous pretexts! Reflect on 80,000 persons annually taken off! There is something in the horror of it that surpasses all bounds of imagination." – Prime

Minister William Pitt the Younger, 1792 Before slavery, what?

"My view is that there are six or seven of us here who had the admission down, but we cannot find it in the transcript and there is wordings that imply that there was, but it is not in black and white." – Dr Shiv Pabary

Dr Shiv Pabary was dishonest or intellectually incompetent and recklessly confused.

He lied when he stated that there were six or seven of them there. They couldn't find it in the transcript (probably because the stenographer was not at their secret meetings).

The satanic network is full of thoroughly deluded racist thugs, without objective basis, and it awards itself the monopoly of knowledge, wears charity as a cloak of deceit, and swears by the name of Almighty God never to tell lies, but it lies that it doesn't lie (Songs of David 144).

"Many Scots masters were considered among the most brutal, with life expectancy on their plantations averaging a mere four years. We worked them to death then simply imported more to keep the sugar and thus the money flowing. Unlike centuries of grief and murder, an apology costs nothing. So what does Scotland have to say?" – Herald Scotland, Ian Bell,

columnist, Sunday
28 April 2013
Before slavery, what?

"Agriculture not only gives riches to a nation, but the only riches she can call her own." – Dr Samuel Johnson

"There is wordings that imply that there was, but it is not in black and white." – Dr Shiv Pabary, Chairman of the GDC Committee and Member of the British Empire.

"There is no sin except stupidity." – Oscar Wilde

Dr Shiv Pabary sought the advice of the GDC legal adviser, and Mr David Swinstead promptly gave him the advice that he desired, with some input from the Cambridge-educated lawyer Nicholas Peacock.

"I think I will ask our legal adviser for any advice he may have. My view is that there are six or seven of us here who had the admission down, but we cannot find it in the transcript and there is wordings that imply that there was, but it is not in black and white." – Dr Shiv Pabary

Mr David Swinstead, the allegedly wise legal sage, responded to the moronic request of their Indian, with a camouflage high title, as follows: "Mr Peacock, is it the equivalent of I think what in criminal law is often called an equivocal plea where, for instance into an allegation of assault a guilty plea is entered perhaps by a person representing themselves, and then in evidence they effectively say: 'I was acting in self-defence,' in which case the magistrate may well say: 'I think you should have leave to withdraw your plea of guilty because quite clearly your evidence is that you have a defence, which is of self-defence.' You are making the equivalent submission here, which is an admission has apparently been made but Mr Bamgbelu has said, particularly at page 72, essentially 'the tanks were not in poor condition'?"

Mr David Swinstead talked nonsense with decorum and delivered it in an upper-class English accent. The upper-class English accent is one of the most eloquent accents for talking rot.

Mr David Swinstead reasoned like an imbecile, and he expressed his reasoning worse than an imbecile. To know the exact basis of the immortalised imbecility, one needs to find David Swinstead's mama and ask her to write a short essay titled "My Day." If, unlike Stephanie Twidale and Nicholas Peacock, she could write legibly, the reason why her son has turned out to be so stupid will immediately become apparent.

Those regularly spun are amongst the dullest adult population in the industrialised world.

="To disagree with three-fourths of the British public on all points is one of the first elements of sanity, one of the deepest consolations in all moments of spiritual doubt." – Oscar Wilde

Shepherds did not bring stolen Africans home, and implicitly deceived moron sheep that the gigantic loot from abroad was the yield of their industry, and partly for that reason moron sheep have grossly exaggerated views of the intellect and integrity of their shepherds.

"Mr Peacock, is it the equivalent of I think what in criminal law is often called an equivocal plea where, for instance into an allegation of assault a guilty plea is entered perhaps by a person representing themselves, and then in evidence they effectively say: 'I was acting in self-defence,' in which case the magistrate may well say: 'I think you should have leave to withdraw your plea of guilty because quite clearly your evidence is that you have a defence, which is of self-defence.' You are making the equivalent submission here, which is an admission has apparently been made but Mr Bamgbelu has said, particularly at page 72, essentially 'the tanks were not in poor condition'?" – Mr David Swinstead, 17.06.2008

What Mr David Swinstead seemed to desire to say was: "Nicholas Peacock, as you are Cambridge-educated too, you must know that we are created superior to this goddamn African and our brain is in our skin. You can neither write legibly nor reason logically, and I cannot reason at all. If one were to call a spade a spade, we must agree that we are imposters on stolen land and we lord it over almost all with gigantic affluence whose entire foundation is the yield of several centuries of merciless, racial hatred and naked fraud (slavery). The Negro and even the dull Indian, our chairman, ha ha ha ha ha, who asked for advice that is based entirely upon his thoroughly stupid deductions, do not know because they could not know that we are descendants of thoroughly wretched agricultural labourers from mainland Europe who stole the land of the aboriginal Britons. We have changed our names, but the very tall dwarf sitting with me on the highest table (Dr Anthony Kravitz) hasn't put on camouflage yet. If the midget could discard his mother's tongue, why couldn't he abandon his father's name too? Nicholas, our common ancestors, feudal agricultural labourers from mainland Europe, who for centuries lived off sustenance farming, acquired guns and used them to loot the world, and were immeasurably transformed by the yield of merciless, racial hatred and fraud. We have reinvented ourselves and we fool the foolish with foolishness. The f****** Negro did not admit to the f****** charge about four small plastic cups, but as our Indian is our chairman and a Member of the British Empire, we must conceal his stupidity with plenty of verbosity. Over to you Nicholas; blow some rot!"

Cambridge-educated Nicholas Peacock received the baton of rot from David Swinstead and he stated as follows:

"For the sake of the transcript it ought to be pointed out that these proceedings are not, in fact, as a matter of law, criminal proceedings in any event, they are civil proceedings, and there may be slightly greater flexibility in allowing withdrawal of admissions in civil cases. Plainly an explanation is needed but there is greater degree of flexibility there" (17.06.2008).

Nicholas Peacock, Cambridge-educated lawyer and one of the topmost England's young adults, seemed to desire to say: 'The goddamn Negro may see an opportunity to use this as an appeal point so we must give others something to play with should he go that route. So only for the sake of the transcript, we must pretend as if our Indian was not a moron, and allow the reversal of the admission, which the Negro never admitted, but we can't show our moron Indian up, so the let off is to say that the Negro is not a criminal, it is a civil case, so there should be flexibilty." F****** rot!

Let me tell you about Oxbridge-educated Nicholas Peacock: no brain, natural resources poor, only skin colour that the wearer neither made nor chose, and what else?

Nicholas Peacock, England class barrister, you dishonest and/or recklessly confused, f****** dyslexic, closeted racist thug, descendant of merciless, sadistic savages, racist mass murderers, armed robbers, and thieves who also seemed to suffer from dyspraxia; you cannot write legibly and you cannot spell, and you cannot reason logically, but you went to Cambridge. How? Nicholas Peacock, a top former England young adult and a shepherd of England's young adults.

Nicholas Peacock knew that the Negro did not admit to the brainless charge or he had full access to the fact that the Negro did not admit to the charge, but the merciless, seemingly hereditary racist thug was dishonest and lied or he was recklessly confused.

Nicholas Peacock should go and invoke the spirits of his merciless, racist thug ancestors and ask them where they got all the money from, as their land yielded only food. They should confess that they stole almost everything except the yield of the land.

"Those who have robbed have also lied." – Dr Samuel Johnson corroborating prophet Habakkuk

"Agriculture not only gives riches to a nation, but the only riches she can call her own." – Dr Samuel Johnson

Dr Stephanie Twidale did not see the tanks, and the Negro did not admit to the incompetent racist charges.

For centuries, guns were used to mercilessly destroy millions of fellow human beings, and the inheritors of evil, without objective basis, seem to have awarded themselves the monopoly of knowledge, and associate the gigantic proceeds of merciless, racial hatred and evil trade in millions of stolen human beings with intellect and industry and civilisation. Deluded fools!

William Pitt the Younger was dishonest when he stated that merciless, racist bastards who for centuries used guns to impose terror on fellow human beings based entirely upon skin colour that they neither made, chose, or could change, and mercilessly used force of arms to force millions, including many who were created intellectually superior, to expend their entire life cutting cane and picking cotton.

Nicholas Peacock should go to Peckham in South London and find a bruno with gold teeth and tell him that he is a Cambridge-educated barrister. The bitch is likelier to say "respect man."

Racist shepherds didn't bring stolen Africans home. They deceived moron sheep that the loot from abroad was the yield of virtue.

It is dishonesty to associate the proceeds of centuries of merciless racial hatred and fraud with personal intellect and industry.

"Sometimes people don't want to hear the truth because they don't want their illusions destroyed." – Friedrich Nietzsche

As requested by their dull Indian, Mr David Swinstead gave his final advice on the stupid request as follows: "There is no specific provisions in the Rules to allow a Respondent to apply for change of admission. On the other hand, there is an inherent power that you have to conduct proceedings in a just and reasonable manner, and that inherent power would give you the right to allow Mr Peacock's application. I perhaps incorrectly used the criminal analogy of an equivocal plea in my statement to Mr Peacock because, as he correctly says, these proceedings are more akin to civil proceedings, but equally I simply posed the question to him to give an example of the situation that we appear to be in in this hearing, which is that an admission has been made and when explanation has been given by the Respondent, Mr Bamgbelu, it clearly does not chime with the admission. Whether the admission was made in error or in circumstances of misunderstanding I think you do not need to go to: the point Mr Peacock reasonably says is that there has been a change of advocate, of Counsel; Mr Hurst is neutral on the matter; and I would ask you simply to look at the matter as set out and consider, in general terms, what is fair and just as between parties, and to decide accordingly. That is my advice, unless either party would wish me to say anything further? I should pick up on Mr Peacock's point that he is right to say that these are more akin to civil proceedings. An individual admission to one fact within the whole matter is rather different to an admission to a charge in a magistrate's court or a count on an indictment, and therefore the change of an individual admission perhaps is different in quality to a change of plea in a criminal court, but nevertheless you obviously must decide on balance what you consider to be fair and just in the circumstances of this case. I add this as a rider."

F****** rot!
"The one great principle of English law is to make business for itself." – Charles Dickens
In his final advice to their dull Indian, Mr David Swinstead seemed to mean to say: "Morons, take this giant dose of balderdash and plenty of it as my final advice to you cretins who have not yet worked it out is that the whole show is confidence trickery, and that almost everything was

stolen, including the building where I sit before you, blowing shit!"

"The great enemy of the clear language is INSINCERITY (DISHONESTY). When there is a gap between one's real and one's declared aims, one turns as it were instinctively to long words and exhausted idioms, like a cuttlefish squirting ink. In our age there is no such thing as 'keeping out of politics'. All issues are political issues, and politics itself is a mass of lies, evasions, folly, HATRED and schizophrenia. When the general atmosphere is bad, language must suffer." – George Orwell

Feudal agricultural labourers from mainland Europe dispossessed/robbed aboriginal Britons. They've been transformed and reinvented by slavery.

※ ※ ※ ※ ※ ※ ※

David Morris cross examined the Negro in the council chambers on 20 November 2008:

DAVID MORRIS: I think you have accepted that the x ray tanks were in a poor condition.

NEGRO: The x ray tanks were not— Mrs Twidale did not actually see the tanks, because to see the tanks you have to take the lid off. What she saw was the manual x ray thing. It was not new, but we use it, I accept, from time to time, just occasionally when I am doing RCT and I need a very quick thing; but we have an electric – we had an automatic one as well that we use more.

NEGRO'S PERSPECTIVE:

The Negro's words were the last words upon the matter of four plastic cups in November 2008, and he did not admit to the nonsense. They hate us like mad, but only secretly. The sole basis of their power is money, and the entire foundation of the money is the gigantic yield of merciless racial hatred and fraud. No brain, natural resources poor, only skin colour that the wearer neither made nor chose, and what else? Pure scam!

"Many Scots masters were considered among the most brutal, with life expectancy on their plantations averaging a mere four years. We worked them to death then simply imported more to keep the sugar and thus the money flowing. Unlike centuries of grief and murder, an apology costs

nothing. So what does Scotland have to say?" – Herald Scotland, Ian Bell, columnist, Sunday
28 April 2013

Before slavery, what?

David Morris, England class barrister, former England young adult, and a shepherd of England's young adults, was dishonest as he unrelentingly lied on oath.

Shepherds of morons are likelier to be morons too.

They convince themselves that they are not racist, and actually enjoy acting in the supposed best interest of Negroes, which in delusion may cleanse them of their seemingly hereditary racial hatred.

Ignorant fools!

Ian Sadler seemed to find a dull and dishonest racist barrister (David Morris) who could conceal inherited racial hatred and pretend to be virtuous.

"Of all tyrannies a tyranny 'sincerely' exercised for the good of its victims may be the most oppressive." – C.S. Lewis

Their ancestors destroyed millions of Negroes with guns. Without objective basis, they have awarded themselves the monopoly of knowledge and immortalise lies.

It is a scam! Apart from the yields of agriculture, almost everything was stolen – directly or indirectly. Everything else is a lie!

Before slavery, what?

"Agriculture not only gives riches to a nation, but the only riches she can call her own." – Dr Samuel Johnson

The Industrial Revolution succeeded slavery by centuries, and the gigantic yields of evil (slavery) paid for it.

"The fact is that civilisation requires slaves. The Greeks were quite right there. Unless there are slaves to do the ugly, horrible, uninteresting work, culture and contemplation become almost impossible." – Oscar Wilde

Before slavery, there was only sustenance agriculture, and landowners and serfs, all from mainland Europe.

The satanic network is everywhere. It controls almost everything except intellect. Without objective basis, it awards itself the monopoly of knowledge.

Mr David Morris, English lawyer/barrister: "It is my fault, I should have clarified this with Mr Hill yesterday, but D5 is a report drafted by

Mr Hill in error."

"The English think that incompetence is the same thing as sincerity." – Quentin Crisp

"Truth, Sir, is a cow which will yield such people no more milk, and so they are gone to milk the bull." – Dr Samuel Johnson

Merit was irrelevant within the satanic network, as the loot they shared was the yield of racist evil. Associating evil with virtue is deceit.

If Ian Sadler (English solicitor) and David Morris (English barrister) are not members of the racist, satanic network and/or hereditary racist thugs, they should answer the following unanswerable questions:

Richard Hill produced a report, which based upon disclosed information, was at the request of Stephanie Twidale (TD), and for her use, and he withdrew the reports (visit of 22.07.2004 and follow up of unknown date) more than four years after the alleged visit of 22.07.2004. In his withdrawal statement of 16.10.2008, he stated as follows: "In 2006 the Healthcare Commission carried out a visit to Bedfordshire PCT and I was asked to provide all my practice visit reports. While collating this information, I noticed that some inspection reports were missing, which included an inspection of Mr Bamgbelu's practice on 02.04.2003. Around that time my department moved and it is possible that some reports had been lost during the move. I did locate some of my draft handwritten notes and referred to these to prepare my inspection report dated 22.07.2004 for MR BAMGBELU's practice which at the time, I understood to be a correct and accurate record of my inspection. Following another move to different premises, I went through some of my files and found my correct inspection report dated 02.04.2003 which is exhibited to my September 2008 statement as RWH11."

Richard Hill was an accurate reflection of the intellect and integrity of Sue Gregory: dull, dishonest, and racist.

The statement was almost certainly created for Richard Hill by some of the brightest former England young adults, such as Ian Sadler and David Morris.

Do they (David Morris and Ian Sadler) think it is possible for those who are not members of a racist satanic network to use such a statement in the course of a legal process?

Do they (David Morris and Ian Sadler) agree that by the following statement that was created for Richard Hill by some of the topmost England young adults was based upon dishonesty and/ or reckless confusions: "while collating this information, I noticed that some inspection reports were missing, which included an inspection of Mr Bamgbelu's practice on 02.04.2003"? Richard Hill implied that the report of the lone Negro in their midst was a subset of the set of results that were missing. Under oath, on 18.11.2008, Richard Hill further implied that he was not sure of the number of reports that were allegedly missing. Do they (David Morris and Ian Sadler) think it is possible for those who are not members of a racist satanic network to make such an absurd statement in the course of a legal process?

✳ ✳ ✳ ✳ ✳ ✳

David Morris cross examined Richard Hill on 18.11.2008:
DAVID MORRIS: Just in terms of the April 2003 visit, I think you have mentioned the Health Care Commission and you were asked to provide details of all your practice visit reports back in 2006.
RICHARD HILL: Yes.
DAVID MORRIS: At that time I think some of your inspection visit reports were missing.
RICHARD HILL: Two or three were missing. The reason was and the reason I suspect why that was missing was because we had moved office, I had moved office in 2002, 2004 and 2006 and the problem is that I work for one session a week and I am at the office quite often only once every other week; the other time I'm on the road visiting. What happens is that when there's a move, other people are responsible for putting all my files into boxes and then re-filing them at the other location simply because I'm not there.
DAVID MORRIS: So when we look at the 2003 report that we have behind tab 20, it had got lost and is it the case that this is a contemporaneous document—
RICHARD HILL: Yes.
DAVID MORRIS: —or might it have been a document reconstituted from memory following the loss of an earlier document?
RICHARD HILL: This would have been contemporaneous. Well, when I say contemporaneous, what I would do, without support, would

be to make some notes and then complete it normally the next day. This was carried out of an evening. We try to be flexible. Most of our inspections/visits are carried out at lunch time and most practitioners are happy for that; it means that we can actually have myself and one or two PCT members of staff visit as well so that we can have, if you like, a holistic approach to the whole practice, not just seeing if people comply but trying to sort of find ways in which we can support the practitioner in the future. So it is a multifaceted approach. In this particular case, we visited in the evening because Mr Bamgbelu was finding that much more convenient. I don't know whether that was because he was at dual locations he could only make it in the evening, but we would normally do it lunch time. Unfortunately, in those circumstances you do not get any support because people finish at 5 o'clock and I go straight from practice. I finish in my practice probably mid afternoon and then I arrange for that visit to be carried out in the evening.

DAVID MORRIS: So this visit that you have documented here behind tab 20, you would have had this pro forma with you, would you?

RICHARD HILL: Yes, I would take it with me.

DAVID MORRIS: Because you now have this pro forma, would there be any need to make any notes?

RICHARD HILL: I would make sort of relevant notes which are not covered by these, sort of anything to do with dentist problems, worries, that sort of thing, concerns.

NEGRO'S PERSPECTIVE:

So, only two or three were missing in 2006, but in November 2008, Richard Hill had not ascertained the exact numbers of reports that were missing. Extraordinary!

Do they (David Morris and Ian Sadler) agree that all the allegedly missing reports – a minimum of two and a maximum of three – belonged to the first ever and only Negro dentist in Bedford, and that in some other jurisdictions, only members of the racist satanic network could get away with things like that?

The 02.04.2003 report was allegedly missing and it belonged to the first ever and only Negro dentist in Bedford.

The 22.07.2004 report was allegedly missing, as it was bizarrely created from handwritten draft notes which contained unrelated matters, and it belonged to the first ever and only Negro dentist in Bedford.

The alleged follow up report of the 22.07.2004 visit, of undisclosed date, was allegedly missing, as it was bizarrely created from handwritten draft notes which contained unrelated matters, and it belonged to the first ever and only Negro dentist in Bedford.

Do they (David Morris and Ian Sadler) agree that Richard Hill was dishonest, as he maliciously lied when he stated under oath that he created two separate reports using only handwritten drafts which recorded other matters? Do they (David Morris and Ian Sadler) further agree that in some jurisdictions, only members of the racist satanic network (all for one, one for all) could get away with such? Do they (David Morris and Ian Sadler) also agree that Richard Hill was a very accurate reflection of the intellect and integrity of Sue Gregory (OBE)?

"In 2006 the Healthcare Commission carried out a visit to Bedfordshire PCT and I was asked to provide all my practice visit reports. While collating this information, I noticed that some inspection reports were missing, which included an inspection of Mr Bamgbelu's practice on 02.04.2003. Around that time my department moved and it is possible that some reports had been lost during the move. I did locate some of my draft handwritten notes and referred to these to prepare my inspection report dated 22.07.2004 for MR BAMGBELU's practice which at the time, I understood to be a correct and accurate record of my inspection."
– Richard Hill, 16.10.2008

"I would make sort of relevant notes which are not covered by these, sort of anything to do with dentist problems, worries, that sort of thing, concerns." – Richard Hill, 18.11.2008

Do they (David Morris and Ian Sadler) agree that Richard Hill was dishonest when he stated that he used handwritten drafts, which recorded other matters, to create two separate reports (22.07.2004 and follow up of unknown date)?

Richard Hill was an accurate reflection of the intellect and integrity of Sue Gregory (OBE).

The sole basis of the power displayed is money, and the entire foundation of the money was merciless racial hatred and naked fraud.

"Many Scots masters were considered among the most brutal, with life expectancy on their plantations averaging a mere four years. We worked them to death then simply imported more to keep the sugar and thus the

money flowing. Unlike centuries of grief and murder, an apology costs nothing. So what does Scotland have to say?" – Herald Scotland, Ian Bell, columnist, Sunday 28 April 2013

Do they (David Morris and Ian Sadler) agree that Richard Hill was dishonest when he implied that his dishonesty had basis, and this basis endured for about four years before it died prematurely?

"I did locate some of my draft handwritten notes and referred to these to prepare my inspection report dated 22.07.2004 for MR BAMGBELU's practice which at the time, I understood to be a correct and accurate record of my inspection." – Richard Hill, 16.10.2008

Do they (David Morris and Ian Sadler) know the basis of the accuracy and correctness was dishonesty, and it was not permanent, and it was baseless?

What exactly was the point of the blatantly dishonest, Negrophobic, and mediocre legal process apart from artificially creating jobs for lawyers?

"The one great principle of English law is to make business for itself." – Charles Dickens

"The contents of the 22.07.2004 and 02.04.2003 report differ. The reason that the contents differ is because the hand written notes I used to prepare the 22.07.2004 also had a reference to a difference and dates and notes were mixed up. Having reviewed the documents, it became clear to me that the July 2004 was created in error. The content of the 02.04.2003 report is an accurate reflection of the inspection done at the time and I stand by the contents of the same." – Richard Hill, 16.10.2008

Do they (David Morris and Ian Sadler) agree that Richard Hill expected the contents of the 2003 and 2004 reports to be the same because he created one as a replacement for the other? Do they (David Morris and Ian Sadler) further agree that it was absurd to create two 2004 reports as replacement for a single 2003 report, and only members of the racist satanic network would tell such lies on record or on oath without consequence?

Based upon very proximate observations and direct experiences, it is actual fact and absolute truth that parts of the administration of the English law is mediocre, Negrophobic, and dishonest.

The administration of the law is the meat, as the lawyer is the tyrant's tool.

"Rightful liberty is unobstructed action according to our will within limits drawn around us by the equal rights of others. I do not add 'within the limits of the law' because law is often but the tyrant's will, and always so when it violates the rights of the individual." – President Thomas Jefferson

Descendants of Eastern European Jews are the shepherds of the descendants of serfs. Sheep are fed with the gigantic yields of evil. Before slavery, what?

As the reports of the alleged visits of 22.07.2004 and follow up of undisclosed date are evidently based upon maliciously falsified information, David Morris, Outer Temple Chambers, Strand, London must have lied or displayed reckless confusion when he implicitly (probably as agreed in secret) told Richard Hill to state that he visited another practice on 22.07.2004 and carried out a follow up at the same surgery on an undisclosed date. There was nothing in Strand before slavery, apart from stolen land and some serfs working it for land owners, all of whom were from mainland Europe.

※ ※ ※ ※ ※ ※

David Morris cross examined Richard Hill on 18.11.2008:

DAVID MORRIS: So (a) there was no visit in July 2004.

RICHARD HILL: No, it was April 2003 which we discussed was, again, a pastoral type of visit.

DAVID MORRIS: And (b) the concerns listed there were not relevant to Mr Bamgbelu's practice.

RICHARD HILL: Not at all.

DAVID MORRIS: They were another practice.

RICHARD HILL: They were another practice that did not refer to him. It did in error, but it was not about him.

DAVID MORRIS: But, unfortunately, that synopsis was sent off to the Bedford PCT in the form of John Hooper, Charlotte Dowling and Sue Gregory.

RICHARD HILL: Yes, although I don't think they acted upon that as regards the Dental Reference Service visit. I think these were required more so for the Health Care Commission which is why there was a whole series. Prior to this, a few months earlier, I carried out a similar exercise for Luton PCT, which I also advise, because they had an imminent visit from the Health Care Commission.

NEGRO'S PERSPECTIVE:

Prior to being invited by David Morris to state that he visited another surgery on 22.07.2004 and implicitly carried out a follow up visit at the same surgery on an unknown date, Richard Hill never at any time made such an assertion, as it would have been absurd to do so. David Morris did because he is not a dentist, and some deluded barristers (descendants of feudal agricultural labourers), without objective basis, award themselves the monopoly of knowledge and associate the gigantic yields of centuries of merciless, racist evil with their own personal intellect and industry

Shepherds of morons are likelier to be morons too.

David Morris and Ian Sadler are shepherds of England young adults.

So, David Morris told or invited Richard Hill to state that he visited another surgery in Bedford on 22.07.2004 and implicitly carried out a follow up visit on an unknown date, and the reports of the alleged visits were created as a replacement for the 2003 report, as they were expected to be similar, and they were created from handwritten draft notes which contained other matters.

F****** rot!

"Nothing that you will learn in the course of your studies will be of the slightest possible use to you in after life – save only this – if you work hard and diligently you should be able to detect when a man is talking rot, and that, in my view, is the main, if not the sole, purpose of education." – J.A. Smith, Oxford University Professor, Moral Philosophy

Descendants of Eastern European Jews whose ancestors used to live off sustenance farming in Latvia, Estonia, and places that moved to Britain discarded their true mothers' tongues (language is the first to go in the metamorphosis of the extinction a people) and abandoned their real fathers' names. They are the shepherds of moron sheep, with gigantic yields of several centuries of merciless, racist evil (slavery).

Before slavery, what?

Before slavery, there was only sustenance farming.

Only a day later, on 19.11.2008, in their dull, dishonest, and Negrophobic charade (incompetent art incompetently imitating life), behind Richard Hill's back, David Morris implied that Richard Hill stated that there was a visit to another surgery on 22.07.2004 and he implicitly conducted a follow up inspection at the same surgery on an unknown date. Thuggery is not law!

David Morris cross examined Stephanie Twidale on 19.11.2008:

DAVID MORRIS: Sir, you will recall Mr Hill's evidence was that this is a report mistakenly attributed to Mr Bamgbelu's practice when it in fact relates to something that was a mistake?

THE CHAIRMAN (DR SHIV PABARY, MEMBER OF THE BRITISH EMPIRE): Was this where there was a lot of cancellations? I remember something in evidence.

NEGRO'S PERSPECTIVE:
"Was this where there was a lot of cancellations?" SHIV PABARY, MBE, mediocre and dishonest or confused GDC Judge

DAVID MORRIS: Mr Hill said yesterday that while he made an error and he thought there had been an inspection on 22 July 2004, and in fact that was not right, it referred to another practice. In chatting with Richard Hill, presumably you did before going round, did he mention any previous inspections that he had done?

NEGRO'S PERSPECTIVE:
David Morris ignored the unintelligible gibberish of their imbecile Indian. Kuli olodo!

Some allegedly civilised Christians found guns and used them to mercilessly slaughter millions of Africans, and armed others to slaughter millions more, and worked millions more still to death so that an imbecile Indian could become a chairman and a judge within the GDC in the distant future. Crass! The charade will not endure. The future generations will be too dull to keep the show going seamlessly. Time will unfold the truth.

STEPHANIE TWIDALE: I never spoke to Richard Hill, nor had I ever met him before we arrived at the practice together. It was a classic two people standing outside a building saying: "Are you? Oh yes, right fine" we had never met and we did not speak beforehand. The only people I spoke to beforehand would be John Hooper and some e-mail correspondence with John, with Charlotte Dowling and with the Consultants in public health, Sue Gregory. I didn't actually have any contact with Richard at all.

NEGRO'S PERSPECTIVE:
STEPHANIE TWIDALE couldn't spell or write legibly. She lied under oath. DR ANAND KAMATH-alleged poor records-DEAD!
THE LEGAL ADVISER (MR DAVID SWINSTEAD): Mr Morris, can you make it absolutely clear for everybody that I think you are referring to the document behind divider 21, and it is the Schedule Record of Practice which is the second part, is that right?

NEGRO'S PERSPECTIVE:
The Negro was "everybody."

DAVID MORRIS: That is right, sir.

NEGRO'S PERSPECTIVE:
"That is right, sir." – David Morris
Oyinbo olodo! Oyinbo ode!
Incompetent art incompetently imitated life.

Very polite racist crooks.
No brain, natural resources poor, only skin colour that the wearer neither made nor choose, and what else? Pure scam!

* * * * * *

THE LEGAL ADVISER (MR DAVID SWINSTEAD):
Sorry, do I look behind it?
DAVID MORRIS: Yes, if you look behind tab 21. Richard Hill sent an e-mail to his colleagues at the PCT, Bedford PCT.
THE LEGAL ADVISER (DAVID SWINSTEAD): It is page 3 behind page 21, I think you have said. There is a table and there is a reference

there which I think you suggested to Mr Hill was not actually a report of Mr Bamgbelu's practice, is that right?

DAVID MORRIS: That is right. It was a report, we have the report here.

THE LEGAL ADVISER (DAVID SWINSTEAD): So the Committee understand what the status of D5 is?

DAVID MORRIS: It is my fault, I should have clarified this with Mr Hill yesterday, but D5 is a report drafted by Mr Hill in error, which he accepted yesterday, in error attributing it as an inspection of Mr Bamgbelu's practice at Bromham Road Bedford. When, in fact, it was not, and the substance of the contents were from another practice.

NEGRO'S PERSPECTIVE:
Of course, it was his fault!

David Morris should go to Peckham and find a bruno with gold teeth and tell the bitch that he is a barrister from Strand in London (Strand was agricultural land before slavery; zero building). It is likelier to say, "Respect man."

The satanic network is almost everywhere, and it controls everything except intellect. Without objective basis, it awards itself the monopoly of knowledge.

MERIT was irrelevant within the SATANIC NETWORK, as the LOOT they shared was the yield of RACIST EVIL. Associating EVIL with virtue is deceit.

THE LEGAL ADVISER (MR DAVID SWINSTEAD): Was there a visit to another practice?

DAVID MORRIS: That is how he put it yesterday.

NEGRO'S PERSPECTIVE:
Richard Hill did not put it like that, and it was brainless to do so, as it was absurd to create two 2004 reports from handwritten drafts, which recorded unrelated matters, and use them as a replacement for the allegedly missing report of 2003.

The privileged dullards were too dull to realise that as the reports were created from handwritten drafts which bizarrely also recorded other matters; they must have been missing too.

They lied on oath and did so incompetently. Those that they regularly spin are amongst the dullest adults in the industrialised world. David Morris is a former England young adult; he is a shepherd of England young adults.

Shepherds of morons are likelier to be morons too.

Is Constance Briscoe the only barrister that had ever lied on record? Mr Andrew Hurst was implicitly instructed by the GDC to lie, under oath.

✳ ✳ ✳ ✳ ✳

THE LEGAL ADVISER (DAVID SWINSTEAD): Effectively, so that the address is incorrect because it is a different surgery, is that right?

DAVID MORRIS: Yes. He listed, when being chased for previous inspections he listed it in that schedule, and he accepted yesterday that there was no such visit in 2004.

NEGRO'S PERSPECTIVE:

"There was no such visit in 2004" is an objective statement. It confirms that the 2004 reports are Negrophobic NHS forgeries. The fact that they were bizarrely created from handwritten drafts, which recorded other matters, further confirmed that they were the NHS's Negrophobic forgeries. The facts in support of the NHS's forgeries is further corroborated by the fact that two 2004 reports were created as a replacement for one supposedly missing report.

David Morris and Richard Hill were dishonest, as they unrelentingly lied under oath. There is no evidence, certainly none conclusive, that David Morris was a member of the racist satanic network.

In order to sell hereditary mediocrity and confusion for value, some people join the racist satanic network (all for one, one for all). Secret information sustains their evil network, but since membership of their racist satanic network is neither meritocratic nor open, they are forced to rely upon some truths, some half-truths, and plenty of lies. They wear charity as a cloak of deceit and swear by the name of Almighty God never to tell lies, but they lie that they do not lie (Songs of David 144).

*****

THE CHAIRMAN (DR SHIV PABARY, MEMBER OF THE BRITISH EMPIRE): This was not put to Mr Hill yesterday.

DAVID MORRIS: The actual report was not, but we went through the schedule, but for completeness I should have put it to him yesterday. (To the witness) You have not seen that before and you did not have any discussion with Mr Hill about it?
STEPHANIE TWIDALE: None at all.

NEGRO'S PERSPECTIVE:
Even if Stephanie Twidale, who sought the report that was exclusively created for her, told the truth about the fact that she did not see the report, David Morris implied that seeing a report is the only way of knowing about a report, and Stephanie Twidale (TD) couldn't admit that she had discussions about reports with Richard Hill when she had already lied unrelentingly under oath that she did not have any contact with Richard Hill before meeting him in front of the surgery of the first ever and only Negro dentist in Bedford.

David Morris and Stephanie Twidale maliciously told Negrophobic lies under oath.

The following is an email from Dr Sue Gregory to Dr Stephanie Twidale, Dr Richard Hill, and Mrs Charlotte Dowling Goodson: "Dear Stephanie, Just to confirm that I have spoken to Richard Hill and he will join you for the DRS visit on Thursday 22nd February to Mr Bamgbelu's Bedford Practice, commencing at 9 a.m. We will endeavour to share any issues the PCT may have with you PRIOR to the 22nd. Kind regards, Sue" (30.11.2006).

Stephanie Twidale was dishonest, as she unrelentingly lied under oath. Did the GDC plant racists in the mediocre and corrupt council to guard and guide the lies of the racist cougar with three-fourths deflated, humungous mammary glands with no milk?

"Truth, Sir, is a cow which will yield such people no more milk, and so they are gone to milk the bull." – Dr Samuel Johnson

Stephanie Twidale has no milk left, and if she had any, it would have been very likkle. She is an ugly, racist bas****, with an uglier, huge ass which was made uglier still by what appeared to be a thoroughly ugly G-string, at nearly her eighth decade.

It is very depressing to see someone cast off youth almost unworn. It usually means they try to dress up in it much later when it doesn't suit them anymore.

Stephanie Twidale was an accurate reflection of the intellect and integrity of Sue Gregory.

Before slavery, what?

"Agriculture not only gives riches to a nation, but the only riches she can call her own." – Dr Samuel Johnson

"Those who have robbed have also lied." – Dr Samuel Johnson corroborating prophet Habakkuk

Descendants of Eastern European Jews are the shepherds of descendants of serfs. Sheep are feed with GIGANTIC yields of EVIL. Before slavery what?

About two years later, under oath, on 20.11.2008, Charlotte Dowling Goodson corroborated the statements in Sue Gregory's correspondence of 30.11.2006.

* * * * * * *

David Morris cross examined Charlotte Dowling Goodson on 20.11.2008:

DAVID MORRIS: Referring to, "Stephanie Twidale calling us a few weeks ago and she wanted to know if there had been a dental inspection there at all (I think that's Bedfordshire) and I didn't know the answer. Cue Richard, have you carried out an inspection at this practice. Please could you advise Stephanie when she contacts you." That is the next time this matter arose, is that right?

CHARLOTTE DOWLING GOODSON: That is correct, yes.

DAVID MORRIS: And then I think in response to that, do we get an e mail from Richard Hill, which we have behind tab 21 in volume 1.

CHARLOTTE DOWLING GOODSON: Sorry, can I have the tab again.

DAVID MORRIS: Tab 21. From Richard Hill 6 September 06 to you and others at Bedford; record of practice visits, and we have the entry on that schedule for July 2004, all right?

CHARLOTTE DOWLING GOODSON: Yes.

DAVID MORRIS: And did you, as part of his process then . . . well, I can see the concerns that were raised in that column: no risk assessment, no COSSH, Kavoclave type autoclave, why that shouldn't be used, no other members of practice staff present at visits, and could not be questioned regarding cross infection control by the practice. But did you, as part of this process, receive a copy of what was purported to be the visit record for that date, 22 July 04?

CHARLOTTE DOWLING GOODSON: Not at that time, but we did get copies of the reports and for these visits at a later date. We had been requesting them.

DAVID MORRIS: That is D5, if you can have a look at that, please. (Handed)

CHARLOTTE DOWLING GOODSON: Thank you

(Perused document).

DAVID MORRIS: And I think if I can take you to the feedback, final page, page 5, summary of these concerns: "The practice uses a Kavoclave type autoclave. This is not acceptable. There is also a large turnover of staff and I am not satisfied that staff training is at an acceptable level and have concerns over the cross infection control procedures," and the essential action points set out there. So you would have received that, and that would have informed your concerns at that time about that practice?

CHARLOTTE DOWLING GOODSON: This report was received at a later time. I did not receive it until 2004.

DAVID MORRIS: No.

CHARLOTTE DOWLING GOODSON: But what I also I received was part of the decision making process, and prioritising the practice for an inspection by the DRS.

DAVID MORRIS: And would those concerns, informed in part by that report, have been fed through to Stephanie Twidale prior to her conducting her inspection in February 07?

CHARLOTTE DOWLING GOODSON: I can't remember if I passed them on. I think Richard Hill would have shared those issues with Stephanie as part of the discussion prior to the visit, and that is part of the reason why Richard went with Stephanie to undertake the visit with her.

DAVID MORRIS: It would have made a lot of sense for the information in that report to have been passed on and fed through as necessary preliminary material prior to inspection?

CHARLOTTE DOWLING GOODSON: Yes, it would have been.

DAVID MORRIS: And do you appreciate that now, very recently, Mr. Hill has realised that that report, relating to Mr. Bamgbelu's practice, in fact was an error, in as much as the concerns in it related to wholly different matters?

CHARLOTTE DOWLING GOODSON: No, I was not aware of that.

NEGRO'S PERSPECTIVE:

Sue Gregory's correspondence of 30.11.2006 and Charlotte Dowling Goodson's testimony under oath about a year later on 20.11.2008 do not fit seamlessly with Stephanie Twidale's unrelenting dishonesty under oath and on record.

Stephanie Twidale (TD) was exceedingly dull. She couldn't have achieved such a high level of dullness from nature; the ugly, old bat, a f******* merciless, racist thug, must have been created dull by Almighty God and born duller by her mummy!

"Why, Sir, Sherry is dull, naturally dull, but it must have taken him a great deal of pain to become what we now see him. Such an excess stupidity, Sir, is not in Nature." – Dr Samuel Johnson

"Sir, he was dull in company, dull in his closet, dull everywhere. He was dull in a new way, and that made many people think him great." – Dr Samuel Johnson Oyinbo olodo! Oyinbo ode!

"Dear Stephanie, Just to confirm that I have spoken to Richard Hill and he will join you for the DRS visit on Thursday 22nd February to Mr Bamgbelu's Bedford Practice, commencing at 9 a.m. We will endeavour to share any issues the PCT may have with you PRIOR to the 22nd. Kind regards, Sue." – 30.11.2006

"I can't remember if I passed them on. I think Richard Hill would have shared those issues with Stephanie as part of the discussion prior to the visit, and that is part of the reason why Richard went with Stephanie to undertake the visit with her." –

Charlotte Dowling Goodson, 20.11.2008

Stephanie Twidale (TD), the merciless, seemingly hereditary racist thug, seemed too dull to realise that if she was given Richard Hill's contact details in the summer of 2006, and he was advised to expect to hear from her, it must be absurd that she had discussions with others based upon information which could only have come from Richard Hill, and those she had discussions with included fourth-rate polytechnic university educated England young adults or former England young adults, descendants of thoroughly wretched, feudal agricultural labourers (serfs) from mainland Europe who were immeasurably transformed the gigantic yields of slavery who have reinvented themselves on stolen land, and fool the foolish.

The descendants of wretched, feudal agricultural labourers (serfs) from the mainland were immeasurably transformed the gigantic yields of slavery.

"So you have got some recollection of being told that Richard Hill had been there some months before?" – David Morris

Again, Stephanie Twidale was dishonest, and she maliciously lied or she was maliciously lied to by Sue Gregory and others when she stated as follows under oath or otherwise on record: "Yes please we would like a surgery inspection. At the point at which I was informed that Richard Hill had been there some months before hand and had some concerns."

"Having discussed with the PCT they told me that Mr Hill had made previous visits not that long before from which there had been some queries, and they felt perhaps it would be sensible for Mr Hill to come along as well with me to be a second person and follow up on his previous visits to the practice."

"I spoke to Dr Sue Gregory, Consultant in Dental Public Health at the Bedfordshire PCT to impart the information and was informed that Richard Hill, Dental Practice adviser to Bedfordshire PCT, had carried out a previous Surgery inspection at Bromham Road that had raised some concerns."

"Then I know it came through that Richard Hill had been in before about 6 months ago, I think they said, and it was probably sensible for him to go as the second person, a second appropriate second person to do a follow up. The actual timings of bits of those I am afraid I can't REMEMBER."

"At the point at which I was informed that Richard Hill had been there some months before hand and had some concerns."

Sue Gregory, the seemingly closeted racist cougar, was the cardinal of evil, and Stephanie Twidale was a very accurate reflection of her intellect and integrity.

They are descendants of merciless, evil, racist murderers, armed robbers, and thieves – stealers, carriers, and sellers of millions of kidnapped and stolen human beings, not for a little while, but for several centuries of merciless, racist terrorism. Those who will steal human beings will steal anything. Whenever they merciless slaughtered, they dispossessed, and wherever they robbed, they took possession. They were the murderous cowards, armed robbers, and thieves that the prophet spoke about.

"Those who have robbed have also lied." – Dr Samuel Johnson corroborating prophet Habakkuk

"I know of no evil that has ever existed, nor can imagine any evil to exist, worse than the tearing of eighty thousand persons annually from their native land, by a combination of the most civilised nations inhabiting the most enlightened part of the globe, but more especially under the sanction of the laws of that Nation which calls herself the most free and the most happy of them all." – Prime Minister William Pitt the Younger

"The grand object of all European traders in kidnapped and stolen Africans was - money, money, money; money was their god! In Africa, the poor wretched natives, blessed with the most fertile and luxuriant soil, are rendered so much the more miserable by the Christians' (European traders in stolen Africans) abominable traffic for slaves and the horrid cruelty and treachery of the petty [African] Kings. The Africans kings were encouraged by their European (Christian) customers who carry them strong liquors to enflame their madness and powder and bad firearms to furnish them with the hellish means of killing and kidnapping. But enough - it is a subject that sours my blood." – Ignatius Sancho, 1778

"Many Scots masters were considered among the most brutal, with life expectancy on their plantations averaging a mere four years. We worked them to death then simply imported more to keep the sugar and thus the money flowing. Unlike centuries of grief and murder, an apology costs nothing. So what does Scotland have to say?" – Herald Scotland, Ian Bell, columnist, Sunday 28 April 2013

Merciless, racist bastards! They are no longer here, but it'd be naïve not to expect their merciless, sadistic genes to continue to flow through the veins of some of those who remain here.

"I never spoke to Richard Hill, nor had I ever met him before we arrived at the practice together. It was a classic two people standing outside a building saying: 'Are you? Oh yes, right fine.' We had never met and we did not speak beforehand. The only people I spoke to beforehand would be John Hooper and some e-mail correspondence with John, with Charlotte Dowling and with the Consultants in public health, Sue Gregory. I didn't actually have any contact with Richard at all." – Stephanie Twidale

Stephanie Twidale, the ugly mammie or mumsie with a gigantic, very ugly ass and three-fourths deflated mammary glands with no milk, had the beautiful, peculiar, aromatic scent of an old lady at the starting of mummification, in readiness for eternity.

Stephanie Twidale (TD) was dishonest, and she lied when she implied that she did not contact Richard Hill at all, despite acknowledging that she was given his contact details in the summer of 2006.

Stephanie Twidale (TD) was dishonest and lied when she implied that she did not have any contact with Richard Hill in 2006, including after she received Sue Gregory's correspondence of 30.11.2006.

Stephanie Twidale was an accurate reflection of the intellect and integrity of Sue Gregory.

Stephanie Twidale was dishonest and lied when she stated, under oath, that she did not have any contact with Richard Hill in 2007 prior to their joint inspection of the surgery of the first ever and only Negro dentist in Bedford.

"Dear Richard, Just to confirm that I have agreed with John Hooper that we go ahead with the Surgery inspection part of the DRS monitoring programme as arranged for 9.00am on Thursday 22 Feb. However the patient and record card/radiograph examination part of the process will now be delayed until after April, as Mr Bamgbelu has already exceeded his UDA target for the current year. I spoke to Mr Bamgbelu this afternoon, and he has asked that I arrange that date with him at the visit next week. I am assuming that I will see you at the practice at 9.00am, as arranged. Di you want to meet up outside first, or should we go in independently? It might look as if we are 'ganging up' if we met first. Also I gather that parking is a problem. If you need to discuss further, please phone xxxxxxxxx or xxxxxxxxxxxx (2 phone numbers)." – Stephanie Twidale's email to Richard Hill on 15.02.2007

Dr Stephanie Twidale's email of 09.02.2007 (prior to visiting the surgery of the first ever and only Negro dentist in Bedford on 22.02.2007) to Mr John Hooper, copied to Dr Richard Hill, Dr Sue Gregory, and Dr Steven Claydon, stated, "John, I telephoned Mr Bamgbelu this morning to confirm the arrangements for the New style monitoring visit (surgery inspection, patient examinations radiograph/ record card checks) due on Thu 22 Feb. This is our normal procedure, 2 weeks beforehand. Mr Bamgbelu told me that there would be no patients to examine, as he is 'already 100 UDAs over his target, so is doing no more NHS work until 01 April.' He refuses to get four patients in for me to see, even if he does not treat them himself that day – he tells me I am welcome to see private patients, whom he is continuing to treat – but of course that is not part of our remit. He is apparently still expecting me to come to do the Surgery Inspection at 0900 –Richard Hill is accompanying me for that. I would also be able to do the radiograph/record card check part of the process – but no patients would be seen. I imagine you would be unhappy with that situation – I certainly am – the onus is on you as PCT I am afraid to decide what to do now. We could put the whole thing off again until April or even do the surg insp now, and patients in April – records/rads could be done at either visit. However this was flagged up by yourselves as a priority, and he has already had it postponed once from January, because he 'booked it for the wrong practice,' and wasn't in Bedford on the day originally arranged. I have been in negotiations over this whole priority visit since August, and I feel he is just putting us off again. Stephanie."

Stephanie Twidale (TD) was a merciless, racist perjurer, a mere descendant of thoroughly wretched agricultural labourers (serfs) from mainland Europe who stole aborigine land (from the native Britons). They were transformed by the gigantic yields of several centuries of the merciless evil which slavery was. They have reinvented themselves with stolen money on stolen land and full the foolish with foolishness. Oyinbo olodo! Oyinbo ode!

"It was in 1066 that William the Conqueror occupied Britain, stole our land and gained control by granting it to his Norman friends, thus creating a feudal system we have not yet fully escaped." – Tony Benn

Normans stole from others what others had stolen from others. Genetically pure Britons are extinct; all were dispossessed, robbed, and slaughtered.

"All have taken what had other owners, and all have had recourse to arms rather than quit the prey on which they had fastened." Dr Samuel Johnson

Before slavery, what?

"Those who have robbed have also lied." – Dr Samuel Johnson corroborating prophet Habakkuk

DAVID MORRIS: The question you posed as reported in D4, an e-mail from John Hooper, whether or not there had been a dental inspection before, you never got an answer to?

STEPHANIE TWIDALE: I got an answer at some stage, but I can't remember exactly where. The question I was asking at that point from John Hooper in the very early stage was quite simply: "Do you just need the SP2?" In other words patients and record card examinations carrying out, in other words is that the reason why you have brought this forward for an urgent visit as opposed to a routine visit which could have taken a year for me to get round to it with the work load we had at that stage or: "do you need anything else in particular? If it is anything to do with the practice, do you need me to do a surgery inspection. Is that part of what you are looking for me to do?" I eventually got an answer that said: "Yes, please we would like a surgery inspection." At the point at which I was informed that Richard Hill had been there some months before hand and had some concerns. I don't think that at that stage, but I am relying on memory here, my memory is it came in when the decision was made that Richard Hill would be the person to accompany me on the visit. As the PCT would rather he did it as he had been there before, rather than the consultant who was in public health, as they felt it was not appropriate for her and while there was a second DRO going to accompany me. That is my memory of it.

NEGRO'S PERSPECTIVE:

Stephanie Twidale (TD), the merciless, seemingly hereditary racist cougar, employed tortuous verbosity to mesmerise the cretins that sat before her. I mean, Shiv Pabary, Member of the British Empire, who was the chairman of the Negrophobic charade in the "fish and chips" GDC, was so dull, he stated as follows: "There is wordings that imply that there was, but it is not in black and white."

OYINBO OLE: WHITE THIEVES: HABAKKUK

Nigeria: Shell's docile cash cow since 1956.

Then, racist white bastards carried and sold millions of stolen children of defenceless poor people; now, they carry natural resources from AFRICA.

30% of the known natural resources reserve in the world are in AFRICA, and the descendants of carriers and sellers of millions of stolen children of defenceless people are directly or indirectly in charge.

Then, racist white bastards carried the children away from their food; now they carry food away from other people's children.

The visible chains were removed; only fools expect the true chains to be voluntarily removed.

The carrying trade did not end, only what was being carried changed. The carrying trade is more profitable now than then.

Then, they carried stolen children; now, they carry natural resources.

"Moderation is a virtue only among those who are thought to have found alternatives." Henry Kissinger

He is watching them – Proverbs 15:3

"There is no sin except stupidity." – Oscar Wilde

"I got an answer at some stage, but I can't remember exactly where. The question I was asking at that point from John Hooper in the very early stage was quite simply: 'Do you just need the SP2?' In other words patients and record card examinations carrying out, in other words is that the reason why you have brought this forward for an urgent visit as opposed to a routine visit which could have taken a year for me to get round to it with the work load we had at that stage or: 'do you need anything else in particular? If it is anything to do with the practice, do you need me to do a surgery inspection. Is that part of what you are looking for me to do?' I eventually got an answer that said: 'Yes, please we would like a surgery inspection.'" – Stephanie Twidale

"The great enemy of the clear language is INSINCERITY (DISHONESTY). When there is a gap between one's real and one's declared aims, one turns as it were instinctively to long words and exhausted idioms, like a cuttlefish squirting ink. In our age there is no such thing as 'keeping out of politics'. All issues are political issues, and politics itself is a mass of lies, evasions, folly, HATRED and schizophrenia. When the general atmosphere is bad, language must suffer." – George Orwell

What exceedingly irritating nonsense by a merciless, racist, ugly, and thoroughly wretched old bat who would be considerably diminished as a human being without her most favourable skin colour, which she neither made nor chose, but wore as if it were a first-class degree from Oxford University.

"The first class at Oxford where I have examined is an overrated mark." – Lord Dacre (Hugh Trevor-Roper), 1981

Who the f*** does Stephanie Twidale think she is? A brainless, racist, and dishonest descendant of thoroughly wretched, feudal agricultural labourers from mainland Europe who lived off the land before they found guns and used them to loot and destroy the world. They were immeasurably transformed by the merciless evil of slavery. They have reinvented themselves and fool the foolish with foolishness.

Before slavery, what?

What Stephanie Twidale actually stated, as alleged by the NHS: "Richard (Hill), Stephanie Twidale called us a few weeks ago about DRS visits and Charlotte prioritised Mr Bamgbelu's practice; Stephanie has been in touch a few times as her colleagues had highlighted issues from a similar practice in Northants and they would like to review report etc etc prior to visiting. She also wanted to know if there has been a dental inspection there at all and I did not know the answer . . ." (NHS, 15.08.2006).

The merciless, closeted racist cougar was obsessed with the first ever and only Negro dentist in Bedford.

The Negro's surgery was prioritised during one of the calls of the merciless, racist bastard. She called a few times only about the Negro. Her colleagues, pencil pushers like her who have failed in almost everything and everywhere, had become inspectors or teachers.

"He who can, does. He who cannot teaches." – George Bernard Shaw

"They," the envious, racist pencil pushers who had nearly failed or just failed in clinical dentistry, and the descendants of wretched, feudal agricultural labourers (serfs) from mainland Europe, had parked their liabilities at the till of other people's money.

"They would like to review report etc etc prior to visiting." – NHS, 15.08.2006

"Et cetera" is a very wide world. "Et cetera, et cetera" is a very, very wide world! Merciless racist bastards! Descendants of more merciless, racist bastards!

"American South is still taken as barbarism's benchmark. Few realise that the behaviour of Scots busy getting rich in the slaveholders' empire was actually worse – (routinely worse) – than the worst of the cottonocracy. You need only count the corpses. By the time slavery was brought to an end in America, the country's 400,000 trafficked people had grown to a population of four million. In the British West Indies, only 670,000 survived from two million imported souls. In the American South, slaves were valuable and bred. We worked them to death then simply imported more to keep the sugar and thus the money flowing. Unlike centuries of grief and murder, an apology costs nothing. So what does Scotland have to say?" – Herald Scotland, Ian Bell, columnist, Sunday 28 April 2013
Before slavery, what?
"Agriculture not only gives riches to a nation, but the only riches she can call her own." – Dr Samuel Johnson

"She also wanted to know if there has been a dental inspection there at all and I did not know the answer . . ." – NHS, 15.08.2006

Why did she want to know whether "there has been a dental inspection there at all"?
Envy!

Dr. Olayinka Bamgbelu

"Envy is weak." Yul Brynner

"The wicked envy and hate; it is their way of admiring." – Victor Hugo

DROs (Dental Reference Officers) do not inspect surgeries, and it was against the rules to do such an inspection with a DPA (Dental Practice Adviser). The ugly, racist old bat was looking for any opportunity to f*** the lone Negro in their midst.
Low life rubbish!
Idiot!
Apart from skin colour, what?
Before slavery, what?
On 15.08.2006, I had superior paper qualifications to those of Stephanie Twidale (TD). I had two thriving practices and considerably wider experiences in clinical dentistry than the dull, dishonest, and closeted racist thug – a descendant of evil human being stealers, carriers, and sellers. Those who would steal human beings will steal anything.

"The grand object of all European traders in kidnapped and stolen Africans was - money, money, money; money was their god! In Africa, the poor wretched natives, blessed with the most fertile and luxuriant soil, are rendered so much the more miserable by the Christians' (European traders in stolen Africans) abominable traffic for slaves and the horrid cruelty and treachery of the petty [African] Kings. The Africans kings were encouraged by their European (Christian) customers who carry them strong liquors to enflame their madness and powder and bad firearms to furnish them with the hellish means of killing and kidnapping. But enough - it is a subject that sours my blood." – Ignatius Sancho, 1778

"I know of no evil that has ever existed, nor can imagine any evil to exist, worse than the tearing of eighty thousand persons annually from their native land, by a combination of the most civilised nations inhabiting the most enlightened part of the globe, but more especially under the sanction of the laws of that Nation which calls herself the most free and the most happy of them all." – Prime Minister William Pitt the Younger, 1792

The evil, sadistic savages are no longer here, but their sadistic genes continue to flow through the veins of some of those whose remain here.

Stephanie Twidale (TD): the dull, dishonest, and seemingly hereditary racist bastard was given the platform to express innate, latent, but extremely potent racial hatred. She has picked on the wrong person. I am very familiar with the detailed history of her feudal agricultural labourer ancestors from the mainland. The f****** racist, wretched barbarians who were immeasurably transformed by the gigantic yields of evil (which slavery was) have reinvented themselves on stolen land.

Sir Winston Churchill implied that the average Briton was a moron.

"The best argument against democracy is a five-minute conversation with the average voter." – Sir Winston Churchill

Stephanie Twidale (TD) and Sue Gregory (OBE) were shepherds of England's young adults. Awon olodo!
In corroborating allegations by a racist NHS nurse, in 2008, the GDC went back 13 years, 1996, and found that Kavoklave wasn't autoclave!
WHITE MORONS: IGNORANT DESCENDANTS OF THIEVES AND OWNERS OF STOLEN CHILDREN OF DEFENCELESS POOR PEOPLE.
Before slavery, what?
Which part of the GDC, 37, Wimpole Street, London, preceded the barbarously racist traffic in millions of stolen children: The building of its chattels?
"The truth allows no choice." Dr Samuel Johnson
OYINBO OLE: RACIST DESCENDANTS OF PROFESSIONAL THIEVES: HABAKKUK.
He is watching them – Proverbs 15:3; Habakkuk.

Andrew Hurst cross examined Richard Hill on 18.11.2008:

ANDREW HURST: Thank you. Now obviously during the course of the run up to the visit of 22 February there was some communication between you and Stephanie Twidale.
RICHARD HILL: Yes.

NEGRO'S PERSPECTIVE:

So, Stephanie Twidale (TD) was dishonest as she maliciously lied again when she stated that she did not have any contact with Richard Hill prior to the inspection of the first ever and only Negro dentist in Bedford on 22.02.2007

Stephanie Twidale was the accurate reflection of the intellect and integrity of Sue Gregory.
Territorial defence: Descendants of thoroughly wretched, feudal agricultural labourers defending stolen land. With her gigantic three-fourths deflated mammary glands with little or no milk or with what?

Stephanie Twidale (TD) seemed too dull and too weak, and too old and too ugly, to defend the poultry of free-range chicks against foxes at night. The English channels were the real defence.

"In the summer of 1940, the British Isles stood isolated and alone facing the might of seemingly unstoppable German war machine that had compelled France to submit and had driven the British expeditionary force off the continent. Never had the United Kingdom been a state of such uncertainty and possible peril. Fortunately, the full breadth of the English Channel held back Hitler's armies and his ambition. Not so for the Channel Island, which stand just a few miles from the French coast."
– Simon Hamon

"If the Almighty were to rebuild the world and asked for my advice, I would have the English channels round every country. And the atmosphere would be such that anything which attempted to fly would be set on fire." – Sir Winston Churchill

Deluded paper tigers: Superiority is their birth right.

Their hairs stand on end when they are challenged by our people; we and our type are the only ones racist white bastards will beat up without the support of the YANKS.

"England will fight to the last American." American saying.

Those who need a real fight should forcibly evict Putin from Crimea; he forcibly stole it.
"Ethical foreign policy." Robin Cook

CHAPTER 17

BEDFORD, ENGLAND: District Judge, which part of our County Court preceded the barbarously racist traffic in millions of stolen children of defenceless poor people: The building or its chattels?

Ignorance is bliss.

OYINBO OLE: RIGHTEOUS DESCENDANTS OF THIEVES: HABAKKUK

"Those who know the least obey the best." George Farquhar

Fake righteousness and deceptively schooled civilised decorum were preceded by several centuries of merciless racist evil: The barbarously racist traffic in millions of stolen children of defenceless poor people - Habakkuk.

OYINBO OLE: STRAIGHT FACED WHITE THIEVES: HABAKKUK

"England is like a prostitute who, having sold her body all her life, decides to quit and close her business, and then tells everybody she wants to be chaste and protect her flesh as if it were jade." He Manzi, Chinese politician

Their ancestors were THIEVES; they know - Habakkuk.

Then, almost everything was stolen - Habakkuk

OUR EMPIRE OF STOLEN AFFLUENCE.

"Affluence is not a birthright." David Cameron

OYINBO OLE: WHITE THIEVES: HABAKKUK

Affluence did not evolve; Then, it was actively and deliberately stolen.

OYINBO OLE: WHITE THIEVES: HABAKKUK

Then, racist white bastards carried and sold millions of stolen children of defenceless poor people; now, they carry natural resources.

SUBSTITUTION: FRAUDULENT EMANCIPATION.

"Moderation is a virtue only among those who are thought to have found alternatives." Henry Kissinger

OYINBO OLE: WHITE THIEVES: HABAKKUK

There are no oil wells or gas fields in KEMPSTON; the highly luxuriant soil of KEMPSTON yields only food

NIGERIA: SHELL'S DOCILE CASH COW

Babies with huge oil wells ad gas fields near their houses eat 1.5/day in NIGERIA; a semi-illiterate former NOrwich Solicitor whose white father and mother have never seen crude oil is our District Judge in BEDFORD

OYINBO OLE: WHITE THIEVES: HABAKKUK

Then, the white ancestors of his white father and mother were fed like battery hens with the yields of stolen children of defenceless poor people - Habakkuk

An ignorant racist leech; a righteous descendant of industrial-scale professional THIEVES and owners of stolen children of defenceless poor people - Habakkuk.

OYINBO OLE: RIGHTEOUS WHITE THIEVES: HABAKKUK

* * * * *

NORTHAMPTON, ENGLAND: Based on available evidence, GDC-WITNESS, Dr Geraint Evans, Postgraduate Tutor, Oxford, unrelentingly lied under implied oath - Habakkuk 1:4; John 8:44; John 10:10.

A RACIST WHITE CROOK.

CREEPING NORTH KOREA.

FACTS ARE SACRED.

CORBY, ENGLAND: Based on available evidence, GDC-WITNESS, Dr George Rothnie unrelentingly lied under implied oath - Habakkuk 1:4; John 8:44; John 10:10.

A RACIST WHITE CROOK.

CREEPING NORTH KOREA.

FACTS ARE SACRED.

CORBY, ENGLAND: Based on available evidence, GDC-WITNESS, Dr Kevin Atkinson, Scottish Ken, unrelentingly lied under oath - Habakkuk 1:4; John 8:44; John 10:10.

A RACIST WHITE CROOK.

CREEPING NORTH KOREA.

FACTS ARE SACRED.

OXFORD, ENGLAND: Based on available evidence, GDC-WITNESS, British Soldier - Territorial Defence, Dr Stephanie Twidale

(TD) unrelentingly lied under oath - Habakkuk 1:4; John 8:44; John 10:10.

A RACIST WHITE CROOK.

CREEPING NORTH KOREA.

FACTS ARE SACRED.

WOLLASTON, ENGLAND: Based on available evidence, GDC-WITNESS, Ms Rachael Bishop, Senior NHS Nurse, unrelentingly lied under oath - Habakkuk 1:4; John 8:44; John 10:10.

A RACIST WHITE CROOK.

CREEPING NORTH KOREA.

FACTS ARE SACRED.

BEDFORD, ENGLAND: Based on available evidence, GDC-INSIDER, Dr Sue Gregory, Officer of the Most Excellent Order of our Empire unrelentingly lied under implied oath - Habakkuk 1:4; John 8:44; John 10:10.

A RACIST WHITE CROOK.

CREEPING NORTH KOREA.

FACTS ARE SACRED.

BEDFORD, ENGLAND: Based on available evidence, GDC-WITNESS, Freemason, Brother, Dr Richard William Hill fabricated reports and unrelentingly lied under oath - Habakkuk 1:4; John 8:44; John 10:10.

A RACIST WHITE CROOK.

CREEPING NORTH KOREA.

FACTS ARE SACRED.

A bastardised, unashamedly mediocre, indiscreetly dishonest, vindictive, potently weaponised, and institutionally RACIST system that his overseen by MASONS (Mediocre Mafia) - Habakkuk.

Then and now, in jurisdictions where the satanic network (Antichrist Racist Freemason) is in charge, their members have power to tell lies under oath.

"The supreme vice is shallowness." Wilde

Antichrist Racist Freemasons wear vulgar Pharisees' charitable works as cloaks of deceit, and they use very expensive aprons to decorate the temples of their powerless and useless fertility tools; they have informal access to some very powerful white Judges – Habakkuk 1:4.

"The good Samaritan had money." Mrs Margaret Thatcher (1925 – 2013).

Presumably, the Good Samaritans money was the yield of transparent virtue.

He told the righteous Jew to sell the yields of virtue, give the proceeds to the poor, and follow Him; He'd have told the rich Pharisee to return the yields of vice to the rightful owners – Matthew 19:21.

The Grand Antichrist Masons' Temple to Baal, 60 Great Queen St, Holborn, London WC2B 5AZ, was built in the 1700s (18th century), at a height of the barbarously racist traffic in millions of stolen children of defenceless poor people – Habakkuk.

Righteousness without equitable reparation is continuing racist fraud.

Deluded and conceited, like the Pharisees, they baselessly awarded themselves the monopoly knowledge and become impervious and intolerant to other views, and they usurped power, their job is to interpret the laws prescribed by the servants of the people, but they impose their will with illegal parallel power (unelected). They lie to their duller children that they're geniuses, and they kill all those who know they're not – Matthew 2:16.

He jailed him only because he spoke; the lunatic Jew removed John's head when he refused to stop speaking – Matthew 14.

He was lynched like Gadhafi and was crucified only because He spoke: He disclosed pictures His unbounded painted.

Then, like Herod, MBS and Kim, they used to butcher those who stated and/or printed what they did not want their moron sheep to know. The last decapitation in England was in 1827, and beheading was removed from the statute book in 1973, and the same year (1973), Kenneth Baker banned caning.

Why remove the heads of your enemies if it is illegal to flog them?

They lied to their duller children that they are geniuses, when, in fact, the power to economically strangulate and/or inflict bodily sufferings on their enemies is the principal leverage of the hands-off racist killers; they will lose, all the time, on a colour-blind and level playing field – Matthew 26, 27.

They lied to their moron sheep that they were geniuses, and they killed all those who knew that they were brainless racist bastards. Their sole objective is to shepherd their moron sheep unchallenged.

"Of black men, the numbers are too great who are now repining under English cruelty." Dr Samuel Johnson.

https://www.facebook.com/rotimi.osunsan/videos/3088536551193798

https://www.youtube.com/watch?v=BlpH4hG7m1A&feature=youtu.be

"They may not have been well written from a grammatical point of view, but I am confident I had not forgotten any of the facts." Dr Geraint Evans, Postgraduate Tutor, Oxford.

Northampton England, Rowtree Dental Care: Based on available evidence, Geraint Evans, Welsh Dunce, GDC-WITNESS, unrelentingly lied under oath – Habakkuk 1:4; John 8:44: John 10:10.

A RACIST WHITE CROOK.

Facts are sacred.

"Freedom to report the truth is a basic right to which the court gives a high level of protection, and the author's right to his story includes the right to tell it as he wishes." Lord Toulson

"It is incumbent upon the court and all those professionals involved to conclude court proceedings as quickly as possible. This hopefully ensures that a child has stability, love and affection and the parents working together to ensure that he has the best opportunity of developing academically and emotional."District Judge Paul Ayers, Senior Vice President of the Association of Her Majesty's District Judges – proofed and approved Judgement

"Yes, Sir, it does her honour, but it would do nobody else honour. I have indeed, not read it all. But when I take up the end of a web, and find it packthread, I do not expect, by looking further, to find embroidery." Dr Samuel Johnson

OUR SEMI-ILLITERATE RACIST FREEMASON YOUR HONOUR.

A CLOSETED RACIST BRAINLESS WHITE MAN.

The only evidence of the purportedly higher IQ of the incontrovertibly functional semi-illiterate white man is stolen affluence that his ancestors crossed the English Channels, without luggage or decent shoes to latch onto. They changed their names, blended, and deceived the undiscerning that their ancestors were aboriginal Britons who evolved from gorillas in Luton.

Descendants of aliens (genetic aliens) oppress, we, the descendants of the robbed with the yields of the robbery.

"All have taken what had other owners, and all have had recourse to arms rather than quit the prey they were fastened to." Dr Samuel Johnson

Everything is subjectively assumed in favour of his indisputably superior skin colour; he neither made nor chose it - Apartheid by stealth.

The last time he passed through a colour-blind and transparently objective filter system was when he studied 5th rate law at Polytechnic, and it shows.

A CLOSETED RACIST WHITE DUNCE.

Facts are sacred.

An impostor and an expert of deception; he has coasted along for decades, seemingly guided and guarded by the AntiChrist Racist Quasi-Religion (Mediocre Mafia/ New Pharisees), and has sold confusion to the undiscerning in exchange for valuable consideration.

In an open dialogue former Justice Ruth Bader Ginsburg (1933 - 2020), Lady Hale lamented funding.

My Lady, what's the value of several layers of unashamed mediocrity and confusion?

New Herod, Matthew 2:16: They lie to their stupider children that they're geniuses; they 'kill' we, their enemies, who know that they're brainless racist bastards.

Deluded intellectual cowards: They want superiority, their baseless birthright; they don't want Freedom of Expression because they don't want their simpler children to know about what they do to our people - Habakkuk.

A typical English man seemed to want to eat his cake and have it: Reductio ad absurdum - A logical fallacy.

"A typical English man, usually violent and always dull." Wilde

Matthew 19:21: He told the righteous Jew to sell the yields of transparent virtue and give the proceeds to the poor. Had the Jew been a scammer who sold confusion for cash, Christ would have told him to return the cash to the scammed, and sin no more.

The Good Samaritan had money." Mrs Margaret Thatcher (1925 -2013).

The money of the Good Samaritan was, presumably, the yield of transparent virtue.

Half-educated school dropouts and their superiors decorate the temples of their powerless and useless fertility tools with expensive aprons, and have informal access to some very powerful white Judges - Habakkuk 1:4.

They want a segregated world (Prince Hall's Mason), in terms of opportunities and rights, where human beings are graded according to the colour of the skin that they neither made nor chose; a world based on the embroidery on the aprons they use to decorate the temples of their powerless and useless fertility tools.

Based on very proximate observations and direct experiences, the natural instinct of some white privileged dullards is Apartheid by stealth.

They do vulgar Pharisees' charitable works in exchange for what?

Their offer is not a good deal - Matthew 4:9.

Brother Jimmy Savile did not fix anything for NOTHING.

Google: Freemasonry, intellectually flawed.

When Freedom of Expression becomes a basic right, we shall show the closeted racist dim-wits what they could't see in the supernatural thing that they're looking at.

The Grand Masons' Temple to Baal, 60 Great Queen St, Holborn, London WC2B 5AZ, was built in the 1700s (18th Century), at a height of the barbarously racist traffic in millions of stolen children of defenceless poor people - Habakkuk.

Righteousness without equitable reparation is continuing racist fraud.

Then, Judges, nearly all, were MASONS; some of them were thicker than a gross of planks.

Charitable AntiChrist Racist Freemasonry Quasi-Religion teaches its members the cultist-like, and quasi-voodoo, handshake, not grammar; the former is considerably easier to master.

Based on available evidence, Dr Richard Dawkins and OECD implied that all the children of District Judge Paul Ayers, Senior Vice President of the Association of Her Majesty's District Judges should be duller than their white father.

Facts are sacred.

"Natural selections will not remove ignorance from future generations." Dr Richard Dawkins

England's young people are near the bottom of the global league table for basic skills. OECD finds 16- to 24-year-olds have literacy and numeracy levels no better than those of their grandparents' generation

England is the only country in the developed world where the generation approaching retirement is more literate and numerate than the youngest adults, according to the first skills survey by the Organisation for Economic Co-operation and Development.

In a stark assessment of the success and failure of the 720-million-strong adult workforce across the wealthier economies, the economic thinktank warns that in England, adults aged 55 to 65 perform better than 16- to 24-year-olds at foundation levels of literacy and numeracy. The survey did not include people from Scotland or Wales.

The OECD study also finds that a quarter of adults in England have the maths skills of a 10-year-old. About 8.5 million adults, 24.1% of the population, have such basic levels of numeracy that they can manage only one-step tasks in arithmetic, sorting numbers or reading graphs. This is worse than the average in the developed world, where an average of 19% of people were found to have a similarly poor skill base.

Just as it was at Professor Stephen Hawking's schools, then, at the University of Lagos, the brightest students did not attend lectures at the Faculty of Law.

"In my school, the brightest boys did math and physics, the less bright did physics and chemistry, and the least bright did biology. I wanted to do math and physics, but my father made me do chemistry because he thought there would be no jobs for mathematicians." Dr Stephen Hawking

They secretly hate Freedom of Expression because they don't want their people to know about what they, secretly, do to our people.

Oxford, England: GDC-Witness, Dr Stephanie Twidale (TD), British Army Officer - Territorial Defence, unrelentingly lied under oath - Habakkuk 1:4; John 8:44; John 10:10.

A RACIST WHITE CROOK.

Her white ancestors lied too; they were industrial-scale professional THIEVES and owners of stolen children of defenceless poor people - Habakkuk.

OYINBO OLE: WHITE THIEVES: HABAKKUK.

Unlike her little brother, age saved the child's sister from the Closeted-Racist-Dylan–Roof-Freemason-Judge. She thanks her stars that the incontrovertibly functional semi-illiterate, closeted racist white man did not have anything to do with her education.
In her GCSE, she gained the following grades:
English Language A*
English Literature A*
Mathematics A*
Additional Mathematics A*
Physics A*
Chemistry A*
Biology A*
History A*
Latin A
Spanish A
Advanced Level Mathematics A
The academic height that the white father and mother of the closeted racist white District Judge cannot know, and which the natural talents of his own children will not exploit.
The brain isn't skin colour; then, we were robbed with guns.
The child sister has since gained a First Class Science Degree from one of the topmost Universities in the UK, and she's gainfully engaged, batting for her Country. Christ saved her from the evil clutches of the Closeted Racist Freemason Thugs.
It's plainly deductible that the white children of the white Senior Vice President of the Association of Her Majesty's District Judges were inferiorly created by Almighty God, certainly intellectually - OECD.
Facts are sacred.
"The truth allows no choice." Dr Samuel Johnson.

BEDFORD, ENGLAND: Based on available evidence, GDC-WITNESS, Freemason, Brother, Dr Richard William Hill fabricated reports and unrelentingly lied under oath - Habakkuk 1:4; John 8:44; John 10:10.

A RACIST WHITE CROOK.

Facts are sacred.

English law is equal; its administration isn't.

Based on available evidence, the administration of English law is a very potent weapon of a raging but latent RACE WAR.

"All sections of the UK Society are institutionally racist." Sir Bernard Hogan-Howe.

The former Chief of the Metropolitan Police had access to a lot of classified information.

"By definition therefore there needs to be a contact order for Mr B so that he knows when he is going to see his son. It is absolutely essential that this occurs and mother agrees with that. She said so several times in her evidence. Mrs Waller agreed that not only should a child have the opportunity of developing relationship with both parents, any sibling should also be there so that inter- sibling relationship could be fostered and nurtured. Obviously in this particular case the children reside in different places. That immediately puts a strain on the children having limited contact with each other. F's sister is very much older than him and she will be further advanced into her adult life. Thus it is not a matter that that sibling relationship can only be fostered by the children being together. Indeed as we all know absence sometimes makes the heart grow fonder. F should have an opportunity of seeing his sister. Wherever he does that it should be done in a friendly and loving environment. If the time comes that his sister goes to university of course his contact with her will be restricted to the time that she is home from university. In years to come when they have both grown up, with their own family they will see less of each other. But it doesn't mean that they don't still love and adore each other as much as they would if they saw each other every day." The Senior Vice President of the Association of Her Majesty's District Judges – proofed and approved Judgement.

https://www.youtube.com/watch?v=BlpH4hG7m1A

Shocking!

"Why, that is, because, dearest, you are a dunce." Habakkuk.

A scatter-head plebeian; an overpromoted polytechnic university educated racist bastard. A righteous descendant of industrial-scale professional THIEVES and owners of stolen children of defenceless people (Kamala's ancestors) - Habakkuk.

OYINBO OLE: WHITE THIEVES: HABAKKUK.

The white father and mother of the Senior Vice President of the Association of Her Majesty's District Judges did not care, had they, he'd not have approved and immortalised excessive stupidity at 16, and he'd be a properly educated lawyer, privately educated Anthony Blair, Anthony Julius, Geoff Hoon and Rabinder Singh's class, and he might practice proper law in STRAND.

It's plainly deductible that the white father and mother of the Senior Vice President of the Association of Her Majesty's District Judges couldn't afford to pay for qualitative education; why should we have to come from very far AFRICA to pay for his misfortune and part of its tell-tale signs (sequelae)?

* * * * * **

Andrew Hurst cross examined Richard Hill on 18.11.2008:

ANDREW HURST: Can you remember when you were first asked to

accompany Stephanie Twidale to undertake that practice inspection?
RICHARD HILL: A date?

NEGRO'S PERSPECTIVE:
"A date?" What else could it be?
****

ANDREW HURST: Time of year? The year, first of all. How long before approximately February 2007 would you have been aware that you were to be asked to do this?
RICHARD HILL: I would say it was probably in the autumn, sometime in the autumn, when it was flagged up.
ANDREW HURST: Of the preceding year.
RICHARD HILL: Of the preceding year. I can't be entirely certain about that date because it was not something – I wasn't emailed or I wasn't sent any documentation. I was just asked by the Consultant in Dental Public Health would I undertake the visit along with the Dental Reference Officer.

NEGRO'S PERSPECTIVE:

Time of year is date, isn't it?
I was the only Negro in the Council Chamber, 37, Wimpole Street, London. They want to kill me, albeit hands-off. He has showed me things about them, and things about Himself that will disrupt normal order: He is who is says He is, and you may do whatever you like, He will get what He wants – Proverbs 16:33.
"God throws dice…" Professor Stephen Hawking
"The supreme vice is shallowness." Wilde
"The God delusion." Dr Clinton Richard Dawkins
CONFLICT OF INTEREST: If one's ancestors were merciless racist murderers, industrial-scale professional thieves, and owners of stolen children of defenceless poor people, one would sleep easier if there were no transparently just God.

He is watching them – Habakkuk; Proverbs 15:3.
The nemesis is not extinct; the fact that it tarries isn't proof that it will never me.

Satanic Network

In his book, 'The God Delusion'. Clinton Richard Dawkins implied that Thomas Jefferson was an atheist.

Writing about the Christ that one believes doesn't exist is business, a very profitable business, by far more profitable than biology. Oxford University Professor were not paid loads of money before COVID, and COVID is wiping out trillions of dollars from the world's economy.

He who merely spoke and the world became can speak again, and it will perish, including COVID

Some people are controlled by demons; they don't know.

A deluded descendant of THIEVES and owners of stolen children of defenceless people - Habakkuk.

"Indeed, I tremble for my country when reflect that God is just: that his justice cannot sleep for ever: that considering numbers, nature and natural means only, a revolution of the wheel of fortune, an exchange of situation, is among possible events: that it may become probable by supernatural interference!" Thomas Jefferson

"The first-class at Oxford, where I have examined, is an overrated mark." Hugh Trevor Roper

If Oxford University Educated Clinton Richard Dawkins, FRS, FRSL, could prove that District Judge Paul Ayers, Senior Vice President of the Association of Her Majesty's District Judges was not a functional semi-illiterate and an incompetent liar, and if he could prove that GDC-Witness, Ms Rachael Bishop, Senior NHS Nurse, did not unrelentingly tell lies under oath, and if he could prove that Dr Richard William Hill, Postgraduate Tutor - NHS, did not fabricate reports and unrelentingly told lies under oath, and if he could prove that Stephen Henderson, LLM, Head of MDDUS, was not a functional semi-illiterate closeted racist thug who unrelentingly deviated from the truth on record, and if he could prove that GDC-INSIDER, Dr Sue Gregory (OBE), Officer of the Most Excellent Order of our Empire, did not unrelentingly tell lies under implied oath, and if he could prove that GDC-WITNESS, GDC-Witness, Stephanie Twidale, British Army Officer - Territorial Defence, did not unrelentingly tell lies under oath, and if he could prove that

Geraint Evans, Postgraduate Tutor, did not unrelentingly tell lies under implied oath, and if he could prove that Kevin Atkinson, Postgraduate Tutor did not unrelentingly tell lies under oath, and if he could prove that Dr George Rothnie, Deputy Postgraduate Dean, did not deviate from the truth under implied oath, he would confirm the belief of billions, which is that Antichrist Freemasonry Quasi Religion, Antichrist Judaism, Antichrist Islam, and motley assemblies of exotic religions and FAITHS under the common umbrella of the Governor of the Church of England and commander of THE FAITH are not intellectually flawed Satanic Mumbo Jumbo; it will also confirm that reason and vision have boundaries. If reasoning and vision have boundaries, He must have lied when, before the Council, He disclosed the pictures His purportedly unbounded mind painted, and He must have also lied when He audaciously stated: "I am the way and the truth and the life. No one comes to the Father except through me." - John 14:6.

If He told the truth before the Council, everything that is not aligned to John 14:6 is travelling in the wrong direction.

Ignorance is bliss.

"I do not approve of anything that tampers with natural ignorance. Ignorance is like a delicate exotic fruit; touch it and the bloom is gone. The whole theory of modern education is radically unsound. Fortunately, in England, at any rate, education produces no effect whatsoever. If it did, it would prove a serious danger to the upper classes, and probably lead to acts of violence in Grosvenor Square." Wilde

If Oxford University Educated Clinton Richard Dawkins, FRS, FRSL stands where He can come, with unalloyed FAITH, he will see what we see; he has time.

Dr Stephen Hawking's time has elapsed: He lived in delusional darkness, and he has progressed to eternal darkness; body and spirit.

Dr Clinton Richard Dawkins, FRS, FRSL, you have time, don't blow it.

'The God Delusion', Oxford University Educated Clinton Richard Dawkins, FRS, FRSL, Christ, the only righteous Judge, doesn't give a f*** about the 5HYT you write to supplement the money you blow on Lala. You and Lala must leave; He is immortal. Prophet Mohammed is dead; may he rest in peace. He, and only He, will judge the living and the dead – Matthew 25: 31-46

"The truth allows no choice." Dr Samuel Johnson.

Based on available evidence, the administration of English law is a weapon of latent but very potent race war.

"Those who have the power to do wrong with impunity seldom wait long for the will." Dr Samuel Johnson

"To disagree with three – fourths of the British public on all points is one of the first elements of sanity, one of the deepest consolations in all moments of spiritual doubt." Oscar Wilde

※ ※ ※ ※ ※ ※

Richard Hill was dishonest, as he lied that he was not emailed about the merciless lynching of the lone Negro in their midst, the first ever and only Negro dentist in Bedford.

In an email of 30.11.2006 to Stephanie Twidale (TD), Sue Gregory (OBE) stated as follows: "Dear Stephanie, Just to confirm that I have spoken to Richard Hill and he will join you for the DRS visit on Thursday 22nd February to Mr Bamgbelu's Bedford Practice, commencing at 9 a.m. We will endeavour to share any issues the PCT may have with you PRIOR to the 22nd. Kind regards, Sue."

So, Richard Hill was dishonest again as he maliciously lied under oath when he stated, "I can't be entirely certain about that date because it was not something – I wasn't emailed or I wasn't sent any documentation."

"Lies are told all the time." Sir Michael Havers, Attorney General, 1990 – Habakkuk 1:4; John 8:44; John 10:10.

Based upon the same fact, Stephanie Twidale lied under oath when she stated that she did not have any contact with Richard Hill prior to the visit of 22.02.2007.

It is a fact and the absolute truth that parts of the administration of the English law is mediocre, Negrophobic, and dishonest.

"The one great principle of the English law is to make business for itself." – Charles Dickens

Richard Hill was an accurate reflection of the intellect and integrity of Sue Gregory.

It will be extraordinary if the NHS told Stephanie Twidale (TD) why Richard Hill would be asked to conduct the joint inspection of 22.02.2007.

Stephanie Twidale stated on oath or otherwise on record that prior to the joint inspection of 22.02.2007, the NHS informed her as follows:

"Yes please we would like a surgery inspection. At the point at which I was informed that Richard Hill had been there some months before hand and had some concerns."

"Having discussed with the PCT they told me that Mr Hill had made previous visits not that long before from which there had been some queries, and they felt perhaps it would be sensible for Mr Hill to come along as well with me to be a second person and follow up on his previous visits to the practice."

"I spoke to Dr Sue Gregory, Consultant in Dental Public Health at the Bedfordshire PCT to impart the information and was informed that Richard Hill, Dental Practice adviser to Bedfordshire PCT, had carried out a previous Surgery inspection at Bromham Road that had raised some concerns."

"Then I know it came through that Richard Hill had been in before about 6 months ago, I think they said, and it was probably sensible for him to go as the second person, a second appropriate second person to do a follow up. The actual timings of bits of those I am afraid I can't REMEMBER."

"At the point at which I was informed that Richard Hill had been there some months before hand and had some concerns." It would be extraordinary, wouldn't it, that the NHS gave Stephanie Twidale all the information supra and Richard Hill knew nothing of it?

It is a fact and the absolute truth that Richard Hill unrelentingly lied under oath. He is a descendant of thoroughly wretched, feudal agricultural labourers from mainland Europe who stole the land of the aborigines (the Native Britons) and who were later immeasurably transformed by the gigantic yields of several centuries of the merciless, racist evil which slavery was. They have reinvented themselves on stolen land and fool the foolish with foolishness.

* * * * *

ANDREW HURST: Just looking at that a little bit more closely, can you remember what the practice inspection was to address? What sort of inspection was it to be?

RICHARD HILL: It's part of a routine process. Since the new contract came into effect which was in April 2006—

ANDREW HURST: Is that the General Dental Services contract?

RICHARD HILL: Yes, I will refer to it as new GDS, if you like, for the purposes of clarity – is that the system of monitoring by the Dental Practice Board for the Primary Care Trusts changed. If we remember what happened before, patients were selected at random or sometimes targeted by the Board and they were examined by a Dental Reference Officer normally in a dedicated centre and that was it. The purpose of it, yes, it was a certain amount of Quality Assurance, but there was also a large probity element in that, making sure that what had been claimed for had been done. Now, with the new contract, the new GDS, it changed to the extent that there was a greater degree of monitoring, a more Clinical Governance Quality Assurance role was introduced. So it was really very much a sort of three pronged approach towards it. Firstly, there would be a practice visit. I will call this one an inspection. I will clarify it in those terms because the Dental Reference Officer's visit is an inspection; it has a more policing function. Secondly, there would be four patients which the practitioner would themselves choose based upon the complexity of the treatment. Treatments are in three bands, what we can describe, I suppose, as simple, intermediate and more advanced, Bands 1, 2 and 3. There would be one Band 1, two Band 2s and a Band 3 selected; the practitioner would choose those and those patients would then be inspected by the Dental Reference Officer, not my function at all. The third one would be a record check, eight records selected by the Dental Practice Board to be checked by the Dental Reference Officer. Then the practitioner would have feedback on all of this. There would be a report compiled for each practice which would then relate to each performer within the practice and so the provider, which is, if you like, the principal of the practice, shall we say for want of a better word, would then get the feedback and they could make any necessary changes. So we are moving from a situation which was perhaps more probity based to one which is more Quality Assurance and, if you like, to use for a better phrase, bottoming up, raising standards in a more consensual fashion. So this inspection was, if you like, just one of the three, but my involvement in the other ones, I wouldn't necessarily have any involvement in the other two parts of it.

NEGRO'S PERSPECTIVE:

OYINBO OLE:
IGNORANT DESCENDANTS OF THIEVES AND OWNERS OF INDUSTRIAL-SCALE PROFESSIONAL THIEVES AND OWNERS OF STOLEN CHILDREN OF DEFENCELESS PEOPLE - HABAKKUK.

"She is better employed at her toilet, than using her pen. It is better she should be reddening her own cheeks, than blackening other people's characters." Dr Samuel Johnson

BRAINLESS NONSENSE: IMMORTAL STUPIDITY.

"Yes, Sir, it does her honour, but it would do nobody else honour. I

have indeed, not read it all. But when I take up the end of a web, and find it packthread, I do not expect, by looking further, to find embroidery."
Dr Samuel Johnson

Tortuous gibberish!

"The great enemy of the clear language is INSINCERITY (DISHONESTY). When there is a gap between one's real and one's declared aims, one turns as it were instinctively to long words and exhausted idioms, like a cuttlefish squirting ink. In our age there is no such thing as 'keeping out of politics'. All tissues are political issues, and politics itself is a mass of lies, evasions, folly, HATRED and schizophrenia. When the general atmosphere is bad, language must suffer." – George Orwell

Those regularly spun are amongst the dullest adult population in the industrialised world.

Richard Hill, Dental Practice Adviser (DPA), was a shepherd of England's young adults.

Shepherds of morons are likelier to be morons too.

✳ ✳ ✳ ✳ ✳

ANDREW HURST: So necessarily then, when it comes to what you are actually going to look at when you turn up at the relevant surgery, you are going to be looking at an inspection of the premises as they are, how they appear and whether they meet the relevant standards.
RICHARD HILL: That's correct. I mean, I must say that the ambit of the Dental Reference Service inspection is far, far greater than the Dental Practice Adviser sheet, as we can see from the documents; it goes much, much further. I mean, our visits, and I will use that terminology correctly, our visits are normally about 30 to 45 minutes, whereas a Dental Reference Officer visit is going to be much longer. I think in the case of 22 February 2007, it was something like five hours and that seems

to be, from what I have heard, quite normal.

ANDREW HURST: You were asked to assist Stephanie Twidale and obviously she is going to give her evidence after you, so she will be able to give evidence as to things from her perspective, but did you understand why you particularly had been asked to assist Stephanie Twidale?

RICHARD HILL: No. It is, as I mention in my statement, unusual for a Dental Practice Adviser to attend on a DRO visit. I was simply asked and part of my contract is to act in accordance with the wishes of the senior managers of the PCT.

NEGRO'S PERSPECTIVE:
It should be extraordinary, shouldn't it, that Richard Hill was reluctant to conduct the follow up inspection early in 2007 after the concerns that he identified in 2003 and 2004 which had allegedly not been resolved at follow up, and coupled with Sue Gregory's email of 18.05.2005?

Thoroughly absurd! They were a network of merciless, racist bastards, the likes of those who systematically murdered Dr Anand Kamath, albeit hands off.

He knew that the inspection and reports of April 02, 2003, July 22, 2004 and the follow up of undisclosed date, were FORGERIES, and he was very reluctant of being part of the NEGRO lynching; he had a conscience but not a lot.

The fabricated reports of July 22, 2004 and the follow up of undisclosed date were abruptly withdrawn on October 16, 2008, more than four years after the fictitious inspection, and after it had been used to destroy the dentistry career of the first ever Negro dentist since He merely spoke and the Universe became, and albeit after I informed the Medical Protection Society (MPS) that I was not in Switzerland on July 22, 2004, and my surgery was shut, and I had evidence.

"Coincidence is Christ's (GOD's) way of remaining anonymous." Albert Einstein

I am an infant, and I have seen beyond vision, not through righteousness, as I am a sinner; only through the unsolicited kindness of Christ - Roman 11.

The older ones will dream dreams and the younger ones will see vision, and as visions are clearer than dreams, it's plainly deducible that the younger ones are closer to God - Acts 2:17

What I am looking at is beyond vision, I must be an infant. I'd love to be a foetus so that I can see clearer still, as only the pure in spirit shall see God – Matthew 5.

We are FORKED: His Knight attacks our Queen and King simultaneously, and only our Queen can move; the checkmate, isn't it.

Only fools believe that what they cannot see is not there.

What I can see is more than enough to make me believe all that I cannot see.

If Dr Clinton Richard Dawkins FRS, FRSL, could prove that the NHS reports of April 02, 2003, July 22, 20004, the follow up report of undisclosed date and the withdrawal statement of fabrications, of October 16, 2008, were not incompetent fabrications motivated by uncontrollable, seemingly, hereditary RACIAL HATRED, he would confirm the belief of billions, which is that Antichrist Freemasonry Quasi Religion, Antichrist Judaism, Antichrist Islam, and motley assemblies of exotic religions and FAITHS under the common umbrella of the Governor of the Church of England and commander of THE FAITH are not intellectually flawed Satanic Mumbo Jumbo; the author of 'The God Delusion' will also confirm that reasoning and vision have boundaries. If reasoning and vision have boundaries, He must have lied when, before the Council, He disclosed the pictures His purportedly unbounded mind painted, and He must have also lied when He audaciously stated: "I am the way and the truth and the life. No one comes to the Father except through me." - John 14:6.

If He told the truth before the Council, everything that is not aligned to John 14:6 is travelling in the wrong direction.

CONFLICT OF INTEREST: An ignorant biologist; a closeted racist descendant of industrial-scale professional THIEVES and owners of stolen children of defenceless people – Habakkuk.

If He is who He says He is, He must be transparently just, and we are all in deep 5HYT – Matthew 25: 31- 46.

Only the very few He has chosen, not through righteousness, but only through his unsolicited kindness, will survive His objective and transparent scrutiny, and He will, vividly reveal Himself to those He has chosen – Romans 11.

Ignorance is bliss.

They mercilessly persecute our people for the dark coat that we neither made nor chose, and cannot change, and they steal the yields of our Christ granted talents.
He is watching them – Proverbs 15:3; Habakkuk
The blame is His who made and chose our dark coat; our people should be blameless.
The sole basis of their power is money. There was no money anywhere before slavery. There was only sustenance agriculture. The gigantic yields of the merciless, evil trade in millions of stolen human beings (and the merciless working of millions more to death) immeasurably transformed the lives of the wretched barbarians. They have reinvented themselves on stolen land with the yields of evil.
Before slavery, what?

* * * * *

ANDREW HURST: But you had had dealings with Mr Bamgbelu before.
RICHARD HILL: Yes, as with every other practice within the PCT.
ANDREW HURST: Although these are not within the Committee's bundle, is it right that you were asked by a colleague at the PCT to provide your previous practice inspection reports or visit reports so that Ms Twidale would have them in advance. Is that right?

RICHARD HILL: I don't think so, no. I think that's a wrong reading of it. I don't think that we did anything of the sort. I don't think she read any of those – in my knowledge, according to my knowledge, I don't believe there was any of that. It would come as a surprise to me if it was. I think, after all, you would not wish to go into a Dental Reference practice in any way prejudiced. You want to go in with an open mind and you need to see things as they are, not from what you have read.

NEGRO'S PERSPECTIVE:

Stephanie Twidale (TD) stated that the NHS advised her as follows: "Yes please we would like a surgery inspection. At the point at which I was informed that Richard Hill had been there some months before hand and had some concerns."

"Having discussed with the PCT they told me that Mr Hill had made previous visits not that long before from which there had been some queries, and they felt perhaps it would be sensible for Mr Hill to come along as well with me to be a second person and follow up on his previous visits to the practice."

"I spoke to Dr Sue Gregory, Consultant in Dental Public Health at the Bedfordshire PCT to impart the information and was informed that Richard Hill, Dental Practice adviser to Bedfordshire PCT, had carried out a previous Surgery inspection at Bromham Road that had raised some concerns."

"Then I know it came through that Richard Hill had been in before about 6 months ago, I think they said, and it was probably sensible for him to go as the second person, a second appropriate second person to do a follow up. The actual timings of bits of those I am afraid I can't REMEMBER."

"At the point at which I was informed that Richard Hill had been there some months before hand and had some concerns."

Stephanie Twidale's statement, albeit pure fiction, corroborated Sue Gregory's (OBE) – the cardinal of merciless, racist evil – email of 30.11.2006, and concomitantly corroborated Charlotte Dowling Goodson's testimony under oath about two years later on 20.11.2008.

So, Richard Hill was confused or dishonest when he stated as follows: "I don't think so, no. I think that's a wrong reading of it. I don't think that we did anything of the sort. I don't think she read any of those – in my knowledge, according to my knowledge, I don't believe there was any of that. It would come as a surprise to me if it was. I think, after all, you would not wish to go into a Dental Reference practice in any way prejudiced. You want to go in with an open mind and you need to see things as they are, not from what you have read."

Reading is not the only means of knowing about a fact. The Right Honourable David Blunkett did not read a lot but knew a lot.

Stephanie Twidale (TD) wanted to review a report prior to visiting. Richard Hill created the reports of 22.07.2004 and follow up of unknown date for that purpose.

Stephanie Twidale lied on oath that she did not have any contact with Richard Hill prior to the inspection of 22.02.2007. Richard Hill confirmed under oath that Stephanie Twidale lied about that fact.

Those regularly spun are amongst the dullest adult population in the industrialised world - OECD.

✱ ✱ ✱ ✱ ✱ ✱

ANDREW HURST: It was a bad question because there were two questions in one, so perhaps I ought to go back and break it down. First of all, did you provide the previous reports of your visits in advance of the practice inspection in February?
RICHARD HILL: I'm not aware of them being provided for that purpose.

NEGRO'S PERSPECTIVE:

Richard Hill was dishonest, as he lied under oath.
What exactly was the point of mediocre, confused, and racist GDC

that seemed to allow only Caucasians to tell naked lies, and indiscreetly? Sue Gregory (OBE) was the cardinal of merciless, racist evil. Richard Hill was an accurate reflection of the intellect and integrity of Sue Gregory.

On 15.08.2006, the NHS asked Richard Hill for reports because Stephanie Twidale (TD) wanted to review them prior to visiting. On 06.09.2006, Richard Hill produced reports for that purpose. About four years later, he withdrew the reports in their entirety. The withdrawal statement is another NHS forgery. It remains live and valid.

✱ ✱ ✱ ✱ ✱ ✱

ANDREW HURST: Well, again, is it that you provided them and then we can discuss what the reason was?

RICHARD HILL: They were provided but then, again, they would be within the practitioner's file so there would be ready access to them.

NEGRO'S PERSPECTIVE:
Richard Hill was dishonest, as he lied under oath. Those regularly spun are amongst the dullest adult population in the industrialised world.

Richard Hill spun rot to rot.

"Nothing that you will learn in the course of your studies will be of the slightest possible use to you in after life – save only this – if you work hard and diligently you should be able to detect when a man is talking rot, and that, in my view, is the main, if not the sole, purpose of education." – J.A. Smith, Oxford University Professor, Moral Philosophy

If they (the alleged reports) were in the practitioner's file, the NHS would not ask Richard Hill for them.

"Richard (Hill), Stephanie Twidale called us a few weeks ago about DRS visits and Charlotte prioritised Mr Bamgbelu's practice; Stephanie has been in touch a few times as her colleagues had highlighted issues from a similar practice in Northants and they would like to review report etc etc prior to visiting. She also wanted to know if there has been a dental inspection there at all and I did not know the answer . . . Cue Richard have you carried out an inspection at this practice, please could you advise Stephanie when she contacts you, and would it be possible to see our reports so we can be more pro active with any other queries. Thanks. With kind regards, John Hooper." – 15.08.2006.

So, if the alleged reports were in the practitioner's file, John Hooper of the NHS would not ask for them, and if he did because he did not know that they were in the practitioner's file, it wouldn't take three weeks to retrieve them (15.08.2006 – 06.09.2006). Richard Hill lied. In order to tell lies on oath without consequence, some people join the satanic network (all for one, one for all). They do charity and/or pay protection money. Some of them are dullards. Information gathered by England's young adult and former England young adults fuels merciless, racist evil. They swear by the grace of Almighty God never to tell lies, but they lie that they do not lie (Songs of David 144).

✳ ✳ ✳ ✳ ✳

ANDREW HURST: So you did provide them but for the purpose—
RICHARD HILL: Indirectly, I would say. I do not recall whatsoever being asked to do so for the purpose of the visit.

NEGRO'S PERSPECTIVE:
Richard Hill was dishonest. He lied on oath.
Parts of the administration of the English law are anarchical, mediocre, Negrophobic, and corrupt. Those that they regularly spin are amongst the dullest adult population in the industrialised world.
By the NHS correspondence of 15.08.2006, Richard Hill was asked to provide reports for the purpose of the joint inspection she conducted at the surgery of the first ever and only Negro dentist in Bedford on 22.02.2007.
Sue Gregory's correspondence of 30.11.2006 corroborated the fact and Charlotte Dowling Goodson's testimony on oath about two years later (on 20.11.2008) further corroborated the fact. Stephanie Twidale's several discussions with the NHS were based upon the racist forgeries (the NHS reports of 22.07.2004 and follow up of unknown date).
The legal process was chaos. It was pure anarchy, and things will get

worse as the future generations will be duller.

*****

THE CHAIRMAN (DR SHIV PABARY, MEMBER OF THE BRITISH EMPIRE): I think what is trying to be established is did you provide them or are you saying that the PCT would have had access to them anyway?
RICHARD HILL: Yes, the PCT would have access.

NEGRO'S PERSPECTIVE:
Their dull Indian with the camouflage title was an exceedingly dull judge!

The same brain that Dr Shiv Pabary used to reason rot was the same brain that he used to state as follows, implicitly under oath:

"I think I will ask our legal adviser for any advice he may have. My view is that there are six or seven of us here who had the admission down, but we cannot find it in the transcript and there is wordings that imply that there was, but it is not in black and white. It might be useful to clarify that by recalling Mr Bamgbelu and see. As to second matter, I think it will help the Committee if there is confusion with the situation with the nurse taking the waste out. We are happy to hear that if it is okay" (Dr Shiv Pabary, 17.06.2009).

Their very dull Indian was a racist, satanic tool with a camouflage title.

"There is no sin except stupidity." – Oscar Wilde

Sir Winston Churchill, in corroboration with statements by Oscar Wilde and George Bernard Shaw, and the more recent objective assessment by the OECD, implied that the average Briton was a moron.

"The best argument against democracy is a five-minute conversation with the average voter." – Sir Winston Churchill

"He (the Briton) is a barbarian, and believes that the customs of his tribe and Island are the laws of nature." – George Bernard Shaw

"A typical English man, always dull and usually violent." – George Bernard Shaw
"To disagree with three-fourths of the British public on all points is one of the first elements of sanity, one of the deepest consolations in all moments of spiritual doubt." – Oscar Wilde"

Dr Sue Gregory, Dr Helen Falcon, Dr Shiv Pabary, and their type are shepherds of England's young adults.
Shepherds of morons are likelier to be morons too.
Very high privileged shepherds of morons who have swallowed tablets or other hallucinogenic chemicals shouldn't insert any organ in the mouth of pigs; they should insert their balls, the two together, into the mouth of live/pacu fish, the organ grinder.
If the bottommost part of a whole is world class bottommost, the topmost part of that whole is unlikely to be world class topmost.
"Sometimes people don't want to hear the truth because they don't want their illusions destroyed." – Friedrich Nietzsche
The sole basis of the power displayed is money. The entire foundation of the money is several centuries of merciless, racist evil and naked fraud (slavery).

"Many Scots masters were considered among the most brutal, with life expectancy on their plantations averaging a mere four years. We worked them to death then simply imported more to keep the sugar and thus the money flowing. Unlike centuries of grief and murder, an apology costs nothing. So what does Scotland have to say?" – Herald Scotland, Ian Bell, columnist, Sunday 28 April 2013

"The grand object of all European traders in kidnapped and stolen Africans was - money, money, money; money was their god! In Africa, the poor wretched natives, blessed with the most fertile and luxuriant soil, are rendered so much the more miserable by the Christians' (European traders in stolen Africans) abominable traffic for slaves and the horrid cruelty and treachery of the petty [African] Kings. The Africans kings were encouraged by their European (Christians) customers who carry them strong liquors to enflame their madness and powder and bad firearms to furnish them with the hellish means of killing and kidnapping. But enough - it is a subject that sours my blood." – Ignatius Sancho, 1778

"I know of no evil that has ever existed, nor can imagine any evil to exist, worse than the tearing of eighty thousand persons annually from their native land, by a combination of the most civilised nations inhabiting the most enlightened part of the globe, but more especially under the sanction of the laws of that Nation which calls herself the most free and the most happy of them all." – Prime Minister William Pitt the Younger Before slavery, what?

"Agriculture not only gives riches to a nation, but the only riches she can call her own." – Dr Samuel Johnson

"Those who have robbed have also lied." – Dr Samuel Johnson corroborating prophet Habakkuk

* * * * *

If the PCT (NHS) had access to them, the NHS would not ask for them by its correspondence of 15.08.2006:

"Richard (Hill), Stephanie Twidale called us a few weeks ago about DRS visits and Charlotte prioritised Mr Bamgbelu's practice; Stephanie has been in touch a few times as her colleagues had highlighted issues from a similar practice in Northants and they would like to review report etc etc prior to visiting. She also wanted to know if there has been a dental inspection there at all and I did not know the answer . . . Cue Richard have you carried out an inspection at this practice, please could you advise Stephanie when she contacts you, and would it be possible to see our reports so we can be more pro active with any other queries. Thanks. With kind regards, John Hooper."

If PCT had them (reports) or had access to them (reports) and could have provided them to Sue Gregory (and Charlotte Dowling Goodson would have access to them too), they would not need to ask Richard Hill for the reports (racist forgeries) and wait for him to provide them. They are incompetent liars and hereditary racist thugs.

"Richard has done visits to Bamgbelu, he would have to provide you with reports of his visits." – Sue Gregory, 15.08.2006

"I can't remember if I passed them on. I think Richard Hill would have shared those issues with Stephanie as part of the discussion prior to the visit, and that is part of the reason why Richard went with Stephanie to undertake the visit with her." – Charlotte Dowling Goodson, 20.11.2008

DAVID MORRIS: And did you, as part of his process then . . . well, I can see the concerns that were raised in that column: no risk assessment, no COSSH, Kavoclave type autoclave, why that shouldn't be used, no other members of practice staff present at visits, and could not be questioned regarding cross infection control by the practice. But did you, as part of this process, receive a copy of what was purported to be the visit record for that date, 22 July 04?

RICHARD HILL: Not at that time, but we did get copies of the reports and for these visits at a later date. We had been requesting them.

ANDREW HURST: So the PCT could have provided them.

RICHARD HILL: That's right. They would have access to them.

NEGRO'S PERSPECTIVE:

Andrew Hurst, the England class barrister, was a moron. Some barristers go on to become judges within one of the least literate countries in the industrialised world.

Andrew Hurst, England class barrister and former England young adult, had access to all available information.

If the PCT (NHS) "could have provided them," it means they had them. If the PCT (NHS) had them, they wouldn't ask for them, and similarly, if the PCT had them, Sue Gregory would not ask for them, and Charlotte Dowling Goodson would not have been requesting them.

Andrew Hurst, a topmost England young adult or former England young adult, is part of the conclusive evidence that the past was stolen with guns and not with brains.

"England young adults are amongst the least literate and numerate in the industrialised world." – The OECD

If the bottommost part of a whole is world class bottommost, it is unlikely that the topmost part of that whole is first class topmost.

Oyinbo olodo! Oyinbo ode!

"We had been requesting them." – Charlotte Dowling Goodson

"Richard has done visits to Bamgbelu, he would have to provide you with reports of his visits." – Sue Gregory, 15.08.2006

"She also wanted to know if there has been a dental inspection there at all and I did not know the answer . . . Cue Richard have you carried out an inspection at this practice, please could you advise Stephanie when she contacts you, and would it be possible to see our reports so we can be more pro active with any other queries." – NHS, 15.08.2006

No brain, natural resources poor, only skin colour that the wearer neither made nor chose, and what else? Pure scam!

The descendants of wretched, feudal agricultural labourers (serfs) from mainland Europe were immeasurably transformed by the gigantic yields of centuries of the merciless, racist evil which slavery was. They have reinvented themselves and fool the foolish – and only the foolish.

Before slavery, what?

Before GIGANTIC yields of SLAVERY there was only feudal agriculture. Yields of EVIL, not agriculture was the magnet for Eastern European Jews.

※ ※ ※ ※ ※ ※

ANDREW HURST: The question was did you provide them specifically.

RICHARD HILL: For that purpose?

NEGRO'S PERSPECTIVE:
What the England class imbecile barrister stated under oath was stupid; what he intended to state was blatantly dishonest. He had access to full and accurate information and knew or had full access to the fact that Richard Hill unrelentingly lied under oath.

ANDREW HURST: Yes.
RICHARD HILL: No, is the answer to that.

NEGRO'S PERSPECTIVE:
Andrew Hurst was dishonest, as he had access to full and accurate information. Richard Hill unrelentingly lied under oath.
ANDREW HURST: Not for that purpose, did you provide them at all? Were you asked for them?
RICHARD HILL: I provided all inspection sheets previously, but not for that purpose – well, as a matter of routine. I mean, part of the reason why we do so was obviously because there was going to be a Health Care Commission inspection or visit to the PCT which is done on a regular basis. But I was not aware of those being passed to the Dental Reference Officer. They may have been, I don't know, but I was not aware of that.

NEGRO'S PERSPECTIVE:
Richard Hill lied again under oath. His kindred knew that he lied, but he seemingly dishonestly feigned ignorance.
ANDREW HURST: So you are not aware of the reason, but you did provide—
RICHARD HILL: No, but they were provided as part of the routine monitoring, that's all. But, as I said, they might have been shown to the Dental Reference Officer. I'm not aware of it.

NEGRO'S PERSPECTIVE:
Andrew Hurst was dishonest, and he feigned ignorance as he knew that Richard Hill unrelentingly lied under oath in their racist "plantation" justice.

The request from the NHS was explicit: "Richard (Hill), Stephanie Twidale called us a few weeks ago about DRS visits and Charlotte prioritised Mr Bamgbelu's practice; Stephanie has been in touch a few times as her colleagues had highlighted issues from a similar practice in Northants and they would like to review report etc etc prior to visiting. She also wanted to know if there has been a dental inspection there at all and I did not know the answer . . . Cue Richard have you carried out an inspection at this practice, please could you advise Stephanie when she contacts you, and would it be possible to see our reports so we can be more pro active with any other queries. Thanks. With kind regards, John Hooper" (15.08.2006).

The further implied request by Sue Gregory was explicit. In her response to John Hooper's (NHS) correspondence above, which she also sent to Richard Hill and Charlotte Dowling Goodson, Sue Gregory (OBE) implied that she was aware of reports but had not seen any and did not have any. Sue Gregory (OBE) was dishonest and/or confused. Sue Gregory (OBE) is part of the evidence that many of the kidnapped and stolen Africans that Sue Gregory's ancestors used guns to slaughter and armed others to use guns to slaughter, and many of those that the merciless, racist bastards worked to death on plantations, were created intellectually superior by Almighty God - Habakkuk.

No brain, natural resources poor, only skin colour that the wearer neither made nor chose, and what else? It's a scam!

ANDREW HURST: We can ask her later.
RICHARD HILL: It's not a matter that I actually discussed with her either.
ANDREW HURST: Thank you. Now obviously during the course of the run up to the visit of 22 February there was some communication between you and Stephanie Twidale.
RICHARD HILL: Yes.

NEGRO'S PERSPECTIVE:
Again, Richard Hill confirmed that Stephanie Twidale maliciously lied

when she stated that she did not have any contact with Richard Hill prior to their joint inspection of the surgery of the first ever and only Negro dentist in Bedford.

Richard Hill and Stephanie Twidale are the accurate reflection of the intellect and integrity of Sue Gregory (OBE).

It is dishonesty and a distortion of historical facts to directly associate the gigantic proceeds of several centuries of merciless, racist evil and fraud (slavery) with personal intellect and industry.

Before GIGANTIC yields of SLAVERY there was only feudal agriculture. Yields of EVIL, not agriculture, were the magnet for Eastern European Jews.

✻ ✻ ✻ ✻ ✻ ✻ ✻

Dialogue between Dr Shiv Pabary, Member of the British Empire, and Dr Stephanie Twidale (Territorial Defence or TD):

THE CHAIRMAN (DR SHIV PABARY): Just to clarify that, prior to your visit to Mr Bamgbelu's practice you had not seen any practice visit reports?

STEPHANIE TWIDALE: Nothing at all.

NEGRO'S PERSPECTIVE:

Dr Shiv Pabary, Member of the British Empire, was dishonest and/or recklessly confused when he implied that seeing a report was the only way of knowing about the contents of a report.

F****** rot! Kuli rot!

"Nothing that you will learn in the course of your studies will be of the slightest possible use to you in after life – save only this – if you work hard and diligently you should be able to detect when a man is talking rot, and that, in my view, is the main, if not the sole, purpose of education." – J.A. Smith, Oxford University Professor, Moral Philosophy

The Right Honourable David Blunkett, former Home Secretary, did not see anything, but he knew a lot.

It is verifiable, fact and absolute truth that Stephanie Twidale (TD) was a racist thug and a Negrophobic perjurer, but only for argument's sake one should assume that the racist cougar with the gigantic, ugly ass, which was made uglier by what seemed to be a G-string (libido killer), did not see a report prior to visiting the surgery of the first ever and only Negro dentist in Bedford since He merely spoke, and the world became.

Stephanie Twidale confirmed that in the summer of 2006 she asked to see reports prior to visiting the surgery of the first ever and only Negro dentist in Bedford on 22.02.2007.

"Richard (Hill), Stephanie Twidale called us a few weeks ago about DRS visits and Charlotte prioritised Mr Bamgbelu's practice; Stephanie has been in touch a few times as her colleagues had highlighted issues from a similar practice in Northants and they would like to review report etc etc prior to visiting. She also wanted to know if there has been a dental inspection there at all and I did not know the answer . . . Cue Richard have you carried out an inspection at this practice, please could you advise Stephanie when she contacts you, and would it be possible to see our reports so we can be more pro active with any other queries. Thanks. With kind regards, John Hooper" (15.08.2006).

"I never spoke to Richard Hill, nor had I ever met him before we arrived at the practice together. It was a classic example of two people standing outside a building saying: 'Are you? Oh yes right fine.' We had never met and we did not speak beforehand. The only people I spoke with beforehand would be John Hooper and some email correspondence with John, with Charlotte Dowling and with the Consultant in public health, Sue Gregory. I actually didn't have any contact with Richard at all." – Stephanie Twidale, under oath, on 19.11.2008

Stephanie Twidale confirmed that she had several discussions with Sue Gregory (the cardinal of merciless, exceedingly destructive, racist evil) prior to visiting the surgery of the first ever and only Negro dentist in Bedford.

"Dear Stephanie, Just to confirm that I have spoken to Richard Hill and he will join you for the DRS visit on Thursday 22nd February to Mr Bamgbelu's Bedford Practice, commencing at 9 a.m. We will endeavour to share any issues the PCT may have with you PRIOR to the 22nd. Kind regards, Sue." – 30.11.2006

"I spoke to Dr Sue Gregory, Consultant in Dental Public Health at the Bedfordshire PCT to impart the information and was informed that Richard Hill, Dental Practice adviser to Bedfordshire PCT, had carried out a previous Surgery inspection at Bromham Road that had raised some concerns." – Stephanie Twidale, 03.09.2008

Unbeknownst to the first ever and only Negro dentist in Bedford, on 30.11.2006 and 03.09.2008 two of the NHS's falsified reports were live, valid, and accessible, but only to white people: the falsified NHS racist report of 22.07.2004 and the concomitantly forged follow up report of undisclosed date. The reports were abruptly withdrawn more than four years after the first of the alleged visits.

Stephanie Twidale confirmed that she had several discussions with Charlotte Dowling Goodson (one of the disciples of Sue Gregory, OBE) prior to visiting the surgery of the first ever and only Negro dentist in Bedford: "I can't remember if I passed them on (Stephanie Twidale). I think Richard would have shared those issues with Stephanie as part of the discussion prior to the visit, and that is part of the reason why Richard went with Stephanie to undertake the visit with her" (Charlotte Dowling Goodson under oath on 20.11.2008).

Stephanie Twidale confirmed that she had several other discussions with Sue Gregory and some of her disciples (Charlotte Dowling Goodson and John Hooper) prior to visiting the surgery of the first ever and only Negro dentist in Bedford when she stated as follows: "Yes please we would like a surgery inspection. At the point at which I was informed that Richard Hill had been there some months before hand and had some concerns."

"Having discussed with the PCT they told me that Mr Hill had made previous visits not that long before from which there had been some queries, and they felt perhaps it would be sensible for Mr Hill to come along as well with me to be a second person and follow up on his previous visits to the practice."

"I spoke to Dr Sue Gregory, Consultant in Dental Public Health at the Bedfordshire PCT to impart the information and was informed that Richard Hill, Dental Practice adviser to Bedfordshire PCT, had carried out a previous Surgery inspection at Bromham Road that had raised some concerns."

"Then I know it came through that Richard Hill had been in before about 6 months ago, I think they said, and it was probably sensible for him to go as the second person, a second appropriate second person to do a follow up. The actual timings of bits of those I am afraid I can't REMEMBER."

"At the point at which I was informed that Richard Hill had been there some months before hand and had some concerns."

By her statement supra, in their entirety, Stephanie Twidale was dishonest and maliciously lied or she was maliciously lied to by Sue Gregory (OBE) and her seemingly hereditary racist disciples.

✳ ✳ ✳ ✳ ✳ ✳

THE CHAIRMAN (DR SHIV PABARY): Nor had you had discussions with Mr Hill about any concerns?

STEPHANIE TWIDALE: Nothing at all, nothing at all. We would normally as a Reference Officer try and work in that way if at all possible.

NEGRO'S PERSPECTIVE:
Moron Indian, albeit Member of the British Empire; how could Stephanie Twidale admit under oath that she had discussions with Richard Hill prior to visiting the surgery of the first ever and only Negro dentist on 22.02.2007, when she had lied under the same oath that she did not have any contact with Richard Hill prior to the inspection of the Negro's surgery on 22.02.2007?

"I actually didn't have any contact with Richard at all." – Stephanie

Twidale, under oath, on 19.11.2008

Dr Shiv Pabary, the chairman of the GDC Committee, seemed exceedingly dull. He couldn't have acquired such a high level of dullness from nature – Almighty God must have created him dull and he must have been born duller.
Shocking!
"Why, that is, because, dearest, you are a dunce." – Dr Samuel Johnson

"Sir, he was dull in company, dull in his closet, dull everywhere. He was dull in a new way, and that made many people think him great." – Dr Samuel Johnson

"Why, Sir, Sherry is dull, naturally dull, but it must have taken him a great deal of pain to become what we now see him. Such an excess stupidity, Sir, is not in Nature." – Dr Samuel Johnson

CHAPTER 18

Sue Gregory (OBE) was the empress of privileged dullards and the cardinal of merciless racist evil; she is a descendant of human being stealers, carriers, and sellers - Habakkuk.

No brain, natural resources poor, only skin colour that the wearer neither made nor chose, and what else? Pure scam!

Before the GIGANTIC yields of SLAVERY there was only feudal agriculture. Yields of EVIL, not agriculture, were the magnet for Eastern European Jews

An NHS statement of 30.07.2007, which was jointly created by Charlotte Dowling Goodson, is as follows:

"Termination of Dr O Bamgbelu's General Dental Services Contract. This decision was made against a history of non compliance with legislation, significant numbers of patient complaints, numerous visits by Bedfordshire Health Authority and Bedfordshire PCT's Dental Practice advisor with little improvement and a recent visit by the Dental Reference Service, which revealed a number of serious concerns: These concerns varied from: A poster was displayed which could give the impression that NHS treatment was inferior, and possibly dangerous. A dental chair covering was torn in several places and seams were unstitched. The window sill was being used as additional work surface, but the paint was cracked making it impossible to clean thoroughly. Several hand instruments had cements adhering to them. Some surgical instruments were unbagged, and loose in drawers and cupboards. Several were rusty."

The statement is an incompetent racist fabrication.
Facts are sacred.
Unbeknownst to the lone Negro in their midst, who was the first ever

and only Negro dentist in Bedford, since he merely spoke and the universe became, on 30.07.2007, when the NHS produced the statement that was based upon falsified information, three further NHS forgeries were live, valid, and accessible to white people:

1) The falsified NHS report of 22.07.2004
2) The falsified follow up visit report of undisclosed date
3) The falsified email address for the first ever and only Negro dentist in Bedford.
The privileged dullards withdrew their incompetently forged reports more than four years later. The incompetent dishonesty which is the withdrawal statement of 16.10.2008 remains live and valid.

"This decision was made against a history of non compliance with legislation." – Charlotte Dowling Goodson and Richard Hill, as instructed by the NHS, 30.07.2007

As instructed by the NHS of Mediocre Great England, Charlotte Dowling Goodson and Richard Hill were dishonest, as their statement supra was in its entirety founded upon merciless, racist lies.

If Charlotte Dowling Goodson and Richard Hill could prove that they were not dishonest, they must sue the Negro.
Grossly overrated rubbish!
No brain, natural resources poor, only skin colour that the wearer neither made nor chose, and what else? Pure scam!
Those that they shepherd and regularly spin are amongst the dullest adult population in the industrialised world.
England young adults are amongst the least literate and numerate in the industrialised world. OECD
Are shepherds of morons, morons too?
These are the facts:

Just before Christmas 1995, I was admitted onto the Bedfordshire NHS list. From thence, I became the first ever and only Negro to practice dentistry in Bedford since He merely spoke, and the universe became. I started work at the practice in the New Year, on 08.01.996. It was an existing concern. My predecessor warned me to expert racism, as people were not used to Negroes being dentists. Some of my Black Caribbean patients openly stated that they did not realise that black people could be dentists, and other commented that I was brave to practice dentistry in almost purely white part of Bedford. They seemed to have been systematically brainwashed. I travel by faith, so I am bound to travel light and safe.

Richard Hill visited my newly acquired practice two weeks later, on 22.01.1996. He made some recommendations about structural changes, which I fully acceded to. He came again in April, July, and November 1996, and came again in April 1997. All his reports were good. He allegedly produced a report, six years later, in 2003. The report of the alleged visit was revealed to the Negro more than five years later, in October 2008, and only after the mediocre, Negrophobic, and dishonest GDC of Mediocre Great England had charged the Negro with the content of the report. The NHS alleged that it visited the surgery of the Negro again on two occasions: 22.07.2004 and a follow up on an undisclosed date. The NHS maliciously told racist lies.

The NHS's racist forgeries were completely withdrawn more than four years after the alleged visit of 22.07.2004.

They were all white.

The GDC charge of 2008, in relation to the alleged visit and report of 2003, is as follows:
"On 2 April 2003 Bedford PCT undertook a routine practice inspection of the Bedford Practice that identified concerns."
The Negro was found guilty of the charge that was based upon alleged 2003 concerns, which were revealed to him more than five years later, after the GDC had charged him with the offence that he was unaware of.
Pretty extraordinary, beautiful nonsense!
The dishonest and racist GDC of Mediocre Great England (MGE) seemed too dull to realise the glaring absurdity in the stupid charge for the retrospective alleged concern.
"There is no sin except stupidity." – Oscar Wilde

The alleged concerns, which Richard Hill allegedly identified in 2003, were revealed to the Negro almost six years later, in October 2008. Furthermore, they were revealed to the Negro after he was charged by the crooked and racist council about the offence that he was unaware of.

Pretty extraordinary!

"Those who have the power to do wrong with impunity seldom wait long for the will." Dr Samuel Johnson

Modular education in far-right factory schools, which England young adults and former England young adults within the crooked and racist council of Mediocre Great England (MGE) were exposed to, did not make the brainless morons realise that an alleged concern which was revealed to the Negro more than five years after the alleged concerns were allegedly identified was one of the full definitions of a racist forgery.

The mummified alleged concerns, which the crooked and racist council exhumed more than five years after they were allegedly identified, concerned only COSSH and risk assessment.

There were no concerns; there were only merciless, racist forgeries and thuggery by some descendants of human being stealers, carriers, and sellers. Those who would steal, carry, and sell human beings, including children, would do anything.

Richard Hill confirmed under oath that the crooked and racist council of Mediocre Great England (MGE) lied about the mummified alleged concerns from 2003, which were revealed to the Negro in October 2008 after the GDC had charged him with them, and which he was found guilty of in 2009.

"Had there been any problem, I would be asked by the PCT to visit the practice and carry out a formal inspection in that situation. That's normally along with a colleague, so it's a proper and formal procedure. But I have no record of being told that there were any concerns." – Richard Hill, under oath, at the GDC hearing of 18.11.2008

The sole basis of the merciless, racist power displayed is money. The entire foundation of the money is forged with the proceeds of several centuries of merciless, racist evil and naked fraud (slavery).

Before slavery, what?

"Agriculture not only gives riches to a nation, but the only riches she can call her own." – Dr Samuel Johnson

"Iain Whyte, author of Scotland and the Abolition of Slavery, insists we have at times ignored our guilty past. He said: 'For many years Scotland's historians harboured the illusion that our nation had little to do with the slave trade or plantation slavery.

"'We swept it under the carpet. This was remarkable in the light of Glasgow's wealth coming from tobacco, sugar and cotton, and Jamaica Streets being found in a number of Scottish towns and cities.

"'It is healthy we are now recognising Scotland was very much involved.'

"The industries, which saw Glasgow and much of the country flourish, were built on the back of slavery. There were familiar names such as Scot Lyle of Tate and Lyle fame whose fortune was built on slavery. Ewing from Glasgow was the richest sugar producer in Jamaica.

"The stunning Inveresk Lodge in Edinburgh, now open to the public, was bought by James Wedderburn with money earned from 27 years in Jamaica as a notorious slaver.

"The Wee Free Church was founded using profits and donations from the slave trade. Even our schools have a dark history. Bathgate Academy was built from money willed by John Newland, a renowned slave master and Dollar Academy has a similar foundation.

"For many years, the goods and profits from West Indian slavery were unloaded at Kingston docks in Glasgow. Leith in Edinburgh and Glasgow were popular ports from which ambitious Scottish men sailed to make their fortunes as slave masters." – Ian Bell, Herald Scotland, 28.04.2013

The proceeds of centuries of merciless, racial hatred and fraud kick-started the industrial revolution in Europe and brought European slave merchants and traders great wealth.

The satanic network is everywhere. It controls almost everything except intellect. Without objective basis, it awards itself the monopoly of knowledge.

Before slavery, there were no houses in the current Wimpole Street area, and there was certainly no council. There were only farmlands that were stolen from native Britons by mainland Europeans, and the stolen lands were worked by wretched, feudal agricultural labourers, most of them from mainland Europe. The thoroughly wretched serfs were transformed by several centuries of the merciless, racist evil which slavery was, and they have reinvented themselves on stolen land with the gigantic loot whose foundation is merciless, racist evil (slavery). Everything else is a lie.

"It was our arms in the river of Cameroon, put into the hands of the trader, that furnished him with the means of pushing his trade; and I have no more doubt that they are British arms, put into the hands of Africans, which promote universal war and desolation that I can doubt their having done so in that individual instance. I have shown how great is the enormity of this evil, even on the supposition that we take only convicts and prisoners of war. But take the subject in another way, and how does it stand? Think of 80,000 persons carried out of their native country by we know not what means! For crimes imputed! For light or inconsiderable faults! For debts perhaps! For crime of witchcraft! Or a thousand other weak or scandalous pretexts! Reflect on 80,000 persons annually taken off! There is something in the horror of it that surpasses all bounds of imagination." – Prime Minister William Pitt the Younger, 1792

"The grand object of all European traders in kidnapped and stolen Africans was - money, money, money; money was their god! In Africa, the poor wretched natives, blessed with the most fertile and luxuriant soil, are rendered so much the more miserable by the Christians' (European traders in stolen Africans) abominable traffic for slaves and the horrid cruelty and treachery of the petty [African] Kings. The Africans kings were encouraged by their European (Christian) customers who carry them strong liquors to enflame their madness and powder and bad fire-arms to furnish them with the hellish means of killing and kidnapping. But enough - it is a subject that sours my blood." – Ignatius Sancho, 1778

"Many Scots masters were considered among the most brutal, with life expectancy on their plantations averaging a mere four years. We worked them to death then simply imported more to keep the sugar and thus the money flowing. Unlike centuries of grief and murder, an apology costs nothing. So what does Scotland have to say?" – Herald Scotland, Ian Bell, columnist, Sunday 28 April 2013

"Those who have robbed have also lied." – Dr Samuel Johnson corroborating prophet Habakkuk

* * * * *

"Significant numbers of patient complaints." – Charlotte Dowling Goodson and Richard Hill as instructed by the NHS, 30.07.2007

The statement by the NHS was in its entirety founded upon dishonesty—purified racist dishonesty.

Seemingly irreversibly educationally damaged, hereditary racist thugs are deluded. They associate the proceeds of centuries of merciless, racist evil, armed robbery, and stealing (including stealing, carrying, and selling millions of stolen human beings) with personal intellect and integrity. It's a lie.

Before slavery, what?

Oyinbo olodo! Oyinbo ode!

"Those who have robbed have also lied." – Dr Samuel Johnson corroborating prophet Habakkuk

These are the facts:

The last alleged patient complaint was in 1996. A significant proportion of the alleged complaints were oral, and were disclosed about thirteen years later, in 2008. I had never heard of all or nearly all of the alleged complaints from more than thirteen years prior.

The mediocre and corrupt council of Mediocre Great England (MGE) desired to use the mummified, unsubstantiated allegations to create a pattern with the 2007 allegations by the blatantly dishonest and racist NHS nurse (probably a member of the BNP) in 2008.

The moron council of Mediocre Great England was seemingly run by England's young adults and former young England adults – all products of far-right factories (pretend schools) within one of the least literate countries in the industrialised world -OECD.

The senior NHS nurse unrelentingly lied under oath in their "fish and chips" legal process. To read more about the mediocre GDC, Google: The White Judge Lied.

The NHS and the former England young adults that it instructed

(Richard Hill and Charlotte Dowling Goodson) were recklessly dishonest, racist, and intellectually incompetent. They immortalised blatant, racist dishonesty.

Before slavery, what?

"Numerous visits by Bedfordshire Health Authority Dental Practice advisor with little improvement." – Richard Hill and Charlotte Dowling Goodson, as instructed by the NHS, 30.07.2007

The NHS statement in its entirety was founded upon blatant dishonesty. Dishonesty on record is a very accurate measure of intelligence.

The statement was disclosed to me more than a year after it was created.

Charlotte Dowling Goodson and her type are "fish and chips" gals—descendants of thoroughly wretched agricultural labourers from mainland Europe. Wretched serfs were immeasurably transformed by the gigantic yields of centuries of merciless, racist evil; their descendants have reinvented themselves on stolen land. Charlotte Dowling Goodson and her type – sensuous and tasteless looking racist cougars, with three-fourths of their gigantic, ugly, mammary glands completely deflated (goddamn libido killers) – are grossly overrated rubbish who are not in tune with reality, and associate gigantic yields of centuries of merciless, racist evil and naked fraud with personal intellect and industry.

The precociously wrinkling racist cougars, with gigantic, muscular-looking ugly asses, have no milk in their seemingly wrinkled and uglier boobs, only blood and fat!

"Truth, Sir, is a cow which will yield such people no more milk, and so they are gone to milk the bull." – Dr Samuel Johnson

The rumour is that Richard Hill was a she-man with no children, as the ass hole which such people allegedly prefer is not a birth canal. They rarely have children unless they do "both." If Charlotte Dowling Goodson, her spouse, and their children could prove that the racist cougar was not dishonest, they must sue the Negro.

Charlotte Dowling Goodson and her type are exceedingly lucky that divine providence favoured them with the most favourable skin colour.

Apart from skin, what?

Like Helen Falcon, Sue Gregory, Richard Hill, and Charlotte Dowling Goodson are shepherds of England's young adults.

"FAILING SCHOOLS AND A BATTLE FOR BRITAIN: This was the day the British education establishment's 50-year betrayal of the Nation's children lay starkly exposed in all its ignominy. After testing 166,000 people in 24 education systems, the Organisation for Economic Cooperation and Development (OECD) finds that England young adults are amongst the least literate and numerate in the industrialised world." – The Daily Mail, 09.01.2013

Shepherds of morons are likelier to be morons too.

In 2020, Bedfordshire yields only food. In 1720, Bedfordshire yielded only food. Then, the people of Bedfordshire were fed like battery hens with the proceeds of evil, merciless, racial hatred and naked fraud (slavery). Then also, shepherds deceived moron sheep that they were paragons of wisdom who fed sheep with the yields of virtue. They did not bring millions of stolen Africans home.

Before slavery, what?

"I know of no evil that has ever existed, nor can imagine any evil to exist, worse than the tearing of eighty thousand persons annually from their native land, by a combination of the most civilised nations inhabiting the most enlightened part of the globe, but more especially under the sanction of the laws of that Nation which calls herself the most free and the most happy of them all." – Prime Minister William Pitt the Younger

The facts are as follows: Richard Hill visited the surgery of the first ever and only Negro dentist in Bedford on 22.01.1996, only two weeks after he took over an ongoing concern. He made some recommendations, which the Negro fully acceded to. He visited again in April, July, and November 1996, and April 1997. He produced reports, which were all good. He allegedly visited again in 2003, and allegedly produced a report. The report was revealed to me more than five years later, but only after the crooked, racist, and mediocre council had charged me with the contents, which essentially said that I did not have COSSH and risk assessment in 2003. The crooked, racist, and mediocre council did not detect the glaring absurdity in the fact that the alleged concerns were revealed to the first ever and only Negro dentist in Bedford more than five years after the alleged concerns were identified. The dull, dishonest, and racist council did not realise that an alleged concern which was revealed more than five years after the alleged concern was the evidence of the fact that there was no concern.

Oyinbo olodo! Oyinbo ode!

Before slavery, there was only sustenance agriculture, and there were no houses. There were farmlands that were stolen from aborigines by mainland Europeans and worked by serfs, oftener also from mainland Europe. The gigantic yields of the merciless, racist evil which slavery was immeasurably transformed the lives of the descendants of wretched agricultural labourers. They have reinvented themselves on stolen land, but many retain the intellects of their serf ancestors.

"Numerous visits by Bedfordshire PCT's Dental Practice advisor with little improvement." – Charlotte Dowling Goodson and Richard Hill, as instructed by the NHS

The statement as implicitly instructed by the NHS was founded on dishonesty.

The Bedfordshire PCT Dental Practice Advisor did not visit the practice of the first ever and only Negro dentist in Bedford. Numerous visits of a practice that was never visited by Bedfordshire PCT's Dental Practice advisor was typical brainless nonsense by former England young adults propped up by crude oil and gas money in the same way as their merciless, racist thug, armed robber, and thieving ancestors were for centuries sustained by the proceeds of the extremely nasty, vicious evil which slavery was.

The imbecile former England young adults (Richard Hill and Charlotte Dowling Goodson) reasoned like imbeciles and expressed their reasoning worse than imbeciles. No brain, natural resources poor, only skin colour that the wearer neither made nor chose, and what else? Pure scam!

Before slavery, what?

"Agriculture not only gives riches to a nation, but the only riches she can call her own." – Dr Samuel Johnson

The Bedfordshire PCT Dental Practice Advisor confirmed that he did not visit the practice of the first ever and only Negro dentist in Bedford.

Charlotte Dowling Goodson seemed exceedingly lucky that divine providence favoured her with the most favourable skin colour. Some people accurately foresaw that direct descendants of thoroughly wretched agricultural labourers from mainland Europe with the inherited intellects of serfs would become NHS managers in the distant future, so when they found guns, they used them to loot and destroy the world so that intellectually ungifted morons like Charlotte Dowling Goodson could thrive in the distant future. Whenever the merciless, racist bastards slaughtered, they dispossessed, and wherever they robbed, they took possession. The merciless, sadistic savages are no longer here, but based upon very proximate observations and direct experiences, it is the Negro's honest belief that their sadistic genes continue to flow through the veins of some of those who remain here.

Charlotte Dowling Goodson and Richard Hill were so dull, they seemed even duller than Dr Shiv Pabary, Member of the British Empire and a chairman of a committee within the mediocre, Negrophobic, and crooked GDC, and duller still than a quality Care Quality Commission (CQC) manager of Mediocre Great England (MGE).

"I think I will ask our legal adviser for any advice he may have. My view is that there are six or seven of us here who had the admission down, but we cannot find it in the transcript and there is wordings that imply that there was, but it is not in black and white. It might be useful to clarify that by recalling Mr Bamgbelu and see. As to second matter, I think it will help the Committee if there is confusion with the situation with the nurse taking the waste out. We are happy to hear that if it is okay."
– Dr Shiv Pabary, Member of the British Empire and a chairman of a committee within the mediocre, Negrophobic, and crooked GDC

"Yes, Sir, it does her honour, but it would do nobody else honour. I have indeed, not read it all. But when I take up the end of a web, and find it packthread, I do not expect, by looking further, to find embroidery."
Dr Samuel Johnson

A brainless Indian. A scatter-head Uncle Tom. A white woman's stooge.

Based on very proximate observations and direct experiences, the Indian is happy with any position underneath a white woman, if he's above all Negroes in the pecking order.

"One witness at a Royal Commission in 1897 said the ambition of Indians in Trinidad was, 'to buy a cow, then a shop, and say, "we are no ni***** to work in cane fields." 'The World Is What It Is by Patrick French, 'The Authorised Biography of V.S. Naipaul.

Wed, 2 Sep 2015 8:31
RE: Outstanding statutory annual registration fee invoice: payment due – FINAL REMINDER
From cqc (NHS SHARED BUSINESS SERVICES LTD (BRISTOL)) SBS-B.cqc@nhs.net To adeolacole adeolacole@aol.com

Hello,

Thank you for your below email

Please be advise a invoice is raised by Care Quality Commission for an annual registration and raised for Primary care (Dental Service) - 3 locations as below

1-219061210 52 BROMHAM ROAD BEDFORD BEDFORDSHIRE MK40 2QG

1-219061275 24 PARK ROAD WELLINGBOROUGH NORTHAMPTONSHIRE NN8 4PW

1-219061290 226 ABINGTON AVENUE ABINGTON NORTHAMPTON NORTHAMPTONSHIRE NN1 4PR

Kindly provide the payment details as the invoice is overdue by several days.

If any query please let me know

Thanks and Regards, Kanchan Jaisinghani
Collections
Debt Management Team
Shared Business Services
Tel 0303-123-1155
Fax 0117-933-8890
E-mail: sbs-b.cqc@nhs.net
Website: www.sbs.nhs.uk
Government Business Award Winner
Central Government Supplier of the Year 2011

Sir Major was a winner too, as he used to bang Egg Winner!

The sole purpose of the racist network is to destroy. The sole basis of their power is money. Bedfordshire yielded only food and yields only food.

Before slavery, what?

Made-in-Birmingham guns, not brains, were the tools of the merciless, racist thugs and slave traders. Before slavery, there was only feudal agriculture, almost everything else was stolen.

"Agriculture not only gives riches to a nation, but the only riches she can call her own." – Dr Samuel Johnson

"It was our arms in the river of Cameroon, put into the hands of the trader, that furnished him with the means of pushing his trade; and I have no more doubt that they are British arms, put into the hands of Africans, which promote universal war and desolation that I can doubt their having done so in that individual instance. I have shown how great is the enormity of this evil, even on the supposition that we take only convicts and prisoners of war. But take the subject in another way, and how does it stand? Think of 80,000 persons carried out of their native country by we know not what means! For crimes imputed! For light or inconsiderable faults! For debts perhaps! For crime of witchcraft! Or a thousand other weak or scandalous pretexts! Reflect on 80,000 persons annually taken off! There is something in the horror of it that surpasses all bounds of imagination." – Prime Minister William Pitt the Younger, 1792

Before the GIGANTIC yields of SLAVERY, there was only feudal agriculture. Proceeds of EVIL, not agriculture, were the magnet for Eastern Jews.

MERIT was not relevant within the SATANIC NETWORK, as the LOOTS they used to share were the GIGANTIC proceeds of RACIST EVIL and FRAUD.

They have repackaged themselves as being highly enlightened, civilised, and righteous.

Descendants of Alphonse Gabriel fool fools that they're Archangel Gabriel.

Dr. Olayinka Bamgbelu

"To deny or belittle this good is, in this dangerous century when the resources and pretensions of power continue to enlarge, a desperate error of intellectual abstraction. More than this, it is a self-fulfilling error, which encourages us to give up the struggle against bad laws and class bound procedures and to disarm ourselves before power. It is to throw away a whole inheritance of struggle about the law and within the forms of law, whose continuity can never be fractured without bringing men and women into immediate danger." - E. P Thompson

CHAPTER 19

Stephanie Twidale, the wrinkling, extremely ugly cougar, with three-fourths deflated, gigantic mammary glands, was a racist thug. God blessed her with fairer skin, which is the most favourable skin colour, but cursed her with a dark black brain. She was exceedingly dull, and lied unrelentingly on record. Dishonesty on record is one of the most accurate measures of intelligence.

Stephanie Twidale lied unrelentingly while under oath, and she recognised the importance of statements under oath. If she could lie under oath, it would be reasonable to state that she will lie anywhere.

"I think at this stage I would wish to take technical advice on that before I wish to on oath comment further." – Dr Stephanie Twidale, 19.11.2008

Racial hatred displayed as dishonesty is likelier to be part of the genetic inheritances of Stephanie Twidale, a direct descendant of merciless, racist thugs, armed robbers, and thieves – stealers, carriers, sellers, and exploiters of millions of stolen human beings, including children. Those who would steal human beings will steal anything.

"I know of no evil that has ever existed, nor can imagine any evil to exist, worse than the tearing of eighty thousand persons annually from their native land, by a combination of the most civilised nations inhabiting the most enlightened part of the globe, but more especially under the sanction of the laws of that Nation which calls herself the most free and the most happy of them all." – Prime Minister William Pitt the Younger

"Many Scots masters were considered among the most brutal, with life expectancy on their plantations averaging a mere four years. We worked them to death then simply imported more to keep the sugar and thus the money flowing. Unlike centuries of grief and murder, an apology costs nothing. So what does Scotland have to say?" – Herald Scotland, Ian Bell, columnist, Sunday 28 April 2013 Before slavery, what?

It is actual fact and absolute truth that Stephanie Twidale was dishonest, as she lied under oath when she stated that she did not have any contact with Richard Hill prior to their joint inspection of the surgery of the first ever and only Negro dentist in Bedford. The scatter head racist cougar did not disclose her contacts with him in 2006, but disclosed some of her contacts with him in 2007. Irrespective of these facts, Stephanie Twidale lied on oath that she did not have any contacts with Richard Hill prior to visiting the surgery of the first ever and only Negro dentist in Bedford. The brainless big gal seemed to wear the skin colour that she neither made nor chose as if it were a first class degree from Oxford University; she seemed thoroughly stupid. Only stupid people immortalise mendacity for eternity. Oyinbo olodo! Oyinbo ode!

"There is no sin except stupidity." – Oscar Wilde

Richard Hill confirmed under oath that Stephanie Twidale lied under oath.

Andrew Hurst (GDC counsel) cross examined Richard Hill on 18.11.2008:

ANDREW HURST: Thank you. Now obviously during the course of the run up to the visit of 22 February there was some communication between you and Stephanie Twidale.

RICHARD HILL: Yes.

NEGRO'S PERSPECTIVE:
So, Stephanie Twidale was dishonest, as she lied under oath. Not all liars are racists, but all racists are malicious liars. Stephanie Twidale is part of the UK society.

"All sections of UK society are institutionally racist." – Sir Bernard Hogan-Howe, London Metropolitan Police

Almost everything is inherited. Stephanie Twidale must have inherited dullness and dishonesty from her own mother and father.

If Stephanie Twidale and/or her spouse and their children could prove that their matriarch, a nasty, racist cougar, was not dishonest, they must sue the Negro. When dishonesty and dullness (double D) copulate, insanity is their offspring.

Stephanie Twidale: a descendant of thoroughly wretched, feudal agricultural labourers (serfs), almost certainly from mainland Europe, who stole the land of aboriginal Britons and who were immeasurably transformed by the gigantic yields of the merciless, racist evil which slavery was. The descendants of aliens have reinvented themselves with the yields of racist evil, and fool the foolish with foolishness.

Apart from Dr Shiv Pabary, the dull, dishonest, and/or confused chairman of the GDC Committee, fifty percent of the members of the committee acknowledged that they were friends and/or neighbours of Stephanie Twidale. There is no evidence, certainly none conclusive, that the mediocre and crooked council planted people in the GDC to smooth the path of the seemingly hereditary racist thug. Dr Catherine Brady belatedly declared her interest, and withdrew from the committee on the second day of the hearing. The GDC was aware of the fact that they would invite Stephanie Twidale and Kevin Atkinson to testify against the Negro prior to the commencement of the hearing.

Stephanie Twidale and Kevin Atkinson unrelentingly lied under oath. Stephanie Twidale was an accurate reflection of the intellect and integrity of Sue Gregory.

The intellectually impotent racist thugs, descendants of wretched serfs (agricultural labourers) who were immeasurably transformed by centuries of the gigantic yields of merciless, racist evil, believed that the Negro treated only emergency patients, so they seemingly subconsciously created what they believed. God Almighty blessed them with fairer skin, the most favourable skin colour, but cursed them with dark black brains. No brain, natural resources poor, only skin colour that the wearer neither made nor chose, and what else? Pure scam!

Stephanie Twidale was dishonest, and she lied under oath when she stated as follows: "When we first arrived at the practice Mr Bamgbelu was seeing an emergency patient. Whilst Mr Bamgbelu was with the patient in his surgery, Mr Hill and I walked around and inspected the waiting areas."

The statement is untrue. Stephanie Twidale, a descendant of stealers, carriers, and sellers of stolen human beings, including children, maliciously lied under oath. If Stephanie Twidale or her spouse and their children could prove that their matriarch was not a racist thug and malicious perjurer, they must sue the Negro.

Stephanie Twidale further stated as follows under oath:

"If I REMEMBER, we arrived and Mr Bamgbelu had a patient I think in the chair, or shortly after. So I THINK we arrived."

NEGRO'S PERSPECTIVE:
Shocking!
"Why, that is, because, dearest, you are a dunce." Dr Samuel Johnson.
Alzheimer's disease is considerably more common than ordinarily realised.

She lied or she was recklessly confused. Lunatic, seemingly hereditary, racist cougar! F****** rotter blower!

"Nothing that you will learn in the course of your studies will be of the slightest possible use to you in after life – save only this – if you work hard and diligently you should be able to detect when a man is talking rot, and that, in my view, is the main, if not the sole, purpose of education." – J.A. Smith, Oxford University Professor, Moral Philosophy

The charade will not endure. It's glaringly obvious; the future generations will be duller, and too dull to keep the "show" going seamlessly.

Stephanie Twidale further stated as follows under oath: "One of the other things that he did also comment to me was in one of my telephone conversations with him he did tell me that he had had a practice inspection within the previous year, which was something I was not aware of."

Stephanie Twidale was a racist lunatic. The NHS seemed racist as it maliciously sent racist lunatics such as Stephanie Twidale to inspect the surgery of the first ever and only Negro dentist in Bedford instead of sending her to Broadmoor.

The Negro had an inspection at his Wellingborough practice in the last year. Stephanie Twidale confirmed that fact when she stated as follows under oath: "Stephanie has been in touch a few times as her colleagues had highlighted issues from a similar practice in Northants and they would like to review report etc etc prior to visiting" (NHS, 15.08.2006).

"I stated in my witness statement, and re-iterated during the evidence today, that I had never met Mr Bamgbelu before the visit, and knew nothing about him other than the fact that he had another practice in

NORTHANTS PCT, which had been inspected earlier in the year by 2 DRO colleagues, where some problems had been found. I was informed later by Beds PCT that Mr Hill had inspected previously, but I was told nothing of the content of the report. I would not wish to have prior knowledge of previous reports, as that could possibly have made it harder for me to issue a fully independent report." – Stephanie Twidale, under oath, 19.11.2008

Stephanie Twidale was intellectually incompetent, dishonest, and racist. The ugly, wrinkling, postmenopausal, racist cougar with three-fourths deflated, gigantic mammary glands had no milk in her ugly boobs, only blood. Goddamn libido killer!

"Truth, Sir, is a cow which will yield such people no more milk, and so they are gone to milk the bull." – Dr Samuel Johnson

Like Stephanie Twidale, the cow had no milk, but the bull will yield blood. Stephanie Twidale was a racist lunatic—a big time psycho! Oyinbo olodo! Oyinbo ode!

Stephanie Twidale maliciously lied when she implied under oath that on 23.08.2006 she was not aware of the fact that the Negro served the NHS from more than one location. The ugly, ill-favoured woman maliciously lied with reckless abandon, as she might have seen or heard her own parents lie.

Stephanie Twidale maliciously lied, or she was maliciously lied to by Sue Gregory and her disciples. They were racist thugs and cowards – the descendants of stealers, carriers, and sellers of stolen human beings. Those who would steal human beings would steal anything, as stealing, carrying, and selling stolen human beings is evil – Ne plus ultra.

Those who stole human beings would have stolen anything, as stealing, carrying and selling stolen human beings was evil – Ne plus ultra.

"Yes please we would like a surgery inspection. At the point at which I was informed that Richard Hill had been there some months before hand and had some concerns."

"Having discussed with the PCT they told me that Mr Hill had made previous visits not that long before from which there had been some queries, and they felt perhaps it would be sensible for Mr Hill to come along as well with me to be a second person and follow up on his previous visits to the practice."

"I spoke to Dr Sue Gregory, Consultant in Dental Public Health at the Bedfordshire PCT to impart the information and was informed that Richard Hill, Dental Practice adviser to Bedfordshire PCT, had carried out a previous Surgery inspection at Bromham Road that had raised some concerns."

"Then I know it came through that Richard Hill had been in before about 6 months ago, I think they said, and it was probably sensible for him to go as the second person, a second appropriate second person to do a follow up. The actual timings of bits of those I am afraid I can't REMEMBER."

"At the point at which I was informed that Richard Hill had been there some months before hand and had some concerns."

Every letter, word, and sentence supra by Stephanie Twidale is a lie, and will forever be lies. Even the punctuation marks are accomplices and/or secondary participants in racist dishonesty.

Stephanie Twidale is an irreversible racist thug and a very hard Negrophobic liar. Negroes should approach her with caution.

On 19.11.2008, Stephanie Twidale maliciously lied under oath when she told the council's judge, Mr Jaques Lee, that she did not have prior knowledge of the termination of the NHS contract of the first ever and only Negro dentist in Bedford. She lied under oath. She is a brainless, racist thug who might have been deceived at home and at school that the brain in the skin.

Mr Jaques Lee questioned Stephanie Twidale under oath in the council chambers on 19.11.2008:

THE CHAIRMAN (DR SHIV PABARY, MEMBER OF THE BRITISH EMPIRE): Mr Lee, do you have any questions?

MR JAQUES LEE: Good afternoon.

STEPHANIE TWIDALE (TD): Good afternoon.

MR JAQUES LEE: I do not have too many questions, as half of them have already been asked. You told us that you were asked to carry out this urgent inspection on this surgery?

STEPHANIE TWIDALE (TD): Yes.

MR JAQUES LEE: For various reasons the inspection did not take place for several months?

STEPHANIE TWIDALE (TD): No.

MR JAQUES LEE: Even then it was half an inspection without the patients?

STEPHANIE TWIDALE (TD): Yes.

MR JAQUES LEE: Would you say this is the normal length of time it takes to arrange an appointment?

STEPHANIE TWIDALE (TD): Sadly it could be. In the early days of the new organisation, the new regulation, the new systems, we basically had every Primary Care Trust in the country asking for routine and in some cases most Primary Care Trusts coming up with a handful of urgent visits that they wanted seen. At that point in time we had about 50 something dental officers with several who had just retired and nobody was replaced. So, we were all doing a really massive work load. The problem would be that when I received that first e-mail in the July my own diary would have been full for the next two to three months with visits that are already booked to other practices, because we always did try to give practitioners two to three months notice, so that there was no question that they had to cancel patients and they could arrange and choose their patients to come in to be seen. If it was a surgery inspection they had time to get their paperwork and everything ready. The PCT's did have to have it explained to them that unless they wanted a very, very urgent inspection, something that they wanted doing very rapidly in which case one of the senior managements dental officers would have dropped everything and probably gone and done it, but it was going to take three or four months. So it was then a question of the first phone call to the practitioner, an initial letter advising that we were going to get a phone call and then explaining what we were doing and saying ok can we now look at your appointment book and my diary. I am looking so many weeks ahead. In the case particularly of Mr Bamgbelu only being part time at that practice, we had to look at a particular day that he was there. My memory was that he was not there every day. Looking at his appointment book and we did try not to cancel patients, so unless the PCT really say they wanted somebody in there within the next couple of weeks, the usual response was you must be joking we have not got anybody to do it I am afraid. Then it was not unusual. This would have been August through to, I think, January was the original date, five months. Not ideal, but that is the way it was I am afraid. What urgent meant that I did not ring up any other of my large list of several hundred routine practices to go to book any more of those in, so I have actually got urgents, lets get these booked as soon as we can.

NEGRO'S PERSPECTIVE:
Stephanie Twidale talked a lot of rot. She was dull. She was a postmenopausal cougar. She was ugly. She was dishonest. She was racist. Everything about her was bad. She was a racist devil, and a direct descendant of racist devils. Negroes should never approach her or look in her eyes. She was the reincarnation of the merciless, racist murderers of old.

"Many Scots masters were considered among the most brutal, with life expectancy on their plantations averaging a mere four years. We worked them to death then simply imported more to keep the sugar and thus the money flowing. Unlike centuries of grief and murder, an apology cost nothing. So, what does Scotland have to say?" – Herald Scotland, Ian Bell, columnist, Sunday 28 April 2013

Stephanie Twidale talked nonsense with an upper-class accent and civilised decorum.

"The great enemy of the clear language is INSINCERITY (DISHONESTY). When there is a gap between one's real and one's declared aims, one turns as it were instinctively to long words and exhausted idioms, like a cuttlefish squirting ink. In our age there is no such thing as 'keeping out of politics'. All issues are political issues, and politics itself is a mass of lies, evasions, folly, HATRED and schizophrenia. When the general atmosphere is bad, language must suffer." – George Orwell

"Nothing that you will learn in the course of your studies will be of the slightest possible use to you in after life – save only this – if you work hard and diligently you should be able to detect when a man is talking rot, and that, in my view, is the main, if not the sole, purpose of education." – J.A. Smith, Oxford University Professor, Moral Philosophy

MR JAQUES LEE: Another thing, when you have written your report obviously it is distributed. Is it your responsibility to follow it up to make sure that any deficiencies that you have discovered are seen to, dealt with?

STEPHANIE TWIDALE (TD): No, our report goes to the Primary Care Trust and that is the end of our involvement with that particular practitioner. Our standard default is in those days at that stage was three years for another surgery inspection or a patient examination, unless we indicated to the Primary Care Trust that we felt that something quicker than three years would be appropriate. Again, we would simply say to the Primary Care Trust you might like to visit a particular practice and look at perhaps a particular aspect a little bit earlier than three years. But we would not go back ourselves, it would simply be left to the Primary Care trust to decide how to deal with it. We simply produce a report and send it to the PCT end of story.

NEGRO'S PERSPECTIVE:

There was an end to the story. Stephanie Twidale was a racist thug and a liar. The sole basis of the power that she displayed is money. The entire foundation stones of the relative opulence were laid with the proceeds of merciless evil, sadism, and savagery: Several centuries of the evilest terrorism the world will ever know - Habakkuk.

Before slavery, there was only agriculture; almost everything else was stolen with guns against unarmed and defenceless peoples.

"It was our arms in the river of Cameroon, put into the hands of the trader, that furnished him with the means of pushing his trade; and I have no more doubt that they are British arms, put into the hands of Africans, which promote universal war and desolation that I can doubt their having done so in that individual instance. I have shown how great is the enormity of this evil, even on the supposition that we take only convicts and prisoners of war. But take the subject in another way, and how does it stand? Think of 80,000 persons carried out of their native country by we know not what means! For crimes imputed! For light or inconsiderable faults! For debts perhaps! For crime of witchcraft! Or a thousand other weak or scandalous pretexts! Reflect on 80,000 persons annually taken off! There is something in the horror of it that surpasses all bounds of imagination." – Prime

Minister William Pitt the Younger, 1792

Before slavery, there was only feudal agriculture.

"Agriculture not only gives riches to a nation, but the only riches she can call her own." – Dr Samuel Johnson

"Those who have robbed have also lied." – Dr Samuel Johnson corroborating prophet Habakkuk Before slavery, what?

* * * * *

MR JAQUES LEE: You have no feedback as to what the state of play is as of now?

STEPHANIE TWIDALE (TD): Absolutely none, other than the fact that my second visit to see patients and examine the records was cancelled. I was told by the Primary Care Trust that that visit would no longer go ahead because they had cancelled Mr Bamgbelu's contract. But I had no knowledge as to why, and I do not know why. I was simply told it was not going ahead and I just said fine and closed my paper work down as it was cancelled.

MR JAQUES LEE: Thank you very much.

NEGRO'S PERSPECTIVE:
Stephanie Twidale, the seemingly hereditary racist cougar with the gigantic, very muscular looking ugly ass, which was made uglier by what appeared to be a G-string, maliciously lied when she stated under oath as follows: "Absolutely none, other than the fact that my second visit to see

patients and examine the records was cancelled. I was told by the Primary Care Trust that that visit would no longer go ahead because they had cancelled Mr Bamgbelu's contract. But I had no knowledge as to why, and I do not know why. I was simply told it was not going ahead and I just said fine and closed my paper work down as it was cancelled."

The closeted racist cougar lied; she was an incompetent liar.

Mendacem memorem esse oportet.

Stephanie Twidale unrelentingly lied under oath: Persecutory Negrophobia and Negrophobic Perjury.

On 22.03.2007, about a month before the first ever and only Negro dentist in Bedford was sent a termination letter, Stephanie Twidale accurately foresaw the termination. Most of real communication is oftener off record. Correspondence on record is almost always incompetent art that incompetently imitates life.

In an email of 22.03.2007 to her fellow pencil pushers – nearly all of whom seemed to have failed or nearly failed or just passed in everything and everywhere – the very ugly, dull, dishonest, and racist postmenopausal cougar stated as follows to Dr Steve Claydon: "Steve, I am still awaiting confirmation from Beds PCT that they have communicated with him to insist on the rest of the NSM process going ahead in May as arranged. After this though, although I am happy to do this myself, with you along – I wonder whether it might be better all round for another DRO to go? Not trying to 'chicken out' at all – I would actually like to see what the clinical side of his practice is like – but might he see it as antagonistic to send along the same DRO he has already made his comment clear about. Would I have any chance of any sensible feedback? NOT THAT WE PROBABLY WOULD ANYWAY, FROM THE WAY HE WAS AT THE SI!!!! (SURGERY INSPECTION) OF COURSE, THEY MIGHT HAVE TERMINATED HIS CONTRACT BY THEN, WHICH WOULD SOLVE ALL THE PROBLEMS! Charlotte Dowling is still away until next week. I await your comments/advice." Stephanie.

They were all white, and the sole basis of their power was MONEY; it was stolen.

Before slavery, what?

Charlotte Dowling Goodson, the intellectually very dull Business Studies graduate, did not receive the report of Stephanie Twidale until about 19.04.2007, but Stephanie Twidale had received my handwritten letter, which seemed to wound the merciless, racist bas***. She was deluded to associate the gigantic proceeds of several continuous centuries of racist evil (slavery) with personal intellect and industry. It is a lie! Before slavery, the land yielded only food; almost everything else was stolen with guns from unarmed and defenceless peoples.

On 17 April 2007, Mrs Charlotte Dowling contacted Dr Stephanie Twidale by email and she stated: "I haven't received the report yet. Did you send it to me or Richard?"

On 19 April 2007 Mrs Charlotte Dowling Goodson contacted Dr Stephanie Twidale again by email: "It's not a problem. I've got a copy now and it does make interesting reading!"

It is very important to note that that by 19 April 2007, Charlotte Dowling Goodson had received the report, and she sent an email of that date (19.04.2007) to Dr Stephanie Twidale: "Hi Stephanie. It is not a problem. I've got the copy now and it does make interesting reading! We haven't written to him about the remainder of the visit as we are about to give notice to terminate his contract for failure to address a remedial notice that was issued in December 2006. Please therefore assume that you would not need to visit him again, at least not at his Bedford practice. Should this change for any reason then I will contact you. Many thanks for the report."

Unbeknownst to the first ever and only Negro dentist in Bedford, on 22.03.2007, 17.04.2007, and 19.04.2007, three NHS racist forgeries were live, valid, and accessible: the forged NHS report of 22.07.2004, the forged follow up report of unknown date, and the forged email address.

Those that they regularly spin are amongst the dullest adult population in the industrialised world.

It is actual fact and absolute truth that Sir Winston Churchill implied that the average British adult was a moron. More than sixty years later, the OECD corroborated the proximate observations when it objectively assessed some British young adults.

"The best argument against democracy is a five-minute conversation with the average voter." – Sir Winston Churchill

"FAILING SCHOOLS AND A BATTLE FOR BRITAIN: This was

the day the British education establishment's 50-year betrayal of the Nation's children lay starkly exposed in all its ignominy. After testing 166,000 people in 24 education systems, the Organisation for Economic Cooperation and Development (OECD) finds that England young adults are amongst the least literate and numerate in the industrialised world." – The Daily Mail, 09.01.2013

Sue Gregory, Stephanie Twidale, and Charlotte Dowling Goodson are shepherds of England's young adults. Shepherds of morons are likelier to be morons too.

Eastern European Jews were not drawn to Britain by agriculture; GIGANTIC yields of merciless, racist evil were the magnet. Before slavery what?

On 15.09.2008, Charlotte Dowling Goodson stated that in the summer of 2006 (July/August), she chose the surgery of the first ever and only Negro in Bedford as priority because of information from a completely different area where he had a practice, and the associated email from Sue Gregory, the Empress of Morons. What a load of brainless nonsense by a seemingly hereditary racist thug – a descendant of stealers, carriers, and sellers of human beings.

"I wanted Mr Bamgbelu's practice at 52 Bromham Road, Bedford to be inspected as a priority because I was aware of the history of concerns that had been raised involving Mr Bamgbelu's practice because of an email I received on 18.05.2005 from Sue Gregory, Consultant in Dental Public Health. Until I received this email, I was unaware of any continuing concerns with Mr Bamgbelu's practice in Northants." – Signed statement of Mrs Charlotte Dowling, Head of Primary Care Contracting, 15.09.2008

Charlotte Dowling Goodson employed the English language like a semi-illiterate Bangladeshi who was in the UK to do a three months crash course in hospitality.

In July/August 2006, Charlotte Dowling Goodson wanted the surgery of the first ever and only Negro dentist inspected as a priority because of an email she received more than a year prior. She stated that only to rope their racist empress into their nonsense.

Charlotte Dowling Goodson's brainless nonsense unpicked: If Sue Gregory's email of 18.05.2005 induced the prioritisation more than a year later (July/August 2006), and the Negro was not contacted at all in 2005, 2006, or 2007 about the alleged concern, the statement does not make sense at all. Charlotte Dowling Goodson was a dunce former England young adult and a shepherd of England's young adults. It seemed extraordinary that the Bedfordshire 2003 and 2004 visits and reports did not give cause for concern. Even if the reports were not available, the alleged NHS Data Base would have revealed that the visits took place, and the reports should have been sought. They were incompetent liars and racist thugs. The brain is not in the skin. There was nothing in Bedfordshire before slavery, apart from feudal agriculture. Jews of Eastern European extraction that seem to be running the show, and other mainland Europeans, were not attracted to Britain by fertile land and temperate climate; they were attracted to Britain by the gigantic yields of several centuries of the merciless, racist evil which slavery was.

Before slavery, what?

The descendants of extremely nasty crooks like Bernard Madoff have transformed into Mother Teresa, but they have not returned the gigantic loot.

"Many Scots masters were considered among the most brutal, with life expectancy on their plantations averaging a mere four years. We worked them to death then simply imported more to keep the sugar and thus the money flowing. Unlike centuries of grief and murder, an apology costs nothing. So what does Scotland have to say?" – Herald Scotland, Ian Bell, columnist, Sunday 28 April 2013

"As hard-hearted as a Scot of Scotland." – English saying

"Scotsmen tak a' they can get and a little more if they can." – Scottish saying Before slavery, what?

Under oath on 18.11.2008, Richard Hill implied that prior to the inspection of 22.02.2007, he was not aware of any concerns: "Had there been any problem, I would be asked by the PCT to visit the practice and carry out a formal inspection in that situation. That's normally along with a colleague, so it's a proper and formal procedure. But I have no record of being told that there were any concerns."

The statement by Richard Hill corroborates the following facts: Even if he did not have the 2003 report, as the visit was allegedly on the alleged NHS Data Base, he must have been aware of it.

The 2004 reports were also allegedly missing, but Richard Hill alleged that he found his alleged handwritten drafts, which recorded other matters, and he magically used them to reconstitute entire reports. Nevertheless, as the visit was allegedly on the alleged NHS Data Base, he must have been aware of it.

Richard Hill was dishonest and/or was recklessly confused. Richard Hill was an accurate reflection of the intellect and integrity of Sue Gregory.

Charlotte Dowling Goodson, former England young adult: "The reason I decided to have Mr Bamgbelu's practice inspected at Bromham Road as a priority was not only because of the history of previous concerns, but it was to ensure that any problems that had arisen in the past with Mr Bamgbelu's practice had been resolved" (15.09.2008).

Imbecile England young adult!

Oyinbo olodo! Oyinbo ode!
Which history and since when?

"History will favour me, for I intend to write it." Churchill

In the same report, Charlotte Dowling Goodson, the dull, dishonest, and racist England young adult, also stated, "I wanted Mr Bamgbelu's practice at 52 Bromham Road, Bedford to be inspected as a priority because I was aware of the history of concerns that had been raised involving Mr Bamgbelu's practice because of an email I received on 18.05.2005 from Sue Gregory, Consultant in Dental Public Health. Until I received this email, I was unaware of any continuing concerns with Mr Bamgbelu's practice in Northants."

Charlotte Dowling Goodson, a top England young adult, seemed too dull to detect the absurdity in her brainless construction. She received Sue Gregory's email on 18.05.2005 and picked the Negro as a priority more than a year later. "Priority" and "delay" are not synonymous words.

"Richard (Hill), Stephanie Twidale called us a few weeks ago about DRS visits and Charlotte prioritised Mr Bamgbelu's practice..." – NHS, 15.08.2006

"The reason I decided to have Mr Bamgbelu's practice inspected at Bromham Road as a priority was not only because of the history of previous concerns..." – Charlotte Dowling Goodson, NHS manager,

15.08.2006

Which previous concerns was the racist cretin talking about? Only Richard Hill had ever been to my practice, and he stated that there was no concern: "Had there been any problem, I would be asked by the PCT to visit the practice and carry out a formal inspection in that situation. That's normally along with a colleague, so it's a proper and formal procedure. But I have no record of being told that there were any concerns."

Richard Hill's statement under oath corroborated his earlier signed statement – where he stated that he did not visit the surgery of the first ever Negro dentist in Bedford between 2003 and 2007.

"I did not undertake any further inspections at Mr Bamgbelu's practice between 2003 and 2007." – Richard Hill, 16.10.2008

Charlotte Dowling Goodson, the polytechnic university-educated Business Studies graduate, seemed too dull to detect the absurdities in her brainless construction. If there were problems in 2005 which Sue Gregory (OBE) communicated to her, it seemed extraordinary that the Negro was contacted. She maliciously lied or she was recklessly confused.

The sole basis of the power displayed by Charlotte Dowling Goodson was money. The entire foundation of the money was the merciless, racist evil which slavery was.

There were three alleged reports which had concerns: the report of 02.04.2003, the report of 22.07.2004, and the report of the follow up visit of undisclosed date. Irrespective of the alleged facts, Richard Hill did not visit the surgery of the first ever and only Negro dentist in Bedford.

The 02.04.2003 report was missing, so Richard Hill, as implicitly instructed by the NHS, created two separate 2004 reports which were also missing from allegedly handwritten drafts for 2004 visits which contained other matters. The handwritten draft for 2003 was implicitly missing too.

Reductio ad absurdum!

Sue Gregory and Richard Hill: very powerful, intellectually impotent nonentities. No brain, natural resources poor, only skin colour that the wearer neither made nor chose, and what else? Pure scam! The future generations will be too dull to keep the charade going seamlessly. Time will unfold the truth.

"Nothing that you will learn in the course of your studies will be of the slightest possible use to you in after life – save only this – if you work hard and diligently you should be able to detect when a man is talking rot, and that, in my view, is the main, if not the sole, purpose of education." – J.A. Smith, Oxford University Professor, Moral Philosophy

Those regularly spun are amongst the dullest adult populations in the industrialised world.

"I, RICHARD HILL, c/o Bedfordshire Primary Care Trust, Gilbert Hitchcock House, 21 Kimbolton Road, Bedford, MK40 2AW WILL SAY AS FOLLOWS: I make this statement supplemental to my statement dated 23.09.2008. I attach as Exhibit SRWH1 a copy of my report dated 22.07.2004, I attach a synopsis of practice visits that makes reference to a practice visit to MR BAMGBELU's practice at 52, Bromham Road, Bedford, MK40 2QG in July 2004. The document is incorrect in recording that the inspection took place in 2004. No such inspection in fact took place. In 2006 the Healthcare Commission carried out a visit to Bedfordshire PCT and I was asked to provide all my practice visit reports. While collating this information, I noticed that some inspection reports were missing, which included an inspection of Mr Bamgbelu's practice on 02.04.2003. Around that time my department moved and it is possible that some reports had been lost during the move. I did locate some of my draft handwritten notes and referred to these to prepare my inspection report dated 22.07.2004 for MR BAMGBELU's practice which at the time, I understood to be a correct and accurate record of my inspection. Following another move to different premises, I went through some of my files and found my correct inspection report dated which is exhibited to my September 2008 statement as RWH11. The contents of the 22.07.2004 and 02.04.2003 report differ. The reason that the contents differ is because the hand written notes I used to prepare the 22.07.2004 also had a reference to a difference and dates and notes were mixed up. Having reviewed the documents, it became clear to me that the July 2004 was created in error. The content of the 02.04.2003 report is an accurate reflection of the inspection done at the time and I stand by the contents of the same."

"I wanted Mr Bamgbelu's practice at 52 Bromham Road, Bedford to be inspected as a priority because I was aware of the history of concerns that had been raised involving Mr Bamgbelu's practice because of an email I received on 18.05.2005 from Sue Gregory, Consultant in Dental Public Health. Until I received this email, I was unaware of any continuing concerns with Mr Bamgbelu's practice in Northants." – Signed statement of Mrs Charlotte Dowling, Head of Primary Care Contracting, 15.09.2008

The entire statement was incompetent spin by a fifth-rate polytechnic university-educated NHS madam: Charlotte Dowling Goodson.

Charlotte Dowling Goodson was a crooked NHS madam for Bedfordshire; she chose the surgery of the first ever and only Negro dentist in Bedford as priority in July/August 2006 because she received an email from their more crooked and intellectually incompetent empress – dmf Sue Gregory – more than a year earlier, on 18.05.2005. Brainless nonsense!

"Nothing that you will learn in the course of your studies will be of the slightest possible use to you in after life – save only this – if you work hard and diligently you should be able to detect when a man is talking rot, and that, in my view, is the main, if not the sole, purpose of education." – J.A. Smith, Oxford University Professor, Moral Philosophy

Those regularly spun are amongst the dullest adult population in the industrialised world. Irrespective of the gigantic yields of centuries of merciless racial hatred and fraud, England young adults are amongst the dullest in the industrialised world.

It is actual fact and absolute truth that Sir Winston Churchill implied that the average Briton was a moron. More than sixty years later, the

OECD seamlessly corroborated the proximate observation of the great man.

"The best argument against democracy is a five-minute conversation with the average voter." – Sir Winston Churchill

Shepherds of morons are likelier to be morons too.

Sue Gregory and Charlotte Dowling Goodson are sections of the UK society, and shepherds of England's young adults. Oyinbo olodo! Oyinbo ode!

"All sections of UK society are institutionally racist." – Sir Bernard Hogan-Howe, London Metropolitan Police Chief

Charlotte Dowling Goodson was allegedly not aware of alleged continuing concerns in another primary care trust, and that reasonably implied that there had been previous concerns in that trust which she was aware of. If that were the case, what did she do about it? Why did she not prioritise the surgery of the first ever Negro dentist in Bedford in the same way? Charlotte Dowling Goodson reasoned like someone who had been lied to at home and at school that the brain is in the skin. If her parents brought her up to believe that, they lied to her.

Almost everything was stolen.

"Many Scots masters were considered among the most brutal, with life expectancy on their plantations averaging a mere four years. We worked them to death then simply imported more to keep the sugar and thus the money flowing. Unlike centuries of grief and murder, an apology costs nothing. So what does Scotland have to say?" – Herald Scotland, Ian Bell, columnist, Sunday 28 April 2013

"I know of no evil that has ever existed, nor can imagine any evil to exist, worse than the tearing of eighty thousand persons annually from their native land, by a combination of the most civilised nations inhabiting the most enlightened part of the globe, but more especially under the sanction of the laws of that Nation which calls herself the most free and the most happy of them all." – Prime Minister William Pitt the Younger

Before slavery, what?

"Those who have robbed have also lied." – Dr Samuel Johnson corroborating prophet Habakkuk

The brightest, stolen and sold AFRICANS in the Americas, West Indies and Africa -genes were wiped out. Illogical to voluntarily produce children in HELL.

Millions were raped, over several centuries of the evilest terrorism the world will ever know.

CHAPTER 20

Seemingly with the full knowledge and tacit approval of Sue Gregory on 09.03.2007, Charlotte Dowling Goodson sent an email to the merciless, racist mob or Bedford Mafia. The email concerned the first ever and only Negro dentist in Bedford.

Charlotte Dowling Goodson's email of 09.03.2007 was sent to Julie Wilkinson and the rest of their racist gang: "Further to our discussion earlier on this afternoon I've checked with the contract about our next steps following Mr Bamgbelu's failure to comply with our CG arrangements. As the remedial notice was issued under the clauses 329 to 336, clause 332 states that where we are satisfied that he hasn't taken the required steps by the end of the notice period, then we may terminate his contract with effect from such date as we may specify in a further notice. It is an extreme course of action but we may wish to consider it in the light of all other issues". I'm proposing to write to him saying that as he has failed to remedy the breach we are considering whether to terminate is contract. Is everyone OK with that? I think it would send a clear message that we are to be taken seriously, but I don't think that we should do it?"

"By all other issues," the hereditary racist thugs, descendants of merciless, evil, racist murderers, armed robbers, and thieves, referred to incompetent lies, chief of which were the forged NHS reports of 22.07.2004 (visit and follow up), which were live and valid on 09.03.2007. Intellectually impotent descendants of wretched feudal agricultural labourers (serfs) from mainland Europe, who were immeasurably transformed by the gigantic yields of centuries of merciless, racist evil and naked fraud, have reinvented themselves on stolen land and fool the foolish. Their incompetent art incompetently imitated life. The seemingly hereditary morons seemed oblivious to the infinite reasoning power of the supreme power that Hawking alluded to.

Shepherds didn't bring stolen AFRICANS home; deceived dull sheep that they were paragon of wisdom who, like Mother Teresa, did good work abroad.

The following was what the cretin former England young adult, Charlotte Dowling Goodson, tried to spin.

The moron (Charlotte Dowling Goodson) who did very soft business studies at a polytechnic university did not know that some people sincerely believed that she was sensuous, but tasteless, brainless sh**.

Before slavery, what?

Apart from white skin, what?

In April 2006, the PCT was granted power, and they were determined to destroy the first ever and only Negro dentist in Bedford. So, they prepared the way for the merciless, racist destruction of a fellow human being and his children in the same way their ancestors did during several centuries of merciless, racist tyranny, when millions of kidnapped and stolen Africans were worked to death or slaughtered.

"Many Scots masters were considered among the most brutal, with life expectancy on their plantations averaging a mere four years. We worked them to death then simply imported more to keep the sugar and thus the money flowing. Unlike centuries of grief and murder, an apology costs nothing. So what does Scotland have to say?" – Herald Scotland, Ian Bell, columnist, Sunday 28 April 2013

"I know of no evil that has ever existed, nor can imagine any evil to exist, worse than the tearing of eighty thousand persons annually from their native land, by a combination of the most civilised nations inhabiting the most enlightened part of the globe, but more especially under the sanction of the laws of that Nation which calls herself the most free and the most happy of them all." – Prime Minister William Pitt the Younger

So, like their merciless, racist thug, armed robber, and thieving ancestors, they (Charlotte Dowling Goodson, Sue Gregory, Richard Hill, and other members of their gang) went about their business as follows: on 07.07.2006, very close to midnight, Steven Claydon, Dental Reference Officer (DRO), emailed a fellow pencil pusher who seemed to have failed or nearly failed or just passed in almost everything and almost everywhere ("He who can, does. He who cannot, teaches," stated George Bernard Shaw) that the PCT had requested an urgent patients and record cards inspection of the surgery of the first ever and only Negro dentist in Bedford.

> From: Claydon Steven (DRO)
> Sent: 07 July 2006 22:54
> To: Twidale Stephanie (DRO)
> Cc: Moseley, Kevin (DRO); Evans Keith (DRO); NHSBSA DPD Helpdesk; Claydon Steven (DRO) Subject: Priority 5GD Bedford PCT
> Dear Stephanie
> I enclose the two SV 16s for Bedford PCT. These are urgent practice visits at the request of the PCT. The rest of the PCT has been allocated to Keith Evans.
> Please contact me if a provider proves difficult to appoint / visit.
> If you believe your return should be different to the default 3 years please inform me.
> Please let me know if you have any concerns/ problems with this.
> Kind regards, Steve

The email is incompetent art that incompetently imitated life. Steven Claydon is a former England young adult and a shepherd of England young adults.

"FAILING SCHOOLS AND A BATTLE FOR BRITAIN: This was the day the British education establishment's 50-year betrayal of the Nation's children lay starkly exposed in all its ignominy. After testing 166,000 people in 24 education systems, the Organisation for Economic Cooperation and Development (OECD) finds that England young adults are amongst the least literate and numerate in the industrialised world." – The Daily Mail, 09.01.2013

Shepherds of morons are likelier to be morons too.

Ignoring the cumbersome, uneducated grammar of Steve Claydon, in his seemingly artificially created email (a former England young adult and a shepherd of England young adults), he was dishonest because he lied or was lied to about the fact expressed in his email to Stephanie Twidale (TD) on 07.07.2007, at six minutes before 11 p.m. In the African bush, the seventh day of the seventh month at 11 p.m. is when witches and wizards come out in the African bush and eat each other, like the ancestors of Steven Claydon used to do.

Steven Claydon: seemingly crooked, direct descendant of goddamn cannibals!

"Ancient Britons were cannibals. So now we can admit the truth: that other 'gentle native peoples' ate each other." – Damian Thompson, Telegraph

Goddamn cannibals: After tens of thousands of years of roasting and eating other people children's gizzards, barbarian and rabbit hunters who used to live off the land found guns, then Africa and Africans, and they instantly mutated to economic cannibals. They are still in Africa. Then, they carried and sold millions of stolen children of unarmed defenceless people; now, they carry natural resources – Habakkuk.

OYINBO OLE: WHITE THIEVES: HABAKKUK
Substitution is fraudulent emancipation.
Nothing has changed, economic cannibalism continues: Then, they carried millions of stolen children from their food, now, they carry trillions of dollars from natural resources rich Africa: 30% of the known natural resources reserve is in Africa.
"Moderation is a virtue only among those who are thought to have found alternatives." Henry Kissinger

The fact was a DRO (Dental Reference Officer) would not normally inspect surgeries, but they were determined to f**k the first ever and only Negro dentist Bedford, so they started with the "opening gambit," which was that they had received an urgent request from the PCT for a patient and record cards inspection of the surgery of the first ever and only Negro dentist in Bedford. Based upon accessible information, it is my honest belief that Steven Claydon was dishonest, as he maliciously lied. The urgent inspection request was never disclosed, and all the statements by the PCT contradicted the statement by Steven Claydon. Steven Claydon and Stephanie Twidale were very close colleagues, and Stephanie Twidale (TD) unrelentingly lied under oath.

"Show me your friends, and I will tell you who you are."

"Walk with the wise and become wise, for a companion of fools suffers harm." – Proverbs 13:20.

Charlotte Dowling Goodson chose the surgery of the first ever and only Negro dentist as priority. The reasons, albeit confused that she gave for doing so, were at variance with what Steven Claydon stated, which further confirmed that he was dishonest and lied.

The illogical reasons given by Charlotte Dowling Goodson for picking the surgery of the first ever and only Negro dentist in Bedford as priority has been fully dealt with in other parts of this book, but for further clarity, they are as follows: "I wanted Mr Bamgbelu's practice at 52 Bromham Road, Bedford to be inspected as a priority because I was aware of the history of concerns that had been raised involving Mr Bamgbelu's practice because of an email I received on 18.05.2005 from Sue Gregory, Consultant in Dental Public Health. Until I received this email, I was unaware of any continuing concerns with Mr Bamgbelu's practice in Northants" (signed statement of Mrs Charlotte Dowling, Head of Primary Care Contracting, 15.09.2008).

"The reason I decided to have Mr Bamgbelu's practice inspected at Bromham Road as a priority was not only because of the history of previous concerns, but it was to ensure that any problems that had arisen in the past with Mr Bamgbelu's practice had been resolved." – 15.09.2008.

There was no mention of record card and patients' inspection, which confirmed that Steven Claydon maliciously lied or he was recklessly confused when he alleged that the PCT sent him an alleged urgent request for a patients and record card inspection. The alleged request was never disclosed. Descendants of thoroughly wretched, feudal agricultural labourers from mainland Europe were immeasurably transformed by the gigantic yields of centuries of merciless, racist evil. They have reinvented themselves on stolen land and fool the foolish.

Deluded Steven Claydon, Stephanie Twidale (TD), and their type – descendants of stealers, carriers, and sellers of stolen human beings (those who would steal and sell human beings will steal anything) – associate the gigantic yields of merciless, racist evil with their personal intellect and industry.

Deluded f****** fools!

Before slavery, what?

I had never had the type of practice inspection described by Stephen Claydon in my practice before, and there was no reason for it, and there was no evidence that the PCT made such a request. Steven Claydon, probably a white supremacist, was dishonest or was recklessly confused when he stated, "I enclose the two SV 16s for Bedford PCT. These are urgent practice visits at the request of the PCT."

Steven Claydon was significant only because of his skin colour and the fact that he was born in a relatively rich country. His brain was not good, and like Stephanie Twidale he lied on record and did so incompetently. There are no oil well or gas fields anywhere near where Steven Claydon was born. The land yields only food as it did before slavery. Steven Claydon should invoke the spirits of his ancestors and ask them where they got the money from. The merciless, racist thugs, armed robbers, and thieves (stealers, sellers, and carriers of millions of stolen human beings) should confess that they stole it. Whenever they slaughtered and armed others to slaughter, they dispossessed, and wherever they robbed, they took possession.

The NHS email of 15.08.2006 confirmed that it desired and requested for a practice inspection only, and that the request did not precede Stephanie Twidale's several calls to the NHS.

"Richard (Hill), Stephanie Twidale called us a few weeks ago about DRS visits and Charlotte prioritised Mr Bamgbelu's practice; Stephanie has been in touch a few times as her colleagues had highlighted issues from a similar practice in Northants and they would like to review report etc etc prior to visiting. She also wanted to know if there has been a dental inspection there at all and I did not know the answer . . . Cue Richard have you carried out an inspection at this practice, please could you advise Stephanie when she contacts you, and would it be possible to see our reports so we can be more pro active with any other queries. Thanks. With kind regards, John Hooper." – 15.08.2006

Under oath on 19.11.2008, Stephanie Twidale unrelentingly lied and employed tortuous verbosity to mesmerise the receptive audience who sat before her. In the council chambers at 37 Wimpole Street, London, incompetent art incompetently imitated life.

✼ ✼ ✼ ✼ ✼ ✼ ✼

David Morris cross examined Stephanie Twidale in the council chamber on 19.11.2008:

DAVID MORRIS: Looking at this, you called and then it was Charlotte Dowling who prioritised Mr Bamgbelu's practice?

STEPHANIE TWIDALE (TD): No, the practice had already been prioritised. I had already received a request from my line manager, this would have come into the Dental Reference Service as a request from Bedford. I can't remember at the time it came in if it was even Bedfordshire, because PCT's all change names around that stage, for could they please have urgent visits to two practices in and around Bedford. That would have been parcelled out to Stephen Claydon who was the Midlands Team Manager, Bedfordshire was his area, and then that was passed on down to me. Having received that I then looked at it and thought "urgent" for both of them and rang the PCT and asked actually about both the practices, what did they require? Did they require just the patients and records, because that was what I had been asked for. Was that going to satisfy whatever their reason was for asking for an urgent visit over and above their routine ones, and did they need a practice inspection at the time while I was there? It was something we were more or less offering to the PCT at that point, if their practice advisers were behind with inspections to say: "Would you like us to do it while we are there?" to save pestering the dentist again with another turning up some time later.

NEGRO'S PERSPECTIVE:
Only stupid people immortalise mendacity. Stephanie Twidale (TD) was so dull she could not have acquired such a high level of dullness from nature; she must have been born with it. Oyinbo olodo! Oyinbo ode!

"Nothing that you will learn in the course of your studies will be of the slightest possible use to you in after life – save only this – if you work hard and diligently you should be able to detect when a man is talking rot, and that, in my view, is the main, if not the sole, purpose of education." – J.A. Smith, Oxford University Professor, Moral Philosophy

"The great enemy of the clear language is INSINCERITY (DISHONESTY). When there is a gap between one's real and one's declared aims, one turns as it were instinctively to long words and exhausted idioms, like a cuttlefish squirting ink. In our age there is no such thing as 'keeping out of politics'. All issues are political issues, and politics itself is a mass of lies, evasions, folly, HATRED and schizophrenia. When the general atmosphere is bad, language must suffer." – George Orwell

"No, the practice had already been prioritised. I had already received a request from my line manager, this would have come into the Dental Reference Service as a request from Bedford." –
Stephanie Twidale (TD)

The crooked, seemingly hereditary racist cougar was contacted by Steven Claydon, her fellow pencil pusher, just before midnight on 07.07.2006. The alleged request by the NHS was at variance with the statements by the NHS, and it was never disclosed.

"I can't remember at the time it came in if it was even Bedfordshire, because PCT's all change names around that stage, for could they please have urgent visits to two practices in and around Bedford." – Stephanie Twidale (TD)

Stephanie Twidale, the well-worn, ugly, racist cougar with three-fourths deflated mammary glands with no milk, but only blood and fat, reasoned like an imbecile, and she expressed her reasoning worse than an imbecile. "In and around Bedford" bulks up nonsense talk and fools the foolish with foolishness.

"Truth, Sir, is a cow which will yield such people no more milk, and so they are gone to milk the bull." – Dr Samuel Johnson

Stephanie Twidale (TD) unrelentingly lied under oath; she almost certainly lied again when she implied that she was unaware of the fact that the PCT came into being in April 2006, and the tortuous gibberish by the cougar with the muscular looking, gigantic, ugly ass was irrelevant to the question that she was asked under oath.

"In examinations those who do not wish to know ask questions of those who cannot tell." – Sir Walter Raleigh

"That would have been parcelled out to Stephen Claydon who was the Midlands Team Manager, Bedfordshire was his area, and then that was passed on down to me." – Stephanie Twidale (TD)

They were all white, and they were all incompetent liars and RACIST thugs.

The f***** parcel was never disclosed; it was a f****** racist forgery by merciless, hereditary racist thugs. After all, some of Steven Claydon's and Stephanie Twidale's direct ancestors were merciless, racist thugs, armed robbers, and thieves – stealers, carriers, and sellers of stolen human beings.

Before slavery, what?

"Agriculture not only gives riches to a nation, but the only riches she can call her own." – Dr Samuel Johnson

"Having received that I then looked at it and thought 'urgent' for both of them and rang the PCT and asked actually about both the practices, what did they require? Did they require just the patients and records, because that was what I had been asked for. Did they require just the patients and records, because that was what I had been asked for. Was that going to satisfy whatever their reason was for asking for an urgent visit over and above their routine ones, and did they need a practice inspection at the time while I was there? It was something we were more or less offering to the PCT at that point, if their practice advisers were behind with inspections to say: 'Would you like us to do it while we are there?' to save pestering the dentist again with another turning up some time later." – Stephanie Twidale (TD).

F****** rot!

Stephanie Twidale (TD) unrelentingly lied on oath. Dishonesty on oath is a very accurate measure of intelligence.

Her statement is at variance with the statement that she made to the NHS, which she confirmed on oath. According to the NHS, it was during one of the dull, dishonest, racist cougar's (Stephanie Twidale's) calls to the NHS that the surgery of the first ever and only Negro dentist in Bedford was picked as priority. According to the NHS, the racist cougar also stated that her pencil pushing colleagues had inspected the surgery in Wellingborough where they found some issues, and they would like to review previous reports and etc. etc. before visiting the surgery of the Negro. She also wanted to know if there had ever been inspection at my practice.

Stephanie Twidale (TD): No brain, natural resources poor, only skin colour that the wearer neither made nor chose, and what else? Pure scam!

"Richard (Hill), Stephanie Twidale called us a few weeks ago about DRS visits and Charlotte prioritised Mr Bamgbelu's practice; Stephanie has been in touch a few times as her colleagues had highlighted issues from a similar practice in Northants and they would like to review report etc etc prior to visiting. She also wanted to know if there has been a dental inspection there at all and I did not know the answer . . . Cue Richard have you carried out an inspection at this practice, please could you advise Stephanie when she contacts you, and would it be possible to see our reports so we can be more pro active with any other queries. Thanks. With kind regards, John Hooper." – 15.08.2006

Three weeks after the email, Richard Hill produced the reports of 2004 (visit and follow up).

Richard Hill alleged that his allegedly correct report of 02.04.2003 was missing, and implicitly its handwritten draft was missing too, but he found the handwritten drafts of the implicitly missing 2004 reports (visit and follow up) and he used them to create two reports of two different dates as replacements for a single missing report for 2003. Grossly absurd! Incompetent mendacity! The very dull former England young adult further alleged that the handwritten notes that he used to create the two 2004 reports (visit and follow up) contained other matters.

Brainless nonsense!

It was f****** rot by a she-man-looking man who walked in short strides and wiggled his ass from side to side as he did so.

Richard Hill released the NHS reports of 22.07.2004 and follow up of unknown date on 06.09.2006. They were NHS forgeries. They were completely withdrawn, albeit more than four years after the alleged visit of 22.07.2004. The withdrawal statement of 16.10.2008 is a continuing NHS forgery; it remains live and valid.

Theirs is unilateral anarchy!

Unilateral anarchy is one of the fullest definitions of terrorism.

"Fight like hell." President Trump

On 27.12.2006, the NHS sent the Negro a Remedial Notice, which was essentially incompetent art that incompetently imitated life. In it the NHS ordered that the first ever and only Negro dentist in Bedford complete the parts (it did not state what the parts were and did not include paperwork about the parts in the notice) by 31.03.2007 and agree to do the parts by signing a PQIP by 24.01.2007. That was the opening "gambit" of the seemingly hereditary racist thugs. Sue Gregory was implicitly their "cardinal."

They are the descendants of thoroughly wretched, feudal agricultural labourers from mainland Europe; they were immeasurably transformed by the gigantic yields of centuries of merciless, racist evil, armed robbery, and stealing – stealers, carriers, and sellers of stolen human beings. They have reinvented themselves with stolen money on stolen land, and foolishly fool the foolish with foolishness.

"American South is still taken as barbarism's benchmark. Few realise that the behaviour of Scots busy getting rich in the slave-holders' empire was actually worse (routinely worse) than the worst of the cottonocracy. You need only count the corpses. By the time slavery was brought to an end in America, the country's 400,000 trafficked people had grown to a population of four million. In the British West Indies, only 670,000 survived from two million imported souls. In the American South, slaves were valuable and bred. We worked them to death then simply imported more to keep the sugar and thus the money flowing. Unlike centuries of grief and murder, an apology cost nothing. So, what does Scotland have to say?" – Ian Bell, "Time for Scots to say sorry for slavery," Herald Scotland, Sunday 28 April 2013

Gigantic yields of sadistic, racist evil were the magnet that pulled Eastern Europe Jews to Britain. Before SLAVERY what? Feudal agriculture!
Before slavery, what?
"Agriculture not only gives riches to a nation, but the only riches she can call her own." – Dr Samuel Johnson

On 05.01.2007, I received the PQIP form from the NHS in an envelope marked 03.01.2007. There was no accompanying letter. I filled out the form and faxed it to the NHS. About two years later, the GDC charged me with dishonesty for stating that I sent the PQIP form by fax, when I hadn't. It was the charge that made me realise that the NHS did not receive my fax. The dull, dishonest, and racist GDC disseminated the brainless rot to the whole world. The GDC was dishonest and intellectually incompetent.

The GDC, manned by England's young adults and former England young adults, were unilateral anarchists, which is one of the fullest definitions of terrorism. The sole basis of the power displayed is money. The foundation stones of the money were forged with the proceeds of several centuries of merciless, racist evil, armed robbery, thieving, and stealing, using guns and arming others to use guns to slaughter millions of unarmed and defenceless human beings and robbing them of all their possessions, including their lives. Merciless, cowards and racist bastards!

Prior to slavery, there were no houses in the Wimpole Street area. There were only farmlands worked by thoroughly wretched agricultural labourers (serfs), mainly from mainland Europe, and they toiled on stolen lands for landowners, also from mainland Europe, who had used violence to dispossess the aborigines.
"It was in 1066 that William the Conqueror occupied Britain, stole our land and gained control by granting it to his Norman friends, thus creating a feudal system we have not yet fully escaped." – Tony Benn

Normans stole from others what others had stolen from others.

"All have taken what had other owners, and all have had recourse to arms rather than quit the prey on which they were fastened." Dr Samuel Johnson

Genetically pure Britons are extinct; all were dispossessed, robbed, and slaughtered. Tony Benn was dishonest, or he was confused when he implied that he was genetically an aboriginal Briton. Genetically pure aboriginal Britons are extinct. They were dispossessed and robbed of their land by a motley assembly of mainland Europeans – hereditary serfs or descendants of feudal agricultural labourers – who were hugely transformed by the gigantic gains of slavery. They have reinvented themselves.

"Iain Whyte, author of Scotland and the Abolition of Slavery, insists we have at times ignored our guilty past.
"He said: 'For many years Scotland's historians harboured the illusion that our nation had little to do with the slave trade or plantation slavery.
"'We swept it under the carpet. This was remarkable in the light of Glasgow's wealth coming from tobacco, sugar and cotton, and Jamaica Streets being found in a number of Scottish towns and cities.
"'It is healthy we are now recognising Scotland was very much involved.'
"The industries, which saw Glasgow and much of the country flourish, were built on the back of slavery.
"There were familiar names such as Scot Lyle of Tate and Lyle fame whose fortune was built on slavery. Ewing from Glasgow was the richest sugar producer in Jamaica.
"The stunning Inveresk Lodge in Edinburgh, now open to the public, was bought by James Wedderburn with money earned from 27 years in Jamaica as a notorious slaver.
"The Wee Free Church was founded using profits and donations from the slave trade. Even our schools have a dark history. Bathgate Academy was built from money willed by John Newland, a renowned slave master and Dollar Academy has a similar foundation.
"For many years, the goods and profits from West Indian slavery were

unloaded at Kingston docks in Glasgow.

"Leith in Edinburgh and Glasgow were popular ports from which ambitious Scottish men sailed to make their fortunes as slave masters." – Herald Scotland, Ian Bell, Sunday 28 April 2013

The proceeds of merciless racist evil and fraud were used to build cathedrals and courts, and councils and castles. Almost everything was stolen.

The proceeds of centuries of merciless, racial hatred and fraud kick-started the industrial revolution in Europe and brought European slave merchants and traders, great wealth.

The satanic network is everywhere. It controls almost everything except intellect. Without objective basis, it awards itself the monopoly of knowledge.

"Those who have robbed have also lied." – Dr Samuel Johnson corroborating prophet Habakkuk Before slavery, what?

"Agriculture not only gives riches to a nation, but the only riches she can call her own." – Dr Samuel Johnson

The Negro replied to the NHS letter of 27.12.2006 as follows: "Dear Charlotte Dowling, Thank you for your letter of 27.12.2006, which came to hand yesterday. I would be very happy to sign up to the PQIP as requested. I cannot recall receiving or refusing your request to sign the legal document. I work only part time in Bedford. Only 25% of my UDA commitments are carried out at the Bedford Practice. We have now completed our allocated UDA, with three months to spare. We have the will and the capacity to see more NHS patients (new and old) with your assistance and support. Your prompt cooperation is very essential. I would look forward to receiving from you. Sincerely and with gratitude yours, Ola."

On 11.01.2007, the NHS contacted the first ever and only Negro dentist in Bedford by surface mail as follows: "Dear Dr Bamgbelu, RE: PQIP. Thank you for your letter of 03.01.2007 which confirms your willingness to participate in the PQIP. Jan Ferdinando has emailed you the sign up sheet which must be completed and returned to her by 24.01.2007. Yours sincerely,

Charlotte Dowling. Head of Primary are Contracting."

The letter of 11.01.2007 by Charlotte Dowling Goodson overrode its predecessor. In the letter, Charlotte Dowling Goodson confirmed the

Negro's willingness to participate in the PQIP. The brainless, sensuous but tasteless, former England young adult implicitly sectionalised the order. She asked the first ever and only Negro dentist in Bedford to expect to receive the PQIP form by email from Jan Ferdinando, and that the Negro should complete it and return it by 24.01.2007, which should fully fulfil the first part of the order.

Correspondingly, on 04.01.2007, Charlotte Dowling Goodson gave Jan Ferdinando the Negro's email address, albeit a wrong one: "Hi Jan, I've just spoken to Dr Bamgbelu about PQIP. Can you email the info to him on adeola@aol.com? This may be the best way to communicate with him as his post is often taken in by estate agents below and occasionally gets lost. Thanks, Charlotte."

The email address that Charlotte Dowling Goodson gave to Jan Ferdinando was another of the NHS's racist forgeries. Despite stating that it was the best way and safest route of contacting the first ever and only Negro dentist in Bedford, she never employed it.

Charlotte Dowling Goodson was so dull; hers was almost certainly hereditary dullness as such a very high level of dullness does not ordinarily exist in nature. She must have been created dull by Almighty God and born duller by her mother. If she told Jan Ferdinando that email was the best way of contacting the Negro, it is very important to note that the racist thug did not say that the Negro told her that. It did not occur to the moronic England former young adult that it was absurd that she never employed the allegedly best way of communicating with the first ever and only Negro dentist in Bedford, including on 11.01.2007, which was only a week later.

"Why, Sir, Sherry is dull, naturally dull, but it must have taken him a great deal of pain to become what we now see him. Such an excess stupidity, Sir, is not in Nature." – Dr Samuel Johnson

In corroboration of her dishonesty, Charlotte Dowling further stated: "You gave me your email address as this was a more secure route to send important information to you" (11.05.2007).

Charlotte Dowling Goodson maliciously lied again when she stated that the first ever and only Negro dentist in Bedford told her that email was a more secure route of contacting him. After giving the falsified email address to the moronic England class NHS manager, Jan Ferdinando, Charlotte Dowling Goodson, the sensuous but tasteless, seemingly hereditary racist cougar sent letters only by surface mail to the first ever and only Negro dentist in Bedford – on 11.01.2007, 27.04.2007, 11.05.2007, 14.06.2007, 28.06.2007, and 10.07.2007. She never employed the email address which she stated was the best way and most secure route of contacting the first ever and only Negro dentist in Bedford.

Charlotte Dowling Goodson should go to any burial ground in Bedfordshire and invoke the spirits of her ancestors, and when she has done so, she should ask them where they got all the money from, as then and now, the land yielded and yields only food. They should tell her that they used guns, not brains, to loot and destroy the world, and that they were merciless, racist thugs and evil murderers, armed robbers, and thieves. Whenever they slaughtered, they dispossessed, and wherever they robbed, they took possession. They were merciless, racist bastards and cowards who were the world champions at using guns to slaughter millions of unarmed and defenceless people and arming others to mercilessly slaughter unarmed and defenceless Africans during several centuries of merciless racist tyranny. Those who like fighting with guns should go and use guns to evict Mr Putin from Crimea – even mighty America wouldn't dare.

Charlotte Dowling Goodson maliciously lied. Dishonesty on record is a very accurate measure of intelligence.

If Dr Richard Dawkins and Dr Stephen Hawking are accurate in their assertions, Charlotte Dowling Goodson's children and all her descendants will be considerably duller than their matriarch, as things will get considerably worse.

"Natural selection will not remove ignorance from the future generations." – Dr Richard Dawkins

"The increase of entropy (disorderliness) is what distinguishes the past from the future, giving a direction to time." – Dr Stephen Hawking, A Brief History of Time

Increasing disorderliness is part of the evidence of accelerating extinction.

"Or in other words, why does disorder increase in the same direction of time as that in which the universe expands?" – Dr Stephen Hawking, A Brief History of Time

Because it is acceleration towards extinction.

Before SLAVERY, there was ONLY feudal agriculture. GIGANTIC yields of centuries of merciless, RACIST evil, not agriculture, lured JEWS to Britain.

In order to impose their seemingly hereditary racist machinations upon the first ever and only Negro dentist in Bedford, they needed to create an inspection report that would fit seamlessly with the other NHS forged reports, particularly the imbecilic, racist forgeries of 22.07.2004 and follow up of undisclosed date. In order to give credibility to racial hatred that was guarded by dishonesty, the NHS recruited Stephanie Twidale (TD), and she was meant to create a racist report which fitted seamlessly with the NHS's racist forgeries of 22.07.2004 and the follow up of undisclosed date. She labelled the 22.02.2007 visit to the surgery of the first ever and only Negro dentist in Bedford – a follow up of the dishonest NHS visit of 22.07.2004 and the follow up of unknown date.

"Having discussed with the PCT they told me that Mr Hill had made previous visits not that long before from which there had been some queries, and they felt perhaps it would be sensible for Mr Hill to come along as well with me to be a second person and follow up on his previous visits to the practice." – Stephanie Twidale (TD)

Stephanie Twidale (TD) was exceedingly dull, dishonest, and racist. She unrelentingly lied under oath. It is not the truth that exceedingly dull Territorial Defence Officers can lie under oath, even in the Third World, including Bobby's Zimbabwe.

In an email of 15.03.2007, Charlotte Dowling Goodson stated as follows: "Having spoken to Sue (Consultant DPH) she thinks that we should terminate his contract. This is against the background of our other concerns about him/the premises."

Sue Gregory (OBE) and Charlotte Dowling Goodson reasoned like imbeciles and expressed their reasoning worse than imbeciles. They allowed seemingly hereditary, uncontrollable racial hatred and uneducated prejudices to becloud their objective reasoning and judgements. They were recklessly intellectually incompetent, shallow, and stupid. No brain, natural resources poor, only skin colour that the wearer neither made nor chose, and what else? Pure scam!

"Shallowness is the supreme vice." – Oscar Wilde

"There is no sin except stupidity." – Oscar Wilde

The sole basis of the power of Sue Gregory (OBE) is money. The entire foundation of the money was the yield of centuries of merciless racial hatred and naked fraud – stealing, carrying, and selling millions of stolen human beings at gun point by allegedly "civilised" Christians. Before slavery, there was only feudal agriculture; almost everything else was stolen with guns against unarmed and defenceless peoples in almost every square inch of the unarmed and defenceless world. Whenever the ancestors of Sue Gregory (TD) used guns and armed others to use guns to slaughter, they robbed, and wherever they dispossessed, they took possession. They were cowards and thieves.

"It was our arms in the river of Cameroon, put into the hands of the trader, that furnished him with the means of pushing his trade; and I have no more doubt that they are British arms, put into the hands of Africans, which promote universal war and desolation that I can doubt their having done so in that individual instance. I have shown how great is the enormity of this evil, even on the supposition that we take only convicts and prisoners of war. But take the subject in another way, and how does it stand? Think of 80,000 persons carried out of their native country by we know not what means! For crimes imputed! For light or inconsiderable faults! For debts perhaps! For crime of witchcraft! Or a thousand other weak or scandalous pretexts! Reflect on 80,000 persons annually taken off! There is something in the horror of it that surpasses all bounds of imagination." – Prime Minister William Pitt the Younger, 1792

"Need for an Autoclave for sterilisation as opposed to the Kavoclave that was in sole use," GDC. Brainless nonsense! Before SLAVERY what?

In November 2008, the dull, dishonest, vindictive, and racist GDC charged the Negro for using a Kavoklave only in January and February 1996. Their own kindred used the autoclave for several years before then, but she was spared; one rule for whites and another for blacks.

"No advance in wealth, no softening of manners, no reform or revolution has ever brought human equality a millimeter nearer." – George Orwell

The first ever and only Negro dentist in Bedford, since He merely spoke and the world became, took over the practice, an ongoing concern, on 18.12.1995, and hell broke loose. He started work there on 08.01.1996. Only two weeks later, on 22.01.1996, he was asked to replace the Kavoklave autoclave as soon as practicably possible. Their own kindred, the Negro's predecessor at the practice, had used it for several years. The first ever and only Negro dentist in Bedford replaced the Kavoklave autoclave in February 1996. The crooked, vindictive, mediocre, and racist council charged the Negro for using a Kavoklave instead of an autoclave almost thirteen years later, in November 2008, and he was found guilty for it. The General Dental Council, 37 Wimpole Street, London, was dishonest, mediocre, vindictive, and racist.

The very shallow council seemed afflicted by the evil spirit of confusion and consumed by uneducated prejudice, which compounded seemingly hereditary racial hatred. The moron council did not know that a Kavoklave is an autoclave. They are the descendants of thoroughly wretched, feudal agricultural labourers from mainland Europe (serfs) who were immeasurably transformed by the gigantic yields of several centuries of merciless racist evil. They have reinvented themselves with stolen money on stolen land, and fool the foolish with foolishness.

No brain, natural resources poor, only skin colour that the wearer neither made nor chose, and what else? Pure scam!

Before slavery, what?

"Having spoken to Sue (Consultant DPH) she thinks that we should terminate his contract. This is against the background of our other concerns about him/the premises." – Charlotte Dowling Goodson, 15.03.2007

Sue Gregory (OBE), seemingly propped up by crude oil and gas money in exactly the same way as her merciless, racist murderer, armed robber, and thieving ancestors were sustained by the proceeds of the sadistic evil which slavery was, was too dull and too stupid to discern the following: On 18.05.2005, Sue Gregory (OBE), the dull, crooked, and racist cougar sent an email to her disciples based entirely upon adverse information about the first ever and only Negro dentist in Wellingborough that she received from Victoria Harrison, a duller and uglier, mainly manly racist cougar, with a gigantic, muscular looking ass and humungous, four-fifths deflated mammary glands with little milk (see Helen Falcon (Community Dentist): Racist Empress of Privileged Dullards by Yinka Bamgbelu).

"To disagree with three-fourths of the British public on all points is one of the first elements of sanity, one of the deepest consolations in all moments of spiritual doubt." – Oscar Wilde

"The English think that incompetence is the same thing as sincerity." – Quentin Crisp

"Truth, Sir, is a cow which will yield such people no more milk, and so they are gone to milk the bull." – Dr Samuel Johnson

In her email of 18.05.2005, Sue Gregory asked to see previous reports of visits to the surgery of the first ever and only Negro dentist in Bedford. More than a year later, the thoroughly stupid and racist big gal implied that she was aware of reports, emphasis on pleura, but hadn't seen one and didn't have one.

"Dear John, I know Richard has done practice visits to Bamgbelu in the past, he will need to let you have the details." –
Sue Gregory (OBE), 15.08.2006

"In the past" implied that the intellectually incompetent, racist cougar did not know when the alleged visits took place; again, emphasis on pleura. According to the later statements by Richard Hill, Sue Gregory maliciously told racist lies on record or she was lied to by her disciples, when she stated, "I know Richard has done practice visits to Bamgbelu in the past, he will need to let you have the details."

Richard Hill contradicted Sue Gregory and confirmed that she maliciously told racist lies or she was recklessly confused or she was deceived when he stated as follows: "I did not undertake any further inspections at Mr Bamgbelu's practice between 2003 and 2007."

Richard Hill visited the surgery of the first ever and only Negro dentist in Bedford only once in 2003. He allegedly produced a report. The Negro knew about the report more than five years later when it was disclosed to him, as its content was part of the crooked, mediocre, and racist council's charges against the Negro.

It seemed pretty extraordinary that the crooked, mediocre, and racist council within one of the least literate countries in the industrialised world did not realise that a concern that was disclosed almost six years after the alleged concern was a racist forgery or at best it was not a concern at all. No brain, natural resources poor, only skin colour that the wearer neither made nor chose, and what else? Pure scam!

Before slavery, what?

To read more, Google by THE WHITE JUDGE LIED by Yinka Bamgbelu.

Upon the release of the NHS's racist forgeries of 22.07.2004 and follow up of undisclosed date, Sue Gregory became orientated. The reports were withdrawn in their entirety more than four years later. They were the sole basis of Charlotte Dowling Goodson's statement of 15.03.2007, and they were also the sole basis of the originally clueless Sue Gregory's email of 30.11.2006.

"Having spoken to Sue (Consultant DPH) she thinks that we should terminate his contract. This is against the background of our other concerns about him/the premises." – Charlotte Dowling Goodson,

Dr. Olayinka Bamgbelu

15.03.2007

"Dear Stephanie, Just to confirm that I have spoken to Richard Hill and he will join you for the DRS visit on Thursday 22nd February to Mr Bamgbelu's Bedford Practice, commencing at 9 a.m. We will endeavour to share any issues the PCT may have with you PRIOR to the 22nd. Kind regards, Sue." – 30.11.2006

Dr Richard Hill's report surfaced on 06.09.2006 in an email sent to Mr John Hooper, Mrs Charlotte Dowling Goodson, and Dr Sue Gregory. The email stated: "Record of Practice VisitsBedford PCT. Dear John, Please find attached the record of practice visits that you were chasing up. Sorry for the delay! As you can see, the great majority of practices are not a cause for concern. However, we will need to focus particularly on the Bamgbelu and the alpha practices. Perhaps also beta practice in delta and the gamma practice are worthy of closer attention. Regards, Richard" (NHS email of 06.09.2006).

"RECORD OF PRACTICE VISITS: BEDFORD PCT. DENTIST: Mr O Bamgbelu. ADDRESS: Grey Friars Dental Practice 52 Bromham Road Bedford MK40 2QG. Telephone No: 01234300505. Visit Date: JULY 2004. CONCERNS: No risk assessment, no CoSSH, A Kavoclave type autoclave was present in the surgery. This type of autoclave should not be used as the cycle can be broken into before sterilisation is complete. No other member of staff were present at the visit so could not be questioned as regards the methods of cross infection control used by practice." – NHS report of 22.07.2004

"OUTSTANDING ISSUES: Even though the necessary documents have now been seen. I continue to have concerns as to the cross-infection control procedures in the practice." – NHS follow up visit report of undisclosed date

The reports in their entirety were merciless, racist NHS forgeries. They were completely withdrawn, albeit more than four years later. The NHS withdrawal statement of 16.10.2008 is another NHS racist forgery, which remains live and valid.

Jews with camouflage English names seemed to be the shepherds of morons, and they seem to control things from behind the scenes.

Jews with camouflage English names seem to be the shepherds of England young adults and England's former young adults.

"FAILING SCHOOLS AND A BATTLE FOR BRITAIN: This was the day the British education establishment's 50-year betrayal of the Nation's children lay starkly exposed in all its ignominy. After testing 166,000 people in 24 education systems, the Organisation for Economic Cooperation and Development (OECD) finds that England young adults are amongst the least literate and numerate in the industrialised world." – The Daily Mail, 09.01.2013

Shepherds of morons are likelier to be morons too.

Before SLAVERY, there was ONLY feudal agriculture. GIGANTIC yields of centuries of merciless, RACIST evil, not agriculture, lured JEWS to Britain

"When we consider the vastness of the continent of Africa; when we reflect how all other countries have for some centuries past been advancing in happiness and civilisation; when we think how in this same period all improvement in Africa has been defeated by her intercourse with Britain; when we reflect that it was we ourselves that have degraded them to that wretched brutishness and barbarity which we now plead as the justification for our guilt; how the slave trade has enslaved their minds, blackened their character, and sunk them so low in the scale of animal beings that some think apes are of a higher class, and fancy the Orang –outang has given them the go-by. What mortification must we feel at having so long neglected to think of our guilt or attempt at reparation! It seems indeed, as if we had determined to forbear from all interference until the measure of folly and wickedness was so full and complete, until the policy which eventually belongs to vice was become so plain and glaring that not an individual in this country should refuse to join the abolition. It seems as if we had waited until the persons most interested should be tired out with the folly nefariousness of the trade and should unite in petitioning against it." – William Wilberforce, 1789

"The grand object of all European traders in kidnapped and stolen Africans was - money, money, money; money was their god! In Africa, the poor wretched natives, blessed with the most fertile and luxuriant soil, are rendered so much the more miserable by the Christians' (European traders in stolen Africans) abominable traffic for slaves and the horrid cruelty and treachery of the petty [African] Kings. The Africans kings were encouraged by their European (Christian) customers who carry them strong liquors to enflame their madness and powder and bad firearms to furnish them with the hellish means of killing and kidnapping. But enough
- it is a subject that sours my blood." – Ignatius Sancho, 1778

It is distorted reasoning to associate GIGANTIC yields of centuries of merciless, racist evil (SLAVERY) with personal intellect and industry
"Many Scots masters were considered among the most brutal, with life expectancy on their plantations averaging a mere four years. We worked them to death then simply imported more to keep the sugar and thus the money flowing. Unlike centuries of grief and murder, an apology costs nothing. So what does Scotland have to say?" – Herald Scotland, Ian Bell, columnist, Sunday 28 April 2013
The thoroughly wretched descendants of thoroughly wretched, feudal agricultural labourers from mainland Europe (serfs) were immeasurably transformed by the gigantic yields of several continuous centuries of the merciless racist evil which slavery was. They have reinvented themselves on stolen land with the gigantic yields of centuries of merciless, racist evil, and fool the foolish with foolishness.
As shepherds didn't bring STOLEN AFRICANS home, moron sheep believed that shepherds were saintly Mother Teresa who did virtuous work abroad.
Before slavery, what?
"Agriculture not only gives riches to a nation, but the only riches she can call her own." – Dr Samuel Johnson
"Those who have robbed have also lied." – Dr Samuel Johnson corroborating prophet Habakkuk

"To disagree with three-fourths of the British public on all points is one of the first elements of sanity, one of the deepest consolations in all moments of spiritual doubt." – Oscar Wilde

OYINBO OLE WHITE THIEVES: HABAKKUK

Some of the biggest building in BEDFORD have been emptied by COVID except Bedford County Court and Bedford Masonic Centre amongst many others.

There were LAWS then.
Based on available evidence, then, the yields of millions of stolen and destroyed lives of the children of defenceless poor people were used to build MAGNIFICENT COURTS and pay the wages of Judges who sent those who stole money to prisons built with stolen money - Habakkuk.

OYINBO OLE: WHITE THIEVES: HABAKKUK.
 Based on available evidence, the Grand Masons Temple to Baal, 60 Great Queen St, Holborn, London WC2B 5AZ, was built in the 1700s (18th century) at height of barbarously racist traffic in millions of stolen children of defenceless people - Habakkuk

Based on available evidence, Bedford County Court and Bedfordshire Masonic Centre were preceded by European commerce in millions of stolen children of unarmed and defenceless people - Habakkuk.

Facts are sacred.

"The truth allows no choice." Dr Samuel Johnson

OYINBO OLE: WHITE THIEVES; HABAKKUK.

"Time for Scots to say sorry for slavery
Herald Scotland:
Ian Bell, Columnist / Sunday 28 April 2013 / Opinion
Sunday 28 April 2013
According to the American founding father, the son of a Caithness Kirk minister had about him of "an air of great simplicity and honesty". The likes of James Boswell and Laurence Sterne also enjoyed the merchant's

company.

To his contemporaries, he was, as the author Adam Hochschild has written, "'a wise, thoughtful man who embodied the Scottish virtues of frugality, sobriety, and hard work'". Oswald was a scholar of theology, philosophy, and history. He collected art, particularly Rubens and Rembrandt, and gave handsomely to charity. Oswald, who learned his trade in Glasgow, also represented Britain in negotiations with the Americans after their war of liberation. He was the cosmopolitan epitome of Enlightenment success. But when he wasn't busy with good works, Oswald waded in blood. The precise number of deaths that can be laid at his door is impossible to calculate. As the leading figure in Grant, Oswald & Co, he had investments in each corner of the "'triangular trade'". In his own name, Oswald trafficked at least 13,000 Africans, although he never set foot on their continent. By the time he bought Auchincruive House and 100,000 acres in Ayrshire in 1764, he was worth £500,000. Writing in 2005, Hochschild thought this was ""roughly equivalent"" to $68 million (about £44m). This is conservative.

Oswald was remarkable, but not unique. Where Glasgow and its merchants in sugar, tobacco, and human life are concerned, there are plenty of names and no shortage of monuments: Dennistoun, Campbell, Glassford, Cochrane, Buchanan, Hamilton, Bogle, Ewing, Donald, Speirs, Dunlop. One way to understand what they wrought is simple: take pleasure in the city"s architecture today and you are likely to be admiring the fruits of slavery.

Glasgow is not alone in that. London, Liverpool and Bristol also have their stories to tell. Edinburgh's once-great banks grew from foundations built on bones. The first Scottish venture into slavery set out from the capital in 1695. Montrose, Dumfries, Greenock and Port Glasgow each tried their hands. In the language of the present age, they were all in it together.

When commerce was coursing around the triangle, most of polite Scotland was implicated. The nobility (and country) rendered bankrupt in 1700 in the aftermath of the Darien Venture was by the mid-1760s contemplating big elegant townhouses and 100,000-acre estates. You could call that a reversal of fortune. Contrary to self-serving myth, it did not happen because of "'frugality, sobriety, and hard work'".

Certain things need to be remembered about Scotland and slavery. One is that the mercantile class got stinking rich twice over: despite fortunes made from stolen lives, they were quick to demand compensation when slavery was ended in 1833. Britain's government decided that £20m, a staggering sum, could be raised. In his 2010 book, The Price of Emancipation, Nicholas Draper reckons Glasgow's mob got £400,000 – in modern terms, hundreds of millions.

Compensation cases also demonstrated that Scots were not merely following an English lead. According to Draper, a country with 10% of the British population accounted for at least 15% of absentee slavers. By another estimate, 30% of Jamaican plantations were run by Scots. For all the pride taken in the abolitionist societies of Glasgow and Edinburgh, the slave-holders did not suffer because of abolition. They were '"compensated"'.

And that wasn't the worst of it. Thanks to Hollywood movies, the slave economy of the American South is still taken as barbarism's benchmark. Few realise that the behaviour of Scots busy getting rich in the slave-holders" empire was actually worse – routinely worse – than the worst of the cottonocracy. You need only count the corpses................"

OYINBO OLE: WHITE THIEVES: HABAKKUK.

BEDFORD, ENGLAND: District Judge, which part of our County Court preceded the barbarously racist traffic in millions of stolen children of defenceless poor people: The building or its chattels?

Ignorance is bliss.

OYINBO OLE: RIGHTEOUS DESCENDANTS OF THIEVES: HABAKKUK

"Those who know the least obey the best." George Farquhar.

Fake righteousness and deceptively schooled civilised decorum were preceded by several centuries of merciless racist evil: The barbarously racist traffic in millions of stolen children of defenceless poor people - Habakkuk.

OYINBO OLE: STRAIGHT FACED WHITE THIEVES: HABAKKUK

"England is like a prostitute who, having sold her body all her life, decides to quit and close her business, and then tells everybody she wants to be chaste and protect her flesh as if it were jade." He Manzi, Chinese politician

Their ancestors were THIEVES; they know - Habakkuk.

Then, almost everything was stolen - Habakkuk

OUR EMPIRE OF STOLEN AFFLUENCE.

"Affluence is not a birthright." David Cameron

OYINBO OLE: WHITE THIEVES: HABAKKUK

Affluence did not evolve; Then, it was actively and deliberately stolen.

OYINBO OLE: WHITE THIEVES: HABAKKUK

Then, racist white bastards carried and sold millions of stolen children of defenceless poor people; now, they carry natural resources - Habakkuk.

SUBSTITUTION: FRAUDULENT EMANCIPATION.

"Moderation is a virtue only among those who are thought to have found alternatives." Henry Kissinger

OYINBO OLE: WHITE THIEVES: HABAKKUK

There are no oil wells or gas fields in KEMPSTON; the highly luxuriant soil of KEMPSTON yields only food

NIGERIA: SHELL'S DOCILE CASH COW

Babies with huge oil wells ad gas fields near their houses eat 1.5/day in NIGERIA; a semi-illiterate former debt-collector Solicitor, in Norwich, whose white father and mother have never seen crude oil is our District Judge in BEDFORD.

OYINBO OLE: WHITE THIEVES: HABAKKUK

Then, the white ancestors of his white father and mother were fed like battery hens with the yields of stolen children of defenceless poor people - Habakkuk

An ignorant racist leech; a righteous descendant of industrial-scale professional THIEVES and owners of stolen children of defenceless poor people - Habakkuk.

OYINBO OLE: RIGHTEOUS WHITE THIEVES: HABAKKUK

* * * * *

NORTHAMPTON, ENGLAND: Based on available evidence, GDC-WITNESS, Dr Geraint Evans, Postgraduate Tutor, Oxford, unrelentingly lied under implied oath - Habakkuk 1:4; John 8:44; John 10:10.

A RACIST WHITE CROOK.

CREEPING NORTH KOREA.

FACTS ARE SACRED.

CORBY, ENGLAND: Based on available evidence, GDC-WITNESS, Dr George Rothnie unrelentingly lied under implied oath - Habakkuk 1:4; John 8:44; John 10:10.

A RACIST WHITE CROOK.

CREEPING NORTH KOREA.

FACTS ARE SACRED.

CORBY, ENGLAND: Based on available evidence, GDC-WITNESS, Dr Kevin Atkinson, Scottish Ken, unrelentingly lied under oath - Habakkuk 1:4; John 8:44; John 10:10.

A RACIST WHITE CROOK.

CREEPING NORTH KOREA.

FACTS ARE SACRED.

OXFORD, ENGLAND: Based on available evidence, GDC-WITNESS, British Soldier - Territorial Defence, Dr Stephanie Twidale (TD) unrelentingly lied under oath - Habakkuk 1:4; John 8:44; John 10:10.

A RACIST WHITE CROOK.

CREEPING NORTH KOREA.

FACTS ARE SACRED.

WOLLASTON, ENGLAND: Based on available evidence, GDC-WITNESS, Ms Rachael Bishop, Senior NHS Nurse, unrelentingly lied under oath - Habakkuk 1:4; John 8:44; John 10:10.

A RACIST WHITE CROOK.

CREEPING NORTH KOREA.

FACTS ARE SACRED.

Satanic Network

BEDFORD, ENGLAND: Based on available evidence, GDC-INSIDER, Dr Sue Gregory, Officer of the Most Excellent Order of our Empire unrelentingly lied under implied oath - Habakkuk 1:4; John 8:44; John 10:10.

A RACIST WHITE CROOK.

CREEPING NORTH KOREA.

FACTS ARE SACRED.

BEDFORD, ENGLAND: Based on available evidence, GDC-WITNESS, Freemason, Brother, Dr Richard William Hill fabricated reports and unrelentingly lied under oath - Habakkuk 1:4; John 8:44; John 10:10.

A RACIST WHITE CROOK.

CREEPING NORTH KOREA.

FACTS ARE SACRED.

A bastardised, unashamedly mediocre, indiscreetly dishonest, vindictive, potently weaponised, and institutionally RACIST system that his overseen by MASONS (Mediocre Mafia) - Habakkuk.

Then and now, in jurisdictions where the satanic network (Antichrist Racist Freemason) is in charge, their members have power to tell lies under oath.

"The supreme vice is shallowness." Wilde

Antichrist Racist Freemasons wear vulgar Pharisees' charitable works as cloaks of deceit, and they use very expensive aprons to decorate the temples of their powerless and useless fertility tools; they have informal access to some very powerful white Judges – Habakkuk 1:4.

"The good Samaritan had money." Mrs Margaret Thatcher (1925 – 2013).

Presumably, the Good Samaritans money was the yield of transparent virtue.

He told the righteous Jew to sell the yields of virtue, give the proceeds to the poor, and follow Him; He'd have told the rich Pharisee to return the yields of vice to the rightful owners – Matthew 19:21.

The Grand Antichrist Masons' Temple to Baal, 60 Great Queen St, Holborn, London WC2B 5AZ, was built in the 1700s (18th century), at a height of the barbarously racist traffic in millions of stolen children of defenceless poor people – Habakkuk.

Facts are sacred; they can't be overstated.

Righteousness without equitable reparation is continuing racist fraud.

Deluded and conceited, like the Pharisees, they baselessly awarded themselves the monopoly knowledge and become impervious and intolerant to other views, and they usurped power, their job is to interpret the laws prescribed by the servants of the people, but they impose their will with illegal parallel power (unelected). They lie to their duller children that they're geniuses, and they kill all those who know they're not – Matthew 2:16.

He jailed him only because he spoke; the lunatic Jew removed John's head when he refused to stop speaking – Matthew 14.

He was lynched like Gadhafi and was crucified only because He spoke: He disclosed pictures His unbounded painted.

Then, like Herod, MBS and Kim, they used to butcher those who stated and/or printed what they did not want their moron sheep to know. The last decapitation in England was in 1827, and beheading was removed from the statute book in 1973, and the same year (1973), Kenneth Baker banned caning.

Why remove the heads of your enemies if it is illegal to flog them?

They lied to their duller children that they are geniuses, when, in fact, the power to economically strangulate and/or inflict bodily sufferings on their enemies is the principal leverage of the hands-off racist killers; they will lose, all the time, on a colour-blind and level playing field – Matthew 26, 27.

They lied to their moron sheep that they were geniuses, and they killed all those who knew that they were brainless racist bastards. Their sole objective is to shepherd their moron sheep unchallenged.

"Of black men, the numbers are too great who are now repining under English cruelty." Dr Samuel Johnson.

https://www.facebook.com/rotimi.osunsan/videos/3088536551193798

https://www.youtube.com/watch?v=BlpH4hG7m1A&feature=youtu.be

"They may not have been well written from a grammatical point of view, but I am confident I had not forgotten any of the facts." Dr Geraint Evans, Postgraduate Tutor, Oxford.

Northampton England, Rowtree Dental Care: Based on available evidence, Geraint Evans, Welsh Dunce, GDC-WITNESS, unrelentingly lied under oath – Habakkuk 1:4; John 8:44: John 10:10.

A RACIST WHITE CROOK.

Facts are sacred.

"Freedom to report the truth is a basic right to which the court gives a high level of protection, and the author's right to his story includes the right to tell it as he wishes." Lord Toulson

"It is incumbent upon the court and all those professionals involved to conclude court proceedings as quickly as possible. This hopefully ensures that a child has stability, love and affection and the parents working together to ensure that he has the best opportunity of developing academically and emotional."District Judge Paul Ayers, Senior Vice President of the Association of Her Majesty's District Judges – proofed and approved Judgement

"Yes, Sir, it does her honour, but it would do nobody else honour. I have indeed, not read it all. But when I take up the end of a web, and find it packthread, I do not expect, by looking further, to find embroidery." Dr Samuel Johnson

OUR SEMI-ILLITERATE RACIST FREEMASON YOUR HONOUR.

A CLOSETED RACIST BRAINLESS WHITE MAN.

The only evidence of the purportedly higher IQ of the incontrovertibly functional semi-illiterate white man is stolen affluence that his ancestors crossed the English Channels, without luggage or decent shoes to latch onto. They changed their names, blended, and deceived the undiscerning that their ancestors were aboriginal Britons who evolved from gorillas in Luton.

Descendants of aliens (genetic aliens) oppress, we, the descendants of the robbed with the yields of the robbery.

"All have taken what had other owners, and all have had recourse to arms rather than quit the prey they were fastened to." Dr Samuel Johnson

Everything is subjectively assumed in favour of his indisputably superior skin colour; he neither made nor chose it - Apartheid by stealth.

The last time he passed through a colour-blind and transparently objective filter system was when he studied 5th rate law at Polytechnic, and it shows.

A CLOSETED RACIST WHITE DUNCE.

Facts are sacred.

An impostor and an expert of deception; he has coasted along for decades, seemingly guided and guarded by the AntiChrist Racist Quasi-Religion (Mediocre Mafia/ New Pharisees), and has sold confusion to the undiscerning in exchange for valuable consideration.

In an open dialogue former Justice Ruth Bader Ginsburg (1933 - 2020), Lady Hale lamented funding.

My Lady, what's the value of several layers of unashamed mediocrity and confusion?

New Herod, Matthew 2:16: They lie to their stupider children that they're geniuses; they 'kill' we, their enemies, who know that they're brainless racist bastards.

Deluded intellectual cowards: They want superiority, their baseless birthright; they don't want Freedom of Expression because they don't want their simpler children to know about what they do to our people - Habakkuk.

A typical English man seemed to want to eat his cake and have it: Reductio ad absurdum - A logical fallacy.

"A typical English man, usually violent and always dull." Wilde

Matthew 19:21: He told the righteous Jew to sell the yields of transparent virtue and give the proceeds to the poor. Had the Jew been a scammer who sold confusion for cash, Christ would have told him to return the cash to the scammed, and sin no more.

The Good Samaritan had money." Mrs Margaret Thatcher (1925 -2013).

The money of the Good Samaritan was, presumably, the yield of transparent virtue.

Half-educated school dropouts and their superiors decorate the temples of their powerless and useless fertility tools with expensive aprons, and have informal access to some very powerful white Judges - Habakkuk 1:4.

They want a segregated world (Prince Hall's Mason), in terms of opportunities and rights, where human beings are graded according to the colour of the skin that they neither made nor chose; a world based on the embroidery on the aprons they use to decorate the temples of their powerless and useless fertility tools.

Based on very proximate observations and direct experiences, the natural instinct of some white privileged dullards is Apartheid by stealth.

They do vulgar Pharisees' charitable works in exchange for what?

Their offer is not a good deal - Matthew 4:9.

Brother Jimmy Savile did not fix anything for NOTHING.

Google: Freemasonry, intellectually flawed.

When Freedom of Expression becomes a basic right, we shall show the closeted racist dim-wits what they could't see in the supernatural thing that they're looking at.

The Grand Masons' Temple to Baal, 60 Great Queen St, Holborn, London WC2B 5AZ, was built in the 1700s (18th Century), at a height of the barbarously racist traffic in millions of stolen children of defenceless poor people - Habakkuk.

Righteousness without equitable reparation is continuing racist fraud.

Then, Judges, nearly all, were MASONS; some of them were thicker than a gross of planks.

Charitable AntiChrist Racist Freemasonry Quasi-Religion teaches its members the cultist-like, and quasi-voodoo, handshake, not grammar; the former is considerably easier to master.

Based on available evidence, Dr Richard Dawkins and OECD implied that all the children of District Judge Paul Ayers, Senior Vice President of the Association of Her Majesty's District Judges should be duller than their white father.

Facts are sacred.

"Natural selections will not remove ignorance from future generations." Dr Richard Dawkins

England's young people are near the bottom of the global league table for basic skills. OECD finds 16- to 24-year-olds have literacy and numeracy levels no better than those of their grandparents' generation

England is the only country in the developed world where the generation approaching retirement is more literate and numerate than the youngest adults, according to the first skills survey by the Organisation for Economic Co-operation and Development.

In a stark assessment of the success and failure of the 720-million-strong adult workforce across the wealthier economies, the economic thinktank warns that in England, adults aged 55 to 65 perform better than 16- to 24-year-olds at foundation levels of literacy and numeracy. The survey did not include people from Scotland or Wales.

The OECD study also finds that a quarter of adults in England have the maths skills of a 10-year-old. About 8.5 million adults, 24.1% of the population, have such basic levels of numeracy that they can manage only one-step tasks in arithmetic, sorting numbers or reading graphs. This is worse than the average in the developed world, where an average of 19%

of people were found to have a similarly poor skill base.

Just as it was at Professor Stephen Hawking's schools, then, at the University of Lagos, the brightest students did not attend lectures at the Faculty of Law.

"In my school, the brightest boys did math and physics, the less bright did physics and chemistry, and the least bright did biology. I wanted to do math and physics, but my father made me do chemistry because he thought there would be no jobs for mathematicians." Dr Stephen Hawking

They secretly hate Freedom of Expression because they don't want their people to know about what they, secretly, do to our people.

Oxford, England: GDC-Witness, Dr Stephanie Twidale (TD), British Army Officer - Territorial Defence, unrelentingly lied under oath - Habakkuk 1:4; John 8:44; John 10:10.

A RACIST WHITE CROOK.

Her white ancestors lied too; they were industrial-scale professional THIEVES and owners of stolen children of defenceless poor people - Habakkuk.

OYINBO OLE: WHITE THIEVES: HABAKKUK.

Unlike her little brother, age saved the child's sister from the Closeted-Racist-Dylan–Roof-Freemason-Judge. She thanks her stars that the incontrovertibly functional semi-illiterate, closeted racist white man did not have anything to do with her education.
In her GCSE, she gained the following grades:
English Language A*
English Literature A*
Mathematics A*
Additional Mathematics A*
Physics A*

Chemistry A*
Biology A*
History A*
Latin A
Spanish A
Advanced Level Mathematics A

The academic height that the white father and mother of the closeted racist white District Judge cannot know, and which the natural talents of his own children will not exploit.

The brain isn't skin colour; then, we were robbed with guns.

The child sister has since gained a First Class Science Degree from one of the topmost Universities in the UK , and she's gainfully engaged, batting for her Country. Christ saved her from the evil clutches of the Closeted Racist Freemason Thugs.

It's plainly deductible that the white children of the white Senior Vice President of the Association of Her Majesty's District Judges were inferiorly created by Almighty God, certainly intellectually - OECD.

Facts are sacred.

"The truth allows no choice." Dr Samuel Johnson.

BEDFORD, ENGLAND: Based on available evidence, GDC-WITNESS, Freemason, Brother, Dr Richard William Hill fabricated reports and unrelentingly lied under oath - Habakkuk 1:4; John 8:44; John 10:10.

A RACIST WHITE CROOK.

Facts are sacred.

English law is equal; its administration isn't.

Based on available evidence, the administration of English law is a very potent weapon of a raging but latent RACE WAR.

"All sections of the UK Society are institutionally racist." Sir Bernard Hogan-Howe.

The former Chief of the Metropolitan Police had access to a lot of classified information.

"By definition therefore there needs to be a contact order for Mr B so that he knows when he is going to see his son. It is absolutely essential that this occurs and mother agrees with that. She said so several times in her evidence. Mrs Waller agreed that not only should a child have the opportunity of developing relationship with both parents, any sibling should also be there so that inter- sibling relationship could be fostered and nurtured. Obviously in this particular case the children reside in different places. That immediately puts a strain on the children having limited contact with each other. F's sister is very much older than him and she will be further advanced into her adult life. Thus it is not a matter that that sibling relationship can only be fostered by the children being together. Indeed as we all know absence sometimes makes the heart grow fonder. F should have an opportunity of seeing his sister. Wherever he does that it should be done in a friendly and loving environment. If the time comes that his sister goes to university of course his contact with her will be restricted to the time that she is home from university. In years to come when they have both grown up, with their own family they will see less of each other. But it doesn't mean that they don't still love and adore each other as much as they would if they saw each other every day." The Senior Vice President of the Association of Her Majesty's District Judges – proofed and approved Judgement.

https://www.youtube.com/watch?v=BlpH4hG7m1A

Shocking!

"Why, that is, because, dearest, you are a dunce." Habakkuk.

A scatter-head plebeian; an overpromoted polytechnic university educated racist bastard. A righteous descendant of industrial-scale professional THIEVES and owners of stolen children of defenceless people (Kamala's ancestors) - Habakkuk.

OYINBO OLE: WHITE THIEVES: HABAKKUK.

The white father and mother of the Senior Vice President of the Association of Her Majesty's District Judges did not care, had they, he'd not have approved and immortalised excessive stupidity at 16, and he'd be a properly educated lawyer, privately educated Anthony Blair, Anthony Julius, Geoff Hoon and Rabinder Singh's class, and he might practice proper law in STRAND.

It's plainly deductible that the white father and mother of the Senior Vice President of the Association of Her Majesty's District Judges couldn't afford to pay for qualitative-education; why should we have to come from very far AFRICA to pay for his misfortune and part of its tell-tale signs (sequelae)?

"To deny or belittle this good is, in this dangerous century when the resources and pretensions of power continue to enlarge, a desperate error of intellectual abstraction. More than this, it is a self-fulfilling error, which encourages us to give up the struggle against bad laws and class bound procedures and to disarm ourselves before power. It is to throw away a whole inheritance of struggle about the law and within the forms of law, whose continuity can never be fractured without bringing men and women into immediate danger." - E. P Thompson

I remain yours, ever so sincerely,
Abiodun Olayinka Bamgbelu

The author attended the University of Lagos. He is a Fellow of the Royal College of Surgeon, Dental Surgery (Oral Surgery and Medicine). He practiced dentistry for several decades.

Review Requested:

If you loved this book, would you please provide a review at Amazon.com?

www.ingramcontent.com/pod-product-compliance
Lightning Source LLC
Chambersburg PA
CBHW071425070526
44578CB00001B/3